Also by Dr Bob Rotella

Golf Is Not a Game of Perfect
Golf Is a Game of Confidence
The Golf of Your Dreams
Life Is Not a Game of Perfect

PUTTING OUT OF YOUR MIND

DR BOB ROTELLA
WITH BOB CULLEN

POCKET BOOKS

LONDON • SYDNEY • NEW YORK • TORONTO

This edition first published by Pocket Books, 2005
An imprint of Simon & Schuster UK Ltd
A Viacom Company

Copyright © Robert J. Rotella, 2001

This book is copyright under the Berne Convention.
No reproduction without permission.
All rights reserved.

The right of Robert J. Rotella to be identified as the author of this work has been asserted by him in accordance with sections 77 and 78 of the Copyright, Designs and Patents Act, 1988.

3 5 7 9 10 8 6 4 2

Simon & Schuster UK Ltd
Africa House
64–78 Kingsway
London WC2B 6AH

www.simonsays.co.uk

Simon & Schuster Australia
Sydney

A CIP catalogue record for this book is available from the British Library

ISBN 1-4165-0199-1

Printed and bound in Great Britain by
Bookmarque Ltd, Croydon, Surrey

Introduction

by Brad Faxon

WHEN I FIRST ENCOUNTERED DR. BOB ROTELLA, GOLFERS SPOKE OF psychologists in whispers, if they spoke about them at all.

In 1979, my first year at Furman University, one of my new classmates was a tennis player from Charlottesville, Virginia, named Frank Taylor. Frank had a book on athletic motivation, one of the first published works that made an effort to apply the science of psychology to sports. It was by two University of Virginia faculty members, Dr. Linda Bunker and Dr. Bob Rotella. I was intrigued. I read it and it helped me. I had a good career at Furman, becoming an All-American and a member of the Walker Cup team.

In 1983, I turned pro. On the PGA Tour in those days, players who talked to psychologists still didn't advertise the fact. But one day I played a practice round with Denis Watson. Denis, at the time, had risen suddenly out of the pack of Tour players to become one of the leading money winners. As we walked off the 18th green, I asked him what was behind his rapid improvement. He looked at me almost shyly. He confided that he had gone to see a sports psychologist in Virginia who had taught him better approaches to the mental side of the game.

"Bob Rotella?" I asked him.

Denis was startled that I knew the name. I told him I had read one of Rotella's books. I asked him about what Rotella had said that had helped him so much.

"Everything," Denis replied.

That was enough to persuade me to go to Charlottesville myself. Bob and I hit it off right away. We have been working together ever since, and Bob has become more than a consultant to me. He's become a friend and an important person in my life. Bob's ideas did not affect my game as suddenly or dramatically as they did Denis's. But they helped me, particularly in putting.

In seventeen years, Bob has never tried to change my putting stroke. To me, that makes sense. Golf has seen a tremendous variety of putting strokes and styles. If I close my eyes, I can see pictures of the great players putting—the crouching Nicklaus, the knock-kneed Palmer, the upright and flowing Crenshaw, and the determined and robotic Watson. They're all different. Tiger Woods, the best in the game right now, has a classic stroke. Tiger looks perfect standing over his putter. But there have also been greats such as Isao Aoki, Bobby Locke, and Billy Casper, with peculiar styles that few would dare emulate.

What Bob Rotella knows is that the secret to great putting is not in the stroke. It's in the mind. When you putt, your state of mind is more important than your mechanics.

Some people have a hard time understanding this. Because I am usually among the leaders in the Tour's putting statistics, I'm often asked if there's a secret to great putting. I usually reply that if there were a secret, I'd bottle it and sell it. I'd make a lot of money. I'd make a lot of golfers better putters and happier people.

But while there is no secret, there is a set of ideas—a way of thinking—that can help anyone become a better putter, perhaps even a great one. That's what you're going to find in this book. The good news is that these ideas make sense and they can be learned. I say this because I learned them and they became the foundation of my putting game. If I learned them, you can learn them, too. Maybe you've tried to improve your putting and haven't been successful. That doesn't mean you can't putt. It just means you've been going about it in the wrong way. The ability to putt well is inside you. You just have to get out of your own way and use it.

You're going to encounter concepts in these pages that may be new to you, concepts like trusting yourself, letting go, freeing it up, and loving the challenge of putting. You're going to learn how to develop a putting routine that works under pressure. You're going to find out what it feels like to love putting and to love making putts. You're going to learn some practice games and routines that I and other players use on the Tour. You're going to learn to understand the paradox that is at the heart of putting success: You make more putts when you don't care if you miss.

Judging by the way my pro-am partners generally act on the greens, these ideas may well be radically different from the thoughts you have now. A lot of the amateurs I see don't know how to trust themselves, don't know how to let go. They loathe and fear putting. They try very hard and they care desperately whether the ball goes in the hole. Not coincidentally, they don't putt very well.

If this sounds familiar to you, prepare for a change. If you can read, absorb, and adopt the ideas Bob Rotella teaches, you'll do more than sink a few putts. You'll enhance the pleasure you take from the game. You'll feel that a weight has been lifted from your shoulders.

Bob Rotella's ideas on putting are simple, but that doesn't mean they're easy to assimilate and follow. They may contradict attitudes you've carried around for most of your life. People often look at me in disbelief when I tell them I don't care that much if I miss a putt, that the result isn't as important to me as where my mind was when I stood over the ball. They don't understand what I've learned from Bob: If I can consistently achieve the right state of mind, I will consistently hole more putts.

Of course, if putting in the right frame of mind were easy,

everyone would do it. And then you wouldn't get the competitive advantage you're going to have when you finish this book.

For now, trust me. Bob Rotella is a master in his field. Thanks largely to him, golfers don't whisper about seeing psychologists any more. He has helped me improve as a player and as a putter. He can help you. Since you've got this book in your hands, I'm willing to venture two predictions. One is that you will never need another putting book. And the second is that you will enjoy reading this as much as you will enjoy putting in your next round of golf.

Foreword

by David Duval

ONE OF THE MOST CHALLENGING PUTTS I'VE EVER FACED WAS THE ONE I had on the final green of the 1999 Bob Hope Chrysler Classic. It wasn't the length or the break that made it hard, of course. The putt was only about seven feet, with a little tail at the end. If I'd had it on Thursday, I probably wouldn't have thought very much about it. But this wasn't Thursday. This was Sunday afternoon. It was an eagle putt to win the tournament. And it was for a score of 59, which would be the first sub-60 score anyone on the PGA Tour had ever shot in a final round. I knew that I might never have another chance to set that record. The circumstances surrounding the putt challenged my mind. And putting, I've learned, is all about your mind and your attitude.

Fortunately, I had something to fall back on under pressure, something I'd been taught by Bob Rotella—my putting routine. All that day, I'd been trying to do the same thing with every putt. For the first sixteen holes, it hadn't been so difficult. I'd started the day seven strokes behind the leader, Steve Pate. All I'd been thinking about was hitting the ball close to the flag and making birdie putts. I was hitting it well that day, and the putts I'd had generally weren't very long. It wasn't until I made birdie on the 16th hole to get to 11 under par for the day that I became fully aware of how low my score was. It was then that I realized what I had to do both to win and to shoot 59.

Once I started thinking about those things, the challenge got harder. When I hit my five-iron to the 18th green and saw it roll up close to the hole, it got harder still.

One of the principal elements of my routine is a decisive read. I don't want to second-guess myself. My caddie, Mitch Knox, and I didn't take a long time reading the putt. We both saw the same little break. I told myself to stick with my first instinct, not to waver, and to concentrate on executing my routine. One temptation in such a situation is to try to be too precise. Another is to focus too much on the outcome, on whether the putt falls. I resisted both. If you watched the tournament on TV and wondered what was going through my mind at that moment, here's the answer: I was telling myself not to think about the outcome and not to question what I was doing. I was thinking about preparation and routine. I wanted simply to hit the putt the way I'd hit the other putts that day, the way I'd practiced thousands of putts before.

I did, and it fell.

Some people, I suspect, might be a little disappointed to read this. They want to believe that there's some secret about putting that few players know and even fewer divulge, some act of self-hypnosis or mysticism that I used on that final green. I hear this when people ask me what I do with Bob Rotella. They think there must be something Doc and I discuss that he doesn't disclose in his books or his talks.

There isn't. Doc tells me the same things he'll tell you in this book. They're very simple. But great putters keep it simple.

I first met Bob Rotella when I was in college at Georgia Tech. My coach, Puggy Blackmon, invited him down each year to talk to the golf team. I remember that we worked that first time on routine, on attitude, and on confidence. Nearly a decade later, we're still working on the same things. Great putting isn't something you suddenly "get" and thereafter always have. It's a long-term challenge that you have to work on every day.

Doc didn't concern himself much with the mechanical aspects of my routine. As it happens, I have just a couple of physical keys I concentrate on when I practice. I try to keep my grip pressure light and consistent. I try to make sure the ball is positioned in the same place every time, just inside my left heel. Doc helped me realize that the particular mechanical elements I chose weren't as important as doing them consistently and believing in them.

We worked on ways to build confidence. As you'll read later on, Doc has some firm ideas about practice. He and I both believe that when you practice with a ball and a hole, it's vital to see the ball going into the hole. This means a heavy emphasis on practicing short putts. As a general rule, I spend a little time working on longer putts, to maintain my touch. But I spend hours at a time working on five-footers. As a result, I've become a really good putter from six or eight feet on into the hole. This benefits my whole game. I hit my longer putts more confidently, since I'm not worried about making the next one if I miss. I make birdies when I hit my chips and approach shots close.

We've worked longest on my attitude. This has been a gradual process with me. Some of it I've worked out by myself and some of it I've worked out with the help of Doc's advice. I'm still working on it. By way of an interim report, I can tell you that you must love putting if you want to be a great putter. You must always look forward to the challenge of holing the next putt. At the same time, you can't get wrapped up in putting statistics, or whether other people think you're a great putter, or how many putts fall. Even when you read them and stroke them perfectly, putts can miss for a lot of reasons, beginning with imperfect turf. So you have to set other standards for great putting—following your routine, observing your practice habits, maintaining your attitude. If you can honestly tell yourself that you're meeting those standards, then you're putting well.

I'd been a very good putter when I was a kid. But as I got bigger and was able to hit it longer, I focused more and more on the full swing. In high school and college, I'd characterize myself as a mediocre putter. That, of course, wasn't good enough to take me where I wanted to go in golf. You have to hit the ball well to win on the Tour. But there are a lot of players out there who hit it well. Week in, week out, the Tour becomes a putting contest. You're not going to have any success if you're not a great putter. There's no way around it.

To get from where I was when I turned pro to where I was when I shot 59 took a lot of thought, a lot of time, and a lot of work. Somewhere along the way, I had to shed a fear of failure when I putted. I can't tell you exactly when it happened. But gradually I found that I was coming to enjoy the moments when I walked onto a green and sized up a tough putt. Gradually, I learned to care less about whether that putt went in and more about whether I had done everything I could to give it a chance to go in.

I won't tell you that nowadays I have my mind exactly where it should be on every putt that I make. No golfer does. There are days when you hit it inside ten feet on each of the first six holes and don't make any of the putts. It's very easy to get down on yourself on such days. The difference now is that I can catch myself when my attitude wavers and get it back to where it should be sooner.

If you read this book carefully and absorb what it teaches, you can start to develop those abilities as well. You probably won't shoot 59. But sometime soon, late in a round that means something to you, you may find yourself sinking a putt your opponent was sure you'd miss. Flustered, he might even miss a putt that you thought he'd make. The match will turn. I can tell you from experience, there are few sweeter feelings to be had on a golf course.

The Heart of the Game

Putting—a game within a game—might justly be said to be the most important part of golf.

—BOBBY JONES

As the last twosome approached the 72nd green of the 1998 Nissan Open, not many people in Los Angeles gave my friend and client Billy Mayfair much chance to win. Tiger Woods, playing a group ahead of Billy, had just birdied the final hole to take a one-stroke lead. Tiger was charging. He had birdied three of the last four holes.

The Nissan Open that year was played at Valencia Country Club, and the 18th hole was a long par-5. Billy had not birdied it all week and he did not reach it in two strokes on this occasion. He hit his three-wood into a bunker to the right of the green. But Billy then hit a nice explosion shot to about five feet. He made that putt to force a play-off.

Even then, it was all but assumed that Tiger would win the play-off, which began on the same par-5. Tiger hits the ball much longer than Billy, whose length off the tee is about average for the PGA Tour. Even those who understood that good putting is much more important than length off the tee found reason to favor Tiger: Billy Mayfair has a very unorthodox putting stroke, the kind of stroke that television commentators love to criticize, love to say won't hold up under pressure.

That putting stroke was what initially brought Billy and me together.

Billy grew up in Phoenix. From the time he started playing golf, he enjoyed putting. He had little choice. His parents weren't wealthy and when they dropped him off at a municipal golf course called Papago Park, they couldn't give him money for greens fees or range balls. The only thing a kid could do for free at Papago Park was putt and chip around the big, crowned practice green.

So Billy did, five days a week after school. He developed into a very good putter. Even though he never hit the ball enormous distances, he won a lot of junior tournaments. He won the U.S. Public Links. He won the U.S. Amateur.

He did all of this with the idiosyncratic putting stroke he'd developed at Papago Park. Billy did not take the putter straight back and bring it straight through the ball. He drew the club back outside the target line—the line he intended for the ball to travel as it left the putter blade. As he started his forward stroke, it looked as if he would pull every putt to his left. But at the last instant, Billy straightened his blade until it was perpendicular to the target line. And he made a lot of putts that way, even though the purists who saw him insisted he was cutting the ball, coming across it from right to left.

Billy, of course, didn't grow up knowing many purists at Papago Park. All he knew was that he had a putting stroke that got the ball in the hole. He assumed it was a stroke that went straight up and down the line of the putt. Why wouldn't he?

When Billy got out on the Tour in 1989, he did quite well. He made enough money to keep his playing card in 1989 and moved up to twelfth on the money list in 1990. But then he started to slip. He developed problems with his short game, especially his putting.

One reason, Billy now thinks, is the way Tour courses are equipped. Every one of them has a big practice range with grass tees. On every practice range there is an unlimited supply of fresh golf balls—real ones, not range balls. For a kid from Papago Park who could never afford to hit all the balls he wanted, this was all but irresistible. Billy started to spend more of his practice time working on his full swing.

At the same time, he started to listen to the critics of his putting stroke. There were so many of them he decided they had to be right, and he set about trying to give himself a classic putting stroke, straight back and straight through. This was what he thought he needed to break into the ranks of tournament winners.

A player who starts spending too much time on his full swing and not enough on his wedges and chips will soon find himself facing longer putts for par. Even the best players hit, on average, only thirteen or so greens per round. Five times a round, they have to get up and down, and if their short game isn't sharp they're going to be looking at a lot of six- and seven-foot putts they feel they have to make.

If they do this at the same time they're thinking about changing their putting stroke, thinking about taking the blade straight back and forth, they will soon find themselves in trouble. If you're obsessed with some model of the perfect stroke, the first time you miss a putt you think you should have made, you're going to start having doubts about your stroke. Pretty soon, you'll be riven with doubt, as self-conscious as a teenager wearing a new outfit he thinks the others kids deem ugly. And you'll be just as awkward.

In fact, when Billy first came to see me in 1991, he told me he had developed a case of the yips. His scores were going up. He was in danger of losing his card.

What he had, I thought, was not the yips. It was a case of misplaced priorities and a way of thinking that wasn't working on the putting green. I suggested that Billy stop trying to fix his putting stroke. It had never been broken. In trying to fix it, he'd lost his focus on the true business at hand on the green, which is rolling the ball into the hole. I told him I didn't care whether he cut the ball when he putted. I didn't care whether he stroked his putts standing on his head. I just wanted him to think about his target and let the putt go. I wanted him to rediscover the practice priorities he'd had as a kid and spend more time working on his wedges and his chipping.

Billy did. He went on to win his first Tour event in 1993 and to build a solid career for himself. He won the Tour Championship in 1995 at Southern Hills on some of the fastest greens in the country.

All of that history was on my mind as I watched that Nissan Open play-off begin. I think it was on Billy's, too.

"I knew Tiger would have an advantage on a par-five," he told me later. "But then he drove into the rough and I knew he wasn't going to be able to reach it in two. That meant the hole was probably going to be decided with wedge shots and putts. I thought to myself, 'Okay, Tiger. The game's on my court now.'"

Billy Mayfair reaffirmed, in that moment, his knowledge of one of the abiding truths about putting. The challenge of making a putt to win, to set a personal record, is what golf is all about. That's why professional golfers practice putting as much as they do—because they want to savor the joy of meeting that challenge. The best and smartest of them realize something else as well. Putting is fun.

Billy drove into the fairway and hit his second shot about eighty-five yards from the green. Tiger couldn't reach the green from the rough. He left his second thirty yards away.

Billy's wedge was lovely to watch. It hit about eight feet behind the hole and spun back, coming to rest about six feet away. Tiger hit his pitch past the hole and left himself a fifteen-foot birdie putt.

Tiger's putt was a good one, but it slid past the hole. He sank to his knees, chagrined.

Billy used the time he had while Tiger went through his putting routine. He walked around his putt, checked out everything he could see. But he had known from the time he stepped onto the green what this putt was going to do. It was not quite on the same line as the putt he'd made on the 72nd hole, but it was close. It would be uphill. It would be straight.

"When you're putting really well," he told me later, "you see a line. It's like a baseball player who's hitting really good and says the ball looks like it's barely moving. Your vision is different. I saw my line, just right of dead straight. Uphill. I had a pretty good idea in the back of my mind how hard to hit it."

Billy had the wisdom, as he paced about and continued to inspect the green, not to let anything change this solid first impression. Instead, his observation only strengthened his initial read.

Then it was his turn. There were a lot of things he could have thought about. He could have thought about the fact that he had last won a tournament three seasons before. He could have thought about how impressive Tiger had been ten months previously in winning the Masters by twelve strokes. He could have thought about what would happen on the next hole if he missed his putt. He could have thought about the statistics that show that Tour players make only about half of their six-footers. He could have thought about his nerves.

Fortunately, he didn't. Billy was experienced. He knew that

the nerves that accompany a PGA Tour play-off were not something to fear. They were something to welcome. He knew that all the hours of practice had been spent precisely to help him get to a spot where his nerves would jangle.

"All I really thought about," he told me later, "was making sure that I did my routine and saw my target well. I let the putt go."

His target was just a bit to the right of the center of the hole. When he's putting well, Billy tells me, he seems to see everything in slow motion. The ball leaves the putter blade and rolls like a big, heavy beach ball. It is as if he can see every revolution it makes, watch it bump gently over each blade of grass.

This time, everything went slowly. The ball rolled ponderously but inexorably. It was dead straight. He knew from the instant he struck it that his touch had been good. It was a nice, firm hit. He watched the ball cover the target point he'd chosen and fall into the cup. An instant later, pandemonium erupted and Billy felt a deep sense of satisfaction.

"You don't get too many chances to beat Tiger," he told me. "And when you do have a chance, you want to take it."

I love the way Billy handled the situation. He wanted to beat Tiger Woods. But he was able to discipline his thinking enough to shove that thought out of his field of focus, along with all other distracting ideas. He thought only of seeing the target he wanted and letting the putt roll. That was why he made the putt.

. . .

I RECOUNT THIS story not solely because I enjoy looking back on a triumphant moment for a nice guy who works hard at his game and deserves everything he gets—though I do.

I recount it because it shows so much about the subject of this book—loving putting, enjoying putting, making putts, making putts that matter, making putts to win. In the pages that follow, I'm going to use Billy's story, and the stories of many other golfers, on and off the professional tours, to tell you how to become a good putter, even a great putter.

I offer this assurance to you: If you can absorb the principles in this book and put them into practice the way Billy Mayfair did, you are going to become a much better putter than most of the people around you, unless, by chance, the people around you are the other members of the Ryder Cup team. You're never going to putt worse than decently. And on your good days, you will putt very well indeed.

Most golf instruction books pay scant attention to putting. They start with the fundamentals of the full swing. They add putting as an afterthought. Some of the classics of instructional literature don't even address putting.

I never thought about golf that way, in part because I came to golf after years spent in other sports. As a kid and a college student, I played basketball and lacrosse. As the director of sports psychology at the University of Virginia, I coached athletes in the gamut of intercollegiate sports. Twenty years ago, when golfers started coming to me and asking for help with their game, I was able to look at golf with relatively fresh eyes.

I knew that in any sport, there were fundamental skills that good coaches emphasized in their teaching and insisted their players execute. In basketball, for instance, I knew that every great team had a good attitude, rebounded well, played defense well, and shot free throws well. Those skills separated them from the merely good teams and the less-than-good ones. A merely good team wins on nights when its shooters are hot. Great teams win on nights when they don't shoot well, because they always play defense, rebound, and shoot free throws. And they always take the floor with a good attitude.

When I started studying golfers, it became immediately apparent to me that good putting was the functional equivalent of good defense, good rebounding, and good shooting from the foul line. I noticed that even the great players didn't bring their best swings to the course more than half the time. But the great ones almost always found ways to turn in a low score anyway. They did it with their short game and their putting. When I started working with golfers, I insisted that they spend a lot of time developing imagination and touch with their scoring clubs, their wedges and putters. At the time, this was not a fashionable view among golf instructors. Most instructors had spent their lives trying to figure out the full swing. They were in love with the mechanics of the driver and the seven-iron. That's what they wanted to teach, and that's what they encouraged their pupils to practice.

That emphasis has shifted in the past two decades, though not necessarily because of my influence. It's the simple logic of the game. No matter how skilled you are with the long clubs, you're going to make roughly 40 percent of your shots with your putter. Moreover, on the PGA and LPGA tours, it's very difficult to separate yourself from the pack by improving your ball striking. Everybody out there can hit the ball well when he or she is on. The putting game is the place to look if you want to get a competitive advantage, to shave the stroke or so per round that makes the difference between making cuts and missing cuts, between winning tournaments and not winning them.

The rule applies no matter what type of golf you play. If you're an average male player who keeps a handicap, you generally shoot in the high 80s or low 90s. Once in a while you make a routine par, hitting your driver into the fairway, your iron onto the green, and getting down in two putts. Far more often, you're around the green in regulation figures, but you're not on it. To make par, you need to wedge the ball onto the green and make a putt. Most often, you don't do that. You probably three-putt more often than you get up and down. But if you putted well, your scores would drop.

In fact, good players know that putting accounts for even more of their success or failure than the strokes on the scorecard would indicate. Seve Ballesteros once explained that on days when he felt that his putting was on, when he could count on getting the ball into the hole when he had to, his whole game changed. Off the tee and on his approach shots, good putting gave him a cocky, go-for-broke attitude that was essential to the production of his best shots. He could afford to be cocky because he knew his putter would rescue him when he made a mistake. Conversely, when Seve felt his putting was off, his whole game suffered. He got tight and careful with his long clubs. He started trying to steer the ball. His good shots turned mediocre and his bad shots turned disastrous.

Good putting helps your golf game the way a strong foundation works for a house. If you putt well, it's easier to hit your wedges and chips. If you can hit your wedges and chips, you'll hit your irons more freely. And if you're confident about your irons, it will help your tee shots.

I like to see players not only accept the importance of putting but revel in it. The ideal golfing temperament would instinctively love putting. A golfer with this ideal temperament would feel a quiet surge of joy every time he stepped onto a putting green. He would think, Oh, good! Now we get to putt! This is where I come to life, this is where I can express my imagination and artistry, this is where I can kick some butt!

Very few people manage to maintain that sort of attitude throughout their golfing careers. A lot of kids seem to have it. But there are socialization pressures at work in golf that want them to become cautious, careful, and eventually fearful about their putting. Over the many years of a golfer's life, it's easy to succumb.

All too many players feel a sense of dread as they walk toward a green, much as they might if they were walking into a dentist's office. They think that nothing good can happen to them there. If they've reached the green in regulation figures, they worry about three-putting and wasting the good shots that got them there. If they have a good birdie chance, they worry about blowing it. If they've struggled just to reach the green, big numbers float through their brains.

If you wonder whether this describes you, let me ask a clarifying question. How often do you look at a couple of three-foot putts and find yourself saying to your opponent, "Good-good?"

This kind of thinking can afflict even the greatest of players. Ben Hogan was one example. When he was winning tournaments, Hogan wrote and spoke of putting with equanimity, as an integral part of the game that could be handled with the right measures of practice, concentration, and relaxation. But as he got older, and his ball striking became virtually flawless, Hogan's attitude toward putting changed. He began to see it as an injustice that putting counted for so much in tournament golf. He began to loathe putting. Once, late in his career, Hogan played a pretournament practice round with the young Billy Casper, who was one of the best putters of all time. During the round, Hogan played his usual immaculate shots from tee to green. He made nearly no putts that mattered. Casper, meanwhile, was all over the golf course with his long shots. But he putted brilliantly. When the round was over, Casper had something like a 66 and Hogan something like 71. Hogan owed Casper some money. As he paid off his lost bet, Hogan sourly told Casper, "If you couldn't putt, you'd be selling hot dogs behind the tenth green."

Hogan, perhaps, thought he was putting Casper in his place,

thought he was making the point that he had a much better golf swing than Casper. What he was really saying was, "I can't play this game anymore." Any golfer whose improved ball striking becomes an excuse for hating to putt is in danger of wasting all the time he's devoted to his full swing.

I see this syndrome threatening many of the successful professionals I work with. Typically, they made it to the PGA or LPGA Tour by first learning how to get the ball in the hole. Many of them, like Billy Mayfair, spent much of their childhood hanging around a putting green. Dottie Pepper tells me that when she was a girl, she'd get on her bike on summer mornings just after dawn. She'd go to a golf course near her home called McGregor Links and go out to the 16th green. She knew that the first players wouldn't tee off till the sun had been up for an hour or so. They wouldn't reach the 16th for several hours after that. That gave her lots of time, and she used it to chip, putt, play sand shots, and putt some more. When the first golfers reached the 16th tee, she raked the traps and took off, only to return hours later for more putting in the twilight.

Quite often, as Billy Mayfair did, this kind of player finds that his arrival on the Tour is a great opportunity to work on his full swing, perhaps the best such opportunity he's ever had. He no longer has to devote time to school. There are no restrictions on how many range balls he can hit. He has access to the best swing teachers in the world. Quite commonly, these players become better, more consistent ball strikers at thirty than they were at twenty-two.

But this only puts more pressure on their putting. They can't help noticing that just as much as it did when they were juniors, putting determines success in professional tournaments. Most of them boil down to putting contests. They realize that putting is almost the only culprit keeping them from the success they've dreamed of since they were kids. This can poison their attitude toward putting, turning them from a kid who naturally putted well into a middle-aged man, like Ben Hogan became, who makes sour remarks about someone else's putting success.

My job, with the players I work with personally, as well as with the readers of this book, is to make sure that doesn't happen. It's to help you develop a great putting mind if you've never had one and to help you preserve it if you grew up being a fine putter. It's to help you embark on a lifelong love affair with putting. With such a mind, you can become an excellent putter.

Without it, you might as well stay on the practice range, because your real game is hitting balls. It isn't playing golf. Golf is a game of scoring. If you want to score, you must putt. If you want to score well, you must putt well. It's as simple as that.

Let me assure you, this isn't impossible. All athletic skills have mental and physical components. Some events—the uneven parallel bars, for instance—require highly developed physical skills. Putting isn't a complicated physical skill. Compared to the uneven parallel bars, it's a snap. If you can walk and roll a ball with your hands, or throw it underhand to a partner, you can handle the physical challenge of putting. Putting is primarily a mental challenge, and the mental side of putting requires some effort, some thought, and some discipline. But if you're reading this book, you have all the tools you need. You can do what so many of the greats of the game have done. You can build your game from the green back toward the tee and have the sweet satisfaction of seeing your scores drop as a result. Or you can continue to fear and dread putting.

The choice is yours.

The Putter Jack Nicklaus Sees in the Mirror

You have to feel that you are a great putter to be one. If you start to tell yourself that you can't putt, you can bet your bottom peso that you won't be able to get it in the hole from three feet.

—LEE TREVINO

A FEW YEARS AGO, I WAS INVITED TO SPEAK AT A FUND-RAISING DINner for the golf program at Georgia Tech. Jack Nicklaus, whose son Michael was then attending Tech, was the featured speaker. I was, of course, eager to hear anything he had to say about golf and the way he played it.

One remark Jack made struck both me and the members of the audience. He was speaking about facing a crucial putt on the last hole of a tournament.

"I have never three-putted the last hole of a tournament or missed from inside five feet on the last hole of a tournament," Jack said. He continued with his talk.

That was more than one member of the audience, a man in

his sixties, was able to bear. When question time came, he stood up.

"Uh, Mr. Nicklaus," he said, "I really enjoyed your talk. But the statement you made about never three-putting the last green of a tournament or never missing from inside five feet on the last hole of a tournament—well, I was watching you in the Senior PGA just last month and I distinctly remember you missed a three-footer on the last hole."

"Sir, you're wrong," Jack said firmly. "I have never three-putted the last hole of a tournament or missed inside five feet on the last hole of a tournament."

"But, Mr. Nicklaus," the man objected. "I have it on tape. I could send it to you. Lee Trevino was in the broadcast booth and he said you never used to miss short putts but now you miss them to the right sometimes and then you missed an entire cup to the right—"

"There's no need to send me anything, sir," Jack interrupted him. "I was there. I have never three-putted the last green of a tournament or missed from inside five feet on the last green of a tournament."

Jack finished his talk and headed for the airport where his jet was parked. He has a busy schedule.

But the questioning man lingered, and he approached me. "Dr. Rotella," he said, "what's wrong with Nicklaus? Why can't he just admit it? You're the psychology expert. Can you explain it?"

I asked the man whether he played golf.

"Yes," he said.

"What's your handicap?" I asked.

"About sixteen," he said.

"And if you missed a short putt on the last hole of a tournament, you'd remember it and admit it," I observed.

"Of course," he confirmed.

"So let me get this straight," I said. "You're a sixteen handicap, and Jack Nicklaus is the greatest golfer ever, and you want Jack to think like you?"

The man had no answer.

THE POINT OF the story, of course, is not whether Jack Nicklaus has ever missed a putt on the last hole of a tournament. Of course he has. The point is that Jack's memory works differently from the memories of a lot of golfers.

We are raised in a culture of red marks. When kids take math tests, their papers come back with a red **x** next to the problems they answered incorrectly. The child is taught to review his mistake carefully, to remember it, and not to make it again. And so it goes through life. Quite naturally, therefore, we are people who tend to dwell on our mistakes. We remember them. We replay them in our minds. Once in a while, in some endeavors, I suppose this does some good. If you paint houses for a living, and you climb to the top of your scaffold and discover you've forgotten your paintbrushes, it's probably not a bad thing to remember your carelessness and remind yourself forever after to bring your brushes.

But in putting, as Mark Twain once observed in another context, the inability to forget is infinitely more devastating than the inability to remember. In that sense, Jack Nicklaus was indeed a talented putter. He had selective amnesia. He was able to block from his mind all the missed putts. He kept and replayed the memories of made putts. He was able to retain a firm belief that the next one was going in the hole. He was able to think of himself as a great putter.

Because he thought that way, he was able to *be* a great putter. As William James, the pioneering American psychologist, shrewdly stated in the nineteenth century, people tend to become what they think about themselves. This simple truth is the basis for much of what I do as a sports psychologist.

It also points to the first step in any serious program to make yourself a better putter. You must examine yourself and your attitude toward putting. You have to assess your self-image regarding putting.

Are you the sort of player who gripes and complains all the time about his putting? When you step onto a green, are you glum and fearful, expecting the worst? Do you silently pray that your opponents will concede your next putt? Have you decided that you simply were born without putting talent, and this will be your burden to bear till the end of your golfing days?

If so, you need a new attitude. And the first step in getting a new attitude about putting is to change the way your memory works.

When I suggest this to players, I often hear this objection. "Whoa, Doc. I didn't wake up one morning and decide I was a bad putter just for the heck of it. I'm a realist. I think I'm a bad putter because I've missed a lot of putts! I can't just decide I'm a good putter when I know I'm not."

First of all, it's foolish to evaluate your putting if your mind has been holding you back. You may well have missed some putts in the past. But if you attempted them with a mind full of doubt, if you tried to steer the ball rather than let the stroke happen naturally—in short, if you putted with the wrong attitude—then those misses aren't relevant to the caliber of putter you can be. What would you think of a football coach who told you you weren't fast enough to play if your time trial occurred when you had a sprained ankle? You'd think he was unfair. Yet people routinely decide they're bad putters on the basis of putts they've missed when they've been carrying around a handicap far more damaging than a sprained ankle.

Second, many people use "realism" as an excuse for negative thinking. Jack Nicklaus has undoubtedly missed more putts than your entire Saturday foursome combined. But Jack either chooses not to remember the putts he's missed or he's blessed with a natural tendency to forget them. Jack remembers instead the putts he's made, the putts that will help him be confident the next time he has a critical ten-footer.

In that he's like many other great athletes. Michael Jordan used to say that he never pondered the mistakes he'd made in a basketball game for more than ten or fifteen minutes after the game was over. In that time, he analyzed what went wrong and learned whatever he could learn from it. Then he focused his mind on getting ready for the next game. Other players hung their heads for hours and berated themselves for mistakes. Jordan saw that they were destroying themselves. He never did that.

It's not easy to discipline your mind the way Michael Jordan and Jack Nicklaus did. But the fact that it isn't easy doesn't mean it's impossible. It means that there's something you can do through strength of mind that will separate you from the vast majority of your competitors, just as it did for Nicklaus and Jordan.

There's nothing worse for your putting than dwelling on the putts you've missed. In fact, it's like multiplying the effects of a missed putt. If you lie awake after a bad round, replaying missed putts in your brain, it's psychologically no different from actually going out on a green and missing them again, over and over. You're training yourself to believe that you can't putt.

But, in truth (or reality, if that's a term you prefer) if you've played golf any length of time, you've made a lot of putts. You could remember those putts. How about that twelve-footer that saved par the last time you played? Or the four-footer that you had to make to win a Nassau against your buddies? Or that curling, twenty-foot birdie putt you sank a week ago? Why not remember those?

You can if you choose to. Training the memory is possible. Try this. The next few times you play, make a conscious effort not to add up the three-putts you made or dwell on the five-footer that lipped out. Forget them. They're gone. Instead, pick the best three putts you made in that round. Think about them. The next morning, when you wake up, remember them. Relive them.

If you do that after every round you'll be on your way to developing at least one important part of your golf game into the equal of Jack Nicklaus's.

CHANGING THE WAY you remember is half the battle in changing the way you perceive yourself as a putter. And changing your self-perception is half the battle in developing from a mediocre putter to a great one.

I am constantly amazed at how frequently golfers cripple themselves with poor self-perceptions. They decide that great putters are born, not made. They decide they lost in the genetic lottery. They have no talent, no ability to putt well. From there, it's a short step to thinking that there's not really much point in trying to improve, because they're never going to be good putters. They're comfortable with the way they've always thought on the greens. It hasn't worked for them, of course, but they're used to it, and changing would require effort and effort wouldn't pay off anyway. They take a perverse pride in describing themselves as bad putters. They sit in the grill after their rounds, their wallets lighter, and grouse about how they couldn't buy a putt, can't ever make a putt. They rehash all the putts they've missed, as if to corroborate the thesis that when it comes to putting, they have neither skill nor luck—except for bad luck.

They embody the self-fulfilling prophecy. They persuade themselves that they have no talent at putting, no skill, no luck. And then when they actually putt, their brains naturally assume they have no chance to make it. It's true that they have no chance—no chance to get into the relaxed, confident state of mind that is conducive to good putting.

It's my job to convince such people that even if they haven't had much success in the past with their putting, their perception of themselves should be governed not by what they've done, but by what they'd like to do. But getting this idea across is not easy.

For one thing, many golfers find poor putting to be a convenient rationale for failing to play well. It gives them a tolerable excuse. These are the sorts of people who claim that they hit the ball very well, but they never win, or even play to their potential, because they can't putt. Implicit in what they say is the notion that ball striking is real golf, and putting is a sissy add-on, and if they're not good at the sissy add-on part, well, hey, can Jean-Claude Van Damme do the tango?

They remind me of a guy who grows a scraggly, miserable-looking, unattractive goatee. Then he uses the goatee to explain his inability to get women to go out with him. He'd have dates, he implies, but not many women are hip enough to appreciate his manly growth. In truth, of course, he's afraid that women will reject him even if he looks his best. He maintains the goatee to protect himself from that disconcerting prospect. In much the same way, people can find it useful to cultivate a perception that they are lousy putters.

On the other hand, consider the player who believes he's a great putter. He thinks back pleasantly to the good putts he's made. He never gripes, he never moans. He never lets himself be thrown by something like a bumpy green. When people ask how he's putting, he usually responds, "Great!" If he didn't make a lot of putts in his last round, he'll say, "Great. I feel like I'm due to hole a bunch of them."

Because of such players' self-perception, it's easier for them to stay in practice. They *like* going out on the practice green. It gives them a little chance to show off. It's the same syndrome that explains why people in the best physical condition are the ones most likely to be found in gyms. It's because they like the shape they're in and they like the chance to show off what their bodies can do.

These players tend to be able to monitor their own attitudes the same way an athlete monitors his weight. They catch themselves whenever they find their attitudes souring. They make the necessary adjustment when they're only a little bit off. They have a much easier time getting and staying confident than the player who periodically throws a pity party for himself and wallows in his own bile.

Because of their self-perception, players with good attitudes find it much easier to putt in competition. They don't step up to a long first putt thinking fearfully of a possible three-putt. They step up to a long putt calmly and confidently. When they have a testy little five-footer for par, they don't feel obliged to give themselves a putting seminar before they stroke the ball, in the process tightening their muscles and spoiling their rhythm. They're more likely to step up to the ball, go through their putting routine, and stroke it gracefully and accurately.

Because of their self-perception, they are immune to doubts and fears about their technique. In fact, they tend to think the rest of the world should copy them.

When I was a kid, the greatest putter in the world was probably Bobby Locke, of South Africa. Locke married a woman from my hometown, Rutland, Vermont. In the summers, I'd see him once in a while at the Rutland Country Club, where I caddied. Sometimes I carried his bag or shagged balls for him.

Locke had a very unorthodox, highly personal putting stroke. On his backswing, he flexed his wrists and hooded the face of his putter in a way that you would never see on the Tour today. He liked to think that he could spin the ball different ways for different putts, "hooking" right-to-left putts and "slicing" those that broke the other way. Despite all that, Bobby Locke could putt.

Locke, of course, didn't think his putting style was unorthodox. He thought his putting style was eminently logical and reasonable. He figured it was the rest of the world that had a problem. In that way, he reminds me of Billy Mayfair when Billy is thinking well about his putting.

That's the way good putters see themselves. That's why they're good putters.

I'm not trying to suggest that changing your putting self-image is easy. It's not. It can be difficult. But improving at golf is not supposed to be easy. If it were, golf wouldn't be the game it is. Welcome the fact that it's hard and that most people won't do it. If you need an incentive, consider this: Thinking the way you have always thought will almost certainly assure that you putt the way you have always putted.

Try this bit of mental practice. Spend fifteen minutes each night thinking of nothing but making putts. Relive putts you've made and savor the sight and the feeling again. Think about putts you might have in your next round of golf. See them going in the hole.

As with any visualization exercise, this one won't help you if you don't apply yourself to it wholeheartedly. Try to imagine as richly and precisely as you can how the grass felt under your feet, how the hole looked, how the ball rolled, how it sounded as it plunked into the cup. Remember the way your eyes and brain interacted, the way your body felt as you stroked the putt. If you can do it, fifteen minutes of this is worth as much as or more than the same amount of time practicing actual putts, particularly if you've mastered the physical fundamentals.

Change the way you converse about putting. Banish any gripes and complaints from your vocabulary. Change the subject if someone in the group wants to moan about putting. If someone asks you about your putting, say it's fine. Tell him about a putt you've made or tell him you expect to break out with a bunch of birdie putts any day.

Some people tell me that they're just not comfortable being Little Orphan Annie about their putting. Visualization exercises are a little too touchy-feely for them. They'd rather not talk optimistically about their putting because they think it's boastful, or they're afraid their opponents might mock them if they later miss a putt. Well, you can't be successful at putting if you're letting fear of missed putts dictate your behavior. But if you're the quiet, modest type who was taught not to boast, that's all right. The only rule is that you not entertain negative ideas about your putting. You can cultivate a laconic shrug of the shoulders for use when the conversation turns to your putting, or putting in general.

But on the green, where it counts, make sure you're thinking like Jack Nicklaus and Bobby Locke.

How Good Putters Think

On every putt, see the ball going into the hole with your mind's eye.

—GARY PLAYER

GOLFERS GENERALLY DON'T BECOME MY CLIENTS WHEN THEY'RE PLAYing the best golf of their careers. They come to me when they have problems with their games. Hal Sutton was no exception.

Hal had once been touted as the successor to Jack Nicklaus. He won early in his professional career and, it seemed, easily. At the age of twenty-five, he led the Tour in earnings and captured a major championship, the PGA. But after a time the victories stopped, for many reasons. One of those reasons was putting.

Hal was the sort of player who could hit the ball very accurately. He was usually near the top of the Tour statistics in hitting greens in regulation. But once he got on the green, his

How Good Putters Think • 29

thoughts tended to be less clear, less certain than they were on the tee or in the fairway. If he was fifteen feet away, he told me he felt as if he had one side of his brain telling him to make the putt, while the other was saying, "Don't waste that good drive and good iron shot by three-putting." He'd start to feel the anguish of the three-putt before he'd even hit his first putt. So, of course, his first putts were sometimes timid and cautious. Or, if he'd been timid and cautious on the previous hole, he could be much too bold. When we started working together, Hal already realized he had to get rid of that negative, doubting voice that he was hearing.

As I do with most players, I tried to impress Hal with the importance of a routine for both long shots and putts, a routine that emphasized looking at the target and letting it go—that is, making the stroke freely and confidently. Hal intuitively grasped what I was telling him when it came to long shots. He hunts as a hobby. He could relate what I was telling him to hunting. When he hunted, he saw a target and, without thinking much about it, aimed his gun and fired. That image helped him develop a free, confident routine on the tee and in the fairway.

On the green, it was harder. One day I asked him to try a little experiment. We were in Charlottesville and we went over to the golf course at Keswick Hall, a resort outside of town. I asked Hal to play a round with me using his normal routine for long shots. But on the greens, I wanted him to putt with his eyes not on the ball but on the target.

Hal was skeptical, but he agreed. He tried it on the practice green for half an hour. Then he putted the entire round with this altered routine. Normally, he would line himself and his club up, look at the ball, look at the target, look at the ball again, and stroke the putt. This time, he used the same routine, but instead of returning his eyes to the ball after his look at the target, he kept his gaze fixed on where he wanted the ball to go. He stroked the putt seeing the target, not the ball.

The result is framed and hangs in the grill at Keswick Hall. It's a scorecard showing that Hal set the course record that day with a 63.

Now, I'm not suggesting that anyone can set a course record if he putts with his eyes on the target instead of the ball. Hal never used this method in a tournament. It was an exercise to help him understand the feeling of being focused on the target just as much when he putted as he was when he hit longer shots. I think it's a useful experiment for any golfer to try and I often encourage players I work with to do it. I think it would be very interesting to see what would happen if a group of them gave it a real test in competition. They don't, primarily because they're skittish about the possibility of mishitting or actually whiffing a putt.

The exercise is helpful to a lot of players because it dramatizes the way good putters think. It's a little bit like taking a child's head between your hands and directing his gaze precisely where you want him to look. In this case, it focuses the golfer's attention where it should be—the target.

How Good Putters Think

• • •

LET'S SUPPOSE, FOR a moment, that someone had invented a device that could read minds. You could aim this device at anyone's head, and a computer would print out what the individual was thinking.

Here's what you might see if you aimed this device at the head of someone who sees himself as a poor putter.

My putter blade is a little off line, let's adjust it. . . . If I miss this I'll probably lose the hole. . . . I've already three-putted twice today, don't want to do that again. . . . Dammit, it's only four feet, I SHOULD make it. . . . Of course, last Saturday I blew a three-footer . . . hmm, the ground under my feet feels like it's got a little bit of slope to it . . . could it really be a straight putt? . . . No, God wouldn't give me a straight putt . . . maybe better play it to break bit left. . . . Why am I always the one who has these four-footers to make and why am I always the one who winds up having to pay for the drinks after the round. . . . Is that a pitch mark I see in my line? This club's gotta get a new superintendent. . . . Wonder if I should hit driver on the next tee or go with the three-wood? This one's gonna be fast, it's downhill . . . don't want to roll it too far past if I miss it . . . all right, now concentrate! Make sure you take the club back straight, perfect stroke now, keep your head still, don't peek. . . .

Here's what you might see if you aimed at the head of a good putter facing the same spot.

My target is that little tuft of raised grass on the lip of the cup.

And that's all you'd see.

A lot of people, at this point, would look at this putative computer screen and object. "Wait a minute," they'd say. "That's all he's thinking? What is he, thick?"

No, the good putter is not thick. But he has a mind so quiet and so clear that it might strike many people as a bit obtuse. In our society, we're been educated to revere thought, to revere the conscious mind. And in some endeavors, that's fine. If you're designing the airplane I'm going to fly in next week, for instance, I want you to be very conscious and to think through everything in detail.

But this cultural pressure makes it difficult for some people to clear their minds. I used to ask students to work on this by spending a short period of time trying to focus their minds on something small and simple, like the top of a ballpoint pen. Look at it, think about its function. But think of nothing else for five minutes or ten minutes, or fifteen minutes. You might want to try this exercise. If you can clear your mind to focus only on the tip of the pen, you can clear it to focus on the target or line when you're putting.

In putting, you want to narrow the focus of your thoughts as much as possible, to shut down a lot of the conscious, thinking parts of the brain, the parts that give instructions. Putting is one of those physical tasks that are best left to the less intellectual, less rational parts of the mind. You don't, for instance, start jogging and consciously think, Better increase my respiration, take more breaths per second to increase my oxygen intake. A subconscious part of your brain takes care of your breathing for you. If you're driving along on a highway and you're talking to someone in the seat next to you, you're easily able to continue the conversation while you pull into the passing lane and overtake a truck. A subconscious part of your brain smoothly handles the driving, allowing you to continue your conversation. In fact, you probably drive more smoothly this way than you would if you stopped talking and paid careful attention to your driving. You certainly drive more smoothly this way than you could when you were just sixteen, driving on a highway for the first time, and carefully using your conscious brain to control every movement.

If you're putting, you'll make your best stroke and hole the most putts if you think only of your target. You won't sink all your putts, of course. Not even putting machines can do that. But you'll sink more putts thinking this way than you will any other way.

I don't know precisely why our bodies work this way. They simply do. I see evidence of it quite frequently. Little kids are often great putters because they simply pick up a putter and roll the ball at the hole. They don't know enough to think their way through the stroke, reminding themselves of all the tips they've had and the lessons they've taken. They just roll it. Older golfers sometimes dramatically improve their putting when they reach a stage in life when they don't worry so much about scores or competitions, or anything else for that matter. They just like seeing the ball roll into the hole.

Some folks understand this intuitively because they haven't been exposed to a lot of the theories and ideas and old wives' tales that abound about putting. Some years ago, shortly after I started counseling golfers, I visited my parents, who were just taking up golf. My mother, Laura, asked curiously what it was that I was telling golfers that they found so helpful they paid me for it.

"A lot of it's about putting, Mom," I said. "I help them to think about the target when they're putting."

"Well, for heaven's sake," she said. "What else would they think about?"

"Mom," I told her, "you'd be amazed."

And she would. Even professional golfers are prone to undermine their own putting with thoughts about their stroke, or making the cut, or keeping their card, or not three-putting. I see this fairly often with Tour pros who let their minds wander from the target for the first thirty holes of a tournament. By that time, they're three or four over par and they figure they're not going to make the cut. So they stop being careful, stop being conscious, start thinking only about their targets, and hole a few birdie putts coming in. Sometimes they make enough putts to survive the cut. Then they go back to undermining themselves on Saturday.

They don't mean to undermine themselves, of course. Some of them don't know that dwelling on the results of putts rather than on the simple act of rolling the ball to a target doesn't help them. They don't know that constantly being aware of the score doesn't help them. Or, if they know these things, they haven't developed the mental discipline to shut those thoughts out of their minds when they putt. They might think that if they lose track of the score and don't worry much about whether the ball goes in the hole, they're not trying hard enough, not giving 100 percent. And how can they compete with Tiger Woods if they're not giving 100 percent?

But it's pretty certain Tiger isn't thinking that way. In the clutch, at least, Tiger is thinking of the target. That's why Tiger's become one of the best clutch putters ever to play the game. As he demonstrated on the final day of the 2000 PGA Championship, when the tournament hangs in the balance, Tiger finds ways to make putts he doesn't necessarily make during the earlier rounds.

I have a theory about why this should be the case. Tiger now is exposed to lots of different ideas about putting. I see and hear things that indicate he's listening to them. He'll talk, for instance, on the day before a tournament about how he's been working on the practice green trying to make his ball roll a particular way—a way that supposedly helps it hold its line and find the hole.

But under pressure, we revert to our dominant habits. Tiger's dominant habit, as far as putting was concerned, was planted in his mind at a very early age by his father. Earl Woods has described how he taught Tiger to putt when Tiger was a toddler. Earl had Tiger put a ball in his right hand and roll it to a hole. Then he had Tiger close his eyes and roll it to the hole again.

He asked Tiger what he'd "seen" after he closed his eyes. Tiger would reply that he'd seen a "picture" of the hole.

Earl taught Tiger always to see that mental picture of the hole before he struck the ball with his putter. He taught him not to worry about the mechanics of the stroke, just to make sure he saw that target in his mind's eye before he putted the ball. He knew that Tiger's brain would take care of the rest more often than not.

It was inspired instruction. When Tiger is in clutch situations, when he falls back on his dominant habit, he's focusing tightly on his target, that picture in his mind. That's why he makes so many clutch putts. Part of Butch Harmon's genius is that, while he's worked on Tiger's full swing, he hasn't tried to change the putting concept Tiger got from his father. A lot of coaches might have fiddled with Tiger's stroke to the point that he got a new and less effective dominant habit. They might have kept Tiger from the success he's had.

Orientation toward the target works because the subconscious brain is capable of quick, accurate adjustments. That's what happens when Billy Mayfair is focused on his target. He unconsciously aims a little left, then squares the blade to the real target line just before his putter strikes the ball—sending it where he wants it to go. Suppose, instead, he was consciously thinking of pushing the putter blade straight through the line. His subconscious mind would be overriden and he'd probably pull his putt to the left. His target orientation makes him a good putter.

• • •

A GOOD PUTTER'S target is never simply the hole. He's always trying to putt the ball into the hole, but the hole is much too big to serve as a good target. The smaller the target you have, the better your brain and body can function in trying to get the ball there. On short putts, you should pick out the smallest target you can focus on. It might be a blade of grass or a discoloration on the edge of the hole. It might be a scuff mark on the white liner inside the hole.

I say that the brain and body "can" function well in reacting to a small target, not that they will automatically do so. Some people, as their target gets smaller, tend to get more careful and controlling with their stroke. They can make a free stroke easily if you tell them simply to putt the ball to nothing. But the smaller the target gets, the tighter they get. Putters have to overcome this. They have to discipline themselves to putt as freely to a small target as they do when they putt to nothing.

On breaking putts, the choice of target varies with individuals, but the target generally won't be in or in many cases even near the hole. I'd teach any new player to make all putts straight putts. How do you do this? Suppose you think that the putt will break about four inches from right to left. Since four inches is the approximate diameter of the cup, measure one cup width from the edge of the hole to the right and pick out a blade of grass or a discoloration there. That's your target. Sometimes, with a downhill putt on a dramatic slope, a player will pick the spot on the green that he considers the apex of the ball's curving journey to the hole. Or it might be the point where a putt reaches the crest of a downslope and starts to go downhill. It doesn't matter. Let the slope of the green and gravity break the ball into the hole.

Some very good players I've worked with have individual peculiarities in this aspect of their putting. If Nick Price has a putt he expects to break six inches, he aims six inches from the hole. But he looks at the hole just before he makes his stroke. Padraig Harrington aims at a spot a foot or so in front of the ball. Somehow, Nick's subconscious mind gets the ball started where he's aiming, not where he's looking. Padraig's subconscious mind gets the putt rolling at the right pace even though he's looking at a target only a foot in front of him. The main thing is that they are both oriented to a target.

OCCASIONALLY, OUR PERCEPTIONS work a little differently. Most players tell me that once in a while, when they start to examine a putt, they see a line. This perception has different looks for different people. Some say it reminds them of the tracks in the morning dew that golf balls sometimes make. Some say it's like a thin line. Some see a wide line. I've also had players tell me they imagine a line of buried ball magnets under the green, drawing their ball inexorably toward the cup.

Some people seem to have a little movie projector running in their minds. They see the ball rolling toward its target and into the hole. Some see a fragment of that—the first two feet of the ball's journey, or the last two feet.

All of these sorts of perceptions are fine, as long as whatever they're imagining—the line, the magnets, etc.—leads to a target.

Don't be concerned if you rarely or never see a line, or if your brain doesn't furnish you with a "coming attractions" clip of the putt you're about to make. That doesn't mean you're not a good putter. It simply means that your brain doesn't work as visually as some other people's. Don't try to force yourself to see a line. Picking out a target and believing that it will work is equally effective.

If you do see a line, don't be afraid to use it. It's probably a very good representation of what the ball will actually do. If you see such lines all the time, count your blessings. It can help you putt more decisively.

There's only one problem that orientation to a line can lead to, and it's analogous to the problem some players have when they select a small target and tighten up. A player can be too careful about trying to start the ball out along the line he has imagined. He can try to steer the blade of the putter along the line.

That doesn't work. Steering the putter, being too careful, strips a player of much of his natural ability and accuracy. It interferes with the purity of the interaction between a target and the nervous system. Human beings are wired to putt best when the golfer simply sees the target and reacts to it with as little conscious thought as possible.

Brad Faxon, who's one of the best putters in the world, is one of those people who generally "sees" a line when he examines a putt. But Brad doesn't try to force the ball along this line. He simply lets the putt go and trusts that his subconscious will get it moving along the line he's "seen."

I often compare it to the way athletes in other sports react to targets. A basketball player doesn't leap into the air, eye the basket, and then ponder how best to set his wrist to get off a good shot. He jumps, sees the target, and lets the shot go. A football quarterback, faced with blitzing linebackers, doesn't give himself a lecture on how to throw tight spirals. He looks to where the receiver is going to be, focuses on that spot, and drills the ball there. That's the way good putters operate, too. Putting well is very athletic.

The analogy to basketball and football targets raises another issue. I sometimes hear television commentators talk about trying to lag a long putt into a three-foot circle around the hole. I have never understood the logic behind this idea. Would a basketball player improve his chances of making a three-point shot if he aimed for the backboard instead of the basket? Would a quarterback do well if he threw the ball somewhere in the general direction of his receiver?

Of course not. Yet I often hear golfers being advised that when they're thirty feet or more from the hole, the best thing to do is draw that imaginary circle around the hole and just try to get the ball into it. I can think of only two reasons for the popularity of this idea. One is that golfers found it easier to make a free, confident stroke if they thought that all they had to do was get the ball into a three-foot circle. The other is that the commentators and teachers themselves thought this way when they were playing tournament golf. This makes an ironic sort of sense. If you try to putt into a three-foot circle, you're only going to increase your margin of error. Instead of being a couple of feet from the hole, your first putts are going to end up four and five feet away. You're going to be missing a few of those second putts. And, if you're a tournament golfer and you three-putt very often, you're soon going to be looking for another line of work—like being a television commentator or teacher.

The advocates of the three-foot circle may think what they really mean is that it's smart to play conservatively, especially in the first few rounds of a tournament. A generation ago, that's what some very good golfers did. Their objective in the first round of a U.S. Open, for instance, was not to "shoot themselves out of it" by turning in a 77 or 78. They didn't really start trying to hole all their putts until the back nine on Sunday afternoon.

Whether or not that was sound strategy thirty years ago, it certainly isn't a winning idea today. Golf, like most sports, has gotten more competitive. A player who shoots even par for the first two or three rounds of a professional event, a major championship, or even an elite amateur competition will quite likely be so far behind the leaders that it doesn't matter what he does on the back nine on Sunday. That's the way tournament golf is nowadays. If you aren't trying to hole every putt you have, you are going to lose to someone who is.

To win in golf today, you have to be prepared to go low at every opportunity. By low, I mean shooting not just in the 60s, but the low 60s. Obviously, to go low a player must be in command of his entire game—driving the ball well, hitting greens, sinking putts. Of the three, the last is the most important. Quite often, professional golfers get their swings grooved well enough that they have a chance to go low. The ones who actually do it are the ones who are able to discipline their minds to think only of the target at every putting opportunity. The ones who fail to go low let other thoughts get in their way. They think that they've already gotten three or four under par, so they ought to be careful and preserve their subpar finish. Or they think they're not good enough to shoot a 64 in competition. Or they think they've used up their birdie putts for the day, as if some government bureaucracy had issued each player the same daily quota.

I work with a player named Tripp Isenhour who's had that problem. When Tripp was at Georgia Tech, he was a good, consistent college golfer. He never shot a high round. He didn't shoot many particularly low rounds either. Once he turned pro, though, he found that shooting a couple of rounds of even par was a good way to have weekends off and go broke fast. Tripp actually quit golf in frustration a few years ago and went to work in his family's Christmas tree business in North Carolina.

When he decided to give professional golf another shot,

Tripp and I worked hard on his attitude toward putting, particularly on thinking of the target and only the target. He had to learn that seeing the target and reacting to it meant that he was doing his best. He had to learn to be content with that, even on days when all of his putts didn't fall, and particularly on days when nothing fell on the first four or five holes. Tripp accepted these ideas. That, along with a serious commitment to fitness, practice, and a lot of other good habits, helped improve his game. He made it to the Buy.com Tour after a year's time. He set his sights on the ultimate goal of becoming a winner on the PGA Tour.

I knew he was getting there when he called and let me know how he'd won the Mississippi Golf Coast Open a few months ago. Tripp shot 70-75 and barely made the cut. In the third round, the field faced miserable weather conditions, wet and windy.

But that was the day Tripp discovered that his game was under control and he had a chance to go low. He seized that opportunity.

He birdied five of the first six holes, sinking putts from four feet to thirty feet. He was seeing his target, having no trouble believing in it. His touch was just right.

"Let's keep it going, keep rolling it to the target," he told himself. "Relax and let it happen."

He fended off thoughts of how far under par he was or what the rest of the field was doing, and where he stood in the tournament. Only later that day, after his round was over, would he learn that just one other player managed to break 70. He just kept seeing his target and rolling his ball to it.

Tripp didn't make all his putts that day. In fact, he lipped out six of them. But his mental discipline stayed intact through all eighteen holes. At day's end, he had a 63. He won that tournament on the strength of that low round. And that victory helped assure him of a promotion to the PGA Tour the following year.

The key to all of that was clearing his mind and thinking only of his target.

Gaining Control by Giving Up Control

I would like to be able to knock in as many putts as Billy does, but even more than that, I would like to be able to act like he does when he's doing it—with an air of unconcern as to whether the putt drops or not.

—Arnold Palmer, speaking of Billy Casper

Unless you've steeped yourself in the history of golf, you've probably never heard of Wild Bill Mehlhorn. Obscurity is the fate of poor putters.

In his day, Bill Mehlhorn may have been as good a striker of the golf ball as ever lived. No less an authority than Ben Hogan said Mehlhorn was the best he'd ever seen from tee to green. If Hogan thought Bill Mehlhorn was the best ball striker he'd ever seen, and most people think Hogan was the best ball striker golf has ever seen, where does that put Mehlhorn?

To Hogan, though, the archetypal Bill Mehlhorn hole was a par-4 they played together in a tournament long ago. Mehlhorn drove the ball beautifully on this hole, long and straight. He striped an iron to within two feet of the cup. And he played his fourth shot from a bunker.

No wonder they called him Wild Bill.

In his old age, Mehlhorn reminisced about his golf career. He recalled that he was one of those players who let his skill at hitting the ball put more and more pressure on his putting, since he knew that it was only putting that separated him from Bobby Jones, Gene Sarazen, and Walter Hagen, the leading golfers of his era. He recalled that on the tee and in the fairways, he was always relaxed and confident. But on the greens, he had a different mentality. He played not with confidence but with desperate desire. This desire drove him to think incessantly about his putting stroke, to try to force himself to putt well.

In the end, that drove him out of tournament golf, despite his lovely full swing. It's a syndrome that, if anything, has grown more widespread in the years since Wild Bill Mehlhorn played tournament golf. I've met many players who fight it.

When I meet with new clients on a practice green it's generally quite easy to persuade them that clearing their minds and thinking only of their targets improves their putting. More often than not, a professional golfer with a clear mind and a focus on a target will hole nearly all of his five-footers, lots of ten- to fifteen-footers, and a fair number of even longer putts. He'll turn to me with a pleased smile and say, "Gee, Doc, I putt really well when you're standing here. I never knew it could be this easy."

It's not.

All too often that player who putted so well on the practice

Gaining Control by Giving Up Control • 47

green will come in after his next tournament round with a 73 or 74 next to his name. He'll tell me that he can't understand what happened to his putting. "I was trying hard, really hard, to clear my mind and think only of my target," he will say. "But it didn't work. No matter how much I was grinding away at it, I still couldn't make any putts."

As soon as I hear the word *grinding,* I have a good idea of what went wrong.

Grinding is one of those concepts that is widespread in sport and, unfortunately, inimical to good putting.

Grinding suggests that someone is doing his utmost to succeed. If he's weight training, he's popping capillaries to make sure he gets that last repetition done. If we're talking about football, we're talking about a team that keeps the ball on the ground, blocks fiercely, runs hard, and scores touchdowns by stringing together four-yard gains up the middle. If we're talking about a student, we're talking about someone who might not have the highest SAT scores in his class, but who closes the library every night because he's going to get into medical school no matter what.

And if he's putting, it suggests that he's trying to *will* the ball into the hole.

I generally admire grinders, and I believe in the transcendent importance of will. Free will is a precious, fundamental part of human nature, the part on which all true accomplishment is based. A strong will is very helpful in putting. But it's helpful only when you're behind the ball, preparing to putt. Will helps you discipline yourself to eliminate distractions and pick out a target. Will helps you work on that part of the putting process until you firmly believe in your target, believe that if you roll the ball to it, the ball will go in the hole. Pat Bradley, who has one of the strongest wills I have ever encountered, told me once that she felt as if her mind was burning a line between the ball and the hole.

But the application of will gets trickier when you are standing over the ball, ready to putt it. In fact, I believe that at that point, will can get in the way. The proper role for a strong will at this stage of putting is to support a firm belief in the golfer's mind that all the preparation is done and the ball will go in the hole if he turns control of the action over to his subconscious. But then free will must exit the stage and leave the scene to other actors.

I have heard players say that they will the ball into the hole, and some of them have been successful putters. I believe that their will helps them focus their attention on their targets and eliminate all other thoughts. But if they then continue to try to force themselves, through an act of will, to hit a perfect putt, I think any success they have is a tribute to their innate ability, their concentration, and their belief in their targets. I think they could putt even better if they stopped being so willful when they stroked their putts.

Paul Azinger is a great example. Long before he ever talked to me about his putting, Paul had been an extremely successful player, winning lots of Tour events, a PGA Championship, and contributing to some memorable and emotional Ryder Cup wins. He displayed the strength of his will again when he battled and defeated cancer.

When we started working together, Paul told me that despite all his success, he'd never actually liked the way his putting felt. To him, it wasn't athletic, free, or easy. He felt that he had an artificial stroke, one that he mechanically forced into the pattern he'd been taught was classic—a short backswing, a long follow-through, and a putter head that accelerated through the ball.

I could see that tension, that artificiality, in his stroke. In fact, I could hear it. Forced strokes look different from free strokes, and the contact between putter and ball actually sounds different.

I told Paul that his putting didn't seem to fit with the rest of his game. When he was in a bunker, for instance, he hit beautifully athletic, relaxed shots that had more than once gone into the cup to win a tournament for him. How, I asked him, did he think about his bunker shots?

"It's like night and day from my putting stroke," he said. "I don't think about it. I just look where I want it to go, splash the sand, and it goes there."

Paul did not need me to spell out for him the obvious fact that if he wanted his putting to be as outstanding as his bunker play, he had to attain the same mental state on the greens that he had in the bunkers. He had to become relaxed, even nonchalant at the moment of truth. This can be very tough to do, especially if a golfer has already mastered the idea of picking out a small target. Picking out a minute target makes a lot of golfers want to make their strokes minutely precise. The challenge of putting consists essentially of doing the opposite—picking out a small target and then taking a free, uncontrolled stroke.

I suggested that Paul think about gaining control by giving up control.

This can be a hard concept to grasp. Players are told that putting is crucially important. They're told they can't win if they don't putt well. They understand that both of those statements are true. Then they're told that at the very climax of their putting routines, they can't try very hard. They hear words and phrases like *nonchalant, carefree, don't give a damn*. I tell them to putt as if they didn't care whether they made it or not. Or to putt as if it had been preordained that the ball would fall no matter how they stroked it.

A lot of players respond to that by saying, "Huh?"

I remind them of a few things. How well do they do with four-footers if they're in a stroke-play competition where every putt counts? How well do they do with four-footers when they're out with their friends playing a casual Nassau and someone concedes that four-footer? They miss a lot of the four-footers that count. When they take a casual swipe at the putt that's been conceded, they knock it in with remarkable frequency.

I remind them that even if they could somehow force their

body to do everything perfectly, they still couldn't will the ball into the hole. Putting machines hitting balls on flat greens still miss a fair number of putts. There are just too many variables that are beyond control. The turf can be imperfect. The ball can be imperfect. The wind can gust. Any of these factors can cause a putt to miss.

But the main reason trying too hard doesn't work is that it almost invariably diminishes the chance of making a good stroke. It introduces doubt to the mind. It tightens the muscles. It robs a player of his natural talent and destroys his rhythm and flow.

Sometimes an example from another sport helps golfers see this. In basketball, for example, I've noticed that teams often play better defense when they're on the end of the floor where their bench is. But they play better offense on the opposite end. The reason is that their coach is yelling at them and they hear him. This raises their intensity on defense. Intense defenders are generally better defenders than casual ones.

On offense, the coach's voice can also raise intensity. But that rarely results in more scoring. On the offensive end, a basketball team doesn't need feverish intensity. It needs creativity, boldness, imagination, and confidence. It needs players who keep looking for their shot even when they've missed a few. When the coach is haranguing his players to work harder on offense, he's not going to get more points. He's going to get more turnovers, more missed shots, and more foregone opportunities.

But the coach doesn't stop yelling, often for the worst of reasons. He knows that to most of the people in the stands and the writers on press row, a coach who's always on his feet, always telling his players something, is perceived as an admirable character. He's showing dedication. He's showing he cares. A coach who sits back and says very little during the course of a game had better have a good team. Otherwise, critics will call him lackadaisical.

Each golfer has his own internal coach. And he's tempted to unleash that coach, to tell himself to try his best when he's putting, even though he might know it's counterproductive. That's because we've been conditioned since childhood to believe that losing isn't pleasant. But it's at least acceptable if the athlete gave 100 percent of himself. I've had players tell me that they can live with themselves if they try hard and putt poorly. But they can't sleep at night if they putt poorly and have the sense that they weren't trying hard enough. They don't understand that the only relationship between trying your hardest and doing your best is that if you try your hardest you won't do your best—in putting, at least.

The most persuasive thing I can say to someone who doesn't get this idea is, "Well, if what you've been doing had been working, we wouldn't be talking, would we?" I don't say it to be harsh, but because I know that old and destructive habits of thought are like weeds. They're hard to kill.

Gaining control by giving up control only seems like a contradiction in terms. In fact, it's a fairly common pattern in our lives.

Take, for instance, a teenager. There comes a time in a teen's life when his or her parents have to understand that they can no longer have complete control over their child's life. They can't dictate where she is at every moment, whom she speaks to, what she wears, what she does. If they try to dictate these details, the teenager is likely to rebel and, behind the parents' backs, do exactly what they don't want. Parents of teenagers are much wiser if they relax the reins and trust that the years they spent instilling sense and values into their child's mind will pay off when they give the child some independence.

Putting is like that.

Take, for instance, a public speaker. When an inexperienced speaker is asked to make a presentation before an audience, it's usually because someone admires her mind and figures she has something worthwhile to say, that she's a person of accomplishment. Being an accomplished person, this inexperienced speaker sets out to eliminate the possibility that she'll stand up behind the lectern, open her mouth, and not be able to think of anything to say. She wants desperately to avoid that. So she writes her speech down, word for word. She edits it. She memorizes it. She practices it. And when the time comes to deliver the speech, just to make sure she won't leave anything out or stand up and draw a blank, she brings her text and reads it. And, of course, she reads it so dully that the admirable qualities of mind that caused her to be invited in the first place never come across to her audience.

I'm fortunate in that I once had a teacher, June Dorian, who advised me to approach a public presentation as if I were having a conversation with one person—casual, relaxed, engaged.

Putting is like that, too.

Take, for instance, jazz musicians. Good jazz men relax. They let the music flow. They don't get hung up on playing every note of a song exactly as the composer wrote it. They don't care if being free costs them an occasional riff that doesn't work. They know that if they want the piano to sing, they have to let it go.

Putting is like that, too.

Take for instance, dancing. A lot of people think they can't dance. But they go to a family wedding, have a couple of drinks, start feeling the music, and dance very well. They may wake up the next morning with a hangover. And they may still believe they can't dance. But when the video of the wedding reception is played, the truth is evident. They can dance if they let themselves not care about dancing correctly.

Putting is like that.

Or, consider your signature. If you're signing checks on bill-paying day, the likelihood is that each of your signatures is basically identical to the others. But suppose I were to hand you a blank piece of paper and say, "Here. Sign this paper exactly as you signed those checks. If the signature doesn't seem genuine to an FBI handwriting expert, you owe me $10,000."

The likelihood is that you would try *very* hard to make your signature identical to the one on the checks. And precisely because you were trying hard, it would not be. It would lack the casual flow your signature usually has. The lines would look wiggly, forced. It would look, in short, like a forgery.

Putting is like that.

Still, when I explain all this to a player and urge him to try gaining control by giving up control, the player sometimes gets the sense that I'm suggesting he not care. And how can he not care about a vitally important part of the game he loves, the game he must play well to fulfill his dreams and support his family?

The answer, of course, is that I'm not asking players to stop caring. I'm asking them to give themselves their best chance to make putts. And the best way to do this is to relax a little, perhaps even to pretend they don't care, to remind themselves that even if they miss a crucial putt, the bank is not going to foreclose and their kids will still love them. Minimizing the importance of a putt is much more helpful than maximizing it.

Paul Azinger immediately grasped the idea of gaining control by giving up control. It appealed to him. Some players respond to one idea, others to another. You have to find a way to present an idea in a way that seems to the player instinctive and understandable to him. For Paul, that was "gain control by giving up control."

We started working on a few putting drills. I asked him to keep his eyes on his target as he began to draw his putter back. He did. I asked him to keep in mind the idea of gaining control by giving up control. He did.

"That feels so free, so flowing," he said, pleased.

I could see the difference in his stroke. It was longer, but it didn't look artificial. It looked better. Contact between ball and putter sounded quieter. The ball seemed to roll a foot or two farther than he expected. (I suspect the changes in the sound and the distance the ball traveled were because a free, unforced stroke is more likely to contact the ball precisely on the putter's sweet spot.)

Not long after that, Paul won his first tournament since his bout with cancer. He's playing very well now, and he's near the top of the Tour's putting statistics. He tells me he's putting every putt as if the guys playing with him had already conceded it.

Other players grasp the concept in different ways. When I started working with Nick Price, one of the problems we confronted was that Nick felt his putting stroke was forced on putts in the ten-foot range. But he really liked his stroke and his mind-set when he putted from twenty to forty feet or more.

The reason, of course, was that Nick felt he should make and had to make the ten-footers. He didn't expect to make the longer putts. When he lined them up, he visualized them going into the hole. But he could live with it if they didn't. So he stroked them more casually—and better. It wasn't that he wasn't trying to make them. He was. But he relaxed on the longer putts because he didn't care so much.

Nick and I worked on making him putt as if every putt was a forty-footer. That was one of the stories behind the story when Nick became player of the year in 1994. He was trying to putt everything as if it was a forty-footer.

No one believes he can will the ball into the hole from forty feet. Good putters try to make their forty-footers. But they understand that their efforts will come up against the vagaries of wind and slope, and the imperfections of turf. They understand that the human body and mind aren't precise enough to hole all forty-footers. So they putt the ball as well as they can and they are phlegmatic if it fails to drop.

That's the way I like players to be about all their putts, even the short ones. Take your satisfaction not from whether the putt drops but from whether you got yourself into the right frame of mind before you hit it. Make the putt in your mind. If you do that, you have done all you can. It's up to fate whether the ball actually drops.

That doesn't mean golfers should be careless about their putting. In fact, I appreciate a meticulous putter. But the smart putter is meticulous to a certain point. She's meticulous about the process of preparing for a putt. She has a routine, and she executes that routine.

But at the moment of truth, she stops being meticulous and simply strokes the putt, freely and even nonchalantly. She expects the ball to go in the hole, but she understands that sometimes it won't.

If you'd like a little jargon from modern psychology, try the phrase *process goals*. By process goals, we mean the preparatory things an individual can do to maximize the chance of peak performance in any endeavor, whether it be selling stocks and bonds or making putts. We don't mean results.

To the financial consultant, the process that leads to success involves first preparing himself, from his wardrobe to his knowledge of the market. It involves preparing his presentation. It involves preparing lists of prospects. It involves finding out as much as he can about each prospect before he calls on him. It involves executing his presentation plan.

But once he's gone through this process as well as he can, the successful financial consultant knows that some prospects are going to say yes and some are going to say no. He can't control what the prospect says. He can only control the process he goes through. If the prospect says yes, the consultant is gratified. But if the prospect says no, the successful financial consultant doesn't worry about it. He reviews his performance, checks to make sure he fulfilled his process goals. And if he did, he simply looks forward to the next call, the next prospect. If he has any reaction at all, he thinks, Good. Everyone's got to hear no sometimes. This just brings me that much closer to the prospect who will say yes.

The good putter thinks similarly. If he misses a putt, he reviews his performance. Did he clear his mind of all thoughts but the target? Did he make a free, confident stroke? If he did, he did all he could do. If he still missed, he just mentally shrugs his shoulders. If all putts went in, he figures, golf would be too easy. That miss just makes it all the more likely that he'll make the next one.

The player who hasn't learned to gain control by giving up control doesn't have that edge working for him. He cares much more about the result of his putt than the process that produced it. He's the sort of player who talks to himself a lot on the green, who's got no consistency as a putter. Especially when he misses some putts on the first few holes, he has no discipline. He reacts to missed putts by altering his approach. He fiddles with his grip and his stance. He overreads his putts. He overcontrols his stroke. And he loses, still thinking he can somehow find a way to force himself to hit perfect putts.

Making Putts Routinely

> *If there has been one thing common to all great putters over the years, it has been their determination to stick with one method and one overall game plan through thick and thin.*
>
> —PAUL RUNYAN

IF YOU GO TO A PGA TOUR EVENT WHERE MY FRIEND AND CLIENT Davis Love III is playing, I suggest you stake out the practice green and wait till he arrives. You'll be able to pick up a quick lesson in one of the elements that makes a good putter.

I'm not talking about watching Davis's stroke, though it's a good one. Watch the number of balls he's hitting. A lot of players take three or more balls onto the practice green. They hit one toward a hole, rake the second into place, hit it, and rake the third into place. Not Davis. He always practices putting with a single ball. After he hits it, he walks to it and either hits it again or picks it up and locates another target. Then he repeats the process.

I point this out not because of any inherent magic in using a single ball on the practice green, but because it illustrates Davis's commitment to his putting routine. He wants to practice the same routine he uses on the golf course, and on the golf course, he has only one ball. That devotion to an unvarying routine is one of the hallmarks of a good putter. Davis, who is a very good putter, employs the same routine whenever he putts, whether it's in a practice round or on the final green at the Belfry with the Ryder Cup at stake.

If you continue to watch Davis, you'll soon be able to predict exactly what he will do before he strokes each practice putt. You'll even be able to tell how much time will elapse between each movement he makes. A good putter's routine can be that predictable.

Developing a good routine was one of the first things Davis and I worked on when we met years ago. He was in college, and his father, Davis Love Jr., was concerned that Davis wasn't putting or chipping as well as he needed to. Young Davis wanted to be a great player, but he didn't think he was much of a putter.

I could see otherwise. Davis had talent as a putter. But, as I told him, he was getting in his own way.

In this context, getting in your own way means permitting something extraneous that you generate to interfere with putting your best. If a player is about to putt and he starts silently lecturing himself about taking the putter head straight back along the target line, he's getting in his own way. If he remembers the putts of similar length that he's missed in the past, he's getting in his own way. If he starts wondering whether he can make the cut if he misses the putt, he's getting in his own way. If he starts thinking about how much money is at stake, or whether someone else is making birdies, he's getting in his own way.

Most golfers face a constant battle to stay out of their own way. One of their allies in this struggle is a strong putting routine. A putting routine has two intertwined components. One is the physical activity—taking the grip, taking the stance, practice swings, etc. The second, and more important, component is the mental activity—reading the green, deciding on the line, clearing the mind, putting to make it, and accepting the results.

We are creatures of habit. A good, habitual putting routine helps us stay out of our own way much as a regular exercise habit protects against heart problems. It's not foolproof, but it's the wise thing to do.

It wasn't hard to persuade Davis about this. We just watched some sports on television. If you look closely at them, you can see that successful athletes in many situations similar to a golfer's rely on habit and routine. We watched Michael Jordan of North Carolina and Mark Price of Georgia Tech shoot free throws. They each had a ritual way of taking the ball from the referee, taking their stance, warming up by dribbling or spinning the ball in their hands, taking aim, and letting the shot go. We saw the analogous thing with placekickers in football and servers in tennis.

I pointed out that at the heart of Jordan's and Price's routines, there was something in common. Both Jordan and Price moved decisively at the moment of truth. They looked at the target and let the shot go without delay. It was much the same when we watched Larry Bird win the NBA's three-point shooting contest. Larry grabbed balls off the rack quickly and decisively. He focused on the target and let the shots go without wasting time. There was no sign that he cared about his shooting form.

Davis could see parallels to other sports that he liked. He's an avid fisherman. We talked about how when he saw fish biting at some remove from his boat, Davis simply looked at where he wanted his lure to go and cast it there. He didn't think about wrist cock, or where the pole was aimed. He just saw it and did it. If, one time out of fifteen, the lure didn't go where he was aiming, he didn't reprove himself or start studying his technique. He just cast again.

Davis also likes to hunt. He was reminded of a man who taught trap and skeet-shooting at Sea Island, Georgia, where Davis lived. This expert taught novice shooters not to think about aiming the gun. They had to watch for the target, focus on the target, and fire. It's a fluid motion. The gun is never still until the trigger has been pulled.

Davis still had trouble thinking of himself as a good enough athlete to apply this idea to putting. I had him toss a ball to me. Unconsciously, of course, he tossed it precisely into my hand.

"That shows you're athlete enough to putt," I said. "Now you have to trust that a very smart engineer designed your putter to fit in your hands, to hit the ball straight. You shouldn't have to think about that any more than you think about your hand when you toss me the ball. In fact, you can putt a lot better with your putter than you can rolling the ball with your hand."

Davis set about mastering a routine that captured his athleticism. It took hundreds and hundreds of repetitions before it became unconscious and automatic, but once Davis makes a commitment to something, he sticks to it. That's why he began working with a single ball on the practice green, and why he always practices the same rhythmic core of his routine. He looks at the target. He looks at the ball. And he strokes his putt as soon as his eyes come back to the ball. It's a routine designed to maximize the chance that he will putt with no extraneous thoughts getting in his way.

Not coincidentally, Davis transformed himself from a young man who didn't think he was much of a putter to a mature golfer who is perennially near the top of the Tour's putting statistics.

You are going to have to develop and consistently employ a sound routine if you are going to become the best putter you can be. If you do, I can offer you this guarantee. On your good days, you will putt great. On your bad days, you'll putt pretty well. That's how powerful a good routine is.

Some readers will react to this by thinking, *That's crazy. I play all the time with guys who have elaborate putting routines that they always follow, and they putt poorly and can't break 90!*

Well, then, evidently they are not employing the sort of routine I'm talking about. They may have a set of motions that they execute. They may squat down behind the ball the same way, plumb-bob the same way, take their stance and grip the same way, take the same number of practice strokes, and take the same deep breath on every putt. But the physical elements, as I've mentioned, are only one component of a good routine, and by no means the most important one. Players who move their bodies through a routine but fail to get their minds where they must be are like people who go to church every Sunday but sit there thinking about work, school, sex, or golf—anything but faith and prayer. God, I assume, is less than impressed by that sort of devotion. In the same way, your putting will not be transformed if you adopt a shallow, purely physical routine.

It's the mental part of a routine that's more difficult to master. Anyone can move his body through a prescribed ritual. But the discipline required to be in the right frame of mind on every putt is difficult to achieve and easy to lose. I work with more than one player on the Tour who fights a constant battle to clarify his thoughts, to see only the target, to think only of the target, and then to let the stroke happen.

That's not to say that a consistent physical routine isn't helpful. It is. Body and mind are part of a unified system, and a sound set of physical habits can promote and support sound mental habits.

I almost never try to prescribe the physical routine. I've seen too many good putters whose routines vary widely from one another to think that there's a single correct way. Some plumb-bob. Some don't. Some squat behind the ball. Some don't. Some take their practice strokes standing behind the ball, looking at the hole, swinging perpendicular to the line of the putt. Some take practice strokes parallel to the line of the putt. Some take the same number of practice strokes before every putt. Some take no practice strokes at all. Some take a varying number of practice strokes, depending on how long it takes them to feel that they've rehearsed the correct stroke for the putt they have to make. It doesn't matter. People's styles differ because people differ. The main thing is to have a physical routine that feels comfortable and effective to you. Then stick with it.

At the core of the routine, though, are some physical movements that I think are less open to individual interpretation. When the moment of truth comes, I like to see players look at the target, look at the ball, and let the stroke go, with no delay between those three movements.

When I see a player who looks at the target, looks back at the ball, and then freezes, I can generally guess what's going on in his mind. He's giving himself a lecture on the putting stroke. Or he's trying to remember the latest tip he saw on television. He is getting in his own way. He is also drastically reducing his chance to make the putt. That's because every instant spent frozen over the ball, thinking about technique or anything else but the target, is an instant in which the body can tense up, the nerves and muscles can get less graceful, and the mind can lose its focus. For every instant frozen over the ball, the golfer is less likely to simply see it and do it.

So I like to see a smooth, relaxed cadence to a player's routine at this point. Sometimes I have them murmur to themselves, "Look at the target. Look at the ball. Roll it." It's interesting that when they slur the endings of each of those sentences so that they sound more like "look at the targetlook at the ballroll it," their putting usually becomes still sharper.

Cindy Figg-Currier, who plays on the LPGA Tour, carries a small metronome to the practice green with her. Sometimes, in drills, she sets it up and starts it ticking with a slow, steady beat. She strokes putts to the sound of that metronome. She feels it helps maintain the smoothness of her stroke. It also helps her maintain the right rhythm in her routine.

The physical elements of a good putting routine won't help you, though, if your mental routine is weak.

THE MENTAL ROUTINE can actually begin before a player arrives on the green, when the player begins to read his putt. The eyes and mind of a good player start to process information about a putt almost as soon as his approach shot stops moving. As he strides up the fairway toward the hole, his imagination comes into play. He sees the general contour of the land and he starts to envision how his ball will be affected when he rolls it.

Much has been written over the years about reading putts. Some of it is no doubt valid, but a lot of it is pseudo-science at best. One thing I do know is that I've seen a lot of putts missed because golfers' heads were churning with so much "information" about how to read greens that they were unable to focus on their targets.

Where does the green drain? What's the grain of the grass? What percentage of putts don't break at all? What percentage of golfers underread their putts and what percentage overread them? What's the effect of footprints around the hole? Has the architect built any optical illusions into this green? If you're thinking about this sort of question, you're likely to be filling your mind with thoughts and doubts that won't help you sink your putt.

This leads to an irony. Experience often doesn't help much in reading putts. It's the older, more experienced players who have had time to absorb all the supposedly helpful data about reading greens who tend to become paralyzed by doubt. Kids who are new to the game seem to know better. I attend a fair number of junior golf tournaments, and I can tell you that kids read greens remarkably well. And they know nothing about grain, drainage, or any of the other supposed fine points of reading putts. They just take a look and whack it.

They putt well in that unsophisticated way because they tend to go with their first impression of how the putt will break. If I have a cardinal rule about reading greens, that's it. Your first impression of how a putt will break will be right more often than any other impression you might form.

That doesn't mean you must read the putt the instant you step onto the green. Cindy Figg-Currier has a useful metaphor in this regard. She tells me that she thinks of reading putts as a process similar to focusing a camera. For those of you who can't remember the era before autofocus, you point the camera at the subject and at first get a fuzzy image. You work the focusing ring back and forth until the image is sharp and clear. But after you've done that, you don't keep turning the focusing ring, blurring and sharpening the subject again and again. Once you've got it clear, you stick with it. That's the way you should read putts.

Good putters can take in an enormous amount of information in this process. First of all, there's the memory they have of playing a particular green before. If you play regularly on the same course, over time you become familiar with the greens. When you walk onto the putting surface you may already know how a putt will break. That's fine. Local knowledge is a great advantage.

Players on the PGA Tour, who play a new course every week, try to compensate for local knowledge during their practice rounds early in the week. If you watch a practice round, you'll see that the players generally play their ball into the hole cut on that particular day. But before they leave the green, they'll putt three or four balls to different areas of the putting surface, especially those areas where they anticipate the pins will be cut. Frequently, they'll mark up the green diagrams in their yardage books with little arrows helping them to identify the contours and breaks in a green. Tour caddies pride themselves in stockpiling data about the greens on Tour courses.

That brings up an issue that sometimes confronts amateurs,

especially women—should they read the putts, should the caddie read the putts, or should it be a collaborative process? Women tell me that they frequently encounter unenlightened caddies who assume they can't read greens and start trying to impose their judgments without being asked. The best thing to do with a caddie like that is take him aside and tell him firmly that when you'd like his advice, you'll ask for it.

On the other hand, I've had players tell me they putt better at a club they've never played before if they take a caddie and let him apply his experience and local knowledge to the reading of the putt. That may be so, and I generally tend to believe in whatever works for an individual player.

But keep several things in mind before you decide what role you want a caddie to play in reading your putts. One is that you're not going to get better at reading greens if you let a caddie do it for you, any more than you're going to learn to fly an airplane by sitting in a first-class seat and letting the pilot handle it. Another is that the goal of your reading routine is to come up with a firm, decisive idea of how the putt will break. That's more likely to happen if only one mind is applied to the problem, rather than two. Finally, there is no single correct line for most putts. There are many lines, depending on the speed with which the player hits the ball. A caddie who looks at a putt and tells you "two cups left to right" is merely displaying his ignorance of the game if he doesn't know how hard you plan to hit the ball.

On the Tour, where caddies work for one player only and

can learn that player's idiosyncrasies, effective partnerships are more likely. Glen Day, for instance, has had the same caddie, Dave "Munster" Munce, for more than ten years. Glen generally likes to putt so that the ball dies in the hole. Munster has learned that, and he reads putts accordingly. The two of them have also learned over the years how to trust one another's judgment and how to say the sorts of things that produce a decisive consensus about the way a putt will break. Glen is generally the first to say how he thinks a putt will go. Munster says nothing till Glen has either stated his opinion or asks for Munster's. Nine times out of ten, Munster agrees with Glen's first impression. If Munster disagrees with Glen's impression, Glen starts the process again, and he works it till he arrives at a firm read.

But the partnership between Glen and Munster, I find, tends to be the exception nowadays. Most tour players read their own putts and rarely ask advice from their caddies.

And Tour caddies are the best in their business. What sort of partnership will you achieve with the guy that a caddie master assigns you on a given Saturday? There are going to be days when you get a new, inexperienced caddie or one who simply can't read greens. There are going to be many days when you play a course without caddies. In those circumstances you had better be able to rely on your own green-reading skills.

A related question sometimes arises over whether to watch the putts of other players in your group for clues about how your ball will break. To be sure, good players sometimes go to school on the putts hit by their competitors. But the smart ones are very selective about whom they watch.

Dottie Pepper, for instance, tells me that she sometimes watches a fellow LPGA player's putt to get a clue about the way the green will break her own putt. But she never watches the amateurs whom she plays with in pro-ams before the formal tournament begins. Their putting, she thinks, is so unlike her own that she'll more likely be misled than informed by anything she sees them do.

That's not a bad rule of thumb. A weak player in your foursome, even if he's on your line, is likely to hit the ball with either too much pace or not enough. That's one reason he's a weak player. In either case, the weak player's ball will break differently from the smart, properly paced putt you plan to hit. I've seen a lot of putts missed by players who turn to someone else in their foursome and say, "But yours broke a foot!"

I LIKE TO see players make their reads fairly quickly. Once in a while, with a long putt on a modern green that has some artificial humps, tiers, and ridges, it may be advisable to walk around a putt and see it from both sides of the hole. Do it only if you're certain that you're trying to find a way to get the ball in the hole, not looking for reasons why that's going to be hard to do. And don't do it very often. Most putts aren't that complicated.

That's not to say that you should rush through this phase of your routine. There's an understandable concern among many golfers about the pace of play these days. But it's important to realize that the problem of five-hour rounds doesn't stem from people taking their time going through their putting routines. It stems from people not being ready when it's their turn to play. It stems from course operators who insist that all players take golf carts, then that the carts remain on the cart paths. It stems from people who waste time rereading putts.

Your routine should not waste time, of course. And it must be something you can execute within the time limits allowed by the rules. But once you're confident you're within those parameters, don't let anyone or anything rush you. Go through your routine at a deliberate, comfortable pace. If you adopt a routine such as the one I've described here, you will never have trouble with slow play.

Davis Love plays a brisk round of golf. But Davis is so committed to his routine that he takes pride in stepping away and starting over if he fails to execute the mental portion of it, if he's distracted by thinking of something other than the ball going in the hole. He's got such a disciplined mind that it doesn't happen very often.

Glen Day attracted some unfavorable television commentary a few years ago from people who thought he took too much time. They gave him the nickname "All Day." Glen was smart enough not to let that fluster him. (In fact, when the company that makes his golf balls asked what name he wanted stamped on them, he told them to put "All Day" on each of them.) He goes through his routine at the pace that ensures he makes the most putts he's capable of making. When you think about it, that's a time-saving measure right there.

I don't believe much in tricks or gimmicks in reading putts. I know, for instance, that Bobby Locke liked to pay particular attention to the last few feet of a putt, the terrain it would cover just before it got to the hole. He reasoned that since the ball would be rolling more slowly at that stage of its journey, the contours around the hole were the most critical in trying to get it to break into the cup. That was fine for Locke, but I wouldn't teach a novice golfer to do it. I'd much prefer that the novice keep green reading as simple as possible.

There are a few exceptions. On a shaggy Bermuda green, you may have to remember to play less break than your first impression of the green contours suggested there would be. And in certain parts of the world, like the desert courses of southern California and Arizona, there may be a local peculiarity you have to keep in mind. In Scottsdale, Arizona, for instance, they say that all putts break toward Phoenix. And I've been on some greens out there where the ball looked like it would break one way, or go straight, and didn't, because of the Phoenix rule. So in those circumstances, you have to add a little compensation to your read.

It's no coincidence, though, that while all the Tour players who come to Scottsdale in January for the Phoenix Open know the Phoenix rule and observe it when they read putts, it's quite often a pro based in Scottsdale who wins the tournament. In much the same way, someone raised on the *Poa annua* greens of the West Coast has an edge in California and someone who grew up on Bermuda often wins tournaments played on Bermuda greens. The reason, I think, is that these pros are putting based on their first impressions. The visitors have to take their first impressions and adjust them. And a pure first impression is almost always better than a read produced by second thoughts.

Players who are putting well find it easier to observe this principle than players who aren't. David Duval tells me that when he shot his remarkable 59 in the final round of the Bob Hope Classic a couple of years ago, he barely looked at the final, seven-foot putt he had to make eagle, to win the tournament and to break 60. He just got an instinctive idea of how the ball was going to roll, picked out his target, and hit it there.

I know that few readers of this book will ever stand on the 18th green with a putt to break 60. But they might have putts to break 70, 80, 90, or 100. The principle remains the same. Can you read that putt and make your judgment about how it will break as instinctively as David Duval read his? Can you then stroke it as decisively as he stroked his?

Players who have been missing a lot of putts, of course, often can't tell for certain whether they missed because of a poor read or a poor stroke. They tend to compensate by being extremely careful with their reads. This doesn't work. It doesn't do much for a player's ability to predict how a putt will break. And the doubts and questions that it introduces do nothing at all for the player's putting stroke. Being overly careful with reads almost always leads to doubts and worries—and poor strokes. The player who begins reading too carefully winds up missing more putts. Soon he's not only overreading, he's fiddling with his stroke while playing competitively, trying to fix it. He's so lost he couldn't find water from a bridge.

Some players intuitively understand the advantage of trusting their first impression of a putt, the read that feels instinctive. But many don't. People in our culture have been raised to believe that second and third efforts distinguish winners from losers. They've been raised to check and double-check their math homework to make certain they got it right. If they don't check and double-check their reads, they feel guilty about not giving their best effort.

I have players tell me that they can live with themselves if they read and reread putts, then miss them. They can't live with themselves if they miss after feeling that they haven't tried hard.

"Oh," I say. "I thought we were looking for a way to make putts. Turns out we're looking for a way to avoid feeling guilty."

I tell them that putting is not math homework. Putting is a game, an imaginative, creative, athletic game. You putt best when you're feeling loose, decisive, and confident. Trusting your first impression helps you be that way. Reading and rereading greens makes it harder to get into that effective state of mind.

Sometimes a player will tell me, "Yeah, Doc, but the hole locations out on the Tour are chosen because they're in the places where your first impression is usually wrong. They're subtle. They're hard to read."

That's sometimes true. We've all seen greens on television where player after player misreads the putt the same way. Everyone plays the putt to break left, but it stays straight. Or vice versa.

If I saw evidence that players who reread the greens got that sort of putt in the hole and players who went with their first impression missed it, I might reassess my belief in the value of putting by that instinctive first impression. But I don't. I don't see any evidence that the second and third reads are any more accurate than the first. Everyone misreads certain putts, no matter how many times they read them. And when I walk a practice round with players, I often ask them to verbalize their first impression of a putt so I'll know what it is. It's amazing how accurate that impression is.

But I do see evidence that players plagued by doubt and misgivings about their reads make fewer putts than players who are decisive and confident. Players tell me about that sort of problem all the time.

The bottom line is that your first impression won't always be accurate, though it will be accurate a lot of the time. You're going to misread some putts, you're going to be fooled sometimes by a tricky green. That's the nature of the game. But your second and third impressions won't be any more accurate—indeed they'll be less so. And the stroke you make with two or three impressions rattling around in your brain will almost certainly be less decisive and less confident than the one you make if you go with your instinct.

Reading the green, of course, is not the object of the exercise.

Sinking putts is the object of the exercise. The goal in reading greens is to come to a point of clarity, a moment at which you are certain that you understand the way the ball will roll and you can make the ball roll that way. One way to know whether you're reaching that point is by gauging your reaction to missed putts. Are you shocked and surprised when the ball doesn't go in or doesn't break the way you'd expected? It sounds like a contradiction in terms, but if you're shocked and surprised when you misread a green, then you're doing a pretty good job.

IF YOU'RE EXECUTING a good mental routine, you're going to feel the atmosphere around you change. It won't, of course. But your perceptions of it will.

Players with strong putting routines tell me that they feel as if they're stepping into their own little world. It's almost like going into a bubble. Their awareness of the things around them fades as their focus on the putt they're facing tightens and intensifies. It's a pleasant place, this little world. They have the feeling they love to putt. They take great pleasure from their skill at it. They feel safe, secure, and competent. They don't care what anyone else thinks or might think about the putt they're about to hit. They are immersed in the challenge of putting it into the hole.

The climactic part of a good routine is very simple: putt to make it.

As my mother might say, "Why else would you putt?"

Unfortunately, there are lots of reasons. People putt not to three-putt. They putt to give themselves a good leave for their next putt. They putt not to go too far past the hole. They putt not to leave it short. They putt to make a good roll.

Well, you can buy a good roll in a doughnut shop. And none of those other reasons works very well, either.

Putt to make it. This means you're absolutely absorbed in this moment, no other. Nothing else in the world interests you except making this particular putt. There is no future and no past. You're not dwelling on the good shot you hit to get your ball to this spot. You're not thinking of how you'll feel if you miss. You're just rolling this ball into that hole.

Seve Ballesteros, a two-time Masters champion, once four-putted a green at Augusta. He was asked about it later in the media center. "I putt and miss. I putt and miss. I putt and miss. I putt and make," Seve explained.

People laughed, but it suggested to me something about the way Seve's mind worked. Seve's answer suggested that he was completely in the present moment on each of those putts. He didn't say that the greens at Augusta were slick and treacherous. He didn't ruminate about the iron shot that may have left him with a tough first putt. His attitude hadn't changed from one putt to the next. He wasn't affected by his misses. He had had four putts. He'd tried to make each of them. He'd succeeded on the fourth.

He had done all a golfer can do. That's why, in his prime, he was such a great player.

• • •

GOOD PUTTERS DON'T four-putt very often, but no matter how good you are, you are going to miss some putts, most likely ten or more during every round you play. A smart response to those inevitable misses is the last major element in a good routine. You must be resilient about missed putts. Remember that it's how you respond to your misses that matters, not whether you miss. You can choose to be angry about your misses or you can choose to accept them.

I don't advocate getting angry about missed putts. I've known a few players who could blow up emotionally, recover quickly, and use that anger to help become more focused for the next putt. But that ability is very rare. More often than not, anger is the enemy of focus. A temper tantrum is a form of getting in your own way.

It's important to distinguish between types of anger. If you're angry at yourself because you didn't putt to make it, that's one thing. At least you're focusing on the real mistake. If you vow to do better at focusing your mind for the next putt, a bit of what Sam Snead called "sensible irritation" might actually be helpful.

But if you get angry simply because the ball didn't go in the hole, it can lead to problems. Maybe you'll start to pity yourself because your luck is so bad. Maybe you'll start trying to compensate on the next putt for the way the last one missed—too high, too low, too short, or too long. You'll stop thinking of each putt as a unique entity and start correcting past mistakes on future putts. That's a form of getting in your own way.

I much prefer a player to react calmly to a missed putt—even two of them on the same green. Calmness says it doesn't matter if he missed that putt, because the player knows he's putting well and will soon hole some long ones to make up for the miss. Calmness says a player has too much confidence in his putting to get upset over a miss.

It may help to keep in mind that putting is not supposed to be easy and greens have been designed to make two-putts a challenging goal that no player will always meet. You're human. You're going to make mistakes. Golf is a game of mistakes, and that makes it a game that will beat you up mentally if you let it. You might as well have some compassion for yourself. From compassion comes forgiveness and from forgiveness comes forgetting. The only constructive thing you can do about a missed putt is to forget it. That way, you can be free and confident on the next one.

Your routine after making a putt isn't so problematic. It's fine to be happy if you hole one. Feeling the emotion helps cement the memory in your mind, and you want to remember your successful putts.

You can overdo it, of course. I don't see too many successful players who go bonkers when they hole a long birdie putt, even in a clutch situation. (I see some players, especially on the Senior tour, who do a pretty good imitation of someone going bonkers when they make a long putt, but I suspect these are people who consider it part of their job to entertain the galleries.) Most people who become good at golf have learned that it's best to maintain a low, consistent level of intensity through good shots and bad, because the calmer you are and the quieter you keep yourself, the easier it is to play the game.

Putting in the Clutch

Tension and anxiety cause more misses than lack of care.

—BOBBY JONES

LOTS OF PUTTS CAN BE CALLED CLUTCH PUTTS, BUT I CAN'T RECALL many that carried more pressure than a fifteen-footer that Cindy Figg-Currier faced on the last hole of the LPGA Qualifying School in October 1983.

Cindy, at that time, was just about a year out of the University of Texas. She'd grown up in Mount Pleasant, Michigan, and she'd been playing golf most of her life. Her father, who'd been a schoolteacher, had bought a little golf course called Riverwood when Cindy was six weeks old. When she was a toddler, Cindy's toys were cut-down clubs with electrical tape for grips. The youngest of four kids, she hung around the putting green at Riverwood in the summer, chipping and putting against her older brothers and her sister. She learned the game by imitation, and she learned it the way kids should learn it, from the green back to the tee. By that I mean she learned to get the ball in the hole first, and only later worry about how to get it off the tee and up to the green.

Cindy was a good junior golfer in Michigan, but her swing was raw. When she got to Texas, the other women on the golf team nicknamed her "Trash Queen" because it seemed to them she was always beating them by getting her ball up and down from around the trash basket near the tee box on the next hole.

Harvey Penick, who worked a little bit with the Texas women, wisely saw this as an advantage for Cindy. He encouraged her to build on it, refining the way she hit her chips and pitches, teaching her how to handle different lies and grasses, when to bump and run and when to lob, how to play the wind.

When Cindy graduated from Texas, she had a degree in marketing and a decision to make. Should she get a job? Or should she follow her dream and try to make it on the LPGA Tour?

She decided to give professional golf a chance, but a limited one. She would take three shots at qualifying. But it would be three strikes and you're out. Or, in Cindy's case, three misses at qualifying school and she'd put up the clubs and try something else.

On her first try, in January 1983, she was not ready and failed. She came close on her second attempt, in August of 1983. But that was a vintage year for young women golfers. Among the players who made it through that qualifying school were Julie

Inkster and Rosie Jones. The LPGA recognized that some good players had been squeezed out, so it scheduled another school for October 1983. That would be Cindy's last chance.

The tournament was held at Sweetwater Country Club in Sugarland, Texas, where the LPGA then had its headquarters. Standing on the final tee, Cindy could see the scoreboard. She needed a birdie to qualify, and the 18th was a long par-4 with the approach over water. Cindy hit a good drive. Her second shot, a four-wood, cleared the water and landed on the green, stopping fifteen feet from the hole.

Now, you may think that a fifteen-footer on the 18th green to win a three-dollar bet from your buddies is a pressure putt. You may think that a fifteen-footer on the final hole to win a major championship is a pressure putt. You may agree with Lee Trevino, who once said that real pressure is putting for a hundred dollars when you only have ten in your pocket. But I think all of those pale next to Cindy's challenge—a fifteen-footer to determine the course of the rest of her life.

Her caddie that week was her older brother Marty. And as they walked across the bridge to the green, Marty had an inspiration that should earn him a spot some day in the Caddie Hall of Fame.

"I'll give you all the money I have in my pocket if you make that putt," Marty said.

Cindy smiled then. She still smiles now, telling the story. Marty's offer immediately transformed the emotional context of the putt. It was no longer a fifteen-footer that a young woman either had to make or start looking for a job. It was a game, just like all the games that a cocky kid sister had played with her older brothers on the putting green back in Mount Pleasant—delighting when she won, not caring all that much when she lost.

Cindy, of course, made the putt and got her LPGA Tour card. She still has it, and she's still a great clutch putter. Marty, as it turned out, had about fifty dollars in his pockets that day. Cindy used it to take him out to dinner that night in the Holiday Inn in Sugarland.

UNFORTUNATELY, THE MARTY Figg solution is not a universally applicable tool for taking pressure off putts. It was available only to Cindy, and even to her only once. She and the rest of us have to find another way to cope with putting under pressure, a way that can be used whenever we face a pressure putt, a way that will work time and again.

Fortunately, that way exists. And the power to use it is within you. It consists of developing a strong mental routine and relying on it in the clutch.

The cliché in discussions of pressure is to point out that pressure doesn't really exist. It's something that a golfer invents. After all, the two dollars you stand to lose if you miss that putt on the 18th green isn't going to affect your credit rating. If you miss the fifteen-footer to win the major, you're still going to make a nice check. Even in Cindy Figg-Currier's case, the worst outcome was that she'd have to do what all the rest of her classmates had done, which was use her degree to make her way in the world. None of us is going to starve or die if we miss a putt. We're not going to lose our families, our houses, or anything else that's truly important if we miss the putt. It doesn't have to be important to us. Certainly the ball and the putter don't know whether the next shot is a ten-footer for a birdie to win a tournament or a ten-foot practice putt. And, as I sometimes tell players, a billion Chinese could care less whether their putts fall.

But so what? The fact is that we do care, we do put pressure on ourselves, and pressure can complicate the process of making a putt.

The professionals I work with face severe pressure, pressure so great it can make their hands shake. That's what happened to Jim Carter recently at the Tucson Open.

Jim was a relative latecomer to golf. He never played on a golf course until he was thirteen. He didn't start to play a lot until his family moved to Arizona a few years later. No one gave him a college golf scholarship. He went to Arizona State and tried to walk on to the team. He didn't make it originally, and he used to take his shag bag to an open field at Mesa Community College to practice, trying to get better. "I was behind my peers, and there's so much to learn about golf," he told me.

Jim was in his third year at Arizona State before he qualified for his first trip with the golf team. But once he got a chance to play, he improved rapidly. By his senior year, he won the

NCAA individual championship. He decided to give professional golf a try.

Jim was far from an immediate success. He felt as he had when he got to college, like a novice trying to catch up to peers who had years more experience than he did. He got his Tour card and lost it. He spent four years wandering in the wilderness of the minor league tours. He'd go to qualifying school each fall and terrible things would happen. Once he bogeyed the last four holes in a row and missed the cut by a shot. The next year he bogeyed two of the last three holes to miss by a shot again. "My confidence was shattered," he told me.

We worked on giving Jim a solid putting routine. Every time he putted, Jim tried to get behind the ball, make a brisk, decisive read, take his stance, take two looks at his target, and roll the putt. More important, he sought always to putt from that moment of clarity, that moment when he envisioned the way the ball would roll and believed firmly in it, when he thought of nothing else.

Jim got back to the Tour and stayed there. But over the course of five or so years, he couldn't win a tournament. He was making a living, but the Tour has its hierarchy, and there is a gulf between those who have won and those who haven't, a gulf that involves not just money, but pride and prestige. He wanted badly to win.

His chance finally came in Tucson. Jim led the tournament by two shots as he stood on the tee of the 72nd hole. He wasn't paying attention to the scoreboard, though. In fact, he thought his lead was only one, and that he'd need no worse than a par to stave off Steve Flesch and Len Mattiace, who were his closest pursuers.

The 18th hole in Tucson is a formidable challenge, a long par-4 where the tee shot must be long and straight, landing between two lakes. Then there's a long-iron approach shot and a tricky green. Jim handled the first two shots well, putting a three-iron into the fringe on the back of the green, perhaps twenty feet above the hole.

His situation seemed starkly clear. Get the ball in the hole in two shots and he'd do no worse than tie. Three-putt and the agonizing years of playing without a win would probably continue.

Fortunately, Jim had the sense not to think of the situation in those terms. He thought, instead, about his putting routine. He got behind the ball and found the line he thought it would take. He decided he wanted it to barely plop into the hole as its momentum died. He took two practice strokes to get the feel of the pace he wanted to give the ball. He stepped into his stance, took two looks at the target, and let the putt go.

It didn't go in, sliding by on the left side and stopping about two feet below the hole.

Now Jim felt his hands shaking. Adrenaline was coursing through his system. He felt, he told me later, as if he could have jumped nine feet into the air.

Instead, he relied again on his routine. He told his playing partners he would putt out. And he went through the process again—lining it up, forcing himself to focus on the path he expected the ball to take into the hole, achieving that moment of clarity. He took his practice strokes and took his stance. His hands felt as if they were going to fly off his arms. He took his two looks at the target and stroked the putt. It rolled straight into the center of the hole. Jim felt a rush of pride, relief—and joy. After all the years of struggle, he had finally broken through and won.

I cite this story because it dispels one of the common illusions about golfers who putt well under pressure. It's said that they have ice water in their veins, or they don't feel nervous. That's just media baloney. Great pressure putters have the same nerves, the same glands, and the same emotions that plague the twenty-handicap player in your foursome who always manages to blow the decisive three-footer. It's how they respond to nervous jitters that distinguishes them.

Their routines are the foundation of that response. As I've mentioned, golfers under pressure revert to their dominant habits. If your dominant habit is a routine that gets both your body and mind into position to putt well, you have a big advantage over players who haven't got a sound routine and find themselves trying to invent one in the clutch.

Part of this is physical. As Jim said to me after his Tucson win, going through the same movements he'd gone through uncounted thousands of times was soothing to him. It reminded him that the final putt in the Tucson Open was just a two-footer of the sort he'd made more often than he could remember. It reminded him of all the two-footers he'd made in practice. That's a good feeling to have under pressure. I tell players that they should make all their practice putts feel as if a tournament is on the line, and they should make all their putts with tournaments on the line feel like practice putts. Routine helps them do that.

But the larger part of it is mental. When a player who has a sound routine reverts to his or her dominant mental habit under pressure, it helps dispel distracting thoughts. It helps the player zero in on a target. That helps make the putt.

Dottie Pepper told me about one of the most satisfying putts she ever made, a putt that was critical to her first major championship. It was at the Dinah Shore tournament several years ago. Dottie was fighting it out with Julie Inkster for the title. They came to the final hole, which is a par-5. Dottie was a stroke behind. Julie missed her birdie putt, and Dottie faced a four-footer to force a play-off.

It was the sort of putt that can cause a major attack of nerves. Not too much break, but some. Close enough that you'd expect to make it, but not close enough to tap in. Close enough that you'd know, if you missed it, you'd blown a chance to break through and win a major.

Dottie was nervous, but she had long before determined that whenever she faced a pressure putt, she would rely on her routine. She did with this putt.

"By the time you get to that stage in a tournament, your feel for the greens is very instinctive," Dottie says. As she squatted behind the ball, she didn't have to work very hard to gauge the way it would break or the pace it needed. Her disciplined mind reverted to its dominant habit, striving for that moment of clarity, that feeling of decisiveness.

As it happened, a bug crawled onto the edge of the cup, right where Dottie intended to aim. Sluggishly, it stopped there. Some players would have been distracted, but Dottie wasn't. Her routine, her habitual search to find a target and focus on it, helped her. The bug simply reinforced the target line in Dottie's mind. She went through the rest of her routine aiming at the bug. She stroked the putt into the hole right over it. She won the first play-off hole and, with it, moved into the ranks of the LPGA's elite, its major championship winners.

GOOD PUTTERS LEARN to welcome nervous symptoms, rather than fear them. Nerves are something they don't feel during practice rounds. Nerves are something they feel when the stakes are high. Good players have practiced and competed for years precisely because they wanted to win tournaments where the stakes are high. So to them, nerves are a sign that their goal is approaching. They understand that nerves are a challenge, but they want to meet that challenge head-on.

Dana Quigley worked longer than most players to get to the point where he putted for a championship. Dana, like Jim Carter, was a latecomer to golf. Unlike Jim, he didn't have the advantage of growing up in a warm-weather state like Arizona.

Dana is from New England, where the golf season is pitilessly short. He started playing as a teenager in Rhode Island. He remembers trying out for his high school golf team as a sophomore and shooting 105.

Dana had a passion for golf, but he had other sports. He played basketball and ran track. Golf was a summer game, which he fit in between caddying jobs at the Rhode Island Country Club. He battled a tendency to slice the ball and he had no opportunity to take lessons. But he worked at the game when he could, imitating better players, especially his older brother, Paul. He improved. He made the high school golf team as a junior and by the time he was a senior, he could break 80.

That's nice, but merely shooting in the 70s won't attract hordes of college golf coaches to your door. Dana went to the University of Rhode Island and tried to walk on to the golf team. He didn't make it as a freshman. But he was persistent. He practiced whenever he could in a field by the college gym. Eventually, he made the team. But he never thought he was good enough to play on the Tour. He worked as a house painter and a club pro. He never won anything bigger than the Rhode Island Open. Finally one winter, on a lark, he entered the Tour's qualifying school. To his surprise, he made it.

He went out on the Tour with no confidence in his ability to compete. "I was scared to death of all the other players," he told me. "I drank and partied my way around for five years."

Dana managed to stay on the Tour that long because by that time he'd developed a reliable swing. He guesses that he averaged 30–32 putts a round in those years, which will not win any Tour events. He had a sense that he wasn't accomplishing anything. After five years he quit the Tour and went back to being a club pro.

He had some bumps along the road. He got divorced. He continued to drink. But in his forties, Dana started to pull himself together. He stopped drinking. He began to hone his game again. He won a lot of regional events. As his fiftieth birthday approached, he decided to give tournament golf another try.

He came to see me shortly before he started out trying to qualify for Senior tour events. We worked a lot on his putting routine, because we knew that on the Senior tour, putting is perhaps even more critical than it is on the regular tour. Nearly everyone at the senior level has a reliable swing, and the courses are set up to make it relatively easy to hit and hold greens. So putting becomes the decisive factor. We worked on Dana's routine, particularly on the climactic part of the routine. Dana had to learn to putt to make putts, not to avoid three-putting, which is what he had tended to do for much of his golfing career.

Dana found early success on the senior tour. He qualified for a tournament in Long Island on a Monday, then went out and won the actual event. That earned him the right to play regularly on the Senior tour for a year. But it didn't solve all of his problems with putting and attitude.

He still tended to see himself as slightly inferior to the players who had been consistent winners on the regular tour. That was especially true with his putting. He told me he understood that his peers on the Senior tour saw him as a good putter. He still had trouble seeing himself as a good putter, particularly under pressure.

But Dana is not the sort of man to back away from a challenge. That is a quality typical of good clutch putters. They not only don't back away from the challenge of putting under pressure, they've learned to love it. They love the fact that when they putt under pressure, their minds and bodies are totally engaged, totally committed. It's a feeling they don't get from driving a car or paying a mortgage or anything else in their lives.

Dana kept getting himself into position to win tournaments, into spots where his putts came with enormous pressure. Inevitably, that meant that if he wanted to win, he had to face down some players he'd all but idolized. Players like Tom Watson.

Watson charged hard at Dana in the final round of the TD Waterhouse Championship in Kansas City recently. Dana had had a wonderful tournament, shooting 65 and 67 in the first two rounds for a total of 132. But that wasn't enough to give him the lead. Going into the final day, Jim Colbert, with a 61 and a 69, for 130, was in front. Watson, with a 70–66, was in third. They all played together on the final day.

Dana took the lead for the first time on the back nine, when Colbert hit it in the water on 14. But Watson was playing a marvelous final round. He kept making birdies.

It was Watson's first professional tournament in his hometown, and the crowd of 25,000 was screaming its devotion to him. The ones who weren't pulling loudly for Watson were rooting for Colbert, who went to college at Kansas State. It was, Dana recalled later, like playing in the Ryder Cup—for the visiting team.

Playing the final hole, Dana had a one-stroke lead. He hit his approach to the green well, and got polite applause. Then it was Watson's turn. He hit an eight-iron that covered the flag. Dana couldn't immediately see where it stopped since the green was elevated. But the enormous roar told him Watson had knocked it close.

As he walked onto the green, the situation became clear. Dana was twelve feet away. But Watson was only a foot from the hole. He would have a tap-in birdie. Dana's challenge, then, was clear. He had to hole his own birdie putt or face Watson and the adoring hometown crowd in a play-off.

"You don't take pressure off a putt like that," Dana told me later. "You face it and deal with it."

Dana found out at that moment what his dominant habit was. He read the green and found the line he believed the ball would take. He took his stance and lined the putt up. It was, he figured, a putt that would break slightly from left to right. He settled on the left edge of the cup as his target.

And then he putted to make it. In the past, he might have putted not to three-putt, told himself to make sure he left it close, so that he could be certain of at least being in the play-off. That was how he had thought in the past. But thanks to all the work he'd put in on his putting routine, especially his mental routine, the dominant habit that emerged under pressure was the right one. He putted to make it.

Remember that when a player putts to make it, there is no past, nor is there a future. There is only the present moment, his ball, his club, and his target.

Had the past entered Dana's mind, he might have remembered how he'd fallen off the Tour when Watson was winning major championships. He might have thought about putts he'd missed. Had he thought about the future, he might have thought about a play-off, or the second place check, or any of a hundred other things that might happen. Those are the sorts of things players think about when they succumb to pressure. It's not that they choke. They don't. They simply let themselves be distracted by unhelpful thoughts of either the past or the future.

Dana's mind was firmly locked in the present. He stroked the putt. He remembers how firm and solid it felt. He remembers watching it track the line he'd foreseen, watching it drift a couple of inches to the right, remembers watching it fall into the hole.

Then he remembered all the times as a boy when he'd practiced putting, dreaming that the putt he was stroking was to make a birdie to take a championship from a great player. Finally, Dana thought, that dream had happened. It was a sweet feeling.

And that is how great players distinguish themselves on the green in clutch situations. They don't rely on tricks or gimmicks. They don't have superhuman control of their bodies. They don't avoid the churning stomach, the sweaty brow, the trembling hands. They simply do better than their competitors at enjoying the challenge, following their putting routines, locking their minds in the present, and putting to make it.

Speed:

The Light Is Always Green

The proper mental approach to a long putt is, "I'm going to hole this one by making the ball fall just over the front edge of the cup."

—CARY MIDDLECOFF

ONCE IN A WHILE, I WORK WITH A PLAYER WHO TELLS ME HE HAS NO touch. He rolls the ball way past the hole all the time. Or he leaves it way short. Or he hits it way past on one hole and then, compensating, he leaves it short on the next. Or he can't putt the fast greens at his best friend's club when he's invited for the member-guest. Or he can't adjust to slow, shaggy greens.

When someone tells me this, I usually respond by tossing them a ball. They catch it, and I ask them to toss it back. Without thinking about it, they toss it precisely into my hands.

"That's amazing," I say. "Your toss reached my hand exactly right. I didn't have to reach out for it. It didn't come in hard enough to sting me. I could just catch it."

The player nods, maybe grins a little.

Then I play the same game of toss-and-catch with an unfamiliar object, like an ashtray or a stuffed animal. Instinctively, the player adjusts to the weight of the new object and tosses it the correct distance.

"That shows that you have good touch," I tell him. "Your problem isn't that you don't have touch. Your problem is that you're worrying about speed instead of putting to make it."

And that is true. The last thing you want to do if you're trying to make putts is worry about speed. Your brain, eyes, and nervous system are marvelously equipped to roll the ball at the right pace if you just let them respond naturally. All too often, though, golfers get in their own way on issues of speed. They decide that they don't have touch because they've left some critical putts short or rolled them too long.

Again, I find this kind of harsh self-evaluation both false and damaging, because the test wasn't fair. When I ask these players what their mental state was when they made these speed mistakes, they almost invariably confess that they were putting fearfully, afraid of making a mistake with pace. Well, even the players with the best touch in the world are going to mishit putts when their minds are in that state. I simply ask players not to evaluate their touch until they have some experience putting with the proper attitude. And the proper attitude doesn't worry much about speed.

It's not that speed isn't important in making putts. It is. A player controls just two things when he putts a golf ball—line and pace. There are a few putts, the straight ones, where line is much more important than pace in determining whether the ball goes on the hole. But on breaking putts, the right line has to be married to the right speed. One doesn't work without the other.

If you don't understand this, try a little game that one of the best putters in the world, Brad Faxon, plays on the practice green. Brad takes three balls and finds a putt of about five feet with a moderate break. He then makes the putt at three different speeds. Hit firmly, the ball breaks very little, and the correct line is inside the hole. Hit at medium pace, the ball breaks more, and the correct line is perhaps a couple of inches outside the hole. Hit softly, the ball breaks quite a bit. Brad makes it plop over the side of the cup, dying into the hole.

If you try this game a few times, it will reinforce the knowledge that there is no uniquely correct line for most putts. Line is usually a function of speed, and vice versa. You'll start to see putts a little differently when you line them up. You'll be able to imagine several ways the ball might roll into the hole, and you'll begin selecting not only your line, but your speed.

But, the fact is that Brad Faxon, like nearly all the other good putters I know, never consciously thinks about speed when he's putting. He trusts his touch. When he reads a green and picks out a line, he's also thinking, subconsciously, of a speed that will make that line the correct one. When he strokes the ball, he's thinking about rolling it on the line he's selected, rolling it on the line that will take it into the hole. He lets the speed take care of itself. Nearly all the time, it does.

Now, I understand that Brad has some advantages over the typical amateur golfer. For one thing, he putts a lot. For another, the greens on the Tour tend toward a fairly consistent speed. They're almost always fast but not linoleum-fast. But I don't think Brad has innately better touch than most players. He's just more successful than most at trusting his touch. He tells me speed just happens.

I don't try to prescribe the appropriate speed for players. I know some, like Glen Day, who like to putt the ball so that it dies into the hole. I know others, like David Duval, who believe in hitting the back of the cup with most of their putts. Most players pick different speeds depending on the situation. They try to hit some putts firmly and others softly. There may be times when firmness is the smart option, such as a straight, uphill three-footer on a green that's been spiked up. There may be times when a delicate touch is called for. I don't care what speed a player opts for as long as he's trying to put the ball in the hole.

THE PROPER PACE of a putted ball has engendered more myths and hogwash than almost anything else in golf.

Few people, I suspect, get through their first round of golf without hearing the adage "Never up, never in." It makes it seem as if the goal in putting is not to get the ball in the hole but to roll it past the hole. At least if you roll it past the hole, no one is going to call you "Alice" and question your boldness, your courage, your manhood.

I heard an interesting story about the origin of the "Nice try, Alice" remark that suggests how silly it is. According to this tale, the first time the words were uttered, the golfer was Peter Alliss, who's now a television commentator. He left a putt or two short in the British Open, and some fans sarcastically called out, "Nice try, Alliss." But by the time the words became common in American golf, they'd been subtly changed to "Nice try, Alice." Leaving a putt short had been transformed from simply a mistake to something effeminate. That made American golfers, who tend to be as macho as the next fellows, all the more determined to make sure they never left a putt short.

I'm sorry, but a miss is a miss—whether it runs a foot past the hole or stops a foot short. You get no extra credit for getting the ball past the hole. Good players understand this. They know that if they're trying to roll the ball in the hole softly, it's possible that it will stop a bit short of the hole. If it does, it's a mistake like any other. They go on.

The "never up, never in" concept, mistaken though it is, is nevertheless a model of lucid thinking in comparison to the notion of the green-light putt. The idea of the green-light putt, I suppose, is that this is a putt that the player can safely try to make. This implies that there are red-light putts, putts that are too fast, too slippery to try to make. What is the player supposed to do with them? Try to miss them?

The people who advance the notion that there are "green-light putts" and "red-light putts" tend to be, I find, people whose bad putting forced them into alternative careers as broadcasters. Giving them a microphone and encouraging them to talk about putting is a little bit like going to traffic court, taking all the people convicted of careless driving, and putting them in charge of driver education down at the local high school.

The truth is that every putt is a green-light putt.

That doesn't mean, of course, that you must hit the ball hard on every putt. Take the twenty-footer that Jim Carter had for his third shot on the final hole of the Tucson Open. It was a downhill putt and the green was fast. No sensible player would try to hit that putt hard enough so that the ball banged against the back of the cup as it went in. Obviously, in that case, a miss could roll ten feet past the hole.

But Jim nevertheless putted to make it. He simply tried to give it a pace to make sure that the ball was dying as it approached the hole. As it happened, he rolled it a couple of feet by.

In the course of a normal round, especially on fast greens, there are going to be some putts like that. When he faces them, a smart player may decide to hit his putt just hard enough to get it into the hole. If he does, he also reads more break into the putt, knowing that a slower putt will be affected more by the contour of the green. But he doesn't try to miss, doesn't say to himself, Where do I want to leave this ball for the next putt? He tries to putt the ball into the hole, just as much as he would for an uphill, four-foot par putt.

Occasionally, when I'm teaching amateurs, someone will hear this and say, "Well, that's fine for pros, Doc, but all I'm trying to do in that situation is avoid a three-putt."

Obviously, no one likes to three-putt. But putting to avoid

the three-putt is like trying very carefully to color inside the lines. It eliminates your artistry, your flair, your imagination. It also defeats your own purpose. When a child is told to try very hard to color inside the lines, she generally fails at it, because by trying too hard she robs herself of some of her fine motor skills. When a putter tries very hard not to three-putt, he generally winds up three-putting more often, and for similar reasons. He doesn't get the first putt on line, or he awkwardly leaves it too short or too long. And he will definitely make far fewer of his first putts.

I'm not suggesting that a golfer who putts every first putt to make it, whether it's uphill or downhill, fast or slow, will never three-putt. He will. All golfers do. But he will three-putt less often than the player who's afraid of three-putting. And he will one-putt more often. In the long run, he'll take fewer strokes.

SOME PLAYERS TELL me that their speed problems are not with fast or slow greens per se, but with making the transition from slow greens to fast, or vice versa. And there's no question that this kind of move requires an adjustment. If you're used to putting on shaggy, slow greens and you play a round on a course with fast greens, the stroke you applied to move the ball twenty feet on your regular course may move the ball thirty feet on the new course. Conversely, the stroke that had the ball rattling against the back of the cup on the fast greens of your home course can leave it short on a course with slow greens.

This can also be an issue from one day to the next in tournament play. The trend in setting up courses for tournaments these days is to make the greens as fast and firm as possible. Sometimes the grass is cut so short that it couldn't survive more than a day or so without being allowed to grow. If a course is hosting an event over several days, this means that the greens will likely get faster as the tournament goes on, with the superintendent waiting until the final day to mow them to their fastest possible speed. So tournament players have to be ready to adjust from one day to the next, even though they're on the same course.

Fortunately, the brain can do this for us automatically. You might find that you haven't got a feel for the proper pace on the first green you putt. But after that, your touch is going to get better. It will very quickly be as good as it was on your home course—as long as you keep your mind quiet and offer it no "instruction."

Still, some players don't like to wait for their brains to adjust, and there are a couple of things they can do to facilitate the adaptation. I don't have a problem with a player who gets to a new course early so he can spend some time on the practice green, rolling putts and getting a feel for their speed and the way they break. (Although, as I'll discuss further on, I don't think he should do this while putting to a hole.)

A player can also mentally shift his target backward or forward to help him compensate for a new and unfamiliar green speed. If the putt is downhill and fast, imagine a cup a foot or so short of the real cup, on the line you intend your ball to take.

Putt at that. Conversely, for slow, uphill putts, imagine a cup a foot or so behind your real target and putt at it.

This is not, I think, as effective as simply trusting your instincts and putting to your real target. If, however, you can't bring yourself to do that on a fast green, it's better than the alternative of putting fearfully, trying constantly to "fix" your perceived lack of touch. The best way to deal with speed is to remember that you already have touch. You just have to believe in it and use it.

The Yips

Some day you're going to realize how hard it is to make those putts. All you do now is aim and fire.

—SAM SNEAD, WHO HAD THE YIPS, TO BILLY CASPER, WHO NEVER GOT THEM

I WISH THERE WERE A WAY TO AVOID WRITING THIS CHAPTER. THIS IS a book about how good putters think. The yips are all about how bad putters think. I'm afraid that talking about the yips may be a bit like a high school coach telling his kids to steer clear of a roadhouse on the wrong side of the tracks. The coach may be putting ideas in impressionable minds that otherwise would never be there.

But I know that players do get the yips and want to get rid of them. It's been happening for a long time. The victims are quite often excellent players. In fact, they get the yips in part *because* they're excellent players.

Typically, what happens is this: A boy (yips seem to befall

men more often than women) learns to play the game in a natural way. His goal is simply to get the ball in the hole. He has a good short game, a confident approach to putting. He doesn't always hit the ball straight, but when he gets in trouble, he finds a way to score.

He starts to play golf well. He may start to win tournaments. Then someone says, "You've got a pretty funky swing there. Would you like to straighten it out, make yourself even better?"

The kid decides he would indeed like to perfect his golf swing. So he works at it, taking good advice, practicing long hours. And his swing gets better. By the time he's thirty-five or forty years old, he hits the ball a lot better than he did when he was twenty-two—maybe not quite as long, but a lot straighter. He hits fairways. He hits greens. From a kid who simply loved to play the game, he develops into a man who still loves it, but is a bit of a perfectionist about it.

But he doesn't win any more than he did when he was twenty-two, and it quickly becomes apparent to him why not. Improved ball striking doesn't necessarily lead to improved scoring. To improve his scoring, he has to improve his putting.

So he sets about improving his putting. He approaches it in much the same way he approached his long game. He works on improving his putting stroke. He gets obsessed with it. He's very conscious of things like whether his stroke is long and flowing, whether he keeps the putter blade square to the line, how the ball rolls after he hits it.

He's a perfectionist, and perfectionists are particularly susceptible to the yips. Perfectionists think they're simply setting high standards for themselves—and what's wrong with that? But the perfectionist carries it a step too far. No matter how well he putts, he's not satisfied. He remembers the one that missed instead of the ten or twenty that found the hole. It's not enough for him, in fact, that a putt goes down. It has to be center-cut. And if it isn't, the perfectionist berates himself, tells himself he's a lousy putter. Over time, he starts to believe it. And, as we've seen, people who think they're lousy putters generally become lousy putters.

So the player's putting gets worse. The player can't understand this. He keeps laying more and more pressure on himself to putt better. He starts to brood about the putts he misses, especially the short ones. And then, one day, something snaps. He takes his stance over a short putt. He can't draw the club back. Or, when he does, he can't smoothly stroke the ball. He has the yips.

One of the earliest recorded victims of this syndrome was the great Harry Vardon. By all accounts, Vardon was perhaps the best ball striker in golf history, at least until Ben Hogan came along. Using primitive clubs and balls, he was able to hit it where he wanted it to go with monotonous regularity. And for a number of years he must have been a great putter as well, because he won six British Opens back in the days when the British Open was essentially the only major championship for professionals.

"For many years, it did not so much as enter my head that I

could miss a short putt, except as the result of carelessness," Vardon wrote in his memoirs. "Then I struck a bad patch."

Vardon described this bad patch as the onset of a twitch that caused his right arm to jump and his grip to tighten. He felt helpless to solve the problem, though he recognized it was mostly mental.

"Once you lose your confidence near the hole, you are in a desperate plight," he said. "Especially if you have a reputation to uphold and you know that a putt of two feet counts for as much as the most difficult iron shot."

Vardon died, as far as I know, still suffering from the yips.

Sam Snead was able to pinpoint exactly when the yips struck him. It was late in 1946. Snead was then at the top of his game. He'd won the PGA, the British Open, and a slew of other tournaments. If there had been a world golf ranking system, he might have been first. Snead agreed to play a series of exhibition matches against Bobby Locke that winter in Locke's home country, South Africa.

Locke, who was probably the best putter of his era, gave Snead a humiliating beating on that tour, winning fourteen of the sixteen matches. Of course, he sank a lot of putts to do so. Snead wasn't able to shrug it off or attribute it to Locke's familiarity with the South African greens. He put more and more pressure on himself to match Locke's putting. Before the tour was over, Snead's stroke on short putts had deteriorated to an ugly, nervous jab. He had the yips.

Snead, who was then thirty-four years old, decided that as

middle age approached, something had gone wrong with his nervous system. He tried fixing almost everything about his putting game except the one thing that might have helped, his attitude. He switched putters; that seemed to help for a while. When switching putters no longer worked, he switched to a croquet style, with the putter drawn back between his legs. When the USGA banned that style, he changed to a style he called sidesaddle. And that was how he was putting when his tournament career ended. Snead was a great player, but there's no telling how much better he might have been if he hadn't developed the yips.

As the travails of Snead and Vardon show, the yips are hard to shake once a golfer has them. At an advanced stage, the golfer is so afraid of missing short putts that he all but freezes over the ball, fearful of what his hands will do when he tells them to move. When he finally does putt, his stroke is a jerky parody of his former movement, like one of those primitive silent films where the actors all look like they've got electrodes hidden in their bodies, making all their moves sudden and graceless.

A baseball player named Chuck Knoblauch developed a condition similar to the yips recently, and his symptoms suggest something about the nature of the malady. Knoblauch's problem was making the throw to first base. He got scatter-armed. On television one time, the broadcasters showed a replay of Knoblauch making a bad throw. He was actually looking at his throwing hand as he released the ball, rather than at his target, the first baseman's glove. He was that obsessed with the mechanics of releasing the ball. Putters with the yips, similarly, frequently get obsessed with physical factors like whether their left wrist breaks down during their stroke.

They do this despite the fact that there is no evidence I'm aware of suggesting the existence of a physical condition called the yips. Spasms, tics, and twitches are not an inevitable symptom of an aging nervous system, despite what victims like to imagine. The yips originate in the mind. Their prevention and cure are mental challenges.

The best solution for the yips is making sure you never get them in the first place. And you won't if you practice some of the mental disciplines we've already discussed in this book, disciplines that are integral to good putting.

Some of them have to do with your outlook toward putting. You must not forget that putting is a human endeavor and therefore will never be perfect. You are going to miss some putts, and some of those you miss will be so short they'll embarrass you. You may miss them because you misread them, or you had to putt over a lumpy green, or just because you mishit them. But you will miss them. You have to accept that fact—accept it as soon as each missed putt slides by the hole. Remember, that's part of a good routine.

Your memory can be either a bulwark against the yips or a fifth column in your golf game, subverting your confidence. If you dwell on the putts you miss, if you brood about them at night, you're more likely to develop the yips. If you forget your misses and develop the ability to remember your best putts, your attitude toward putting can get better and better as you age. Instead of developing the yips, you can be a calmer, steadier putter at sixty or seventy than you were at twenty or thirty. After all—who's made more putts, the twenty-year-old or the sixty-year-old? Who's got more great putts to remember?

Putters who develop the yips tend to be players who entertain ideas like, "You should make all your three-footers. . . . You can't afford to miss any par putts. . . ." They're skilled at finding ways to add pressure to the putts they face. They think this will force them to focus, force them to make putts. In reality, of course, it has the opposite effect.

Players who are immune to the yips tend to be players whose thoughts are less about results and more about process. The only thing they tell themselves they should or must do is follow their putting routine on each putt and love the joy of putting to make it. If they do that, they know they're going to hole the most putts they can possibly make. They're content with that.

Players who develop the yips tend to be players who don't understand that good putting is an uncontrolled, subconscious act. They want to guide or steer the ball into the hole. They try consciously to control their putting strokes, to make them perfect. When they stand over putts, they're not seeing the hole or seeing the ball go into the hole. They're seeing their hands, their putter blades, the line they want their blades to travel. They're trying to force their bodies to make their putters follow that path.

That sort of thinking—the conscious, forceful pursuit of putting perfection—overloads the mind and the nervous system the way turning on too many appliances can overload your house's circuit breakers. Something has to give. When it does, the yips are often the result.

Players who get the yips sometimes remind me of classically trained musicians who have been taught to believe that every note must be played exactly as the composer intended and try very diligently to do precisely that. Players who don't get the yips remind me of good jazz musicians, who may not even be able to read music, but who let the rhythm, the joy, and the creativity within themselves flow out when they perform.

The golfing equivalent of playing jazz is imagining the ball going into the hole and making a free, unconscious stroke—seeing it and doing it, as I sometimes tell players. You will never get the yips if you consistently just see it and do it.

Of course, not everyone can be this way all of the time. Even good putters have days when their minds are less clear and less quiet and their strokes are more tentative. They can't quite bring themselves to simply see it and do it. On such days, a good putter might experience a pang of doubt, a prickling feeling of fear. He might, indeed, see the ball missing the hole instead of dropping in. When he does, though, a good putter catches himself. He doesn't allow one mental mistake to build on another. He reverses the negative tendency in his thinking and becomes more casual, less controlled, more reactive. He doesn't allow a pang of doubt to become a full-blown case of the yips, any more than a person who takes care of his health would permit a head cold to develop into pneumonia.

So what if you already have the yips?

I'm sorry to tell you that you can't practice your way out of them. If three-foot putts are your nemesis, you can spend twelve hours a day, seven days a week on the practice green sinking three-foot putts. But no matter how much you practice, if you don't change your attitude, the next time you face a three-footer that really matters to you, you're likely to see the yips return.

It's a little bit like what happened to a catcher named Mackey Sasser for the New York Mets a few years back. Mackey had a yiplike problem throwing the ball back to the pitcher with men on base. He'd pump, pump, pump—but he couldn't pull the trigger, couldn't just take the ball out of his glove and toss it back. It didn't matter how often Mackey practiced throwing the ball back to the pitcher in between games. His problem wasn't that he didn't know how to throw it back, after all. His problem was that he couldn't bring himself to do it in certain situations. So practicing the mechanics didn't help Mackey with his yips and they won't help you with yours.

There are some short-term cures that people have tried. Some players switch putters. Some change their grips. Some go to the long putter. Quite often, these changes bring some temporary relief, as we saw in the case of Sam Snead. That relief usually lasts as long as it takes for the player to begin applying his analytic mind to the question of *why* the new grip, new stroke, or new putter works better than his old way. As soon as he does that, he's applying his conscious mind to the problem of putting the ball in the hole. And when that happens, he's on his way to developing a renewed case of the yips.

But it's not hopeless. It's not true, as someone once said, that once you've had the yips, you've always got them.

The only sure cure is a difficult one. The player has to go back to the mental fundamentals of good putting. He is in a position somewhat analogous to a carpenter who's built a house that just doesn't work. Rather than keep adding joists and beams and buttresses in an effort to make it work, he's got to tear it down and rebuild from the basement up.

For a putter, this means rediscovering a carefree, cocky attitude about putting. It means not caring if you miss a short putt or two, because you know you're a good putter and you'll make up for it down the line. It may mean developing a sense of humor about putting, cultivating the ability to laugh at your own mistakes. It means developing the capacity to accept error and go on. It means developing a short memory for your misses and a long memory for your successes. It means giving up the illusory quest for the perfect stroke. It means committing yourself to a routine that includes seeing the ball going to your target and stroking the ball unconsciously.

If you attend professional golf tournaments, it might help you to follow a good putter for a couple of rounds and notice how often he misses a short putt. It will happen. Then see if you can detect any reaction to that miss beyond a wince or a groan as it slides by. Does the player's routine change on subsequent putts? Does his body language change? Does he start growling at his caddie? I suspect that the answers to all of these questions will be no. Otherwise, the player wouldn't be a good putter. Your reaction to missed putts should be similar.

It's much easier, I know, to write these things than it is to live them. If you have the yips now, you're not going to find it easy to reconstruct your entire mental approach to putting. But that is the only cure. If you can do it, you'll gradually become more confident about your putting, until finally someone in your foursome will remark how solid you are on short putts. And then someone else will say, "Didn't you once have the yips?"

And you'll have to pause for a moment to remember that, yes, you did once have them, just as you had mumps, chicken pox, and other ailments that you've long since forgotten.

New Putters, New Grips, Old Problems

A putter is like a woman. Treat it with care and it will treat you right.

—Gene Sarazen

Gene Sarazen, the first golfer to complete the modern career slam, told the best story about a putter I've ever heard. The year was 1932. Sarazen had a blade putter similar to the one that Bobby Jones had used and called Calamity Jane. Sarazen had customized his version by sawing it off at the neck and welding the blade to the hosel so that it had a bit more loft. (These were the days before the equipment manufacturers followed the Tour in mobile workshops staffed by specialists who work with the pros' clubs. Professional golfers of Sarazen's generation knew how to do this for themselves.) Maybe he should have called it Calamity Gene.

Sarazen took the putter to England with him for the British

Open on the prince's course in Sandwich, adjacent to Royal St. George's. Sarazen played brilliantly in that Open, winning by five shots. His 283 set a scoring record that stood for eighteen years, till Bobby Locke broke it in 1950 at Troon.

In those years, the British Open was played before the U.S. Open each summer, and when Sarazen came home, he still had his own national championship to look forward to. He did something many would think peculiar. He put his favorite putter in a locker and left it there for a few weeks. He pulled it out of the locker just before the U.S. Open began.

Once again, Sarazen was brilliant. Playing at Fresh Meadows Country Club in Flushing, New York, he covered the last 28 holes of the tournament in 100 strokes and won with a 286, tying the Open scoring record.

Why had he put his favorite putter in a locker between tournaments? Sarazen explained it some years later. He knew that he usually need some time to adjust from British greens to American greens or vice versa. He knew that he would miss some putts while he was making that transition. He didn't want to lose faith in his trusty putter. So he put it away and let some lesser club take the blame for the misses he knew he could expect. When he put Calamity Gene back in his bag, it was, to his mind at least, unsullied. And, not coincidentally, he won with it.

Sarazen's little putter ploy worked because it respected one of the psychological rules of putting: If you think the putter you're using will help you, it probably will. Conversely, if you think the putter you're using is worthless, it most likely will be.

The truth, if we define truth objectively, is that it shouldn't matter much which putter a player uses. A good putter can get the ball in the hole with an old shoe if he has to. And any putter you pick up, unless it's been sloppily built or damaged, is going to be a much better instrument for rolling a ball than an old shoe. Its grip, its shaft, and its blade have all been designed to facilitate putting a straight stroke on the ball and making it roll into the hole.

Most of the best putters I know long ago found a putter they liked. Years later, they're still playing with it, or something very similar to it. In fact, I've seen players get quite disconcerted if they sign an endorsement deal with a new equipment company and try to play that company's putter. Even if the new club is essentially the same kind of putter as their old favorite, they're unable to believe in it. Once in a while, you even see someone painting over the brand name on the old putter so that it won't show on television and no one will wonder why he's got a putter from Company A when his bag says Company B, or vice versa.

But I've also known players whose putting responded very well to a change in clubs or a change in grip. And I have been around golf long enough to have a healthy respect for whatever works. I would not have told Gene Sarazen he was deluding himself to think it made a difference to put his British Open putter in storage for a month. I don't tell a modern player who starts sinking putts after changing clubs that he's being foolish.

My primary concern is that a player stand over the ball knowing she's going to make her putt. It pleases me if she came by that confidence by thinking the problem through and adopting a sound mental putting routine. But if her confidence stems from the fact that she dreamed the previous night that her putter had been blessed by the Good Putting Fairy, it's likely to serve her just as well—at least until someone convinces her that fairies don't exist.

I'VE MENTIONED HOW Paul Azinger has worked to develop a mental putting routine that enables him to feel as free and unconscious and target-oriented with his putting as he has always felt with his sand game. One day, in the midst of that process, he happened to be in a pro shop and he saw one of the long-shafted putters, the kind that a player manipulates by sticking the butt end into his body around his sternum and making a pendulum stroke, moving the club with his right hand. It's a club that a lot of players go to when they have lower back problems, because they don't have to bend over to use it and they can, consequently, practice longer with it.

Paul picked up the long club and casually tried it on the floor of the shop. He immediately felt that his putting stroke got longer, more graceful and rhythmic, more natural, more free. He soon started using the long putter in competition, and he was using it when he won the Hawaiian Open, his first Tour victory since his battle with cancer.

Did the long putter help him? Well, I know his putting got

better. I think the more important factor, by far, was the effort Paul was making to get freer with his stroke, to gain control by giving up control. But maybe the switch to the long putter helped him make the mental transition from a feeling that he was forcing his stroke to a feeling that he was simply seeing it and doing it.

In a similar way, I've seen players get good results from switching putting styles, especially by going to the left-hand low, or cross-handed grip. I don't think this is because cross-handed is mechanically superior to the more traditional grip. I think it's because players who try it find that the new grip allows them to putt confidently, freely. They assume that the new grip will prevent a recurrence of the stroke problems they believe have been plaguing them. They start to see it and do it.

Unfortunately, this confidence usually lasts only until they miss a few putts they feel they should have made. At that point, they react by analyzing what went wrong with the new grip, why it failed. At about that time, some teacher or magazine article might "enlighten" them about some of the technical flaws in the cross-handed grip. The players fall back into the same pattern of thought that soured their putting with the old grip. Quite often, they start wondering as they putt which grip they ought to be using.

I don't know anyone who putts well when his mind is occupied by doubts about his grip.

That's why, if a young player asked my advice about putters and grips, I would advise him to pick a putter and a putting style that felt good to him and stick with them. Putting, after all, isn't about which club is best or which grip is best. It's about whose mind can best master the discipline that putting requires.

A player who gets hung up on putters and grips reminds me of an actor who says he can't get into his role as Hamlet because he doesn't like the skull he's been given as a prop for his "To be or not to be" soliloquy. I'd tell him that good actors don't care about their props. They're too busy looking within themselves for the emotions that will make their performance alive and real. In the same way, the golfer obsessed with his putter or his grip is focusing on the props and not on the core of his performance.

The Myth of the Perfect Stroke and the Perfect Roll

> *The fact is that a ball struck with a putter in anything like a normal way will have no spin at all. The contact is not brisk enough to cause the ball to do anything but roll.*
>
> —BOBBY JONES

WHAT I AM ABOUT TO SAY WILL BE AS POPULAR IN SOME QUARTERS AS an assertion that Earth has never been visited by extraterrestrial beings and there are no white alligators in the New York City sewer system. Even though the evidence would support my statement, there are a lot of people who would prefer to think otherwise.

But I'll come out and say it anyway. There is no such thing as perfect putting mechanics. There is no perfect way to roll the ball.

In fact, there are any number of putting strokes and styles and they can all work, depending on the mind of the player who employs them. And a golf ball is designed to roll pretty much the same way no matter how you stroke it. The stories you may have heard or read about the perfect stroke or about "hole-hunting spin" are golf's equivalent of tales about UFOs and albino alligators.

A lot of people believe them, and some of these people are good putters. But in my judgment they're good putters despite believing in those things. They're good putters because they believe in their method and because at the moment of truth, they're not distracted by thoughts of a perfect stroke or a perfect roll. They're focused exclusively on the target.

More typically, golfers get in their own way with thoughts about their stroke or the way the ball rolls. A rabbit could hop out of the hole in the middle of their putting routine and they wouldn't notice. They'd be too busy thinking about taking the clubhead straight up and down the line or putting overspin on the ball to be conscious of the target. And I don't know anyone who lets stroke mechanics or the roll of the ball dominate his mind that way and still putts well.

If you're a player who believes in perfect roll, try this experiment. The next time you're out at your golf course, take a striped range ball over to the practice green. Squat down about twenty feet away from a hole. Roll the ball toward the hole using your hand instead of a club. Try to give it the most violent sidespin you can, like a baseball pitcher throwing a curve ball.

The stripe will allow you to see the ball's spin better than you could with a normal ball. What you'll see is that the sidespin lasts for a few feet at most. Then it dissipates. The ball rolls end over end, as it were. It has topspin.

Then try it with a putter. Hit the ball toward the hole, putting as much sidespin on as you can. You will find that you can't put nearly as much sidespin on the ball with your putter as you could with your fingers. The spin you can put on the ball is infinitesimal. You probably won't even be able to see it.

So what would happen if you were trying to hit the ball straight, with no sidespin?

Right. Sidespin would play no role at all in how the normal putt behaved.

The fact is that the ball is round and it's going to roll in the direction you hit it. High-speed video of golfers' putting strokes confirms this. The films show that sidespin dissipates so quickly that it's basically irrelevant in determining where the ball goes on putts of more than a foot or so. They show that you don't have to worry about overspin. The laws of physics will give the ball overspin if you just hit it toward your target.

I know that some great players of the past, like Locke and Vardon, claimed they could cut or hook putts. Maybe with the lofted putters of their day they could in fact put a little sidespin on the ball. (More likely, they were simply describing what they perceived as the ball curved.) But the evidence is that today's putters on today's greens cannot put any significant sidespin on the ball.

Nor is there any evidence I've seen to support the proposition that a certain kind of spin helps the ball fall in the hole. Speed can help determine whether a putt goes in. A ball rolling slowly is more likely to drop along the edges of the hole than a ball rolling quickly. But by the time the ball reaches the hole on a putt, it's going to be rolling in the direction you hit it, modified by the break of the green. It can't do anything else. Speed and line are the only factors at work in deciding whether it falls.

If, despite this, a golfer stands over a putt and thinks, I want to put overspin on this ball, he's doing two things. First, he's trying to do something entirely superfluous. It's as if the pilot of a jet plane thinks, I know that planes make a lot of noise when they take off, so I'd better make sure this one does. Then he opens the cockpit window and roars like a lion as the plane taxis down the runway. He doesn't need to do that. If he's got the engines running properly, the airplane will make more than enough noise.

Second, and more important, the golfer who's thinking about overspin isn't thinking about his target, any more than the roaring pilot is thinking about his flight plan. He's liable to jab at the ball with an upward, wristy motion, trying to impart overspin. He's going to make fewer putts than he should.

Hey, it's a ball. Balls roll.

IF YOU BELIEVE in perfect putting mechanics, I invite you to think back to one of the most dramatically successful putts in recent golf history, the one from about forty feet that Justin Leonard sank on no. 17 at The Country Club in Brookline to win the 1999 Ryder Cup for the United States.

If you looked at Justin Leonard and believed what you'd read about putting mechanics, then you'd have to conclude that his putt was some kind of mass delusion shared by the American team, the European team, and forty thousand screaming spectators. Because, based on every theory of putting mechanics I've ever heard of, Justin could in no way sink that putt.

Experts on putting mechanics say you have to stand with your eyes directly over the ball in order to see the line properly and stroke the putt along that line. Justin's stance leaves his eyes well inside the target line. The experts say a putter's arms should hang straight down from his shoulders to promote a pendulum stroke. Justin putts with his arms extended away from his body.

How could he hope to sink that putt with such grievously flawed mechanics?

The answer, obviously, is that there's more than one acceptable way to stroke a putt. What matters is where the player's mind is as he strokes it. And I am sure that when he stood over that ball, Justin was thinking only of getting it into the hole.

I'm not suggesting that you adopt Justin Leonard's stance and stroke, or anyone else's for that matter. I am suggesting that your present stance and stroke are probably a lot more effective than you've been led to believe—if your mind is in the right place when you use them.

Golfers today are inundated with information and pseudo-information about the mechanics of putting. The implication in much of it is that a perfect stroke exists and that if you could only attain it, you would putt perfectly. Golfers put stock in this information, I think, because it's more comfortable to believe that their stroke is flawed than that their mind is weak. A flawed stroke, after all, is something that can be blamed on bad instruction or bad coordination. A flawed mental approach edges uncomfortably close to a character issue in some players' minds.

So we have many players in hot pursuit of the perfect putting stroke. The more putts they miss, the more convinced they become that their stroke is to blame. The more information they get about the stroke, the more lost they become in thoughts of mechanics. The more lost they become, the worse they putt. And so it goes.

Let's remember that when we're talking about putting, we're talking about something considerably simpler on a mechanical level than, say, riding a bicycle. Suppose we devised a new athletic event, the suburban biathlon. It would comprise a one-mile bicycle ride to a golf course, followed by a putting contest. During the bike portion of the event, the mechanics would be indeed complex. Contestants would have to steer, balance themselves on two thin wheels, pedal, brake, shift gears, and watch out for traffic—simultaneously! Yet I'd bet that nine out of ten of them would do most of these things subconsciously and naturally, simply keeping their eyes on the road ahead.

These same people, though, would probably turn very conscious and deliberate when they got off their bikes and had to putt. Yet putting a ball along the ground is so much simpler and easier physically than riding a bike. People already know how to do it. They don't have to think about it.

The irony is that the contestants most likely to turn conscious and deliberate when they started to putt would be the experienced golfers. That's because of all the information they've ingested about the putting stroke. That's because of the ethos in the golf world that worships mechanical perfection. There's a strong socialization process at work and it leads to conscious, unsuccessful putting.

You will hear quite often, for instance, that moving the head while you putt is deadly. Yet I remember an incident several years ago at the Walt Disney Tournament. I was working on the practice green with Brad Faxon. A teaching pro Brad knew was standing nearby, having come down to Florida to watch the tournament. This teaching pro had his video camera out, and he noticed Ben Crenshaw practicing near Brad. He prevailed on Brad to invite him inside the ropes. Then he prevailed on Crenshaw to let him tape Crenshaw's practice.

After one of Crenshaw's typically elegant strokes, the teaching pro asked, "What are you working on, Ben?"

"I'm trying to make sure my stroke feels long to short and really leisurely and my head moves a little bit."

In a single, two-second sentence, Crenshaw had contradicted all of the conventional wisdom this pro had learned about putting.

"Because every time I start putting badly, my stroke gets stiff and feels really short to long and, man, I never have any rhythm or flow when I feel like that," Crenshaw replied. "So I'm just trying to get my head moving and my stroke just leisurely going through it."

The teaching pro lowered his video camera, stunned. I have sometimes wondered whether he went home and continued to tell his pupils that the secret to putting well was a short-to-long, accelerating stroke with a still head, or whether he began teaching the opposite. I suspect that he made a valiant effort to suppress what he'd heard and keep on teaching conventional putting mechanics. As I said, there's a strong socialization process at work here.

I am not, in recounting this story, suggesting any particular stroke or head movement. In fact, it's conceivable that Crenshaw was telling the teaching pro what his stroke felt like to him on that day, rather than describing what he was actually doing. Golfers are frequently less than accurate in the way they perceive their own movements.

But the story does illustrate how one of the game's best putters, when he thinks about mechanics, thinks about contradicting so much of what everyone "knows" about putting.

The idea that there is a single correct way to putt is about as valid as the idea that there is a single correct way to write. Where would we be if all of us were told that the only way to write was to copy Shakespeare? We would be without a host of great writers, from Mark Twain to e.e. cummings. The same goes for putting mechanics.

This is why some of the great putters I know make a conscious effort not to think about mechanics at all when they practice. I've seen people ask Brad what part of the stroke he's working on when he practices.

"Nothing," Brad replies.

"Oh, come on," they say. "You must be working on something."

"I am," he says. "I'm working on thinking about nothing mechanical."

IN FACT, THE worst way to try to make a great stroke is by thinking about its mechanics when you putt the ball. As we've seen, the physical work of putting is like riding a bicycle or signing your checks. It's something best left to your subconscious. If you consciously try to guide your putter along a path you've been taught is the correct one, you're reducing the chances that you'll make a smooth, solid, accurate stroke. That's the way the human body works.

On the other hand, if you allow your brain and the nervous system to perform at their best, without interference from your conscious mind, they can do some remarkable things. I know players who have always aimed a little bit left of their targets. They didn't think they were doing it, but they were. However, they didn't hit all their putts left of the hole. As long as they were target-oriented, their brains subconsciously adjusted and altered their strokes enough to send the ball where they wanted it to go.

It's only when such players become conscious and rational about their strokes that they get into trouble. If a player who aims left makes it his business to force the putter to go straight up and down the target line, he's going to miss left. He'll be overriding his subconscious mind's ability to make the adjustment that would have sent the ball toward the target.

If you want to have a flowing, rhythmic, and elegant putting stroke, the last thing to do is think about flow, rhythm, and elegance when you're putting. That will make your stroke tight and strained, more like a jab at the ball. If, on the other hand, you're properly focused on your target, your body will naturally produce the most rhythmic, elegant stroke it can make. I know this because of what I see and hear around Tour practice greens. When a player I'm working with is sharply focused on his target, I can see that his stroke is smooth and flowing. I can tell by what I hear from other players, caddies, and swing teachers that I am not the only one who sees this.

If, after reading this, you nevertheless feel your putting stroke needs work, try this: Go to the practice green and try to make some four-foot putts, the kind that you're probably missing on the golf course. If you can make the four-footers on the practice green but not on the course, then your problem isn't your stroke. If you can't make the four-footers on the practice green, then maybe your mechanics do need work. If so, there are a few things you can do to help prevent your stroke-improvement effort from undermining your putting.

First, go to a good teacher and take a lesson in putting mechanics. Determine the fundamentals you plan to incorporate into your putting game. Commit yourself to staying with them. This means that for the foreseeable future, you are going to putt with the grip, the stance, and the posture you and your teacher agreed on. Players who are constantly fiddling with new grips and postures in an effort to find the perfect stroke can almost never free themselves of mechanical thoughts when they're in competition. Settle on a physical method and stick to it.

Second, practice it off the golf course. I'll talk more in a subsequent chapter about ways to do this. For now, suffice it to say that when you're on a putting green, putting at a hole, you want to be completely focused on getting the ball into that hole. This applies particularly to amateurs whose practice time is limited. A pro might get away with spending an hour on the practice green working on his stroke, because he has an additional hour and fifteen minutes to work on getting the ball into the hole. The amateur rarely has so much time.

Third, don't forget that putting remains more an art than a science. If you immerse yourself in the so-called science of putting, you risk filling your mind with ideas of dubious value (and dubious scientific validity). You risk losing the attitude and habits of mind that characterize great putters.

Imitation of other players can be a better way of improving your stroke. I have clients on the tour who spend time on the practice green pretending they're Ernie Els or Brad Faxon. They think their stroke needs a little of Ernie's and Brad's languid flow. So they imitate them.

This mimics the natural process that kids go through when they pick up a game by watching older people do it. It bypasses all the lectures about mechanics that usually accompany putting lessons and therefore it poses less danger to your mental putting routine.

But if any of the great majority of golfers asked me what I thought they should do about their putting stroke, I'd tell them this: Fall in love with the stroke you have. It's more than good enough to get the ball into the hole.

Practice to Get Better

Around the greens, my father tells me, I was deadly. But, then, I had spent so much time practicing.

—BOBBY LOCKE, SPEAKING OF HIS YOUTH

MY FRIEND AND CLIENT BILL SHEAN HAD A ROUGH TIME ON THE greens during the qualifying rounds of the most recent U.S. Senior Amateur Championship. Bill is a crackerjack senior golfer. In 1998, he won the U.S. Senior Amateur in his first year of eligibility. Nine months later he won the 1999 British Senior Amateur. Not many golfers have simultaneously held British and American national titles. The list includes Tiger Woods, Lee Trevino, Ben Hogan, Bobby Jones, and a few others—not bad company for a guy who sells insurance for a living and plays little or no golf from November to April each year.

To reach the elite level in senior amateur competition, Bill had worked particularly hard on his putting. He reasoned, correctly, that the higher one goes in tournament competition, the more the ball-striking differences among the players diminish and the more putting becomes decisive. He had not thought of himself as a particularly good putter when he was in his early fifties. By the time he reached fifty-five, the age of eligibility for senior amateur tournaments, he had made himself into an excellent one.

But at this championship, the greens were giving Bill trouble. The tournament was held at the Charlotte Country Club in North Carolina, an old Donald Ross layout that had been reworked by Robert Trent Jones. The greens were deep and narrow, with plenty of swales and tiers. And during the early part of the tournament, they were still wet from several days of rain.

Wet greens can be harder to figure than dry ones. Greens don't hold moisture equally over their entire surface. Some areas, because of drainage and exposure to the sun, dry faster than others. That may have been why Bill misjudged a couple of putts badly early in the first round, rolling them eight or ten feet past the hole.

The ensuing three-putts unnerved him. He took forty putts in the first round and forty more in the second round, which was played on a Tuesday morning. He was surprised when his two-round total of 157 made the field of sixty-four golfers for match play. He was barely under the cut line.

Because of the rain delays, there was no overnight break between the end of the qualifying rounds and the first round of match play. Bill had three hours before his first round match. He decided to use that time to practice in an effort to regain confidence in his touch, his ability to judge the pace on the tournament greens.

But Bill did not, as many golfers would, spend those three hours putting several balls to a distant hole on the green. Bill is a golfer who has thought a great deal about how to practice effectively. He knows that one of the guiding principles of effective practice is that you don't putt balls to holes so far away that you can't make the vast majority of the putts you try.

So Bill did what I would recommend to anyone who wants to practice to sharpen his sense of pace, his touch. He putted to the edge of the practice green.

He did this very deliberately. He took a few balls onto the green. He selected lines that offered some complications—sideslopes, downhill, uphill. He putted a single ball along each line he selected. He went through the core of his routine with each one. His goal was to make each ball stop precisely on the border between the green and the fringe. As time passed, his putts started to do so more and more often. Gradually, he rebuilt his confidence in his touch.

When match play began, Bill's putting was transformed. He sank three birdie putts during the early holes, from distances of six to fifteen feet. He felt that he had the ball once again under control—that it would go not only on the line he wanted but the distance he wanted. He started winning matches. Despite having barely made it through qualifying, Bill went all the way to his second U.S. Senior Amateur championship, putting well the entire time.

I TELL THIS story because I think it highlights a few important principles about putting and putting practice.

First, I don't think Bill had to "learn" the speed of the greens at Charlotte Country Club by practicing for three hours. He's an experienced tournament player with a number of USGA events under his belt. He knows how to putt on fast greens. And, as I've said, golfers have already got touch. What they sometimes lack is confidence in their touch. Bill had lost his confidence because he allowed some missed putts early in the event to bother him.

Nor do I think that hours and hours of putting practice are necessary to become a good putter or to maintain your skills. On the contrary, the most important factor in putting well is the confidence that enables the player to see it and do it, simply and subconsciously. Some players can see it and do it the moment they step onto a putting green. They don't need to practice much at all. That's fine with me. But other players either generally or on certain occasions need to practice before they can feel that confidence. Bill Shean is like that. And that's fine, too.

Basically, all that matters is that when you putt in competition, you putt freely and with confidence, seeing your target and letting the stroke go. If you can get to that point with little or no practice, fine. Use the time you save to work on other parts of your game. But if you're the sort of player who builds confidence through practice, do as Bill did. Practice wisely. Practice in ways that build confidence. Practice in ways that reinforce and strengthen your mental routine.

If you practice putting correctly, it should help your game. But I see a lot of golfers, particularly amateurs, who spend a fair amount of time on the practice green and then complain that their putting isn't getting better. They go on to conclude that they just don't have any talent for it, and they give up on becoming good putters. What's really happening is that they're practicing the wrong way. And if you do that, you can get worse.

There are no universally applicable drills or practice programs that will help all players. Just as individuals respond best to different putting stances and grips, individuals need different practice regimens. You have to be your own coach in this regard. You have to experiment a little with different drills and practice routines and find the ones that help your confidence, that help you get ready to putt to make every putt.

I have, however, observed a lot of practice regimens. I think there are a few guidelines that will help most, if not all, putters.

First and foremost, when you practice with a ball and a hole, always putt to make it. This isn't easy to do if you're twenty feet away from the hole and have several balls in front of you. It's very hard in those circumstances to avoid the tendency to get sloppy with your mental routine, to be content with simply rolling balls in the general direction of the hole.

Consequently, a lot of the good players I've seen and worked with emphasize short putts in their practice routines. When David Duval practices putting, he works most of the time from two to six feet. He's not the only one. You might think that putters of David's caliber would practice from longer range because, after all, they're already very good at shorter putts.

But they continually practice short putts, for a number of reasons. Practicing from close range assures them of making most of the putts they try. There's nothing better for your confidence and your putting than seeing balls go in the hole time after time. Second, they know the critical importance of short putts. If you're solid from, say, two to five feet, it makes it so much easier to make your longer putts. You can stroke them more confidently when you know that if by some misfortune you do miss, you're a cinch to sink the next one. Putts in the range of roughly five feet to seven feet are critical because they occur most often in two situations—when a player has hit his approach shot very well and has a chance to make birdie, and when he's missed the green, knocked a chip or pitch fairly close, and needs to save par. Good players will tell you that the difference between low rounds and high ones is usually sinking short birdie putts and getting up and down to save par when they miss greens. To me, short putts are the golfing equivalent of basketball's lay-up shot. The short putt, like the lay-up, is the foundation skill upon which all else is built. It's no coincidence that basketball teams get ready for every game by practicing lay-ups. It's equally true that good golfers make sure their short-putting skills are always honed.

Some players have short putting drills they perform as faithfully each day as brushing their teeth. Dottie Pepper, for example, takes three balls to the practice green and finds a reasonably straight putt to a particular hole. Then she sticks tees in the ground three feet, five feet and seven feet from the hole. She putts till she makes three in a row from three feet. Then she places the balls five feet away and tries to make all three of them. If she misses one, she starts over at three feet. And she keeps on this way until she's made nine putts in a row—three from three feet, three from five feet, and three from seven feet. Some days this takes her ten minutes. Some days it takes an hour. No matter how long it takes, she does it.

The drill does several things for Dottie. First, it enables her to see a lot of putts falling. Even if she doesn't complete the drill on the first try or two, she's going to make the vast majority of the putts she attempts. Second, it makes her feel that her putting is reliable and consistent from seven feet in. Third, it simulates putting under tournament pressure. If you don't believe this, try the drill. If you fail to complete it a few times, and then make eight in a row, I guarantee you're going to feel a little pressure on the ninth putt.

This last element suits Dottie. She likes the feeling of pressure while she practices. It helps her to be calm and free on the golf course. When she steps up to a critical short putt, she feels, This is easy. I did it nine times in a row in practice yesterday.

Other players tell me they don't feel that way. They find that when they're on the course, the memory of practicing under pressure only adds to the pressure they feel with actual putts.

They think, You can't miss this. You'll have wasted all that practice time.

Only a player can judge whether he's like Dottie or not. If you aren't, and you'd prefer to practice without that much pressure, there are other ways to do it. You could simply putt from, say, two, four, and six feet, until you'd made a specified number of each length. Misses wouldn't count. Stewart Cink likes a drill where he places tees in a circle around the cup, mimicking the face of a clock with a diameter of, say, three feet. Then he sinks a putt from every tee.

The main thing is that when you putt with a ball and a hole, you're putting to make every putt and you're making all or nearly all of them.

That's why I think practicing for touch and pace is best done without a hole. When you practice for touch and pace, you're going to have to vary your distance to the target, from perhaps three feet all the way back to forty feet. Especially if you're by yourself and using several balls, you're going to have a hard time putting each one to make it, and you're not going to see the ball go in the hole as often as you should when you practice.

That's why I recommend the drill Bill Shean used, putting to the fringe. If you don't like that, stick a tee in the turf and putt to it. That will simulate practicing for touch the way the pros do on the days before a tournament starts. They putt to tees or to small dots painted on the grass by the superintendent, signifying where the cups are going to be during the tournament.

But I don't see good players spending a lot of practice time working on pace and longer putts, whether it's to the fringe or to a tee, or to a spot painted on the grass. They do it just enough to get a feel for the greens they're playing in a given tournament.

Some players find it hard to get confident unless they feel they've practiced to make sure their alignment is good—that their putter blade is perpendicular to the target line, that their eyes are over the ball, their shoulders are square, etc. These matters all fall under the heading of putting mechanics. If you want to practice them, in my opinion the best place to do so is at home. Find a rug with a straight edge or a straight line in its design. Practice your stroke up and down this line all you like. Use a mirror to check your posture. But do all these things without a golf ball. Remember that when you practice with a ball and a hole, you're practicing putting to make it, not putting to check your alignment or your putter path.

If you want a drill that allows you to use a ball, a club, and a hole, and at the same time indirectly check your alignment, try the chalk line drill. It's the best putting practice tool I know of. There are lots of putting gadgets on the market, all claiming to be the answer to your putting woes and all priced as if they were. For my money, the best practice aid isn't sold through infomercials and isn't carried in golf shops. Nor will you find it advertised in golf magazines. It's in the hardware store, and it costs ten or fifteen dollars. It's the chalk line.

This is a tool that builders use to put lines on the ground to guide them in digging. It's basically a reel of string encased in a plastic shell that includes blue chalk dust.

To work on your putting with a chalk line, find a straight putt of about ten feet on your practice green. Shake the reel to coat the string with chalk dust. Then let out about ten feet of string. Pin one end of the string with a tee or a pencil to your hole. Let the string run along the straight putting line you've selected. Pull it taut and then snap it against the ground. It will leave a faint blue line on the ground. (It's harmless to the turf, by the way.)

Now all you need to do is center a ball on the line and putt it into the hole. You'll be amazed at how often it goes in. Using a chalk line, you can effortlessly sink putt after putt from eight or ten feet.

There's only one way you can mess up the chalk line drill, and that's by consciously trying to steer your putter along the line on the ground. That defeats the purpose. I don't know precisely what the magic of the chalk line is. I only know that the visual aid of the line will allow you to adjust your alignment and your putter blade subconsciously until everything is square. It will enhance your ability to roll the putt precisely along the line to the hole. Of course, you'll have complete trust in that line, because you'll already know that the putt is straight.

I know many pros who work regularly with a chalk line when they're at home, polishing their games before a tournament. I'm sure I'd see it more often on Tour, but some of the superintendents at Tour courses try to discourage its use. They know that once someone lays a chalk line down on the practice green, nearly every golfer in the field is going to want to use it, and they'll get too much wear in that portion of the practice green.

Presumably, though, the superintendent at your course won't have that problem. That's because only a small fraction of the players at most clubs systematically practice putting and even fewer understand the value of the chalk line.

There's only one pitfall with chalk line practice. It works so well that some players get overly fond of it. They stop practicing short putts without the chalk line. Then, in competition, they find themselves missing the chalk line, doubting their ability to putt without it. So use it in conjunction with other putting practice. Over time, you'll find that you will start to "see" a line away from the practice green. That's part of the magic of the chalk line.

I LIKE TO see players turn putting practice into a game. If you've got a friend on the practice green with you, for instance, you might want to try a little variation on the drill of putting to the fringe. The players start at the same point and putt to the same area of fringe. The player closest to the edge gets a point. If he stops his ball precisely on the edge, he gets two points. Points can be translated into nickels, dimes, and quarters if you like to have a small bet going. This kind of game enhances your interest in practice and helps you practice putting under a little pressure.

I'll even relax my rule against practicing longer putts toward a hole if it's part of a game. Brad Faxon, Billy Andrade, and Davis Love III often play a putting green practice game they call "Look and Shoot." Two players find a couple of holes about fifteen feet apart. Each player takes one ball. You putt your ball toward the other guy's hole, trying to make it, and vice versa. There's no time to read the green or take a practice stroke. Each time a player holes his putt, the contestants switch holes. If they miss, they putt the balls back and forth till someone makes one. They keep at it till someone has made five putts.

When it's done properly, the pace of this drill is very brisk. The competing players keep one another from getting too careful. They make sure the opponent has time only to look at the target and react to it. It makes them both putt very athletically.

At the clubs I visit, I've seen countless variations of another game. Everyone in this contest putts toward a hole perhaps thirty feet away. If someone gets the ball in the hole, he instantly wins two units from everyone else in the game. The player whose first putt is farthest from the hole has a choice. He can either attempt his second putt or pass on it. If he passes, he loses one unit to everyone. If he tries and misses, he loses two units to everyone. If he tries and makes it, there's no blood. The loser chooses the next putt and the game starts again.

This is a good practice game because it puts a premium on getting the ball into the hole. It introduces competitive pressure. And if you've got four or five buddies jingling change and making unhelpful remarks about your putting stroke when you line up a four-footer, it helps to develop a routine that insulates you from distractions and pressure.

This kind of game will help you find the seemingly paradoxical place where most good putters' minds reside. They hit practice putts as if they were in a tournament, and they hit tournament putts as if they were practicing.

That is, when they practice, good putters employ their mental routines. They putt to make every putt that involves a hole. Then, when they're in competition, the practice they've put in helps them relax, focus on the target, and stroke their putts freely.

That's effective practice.

A Word About Wedges

Improve your chipping and you automatically improve your scoring.

—Tom Watson

What's a chapter on wedge play doing in a book about putting?

Try a little experiment. Next time you're on a practice green, drop five balls ten feet from a hole. Putt them, putting to make each of them. Count the number that fall. Now take the same five balls and drop them three feet from the hole. Make it hard on yourself. Use the leading edge of your sand wedge to putt them.

I'll bet that more balls go in off the edge of the sand wedge from three feet than drop from ten feet using a proper putter.

And that's why, even though this is a book about putting, I want to say a little bit about wedge play. Give me the average hacker from three feet and you can have Loren Roberts or Brad

Faxon or Ben Crenshaw from ten feet. Despite their considerable skills, they're going to miss more from ten feet than a poor putter will miss from three feet.

Good wedge play makes the difference between a lot of putts from ten feet and a lot of putts from three feet. If you knock your chips and pitches closer to the hole, you're going to make more putts.

Wedge play is one reason why putting statistics don't always show who's the best putter. The statistics count the average number of putts a player makes on greens he's hit in regulation. What they don't reflect is the average length of those putts. A player with mediocre wedge games may be leaving his pitches twenty feet from the hole on short par-4s and on par-5s, both the sorts of holes where a good player is likely to have an approach to the green from about one hundred yards. A player with a better wedge game may be leaving himself an average of ten feet from the hole in those situations. Consequently, he makes more putts.

Good wedge play belongs in that category of fundamental skills I've mentioned already, skills analogous to playing good defense and rebounding in basketball. Just as winning basketball teams make it a priority to play defense and rebound, winning golfers make it a priority to hit their wedges close to, or in the hole.

I've seen improved wedge play elevate a professional's game. It can be the difference between playing on the Buy.com Tour and playing, and winning, on the PGA Tour.

Michael Clark II and I started working together years ago,

when he was playing at Georgia Tech. Mike had a lot of talent. But, as he would be the first to tell you, he didn't have a lot of maturity, or a lot of luck. He didn't practice as much as he should have in college. He didn't play as well as he should have.

When he turned pro, he had a series of injuries. They kept him from climbing the ladder quickly. But they also helped Mike discover persistence, strength of will, and purpose. He kept plugging away at the game, even when the rewards were scant.

As he matured, Mike began to realize that his wedge game was one of the things keeping him from being the player he wanted to be. He was capable of shooting low scores when his swing was in synch. But he wasn't able to use his wedges and chips to prevent a 75 or 76 on days when his swing wasn't working as well.

For Mike, the key to improving his wedge game was unleashing his creativity. He had been taught as a boy to hit a lot of bump-and-run shots. They were the shots he felt most comfortable with, the shots he instinctively wanted to hit in most situations around the green. But in professional golf, the fashion was for high wedge shots. Mike became, in a sense, a victim of fashion. He found himself torn in many situations between the creative bump-and-run shot his instincts told him to hit and the high, fly-it-to-the-hole-and-stop-it shot his peers tended to hit. Indecision, of course, is as fatal in the wedge game as it is in putting.

Gradually, over the past couple of years, Mike found a solution. He started to rely more on the sorts of bump-and-run shots he loved to play as a boy. But he also worked hard on his soft, high wedges, especially from bunkers, so he'd have them when he needed them.

When he went to the Tour qualifying school last year, Mike found that his swing was not where he wanted it to be. He wasn't hitting it too well. But his wedge game saved him. On one of the first holes of the first round, he found himself with a tough little shot to play—over about ten feet of Bermuda rough and then over about fifteen feet of green to the hole. It was slightly uphill. He hesitated. His instinct told him to hit a nine-iron and try to chip it in. He had a second thought, which was a safe wedge into the slope. Mike this time went with his instinct and hit an excellent chip, landing it in the fringe and running it up to the hole. It lipped out, leaving him a tap-in par putt. His confidence got an enormous boost from the knowledge that even with his swing out of whack, he could still score.

Despite having a kinky swing the first three days, Mike managed to shoot 66, 68, and 70. Then he got his swing straightened out, thanks to a tip from his old college coach, Puggy Blackmon. He shot a 63 in the fourth round. He eventually finished eleventh at the school and got his card for the PGA Tour. In his rookie season he won the John Deere Classic and established himself as a player to be reckoned with. And the primary difference in his game was his wedge play and, not coincidentally, his putting.

• • •

IT'S NOT MY purpose here to discuss the mechanics of the various chips and pitches a good golfer must be able to hit. If you have a problem with your short-game mechanics, see a pro, settle on a method, and stick to it.

But I do want to point out some of the ways in which a sound mental routine for wedge play resembles a sound mental routine for putting.

The first and most important is that good chippers and pitchers always try to hole their shots from within a threshold distance, just as good putters always putt to make it. They're not thinking about getting it close or leaving themselves an uphill putt. They're thinking about holing the shot.

Second, the chipping and pitching routine of good players resembles the putting routine at its core. They look at the target, look at the ball, and let the shot go. It's athletic, creative, almost improvisational. Think of a basketball player pulling up and shooting the open jumper in the split second before his defender can adjust. Think of a third baseman scooping up a bunt with his bare hand and throwing on the run toward the outstretched glove at first base. At the critical moment, these athletes simply react to the target without thinking. So does a good wedge player.

Mike Clark told me about a shot he was particularly proud of at the qualifying school. It came in the final round. He'd hit the ball over the green with his second shot on the par-5 16th hole.

He had a delicate pitch back up a slope, a shot he'd have to play like an explosion from the Bermuda rough. Mike simply went through his routine. And at its climax, he started taking the club back as soon as his eyes returned to the ball after his final look at the target. There was no hesitation. He knocked it four feet from the hole.

If you react similarly to your target, you'll be well on your way to solving one of the common problems in wedge play, a problem very similar to the problem of speed in putting. With a wedge, the issue is how far to hit the ball. Many golfers find it's not too hard to chip the ball toward their target. But they tie themselves up trying to make sure they chip it the right distance.

Some years ago, I worked with a pro named Buddy Harston from Lexington Country Club in Lexington, Kentucky. Buddy was unhappy about several aspects of his game, particularly wedge play. I took a look at Buddy's routine. There was a long gap between his last look at the target and the beginning of his swing. I asked him what he was doing during that interval.

Buddy told me he was trying to visualize the shot he was about to hit, starting with the swing he intended to make and finishing with the ball rolling close to the hole.

I told him that the time to visualize was when he was standing behind the ball, planning his shot, not when he was about to execute it. At the core of his routine, I wanted him to look at the target and let the shot go within seconds.

I knew Buddy had been a baseball player in his youth. He

played second base on some teams that reached the College World Series. I asked him how he'd handled the cut-off play responsibilities of a second baseman.

"I went out into the outfield and put my hands up and caught the ball and listened for the shortstop to tell me where to throw," Buddy said. "Then I whirled and threw it there."

"You didn't stop and visualize how you were going to throw it?" I asked.

Buddy understood. "No, of course not. There wasn't time. I just threw it where the shortstop told me to."

"And it went the right distance?"

"Yes."

That, I told him, was how his wedge game would work best, too. I wanted him to get set up, take a last look at the target, and let the shot go without delay. His athletic ability would make sure the ball went the right distance, so long as he was reacting to that target.

Buddy tried it and the results were dramatic. He soon won his first significant championship as a professional, a section PGA competition in Kentucky. He's won many more since then. Today, he's looking forward to a chance to qualify for the Senior PGA tour.

He might make it if he keeps reacting to his target with his wedges and his putter.

There are a couple of nuances in wedge play that differ from putting. The first is the selection of a target during the preshot routine. Some players like to home in on the cup just as they do

A Word About Wedges • 157

in putting. They use the cup as a target on straight chips and pitches. They pick out an imaginary target to the left or right of the cup on shots that will break.

Others envision their shot and see a point on the green where they want the ball to land. They imagine a specific trajectory for the airborne portion of the shot. They foresee how the ball will roll once it lands. So when they chip or pitch, their target is a spot on the green that might be a long way from the hole.

It doesn't matter which way you prefer to do it. If you're not already a confirmed believer in one way or the other, experiment around the practice green. Choose the method that appeals more to you and stick with it.

The second nuance involves your threshold distance. That's the distance within which you always try to hole a shot. You try to make every putt. But you try to hole only those wedges that are played from within your threshold distance. For Tour pros, who wouldn't be where they are without precise control of their wedges, the threshold distance might be 120 yards, which is the distance a professional generally hits a wedge. Whenever he has a shot from that distance or less, he should be thinking about holing it.

For amateurs, whose control is less precise, the threshold distance may be shorter—twenty, thirty, sixty yards. And there may be occasions when you have to adjust it. Suppose, for instance, that you have twenty yards to the green and the hole is cut five yards from the front edge. Your normal threshold distance is fifty yards. In that situation, you might normally be thinking of pitching the ball to the edge of the green and letting it roll in. But let's add a pond to the situation—beginning just in front of you and extending to the very edge of the green. Your wedge control may not be precise enough for you to risk trying to land the ball a couple of feet beyond the water. You may have to aim for a spot deeper on the green and settle for a shot that leaves you beyond the hole, but dry. Such situations, though, are relatively rare. Most of the time, when inside your threshold distance, think about holing it.

And then practice it. While it's possible to be a good putter without spending too much time practicing putting, I don't know many good wedge players who don't work constantly to keep that aspect of their game sharp. They've fallen in love with getting the ball up and down, or chipping it in, and they like practicing it. It's quite common for pros on the Tour to spend an hour and a half every day practicing around the greens.

There's no mystery to how to do this. Walk ten paces out from the edge of your practice green. Circle the green using the new radius you've established. Everything within this circle is your practice area. Within it, you'll find, I hope, a rich variety of short-game situations—tight lies and grassy lies, side slopes and humps, chips and pitches. There should be a practice bunker somewhere within this circle for sand shots. If not, you can always wait till twilight or early morning and use a bunker on the course.

Let your imagination work as you practice. Try a variety of

A Word About Wedges • 159

ways to put the ball in a hole from a given situation. Lob it close, then chip it and let it run to the hole. You'll sharpen both your touch and your sense of what shot best fits a given situation.

If you're a high-handicap player, your wedge game by definition isn't as sharp as a pro's. If it were, you wouldn't have a high handicap. Your practice can help you address some of the common problems that less skilled players have with the short game.

Many amateurs, I know, worry about skulling or chili-dipping their short shots, particularly from tight lies. The best cure for this is practicing from bare dirt. If you practice on a range, it's not hard to find a spot where the grass has been hacked away by someone else. (If you don't practice on a range with grass tees, but you play a lot of golf, it's likely that the grass in your backyard isn't all that lush. That's because you're probably out on the course when you could be laying down fertilizer. Now you can reap a benefit from neglecting your yard. You can find a bare spot there and use it for short-game practice.) Wherever you do it, learn to hit from bare dirt. When you encounter a tight lie on the golf course, it'll seem easy by comparison.

You may be wondering, now that I've suggested practice drills and games for your putting, and I've suggested lots of practice for your short game, when do I expect you to work on your cherished goal of learning to hit a precisely faded seven-iron to a tight pin?

The answer is that I don't. If you're a tournament pro whose business is playing golf, you might have time to work on that sort of shot. But if you make your living off the golf course, you probably don't. Part-time golfers whose practice time is limited ought to spend nearly all of it on three areas—putting, the short game, and whatever club—driver or fairway wood—they rely on for most tee shots.

Until you become proficient from all lies with your wedges, there's nothing wrong with using a putter from tight lies, where that's possible. I've seen some players have good results using the three-wood from the fringe, rather than hitting a traditional chip. That's fine, too. The Scots invented golf, and they use putters anywhere within forty yards of the green.

But you will not be playing your best golf until your wedge game is sharp enough that bad lies don't deter you, until no matter where you find yourself around a green, you have a chip or a pitch that you feel you can put in the hole.

When you reach that level, you'll need fewer putts.

How You'll Putt from Now On

I've always been a good putter and I probably always will be.

—Tom Kite

Now you know what it takes to be a good putter. The question is, how will you apply what you know? What kind of commitment are you prepared to make to it?

I sometimes run into people who have read one of my earlier books, most notably *Golf Is Not a Game of Perfect*. And sometimes one of these readers will say, "The stuff in that book worked great for a while, Doc. I was really playing well. But it doesn't work so well anymore."

When I have a chance to talk with one of these people, it becomes clear that the stuff in the book isn't the problem. Commitment to it is the problem. When the book was fresh in their minds, they trusted their swings, they managed their golf games intelligently, they disposed of anger on the course. They did a lot of things right and their scores showed it. But with time, their old habits of thought reasserted themselves. They started to think about their swing mechanics when they played, and to try to fix them. They started to make foolish strategy choices. They started to let anger affect their next shots. And their scores went up as a result.

Thus the question: How will you apply what you now know about putting? What sort of commitment will you make to it?

The principles of putting in this book will work, but only if you apply them for an extended period of time—say, six months to a year. And they'll continue to work for as long as your commitment stands. They'll stop working if your commitment fades.

Don't think that keeping a commitment to these ideas will be easy. Making a commitment is easy. Keeping it is hard. That's because no system, no set of ideas, will turn you into a putting wizard. Putting isn't wizardry. It's an art, and there are days when it's a capricious art. There are going to be times when you miss putts you think you should have made. There are going to be times when those missed putts will cost you a match or a title you dearly wanted to win.

That's when keeping a commitment begins to get hard. That's when other paths will become tempting. There are always going to be people in the golf world trying to persuade you that their grip, or their putter, or their practice aid, or their stroke is the answer. There are always going to be people telling you that there's no point in trying to be a good putter because you have no talent and it's an impossible, unjust part of the game anyway. If you listen to them, you won't keep your commitment.

If you want to keep your commitment, it will help if you know you're committed to a process, a process that works. The process isn't dependent on how many putts you take on a given hole or round. Those numbers will fluctuate, though the trend will be downward.

If you're the sort of player who adds up his putts at the end of a round and evaluates himself by the number he made, the number of three-putts or whatever, you may need a new way of thinking to buttress your commitment. Instead of asking, How many times did I putt this round?, you need to ask, How many times did I putt without executing my mental routine? How many times did I fail to simply see it and do it? If the answer is never, then the number of putts you actually took is irrelevant (though it will usually be satisfyingly low).

If you'd like to keep a commitment to change the way you putt, you might do well to have some criteria by which you can monitor the way you're thinking. Here are some ideas that might help you:

Do you love putting on whatever sort of green you encounter, fast or slow, grainy or smooth?

Do you welcome the challenge of putting?

Do you take pride in how free and confident you are with your putter?

Do you execute your mental and physical routine on every putt?

Do you refuse to let missed putts bother you? Do you stick with your routine and habits of mind even when putts don't fall on the first nine holes?

Do you always putt to make it?

Do you ever permit your fear of three-putting to dominate your love of one-putting?

When you talk about your putting to others, do you talk about how well you're putting rather than whine or complain?

Do you try to recall the great putts you've made and forget the ones you've missed?

If you're coming up with the wrong answers to those questions, then it's time to reexamine and reinvigorate your commitment.

Don't think of this commitment as a porcelain vase that, once broken, can never be put together again. I don't know of any player whose mind is always where it ought to be. Every player I've ever worked with has had occasions when he's putted in fear or doubt, when he's tried to steer the ball into the hole. Good players recognize when their commitments waver, and they set things right quickly. They constantly recommit themselves.

But while keeping your commitment to good putting won't be easy, neither will it be like keeping a commitment to go to the dentist twice a year. Putting well is fun.

You're going to love the difference thinking well about putting makes in your golf game.

If we could turn that theoretical computer-assisted mind-scanning device I spoke of earlier onto the mind of a good putter, we'd find these kinds of pleasant thoughts:

All right! Safely on the green. Now the fun starts. This is going to be an interesting putt. I can see two breaks. Downhill. A real challenge. Neat! I like the fact that my partner has no doubts that I'm going to make par or better on this hole. I like being the bulwark of our team because I putt well. I like the way the other guys' faces will look when I sink this for a birdie. Okay, now into the routine. . . .

You're going to love knowing that the way you putt and think about putting gives you a big advantage over the rest of the players in your weekly foursome, the ones who are always grumbling about putting and buying new putters. You're going to love seeing a three-foot putt for par and knowing you'll make it. You're going to love being the guy who rescues holes given up for lost with a great putt. You're going to love watching your golf ball roll firmly and boldly across a green full of treacherous waves and currents, and then drop toward the hole like a sailboat making for harbor. You're going to love that moment of clarity, when confusion burns away like a morning fog and you see the line your ball must follow. You're going to love the sound of the ball rattling in the hole.

You're going to love to putt.

Appendix

ROTELLA'S RULES FOR PUTTING

1. No matter how skilled you are with the long clubs, you're going to make roughly 40 percent of your shots with your putter.
2. The putting game is the place to look if you want to get a competitive advantage.
3. The ideal golf temperament instinctively loves putting.
4. In putting, the inability to forget is infinitely more devastating than the inability to remember. There's nothing worse for your putting than dwelling on the putts you've missed.
5. Thinking the way you have always thought will almost certainly assure that you putt the way you have always putted.

6. You'll make your best stroke and hole the most putts if you think only of your target.
7. Orientation toward the target works because the subconscious brain is capable of quick, accurate adjustments.
8. The smaller the target you have, the better the brain and body can function in getting the ball there.
9. Never putt for a three-foot circle. If you aren't trying to hole every putt you have, you are going to lose to someone who is.
10. To gain control, give up control.
11. Devotion to an unvarying routine is one of the hallmarks of a good putter.
12. When the moment of truth comes, look at the target, look at the ball, and let the stroke go without any undue delay between these three movements.
13. Your first impression of how a putt will break will be right more often than any other impression you might form.
14. Putt to make it.
15. More often than not, anger is the enemy of focus.
16. Good players handle pressure putts by developing a strong routine and relying on it in the clutch.
17. Good putters learn to welcome nervous symptoms rather than fear them.
18. The last thing you want to do if you're trying to make putts is worry about speed.
19. You already have touch. You have to believe in it and use it.

20. A miss is a miss, whether it runs a foot past the hole or stops a foot short.
21. Every putt is a green-light putt.
22. The yips originate in the mind. Their prevention and cure are mental challenges.
23. If you think the putter you're using will help you, it probably will.
24. Pick a putter and a putting style that feel good to you and stick with them.
25. There is no such thing as perfect putting mechanics. There is no perfect way to roll the ball.
26. Fall in love with the stroke you have.
27. Practice in ways that build confidence.
28. Practicing for touch and pace is best done without a hole.
29. Good wedge play makes the difference between a lot of putts from ten feet and a lot of putts from three feet.
30. The principles of good putting will work for as long as your commitment to them stands.

Also by *Dr. Bob Rotella*

Golf Is a Game of Confidence
The Golf of Your Dreams
Putting Out of Your Mind
Life Is Not a Game of Perfect

GOLF IS NOT A GAME OF PERFECT

DR. BOB ROTELLA

with Bob Cullen

This edition first published by Pocket Books, 2004
An imprint of Simon & Schuster UK Ltd
A Viacom Company

Copyright © Robert Rotella, 1995

This book is copyright under the Berne Convention.
No reproduction without permission.
All rights reserved.

The right of Robert Rotella to be identified as the author of this work has been asserted by him in accordance with sections 77 and 78 of the Copyright, Designs and Patents Act, 1988.

5 7 9 10 8 6 4

Simon & Schuster UK Ltd
Africa House
64–78 Kingsway
London WC2B 6AH

www.simonsays.co.uk

Simon & Schuster Australia
Sydney

A CIP catalogue record for this book
is available from the British Library

ISBN 0-7434-9247-1

Printed and bound in Great Britain by
Cox & Wyman Ltd, Reading, Berkshire

Foreword to the British Edition

I WAS PARTICULARLY PLEASED TO LEARN THAT THERE WOULD BE A BRITISH edition of *Golf Is Not a Game of Perfect* so that more golfers from these isles could get to know Bob Rotella's unique and down-to-earth brand of mental fitness.

I have worked with Bob for many years and while he has helped to remind me of some of the timeless lessons of golf, he always does so with a fresh eye and a clear focus on what matters most. There are countless 'mind-doctors' and 'gurus' on the tour who spend a lot of time dressing up conventional wisdom and complicating common-sense. Bob Rotella is the real deal, whose virtue is to keep it simple so that I can do the same on the golf-course.

Golf Is Not a Game of Perfect has been one of the most-thumbed books in my golfing library for a long time. I understand that it was originally written nearly ten years ago but the lessons contained within are as important today as they have ever been. Staying positive, overcoming your fear of failure, setting yourself the right goals, avoiding those fatal lapses of concentration and focusing on the next shot instead of the last one are all crucial ways of improving your score, and all are covered here in a really accessible no-nonsense manner.

For most of us, when things aren't going well, rebuilding our swing or changing our putting style is not an option. Nor should it be. A reminder of the basic mental exercises, which the Doc explains so well, goes a long way towards turning things around.

Darren Clarke
March 2004

Introduction

OVER THE PAST THIRTEEN YEARS, I'VE BEEN FORTUNATE ENOUGH TO work with many of the greatest golfers in the world. This book is an effort to share with others who love the game what I've taught some very successful golfers and what they've taught me.

The psychology of great golf is quite plain and logical. Most players with whom I work are at first amazed by the simplicity of what I tell them. They're surprised to find that there is nothing weird or mysterious in what I do. With a bit of relief in their voices, they tell me that the type of thinking I teach strikes them as good common sense.

Sport psychology, as I teach it, is about learning to think in the most effective and efficient way possible every day. It's the psychology of excellence. My job as a coach of mental skills is to help players go where they might not be able to go on their own, given their old ways of thinking.

They may have learned ways of thinking that work on a driving range or a practice green. What I offer is a way of thinking and playing that works under the fire of competitive pressure, that breeds consistency, provides the best chance to "go low," and helps players find a way to win.

The challenge lies not in understanding the concepts I teach, for, as I've said, they're simple and make common sense. The challenge lies in thinking this way every day on every shot.

To meet this challenge, golfers must understand the power within themselves. They must learn to tap this power and let it flow into their golf game.

One of my goals in writing this book is to expose people who love golf to the truth about free will. I am convinced that it is the power of will that separates great golfers from those who never reach their potential.

Though I teach psychology, I have never known for sure where the mind ends and where heart, soul, courage and the human spirit begin. But I do know that it is somewhere in this nexus of mind and spirit, which we call free will, that all great champions find the strength to dream their destinies and to honor their commitments to excellence. All great champions are strong on the inside.

They all learn that competitive golf either builds character or reveals character. They learn to be honest about their thoughts. They learn to relish the game's mental and emotional challenges. They learn to appreciate the value of thinking in an athletic manner. Finally, they learn that golf is a game, and it has to be played.

I also know that it's all too easy, in this age of videotape, for the media to overlook the role of the mind. Television cameras can't take pictures of thoughts. But anyone who plays championship golf will tell you that at least half the battle occurs inside the golfer's mind.

This book will equip you for that challenge. Because I think it's important to learn from the experience of other players, I've drawn lots of illustrations from the history of the game and from conversations I've had with the players I teach. I hope these anecdotes will help readers understand and remember the principles I want to convey. They are the honest truth about golfing excellence.

Read and enjoy.

Contents

	Foreword by Tom Kite	15
1.	On *My* Interpretation of Dreams	19
2.	What Nick Price Learned from William James	30
3.	Train It and Trust It	37
4.	How Stuart Anderson Created His Own Reality	45
5.	The Hot Streak: Staying Out of Your Own Way	49
6.	Rediscovering Old Scottish Wisdom	52
7.	What the Third Eye Sees	60
8.	Your Rod and Staff	68
9.	Let the Short Game Flow	82
10.	What I Learned from Bobby Locke	95
11.	Golf Is Not a Game of Perfect	113
12.	Anyone Can Develop Confidence	125
13.	What Mark Twain and Fred Couples Have in Common	130
14.	Fighting Through Fear	133
15.	What I Learned from Seve Ballesteros	140

16.	Conservative Strategy, Cocky Swing	147
17.	Game Plan	152
18.	Thriving Under Pressure	170
19.	When the Scoreboard Looks at You	184
20.	Competitors	190
21.	Practicing to Improve	195
22.	What I Learned from Paul Runyan	211
	Appendix: Rotella's Rules	219

Foreword

By Tom Kite

THROUGHOUT THE YEARS, THERE HAS BEEN A GREAT DEAL OF DISCUSsion about the game of golf and about improving scores. Invariably, the discussion turns into a debate on exactly how much of the game is physical and how much is mental. Generally, the better a player is, the higher the percentage he will attribute to the mental side. That's reasonable. A beginner, who has very little control over his swing, can't be expected to understand that the game is 80 percent or 90 percent mental. But on the PGA Tour, where all the players can hit quality shots, the mental side is at least 90 percent of the margin between winners and losers. Percentages aside, no matter what a player's handicap, the scores will always be lower if the golfer thinks well.

There have been untold thousands of instruction books written on golf. Most have chapters on the grip, the stance, posture, swing plane, alignment, and the rest of the game's mechanics.

But, given the mental side of the game's importance, far too little has been written on it. There must be reasons for this. Maybe it's because it's impossible to see what a person is thinking. Many times I have had fans tell me how cool I looked on the course, when all I could remember was how scared or nervous I had been. Or, possibly, it's because the top players, those who have found an effective way to think on the course, are very protective of any thoughts that might aid an opponent. Or maybe it's because few people have studied the mental side of golf compared with the vast number who have studied the swing. But for whatever reason, accurate information on the mental side of the game is long overdue. Bob Rotella's book—this book—is it.

I met Doc in 1984 at the Doral Open in Miami. I was in one of those phases where I just couldn't seem to do anything right on the course, and my scores showed it. I hadn't had a top finish for months, and winning a tournament seemed as far away as the moon. But after a couple of meetings early in the week, when Doc did no more than refresh my memory of those great thoughts I usually have when I am playing my best, I went out and actually won the tournament, beating none other than Jack Nicklaus down the stretch. My swing hadn't changed at all in the couple of days since the last event. But I was like a new person. All of a sudden, I could hit shots that I could not even imagine the week before. My patience level increased dramatically. Even my walk was confident. I had a new best friend, and it was me!

In the first twelve years of my life on the PGA Tour, I had established myself as a pretty decent player but had only won five official tournaments. In the ten years since meeting Doc, I have won fourteen tournaments, played on the Ryder Cup team, and won my first major, the U.S. Open. To say that I think Doc has helped make me a better player would be an understatement. I now realize that I must spend as much time working on a good mental approach as I do hitting balls on the practice tee.

But don't let the idea of yet another task scare you! This won't require much hard work on your part. After all, we all have thoughts running through our minds all the time. What Doc can do is show you what thoughts are advantageous and what thoughts are destructive. And one of the really neat things that comes along when you try this approach is that not only do you become a better golfer, athlete, or sales executive, but you learn more about yourself and become a more fulfilled person.

Who says we can't have it all?

1.

On *My* Interpretation of Dreams

I HAVE TWO things in common with Sigmund Freud. I have a couch in my consulting room. And I ask people to tell me about their dreams. But there the resemblance ends.

The couch is in my basement rec room, near the Grounds of the University of Virginia in Charlottesville. The picture frames above it hold not the psychoanalyst's carefully neutral art but a print of a golfer swinging a mid-iron and a flag from the 18th hole at Pebble Beach, signed by Jack Nicklaus, Tom Watson and Tom Kite. A four-and-one-quarter-inch putting cup, sunk into the floor, and a universal gym complete the decor. And no one lies on my couch. They sit, and we talk face to face.

Freud believed dreams were a window into the subconscious mind. From them, he spun a web of theory that, too often, boils down to a belief that people are the victims of circumstances beyond their control—of childhood traumas, parental mistakes, and instinctive impulses.

But the dreams I ask about are not the ones that crept from the unconscious the night before. They are the goals and aspirations a golfer has been carrying around in his or her conscious mind.

The dreams I want to hear of excite some fortunate people from the time they wake up each morning until they fall asleep at night. They are the stuff of passion and tenacity. They might be defined as goals, but goals so bright that no one need write them down to remember them. In fact, the hard task for the professionals I work with is not recalling their dreams, but occasionally putting them out of their minds and taking some time off from their pursuit of them. The dreams I want to hear about are the emotional fuel that helps people take control of their lives and be what they want to be. Time and again, I have heard stories of dreams that are intimately connected to the ability to play great golf. In fact, this is the first mental principle a golfer must learn:

A person with great dreams can achieve great things.

A person with small dreams, or a person without the confidence to pursue his or her dreams, has consigned himself or herself to a life of frustration and mediocrity.

PAT BRADLEY HAD some of the most exciting dreams I have ever heard. When I first met her, in the early 1980s, she had won a number of tournaments, but she wasn't convinced she knew how to win. She wasn't even sure she was innately gifted at golf. As a kid, she had concentrated most of her attention on skiing. She hadn't won many important amateur events, and she hadn't attended a college with a great women's golf team. She was a good player who just slowly and gradually got better, until she was making a good living as a professional.

She sat on my couch and said, "I'm past thirty. I want to win more. I want to win majors. I want to be Player of the Year at least once. And I want to be in the LPGA Hall of Fame."

At that point, I didn't even know what it took to get into the LPGA Hall of Fame. I quickly learned that, in all of sports, it's the hardest Hall of Fame to enter. A golfer has to win thirty tournaments, at least one of them a major. Very few make it.

I said to myself, "Wow. This woman has a great head."

Just talking with her exhilarated me. She was so intense and so excited. She had a quest.

We worked for two days on how she could learn to see herself as a winner, to think effectively, to play one shot at a time, to believe in her putting and herself. We talked periodically thereafter, and still do.

The first year after our visit, she won five tournaments, three of them majors. She nearly won the Grand Slam of women's golf. I attended the one major she lost that year, the U.S. Women's Open in Dayton, Ohio. She lipped out putts on two of the last three holes and lost by a shot or two.

Afterward, we talked, and I told her I was glad I hadn't been carrying a million dollars with me, because I would have bet it all on her to win the Open. That was how impressive her attitude and confidence were that year.

Pat continued to win, and in 1991, with her fourth victory that year, she qualified for the LPGA Hall of Fame. The induction ceremony was at the Ritz-Carlton in Boston, and Pat invited my wife, Darlene, and me. We came into the lobby and saw Pat and her mother, Kathleen. We exchanged hugs.

"Hey, before you leave, we have to talk," she said.

"What do we need to talk about?" I asked.

She looked at me and said, "Where do we go from here? Bob, we've got to find a new dream. What's next?"

Pat is still trying to figure out what comes next. For a while, she thought that the 1996 Olympics would include golf and be played at Augusta National. She had always dreamed of playing at Augusta, and she had always dreamed of being an Olympian. The prospect of doing both fired her up, until the International Olympic Committee dropped the idea.

Now she's searching for a new dream. And she hasn't won since 1991. I know that when she seizes on a new dream, she will win again. Her dreams propel her.

I HEARD SOMETHING similar from Byron Nelson recently. Tom Kite and I were giving a clinic at Las Colinas Country Club, outside of Dallas, and we were flattered that Byron and his wife, Peggy, showed up to listen to what we had to say.

After our presentation, during the question period, Byron raised his hand.

"People have often asked me where my mind was the year I won eleven tournaments in a row," he said. "I've never had a good answer, until now, when I listened to what you and Tom were saying about going after your dreams.

"When I was a young player, my dream was to own a ranch. Golf was the only way I was going to get that ranch. And every tournament I played in, I was going after a piece of it. First I had to buy some property. Then I had to fence it. Then I had to build a house for it. Then furnish the house. Then I had to build barns and corrals. Then animals. Then I had to hire someone to look after it while I was touring. Then I had to put enough money aside to take care of it forever.

"That was what I won tournaments for. It's amazing, but once

I got that ranch all paid for, I pretty much stopped playing. I was all but done as a competitive player."

TOM KITE is a great example of a person who dreamed huge dreams, and kept dreaming them in the face of all kinds of supposed evidence that they were foolish.

A few years ago I was down at the Austin Country Club working with Tom the week before the Tournament of Champions. He had to go inside to take a phone call, and while I waited for him to return, a tall, athletic-looking man walked up to me and introduced myself.

"You're Bob Rotella, aren't you?" he asked. "What are you talking to Kite about? You know, he really thinks you're helping him."

We shook hands, and he identified himself as an old friend and competitor of Tom's from boyhood days.

"I went to high school with Tom and played golf with him," the man said. "Ben Crenshaw was right behind us. Ben won the state championship twice. I won it once. Tom never won it. I thought I was way better than him. He seemed to be always shooting three over par. How did he get so good?"

There was a long answer and a short answer to that question.

The short answer was that Tom had a dream and he never stopped chasing it.

As a boy, he was small, needed glasses, and wasn't even the best junior golfer at his club. His dream seemed so unlikely that when he was fourteen or fifteen, his parents took him to see Lionel and Jay Hebert, the former touring pros. Tom's father wanted the Hebert brothers to tell Tom something discouraging, to tell him how high the odds were against him.

The Heberts, fortunately, demurred. "He'll find out soon enough how hard it is," they said. "Let him go after it."

When Tom and I first met, dreams still motivated him. He wanted to win more tournaments, including majors. He wanted to be player of the year. He wanted to be the leading money winner.

He has fulfilled those dreams. Now he has new ones. Two days after he won the U.S. Open for the first time, he called me up. He knew what would happen when he returned to the Tour. Everyone he met would want to congratulate him. Reporters would want to interview him about the Open. Fans would mob him. Faced with those distractions, a lot of new Open champions have suffered letdowns. Tom was determined not to be one of them. He wanted to test his self-discipline. He wanted to be a player who used the Open as a springboard to even better performance. And he did.

I suspect Tom will attain his new dreams as he did the old ones, because he has always been willing to do what was entailed in the long answer to the question posed by his boyhood rival.

The long answer would have recounted how hard Tom worked, on both the physical and mental aspects of his game, how often he endured failures, how often he bounced back, as he pursued those dreams.

The man I was speaking with had made a common mistake in assessing Tom. He confused golfing potential with certain physical characteristics. Most people carry in their mind an image of a golfer with potential. He is young, tall and lean. He moves with the grace of the natural athlete and probably has excelled at every sport he's ever tried. He can hit the ball over the fence at the end of the practice range.

But while I certainly wouldn't discourage someone with those physical characteristics, I've found that they have little to do with real golfing potential.

Golfing potential depends primarily on a player's attitude, on how well he plays with the wedges and the putter, and on how well he thinks.

It's nice when Tom gives me a little of the credit for his achievements, but the truth is that he had a great attitude before I ever met him. He had a backyard green and sand trap as a boy, where he developed his short game. He refused to believe he couldn't achieve his goals. Those qualities of mind were and are true talent and true potential. I believe that with his mind and attitude, if Tom had decided as a five-year-old that he wanted to be a great basketball player instead of a great golfer, he would have been an All-American in basketball. That's because talent and potential have much more to do with what's inside an athlete's head than with his physical characteristics.

I'm sometimes asked if there is a distinct champion's personality. I see no evidence that there is, because the champions I've worked with cover a broad spectrum of personality types. They come from cities and small towns, poverty and wealth, athletic parents and nonathletic parents. Some are shy and some are gregarious. Tom Kite and Nick Price, if they were in law and accounting instead of in golf, might well find they had few common interests.

But they and other champions all have a few common characteristics. They are all strong-willed, they all have dreams, and they all make a long-term commitment to pursue those dreams.

In fact, I think it's often more difficult for a person branded with what most people perceive as potential to become great than it was for, say, Pat Bradley.

When everyone around you is telling you you have great potential, and they expect you to win all the time, you can quickly start to hate and despise the potential you have, to perceive it as a burden. Val Skinner, one of the players I work with on the LPGA Tour, has struggled with that problem. She came to the tour as the Collegiate Player of the Year, and she hits it a long way. When she didn't win immediately, she got frustrated and critical of herself. She's had to work hard to realize that her physical talent is only one factor in her golfing ability—and not the most important factor.

Most people use only a small percentage of their innate physical ability, anyway. The golfer whose attitude enables him to tap a higher percentage of a relatively modest store of God-given talent can and will beat the one who doesn't know how to maximize what he has.

ON THE OTHER hand, a player with no dreams has little real potential. Not too long ago, a young man from another university came to Charlottesville to see me, looking for help with his golf game. I asked him what his dreams were.

"I don't know," he said. "I'm a pretty talented golfer, a pretty talented student. I do pretty well at both. My dad's got a pretty good company, and I guess after college I can go to work for him and make a pretty good living, so I'm not worried about the future."

The conversation floundered for a while. Finally I asked if there was anything he really loved doing, anything that truly excited him. He perked up immediately.

"Oh, yeah! I love going to see our school play basketball. The team is so awesome, so good, so into it. They're like on a mission, Doc. I'd stay up all night in a tent to get tickets to the games. I go on the road with them."

His school indeed had a successful basketball program. The team had been to the Final Four several times.

I stopped him and told him, "I don't want to break your heart, but you must realize that if your school's golf program was as good as its basketball program, you couldn't play."

He asked why.

"You have talent, but your school recruits basketball players with both talent and attitude," I said. "Your basketball coach dreams of winning national championships. He recruits only players who are totally committed to winning national championships. If you're not, he doesn't want you. Because if you're not, you're not going to work on free throws every day until you become an excellent free-throw shooter. If you're not, you're not going to play defense every night."

Free throws and defense, I said, are like the short game in golf. They require not so much talent as determination and commitment. And they are usually what separates teams that win national championships from aggregations of slam-dunk artists.

I asked how many times that year his golf coach had talked about winning the national championship.

"Not at all," the boy replied. In fact, the team had felt it did very well just to qualify for the NCAA tournament, where it failed to make the cut. They had a party after the tournament was over.

"That's the point," I said. "You have to look at what you're aiming for, because that's going to influence your level of commitment. I guarantee you that guys on your golf team practice when they want to practice. I guarantee that they spend all of their time on the range working on their swings and that no one's ever over at the practice green working on the short game. And I bet most of you spend a lot of time justifying being so-so golfers because you're at a very demanding school, academically, and you spend too much time studying."

He nodded.

I told him it would be harder for him to achieve great things in golf than it would be for his school's basketball players to achieve great things in their sport, because he would have to do it himself. He would have to set his own goals higher than his team's, and commit himself to achvieving them. It would be an individual quest, and sometimes a lonely one.

THAT'S BECAUSE THE world is full of people happy to tell you that your dreams are unrealistic, that you don't have the talent to realize them.

I never do that. Whenever someone introduces me or identifies me as a shrink, I am tempted to correct him. I'm not a shrink. I'm an enlarger. I am not in the business of telling people that they don't have talent, that their dreams are foolish and unattainable. I want to support people's talent. I believe in human abilities.

If someone came to me and said, "I'm forty-five years old, my handicap is 25, and my dream is to make a living on the Senior Tour," I would say, "Fantastic! You're just the kind of person who excites the living daylights out of me. Just the fact that you're shooting 95 and you're talking about being able to shoot 70 every day means you have the kind of mind that has a chance. I live to work with people like you."

I would not guarantee this fictitious duffer more than a chance. The next question would be whether he could keep that dream in front of him for eight or fifteen years. The right thinking can quickly and substantially lower the score of any golfer who has been thinking poorly. But there is no rapid, miraculous way to go from a 25 handicap to scratch, no matter how well a golfer starts to think. Improvement takes patience, persistence and practice.

If a golfer chooses to go after greatness, whether he defines greatness as winning the U.S. Open or winning the championship at his club, he must understand that he will encounter frustration and disappointment along the way. Tom Kite played in and lost more than a dozen U.S. Opens before he finally won one. Big improvements require working and chipping away for years. A golfer has to learn to enjoy the process of striving to improve.

That process, not the end result, enriches life. I want the people I work with to wake up every morning excited, because every day is another opportunity to chase their dreams. I want them to come to the end of their days with smiles on their faces, knowing that they did all they could with what they had.

That's one reason golf is a great game. It gives people that opportunity.

2.

What Nick Price Learned from William James

SEVERAL YEARS AGO, Nick Price came to see me for the first time. I met him at the airport and we drove to my home.

Nick was then in his early thirties. He was a good professional, but not a great one. He had not won a tournament in six years and had never won a major.

He had dreams. He dreamed of winning all the major championships. And his talent was apparent in the very low numbers he sometimes posted—rounds in the mid-sixties and lower.

But he was capable of following a 64 with a 76 and shooting himself out of a tournament. Inconsistency plagued him.

As we talked, it became apparent that Nick had a problem shared by a lot of professionals. His thinking depended on how he played the first few holes. If they went well, he fell into a relaxed, confident and focused frame of mind. Not coincidentally, he shot an excellent round. But if the first few holes went poorly, his concentration was shattered. He might start trying to fix his swing in the middle of the round and become increasingly erratic.

The worst thing that could happen to him, he said, was to hit his approach shot close to the pin on the first hole. If he then missed the putt, he became discouraged and timid. He putted worse. This was the state of mind that accounted for the all-too-frequent 76.

Nick let events control the way he thought, rather than taking control of his thoughts and using them to influence events.

"If you're going to be a victim of the first few holes," I said, "you don't have a prayer. You're like a puppet. You let the first few holes jerk your strings and tell you how you're going to feel and how you're going to think.

"You're going to have to learn to think consistently if you want to score consistently," I went on. "You wouldn't be foolish enough to try a different swing on every shot, would you?"

No, he said.

"It's the same way with your mind," I said. "You're going to have to decide before the round starts how you're going to think, and do it on every shot. You have to choose to think well."

NOT MANY PEOPLE think that their state of mind is a matter of choice. But I believe it is.

Unfortunately, major branches of psychology and psychiatry during this century have helped promote the notion that we are all in some sense victims—victims of insensitive parents, victims of poverty, victims of abuse, victims of implacable genes. Our state of mind, therefore, is someone else's responsibility. This kind of psychology is very appealing to many academics. It gives them endless opportunities to pretend they know what makes an individual miserable and unsuccessful. It appeals as well to a lot of unhappy people. It gives them an excuse for their misery. It permits them to evade the responsibility for their own lives.

But I didn't get into psychology through the normal academic route. I got in via the back door, from the gym. I grew up in Rutland, Vermont, where my father owned a barber shop. As a boy, I wanted nothing more than to play. I played football, basketball and baseball at Mt. St. Joseph Academy in Rutland. I played basketball and lacrosse at Castleton State College, and did well enough that the school recently inducted me into its Hall of Fame.

Golf, then, was only a minor interest. In the summer I carried clubs at the Rutland Country Club, where a neighborhood friend of mine, Joe Gauthier, was caddy master. I played a few rounds a year, on Mondays, just because my friends were doing it.

By the time I became a teenager, coaching fascinated me. I liked to hang around coaches and listen to what they had to say. I was blessed by contact with some excellent mentors. My cousin, Sal Soma, was one of the greatest high-school football coaches in New York state history. He was a good friend of Vince Lombardi, and I hung on every word he said about training and motivating athletes. My next-door neighbor, Bob Gilliam, coached basketball at Kimball Union Academy in New Hampshire. He impressed me with how much fun he had developing a team and getting the players to believe in themselves. My elementary-school basketball coach, Joe Bizzarro, taught me that the team that wins is usually the one that believes in itself. My entire high school experience at Mt. St. Joseph was filled with invaluable lessons. Jim Browne, my high-school basketball coach, was an extremely talented player and coach from Ridgefield Park, New Jersey, who had survived the Korean War. He taught mental and physical toughness; one of his drills cost me a front tooth. But I remember not caring because I loved his approach to the game. Tony Zingali, an assistant football coach who was the backbone of a legendary high-school program, taught us that we had to be mentally disciplined every day in practice if we wanted to be disciplined on game days and that attitude would always win out over ability. My quarterback coach, Funzie Cioffi, who had played for Lombardi at Fordham, passed along the necessity of having and executing a game plan. Bill Merrill, the head baseball coach at Castleton State, lived in my dormitory. We talked for hours about coaching. He taught me that if an athlete or a team wanted to be successful, a way could be found. He proved it with his baseball team. Roy Hill, one of my basketball coaches at Castleton, taught me that an athlete had to stay focused at all times and that the size of your heart was far more important than the size of your body.

I started to coach informally when I was in college. At Christmas break one year, the basketball squad was told that every Friday afternoon it would be working with a busload of retarded children from a nearby institution called the Brandon Training School. I thought, at first, that the basketball team could hardly afford to waste practice time working with retarded kids. But after a while, I started to enjoy doing it. Those youngsters would happily try anything we wanted to teach them—dribbling, shooting, an obstacle course, or tumbling. They always had good attitudes. They were always in good moods.

The varsity athletes I played with had almost everything going right in their lives. They were good-looking, talented guys. But a lot of them focused on the little things that were wrong with their lives. They wanted to be taller, or they wished their families had more money.

In contrast, these retarded kids had almost everything going wrong in their lives. But they focused on the only thing that was going right—their chance to learn to play. And they learned, despite their limitations. It started to hit me that attitude, self-perception and motivation heavily influenced success in life. I realized that happiness had more to do with what you did with what you had than with what you had.

After college, I continued teaching the retarded; and Frank Bizzarro, the brother of my elementary-school basketball coach, gave me a job as an assistant coach at my old high school in Rutland. The more I coached, the more convinced I became that the Xs and Os that obsessed many coaches were rather less important than the attitudes and confidence they instilled in their players. Without confidence, concentration, and composure, teams lose. With confidence, almost any plays would work. So when the chance came to go to graduate school at the University of Connecticut, coach lacrosse at the university and basketball at the university high school, and pursue a degree in sports psychology, I took it. Eventually, I got my doctorate and became director of sports psychology at the University of Virginia. Since 1976, I've had the enormous pleasure of working with the University's athletes in all sports.

As a psychology student, I soon found myself skeptical of a lot of the theories and theorists I read. For one thing, a lot of the theorists were themselves unhappy individuals. I was attracted, on the other hand, to the ideas of people who seemed to have a knack for happiness and success. In particular, I liked the ideas of William James, the most prominent American psychologist of the nineteenth century. Once, at a meeting of the

American Psychological Association, James was asked to identify the most important finding of the first half-century of university research into the workings of the mind. His reply became part of my philosophy:

People by and large become what they think about themselves.

The idea is so simple that it is easy to dismiss. People become what they think about themselves. It's almost all a person needs to know about how to be happy.

If someone came to me and asked me how to be happy, I would reply that it's simple. Just wake up every morning thinking about the wonderful things you are going to do that day. Go to sleep every night thinking about the wonderful events of the past day and the wonderful things you will do tomorrow. Anyone who does that will be happy.

John Wooden, who won nine national basketball championships at UCLA, expressed the same idea; maybe he'd also read William James. Winners and losers, Wooden said, are self-determined. But only the winners are willing to admit it.

That strikes a lot of people as fatuous. But it's quite realistic if you accept another old concept that has unfortunately gone out of style: free will.

I harp on free will with the players I work with. Free will means that a person can think any way he or she wants to think. He can choose to be a happy person or a miserable person. She can choose to think of herself as a great golfer or a born loser.

Free will is the greatest gift anyone could have given us. It means we can, in a real sense, control our own lives.

On the golf course, it means that a player can choose to think about his ball flying true to the pin, or veering into the woods. She can choose whether to think about making a putt or just getting it close.

Every now and then a player says to me something like, "Doc,

I just involuntarily started thinking about hitting the ball into the water. I couldn't do anything about it."

My response is, "No. You can indeed do something about it. You can think about the ball going to the target."

A golfer can and must decide how he will think.

IN NICK PRICE'S case, these ideas meant that Nick could choose to allow a few missed early putts to affect his thinking for an entire round. Or he could choose to think the way he did when those first few putts dropped and he was on his way to a 64. He could think only about what he wanted to achieve on the course, about the ball going to the targets he would select. He could think about scoring well insead of real or imagined flaws in his swing or his putting stroke.

After listening to this for a while, Nick said, "If I had known this is what you were going to talk about, I would have come to see you a long time ago."

"Why didn't you?" I asked.

"Well," he replied, "I was afraid you'd be into something weird. I didn't realize it would be this logical and sensible."

I laughed. At that point, Nick and I were ready to go out to the practice tee and work on how he could control his thoughts and make his game more consistent.

3.

Train It and Trust It

GOLFERS LIKE TOM KITE, Pat Bradley and Nick Price have come to me with exciting dreams and aspirations. But they have encountered obstacles, and they want help overcoming them. A lot of them tell me that they've never worked harder practicing their game, but they're not getting better scores. Almost all of them want help learning to win and to play more consistently.

The high handicappers whom I see in clinics tend to be people tying themselves in knots, physically and mentally. They've read all the books and all the golf magazines and they've been to six different pros, and they can't understand why their games aren't more consistent. Or they say that they hit the ball well on the range, but not on the course.

But, pro or amateur, whatever their specific concerns are, they all know one thing. They're better players than they're showing on the golf course and in tournaments.

38 • GOLF IS NOT A GAME OF PERFECT

This raises one of the essential issues in golf. Why is it that a golfer cannot simply command his body to repeat the motion that has brought success thousands of times on the practice range or the putting green?

The answer has to do with connections between the brain and other parts of the nervous system that we still only vaguely understand.

Having come to golf from other sports, I bring a broader perspective than that of professionals who have devoted their entire careers to the mechanics of the swing. To me, the act of striking a golf ball belongs in that category of sports events in which the player need not react to what another player does, as a batter must react to the pitcher. Major variables are constant and under the golfer's control—the moment the action begins, the position of the ball, and his position in relation to it. Swinging at a golf ball is, in this sense, akin to pitching a baseball, shooting a free throw in basketball, or walking a balance beam in gymnastics.

Consider the baseball pitcher. Greg Maddux of the Atlanta Braves tells me that he pitches best when he virtually forgets about the batter and thinks only of the place he intends his pitch to go, his target.

Consider the free throw. As with the tee shot in golf, nearly everything—the ball, the height of the basket, the distance—is constant, except the movement of the athlete. If you watch the best free-throw shooters, you will notice two things. First, they have routines that they follow on every shot. They may spin the ball in their hands. Then maybe they dribble the ball a precise number of times. They take their stance in the same way every time. They focus on a small piece of the rim. And they let the shot go, without giving much, if any, thought to such things as the angle formed by the right elbow at the point of release.

Train It and Trust It • 39

Or consider the balance beam. If you lay a four-by-four-inch beam on the floor and ask people to walk from one end to the other, it's easy. Most people will instinctively focus their vision and attention on the far end of the beam, their target. And they will walk confidently and casually until they reach it.

Now mount the beam forty feet in the air, with no net underneath. Physically, the task remains the same as it was when the beam was on the floor. Mentally, though, it has changed dramatically. Mounting the beam high in the air introduces a strong fear of failure.

Most people, in such circumstances, will respond by starting to think about mechanical things they didn't worry about when the beam was on the floor. How, exactly, does a person keep his balance? And how does he put one foot in front of the other? Toes in or toes out? Body sideways or facing straight ahead? Eyes on the end of the beam or on the feet? Arms limp or extended to the sides? Their goal will become not falling, rather than getting to the end of the beam. They will stop trusting the body's ability to remain balanced as they negotiate the distance. Thinking that way causes the muscles to tighten and the movement of the body to grow spasmodic and jerky rather than rhythmic and graceful. If you actually conducted the experiment, many people who successfully negotiated the beam when it was on the floor would fall off from forty feet.

In much the same way, a golfer who fears failure—as most amateurs and many professionals do, at least some of the time—tends to think about how he takes the club back, how far he turns, how he cocks his wrists, how he starts the downswing, or other swing mechanics. Inevitably, he will tend to lose whatever grace and rhythm nature has endowed him with, which leads to inconsistent shotmaking with every club, from the driver to the putter.

This suggests a most important principle:

You cannot hit a golf ball consistently well if you think about the mechanics of your swing as you play.

When someone asks me why this is so, I cannot give a scientific reply. Psychologists and other specialists in human performance may one day figure it out. I simply know that the human organism performs a task like the golf swing much better if the athlete looks at a target and reacts rather than looks, thinks and reacts. I don't want to impose religion on anyone, but the only explanation I can come up with for this is that someone created us this way. We are endowed with the most marvelous computer system imaginable, and it is wired to maximize physical performance and grace if a person simply looks at a target and reacts to it.

There is, of course, a time and place for thinking about the mechanics of the golf swing. I am not one of those who try to sell the notion that golf is purely mental and that mechanics don't matter. They do. It is much better to have a good swing than a bad swing. To be successful, a golfer must blend work on mechanics with work on the mental approach to the game. The professional golfers I work with all have swing teachers who help them with their mechanics.

But the time to worry about swing mechanics must be limited, and the place to worry about them is the practice tee and only the practice tee. If you step onto the course with the intention of shooting your best possible score, you cannot think about mechanics. On the golf course, you have to be like the good free-throw shooter who eyes the basket and lets the ball go. You have to be like the person who walks across the balance beam without thinking about how to walk. You have to believe that you've practiced the golf swing enough to have faith in it. To put it concisely:

A golfer must train his swing and then trust it.

When I say this at clinics, someone usually stands up and says that trusting the swing might be all well and good for a Tom Kite or a Nick Price, who has endless hours to practice and who hits the ball almost perfectly almost all of the time. But how can a weekend player who sprays the ball all over the course trust his swing?

I respond that I have seen lots of high handicappers with lots of kinks in their swings, but I almost never see one who improves his play by doubting himself, dwelling on mechanics or trying to correct a swing flaw in the middle of a round. The fact is, most amateurs don't know exactly what breaks down when they swing badly. If they try to correct their swing, they usually wind up compounding the error. They would be far better off forgetting about their swing mechanics, thinking about appropriate targets and strategy, and making up their mind that they will shoot the best score possible with the swing they brought to the course that day.

Yet, this notion of trusting the swing strikes many weekend players as difficult, if not impossible. But how often have they hit the ball well while thinking of mechanics? Why do they fear abandoning the effort to control and guide their swing?

It's just habit, habit that has become comfortable, however ineffective.

The fact is that neither Tom Kite nor Nick Price nor anyone else I work with hits the ball perfectly or even close to perfectly all the time. In fact, over the past ten years I've been working regularly with players who have posted well over two hundred and fifty wins on the PGA Tour, LPGA Tour, and Senior Tour. I can't remember more than a few times when a winning player has told me he or she hit the ball really well for more than two of the four days of a tournament.

Winners learn to accept the swing they bring to the golf course on any given day and to score with it. They win tournaments, as often as not, because they manage to use their short game and their mind to avoid a high round on the day or days when their swing is not what they wanted. If they need to work on their mechanics, they do it after the round is over, or they take a week off and go to the practice tee.

Even Jack Nicklaus had limits in his ability to repair a faulty swing on the course. Tom Kite told me about a round he and Nicklaus played during the PGA Championship. Nicklaus split the fairway with his driver on the first hole. On the second hole, a short par four, he used a 3-wood. The third was a par three. On the fourth hole, he pulled out his driver, but he pull-hooked the ball, almost out of bounds. Tom said it was the worst shot he'd ever seen Nicklaus hit. From that moment until the end of the round, the driver stayed in Jack's bag, even though the championship was being played at Kemper Lakes, a brutally long, 7,200-yard course. Despite its length, Nicklaus played it with the clubs he could trust, his 3-wood and his 1-iron. He saved the driver for the practice tee after the round, where he drove balls until he was satisfied he had worked out the kink that had produced the pull-hook at the fourth hole.

Most golfers, amateur or pro, lack Nicklaus's patience and discipline. Most of them would react to a pull-hook like the one Nicklaus hit on the fourth tee that day by taking the driver out on the next tee and trying to fix their mechanics. They'd start thinking about how fast their hips opened, or when they turned their hands over, or their swing planes. And their score would suffer for it.

Trusting is not instinctive or easy for most golfers. They experience it only sporadically. Maybe they have a club that gives them such a feeling of confidence that they can trust their swing when they use it. They get better results with this club because trust allows them to swing decisively and fluidly. This reinforces their confidence with that particular club. Or they feel trust in the midst of a hot streak.

The challenge, of course, is to trust your swing with every club and score well when your shots are telling you that your swing is not in the slot. It's not easy or instinctive for many people. But this is the way great golfers and all great athletes think.

This was the way Tom Watson played in his prime. The worse he hit it, the more he ripped it. He knew that if he reacted to a bad shot by getting more careful, it would not make his swing better. It would make it tentative—and worse. I've seen him hit it seventy yards left, then seventy yards right and then hit the third one screaming on line to the pin.

At the Nabisco Championships a few years ago, Chip Beck, whom I was working with, shot 63 on Sunday. It was a big breakthrough for him. He had a chance to win if Watson faltered behind him.

Watson could barely put the ball on the golf course down the stretch, but he kept getting up and down. On the last hole, he had a 6-iron approach to a tiny green surrounded by trees, with the pin cut tight to one side. But he knew what to do. Just as he always did, it was one waggle, two waggles, and let it go. And he knocked it stiff. That's why he's been a great player. He knows that no matter what happens, he has to keep trusting. He's gotten away from that in recent years with his putter, but I always expect him to come back, because he knows how to think the way great athletes think.

When great athletes stop trusting, they stop being great. The difference in a player's attitude can be very subtle. A little doubt or a little indecision is sufficient to impair performance.

44 • GOLF IS NOT A GAME OF PERFECT

When great players are playing well, trust becomes a habit. The golfer executes his shots without being aware that he's trusting his swing. He simply picks out a target, envisions the kind of shot he wants to hit, and hits it. Brad Faxon will often hit a draw off the tee on one hole and a fade on the next, depending on the shape of the hole. But he tells me that he never thinks about the mechanics of a draw or fade. He trusts that his body will produce the swing needed for the shot he envisions.

If you don't trust right now, you will have to go through a period of conscious awareness until you learn the difference between the feeling of trust and the absence of trust. You will have to work at developing thoughts and habits that promote trust. You will have to learn to focus your mind on your target and your preshot routine rather than on swing mechanics.

4.

How Stuart Anderson Created His Own Reality

FINE ATHLETES IN every sport know the importance of trusting their mechanical skills. And they do it regardless of the results they achieved on their last attempt.

One of the best stories on the subject that I've ever heard came from Stuart Anderson, a University of Virginia football player who went on to play for several years with the Washington Redskins. Stuart took a seminar I gave on confidence in athletics. I asked him to share with the class what went through his mind when he was thinking confidently.

Stuart replied with a story from his high-school basketball career.

"I was a fifty percent shooter from the floor," he said. "In the first round of the state playoffs during my senior year, I took my first shot and I missed."

Stuart kept missing. He had the worst shooting night of his

life in that game. He missed twenty-odd shots in a row. His team teetered on the edge of elimination.

One of the other students in the seminar asked, "Stuart, why didn't you start passing the ball after you missed, say, ten in a row?"

"Because I'm a shooter. But let me finish the story," Stuart said.

His team scrapped and stayed in the game. With a minute to go, trailing by a point, they stole the ball and called time out. The coach, reasoning that Stuart was irremediably cold that night, diagramed a play to run 55 seconds off the clock and set up a shot for another player, a junior.

"Wait a minute, Coach!" Stuart objected. "I want the shot. Give me the ball!"

The underclassman, it turned out, didn't really want the shot at that stage. So the coach, against his better judgment, changed his plan and called a play to give Stuart the shot.

He got the ball beside the free-throw line, one of his favorite spots. He turned and jumped, absolutely confident. His eyes zeroed in on the rim. He let the shot go.

And in it went. Stuart was the hero. Fans carried him off the floor. The next day, the newspapers headlined his game-winning shot.

After hearing this story, one of my students raised a hand and asked, "How did you stay confident after you missed all those shots?"

"Well, you have to understand. I've always been a fifty percent shooter," Stuart replied. "After I missed one, I figured the next one was likely to go in. After I missed two, I was overdue. By the time I'd missed five, I figured the next one absolutely had to drop. Every time I missed, I figured the odds were increasing in my favor."

"Okay," the student said. "If that's how you think when you miss your first shots, what do you think if you make your first six or seven in a row?"

"That's totally different," Stuart said. "You decide that tonight's your night, you're on a hot streak, and you're going to make everything you look at."

"That's ridiculous," the student said. "You can't have it both ways."

"Of course you can," Stuart said.

Stuart had revealed something very basic about the way good athletes think. They create their own realities. They think however they have to think to maintain their confidence and get the job done. In basketball, this is called the shooter's mentality. In golf, it's even more essential, because there is no one to come off the bench to replace a player who's struggling.

A golfer has to learn to do what Stuart Anderson did, to put aside all thought of past failures and to trust that his next swing will send his shot where he aims it. He has to develop the basketball shooter's mentality.

If he misses a few putts, he has to believe that this only enhances his chances to make the next one. If he hits a tee shot out of bounds, he has to believe that this only means he's gotten the bad swing out of his system. The shot was an accident. It's not the norm.

This may seem, to an outsider, to be absolutely irrational. How can a kid who's just missed twenty-odd shots in a row be confident he's going to make the next one?

The answer is that whether it's irrational or not, it's more effective than the alternative. Would Stuart Anderson have been more likely to make that shot if he had doubted himself? Would it have helped him to start trying to fix some real or imagined flaw in his shooting form?

Of course not. If Stuart had reacted to his missed shots by deciding that there was a kink in his shooting form and trying to fix it in the middle of the game, he would have destroyed his natural grace and rhythm. He would most likely have started shooting airballs.

Many weekend golfers don't even wait for a bad shot to stop trusting their swing. They step onto the first tee thinking of a dozen mechanical concepts they've heard from friends, read about in magazines, or seen on television. Half the time, these dozen mechanical thoughts conflict with one another. They take the driver out and start their backswing thinking about stiff left arms, still heads, full turns, wrist cocks, or pronated hands. Without realizing it, they're doing everything possible to undermine their own game.

Even the weekend players who start off trusting tend to stop doing it after a bad shot or two. They start trying to fix the mechanical problem that led to the bad shot. They would be far better off if they realized that, as human beings, they are highly unlikely to get through eighteen holes without a few bad swings. They are much more likely to play their best if they trust their swings, flawed though they sometimes are. This can be done. A golfer has free will. He can choose how he will think.

If more golfers chose to continue trusting their swings, they might be surprised at how often the brain and body respond by doing things right when it matters most—just as it happened for Stuart Anderson.

5.

The Hot Streak: Staying Out of Your Own Way

MOST GOLFERS, EVEN mid to high handicappers, if they play often, have experienced a string of holes where everything fell into place, and for a while at least, they played the golf they had always sensed they were capable of. For one golden hour, perhaps two, the golf ball went where they wanted it to go and they strung together pars. Then something happened to break the spell—an errant tee shot, a stubbed chip, a three-putt green. They went back to making bogeys. Perhaps they thought that during the hot streak they played over their head.

They did not. The hot streak represents the golfer's true capability. It results, essentially, from trust. The golfer trusts his abilities. He steps up to the ball knowing that he can pick a target and hit it there. He does things unconsciously. The swing repeats itself. It feels effortless.

You can learn a lot from a hot streak.

I've asked many golfers to recall and describe their state of mind during their hot streaks. I have yet to hear one respond that he was thinking of swing mechanics. Most would say that the hot streak enabled them to *stop* thinking about swing mechanics. That's another way of saying they were able to trust their swings.

Players I work with have had some very low rounds and very hot tournaments. David Frost has scored 61 or 62. Nick Price shot 11 under par in a South African tournament. Davis Love III shot a 60 in Hawaii recently. Andrew Magee set the record for a 90-hole tournament in Las Vegas in 1991 with a 329, 31 under par. Tom Kite broke it two years later at Bob Hope's tournament, shooting 325.

The lowest single-round score any of my players ever recorded in an official tournament was Chip Beck's 59 a couple of years ago in Las Vegas.

Chip called me after the round, and naturally, I wanted to know as much as possible about his state of mind that day.

Of course, he had sunk a lot of birdie putts. He had hit lots of fairways and greens. Mentally, he told me, he had a serene feeling of confidence as the round progressed.

"Doc, I stayed out of my way the whole day," he said.

By "staying out of my way," Chip meant that he had not allowed doubts of any kind—particularly doubts about his mechanics—to interfere with his game. He had a plan for each hole, each shot, and he executed that plan. He trusted completely that his mechanics would enable him to do so. He let nothing from his mind interfere with his physical capabilities.

Trusting won't, by itself, turn on a hot streak. But it will make a hot streak much more likely.

If you wish to play your best golf, you can't wait until a few putts fall and a couple of birdies go on the scorecard before you start trusting. You have to start replicating the state of mind you have on a hot streak as soon as you step onto the first tee. No matter what happens during your round, you have to strive to maintain that state of mind.

You have to stay out of your own way.

6.

Rediscovering Old Scottish Wisdom

SHORTLY AFTER I met Tom Kite, he suggested that I start regularly visting him and other players on the PGA Tour. They wanted, Tom said, to keep abreast of all the new discoveries being made in sports psychology.

I had to tell him that most of what passes for discovery in sports psychology really isn't new. There is just the same old wisdom, repeated over and over again, repackaged in new terminology.

The Scots who invented golf knew a lot of what I teach to pros today, and they passed it along to early American golfers. Bobby Jones, for instance, learned the game from a Scottish pro named Stewart Maiden at the East Lake course of the Atlanta Athletic Club, just after the turn of the century. Jones's family lived in a house near the 13th hole of this club, but as a boy, Jones did not take lessons in swing mechanics, as so many children do today. He learned the game playing around the 13th green and by tagging along behind Maiden and imitating his movements.

Jones also learned the psychology of the game from Maiden. In the midst of his great career Jones disclosed what he had been taught in his autobiography, *Down the Fairway*. Jones wrote at length about his swing mechanics in the instructional section of the book. But at the end of this section, he appended:

"One bit of earnest admonition. Stewart Maiden maintains that he cannot think of any of these details, or of any other details, during the execution of a shot—that is, if the shot is to come off. He adds that he does not believe anybody else can think of these or other details and perform a successful shot. I find this to be the case with my own play."

Other great players from American golf's early years figured this out in their own way. Walter Hagen, like Jones, learned the golf swing by imitating, though he did it as a caddie, rather than a member's son. He discovered the essential psychology of the game as a young pro, in 1914. He was working at the Country Club of Rochester, N.Y., and his game impressed the members enough that they passed the hat and paid for his train fare to Chicago, where the U.S. Open was being contested at Midlothian. Hagen, even then, had luxurious appetites. The night before the tournament began, he treated himself to a lobster dinner. But Hagen's purse was not yet commensurate with his tastes and he couldn't afford a place that served truly fresh lobster. The lobster he got was old and bad.

He awoke the next morning with a fierce case of food poisoning. He was almost doubled over with pain. Had he not been afraid of what the members back in Rochester would say if he withdrew, he would not have played. But play he did.

Because of his pain, Hagen could think only of finishing his round. He stopped worrying about the way he was swinging and thought only of putting the ball into play off the tee, getting it onto the green, and getting it in the hole.

He shot 69 and went on to win his first Open.

Sam Snead grew up poor in the hills of Virginia, and started caddying at a nearby resort. Golf fascinated him, but he had no money for clubs or lessons. He whittled sticks into the shape of clubs, found rocks for balls, and practiced in a pasture, seeing how many fence posts he could knock the rock past. Snead had a fine, intuitive sense of his own capabilities. And he soon learned that he knocked the rock farther and straighter when he cleared out his mind and just let his naturally fluid swing occur.

"I found that the best way was just to draw that stick back nice and lazy, not thinking too much about how I was doing what," Snead wrote many years later.

He had to relearn the lesson when he started playing golf professionally in the early 1930s. Snead allowed himself to be convinced that what had worked in the pasture back home wasn't good enough for professional competition. He decided he had to learn to "concentrate," which he took to mean trying very hard to swing absolutely correctly. His first tournament was in Hershey, Pa., near the chocolate factory. On the first tee of his first round, he concentrated fiercely, concentrated so hard that he thought the ball might catch fire. He sliced it into the factory grounds. He concentrated harder. Another slice, deeper into the factory grounds. He was lying four, still on the tee.

Snead's professional career might have aborted right there if he had not had the instinctive wisdom to stop trying to concentrate. He relaxed and let his body swing the club. He drove the green, 345 yards away, made the putt, and went on from there.

Rediscovering Old Scottish Wisdom • 55

• • •

Sometime in the 1940s, though, American golfers began to overemphasize and complicate swing mechanics. They began to forget the wisdom that Stewart Maiden passed along to Bobby Jones and that Walter Hagen and Sam Snead discovered for themselves. This was not, of course, true everywhere. Golf is a sport of individuals and everyone had his own approach to the game. Teachers like Harvey Penick never stopped imparting sound principles about the mental side of golf. But they became a minority.

There were many reasons for this. One, I think, was technology. As motion pictures and stop-action still photography developed, it became possible to record and study the swings of good players in minute detail. You could actually determine whether Byron Nelson pronated or supinated at the top of his backswing. Televised golf and the plethora of magazines and books reinforced the emphasis on mechanics.

Practice ranges came along, and teachers found that they could make a living just standing on the lesson tee and talking about hand positions and body coils and swing planes. They stopped walking the course with their pupils. They stopped teaching rhythm and feel and scoring skills.

Gradually, teaching golf became a big business. Teachers competed for a share of the market by claiming that they, and they alone, had discovered the secret, the mechanical key to the perfect swing. Many in the golf business fought over ownership of the "correct way" to teach the swing, even though, as it happens, almost none of the great golfers swung the club "correctly." Bobby Jones regripped the club at the top of his backswing. Walter Hagen had a forward move that resembled a lunge. Not only that, but the best players, from Jones down through Palmer, Player, Nicklaus and Trevino, have always taken pride in the fact that their swings were a bit idiosyncratic and highly personal. The best players have always had the courage to swing in their own way and ignore teachers who insisted that only a classic swing could win.

Unfortunately, as far as the mental side of the game was concerned, in the 1940s and 1950s a distorted image of Ben Hogan became the model for American golfers. Hogan was badly misperceived. The press and public saw him as a robotic exemplar of swing mechanics. In fact, as Hogan himself wrote, he played his best golf after he stopped being obsessive about swing mechanics. Until 1946, Hogan never fully trusted his swing. He played every round in fear that he could fall out of the groove. He worried about dozens of mechanical details on every stroke.

Around 1946, though, Hogan realized that he had mastered the fundamentals of the swing and didn't need to worry about them so much. He abandoned what he called "this ambitious overthoroughness" in relation to his swing. The results were dramatic. "At about the same time I began to feel that I had the stuff to play creditable golf even when I was not at my best, my shotmaking started to take on a new and more stable consistency," he wrote.

In other words, when he started to trust what he had trained, he played better.

But this was not the Hogan image. The press and the golf publishing houses presented him as a man who became great by obsessive attention to the mechanical details of the golf swing. Everyone heard how Hogan hit bucket after bucket on the practice green. Everyone heard how Hogan developed a "secret move" that cured his hook.

I had a chance to visit Hogan several years ago, and what he said differed substantially from the Hogan image.

"I played by feel," Hogan told me.

He also told me that he didn't start to win major championships until he learned that on any tough course there would always be a few holes that bothered him, where he couldn't use his driver. Once he started using 1-irons in those situations, he started to win. So strategy and course management, not perfect ball-striking, had a lot to do with his success.

A final point about Hogan makes clear the depth of the public misperception. It was brought to my attention by David Frost. Frosty is a native South African, and a couple of years ago he passed along to me an autobiography by the great South African golfer of Hogan's era, Bobby Locke. At the end of the book, Locke presented an all-star team, listing the best player he'd seen with each club in the bag. Hogan didn't make the team for ball-striking. He made it for putting.

That was so at odds with Hogan's image that I asked the great player and teaching pro Paul Runyan about it the next time Paul and I worked together at an instructional clinic. Paul confirmed that Hogan, in his prime, was as good as anybody at putts from five to fifteen feet. On the professional tour, those are the putts that separate the winners from the also-rans, because they are the putts that produce birdies.

When Hogan stopped being a confident putter and started muttering that putts should only count half a stroke, he stopped winning golf tournaments.

I wonder how American golf might have developed if someone had asked Hogan to write a book on golf psychology. Such a book might have caused people to focus, not on his mechanics, but on the nerve he showed in developing a swing that was completely different from those of his peers. It would have highlighted how he steeled his mind and refused to be distracted on the course, and how he developed the inner strength to pursue his dreams through many years of failure.

But no one ever did. And Hogan's perceived obsession with swing mechanics influenced a generation of golfers.

After Hogan, the mantle of superiority in American golf passed briefly to Arnold Palmer and then to Jack Nicklaus. Nicklaus helped reemphasize the importance of the right mental approach to the game. He was a great strategist and thinker on the golf course. He was among the first golfers to talk about visualizing the shot he desired before he swung the club. He insisted on waiting until his mind was relaxed and focused before hitting a shot.

In the past decade, thinking about golf psychology has continued to progress backward toward the wisdom of the old Scots. Jim Flick, one of the best of today's golf teachers, says that a player has to pass through three stages: unconsciously incompetent, consciously competent, and unconsciously competent.

Today's best players strive to stay on that third level. Nick Price wants to think only of his target as he swings. He tells me that he's constantly struck by how much better he swings the more sharply he focuses his mind on his target. Fred Couples says he tries to have no swing thoughts at all. They are the new avatars.

The new breed of golf winners has to have a tougher approach to the game than their predecessors did. In Hogan's day, and even in Nicklaus's, it was often sufficient to play cautiously for the first three-and-a-half days of a tournament, then cut loose on the back nine of the final round, trying to hole everything. Nowadays, winning scores are lower and players have to be free and cocky from the first hole Thursday morning. With that exception, though, not much that today's winning players say about their mental processes would surprise Stewart Maiden.

7.

What the Third Eye Sees

IF THINKING ABOUT swing mechanics can spoil a golf swing, what should a golfer think about as he stands over the ball?

A Ben Hogan story told by members of the Los Angeles Country Club suggests part of the answer. It concerns an exhibition round Hogan once played on their North Course.

Hogan came to the 5th hole, a 476-yard par five on which the green, because of the slope of the land, is not visible from the tee. A cluster of four tall palm trees, planted only a few feet apart, stands immediately behind the green and towers above the horizon.

When Hogan arrived at the tee, he asked his caddie for a target.

"Aim for the palm trees, Mr. Hogan," the caddie replied.

To which Hogan answered, "Which palm tree?"

The story is cited sometimes as an example of Hogan's perfec-

WHAT THE THIRD EYE SEES • 61

tionism. But what it really suggests is Hogan's knowledge of one of the fundamental psychological principles in golf:

Before taking any shot, a golfer must pick out the smallest possible target.

This may seem obvious to some people. But I'm continually amazed by the number of golfers who don't do it. When I'm at a clinic or pro-am with someone who's just sprayed his ball into the next county, I sometimes ask what he was aiming at when he hit the errant shot.

Usually, the reply is something like, "I was aiming down the left side." Or "down the middle." Or people might say, "I don't know what I was aiming at. I just knew I didn't want to miss left."

That's not good enough. Aiming down the middle is the equivalent of trying to go to Los Angeles by flying to an airport somewhere in California.

The brain and nervous system respond best when the eyes focus on the smallest possible target. Why this is so is not important. It just happens to be the way the human system works. Perhaps it has to do with the evolutionary advantage enjoyed by those cavemen who focused on the hearts of attacking tigers, as opposed to those cavemen who merely looked in the tiger's general direction and hurled their spears.

It is true in virtually every sport. We teach basketball players to look, not at the backboard, nor even the rim, but at the net loop in back of the rim. We teach quarterbacks to aim, not at the receiver, nor even his number, but at his hands.

The smaller the target, the sharper the athlete's focus, the better his concentration, and the better the results. When an athlete locks his eyes and mind onto a small target, the ball naturally tends to follow.

Satchel Paige, the old pitcher, used to put bubble gum wrappers on the edge of the plate as he warmed up. Aiming at them sharpened his control.

The small, precise target helps golfers in one obvious way, by making it easier to align the player and his club. But it has another benefit. A golfer needs to have something on his mind if he does not want thoughts about swing mechanics to intrude on his consciousness just as he is preparing to play his shot. The target helps fill that void. It helps prevent distractions.

Nick Price, after we had worked together for a while, told me that once he had picked out a target, he could look back to the ball, but continue to "see" the target in his mind. He has seen his consistency and his success greatly increase as he has committed himself to refusing to hit a shot unless his mind is locked onto the target.

Other good players tell me they feel almost as if they had a third eye on the left side of their head. Their eyes shift down to the ball before they swing. But with that third eye, they still see their target.

Tom Kite, on the other hand, looks at a small target in the distance, thinks about it, but does not see a picture of it when his eye returns to the ball. His mind is just as locked onto the target as Nick Price's. This is merely an individual variation.

Hogan was so aware of the value of a target that he told me one of the worst developments in modern golf was the demise of the shag caddie.

When he practiced, Hogan said, he always had a shag caddie stand precisely where he intended to hit the ball. This brought the target to life. The caddie wanted to field the balls with the least possible effort, catching them on the first or second hop. Hogan took pride in enabling him to do that. It made him pay attention to the target on every practice shot, in terms of both direction and distance. That habit carried over to the golf course.

On the golf course, though, finding a target is not quite so natural or instinctive as it is in, say, basketball. Off the tee, except on par-three holes, the course often presents no obvious targets. And experience, that false friend, tells you that you can't hit a driver precisely enough to bother with a specific target. So golfers are tempted to be sloppy about targets. If they fall prey to the temptation, they tend to hit, not surprisingly, sloppy shots.

Many of the players I work with have found that it's most effective to pick elevated targets—that is, something above the ground. On some courses, trees will serve this function. If you pick a tree as your target, try to focus more narrowly. Make it a specific branch on the tree. You can use a distant church steeple, a radio tower, or anything that presents something small and precise to aim for.

Only if there is no other choice, though, should you pick something like a specific undulation in a fairway. A particular point on the ground is easy to lose track of, and in the middle of your backswing, you might find yourself wondering if the undulation you looked at just before you started to swing is the same undulation you picked out when you were standing behind the ball. And good golf course architects will use undulations to create illusions that can cause you to question your alignment. That's why an elevated target is preferable.

On tee shots and full swings, your target rarely will be at the precise distance you want the ball to travel. You might aim, for instance, at a tree behind the green on a par four, knowing that you can't reach it from the tee. Frequently, your target will not be on a direct line between where your ball is and where you want it to be. A straight hitter, looking from the tee into a fairway that slopes from left to right, will pick a target to the left of center, assuming he wants the ball to wind up in the center of the fairway. He'll allow for the rightward roll he'll get once the ball hits the ground.

If you curve the ball, you need to make allowance for that when you select your targets. I'm not going to tell you that your mind can cure a slice or a hook. If you're a slicer, I don't believe you can stand on the tee, aim at a target on the right, persuade yourself that you're going to draw the ball, and miraculously cure your slice. And, of course, you now know better than to try to cure your swing flaws on the golf course.

So, work with your dominant tendency. If you normally slice the ball twenty yards off line, pick a target twenty yards to the left of where you want the ball to finish. Obviously, it's better to be able to hit the ball straight enough so that you can always aim in the fairway. But the important thing is to adjust. Too many players get obsessed with straightening out a hook or slice that they could simply play with. Without realizing it, they change their goal from shooting their best score to fixing their swing.

There's a limit to this, however. Don't ever aim at a target that would mean severe trouble if you happened to hit the ball straight. From the tee, it's all right to have a target in the rough, but not out of bounds or in a lake. And sometimes, the golf course architect will not let you aim far enough off line to correct for a slice or hook. He'll put the tee in a chute of trees, for example. In such cases, you have to go to a shorter club, one that you can hit straight enough to get out of the chute.

Many of the players I work with also pick an intermediate target on the tee to help them with alignment. This can be an old divot, a bit of paper, or the remnants of a wooden tee. All that matters is that it is precisely on the line between the ball and the target. The player picks both the target and the intermediate target as he stands behind the ball. Then he walks up to the ball with his eye on the intermediate target. He uses it to help align his clubface and his body. Then he forgets it.

Some players find the intermediate target a distraction. They prefer to align themselves using the real target. That's fine, too. Whatever you choose to do, make certain that it clears your mind and makes it easier to trust what you're doing.

LOCKING YOUR MIND onto a small target will help you deal with looming hazards. The brain tries to be an accommodating mechanism. It will try to send the ball in the direction of the last thing you look at or think about. If that happens to be a pond, you can find yourself in severe trouble. So if you're preparing to hit an approach shot over water, or a pitch over a bunker to a pin, it's important that you have an established habit of focusing your mind firmly on your target.

Most tour players have long since learned not to let things like water hazards bother them. More often, their brains get distracted by something like the flag. Fred Couples, in the final round of the 1992 Masters, barely escaped disaster when he hit his tee shot onto the bank in front of the 12th hole. Miraculously, it hung up in the grass and stayed out of Rae's Creek. Couples was able to pitch up to the green and go on to win. He later acknowledged that he had planned to play the 12th safely, by aiming for the left-center of the green. But at the last second, his attention was distracted by that siren flag, fluttering in the breeze on the right and most dangerous side of the green. Not surprisingly, the ball went where his attention did.

This is not a problem peculiar to Couples. Many players have difficulty focusing on their real target when a flag is in their field of vision. I often work with them on this, suggesting that they try to focus on something small, like a fence post in the distance, instead of a flagstick. It helps to develop the discipline they need in pressure situations.

Sometimes even the best players let a hazard distract them from their target. I went to Houston in 1986 to give a talk to some of the touring players. It was a week after the Masters. I was talking about the importance of having your mind focused tightly on the target for every shot you play. Corey Pavin raised his hand and stood up.

"That's what I didn't do at the sixteenth hole on Saturday and Sunday last week," he said.

I asked him to explain.

"Well," he said, "I'm cruising along Thursday, Friday and Saturday. I'm eight under coming into sixteen, with birdie chances ahead of me. I get up to sixteen, and for some reason I tell myself at the last second, 'Don't hit it in the water.'"

Splash.

"I go home that night," Pavin continued, "and I tell myself, 'Make sure you don't do that tomorrow.' On Sunday, I get back to eight under. I'm in position to win the thing, and I get up to sixteen, and all I can do is remember what I did yesterday and think, 'Oh, God, don't do that again today.'"

And splash again. Two mental mistakes and he was out of the hunt in the Masters.

Two things impressed me about what Pavin said. First, it confirmed one of the key attributes of the brain and how it affects your golf game. The brain, at some level, cannot seem to understand the word "don't."

If your last thought before striking the ball is "don't hit it in the pond," the brain is likely to react by telling your muscles to hit it in the pond.

That's why it's doubly important, when facing a hazard, to focus your attention sharply on your target. Obviously, you have to be aware of where the hazards are. But I tell tournament players to think about them only during practice rounds. Take the 1st hole at Augusta. It has a gaping sand trap down the right side and pines on the left. Obviously, a player wants to avoid each of them. But a player who stands on that tee, fighting nerves already, and thinks about where he doesn't want to hit it, only multiplies his chances of hitting it badly. He needs to use his practice rounds to learn where the hazards are and establish the right target for his drive—fade or draw, long or short. Then, when he steps onto the tee in competition, he must think only of that target.

The second thing that impressed me about what Pavin said was his commitment to learning about himself and his game. He didn't care what anyone else, including his peers and competitors, thought. He was intent on learning what he had to know to get better.

8.

Your Rod and Staff

WHEN TOM KITE stepped to the 18th tee at Pebble Beach on Father's Day in 1992, protecting a slim lead in the last round of the U.S. Open, it would not have been overstating things to say he faced a challenging shot.

The wind was howling. The Pacific Ocean lined the left side of the 548-yard fairway. Deep rough stood ready to punish anyone who tried to play safe by pushing the ball down the right side. Add to that the enormous pressure of being on the brink of winning a first major championship.

Bob Toski later told me that he couldn't bear to watch. Sitting at home, watching television, he had to get up and go into the kitchen, asking his wife, Lynn, to let him know what Tom did.

I was nervous as well, but I was more aware than Bob was how much Tom had practiced something that would help him handle this challenging situation.

I was not thinking of practicing drives, though Tom had certainly done that. I was thinking of Tom's preshot routine, an element of his game that he works on constantly.

A sound preshot routine is the rod and staff of the golfer under pressure, a comfort in times of affliction and challenge. It ensures that he gets set up properly, physically and mentally. It blocks out distractions. It helps him to produce his best golf under pressure.

Which is what Tom did that Sunday, smacking a 280-yard drive down the middle of the fairway.

High handicappers often tell me that what they most want to solve are problems of inconsistency. They can't figure out why what feels like the same swing produces a long, straight shot one time and a ball that fades to a splash the next.

I usually respond by asking them to describe their preshot routines. Many of them can't, because they don't have preshot routines. And yet, the pros I work with, who know the golf swing better than anyone, tell me that 80 percent of any golf shot happens before the player takes the club back: when he aims, takes his grip, addresses the ball, and, most important, focuses his mind.

This fact leads to the next fundamental principle:

The foundation of consistency is a sound preshot routine.

The next time you watch a tournament on television, take a look at a player like Tom Kite or Pat Bradley and see if you can break down his or her routine. You will find a remarkable consistency. These golfers strive to repeat the same mental and physical steps before every shot, right down to the number of waggles.

There will always be inconsistency in every golfer's results, as Kite and Bradley would be the first to attest. No one can completely prevent minute variations in the swing that can lead to great disparities in the way the ball flies. But golfers with an effective mental approach to the game know that they can control much better what happens before the swing begins, when the movements are slow, deliberate, and more susceptible to discipline. They seize that advantage by adopting a disciplined, constant preshot routine.

They use this routine for every full shot, be it a wide-open lay-up on a par five or the tightest, most challenging tee shot on the course.

Every player I work with has his or her own variation on the routine. But all sound routines incorporate certain fundamentals. A good routine enables a golfer to be trusting, decisive, and focused on the target. It fits his or her personality.

To develop a reliable routine, a golfer has to decide to follow it and practice it time after time after time until it becomes an ingrained habit that will show up no matter how much pressure he or she is under. You can be sure that under pressure, you will find out what your dominant habit is.

Some players like to begin their routines with a triggering gesture. They may fiddle with the grip on the club, or hoist the club over a shoulder. They may set a hand on the top of the driver as it rests in the bag. It doesn't matter what the gesture is. It simply serves to remind the player that his preshot routine has begun and it is time to focus intently on it. Players whose attention tends to wander on the course may find a triggering gesture particularly helpful.

Other players don't need triggers to start their routines. Just taking the club out of the bag or standing behind the ball and beginning to plan the shot suffices to get their attention. It's a matter of personal preference.

Good players feel that when their routines start, they are stepping into a bubble, a small, private world in which nothing can distract them. Tom Watson once said it feels like going into a room where everything is dim and quiet.

Once their routines are under way, most players assess the distance they want to hit the ball, the wind, the trajectory, if that's a factor, and the appropriate club. The important thing about club selection is decisiveness. If you step up to the ball still uncertain whether you have the right club, your routine is not sound. You have to start over, rethinking the shot until you are convinced you have the right club for it.

Next, pick the target. Most players do this standing behind the ball. Some do it standing next to the ball. It doesn't matter. What's important is that the target be small and precise.

This preaddress phase of the routine is the time to deal with any problems that might be caused by an unusual or unfavorable lie. If the ball is on a downslope, an upslope, or the side of a hill, take a stance next to it, take a practice swing or two, and determine the adjustments in the flex of your knees or the tilt of your shoulders you will have to make to cope with the lie. Think them through at this stage because you don't want to have them occur to you as you prepare to hit the ball. If your lie is flat, of course, this step isn't necessary.

The next step depends on the individual. Some players, when they have picked the target and club, can visualize the ball flying through the air, landing, rolling, and stopping where they want it to stop. They can visualize how their swing will look. These visions are as clear to them as if they were in a movie theater watching them.

Such visualization can help to produce a successful shot. Brad Faxon feels that the vision in his mind dictates to his nerves and muscles the type of swing to execute. If he stands on the tee of a par four that doglegs to the left and demands a high draw, he sees the high draw. That's enough to get his body to produce the swing that makes the ball fly high and curve from right to left. He doesn't have to think consciously at all about the grip, the stance, the swing plane, or any of the other mechanics that most golfers would associate with a high draw.

But you don't have to visualize. A lot of great players don't, because their minds don't work that way. They look at their targets, decide they are going to hit those targets, and how they will work the ball—draw or fade. That suffices. Some players simply focus on the target and know the ball is going there. That gets the job done.

The important thing is that you know the ball is going to the target. If you can't make yourself believe it, pick another club or another target until you can. If you've got a driver in your hands and you can't believe that the ball is going to go where you want it, put it back in the bag and take a 3-wood or an iron.

Instilling this unwavering belief in the shot is one of the fundamentals without which your routine loses its purpose. Remember that the point of the routine is not to go through a physical ritual. It is to get your body aligned properly and your mind in an effective state before every shot.

Val Skinner had an unfortunate experience at the 1994 British Women's Open that illustrates the point. Val arrived in England for the tournament a little jet-lagged, and her first-round score reflected it. But she righted herself in the next two rounds, and by Sunday afternoon, she was three under par, two shots off the lead.

On the 15th hole, though, she made a critical mistake. She drove the ball well, leaving herself an approach shot of 173 yards. There was a slight breeze. Her instinct told her to hit a 5-iron, but she chose to ask her caddie for advice. He said 6. This introduced doubt into her mind about club selection. She hit the shot with a mind infected by doubt and plugged the ball in a trap. She was fortunate to make bogey.

She repeated the mistake at No. 17. This time, her instincts told her to hit a 9-iron for a short approach shot. She asked her caddie again, and he said wedge. Again, she hit before resolving the doubt. Again, she bogeyed the hole.

She walked to the 18th tee angry. And she hit her drive in that frame of mind. It wound up in an unplayable lie, and she finished the tournament with a double-bogey. She fell from third place to ninth in the final four holes.

In each case, she later said, she failed to follow her routine. To a spectator, this would not have been apparent. Physically, she went through all the motions. But she did not follow the mental side of the routine, which required her to dispel any doubt or anger from her mind before she hit the ball.

This is often the hardest part of the routine to execute. It's not enough to go through the motions that set up the body properly. You have to set up the mind as well.

Even the best players, the ones who have learned this principle, understand it, and have practiced it, have to work constantly at it. The game is always tempting them, as it tempted Val Skinner, to hit a shot before their minds are set. Everyone succumbs to the temptation once in a while and strays from the proper routine. The best players recognize when they have done it and renew their commitment to hit shots only when they have executed each step in their mental routine.

So, NOW YOU have assessed the shot, picked the club, picked the target, and adjusted for any lie and stance variations. You may or may not have visualized the shot, but you know the ball is going to the target. Your mind is calm, focused, and decisive.

At about this point, you might want to take practice swings, particularly on shorter touch shots. Whether to take them, when to take them, and how many to take are matters of personal preference. Some of my players stand up next to the ball, take a practice swing, then go behind the ball and visualize the shot. Others prefer to visualize behind the ball, take a practice swing, and then step forward and begin their address. Still others visualize, step up to the ball and take their swings in an alignment parallel to the one they plan to use. The only important thing is that the practice swing or swings leave you feeling comfortable and decisive.

Davis Love III's routine is to visualize the shot, stand next to the ball, then take a practice swing, feeling a high draw or a high fade or whatever he's planning. His practice swing captures the feel of that shot.

The practice swing, improperly used, can inject trouble into your routine. Some people, for instance, feel it's important to take precisely the same number of practice swings before each shot. But if the last swing doesn't feel right, and they step up to the ball anyway, they can't help but have doubts about their ability to execute the shot. They would be better off being flexible about the number of practice swings they take, making certain that the last one feels right and inspires trust in the swing.

Some of the best players are inconsistent about practice swings. Brad Faxon sometimes takes a full practice swing. Sometimes he takes merely an extended waggle. Sometimes he does nothing at all. He knows that the purpose of the routine is not to take a certain number of practice swings, but to set him up properly, mentally and physically, for the shot. So he does what feels right at the time.

The practice swing can be the back door through which

thoughts about swing mechanics invade your routine. Many players, as they take their practice swings, remind themselves of all sorts of mechanical concepts, from keeping their heads still to following through. It is difficult, perhaps impossible, for them to then step up to the ball and banish those thoughts from their minds.

I much prefer that a player take his practice swing with his focus on the target, thinking only of loosening up, feeling the right swing and gaining confidence.

I know that many golfers cannot easily bring themselves to do that. They go through a phase where they simply must think about mechanics on the practice swing. If you fall into that category, my advice is to take at least two practice swings. Let the first one be the one on which you think about mechanics. Once your mechanics feel right, take a final practice swing in which you concentrate only on target and feel.

In the ideal routine, the player takes his grip and his stance unconsciously and correctly. I like to see my players take their grip while they are standing behind the ball, rather than during their address. I don't want to see them fiddling with the grip over the ball.

The best professionals can deal with their grip and stance unconsciously because they recognize their importance and they practice them, sometimes more than they practice hitting golf balls. Many of them have full-length mirrors at home on which they have placed tape to indicate where their hands, shoulders and other checkpoints should be when they set up properly.

Amateurs may not be able to spend as much time on this as professionals, or they may find it boring, but it's still a good idea. The correct grip and stance are so important that if you plan on taking only one golf lesson for the rest of your life, I would recommend that it deal only with grip, stance, alignment, ball position, and developing a routine that enables you to mentally and physically set up properly every time.

Until you reach the stage where you can unconsciously take care of grip, stance, and alignment, you need to be consciously meticulous about your setup. As soon as you've completed setting up, shift gears mentally, stop thinking about mechanics, and focus on the target.

Then the most important part of an exemplary routine begins. It's deceptively simple:

Look at the target, look at the ball, and swing.

The idea that underlies this fundamental principle is the same one behind trusting your swing. Your brain and body work best together when the brain reacts to a target. Once you have completed your setup and locked onto your target, further delay can only be an opportunity for unwanted thoughts and distractions to disturb your concentration and pollute that pure and unconscious reaction.

You will, however, see some professionals who spend a long time with their eyes focused on the ball after they have taken their last look at the target. Jack Nicklaus did this. If it works, it is a sign that the player doing it has a highly disciplined mind. But I wouldn't teach any beginner, or any golfer just developing a routine, to stand over the ball very long once that final look at the target has been taken.

Of course, you don't want to rush your backswing. Your routine at this stage should have a pace that fits your personality, yet has rhythm and flow: Look at the target. Pause. Look at the ball. Pause. Swing.

This core of the routine remains the same for all shots, from drives to putts.

Some players have faster natural rhythm than others. Nick

Price is most effective with a pace that would feel rushed to Davis Love or David Frost. A player has to find a tempo that feels right to him or her.

Individual routines also vary on such things as waggles. Tom Kite has for years had a routine that incorporates several looks and waggles after the address. It works for him and I wouldn't recommend that he try to change it. Tom does the most important thing very well. After his last look at his target, he starts the swing without delay, his mind focused narrowly on his target.

One of the first things I look for when a player I'm working with is having trouble under pressure is the rhythm of this final part of the routine. If the time between the last look at the target and the beginning of the backswing grows any longer on the course than it was on the practice tee, that's a sure sign that the player is not maintaining his or her routine.

UP UNTIL THIS point, most golfers find everything about this pre-shot routine intuitively satisfying. Then it strikes them that there is no place in it for a swing thought. And they panic.

The best swing thought is no swing thought. But I understand that most golfers have been raised with them. So if a player tells me he absolutely must have a swing thought, I let him have one.

But he can have only one per round, and only for shots of 120 yards and longer. Switching from one swing thought to another bogs the mind down hopelessly in mechanics. And from 120 yards and in, it's important that nothing interferes with concentration on distance and the target, on getting the ball into the hole.

Some swing thoughts are more conducive to staying focused on the target and trusting your mechanics than others. "Nice and slow" is a good swing thought. Counting your looks and waggles is a good swing thought.

The swing thought should suggest an effortless motion. There is a big difference, mentally, between "Take it back straight" and "Make sure to make a really straight takeaway." The former is flowing and effortless. The latter is so tight, careful and contrived that it's deadly.

The same is true of almost any swing thought that involves the downswing. Once that club starts forward, you're courting disaster if you try to think about its path and control it.

YOU CAN'T ALLOW yourself to be rushed through any segment of your preshot routine. But a player with a sound and deliberate preshot routine need not be a slow player. In fact, a person with a sound, deliberate routine should be a faster player, because he or she will spend less time in the woods looking for lost balls. And he or she won't spend long chunks of time frozen over the ball, reviewing all the mechanics that someone has said must be executed perfectly.

I advise my professional players to make their routines as short and simple as possible. The best routines are often the simplest and take the least time. It's easier to repeat a simple routine than a long, complex one.

I also advise them to make sure they can execute their routines well within the time allowed by the rules, so that they never need worry about a slow-play penalty.

I never urge a professional to hasten his routine unless I see evidence that indecision, rather than being deliberate, is the cause of the slowness. This happened recently with a young player I've been working with, Glen Day.

Glen was having the best tournament of his rookie season at the Anheuser-Busch Classic in Williamsburg, Va. He had the lead after 36 holes. But then he began playing very slowly. The television network covering the tournament made an issue of it, superimposing a clock on the screen as soon as it was Glen's turn to play. He shot 72 and fell out of the lead.

He called me after the third round, upset about the added pressure this placed on him. I sympathized with him. It's not something the network would probably have done to Jack Nicklaus. But Nicklaus has the wherewithal to retaliate against a televison director who offends him. A rookie doesn't. This, I told Glen, was a fact of life he would just have to put up with.

Then I told him that he had another, better reason to speed things up. When he and I had worked on his routine, he had no trouble making his shots within the time allotted by the rules. But in the tournament, once he got the lead, he started having trouble making up his mind. He read putts two and three times. He changed clubs before approach shots. That was taking up time. More important, it was undermining his confidence. It showed in his score. I told him he ought to trust his first instinct on putts and club selection the next day.

He did, and though he finished second to Mark McCumber, Glen shot 66 and Mark had to sink a couple of great pitch shots on the final holes to beat him.

There is a distinction between being indecisive at the beginning of the routine and being distracted close to the end of the routine. While I want my players to be decisive, a player should never hit a shot if he is distracted and not absolutely ready. If this means backing away from the ball and starting the routine over again, so be it.

This was a point I emphasized to David Frost when we started working together a number of years ago. Frosty thereupon went on to New England for a tournament and called me after the first round.

"Doc, I had to back off from about ten shots today," he said.

"What happened?"

"Well, one time I heard a baby crying. Another time someone jingled change in his pocket. Another time the wind kicked up. But you told me not to hit the ball if my mind wasn't where it should be, and I walked away every time. Should I have had to do it that often?"

"What," I asked, "did you shoot?"

"Sixty-six," David replied.

"I guess you did," I said.

I assured him he would not always have to walk away so often. As his routine became an ingrained habit, he would be less prone to distraction. But the most important thing was that he had played a round free of mental errors, where in the past he probably would have hit two or three bad shots because of lost concentration.

The main reason I see for slow play among amateurs is not players following deliberate routines. Nor is it players who back away occasionally when they are distracted. Slow play may be caused by three types of golfers. People who aren't ready to play when it's their turn because they're too busy chatting, or watching their friends hit, are slow. Indecisive players, second-guessing their club selection, are slow. Players who give themselves swing lessons as they address the ball are slow.

You can begin a sound routine while the other members of your group are hitting their shots. You can figure the yardage and pull the club. You can read the green while others are putting. If you have an unusual lie, you can assess it and take a few practice swings while you're waiting. Then, when it's your turn, you're immediately ready to focus on the target, believe in the shot, set up, look at the target, look at the ball, and swing.

I believe amateurs, even more so than professionals, ought to trust their first instincts regarding club selection or the break of a putt. If your first thought as you walk up to an approach shot is "5-iron," you will be better off ninety-nine times out of a hundred if you hit the 5-iron decisively, rather than waffle about using a 6. If your first thought on a putt is "right lip," you will be better off hitting it there than if you start to consider whether that spike mark six feet from the hole is going to throw your ball off line.

If you do these things and develop a sound, simple routine, you will find that even if you occasionally walk away and restart your routine because something has interfered with your concentration, you will be a faster player.

9.

Let the Short Game Flow

ONCE IN A while, I come across a player I don't help to improve. Almost invariably, this is a player who cannot accept the fact that low scores depend on how well a golfer plays once the ball is within about 120 yards of the hole. This is a player who persists in thinking that golf is about who hits the longest drives or the prettiest 3-irons.

It's not. Everything that happens from the tee to that 120-yard range is almost insignificant compared with what happens thereafter. In fact, I'll occasionally tell a player that I don't care what he does with his long game—whether he focuses on a target and follows a routine or not—as long as he tries what I suggest about wedging, chipping and putting.

A good golfer must not only accept the preeminence of the short game. He must learn to relish getting the ball into the hole, to love it as much or more than mere ball-striking.

This is not a truth that I discovered. Good players have known it for generations. Still, lots of people persist in thinking that the key to improvement is learning to hit tee shots like John Daly's. Nothing could be further from the truth. In fact, the closer a golfer gets to hitting as long as John Daly, the more critical his short game becomes.

Early in 1994, I began to work with Daly. We sat down together and talked for five or six hours.

He told me about his drinking problems, his marital problems, his suspension from the Tour. He told me that he often found himself out on the golf course, thinking not about his game, but about all of his personal problems. He told me that hitting the ball as far as he does put even more pressure on him. If he didn't make birdies, he felt he was wasting his potential. That made him angry at himself. Growing up, he had never learned to deal with anger or any other difficult emotion, except by getting drunk.

I taught John the same philosophy and psychology I teach all of my players. While much of what had happened to him in the past was unfortunate, the only question in front of him now was what the rest of the John Daly story would be. He had, I said, the chance to write his own biography. He could be a hero, overcoming great barriers to success, or he could script a sad ending to his golfing career. But it would be his choice. It is a choice he will struggle with for a long time.

As to golf, I told him to work on his game from 120 yards and in.

In addition to his prodigious length, John has fine touch on the greens—he wouldn't have won the PGA at Crooked Stick in 1991 if he hadn't been sinking a lot of putts from five to fifteen feet out. And he has a natural, loose little flop shot from just off the green.

But he will not win much on the Tour without being excellent from 120 yards and in. These are the shots that will create birdies for him. With John's length, he can hit wedges to the green on most par fours. His success will depend, in large part, on whether he can consistently get the ball close enough to the pin from 120 yards and in to make birdies.

Truth be told, though, I tell the same thing to nearly all the players I work with.

A little while ago, I was talking to another strong young pro at the Players Championship. He had just shot a 73, and he was telling me how long he hit the ball and how much potential everyone tells him he has.

I told him that I didn't look at length off the tee when I assessed potential. I want to know how strong a player's mind is, and how well he plays the scoring game with his wedges and his putter.

To explain what I meant, I had him review his round, stroke by stroke, while I made notes. When he was finished, I added up the totals. Of his 73 strokes, 64 fell into just three categories: drives, wedges and putts. Throw out the 14 drives, and he had played 50 strokes with the wedges or the putter.

Then I asked him how much time he thought he ought to be spending on his 3-iron and how much time he ought to be spending on his short game.

The same thing is true, and even more so, with amateurs, from tournament players down to high handicappers. Their short games may not set up as many birdies as John Daly's can. But a weekend player's short game can save pars and turn double-bogeys into bogeys. A solid short game can turn a hacker who can't hit more than a weak banana ball off the tee into a player who shoots in the low 80s or high 70s.

Someday, I am going to talk Tom Kite into conducting an experiment to prove this. We occasionally do clinics together. As I imagine it, at some clinic, he and I will select someone with a handicap of 20 or so to play a round with Tom. The duffer and Tom will each hit the first three shots on par fives, the first two shots on par fours, and the tee shot on par threes. Then they will switch balls. The duffer will hole out Tom's, and Tom will hole out the duffer's.

I am prepared to bet that the score of the ball Tom takes over from the duffer will be lower than the score of the ball the duffer takes over from Tom.

Look at it another way. Nick Price in 1993 led the Tour in scoring average with just under 69 strokes per round. He hit an average of twelve or thirteen greens per round. Most 20-handicappers I see hit at least four or five greens per round. If they had Nick Price's short game, they'd be shooting in the seventies instead of the nineties. But they botch too many shots from 120 yards and in.

Nick tells me that improving his short game has contributed enormously to the improvement in his general attitude over the past few years. He is so confident in his wedges and his putter that he knows he will score well even on days when he's not swinging well. This gives him peace of mind and helps him maintain the mind-set that has characterized his recent play. He can be patient and trusting.

Good short shots are extremely productive. On the average par four, you can hit an excellent drive, a pretty good approach, and still have lots of work left to make par. Foul up one of the putts and you're looking at a bogey. Conversely, you can hit two bad shots with the longer clubs—say, a drive into the rough and a fat approach—and still save your par with an excellent chip or pitch that stops next to the hole. In terms of scoring, the payoff for a good short shot is much higher than the payoff for a good long shot.

Curtis Strange won the U.S. Open in 1989 even though he hit the ball into nine greenside bunkers in the final round. He got up and down eight times. And yet, he appeared in golf magazines thereafter as an exemplar of the swing. His swing didn't win the Open; if he had had a great swing working, he wouldn't have been in nine bunkers. It was his ability to play sand shots, putt, think and stay patient.

A couple of years ago, John Cook, Brad Faxon and Fred Couples were all in the top eight on the money list, but they were all way down in the rankings on driving accuracy. They won money because they all had great short games.

Pat Bradley, during the years she dominated the LPGA Tour, told me that, in her mind, missing a green didn't matter. She was just as intent on, and confident about, holing chips and pitches as she was on long putts. That's how solid her short game was.

Most amateurs have heard about the importance of the short game. But judging by their actions, most don't believe it. At almost any club I visit, I will find ten players standing on the practice tee, whaling away with woods and long irons, for every one I see at a practice green, refining the touch and the shots that will help him or her score.

There's no small amount of *machismo* involved in this. The long drive connotes strength, power, virility. The short game has connotations of delicacy and femininity. Part of my job as a sports psychologist is to help players get past this.

All I can say is that if you want to score well, attach your ego to how well you think, how well you manage your game, how well you hit your wedges, how well you putt. The long-drive swing won't be in the slot every day. But you can always think well, manage your game well, and play the short game well.

The short game is what a lot of great golfers learn first. Bobby Jones spent countless hours on long summer afternoons and evenings chipping and pitching shots to the 13th green at the Atlanta Athletic Club, then sinking the putts.

"I don't remember any glimmering thought of form or any consciousness of a method in playing a shot," Jones wrote later of those boyhood years. "I seemed merely to hit the ball, which is possibly the best way of playing golf."

Sixty years later, in Spain, Jose-Maria Olazabal had much the same kind of early training. He lived on a golf course where his father was the superintendent, and he spent hours and hours chipping and pitching. In the decades between Jones and Olazabal, dozens of great players learned the game by learning the short game first. Some were caddies, pitching and chipping for penny wagers. Tom Kite's father built a bunker and green in his backyard in which Tom spent countless hours. So did the fathers of Ernie Els and Phil Mickelson.

In fact, I would say that most great players first became good at getting the ball into the hole, at the short game. Then, later, they refined their full swings.

Some modern players had the good fortune to have teachers who understood how to inculcate a short game. Tom Kite has told me about how he and Ben Crenshaw learned from Harvey Penick. Tom or Ben would say, for instance, "Mr. Penick, how do you hit a high lob over a trap and stop it real fast?"

Harvey Penick was smart enough not to fill their heads with a lot of instruction about weakening their grips and not turning their right hands over. He gave them some balls and sent them out to a practice green. He told them to stand behind the bunker and pretend there was a tree growing in it. Then they were to hit balls over the tree. They were to make the tree grow higher until it was the right size to make the ball sit down and stop near the hole. And when they could do that, they were to come and tell him about it.

Eventually, Tom and Ben would come running into the pro shop, proudly announcing that they had completed their assignment. Harvey Penick would go out to the practice green and watch.

And if one of them asked him a question about technique for the high lob, Mr. Penick would reply, "I don't know. Show me again." After they'd demonstrated again, he would say, "It's what you just did."

For the short game, he knew that touch, feel and confidence were paramount. And he knew how to teach them.

How do you develop a good short game if you didn't grow up on a golf course, have a backyard bunker, or have Harvey Penick for a teacher?

First of all, you practice it. The professionals that I work with all do. If you're not spending 70 percent of your practice time on shots from 120 yards in, you're not trying to become the best golfer you can be.

The pros play little games in the practice area. They'll have their caddies take a couple of shag bags and put them ten yards apart, a hundred yards out. Then they'll put a towel midway between the bags. Then they'll shoot at the towel. They get a point for every ball that lands between the bags and three for every one that hits the towel. They lose two points for every ball that lands outside the bags. They frequently change the distance they're hitting, of course. Or they play little up and down games around the practice green, frequently for small bets. A player can't get enough of this kind of practice.

Tom Kite has a couple of excellent short-game practice routines.

In the first, he sends his caddie, Mike Carrick, precisely 40 yards out from the practice tee. Tom then tries to hit to a ball bag at Carrick's feet. As soon as he makes contact with the ball Tom yells out the distance he thinks it will go. He might, for instance, yell, "thirty-eight," if he thinks it will land two yards short of Carrick. When the ball lands, Carrick tells him the exact distance it traveled. If it goes precisely to the target, Carrick simply raises his arms over his head—touchdown.

Once he's handling 40 yards, Tom changes to 50, then 60, then 70, and on up to 120. When he's done that, he starts staggering the distances—first 40, then 80, then 60, then 110. In this way, he sharpens his touch with his wedges.

Tom and I often play a similar game from the practice bunker. I'll stand on the green, 20 yards away, and hold out my hand. Tom has to blast the ball close enough to my hand so that I can catch the ball without moving my feet. When he's done that, I move a few steps closer. And then closer, until, in the final stage, I am squatting on the lip of the bunker, just a few yards from Tom, and he has to feather the ball to me the way he would if he were blasting to a tight pin.

I don't suggest that high handicappers try this with their firstborn children as catchers, at least not at first. I offer it as an illustration of how well a player like Kite hits wedges, and how hard he works to maintain his touch with the short clubs.

The ideal way to develop a good mental approach to golf would be to learn how to think your way around the green, and then let those skills transfer to the long game. From a psychological point of view, the short game requires the same uncluttered mind, the same focus on the target, and the same disciplined routine that the long game requires—only more so.

What do I mean by more so?

First of all, have no swing thoughts whatsoever from 120 yards and in. Think only of the target.

You will use your standard routine for the short game, except that you may want to make a few more practice swings, eyes focused on your target, until the swing feels right and you can trust it completely.

More so than in the long game, you will have shots that require some adjustments in grip and stance. You may have odd lies. Take care of those adjustments with the first couple of practice swings.

Don't hit the shot thinking about making a weight shift, or how far your backswing should go. That kind of thought introduces tension into the body, and tension can ruin a pitch or chip.

Frequently, the pitch shot you face will be shorter than the distance you get from a full swing with your wedge. This poses a problem for many amateurs. One way to combat it is to know what your optimal wedge distance is and lay up to that distance. If you're 260 yards from the green and you can only hit the ball 230 with your fairway wood, it makes no sense to hit that wood if your favorite approach shot is a wedge from 100 yards. Hit a 6 or a 7-iron, then hit the wedge.

But when you do face a wedge from other than your optimal distance, trust your feel. If you've practiced enough, you'll have it. And don't try to get too cute. If your normal swing produces a 100-yard wedge shot, and your distance is 98 yards, don't start thinking about taking two percent off your normal swing. Even professionals can mess themselves up trying to take just a little off their full swings.

Once you've set up, taken your practice swings, and envisioned the shot, don't freeze over the ball. Look at the target. Swing.

For my professional players, 120 yards from the pin is a threshold distance. From within that range, I want them to be thinking about sinking the shot. The hole is their ultimate target. Obviously, this may be asking a little too much of most amateurs. I would not recommend that a 20-handicapper try to hole a 110-yard wedge shot if the flag is tucked on the far edge of the green, close to a pond—because, by definition, 20-handicappers don't hit their wedges that accurately. Facing such a tight and dangerous pin placement from 110 yards, the 20-handicapper should pick a safer target, closer to the middle of the green. The threshold distance for an amateur might be 40, 60, or 80 yards, depending on his or her skills. Every player has to judge that individually. But inside your threshold distance, don't just go for the middle of the green and don't just try to get it close.

From inside your threshold distance, think about holing the shot.

You have to consider how the ball is going to roll once it hits the ground. If the slope of the green is going to make the ball break, you must shift your target accordingly. It may become an imaginary hole two feet to the left of the real hole or five feet right. But whenever possible, you should have your imaginary target be the same distance from the ball as the real target, the hole.

Ninety percent of the players I work with pick a target at the distance they want the ball to travel. This is the way I would teach a youngster to do it. But some players have been brought up to chip or pitch to a landing spot and to think of that as their target. If they have, I don't insist that they change, but I do insist that they commit themselves to spot-chipping every time the same way. The main thing is that the player be thinking about chipping the ball in the hole, not just getting it on the green or getting it close.

There may be occasions when you can't see the hole on a short shot. You might, for instance, be at the bottom of a slope, pitching up to an elevated green. In that situation, think about dropping the ball straight onto the flagstick. This frightens some people. They think the ball will go too long. But the slope of the land causes the ball to pop up higher and land shorter than they expect.

When I first started to work with Davis Love III, he was a student at the University of North Carolina. His father was an old friend of mine from *Golf Digest* schools, and he sent Davis to me for help with the mental side of his game.

As a college student, Davis already had a long, fluid swing and enormous distance. He knew how to hit the short shots, having been taught by his father, who was a master. But his short game wasn't as productive as it would need to be if he wanted to be a successful professional.

I suggested that he approach pitches and chips the way his friend Michael Jordan approached scoring in basketball. Jordan just looked at the basket and shot. I wanted Davis to do the same thing with chips and putts—just look and react. I told him to think of his short game as a run-and-shoot offense.

I threw another metaphor at him, suggesting that it was a lot like playing jazz on the piano. Anyone can learn to put his fingers on the right keys, just as anyone can mechanically place his putter or his wedge in the right spot. But to make beautiful music, a piano player has to let it flow, the way a putter or chipper has to look and react.

Davis also needed to learn to think about holing his short shots. When he first came to me, he was not thinking about getting his chips and pitches into the hole. He was thinking about getting up and down. Sometimes he'd be confident he would. Sometimes he'd be worried he wouldn't. But he was not thinking about the hole.

That had to change before he could win consistently, and it did.

Davis has gotten better every year, and he's become a fine player with his wedge and putter. Of course, I'm particularly happy for him when he wins a tournament with his short game.

A few years ago, at the Tournament of Champions, in the last two rounds, Davis hit something like six fairways and five or six greens. He won the tournament because he had his wedge and putter going so well.

I remember his triumph at the Tournament Players Championship and in particular the way he played the 8th hole at that tournament, a long par three. During the final round, Davis pushed his tee shot a bit and wound up right of the green. He was getting ready to play his second shot when he heard a couple of guys in the gallery behind him making bets about whether he could get up and down. Davis stopped.

He turned toward the bettors and said, "Guys, I'm going to make this shot."

Then he turned around, went through his routine, and holed the pitch for a birdie.

Of course, thinking about the hole doesn't always work quite that well. A few years ago, Brad Faxon got into a sudden-death playoff at the Buick Open. He hit an errant approach and left himself with a nearly impossible shot—from a thin lie, over a bunker to a tight pin. He had to make it to stay alive.

Most players, faced with that shot on national television, would have thought about avoiding disaster. They would have played not to stub it, not to leave the ball in the bunker. They would have been satisfied just getting the ball somewhere on the green.

Not Brad. He took a long, fluid swing and flopped the ball just over the lip of the trap. It trickled down, rolled just over the edge of the cup—and past. Brad fell to the ground, unable to believe it hadn't gone in.

Those are the breaks of the game. The important thing is that Brad had focused sharply on hitting the ball into the hole. If you do that, your misses will be closer and the breaks will, eventually, even out.

Above all in the short game, be decisive. Your model might be Tom Watson's famous chip shot from the deep fringe at the 17th hole at Pebble Beach, the shot that won the U.S. Open in 1982. Bill Rogers, Watson's playing partner, must have taken ten minutes to get the ball from the fringe up to the pin. Watson's mind remained quiet. He took a look at the lie, then returned to stand with his caddie, Bruce Edwards, to wait until it was his turn to play. Then he walked behind the ball, took two practice strokes, decided it felt good, took a last look at the target, and let the shot go.

Most golfers would have hunched over that ball forever, until whatever touch they had was gone. They would have decided that it was good enough just to keep the ball close. Then they would have jabbed at it and sent it skittering past the hole.

But Watson told his caddie he was going to put the ball in the hole. And he did.

10.

What I Learned from Bobby Locke

When I was a boy in Rutland, Vermont, I quite accidentally got to know Bobby Locke, the man widely acclaimed as the greatest putter who ever lived. I had a summer job toting clubs at the Rutland Country Club. Locke, coincidentally, had married a Vermont woman, and he spent a few weeks every summer with her family. The Rutland Country Club was the best course around, and he would come by to play a few rounds or give an exhibition. I got his bag.

Altogether unwittingly, from both his perspective and my own, he began my education in that part of golf which is played between the ears.

Bobby Locke did not, to my eyes anyway, look like much of an athlete. He was pear-shaped, with a thin little mustache, and he still wore plus fours and a long-sleeved shirt with a tie, even though this was around 1960.

Nor did he display the fierce demeanor that I had been led to believe was common to all successful athletes. He was not one to get up at dawn. Most days, he would show up at the course around ten in the morning. He'd hit fifteen or twenty wedges, chip and putt for a few minutes, and then go play. He walked very slowly, so much so that some members grumbled when he was on the course. But I noticed that he never spent very much time over the ball.

After his round, he'd spend a few hours in the bar, drinking something like Pabst Blue Ribbon and telling stories.

Years later, when I read his autobiography, I learned that someone had told him early on in his career that a good player had to be relaxed. Locke said he had set out to cultivate relaxation in everything he did. That certainly described the man I knew in Vermont.

It was not that he did not care about how he played, because he did. When he gave an exhibition, he warmed up more thoroughly. The club had no practice range, so he would take some balls to the first tee. I shagged for him, and I brought my baseball glove with me. He started off hitting high 7-irons with a pronounced draw. I would wait until the last moment, break to my right, and make a running catch off the first or second bounce—looking, I no doubt thought, very much like the Red Sox centerfielder of the future.

"Master Bob!" he called out after I had caught a couple. No one had ever called me "Master" before, but it seemed to go with the way he was dressed, so I came running in.

"Master Bob," he said when I arrived. "My ball always will curve to your right. And I want you to walk, leaving early, to catch it. That makes me look good, and this is my show, Master Bob, not yours."

I went back out and shagged balls his way.

At the close of every exhibition, Locke would answer questions. Whenever someone asked him about his putting secret, he would say:

"Well, you just hit it and listen."

And someone would inevitably say, "What do you mean, hit it and listen?"

And Locke would reply, "You just hit it and listen."

Then some genius would ask, "Yeah, but don't you want to see if you make it?"

And Locke would respond, "I don't have to see if I make it. I can hear it."

Then some real genius would pipe up, "Well, if you miss it, don't you want to see how it will break coming back?"

And Locke would say, "Why would I want to see it if I miss it?"

The point, I now realize, was that he wanted nothing to impair his confidence.

He didn't want to dwell on the putts that he missed, because that would only make it harder to be certain that the next one was going in. And that was one thing Locke insisted upon. Putting was about confidence. "Hitting a putt in doubt is fatal in most cases," he wrote in his autobiography. Locke had to be certain that the putt was going in. Looking back, I can believe that he was.

PHYSICALLY, PUTTING IS the simplest of all the golf strokes. Anyone who can toss a beanbag underhanded into a wastebasket has the required coordination.

The style of the stroke is unimportant. There have been great wrist putters and great shoulder putters. There are good putters who putt cross-handed. Johnny Miller won the AT&T Pro-Am at

Pebble Beach in 1994 with something he called the claw grip. Bernhard Langer won the Masters in 1993 putting with one hand clasped to his forearm.

Yet, you can still find teachers who will dissect the "proper" stroke and grip at great length and insist that their pupils master these mechanics.

I don't think there is a classic putting stroke. Locke took the putter back a little to the inside of the target line, with a closed stance and a slightly hooded clubface, to put overspin on the ball. All of those things were wrong, if you go by the conventional wisdom about putting mechanics.

Brad Faxon told me a story about a friend of his who is a teaching pro and Ben Crenshaw. The teacher called Faxon and asked for help in getting inside the ropes at a tournament practice green, so that he could videotape Crenshaw's putting stroke. Faxon agreed.

Crenshaw, as usual, was friendly and accommodating as the teacher taped his practice putts. The teacher got more comfortable.

"Ben, will you tell me what you're working on while I have the tape running?" he asked.

Crenshaw obliged.

"I'm trying to make sure my head and my knees move a little and my stroke feels longer," he said. "Because when it feels like that, I always putt real well. But every once in a while, you start getting a little careful, and you try to make sure your head stays still. And if your head stays too still, you lose your feel and you start putting badly. You can never putt well without feel."

The teacher was dumbfounded. The best putter in the world had just denied one of the tenets he held sacred about the mechanics of putting, the still head.

The point is not that the head should move and the stroke

should be long. Or that the head should be still and the stroke short. The point is that what's important is not the mechanics of Crenshaw's stroke, but his feel for it, his belief in it, his trust that it will make the ball go in the hole. When doubts started to erode this confidence, he had to catch himself and get back that feeling of trust.

Attitude is what makes a great putter.

Putting is largely mental, and you have control over your mind and attitude. To become a good putter, you must make a commitment to good thinking. You have to fill your mind with thoughts that will help you, not excuses for poor putting. You have to decide that, come what may, you love putting and you're glad that every hole gives you a chance to use your putter, because that's where you've got a big advantage over all the players who dread putting.

Nick Price, when he was dominating the tour in the summer of 1994, told me he was so confident when he stepped up to a straight putt he almost felt as if he were cheating. That kind of confidence guaranteed that he would make a lot of putts.

The late Davis Love, Jr., once told me an illustrative story about putting attitude. Love had himself been a touring pro, and for a while in the 1950s he cut expenses by sharing a motel room with another young pro, Gary Player.

Their first tournament together was on a course down South with very slow Bermuda greens. This occurred before the development of the modern, hybrid Bermudas, and the greens on this course were like shag rugs. Love thought they were the worst he'd ever played on. But every night, Player would come back to the room and talk about how much he loved slow, shaggy Bermuda greens.

The next week, they drove north to a course with bent-grass greens, which the superintendent had shaved until they were like linoleum. Player, of course, came back to the room talking about how much he loved to play fast, bent-grass greens, the faster the better. Love couldn't stand the contradiction.

"Which is it, Gary? Do you love slow, Bermuda greens" he asked, "or fast, bent greens?"

"You just have to love whatever greens you're playing on," Player replied.

To someone unfamiliar with the way great athletes think, Player's attitude would seem to verge on foolishness. A golfer might like fast greens or slow greens or medium greens, but he cannot rationally like fast greens one week and slow greens the next. And only a fool could stand over a twenty-foot putt and be absolutely confident of holing it, when he has a lifetime of experience to prove that his chances of doing so are really about one in ten.

But this kind of foolishness is precisely what all great putters have in common.

Losing that foolishness is what happens to players when they get what are commonly called the yips.

There is no neurological basis for the yips. Nothing about the physical aging process dictates that a golfer cannot putt as well at sixty as he did at twenty.

The great players usually start out as confident putters, even bold putters. But over the years, even the great ones have trouble maintaining this attitude. Maybe playing for years with major championships on the line inevitably produces memories of missed putts in crucial situations. After a while, those memories become so burdensome that the golfer can't keep them out of his mind as he stands on the green. Then he loses the instinct to look at the hole, look at the ball, let the putt go, and know that it's going in.

In other cases, a player's ball-striking actually improves as he gets older. Then it becomes agonizingly apparent that the only thing that is keeping him from winning is his putting, particularly his short putts. That places enormous pressure on his putting, pressure that did not exist when he was younger and could blame other flaws in his game for his bad rounds. Little doubts and smidgens of indecision creep into his mind as he putts.

Then, perhaps, the problem becomes public knowledge. People hear that Hogan can't putt anymore, or Snead can't putt anymore, or Watson can't putt anymore. Golf magazines write about it. Johnny Miller talks about it. That multiplies the pressure. Pretty soon, the only thing the golfer can think about when he stands over an important four-footer is, "The whole world knows I can't make this kind of putt anymore."

At this point, fear infects the player's mind, and fear destroys putting. A good putting attitude is free of fear. A good putting attitude blends ideas that almost seem contradictory. The golfer has to believe the putt will go in the hole, but he must not care if he misses. He has to try enough to maintain a disciplined routine focused on sinking the putt, but not try so hard that he tightens up. He has to find a balance between determination and nonchalance.

Arnold Palmer, in his prime, instinctively had that balanced attitude toward putting. A few years ago, he and I were speaking at a corporate golf outing in New York. I was talking to the duffers in the audience, or so I thought, when I made some comments about nerves and putting. I told them that golfers don't physically lose their nerve on the greens. They simply start buying the myth that age brings on the yips. Then they lose the habit of looking at the hole and reacting to it with confidence.

"That's exactly my problem!"

It was Palmer, breaking in, unable to contain himself. "That's what I'm doing!"

Palmer went on for ten minutes. In his youth, he said, he had been decisive, even bold on the greens. But he wasn't any longer. He had become careful and tentative. He had to get back to being decisive.

I respected him enormously for speaking publicly about it. Upon reflection, I was not surprised that he did. Playing golf well demands honesty. Palmer would not have become great if he had been in the habit of deluding himself. I think that this willingness to confront the problems in his mental game and not to blame them on the inevitable onslaught of the yips is one reason he will keep winning the occasional Skins Game to supplement his Social Security checks.

Unlike Palmer, most players have their putting confidence spoiled well before they become champions. There is a process of socialization at work. As kids of twelve or thirteen, I think most golfers, if they have any athletic talent, are instinctively good putters. Like the young Bobby Jones, the good natural putter begins by simply walking up to the ball and rapping it at the hole.

But eventually, the good young putter will miss a five-footer. And when he does, some well-meaning adult will tell him that he missed it because he was too casual. He will tell him that putting is hard. He will tell him to size up every five-foot putt as if he were buying the putting surface instead of playing on it. And the youngster will start to tighten up and get careful with his putts, the way the 20-handicappers at the club do. More often than not, he'll be on his way to having a 20 handicap himself.

But kids, before their attitudes are spoiled, have a confident approach to putts. A few years ago, I was watching the Buick Open. Brad Faxon had a six-footer to win the tournament. My daughter, Casey, who was about nine years old, walked into the room and noticed that the adults were all nervous. She asked why, and I explained the situation.

"Oh, that's nothing," she said, mystified by our attitudes. "Brad always makes those." She left the room, supremely confident in Brad. And Brad made it.

Brad doesn't always make them, but any golfer will make more putts if he can get close to Casey's attitude.

I remember once watching, along with Tom Kite's mother, as Ben Crenshaw sank a few long putts to win a tournament.

"That's nothing compared to the way he used to putt," Mrs. Kite said. "When Ben was a boy, he'd just walk up to the ball and hit it. He generally didn't even bother to squat down behind it and read the green. And he sank putts from all over."

Over the years, Ben has gotten more deliberate and careful. And though he's still very relaxed on the green compared with most golfers, and he's still a wonderful putter, I'd love to know whether he's any better now than he was when he was a teenager.

WHEN TOURING PROS come to me for help with their putting, we begin as we begin for all shots, by establishing a good routine. All routines have personal variations, of course, and the putting routine differs somewhat from the full-swing and short-game routines because it has to allow for reading the green.

You might, as you read the putt, want to walk around the cup if this helps you see the whole putt. But I don't like to see golfers pace off the distance between the ball and the hole. This promotes an analytical, mechanical approach to something that must be based on feel. If you plumb-bob, which some touring pros do, insert it into your routine at this stage.

The important thing is that you commit yourself completely to the read you make. A decisive attitude is much more important in putting than reading the minute breaks and the grain of the grass.

It's easy to fall into the trap of overreading a putt. Frequently I find that players would do better if they didn't bother trying to read putts at all, if they walked onto the green, looked quickly at the line, and hit the ball.

Blaine McAllister did just that a short time ago in the B.C. Open. He came to the final green brimming with confidence, tied for the lead in the tournament. He had an eight-footer left. He was so confident that he didn't bother to line it up. He just walked up to it and hit it in the hole, for the win.

When we talked on the phone afterward, Blaine was still overjoyed by the confidence he'd displayed. I told him it was a good thing he'd let that confidence dictate his putting. A lot of players would have analyzed that eight-footer until it looked like a freeway interchange. They would have found it impossible to believe that such an important putt could be straight; they'd have read the green until they found a break. Then they would get tentative and leave the ball either short or long. They'd have left themselves a three-footer to tie and gotten even more nervous. It happens all the time. People who overread are, as Billy Casper once said, often really looking for a way to miss rather than a way to make the putt. And they forget a most important principle:

It's more important to be decisive about a read than correct.

ONCE YOU'VE MADE a decisive read, you need to think about, or visualize, the line of the putt. As with full shots, this step depends on individual idiosyncrasies. Some golfers can envision the line of the putt as clearly as they can see a yellow line painted down the middle of a highway. Others don't see anything in their mind's eye. But they nevertheless convince themselves that the line is right and the putt will drop. That's all that's important.

Next, for most players, it's time to pick out a target. There are no intermediate targets in putting, because an intermediate target might confuse you about how hard to hit it. For a straight putt, obviously, you use the cup for your target, but not the whole cup. Pick a particular spot in the cup.

For breaking putts, you will have to improvise a target. The idea is to try to make all putts seem straight. If you think the putt will break two feet to the right, pick out something two feet to the left of the hole—a spike mark, a discolored blade of grass, or a grain of sand. This can be difficult on courses with excellent, uniform greens, and you may have to settle for a spot in the grass. Or, you can just imagine a hole at the end of the line on which your putt will start.

On uphill and downhill putts, your imaginary target may be a foot or two in front of or behind the hole. Occasionally it will be even further than that. There are greens with humps and ridges, and the right target may be a spot at the crest of a ridge, from which gravity will pull the ball down to the hole.

Once you have selected your target, focus on it exclusively. Don't let your eyes wander to the cup.

There can be individual variations. Brad Faxon concentrates on the entire path of the putt, rather than an imaginary hole-high target, from the time he reads the putt until the time he strikes the ball.

Speed is a critical factor, especially on slick greens, but I don't advise players to think too much about it. The best putters don't.

Faxon, who consistently ranks near the top of the PGA putting statistics, tells me he never thinks about speed. He goes entirely by instinct, an instinct honed, of course, by a lot of practice and playing experience.

There is a way of thinking that can help you get the speed right. For a downhill putt, tell yourself that you want the ball to barely make it over the front lip of the cup on its last rotation. For an uphill putt, you might think of hitting the ball so it strikes the back of the cup as it goes down.

As far as speed is concerned, I have no quarrel with players who try to make their putts die in the hole. Many of the greatest players in the game did that. Other players believe in putting firmly, so the ball bounces off the back of the cup, particularly on short putts. I don't care which method a putter chooses, as long as he's focused on putting the ball in the hole.

If you miss short very often, it may be a sign of tentativeness and indecision. People who leave it short due to fear are afraid of running it too far past the hole and missing the return putt. If that's why someone is leaving putts short, it's a problem to be corrected.

But remember that the goal is neither to hit them firm nor to have them die at the hole, but to sink them. Don't be distracted from this objective by concerns about missing short or missing close.

A few years ago, the basketball coach at James Madison University, Lou Campanelli, called me. He asked if I could help one of his players, a senior who had previously been a good free-throw shooter. In his final season, Lou said, this kid was breaking the backboard with every free throw he attempted. He was still a fine field-goal shooter, but his free-throw percentage was way down. Every shot he took was long.

I went to talk to the young man and asked him when his free-throw problem started.

"I don't know," he said. "The first game of the year, I guess."

Anything prior to that, I prodded.

"Well, in the NCAA tournament last year," he said, "we were playing North Carolina and we had a chance to upset them. Inside the last minute, it was a one-point game. I went to the free-throw line with a one-and-one. And I shot an airball. They brought it inbounds, but after about ten seconds we stole it. I had the ball and the whole North Carolina team attacked me. I thought, my gosh, they want me on the line.

"I thought I was composed, but as soon as I was set to shoot, the North Carolina fans started chanting: 'Airball.' That really got to me, and I barely ticked the rim with my shot. North Carolina went on to win the game.

"I had let myself down and I had let my teammates down. Before I left the locker room, I made a commitment to myself that I would never shoot an airball again."

"Congratulations," I said. "Keep on doing what you're doing and you'll never shoot another airball. But if you want to make free throws, you have to change your thinking. You have a perfect attitude for avoiding airballs, but a lousy attitude for making free throws. If you want to be a great free-throw shooter, you have to accept an airball now and then."

Golfers can do the analogous thing. In their eagerness to stop leaving their putts short (and being called "Alice") or to stop running them too far past, they can lose focus on the real goal, which is putting the ball into the cup. The putter who is called Alice on the first green runs putts five or ten feet past on the next seventeen holes. Or the putter who runs one way past on the first green becomes tentative. What they don't do is knock anything difficult into the hole.

So, you've read the green decisively and picked out a line or a target. You may at this point in your routine want to take a couple of practice strokes. Take them with your eyes on the target, not the ball, and certainly not on the putter blade. Use them to make sure you feel the right stroke for the distance the ball has to travel. If you look at the ball or the blade, it will only introduce questions into your mind about the path the blade is taking, mechanical questions that divert you from your focus on the target.

The next step is getting yourself aligned and aimed properly. Many of the players I work with use the lettering on their golf balls to aid in doing this. They mark their balls, clean them, and then replace them so that the lettering is precisely in line with the intended line of the putt. Then they take their stances and use the lettering to align the blade of the putter.

Though there's no particular stance or grip that makes for good putting, there is one mechanical point worth mentioning in the alignment process. The eyes see the putt better when they are precisely over the ball. As a golfer develops a putting routine, it's worth practicing this indoors. Put a mirror on the floor and place the ball on it. Adjust your stance until your eyes are right over the ball or just inside it, whichever works better for you.

Once you've aimed yourself, you have to trust that your routine works and you're aimed correctly. Sometimes, a green will have undulations placed purposely by the architect to create optical illusions and confuse players. Don't let them distract you. Be decisive. If you take your stance, look at the target, and start wondering whether you're aimed correctly, you need to walk away and start the process over again, because you can't putt decisively if you're questioning your aim. Don't worry about slowing play down. If you are this meticulous about trusting your routine, you will make up for the lost time in the long run by taking fewer putts.

The heart of the putting routine is analogous to the core of the exemplary routines for full shots and the short game:

Look at the target. Look at the ball. Let the putt go.

Two principles, by now familiar to you, underlie this postulate. One is that your brain and nervous system work best when the brain simply reacts to the target. The other is that the longer a player stands over the ball before he hits the putt, the more likely he is to allow the intrusion of mechanical thoughts or doubts that will corrupt the pure, simple interplay among the target, the brain, and the nervous system.

The "run-and-shoot" attitude that Davis Love III borrowed for his short game from watching Michael Jordan play basketball exemplifies this. The idea is to let the conscious mind step aside and let the subconscious react to the target. Think when you're behind the ball. Don't think when you're over it. Do.

As with the full swing, there is a rhythm to looking at the target, looking at the ball, and letting the putt go. When I begin to work with a player, we spend a lot of time getting this rhythm ingrained in his or her routine. The player strokes one five-footer after another in time with my voice: Look at the target. Short pause. Look at the ball. Short pause. Let it go. It's almost like a mantra.

If a player I've been working with develops putting problems and asks me for help, the first thing I check is his rhythm. Is he following his routine in competition at the same pace he did on the practice green? If he's not, particularly if the pause between looking at the ball and letting the putt go has lengthened, that's a sign that he's not getting himself into a decisive frame of mind before he strokes the putt.

This is especially important on short putts. In every round, a golfer will have some critical putts of three to six feet. And everyone I work with, from high handicappers to the winners of major championships, occasionally has trouble with them.

Short putts remind me of field-goal kicks in football. Kicking field goals has little in common with the elements of football that most coaches like to emphasize: blocking, tackling, running. It's a simple task that comes down not so much to strength as to trust. But so many games are decided by field goals that no sensible coach would send a team onto the field without a good kicker. Similarly, no golfer should approach competition without a confident attitude toward short putts.

You have to begin by committing yourself to liking them. You will not be one of the guys who sit in the locker room complaining about what great scores they'd be shooting if they weren't blowing short putts. You will, instead, be a player who loves holing short putts. You will roll them just as freely as you roll 40-foot putts. You won't try to steer them or overcontrol them.

You can do this, in part, by practicing them. As you practice, emphasize being trusting and decisive with each putt. In most cases, this will mean hitting it firmly. I advise my professionals to do this with all short putts, taking some of the break out of them.

You won't, of course, make all your short putts. But when, inevitably, you miss a short putt, ask yourself why you missed it. Did you misread the green, or get the speed wrong? If so, forget it. But if you missed it because you were afraid of missing it and got tentative and careful, because you really didn't believe you would make it, redouble your effort to be trusting and decisive. If you do, you will still miss some short putts. But you will be a good short putter. You will miss less often.

On long putts, the biggest fallacy I see players falling for is the three-foot target. This is an imaginary circle with a radius of three feet and the hole at the center. Some teachers suggest a player facing a long putt should try only to get the ball inside this circle. This makes no sense. Think about an archer or a pistol shooter. They shoot at an artificial target with a bull's-eye and concentric outer circles. But no matter what the distance, they always aim for the bull's-eye. It gives them the biggest margin of error. Even if they miss it, they're likely to hit something on the target. The same principle applies to putting. Always aim to make it.

It's not hard to be decisive if the ball is going in the hole for you. Anybody who makes a couple of long putts on the first two holes is going to be decisive when he putts on the third green. The hard part is remaining decisive even if the first critical putts of the day don't fall.

This bedeviled Nick Price and a lot of professionals. I've had players tell me that they actually hope they don't hit their approach shots stiff on the first few holes. This sounds incredible, but the fact is they don't want to risk blowing a few makable birdie putts, because they know from experience that if they miss a couple of short birdie putts on the first few holes, their putting will be tentative and ineffective the rest of the day. Responding positively to missed putts is a major challenge.

The question you must ask yourself is not whether you're sinking your putts. The proper question is whether your attitude is giving your putts a chance to go in. If it is, you should be encouraged by missed putts. Sooner or later, since you're doing everything right, putts will start to fall. The law of averages, if you've just missed a few, suggests it will be sooner rather than later.

But if you have to admit to yourself that you have not been trusting and decisive with your putting, then you have a choice. You can let your missed putts make you even more tentative and indecisive for the rest of the day, and hope that geese land on the green and peck your errant putts into the hole. Or you can decide to become even more decisive and trusting in your putting and give yourself a chance to make some.

I recall Tom Watson at the 1982 U.S. Open. Everyone remembers the chip shot he sank at the 17th hole to seal the win. But equally impressive to me was the way he reacted after missing a straight, two-foot putt on the 7th green. He missed it so badly that it didn't even touch the cup. But he refused to get flustered and refused to get tentative.

On the next hole, he buried an 18-footer for birdie, getting back the lost stroke and a share of the lead with Jack Nicklaus. Some time after that, I asked him what had gone through his mind on those two holes. He told me that his miss only showed that even great putters miss an occasional easy one. He was a great putter. He acknowledged that it was disappointing and unfortunate to miss a two-footer in the final round of the U.S. Open. But he reminded himself that if he wanted to continue to be a great putter, he had to give himself a chance on the next hole and the ones after that.

In candor, Watson said, he knew that giving himself a chance would not guarantee that the next birdie putt would fall. But back in the days when he was putting well, that was what he knew he had to do.

11.

Golf Is Not a Game of Perfect

A FEW YEARS ago, Tom Kite and I were in Austin, and we played a round at Lakeway Country Club with a couple of members of the University of Texas golf team. It was a beautiful day and a great match. They all shot between 69 and 73. Afterward, we all sat down for a soda, and it was obvious they were dying to ask a question. So I said, "What's on your mind?"

One of the guys replied, "Tom, we basically hit it as good as you did today. When we missed and hit a bunker, our bunker shots were as good as yours. When we missed a green, we got it up and down like you did. We scored within a shot or two of one another. So how come you're the all-time leading money winner and we're the number three and four golfers at the University of Texas?"

Tom grinned at me and said, "Do you want to tell them?"

"No," I said. "They'll believe it more if it comes from you."

"The difference," Tom said, "is that when you guys get in tournaments, the likelihood is that you'll lose your concentration on four or five shots every round. Over a four-day tournament, even if every lapse costs you just one stroke, that's sixteen to twenty shots a week, and that's the difference between being the leading money winner and losing your card. If one of these lapses costs you two or three strokes, or you get upset and lose concentration on a second shot, you can be talking about twenty-five to thirty strokes a week, and you won't even make the college golf team. Over a career, losing concentration once in a while can mean lots of strokes."

I joined in. "Today, each of you hit a few balls off line, into the rough or the trees. But since it wasn't a tournament round, you didn't let it bother you. You just went over and found the ball, pitched out, wedged up to the green, saved your par and went on. But in the Southwest Conference Tournament, you might hit the same shot and overreact to it. You start telling yourself, 'You're such a jerk,' and 'Why does this always happen in a big tournament?' Before you even hit your next shot, you're convinced you're going to make bogey or double-bogey. And you do."

One of the things Tom, or any successful pro, does best is to accept his bad shots, shrug them off, and concentrate completely on the next one. He has accepted the fact that, as he puts it, "Golf is not a game of perfect."

This does not mean that a pro doesn't strive to eliminate mistakes from his game. He does, unless he wants to savor the joy of Qualifying School once again. But he understands that while striving for perfection is essential, demanding perfection of himself on the golf course is deadly.

Of all the tournaments Tom Kite has won, one of the most impressive to me was at Bay Hill a few years ago. He and Davis

Love both butchered the final hole. Tom hit his approach in the water and Davis flew his over the green. What impressed me was the way Tom responded to the shot that went in the water. He then had to play a long wedge shot over the same water to a tight pin. He could have dwelled on the way he hit the last shot so badly. He could have tried for the middle of the green or even the bunker, just to make sure he didn't make two splashes in a row. Instead, he hit that second wedge stiff, made the putt, and went on to win the playoff.

The television announcers and the golf writers weren't impressed. They don't think a guy who hits his ball into the water on the last hole deserves to win the golf tournament. But I knew how brilliantly Tom had responded to one of the fundamental challenges of the game:

No matter what happens with any shot you hit, accept it. Acceptance is the last step in a sound routine.

When I next talked to Tom, he had almost bought into the attitude of the writers and commentators that there was something wrong with the way he'd won the tournament. I told him that, on the contrary, there was a great deal to admire in it.

Tom had wanted to win, desperately. He had hit a bad shot. But he hadn't reacted by losing his concentration. Instead, he got up and down and went on to win the tournament.

"You know, Tom," I said, "no matter how good you get at this game, a lot of funky, crazy things are going to happen on the golf course. The better you can get at accepting them, the better you're going to get."

Good golfers, I think, have to get over the notion that they only want to win by hitting perfect shots. They have to learn to enjoy winning ugly. And that entails acceptance of all the shots they hit, not just the good ones.

The next week, as it happened, Tom won the TPC with a

display of nearly perfect golf. The writers and commentators all swooned at his feet. But I still like the win at Bay Hill a little better.

I FIND IT amusing and ironic that players like Tom and Nick Price, who are among the best ball strikers in the world, who practice regularly, can learn to accept their bad shots, while the high-handicappers I see in pro-ams and clinics often cannot. If Price or Kite pushes one into the woods, which he occasionally does, he accepts it as something that is going to happen in golf and he calmly plans his next shot. In fact, the best Tour players make a remarkable number of birdies from out of the woods. They know that escape from the woods demands that they become even calmer and more sharply focused than they normally are.

But the high-handicapper, who's got a loop in his swing the size of the Washington Beltway, who practices twice a year if the weather is good, will fume and curse and berate himself if he hits one into the woods. How could he have been so stupid as to slice the ball?

I've had guys in pro-ams turn to me after a tee shot that wiped out two squirrels and a woodpecker and say, "I don't hit the ball that way."

To which I am tempted to reply, "That's funny, I thought I just saw that you did."

No one likes to hit a bad shot. Let's suppose you're on the first tee at your club in the first round of the club championship and you pull-hook your drive into the trees. This can happen to the best of players. At my home course, Farmington Country Club, at the U.S. Senior Amateur in 1993, the eventual winner hit his very first tee shot out of bounds on the first day of qualifying. Did this make him happy? Of course not.

But the question is, does it do any good to get angry?

Getting angry is one of your options. But if you choose to get angry, you are likely to get tighter. That's going to hurt your rhythm and your flow. It will upset you and distract you. It will switch on your analytical mind and your tendency to criticize and analyze anything you do that falls short of perfection. It will start you thinking about the mechanical flaws in your swing and trying to correct them.

You will very likely play worse.

Alternatively, you could train yourself to accept the fact that as a human being, you are prone to mistakes. Golf is a game played by human beings. Therefore, golf is a game of mistakes.

The best golfers strive to minimize mistakes, but they don't expect to eliminate them. And they understand that it's most important to respond well to the mistakes they inevitably make.

Chip Beck has one of the best attitudes toward bad shots. When he hits it into the woods, he walks toward the ball and all he says is, "You gotta love it. This is what golf is all about."

And he's right. Golf is indeed all about recovering from bad shots. It's about getting up and down from sand traps. It's about knowing when it's smart to pitch sideways out of the rough and do your best to save par or bogey with your wedge and putter. It's about the exhilaration that comes from spotting a narrow path through the trees and threading your ball through it to the green. Viewed this way, any round you play will be enjoyable.

But if you bring a smothering perfectionism to the golf course, you will probably leave with a higher handicap and a lousy disposition, because your game will never meet your expectations.

Some good players have developed idiosyncratic ways of diverting the anger that bubbles up within them after a bad shot.

Sherry Steinhauer tells me that she thinks of her memory as a video machine. If she hits a bad shot during the course of a round, she thinks about erasing the tape of that shot. It's a way of putting the mistake out of her mind. Others think of filing the memory of the mistake away somewhere, or changing the channel on the television.

Jack Nicklaus had a few tricks of his own. Nicklaus nearly always selected his own club and generally wanted only silence and a dry towel from his regular caddie, Angelo Argea. But if he hit a bad shot, he might turn to the innocent Angelo and chew him out, saying, "Damn it, why did you let me pick that thing out of the bag?"

Angelo was smart enough not to take it personally. He knew that Nicklaus would play much better if he directed his anger at his caddie rather than at himself.

Arnold Palmer and Bernhard Langer tend to blame their clubs, frequently switching from one set to another and banishing the offending implements to a dark basement. Langer has been known to soak his clubs in a barrel of water overnight as punishment for their betrayal. He did that the week he won his first Masters.

But if you don't happen to have an understanding caddie in your employ, and you don't have an endorsement contract with a manufacturer who is willing to supply an infinite number of clubs, how do you handle anger?

The first thing to do is to throw away your expectations as soon as you step onto the golf course, and just play. It's very difficult to do. But I have never worked with a golfer who could play anywhere close to his potential unless he shed his expectations before the first shot.

Expectations are great if you confine them to long-range considerations. It's fine, for example, to expect that if you work at your game intelligently for an extended period of time, you will improve. But expectations can hurt you if they are narrowly focused on the results of a particular stroke, hole or round.

Golfers in American society, though, tend to be people who are used to getting what they want. Many were born into families of wealth and achievement. Many of those who were not are people who rose to positions of wealth and status because of ambition and hard work. They expect to master golf just as they've mastered everything else in life. If they are competing, they expect to win. If they swing at a golf ball, they expect to hit it well, every time. When their golf fails to meet their expectations, what happens? They begin to judge how well they are doing against how well they expected to do. They get angry at themselves. They tie themselves up in knots.

This is not to say you should not think about hitting every ball to the target and believe that every shot will do just that. You should. But there is a fine difference between believing that the ball will go where you want it to go and expecting that it will and being upset if it doesn't. You have to put expectations out of your mind by the time you get to the first tee.

On the first tee, you should have two immediate goals. One is to have fun. The other involves the process of playing, not the results. This goal is to get your mind where it's supposed to be on every shot. If you do that, you'll shoot the best score you're capable of shooting that day, whether it's 67 or 107.

Having fun shouldn't be so difficult. You are, after all, out in the fresh air. You are playing in what amounts to an emerald park. Clipped grasslands, according to one theorist, have been the most soothing and emotionally satisfying habitat for man since the first humans dropped out of the trees. You are, presumably, in good company, the company of other golfers. You have a chance to strike a little ball and send it flying straight and true against the sky, an act that seems to resonate pleasantly somewhere deep within the human brain. These are the reasons you initially liked golf even though you couldn't play it very well. Savor all of them as you play. Let the joy of the game come to you.

Shooting the best score you're capable of on a given day requires that, to paraphrase something that's become trite, you become your own best friend—or in this case, a good caddie and pro to yourself. Can you imagine someone paying a caddie to berate him after a bad shot in this fashion: "You left that putt short! You're a wimp! No guts!" Can you imagine someone paying a teaching pro to get apoplectic and tell him he's an idiot for slicing the ball? Or to visit his hotel room after a bad round and remind him of all the mistakes he made that day?

No one would do it. Yet, every time I play golf, I see people doing it to themselves.

You have to be nonjudgmental. You have to forgive and forget and be compassionate toward yourself. But in our culture, people, particularly high achievers, are taught to judge themselves harshly. They're taught that being compassionate toward oneself is weak and indulgent. There is a kernel of truth in this. There is a time and place for tough self-evaluation, and you will not improve as a golfer unless you honestly examine your game and work on its weaknesses.

But don't do it on the golf course.

When a shot is done, it's done. The only constructive thing you can do about it is to hit the next shot as well as you can. That requires that you stay optimistic and enthusiastic.

If you must have expectations about results, expect to make some mistakes. Walter Hagen once said that he expected to make seven mistakes per round. When he hit a bad shot, he wasn't bothered. It was just one of the expected seven.

Acceptance allows a golfer to be patient, and patience is one of the necessary virtues in golf. Sometimes, players tell me they are sick and tired of hearing me say that they must be patient and keep believing that if they do all the right things, the results they want will follow. That's just one more thing they have to learn to be patient about.

If you remember to have fun, it shouldn't be too hard. When was the last time you were impatient when you were having fun?

Remember, too, that golf is not a game of justice. A player can practice properly, think properly, and still hit a bad shot. Or he can hit a good shot and watch a bad hop or a gust of wind deposit the ball in a sand trap.

A golfer can't force results to happen. He can only do everything possible to give those results a chance to happen. As Tom Watson once put it, to become a really good golfer, you have to learn how to wait. But you have to learn to wait with confidence.

ON THE TOUR, there are many factors conspiring to raise a player's expectations, to encourage him to demand perfection of himself. When this happens, the work ethic that brought a lot of players to the Tour can become a double-edged sword, driving an individual to grind himself down in a dogged, joyless attempt to meet those expectations. A successful player has to develop the ability to evaluate himself objectively, to work harder when he needs more practice, but to ease up when he's tempted to push too hard.

Scott Verplank won his first PGA tournament, the Western

Open, while he was still an amateur. He expected that his golf could only get better once he finished school and could commit himself totally to golf, practicing as long as he wanted, playing all the time.

It didn't immediately work out that way for him. Performances that would have won or at least finished in the top ten in any amateur tournament didn't make the cut on the Tour. He perceived them as failures. He responded as most good athletes have been taught to do, by working harder. He practiced all the time. He practiced when he shouldn't have, when what he really needed and wanted to do was sit in his hotel room and read a book. And the hard work didn't show up in better results. Eventually, he found himself returning periodically to Oklahoma State and asking the football coach to let him help out with the running backs. It was the only way he could take his mind off golf.

Talking with him before the Buick Open one year, I emphasized the need for him to take it easy on himself. I told him it would be all right to stay in his room and read a book for a few hours instead of going to the practice tee all day. And I asked him to promise me that he would try to have fun.

I returned to Charlottesville to teach. On Thursday evening, I got a call from Scott.

"Gosh, Doc," he said, "I did it! I had fun all day long. And I'm leading! But what was really great was that I missed a five-footer on the first hole and I didn't let it get to me! Made a thirty-five-footer on the second hole."

"I bet you were invited into the press tent afterward," I said.

"Yeah, I was," he replied.

"And I bet that they asked whether Scott Verplank could win his first tournament as a professional."

"Yeah, that's all they talked about."

"Well, if you're not careful, they're going to have you thinking about the results you get instead of having fun. You might go out there fixed on shooting a certain number and keeping the lead and getting in position to win. You have to remember to throw away expectations, to just have fun and see what's the lowest score you can shoot. You have to attend to the process, not concern yourself with the results."

Of course, I would not be telling this story if it didn't have a happy ending. Scott won the tournament, and he called me up on Sunday evening. After telling me what happened, he said he was being interviewed by the golf writer for a newspaper in Dallas, and he was having trouble explaining to him why the idea of having fun had just helped him win a breakthrough golf tournament. Then he put the writer on.

I talked for a while about the necessity to relax, enjoy the game and accept mistakes if a player wants to do his best. The writer still didn't see it. He couldn't understand why having fun could be difficult.

"Try this," I said. "Tomorrow in your paper, ask everyone in Dallas who plays golf to try a two-week experiment. During the first week, after every shot that's less than perfect, they should get disgusted and angry with themselves. And they should stay mad even after they leave the course and go home. I guarantee you every one of your readers will be able to do it.

"The second week, tell them that after every shot, no matter what happens to it, they are not going to be bothered. They are to have fun, stay decisive, and keep ripping the ball to the target. They are going to have a ball no matter what they shoot.

"You can offer a big cash prize to anyone who can do what you ask during the second week, because I guarantee you there won't be many people, if any, who will be honestly able to collect it."

• • •

RETIREES SOMETIMES HAVE a problem analogous to Scott Verplank's. He expected his golf game to improve immediately once he finished school and could play all the time. Retirees often expect to get good after they stop working and don't have to confine their play to weekends.

When it doesn't happen that way, it's often because they forget that golf remains a game. They practice more, but they also raise their expectations every time they step onto the course. They forget how to laugh off mistakes.

Players plagued by perfectionism and unforgiving expectations would do well to remember the common sense their mothers taught them, or would have taught them if they'd paid attention.

Here's what Adela Saraceni told her son, Gene Sarazen, about perfectionism and expectations, just after he lost the 1927 U.S. Open by a single shot:

"Son, everything that happens to you happens for the best. Don't ever forget that. You can't win all the time, son."

Gene Sarazen said this little bit of advice stuck with him and helped him to develop a certain fatalism about his golf that allowed him to accept whatever happened and make the best of it.

If Mrs. Saraceni were around today, I might be out of business.

12.

Anyone Can Develop Confidence

I WILL BE revealing no secrets by stating that good golf requires confidence.

Coaches and athletes in all sports have long recognized that teams don't win and athletes don't perform well without confidence.

All of the ideas and techniques I teach to golfers, from free will to the preshot routine, are intended to produce confidence. Without confidence, you can't trust your physical ability. You can't perform at your best.

But a lot of golfers that I speak to about confidence have misconceptions that hold them back.

They think that confidence is an attribute that they cannot choose to seek and acquire. They think it's something that descends on an athlete, like a revelation from above, after he's performed perfectly for a long time.

Sometimes, a player struggling with this kind of misconception will ask me which comes first, confidence or success. They understand that a player cannot win tournaments without confidence. But they think that you have to win tournaments before you can get confidence.

If that were true, no one would ever win a tournament for the first time.

In fact, anyone can develop confidence if he or she goes about it properly. Confidence isn't something you're born with or something you're given. You control it. Confidence is what you think about yourself and your golf game.

Confidence at the level of any single shot is nothing more than thinking about your ball going to the target. If you're thinking about the ball going to the target, you're confident.

A lot of golfers find this too simple. They have good educations. They've learned how to analyze and question. They want to apply what they know about probability and statistics.

This kind of person might engage me in the following argument:

"Doc, are you confident when you stand over a forty-foot putt that you're going to make it?"

"Yes," I reply.

"Well, then, would you bet me your house that you'll make it?"

"No."

"Then how can you say you're confident?"

The answer is that while I wouldn't bet my house, that doesn't mean I'm not confident.

Being confident doesn't mean that I don't know that 2 percent is a good average on 40-foot putts. It means that when I'm standing over a 40-foot putt, no one is asking me to bet my house, and I'm not thinking about averages. I'm thinking about putting the ball in the hole. And that's all I'm thinking about.

Great athletes think this way. It would never occur to one of them to ask me whether I would bet my house on a 40-foot putt.

People would understand this better, I think, if confidence guaranteed success. It doesn't. Standing on the tee and thinking about your drive going to the target doesn't guarantee that it will go there. It only enhances the chances. If it guaranteed success, people would more readily get the idea. But they try thinking confidently, and as soon as a shot doesn't succeed, they think, "Well, that doesn't work."

But look at it another way. If you're not thinking about your drive going to the target, what are you thinking about? Obviously, you're thinking about it going somewhere else—into a lake, maybe.

And that kind of thinking definitely works, assuming you want to hit the ball in the lake. Negative thinking is almost 100 percent effective.

IN A LARGER sense, your confidence is the sum of all the thoughts you have about yourself as a golfer. You've got to think about what you want your golf game to be. You've got to think about driving it well, wedging it well, being a great bunker player, being a superb putter.

If you are a competitive player, you have to think about winning tournaments, about shooting low scores, about being able to stay cool if you get off to a rocky start and still come in with a good number.

I frequently tell touring players that when they're off the

course, if they can't think about playing great golf, they shouldn't think about golf at all.

By its nature, golf will try to sap your confidence. On every round, even the best golfer will mishit some shots. Over the course of a year, even the best golfer will lose more tournaments than he wins. So, maintaining confidence in golf is like swimming against a current. You have to work hard to stay where you are.

I tell players to try to feel that their confidence is increasing over the course of every round, every tournament and every season. I want them to feel that they are looser and more decisive on the eighteenth tee than they were on the first. I want them to feel more capable of going low on Sunday than they did on Thursday. I want them to feel more likely to win the last tournament of the season than they did in the first. As golfers grow in skills and experience, they must make certain that their confidence grows along with them.

They can do this if they learn to be selective about their thoughts and their memories. They have to learn to monitor their thinking and ask themselves whether an idea that springs to mind is likely to help them or hurt them in the effort to grow more confident.

If it won't help them, they have to make a conscious choice to put that thought out of their mind and turn to one that will enhance their confidence. They have to focus on what they want to happen, be it a particular shot or an entire career. Everyone thinks this way some of the time. Doing it consistently is a habit that requires disciplined effort.

This is what Nick Price has learned to do over the past few years. Nowadays, he tells me, the only thoughts that enter his mind on a golf course are thoughts about what he wants to do —where he wants to place his tee shot, where he wants his approach to land, and how he wants his putts to fall. The prospect of hitting a drive into the woods or running a putt way past the hole simply does not occur to him.

It can sound a little bit like self-deception. But it isn't. It is simply the way that great athletes, or successful people in any field, have trained themselves to think.

13.

What Mark Twain and Fred Couples Have in Common

MARK TWAIN WAS not, as far as I know, much of a golfer. But he had an insight that can help any golfer develop confidence and play better.

The inability to forget, Twain said, is infinitely more devastating than the inability to remember.

Golfers, after they've played for a while, have a vast store of memories that can affect the way they play.

They've hit long, straight drives that rose majestically against an azure sky and dropped to earth in the middle of a clipped, green fairway. They've struck irons that covered the flagstick all the way and settled softly on the green. They've chipped in from the fringe. They've hit 40-foot putts and watched them snake across an undulating green and die in the cup.

They've also topped drives that barely made it off the tee.

They've shanked 7-irons out of bounds. They've left sand shots in a trap. And they've watched, horrified, as putts rolled on past a hole forever.

The question is, as you stand over a ball and prepare to hit it, which shots do you choose to remember?

A lot of players tell me they don't choose—that the memories of bad shots jump, unbidden, into their mind. Others say they have realistic memories, that they recall both the bad and the good.

But a golfer can indeed choose. Free will enables him to develop the kind of memory that promotes good shotmaking: a short-term memory for failure and a long-term memory for success. A golfer can learn to forget the bad shots and remember the good ones.

One way is to permit yourself to enjoy your good shots.

People tend to remember best those events in their lives that are associated with strong emotions, like the birth of a child or the death of a parent.

The problem is that many golfers allow themselves to get very angry at bad shots. That helps plant the memory of the bad shot strongly in their minds.

These same players tend to get very little joy or satisfaction from their good shots. They take them as routine events that cause no particular excitement.

If they thought about it, though, they would realize that a great golf shot is a thing of beauty. They would savor it and celebrate it.

I encourage players to do that. It will help make the game more enjoyable. It will help make the memory of good shots stronger.

Second, golfers often have a problem of perception. If a

player, facing a tee shot, starts to remember shots she's hit out of bounds, is she being realistic? Or is she being unduly harsh on herself?

If she thought about it, she'd probably remember that she's hit far more tee shots in bounds than out of bounds during the course of her golfing career. Remembering one of the good shots, therefore, would be far more realistic than remembering a shot that sliced out of bounds.

But golfers, particularly high-handicappers, often perceive themselves too negatively. They allow the bad shots to dominate their memories.

Good golfers, I've found, frequently have a selective memory that helps them.

The night before the final round of the Masters in 1992, I had dinner with a group of players and teachers that included Fred Couples, who went on to win the tournament.

Fred is not a player I've worked with, but he asked me that night what I thought about his mental game.

"I don't know," I said. "It looks pretty solid to me. What do you try to do?"

"Well, you know, when I come up to a shot, I just pull up my sleeves and shrug my shoulders to try to get them relaxed," Fred said. "And then I try to remember the best shot I ever hit in my life with whatever club I have in my hand. Is that okay?"

"I think that will do just fine, Freddy," I said. "Just fine."

14.

Fighting Through Fear

SEVERAL YEARS AGO, Brad Faxon began talking to me about a difficult challenge. Brad had begun to fear his driver.

Brad is one of the most successful young players on the PGA Tour. He's not overwhelmingly long, but he can hit a drive 280 yards. He's very accurate with his irons. He's a fearless wedge player who will make a long, loose swing to flop the ball onto the green in a tight situation and give it a chance to go into the hole. He's one of the best putters I've seen. And he has an ideal temperament for golf. He's intelligent and easygoing. He loves the game and he likes the people associated with it.

After he graduated from Furman in 1983, Brad quickly established himself as a professional, and by 1985 he was an exempt player on the Tour. Despite this success, he started to have vivid, disquieting thoughts about drivers, or, more precisely, what might happen to the ball after he hit it with a driver. These thoughts occurred not only on the tee. They might come to him at night in his sleep. They might come to him as he sat at the dinner table with his wife. Usually, he could see the golf ball flying 50 yards off course to the right, into trouble or out of bounds, even though his natural shot is a draw.

These thoughts became so persistent that he could no longer stand on a tee with a driver in his hands and even come close to believing that the ball would go to his target. In that mental state, his game off the tee inevitably suffered. In stressful situations, on narrow driving holes, he tightened up and lost his rhythm. If he mishit a driver, it was as if someone had punched him in the solar plexus. All the air, all the energy left his body.

It's important to differentiate between fear and nervousness. Nervousness is a physical state. It's sweat on the palms, adrenaline in the bloodstream. There's nothing wrong with it—it can even help a golfer.

Fear is a mental state. It's being afraid of making a mistake when you swing the club. Fear causes golfers to try to guide or steer the ball, rather than swing freely. That doesn't work. Swinging freely makes the ball go straight. Swinging carefully causes disasters. To play his best, a golfer has to feel that once he's aligned himself and picked his target, it's as if he doesn't care where the ball goes. He is going to trust his swing and let it go.

If fear could plague a golfer as talented and successful as Brad Faxon, it could certainly debilitate the average golfer. And it does.

I've talked to players who can't look at a downhill putt without thinking that they could roll it 10 feet past. They make ugly jabs at the ball. I've talked to players who can't look at a pitch shot over a bunker without thinking about dumping it into the sand.

They chunk a lot of wedges. And there are many, like Brad Faxon, who get fearful when they put a driver in their hands.

On the professional circuit, there have been prominent players whose careers were totally derailed by fear. One year they were contending in major championships. The next year they were staying at home, unwilling even to risk exposing their fear in a tournament.

Sometimes I wish there were a quick, simple answer for them, a psychological parlor trick that would banish their fears and allow them to hit their best shots. There isn't, at least not in most cases. Fighting through fear can take a lot of patient effort. But a golfer who learns to do it has given himself an invaluable lesson.

In Brad's case, we began by trying to decide whether his problem was mental or mechanical. He decided that it was some of both.

There were a few subtle mechanical changes he decided to make in his swing with the driver, changes having largely to do with his posture and his release. He went to work with a teaching pro to make the necessary adjustments.

With a lot of players, this would have been as far as they went. They would have proceeded to try to beat the problem to death on the practice range, hitting bucket after bucket of balls in an effort to fix their mechanics.

But the fact was that even before he made those mechanical changes, Brad could always hit the driver fairly well on the practice range. That suggested that his problem lay mainly in his mind.

We didn't waste time trying to figure out why he was getting these fearful flashes. Anyone who has played golf for a while has inevitably hit some monstrous slices or hooks off the tee.

Images of those shots remain buried in the memory, capable of springing into a golfer's consciousness at the worst possible moments. The fact was, they were springing into Brad's mind. Why they were was hardly relevant.

We reviewed some fundamental ideas. First and foremost, we talked about how free will controls thought. Any golfer can decide what he wants to think about as he contemplates a shot.

So we worked hard on getting Brad to think of what he wanted to happen with the driver rather than what he didn't want to happen. We talked about picking a target and visualizing the ball going to that target. We talked about making this the centerpiece of a mental routine that Brad would repeat on every shot, particularly tee shots.

But it wasn't that easy. Brad still could not make himself feel certain that the ball would go to the target when he hit it with a driver. He needed something to fall back on while he worked on vanquishing his fear.

So for a long time, Brad hit lots of 3-woods off the tee. I told him that whenever he felt doubt or fear about hitting a driver, he should leave it in the bag and hit a 3-wood or a 1-iron instead.

Fortunately, Brad hits an excellent 3-wood. Moreover, the rest of his game—his irons, his chipping and wedging, and his putting—helped him compensate for the loss of distance off the tee. For several years, he was able to stay high on the money list while rarely using a driver.

This didn't really surprise me. Most amateurs, watching the professionals play golf on television, notice their length off the tee first of all. It's glamorous. It's masculine. The weekend players get the idea that this length with the driver is the key to shooting low scores. But the driver is the toughest club to hit consistently. It mercilessly exposes swing flaws and thinking flaws. A lot of weekend players ruin their games with it. They think they have to hit it, and hit it a long way. When they don't, or don't hit it straight, they get tense and mechanical. Their tee shots get worse, and the rest of their game frequently comes apart as well.

In truth, while length off the tee is desirable, it's not nearly as important as keeping the ball in play and chipping and putting well, as Brad demonstrated. Weekend players who have trouble driving would do well to emulate him, hitting a 3-wood or a long iron off the tee and developing a short game they can score with. This would enable them to feel, from the beginning of every hole, that they were following their mental routines and feeling certain about every shot before they swung the club.

Of course, Brad did not want to spot the competition 40 yards off the tee indefinitely. He continued to work hard on thinking about hitting the ball where he wanted it to go. Using a 3-wood helped him maintain this habit. Gradually, he began to be able to do it more often with the driver.

He worked at this all day, not just at the golf course. I told him that he should either think about driving the ball well or not think about it at all, and he made it a habit to think about hitting long, beautiful drives. We made some audio tapes that he could play in the car in which I reminded him of great drives he had hit in critical situations. He tried to develop a long-term memory for his good drives and a short-term memory for the bad ones.

It helped as well that Brad retained a sense of humor about the whole thing. His caddie, Cubby Burke, is an imaginative and irreverent kidder who could have matched insults with the regulars at the Algonquin Round Table, provided, that is, that the Round Table permitted certain epithets common to the golf course. Brad had the good sense not to restrain Cubby, but to let himself be teased. Laughing at the problem helped put it in perspective.

By the time Brad first qualified for the Masters he had, over the course of several years, made a lot of progress. But his Masters debut made him all the more anxious to be done with his driver anxiety once and for all. Augusta National, with its absence of rough, its reachable par fives, and its long par fours, favors the long hitter. Brad was eager to do well his first time out.

The night before the tournament began, we had dinner in the house he had rented for himself and his family. After dinner, we took a walk down the dark, narrow, tree-lined street. I told him to imagine teeing a ball in the street, hitting it with a driver, blasting it straight between the trees and then drawing it into the house at the end of the block.

"Hopefully," I added, "no one will be watching through the windows."

Brad laughed and took a swing in the shadows. Yes, he said, he could see that shot.

He did it a few more times. He laughed some more. Each imaginary shot was perfect. I told him that the only difference on the golf course the next day would be the presence of a ball and a club. His body and mind could work just as well then as they did on that darkened street, unless he let the ball intimidate him.

With that thought in mind, he played well in his first Masters. He felt that he had turned a corner, and in 1992, he won two tournaments.

He learned what all successful athletes sooner or later learn. Courage is fear turned inside out. It is impossible to be courageous if at first you weren't afraid.

Finally, Brad did something that I can take no credit for. He moved from Florida back to his native Rhode Island. He started practicing and playing, between tournaments, at the courses he grew up on, Rhode Island Country Club and Metacomet. He played with friends from high-school days. This change of scenery helped him recapture the attitude toward driving the ball he had had when he was fourteen or fifteen years old, when he couldn't wait to walk onto the tee and bust one. As a kid, he had driven the ball fearlessly. Back home, he completed the process of learning to think that way again.

Nowadays, Brad's biggest problem is the opposite of the old one. He loves hitting the driver again, and he steps onto every tee looking for a reason to pull it out of the bag. Sometimes he uses it when the situation calls for a 3-wood or an iron.

That, however, doesn't strike him as such a bad problem to have.

15.

What I Learned from Seve Ballesteros

A COUPLE OF summers ago, Seve Ballesteros walked up to me at the Westchester Classic and introduced himself. Seve had not been playing well for a year or so.

"Nickie Price says I need to talk to you," Seve began abruptly. "He said you'll teach me how to win again. He said what you teach is the future of golf."

I was flattered, but not so much that I was not startled by Seve Ballesteros admitting that he had lost the knowledge of how to win.

"Once," Seve went on, glumly, *"I was the future of golf. All I ever did for years is what I think you teach. I just saw myself in my mind winning golf tournaments. I saw myself making the shots. I saw myself winning. The year I won the Masters by seven or eight shots, I knew I would win it before the plane landed in America. The only problem was that I walked up the eighteenth fairway without any joy, because I had known I would win before the tournament started."

I winked at him. "Well, I could certainly teach you how to get happy and party."

But Seve was not in a mood to banter. He wanted to explain himself.

It turned out that, in Seve, personality and environment had combined to produce a golfing artist. He grew up poor in Spain, and like Hagen, Nelson, Sarazen and Hogan, he got into the game as a caddie. He started playing with a few mismatched clubs, and he competed ferociously from the outset.

From the beginning, Seve had focused his energy not on his swing, which he picked up instinctively. He was always concerned with the ball, with making the ball move in such a way that it went into the hole. He was the kind of kid who might walk into a sand trap with a cast-off 7-iron and experiment until he found ways to get the ball up to the hole with it.

He had a natural instinct for thinking right. When he went to sleep at night, he saw himself making great shots and winning tournaments.

When he practiced, he told me, he would almost immediately have all of his clubs strewn on the ground beside him. He was not the type to hit one club over and over, seeking to groove a swing. He played imaginary holes on the range, inventing different shots to fit the circumstances his mind conjured up. He might imagine a par five, and hit a driver and a 2-iron. If the 2-iron drifted a little left, he'd pull out his wedge and practice a flop shot.

In his first years as a professional, Seve said, he'd had a feeling of immense control. He felt sometimes as if he controlled not only himself and his ball, but the galleries and his opponents as well.

"You know," he said, "when I first came to America, if I hit the ball in the rough, I didn't care."

He crouched down like a golfer peering under the low branches of a tree at a distant green.

"I just looked for a way, an opening. I didn't care that there was a tree there. I just found the opening, hit the ball over the tree, or around it, or under it, and got the ball in the hole. When I saw an American player hit the ball in the rough and then chip out into the fairway, I laughed. I thought, 'How can they beat me if they do that?'

"Then, around the green, I saw that a lot of them hit a putter from the fringe. They said that if they missed with the putter, they left the ball closer than if they missed with a wedge. I thought that was silly. I used a wedge. I never thought I would miss."

Now, he went on sadly, he had started to resemble those golfers he used to scorn. He pitched sideways out of the rough. He used a putter from the fringe. His whole attitude toward the game had changed and all the joy was gone.

"It used to be that I would come to the eighteenth hole and be sad because there was no more golf left to play," he said. "Now I come to the ninth hole and I'm sad because I still have nine to go. I hate golf like this. I don't want to keep playing if it feels like this."

As we talked, it became apparent that Seve's game had gone sour when he tried to change from the intuitive, imaginative and ball-oriented attitude of his youth to a mechanical, swing-oriented approach. A sincere desire to improve had prompted him to do it, but he had found that it was not easy—and perhaps impossible—to go from being an artist to being a scientist.

"I wanted very much to win the U.S. Open," he said. "People

would tell me that I would have to get a much better, more consistent swing if I wanted to win on a U.S. Open course."

People are always giving unsolicited lessons and tips to leading professionals like Seve. They want to take some of the credit for his successes. In his desire to win an Open, Seve bought the idea that he needed to restructure his swing, to make it more mechanically flawless. He forgot that course management, a stellar short game, good putting and patience win Opens. Of these, the only quality he might have lacked was patience.

So he set out to perfect his swing. He took lessons from some of the game's most renowned teachers of golf mechanics. His swing doctors persuaded him that if he practiced hard enough, he could incorporate half a dozen or more separate changes into his swing and find the Nirvana where all balls are perfectly struck. And periodically, on the range, all of these changes would fall into place and Seve would start hitting beautiful shots.

The trouble was that all of this work on the swing changed his attitude toward the game. Now, if he hit a drive into the rough, his mind did not click into thoughts of how to get the ball through the trees and into the hole. It clicked instead into thoughts of swing mechanics. He felt that he understood his swing now, and he should be able to fix it on the course and make the next shot great.

It didn't work.

"If I hit one bad shot, I started trying to do all things my teacher had been telling me about. Things just got worse and worse," he said. Eventually, he added, the tendency to think mechanically had infected his short game.

He stopped winning tournaments and, after a while, he stopped enjoying the game.

In a corner of his mind, Seve knew what had gone wrong. He

understood that he couldn't think of all those swing changes and still hit the ball.

But then he discovered that it was not easy to go back to the old, instinctive way of thinking on the course.

I told Seve that he had to find his way back to the old Seve. He had to learn again to trust his athletic ability. He had to recapture the attitude of the young Spanish caddie, navigating the golf course with a handful of cast-off clubs, inventing shots to get the ball into the hole.

I talked to him a little about how the body and brain work best together when an athlete simply looks at a target and reacts to it, rather than thinking about the mechanics of his movement.

That struck a chord with Seve.

"You know, when I was a little boy, a caddie, we pitched pennies in the caddie yard. We'd put a club down on the ground and pitch pennies to the club. No one could touch me at it. I was the best. Sometimes, now, I lie in bed in the hotel and throw things at that—what do you call it in the corner?—the trash can. And I never miss. I don't know how I do it. I just do it, like you say."

I was only telling Seve something he had realized himself at some level. He knew he had to recapture the confident focus on the hole that had characterized his best golf. He knew he had to go back to being an artist rather than trying to be a scientist.

"I know what you tell me is right," Seve said. "I know I have to go back to being Seve. But be patient. It's going to take a while. I think I will. But now I have these thoughts in my head, and I can't get rid of them."

He told me that when he stepped on a golf course, where once he had felt completely in control, he now felt lost and in jeopardy. "It feels," he said, "like I'm stepping on clouds and I'm going to fall through."

My conversations with Seve reminded me of how a player can get lost trying to improve. It's not enough to decide to get better and to be willing to work hard at it. A player has to judge carefully whether the improvement nostrums he's being offered are right for him.

Some players with a more natural mechanical bent—the scientists—might have been able to incorporate the changes that Seve tried to make in his swing without losing the ability to trust their mechanics on the golf course and remember that the objective is to get the ball in the hole.

But others, who play by feel—the artists—can hurt themselves trying to do it. Our conversation showed that even a golfer who has won eighty tournaments around the world has to take care to maintain and enhance his mental game, his confidence and his trust no matter what he is doing with his swing. Even such a golfer as Seve needs to find a teacher who recognizes that too much mechanical advice can be harmful.

This is all the more important for amateurs who play once or twice a week. They need to keep their swings simple and their confidence high. They must learn to resist the kind of temptation that can lead to loss of confidence, temptation often garbed as well-meaning advice.

Most golfers assume that once they learn how to think confidently, they can fiddle with their mental approach to the game. They believe they can always go back to the attitude they once had.

But, as Seve learned, it's not always that easy.

I think Seve is on his way back. He's recognized his problem and he's dealing honestly with it. Periodically, I scan the European golf results to see whether he's broken through and started winning again. Recently, I noticed that he had.

As long as he has his dreams and his passion, I expect that he will keep coming back.

16.

Conservative Strategy, Cocky Swing

PERHAPS NO SINGLE shot has misled more golfers than the drive Arnold Palmer hit to the first green in the final round of the U.S. Open at Cherry Hills in 1960.

The first at Cherry Hills then was a 346-yard par four with trees down the left side, a ditch on the right, and thick, U.S. Open rough in front of the green. The course, outside Denver, is a mile high, and balls fly farther at altitude. Palmer decided he could drive the green. In the fourth round, he proved it.

Virtually every American golfer heard the story of that tee shot and how it launched Palmer on the way to a closing 65 that overcame a seven-stroke deficit and won him his only Open title. Palmer's final round burned into the minds of a golfing generation the idea that real men, and real winners, play aggressive, even reckless golf.

But not many people remember what Palmer's effort to drive

the green produced in the first three rounds of that Open: one par, a bogey, and a double-bogey, thanks to drivers hit slightly awry. In other words, Palmer was three over par for No. 1 when he started the fourth round. The final birdie he got by driving the green meant that he had played the hole in two over for the tournament.

Suppose he had decided to play the hole differently that week, hitting a 2-iron off the tee and setting up a wedge into the green. He would, most likely, have done no worse than par each round. Quite possibly he would have sunk a birdie putt or two.

He wouldn't have needed to close with a 65 to win.

That 1960 Open was one of the first to demonstrate an unfortunate truth: listening to television golf commentators can be hazardous to your game.

Television producers want the broadcast to be exciting. They want the drama of bold, reckless shots and swashbuckling players. So when they see a player gamble the way Palmer did, they glorify him. People listen to the broadcasts, and they get the idea that bold, reckless shots pay off.

They don't. At least not often enough to make them worthwhile.

The key to successful strategy and a confident swing for golfers at every level is, instead, quite the opposite.

Hit the shot you know you can hit, not the shot Arnold Palmer would hit, nor even the shot you think you ought to be able to hit.

I teach a conservative strategy and a cocky swing. You want to play each hole in such a way that you're confident you can execute each shot you attempt. That gives you a cocky swing, which is another way of saying that you swing aggressively, that you swing with trust. It produces your best results.

The opposite approach would be a bold strategy and a tentative swing. A bold strategy would have you attempting shots you are not confident you can hit. That leads very quickly to tentative swings, and tentative swings produce bad shots. Bad execution of bold shots produces very high scores.

What does this mean in practice?

A great story from the literature of golf illustrates the point.

The late Tommy Armour won all the major championships available to a professional golfer in his day—the U.S. Open in 1927, the British Open in 1931, and the PGA in 1930. But at that time, golf tournaments paid the winner a thousand dollars or so. A professional golfer who aspired to a decent standard of living had to know how to make money in other ways—in short, to hustle. And Tommy Armour liked to live well.

After his competitive career ended, Armour spent his winters at a posh club in Boca Raton, Florida, giving lessons in golf and gamesmanship to the swells. He took their money in the mornings, giving swing lessons. And he took it in the afternoons, playing exorbitant Nassaus.

"What do you take me for? Jack Benny?" Armour would fulminate when someone on the first tee suggested slightly lower stakes.

One winter day in the locker room, Armour overheard a pupil of his offering to bet some friends that he could break 90, a feat that the pupil had theretofore never threatened to accomplish. Armour's keen instinct for a sure thing was aroused.

Armour offered to back his pupil in the wager, on one condition: that Armour be allowed to walk the course with him during the round and offer advice.

With the stakes set, and set high, the match commenced. The first hole was a long par four. Armour's pupil wound up and sliced a long drive into the rough to the right of the first fairway. They walked to the ball and eyed the green, about 170 yards away, elevated, guarded by a couple of deep traps. The pupil pulled out his 5-iron.

"Put the five-iron back," Armour said. "You're going to play an eight-iron to the fairway thirty yards short of the green and a little left. Then you're going to chip up through the opening to the green. The worst you'll make is five. If you go for the green and mishit that five-iron just a little bit, you're looking at six or seven."

The pupil was smart enough to do as he was told. He played the 8-iron to the spot Armour indicated. He chipped up. He sank the putt for his par. He went on to shoot 79. And Tommy Armour won enough money to live a good while longer in the style to which he was accustomed.

What Armour had done, of course, was to give his student a temporary brain transplant. With Armour making the strategy choices, the student played only shots that were well within his physical capabilities. He aimed at specific targets that Armour selected for him. He felt calm, confident and decisive. He stopped worrying about his swing mechanics, assuming that Armour would correct any flaws that needed correcting. And by doing those things, by acquiring a conservative strategy and a cocky swing, he shot a score he had previously only dreamed of.

This principle applies to golf at the highest levels as well. Tom Watson, in his final round at the 1992 U.S. Open, demonstrated it.

Playing the par-five 18th hole, Watson hit a 3-wood onto the fairway and then a 7-iron, leaving him a full 9-iron to the green. The broadcast crew, expecting his second shot to stop much closer to the green, thought momentarily that he had flubbed it. Of course, he hadn't. Normally, he said later, he laid up closer, with a 5-iron. But earlier in the round, he had partially mishit two short fairway sand-wedge shots. He wanted a full 9-iron into the green because he didn't think he would feel confident with a wedge, particularly a partial wedge.

A lot of golfers, facing that situation, would have tried to bash a driver and a long iron and lay up close to the green. They would have told themselves that they simply have to be able to hit a fairway wedge if they want to consider themselves real golfers. Not Watson. He was perfectly content to leave the wedges in his bag until he had a chance to do some postround practice and restore his confidence with them. So he altered his strategy slightly to give him the shot he wanted. But he altered it in the conservative direction.

He had, in other words, a conservative strategy and a cocky swing.

17.

Game Plan

No FOOTBALL OR basketball coach whom I've ever heard of would send his team into competition without a game plan. Coaches in those sports recognize that an intelligent game plan can take advantage of a team's strengths and camouflage its weaknesses. More important, a good game plan makes the mental side of the game easier. Players don't have to make as many impromptu, possibly emotional decisions. They can instead execute decisions made in advance, calmly, outside the heat of competition.

The same considerations apply to golf:

You must play every significant round with a game plan.

Amateur golfers, particularly high-handicappers, frequently don't understand this. They play spontaneously, making up strategy on the fly. As a result, they make more bad decisions.

A good professional never plays a tournament round without

first examining the course and preparing a plan to play it. The plan encompasses target and club selection for each tee shot, the preferred landing area on every green, and hazards to be avoided. It envisions responses to rain, wind and other weather variables.

The professional plans all this ahead of time because he wants to do as little analyzing and improvising as possible once he's on the course. He wants to leave his mind clear and free to focus on each target.

Once in a while a player has to play a round on a course totally new to him, without time to inspect it beforehand. In such cases, a golfer has to improvise. He should look at hole diagrams on the scorecard, ask a caddie, or ask a member with local knowledge. Even a plan made up at each tee is better than no plan at all. But whenever possible, plan in advance.

The best way to prepare a plan is to walk or mentally review each hole backward. Standing on the green and looking back toward the tee usually reveals much more about a hole than standing on the tee and looking at the green. It shows more of the tricks and deceptions that the architect may have built into the hole. And it forces you to think strategically about where you want your ball to land on the green, what club would be best for landing it there, and what kind of tee shot will set this up.

Consider perhaps the most familiar stretch of holes in tournament golf, Nos. 10-13 at Augusta National, the holes encompassing Amen Corner. What do you learn from examining each hole backward? This is what I see when I walk them with a player preparing for the Masters:

No. 10 is a long, downhill par four, a slight dogleg left, 485 yards from the tournament tees. Standing on the 10th green and facing the tee, you immediately notice that the green itself slopes to the left into a downslope that is very hard to chip back from. Next, you notice how tough the shot can be from the bunker that protects the front right corner of the green; you might have as much as 50 yards of carry from the far end of the bunker to the far end of the green.

For a professional, the biggest discovery gleaned from standing on the green is how much the hole favors a tee shot played down the left side. This isn't so apparent from the tee. But from the green you see that the downslope in the fairway is much more significant on the left side. A drive drawn around the corner and down the left side can make the hole play almost a hundred yards shorter than a tee shot blocked down the right side.

Hitting the left side of the fairway leaves a professional with a 6- or 7-iron, while the approach from the right can be a long iron or a fairway wood from a sidehill lie that makes you feel as if you're standing on your ear. So, for a professional or a first-class amateur with good length, the game plan is very likely going to be to draw a drive down the left side.

Every game plan, of course, must be tailored to the individual's strengths and preferences. It must be based on an honest appraisal of a player's skills, and it can change from one year to the next, or one round to the next, depending on changes in those skills. I would never prescribe to a player the strategy he or she ought to use on a given hole. If one of my players told me he just felt better hitting the ball down the right side at No. 10, that would be fine with me. My concern is that the player has a plan, that he believes in the plan, and that he follows the plan.

For a typical member at Augusta National, or an amateur lucky enough to be invited to play there, the calculations on No. 10 would be somewhat different. He would still take note of the leftward slope of the green, especially if he likes to putt from below the hole. He would definitely pay attention to the potential problem caused by the right bunker. He would want to avoid at all costs a long, faded approach shot that fell short, slid into that bunker and left him with perhaps the most difficult of all shots for amateurs, the long bunker shot to a green that slopes away.

He would also take note of the trees on either side of the fairway, trees that rarely come into play at the Masters, but which could certainly threaten to catch a drive a weekend player might hit, particularly if he swung hard, trying for distance. Finally, he would note the large bunker in the middle of the fairway, about a hundred yards short of the green. It rarely affects a Masters golfer, but if the amateur laid up, he would be safest to lay up short of that bunker.

From these observations, the intelligent amateur might well conclude that he must play this hole as a short par five rather than a long par four. He would want to hit his first ball somewhere into the fairway and his second shot short of the big fairway trap, a total distance of perhaps 360 yards. That would leave him an easy wedge or 9-iron to the green, with a chance to sink a putt for a par and a realistic plan to make no worse than five on the hole. That's not bad, considering that the Masters field averages about 4.2 strokes here.

By working backward, the amateur can then make an informed decision about the club to use off the tee. If he merely stood on the tee, without a plan, he would probably decide to bust his driver as far as he could, given the length of the hole. But by working the hole backward and planning a strategy, he might come to a different conclusion. If he can hit a fairway wood or even a 3-iron somewhere into the fairway, he has only a comfortable mid-iron left to his lay-up position. The obvious call, if he wants a conservative strategy and a cocky swing, is to leave the driver in the bag and play something he knows will get the ball into the fairway, 200 yards or so out. Then he can count on a 6- or 7-iron to the lay-up spot.

If he risks the driver and hits it well, say, 240 yards down the middle, what has he gained? He's still looking at a 245-yard shot to the green, (assuming, for the sake of illustration, that he's playing this hole from the tournament tees). This shot is beyond the capability of most amateurs. If he misses the second shot right, he's looking at that difficult long bunker shot. If he decides to lay up, all he's accomplished with his driver is to reduce his lay-up club from a 6-iron to a 9-iron. The reward does not justify the risk.

The same goes for most amateurs playing long par fours on any course. A lot of them have no chance of reaching par-four holes that are over 430 yards. They could easily reach the greens on all these holes with a couple of smooth 5-irons and a wedge. Yet they consistently pull the driver out of the bag and get themselves into trouble, turning a hole that could be a routine bogey and occasional par into a 6, a 7, or an 8.

Too many players at all levels try to rip a driver on nearly every tee. A professional might tell you that he truly has confidence in his driver. And sometimes that's justified. A Tom Kite or a Nick Price can play a precision shot with a driver. But a weekend player, if he or she is honest, will generally admit that the driver comes out of the bag because the driver is fun. It appeals to the ego to hit, occasionally, a drive that impresses the rest of the foursome. So even if he recognizes that he might score better if he never carried a driver, he keeps using it.

If that's what you want to do, fine. Just don't get angry when you get punished for it, because you're going to get punished severely on most courses. Instead of a third wedge, you might want to carry a chain saw.

If your objective is to shoot the best score you can, you might do well to remember why Jack Nicklaus, Ben Hogan and Nick Faldo hit lots of 1-irons and 3-woods off the tee. Even if the longest club you can hit confidently onto the fairway is a 5-iron, you'd be better off using it if your purpose is to score.

This is doubly true on short par fours. A good architect will tempt a player on one of these short holes to hit the ball a long way, thinking to drive the green or set up a very short second shot. But the architect, if he's good, will build lots of trouble into the hole where even slightly errant drives would land. The smart choice is usually to hit an iron or fairway wood off the tee, leaving a full wedge for the second shot.

No. 11 AT Augusta is another long par four, 455 yards. Standing on its green, the first thing you notice is the little pond in front of the left side of the green. This will influence the way you play the hole. No matter where the flag is, and on Sunday at the Masters it is always near the pond, you want your second shot to stay safely away from the water.

This might seem, at first blush, to be negative thinking. Why not ignore the pond and fire at the flag, even if it's on the left side? Isn't that positive thinking?

Positive thinking, in my opinion, does not mean taking a rip at every risky shot the course presents. It is, rather, the development and execution of an intelligent strategy that weighs risks and rewards and gives a player a chance to shoot his best possible score.

I tell my professional players that going for the flag depends on the distance. With a wedge in their hands, they should always go for it. Indeed, they should go for the hole. No one makes it to the Tour without being at least that good with the wedge. Between 120 and 170 yards is a gray area for most professionals. They must consider the wind, the speed of the greens, how they feel, and the potential penalty for a slightly missed shot before they decide whether to aim for the pin. If, for instance, the penalty for missing is likely to be no worse than a routine bunker shot, especially from the uniform, groomed bunkers at Augusta, a professional might go for the pin. If the penalty is a wet ball and a stroke penalty, he'll probably aim for the middle of the green. From 170 yards out or farther, I advise professionals to always shoot for the fattest or safest part of the green, regardless of where the flag is. Once in a while, I see someone knock it close to a tight pin from 200 or 250 yards. Invariably, the television announcer will praise his boldness for going for the flag from that distance. In fact, what usually happened is that the player aimed for the middle of the green and mishit it.

On No. 11, the safe side is obviously the right side. In fact, closer observation of the green area shows that there is a spacious area of manicured fairway grass to the right of the green. This is the area from which Larry Mize chipped in to beat Greg Norman in their 1987 playoff. You could even putt from there if you trusted your putter.

The professionals who get in trouble with the pond on No. 11 are usually players who don't feel confident about their putting and chipping. They are afraid they will need three to get down unless they get their second shots close to the pin. You can be a genius at course management if you're really cocky with your wedge and putter.

For weekend players looking backward at No. 11, the calculations would again be somewhat different. The hole would be too long for some of them to reach in two, and they would do best to devise a plan for the first two shots that would leave them their most comfortable pitching distance. Their target as they approach the green would depend on their personal threshold distance. Inside the threshold distance, they would go for the flag. Beyond it, they would shoot for the right side of the green, taking the pond out of play. Looking at a long iron into the green, an amateur might well aim for the right edge, planning to rely on his short game to get up and down if he hits the fairway area to the right of the green. This strategy takes the pond out of play.

No. 12, although only 155 yards long, is another hole that rewards a backward examination. From the green, the perils of Rae's Creek are more apparent than they are from the tee. The green, which simply looks wide from the tee, shows itself to be terribly shallow once you're standing on it. And it is easier to see that the creek, which looks from the tee to flow perpendicular to the line of the shot, in fact bends away from the tee on the right side of the green. This means that there is almost no margin for error on the right. A few yards too long, and the ball is bunkered, raising the possibility that the ensuing sand shot will roll back over the green and into the water. A few yards too short, and the ball is lost, unless you are Fred Couples in 1992 and the gods are smiling down on you. (And you have the ability and presence of mind to get it up and down from the bank as he did.)

Therefore, most professionals always aim for the left center of the green at No. 12, where the margin for error is greater. Of course, the pin is always cut on the right side on Sunday, but most feel that going for it is not worth the risk.

A good game plan has to be flexible for holes like this. You can't plan on the club to use until you have a chance to assess the wind. (Of course, No. 12 is a great hole because it's so hard to figure out what the wind is doing.) When Tom Kite plans his Masters round, he will typically decide to use a 6-iron or a 7-iron at No. 12, depending on the wind. The important thing to plan on here is making a decisive club selection when the time comes. Once you make up your mind, you have to believe in your decision.

Good golf courses like Augusta National are full of sucker pin placements analogous to the right-side position on No. 12. A good player learns to resist them. A few years ago, when the PGA Championship was being played at Shoal Creek, I was walking during a practice round with Tom Kite and Gary Player. They got to the 16th, a fairly long par three with a big green shaped liked a distended kidney. The closer section of the kidney was reasonably wide and accommodating, but the far section was very tight, guarded by sand and heavy rough. It was obvious that when the tournament started, particularly during the closing rounds, the pin would be cut in the far section and that a lot of bogeys would be made there by players trying to reach that flag with a long iron.

"I don't care where they put the pin," Player told his partners. "I'm aiming right there." And he pointed to the fat part of the green. As it turned out, he played that hole in two under par for the tournament, better than virtually everyone else in the field. He made one birdie by holing a 90-foot putt that rolled partly through the fringe. Player had, as he usually does, a smart game plan. He played conservatively and carried a cocky putter.

The weekend player's plan for No. 12 at Augusta will be the same as the professional's, except perhaps for club selection.

The hole really doesn't offer much choice. But there are longer par threes on other courses that do.

The most famous example is No. 16 at Cypress Point, which plays 220 or 230 yards from tee to green, almost all of it over the Pacific Ocean. Examining the hole backward shows an alternative route. Aim at the hulk of a dead cypress tree well to the left of the green, and the carry over the water is only 140 yards to a broad fairway. A reasonable 7-iron (assuming the wind is not blowing in your face) will leave a simple pitch of 60 or 70 yards to the green.

Which route would you take? It depends, of course, on your game. If you had a dependable club that could carry 220 yards, even into the wind, you would go for the green. But as Allister Mackenzie knew well when he designed Cypress Point, most amateurs don't consistently carry the ball that far. A lot of them might think they do, but they're probably confusing carry with total driving distance, which includes roll. And the penalty for hitting a little short at No. 16 is severe. The ball bounces off the cliff on the far side of the inlet and becomes a toy for the seals. You're still on the tee, preparing to hit your third shot.

I'm certainly not going to tell players fortunate enough to get a chance to play Cypress Point that they should not pull out their drivers or 3-woods and have a go at No. 16. But if they played the course frequently, or in competition, the intelligent plan for a lot of them would be to aim for the dead cypress tree and the fairway to the left of the green and take the safe route, playing for a possible par and a fairly certain bogey. This is not negative thinking. It's honest thinking. If you honestly assess your game and determine that you will hit the 7-iron successfully nine out of ten times and hit the driver to the green one time in ten, the risk-reward calculation is obvious. It would only be negative thinking if you then let yourself lose confidence in your ability to hit the 7-iron.

Your course might have an analogous, if less spectacular, long par three. There might be out-of-bounds markers running down one side of the hole. There might be a pond or creek in front of the green. In such cases, the smart game plan for a weekend player could be to lay up with a medium iron, pitch onto the green, and take double-bogey or triple-bogey out of the equation. On the other hand, if the hole is wide open, the smart plan might be to bang away with the driver. The point is to think about these things ahead of time, when you can make your decision coldly and rationally.

No. 13 at Augusta, at 485 yards, is probably the toughest short par five the touring pros will see all year. I've never told a player whether his game plan should have him go for a par-five green in two or not. It's a decision that the individual has to make, based on the hole and the strengths and weaknesses of his own game. Some players hit long irons exceptionally well. Others don't. The length of the tee shot obviously plays a critical role. Most professionals' game plans for par fives establish a threshold distance. If their second shot would be shorter than, say, 230 yards, they go for it. If it is longer, they lay up.

In general, on par-five decisions, I tell players to ask themselves whether the risks they are taking in trying to reach the green in two are worth the reward. If the second shot misses the green, can it go out of bounds or into a water hazard? Or is a greenside bunker the worst penalty the course is likely to exact for a miss? I hate bumping into a player after a round and hearing him say, "God, if I had just not double-bogeyed that par five, I'd be leading." Players who carefully balance risk against reward rarely have to say that. For a professional, a birdie is or should be almost as likely from a comfortable lay-up position as it is from a spot on the edge of the green, 40 feet from the hole.

That's the calculation Chip Beck made in the 1993 Masters on another par five, No. 15. I had worked with Chip for four or five years, although we had stopped some time before this tournament. Chip has a great attitude toward the game and its adversities.

I have told him, as I tell all the players I work with, to be prepared for second-guessing. I learned playing quarterback for my high-school football team that if you call an audible and it works, fans and writers call you a genius. If it fails, they call you a dope. You have to know yourself well enough to shrug off either appellation. If Chip had gone for the green in two, sunk the eagle putt, and won the tournament, the writers and the television commentators would have canonized him. And if he hit a wood into the water or plugged it into the lip of the bunker on the right, they would have said that he got impatient and lost his composure. I tell players not to let this kind of baloney, whether positive or negative, surprise, disturb or gratify them. They should accept the fact that it comes with the territory for a contender in major championships. They should be glad that they're in that territory.

Chip was obviously very close to his threshold distance on No. 15 that Sunday. His lie was not helpful. It was downhill, on the back side of a mound, which makes it harder to control the ball. The pin was back right, meaning that if he managed to get the ball over the pond and into the bunker on the right, he'd still very likely make only a par. So he chose to lay up. It was not that he wanted to settle for par and protect second place.

He wanted the birdie. He just calculated that he had a better chance to make it using his wedge and putter. As it happened, he made par.

But, Chip made the right decision, despite what you might have heard from your newspaper's golf expert or the sports maven on the eleven o'clock news. If his wedge shot had landed a few feet shorter and he had made his birdie, those same people would have been saying what a great course manager he was and praised his patience.

Anyone who doubted Chip's nerve had obviously forgotten what happened on No. 13 a few minutes earlier. He hit a beautiful wood over Rae's Creek and into the green, stopping 25 feet away. Bernhard Langer then hit a 3-iron a foot inside him, with the same line. Chip's eagle putt lipped out. Langer, able to study the line and speed by watching Chip's ball, made his three.

That and a few other putts like it made the difference in the tournament. Langer's went in and Chip's didn't.

With all that said, No. 13 is short enough so that virtually everyone in the Masters field can reach it in two, given a decent drive. Standing on the green and looking backward helps plan how to do it. The first thing you notice is Rae's Creek, winding down the left side of the fairway and curling in front of the green. Then you notice the steep cant of the fairway in the area from which the second shot is likely to be played. The ball will be well above the golfer's feet on that shot, which may make it harder for him to hold the green. After looking at the hole this way, a lot of smart players decide not to flirt with the water on the left and to play a little right instead, toward where the spotters usually stand on this hole. The temptation on the tee is to try to burn the drive down the left side and draw it. You can set up a very short second shot this way, but you can also get into a lot of trouble.

For a professional, the most important thing for both the tee shot and the second shot is being decisive. He must pick a target, pick a club, and believe in both. I spend a lot of time prior to the Masters with my players' caddies. I tell them to support whatever club decision their players make, not allowing any doubts to slip out. In other words, if the player stands in the fairway at No. 13 and says 4-iron, and the caddie thinks the 3-iron would be better, I want the caddie to say that 4-iron is exactly what he was thinking.

For the weekend player, this kind of consideration is largely irrelevant. Even if he busts his drive 250 yards, he's still looking at a 235-yard approach over Rae's Creek. He's better off thinking about the distance from which his third shot will be most comfortable. In a lot of cases, this will not mean laying up close to the creek. It will mean laying up well back of the creek, leaving a full wedge shot in. And that raises the issue of what to hit off the tee, just as it did on No. 10. In a lot of cases, amateurs would be better off hitting a 3-wood or a long iron rather than reflexively pulling out the driver. This applies to many par fives played from the white tees, in the range of 470–520 yards. Unless a player can realistically plan on reaching the green in two, what's the point of hitting a driver?

Weekend players generally would do well to spend time practicing with a long iron or fairway wood until they have a club they know they can hit 200 yards into the fairway. It will make the game a lot easier for them.

PROBLEMS OF STRATEGY at Amen Corner, as on any good course, require detailed knowledge of yardages to solve. In recent years, with more courses posting yardages on sprinkler heads in the fairway, amateurs have tended to become complacent about yardages, figuring that there will always be a nearby sprinkler head to tell them the distance left to the middle (or front, depending on the course) of the green. That's true, as far as it goes. But sprinkler heads and 150-yard markers won't give a golfer many of the distances he needs. Only walking the course and annotating your own scorecard will do that, and when I talk to professional or college players, I stress the necessity of doing so.

On many holes, for instance, you need to know the precise distance between the tee and a particular hazard like a tree, trap or creek, or to the corner of a dogleg. On par fives, you need to take into account the distance from points in the tee-shot landing area to the ideal lay-up position. Unless you know these distances, you will face an extra and unnecessary element of doubt as you prepare to hit your shots. And doubt is the last thing you want floating through your mind as you prepare to hit the ball.

Your game plan must also prepare you for adversity. No matter how carefully you study the course and plan your targets, you are not going to hit everything perfectly. And even if you hit it perfectly, golf courses are full of bad bounces. Some of your tee shots are going to land in fairway traps. Some of your approach shots will also find sand. Once in a while you'll be in the woods, and once in a while you'll be in the water.

Your plan has to prepare you for all contingencies, so you're ready for the best happening and ready for the worst. Let's suppose that you are about to play in a club championship, and the 1st hole, a 370-yard par four, has a deep-lipped fairway trap 235 yards out from the tee on the left side and out-of-bounds on the right. You decide that you'll hit a 3-wood off the tee, aiming for the left center. You choose the 3-wood because you can't normally hit it 235 yards and you rarely slice this club enough to go out of bounds. Four rounds out of five, your choice will work out fine. But one round out of five you might block it right, past the white stakes. Or you might really catch it pure and see it trickle into the fairway trap.

If you haven't planned for either eventuality, you might get all upset and kick away your chances right there. But if you've prepared, you will know that in the event of an out-of-bounds tee shot the only effective thing to do is to realize that all players occasionally block a ball, forget about it, tee up a new ball, and swing more freely than you did on the first shot. In the event of hitting the fairway trap, you'll have already decided that if you're within five yards of the lip, you can't reach the green, and you'll take out a sand wedge and rely on your short game to salvage par. If you're more than five yards from the lip, you'll take out an 8-iron and go for the green. The important thing is to be prepared for both bad shots and the bad breaks the course can dish out even on good shots. When they happen, as they inevitably will, you'll maintain your equilibrium.

Doing this helped Tom Kite win the U.S. Open in 1992. Three years previously, at Oak Hill, he let a bad hole upset him. This was the 5th, and it happened when he was leading. He hit a shot in the water, pitched up, and had a putt for a bogey. As he later described it to me, he still felt positive and confident and knew he was going to make it. But two feet from the hole, the ball caught a subtle break that he hadn't foreseen and slid past. He was really shocked. Rather than mark the ball, collect himself, and adhere to his routine, he walked up to the next putt quickly and missed it. That turned the hole into a triple-bogey and really hurt his chance to win that Open.

In 1992, as he prepared for the Open at Pebble Beach, I asked Tom every day whether he was prepared to miss a two-foot putt and not let it bother him. He told me he was.

He proved it Sunday on the 4th hole. Everyone remembers the chip he holed for a birdie at No. 7 to take the lead. But to me, what happened at No. 4 was equally important.

The 4th at Pebble Beach is a very short par four, only 327 yards from the back tees. It's one of the holes a good player wants to birdie, because he knows he's likely to need that cushion as he plays the much tougher holes ahead. Tom hit two good shots at No. 4, a 4-wood and a sand wedge, but his approach hit a hard spot on the slick, wind-dried green and bounced into a bunker. He exploded out, missed his par putt, and had a tricky short putt for bogey. He missed it and took double-bogey.

But this time, he had learned his lesson and was better prepared. He never let his thoughts get ahead of his position on the course. He never let himself wonder whether those two wasted strokes had cost him his chance at the Open. He kept his attention focused tightly on every ensuing shot as it came up. He stayed with his game plan and his routine. And he won his richly deserved major championship.

YOUR GAME PLAN must always have flexibility. You must think in advance about what you will do if the wind blows strongly. In this case, you might hit more low irons off the tees into the wind rather than taking a chance on a wood hit up into the wind. You might hit a driver instead of a shorter club on a par five with the wind at your back, if the wind gives you a good chance to reach the hole in two. If it rains, or the course is soggy, your shots will get less carry and much less roll. You have to alter your plan accordingly. You may want to use longer clubs off the tee and go for more pins in marginal situations.

But in general, I recommend altering your game plan only in

a conservative direction. I don't like to see players under pressure make bolder and more aggressive choices than their plan calls for, especially in medal play. Too often, the new choice winds up costing them more strokes. Any time you're not sure, make the more conservative choice.

18.

Thriving Under Pressure

MOST GOLFERS TAKE up the game casually. As beginners, they're just trying to learn how to hit the ball, and their only opposition is the game itself.

But sooner or later, most move on to another level, the level of competition and pressure. They join a foursome that plays for a few dollars a side. They enter club tournaments. At higher levels, they try to make their living as professionals. And at the highest level, they try to engrave their names on the trophies awarded at major championships.

When they step up to this level, they often find that they perceive the game very differently. The grass is still green and the ball is still white. But fairways that once looked wide and inviting turn tight and menacing. Putts that once seemed short and straight start to writhe like snakes.

At their first exposure to competitive pressure, not to put too fine a point on it, a lot of players choke. They don't produce anything resembling the kind of golf they play when they're completely relaxed.

To deal with choking, let's first define it.

A golfer chokes when he lets anger, doubt, fear or some other extraneous factor distract him before a shot.

Distracted, the golfer then fails to do one or more of the things he normally does. He fails to follow his routine, particularly his mental routine. He forgets his game plan. He fails to accept his shots. Quite often under pressure, a distracting doubt or fear turns on the conscious mind. The golfer stops trusting his swing. He starts going through a checklist of errors to avoid. He gets tight and careful. When he's tight and careful, his body must work against gravity, rhythm and flow. His muscles get spastic, his feet get stiff, and he loses his natural grace and tempo. He hits a bad shot, relative to his ability.

That's all that choking really is.

It's important to dispose of a few common misconceptions.

First of all, choking is not synonymous with being nervous. The fact is that, at one time or another, all golfers are nervous. I visited Jack Nicklaus some years ago, and I remember vividly what he told me about nerves. Nicklaus wanted to be nervous. He liked being nervous. One of the symptoms that he noticed as he aged and his performance level started to decline was that he didn't get nervous often enough.

"I don't know how you play well unless you're nervous," he said. "Nowadays, I don't get nervous unless I'm in a major and in a position to win. If I could only learn to concentrate when I'm not nervous, so I could get in position to win, then I'd be fine."

Nicklaus understood what most great athletes do—being nervous can help performance. Bill Russell, the great Boston Celtic center, wrote in his memoirs that he always felt confident the Celtics would win a big game if he threw up in the locker room before it started. A nervous stomach meant, to Russell, that he was interested and excited. If he didn't vomit, he was afraid his performance would be flat.

Being nervous produces adrenaline. Being very nervous can produce a great gush of adrenaline. That can cause the heart to pound. It can cause the hands to shake.

In a young golfer, or an older golfer who hasn't learned how to handle it, this gush of adrenaline can be devastating. He stands over a shot or a putt and feels the trembling hands and the furiously beating heart. He doesn't understand that this is simply a natural reaction to the situation. It's the way the body is wired. He begins to think, "What the heck is wrong with me?"

And that thought introduces doubt and fear, which, as we have seen, are the termites that destroy the foundation of the successful stroke. He or she may try to still the heart and hands, which makes the body stiff. He or she forgets to trust. He blames the ensuing bad shot or putt on shaking hands, not on being distracted by shaking hands.

Many players, including Val Skinner, one of the LPGA players I work with, have had to learn to handle this challenge. Under pressure, particularly on the greens, Val's hands would start to shake because of the intensity she brings to the game. She worried about this until I told her about all the critical putts that good golfers have made with shaking hands. Then she started to accept and welcome the physical symptoms of stress as a normal part of the human condition.

The successful golfer either has learned, or instinctively understands, that the pounding heart and the trembling hands are nothing to worry about. They are, at worst, another factor to be accounted for, like a following wind. They may cause an iron shot to carry 10 or 20 yards longer than it normally would. But they will not, of themselves, destroy the swing.

The successful golfer knows that rather than concern himself with stilling the hands and quieting the heart, he must focus the mind, blocking out distractions and attending to routine and strategy just as meticulously as if this were a practice round, on his home course at twilight, with no one else around. The body can and probably will stay excited. The mind must not.

Successful golfers, like Nicklaus, welcome the onset of nervous symptoms. That's why they got into competition in the first place—because winning was important to them and overcoming the emotional challenges of competitive golf gave them a great feeling of accomplishment. They play tournament golf precisely because it makes them nervous.

I sometimes tell young players that being nervous on the golf course is a little bit like being nervous the first time you make love with someone you really care about. Nearly everyone is nervous in that situation, but nerves are part of what makes the experience so exhilarating. If it didn't make you nervous, it wouldn't be so gratifying. In fact, it might be a little boring. Ask any prostitute.

So, choking is not being nervous. Choking is also not synonymous with making a bad shot in a pressure situation. Hitting a golf ball precisely is a complicated task. No human being can do it well all the time. A player can do everything right, mentally, and still miss a two-footer on the 18th hole of an important match. In golf, that simply happens sometimes. It's not necessarily due to choking. If the putt or shot is missed in spite of good thinking, the golfer simply has to accept his misfortune as part of the game, and move on.

Choking is also not the inevitable by-product of a flawed

swing, although you often hear golfers talk about trying to learn a swing that will "hold up under pressure." If a swing is good enough to repeat itself on the practice tee, it is good enough to repeat itself on the golf course, as long as the golfer's thoughts remain consistent. Swings don't hold up under pressure. People do.

And, finally, choking is not synonymous with having a flawed character. Some nasty, miserable people have triumphed under pressure. And some of the finest, most admirable human beings in the world have choked in tight situations. If you play golf long enough, you are bound to encounter some pressure situations in which you will perform at less than your best. They will help you learn how to cope with pressure, which is a skill that must be learned, and, once learned, constantly maintained.

I've already spoken of some examples of choking. We've seen how Corey Pavin let the pond on No. 16 at Augusta distract him from his target and ruin his chances at the 1986 Masters. And we've seen how Tom Kite let a missed putt cause him to abort his routine and miss a two-foot comeback putt at the U.S. Open in 1989. These are two of the toughest minds I've ever known. I could cite dozens of other examples. Raymond Floyd blew a big lead and lost the Senior PGA Championship on the final nine holes in 1994. Afterward, he told the press that he realized that under pressure, he'd been altering his setup a little, causing blocked shots.

Each of them, it should be noted, learned from the experience and went on to become a better player. Choking is not a congenital, incurable disease. It can be overcome if the golfer intelligently analyzes what went wrong in a particular situation and takes steps to correct it.

. . .

THE U.S. OPEN is perhaps our greatest laboratory for the study of performance under pressure. Golfers can quibble about whether the Masters is more lucrative or the British Open more prestigious. But no other tournament offers quite the cauldron of distractions as our Open. The sheer, overwhelming desire to win the title is itself a distraction. So is the fear of getting into contention or into the lead and then failing to capitalize. The U.S. Golf Association lets the rough grow and pinch the fairways to provide another source of doubt. It shaves the greens to make it all the more difficult to ignore any tremor in the hands. The finishing holes are invariably among the longest and most testing in golf. Not surprisingly, the history of the Open is rich in stories of golfers, many of them great golfers, who fell in the stretch with an apple stuck in their throat.

I say this knowing that I am putting myself into the position of the second-guesser in his armchair, whom I generally detest. I do not mean to besmirch anyone's character. I don't mean to gainsay the tremendous achievement of simply getting into position to blow an Open. Those who have gained such position are the warriors who dared to enter the arena, and they deserve admiration. I simply note that even the greatest players are human, human beings commit mental mistakes, and all golfers can learn from the study of those mistakes.

Arnold Palmer, who won the Open so dramatically in 1960, blew it just as dramatically in 1966 at the Olympic Club in San Francisco. Most golfers know the outlines of that story. Palmer made the turn in the final round seven strokes ahead of Billy Casper. He wound up losing the tournament to Casper in a playoff the next day.

I admire Arnold Palmer a great deal. My favorite story about him suggests how loose and trusting he was in his prime. It occurred in 1962, at the Colonial. Palmer was in a playoff with

Johnny Pott when he hit a ball into a bunker on the 9th hole. He was about to hit his recovery shot when he heard a small boy's voice, followed quickly by the sound of a mother hissing at the boy to hush. Palmer turned around and saw the two, the boy looking chagrined and the mother embarrassed. Palmer just laughed, turned back to the ball, and addressed the shot again. Just as he was about to swing, he heard another sound. This time, the mortified boy was sobbing. Palmer backed off again and again smiled at the child. Then he addressed the ball a third time. He heard a gagging sound. He turned around and saw that by this time the mother had clamped a hand over the boy's mouth.

"Hey, it's okay," Palmer said. "Don't choke him. This isn't that important."

Whereupon he blasted out of the trap and went on to win the playoff.

But four years later, Palmer was being supplanted as the best golfer in the world by Jack Nicklaus, and he desperately wanted to win the Open. He was not quite so loose.

As it happens, I have taught at clinics several times with a pro named Mike Reasor, who was Palmer's caddie during that Open. From Reasor's account, and what Palmer himself has written, it's possible to reconstruct much of what went through Palmer's mind that Sunday in San Francisco.

Palmer gave one standing instruction to his caddie that day. If his swing tempo got too fast, he wanted Reasor to tell him. Reasor was himself a top-flight golfer, a member of the Brigham Young University team. And he noticed on the 7th hole of the final round that Palmer's tempo was quickening. But, he reasoned, who was he to correct the best player in golf, a man leading the Open by seven strokes? Reasor kept his counsel for the time being.

Palmer has written that as he stood on the 10th tee, he was so confident of victory that he stopped thinking about the shot immediately ahead of him and started thinking about breaking the Open scoring record of 276, set by Ben Hogan in 1948. Palmer already held the British Open scoring record. The thought of holding both records simultaneously enchanted him. Distracted by that thought, he lost a stroke to Casper on No. 10.

At No. 11, he hit his tee shot into the right rough. Reasor was trailing eight or ten paces behind Palmer as they set off from the 11th tee. He had noticed that the swing was getting even quicker. He decided to tell Palmer.

"I called out, 'Arnold,' and he stopped and looked around," Reasor recalled. "I told him his swing had gotten way faster. He made an attempt thereafter to gear it down, but it was difficult. Trying to slow it down took away his free flow and put tension in the swing."

Palmer had already committed, in retrospect, two of the common mental mistakes a golfer makes under pressure. He had let his thoughts drift into the future. He had started to dwell on the score he was shooting and the Open record. Then, he compounded the error by introducing a new, mechanical thought, about swing tempo. As I've mentioned, tempo is one of the least harmful swing thoughts a golfer can have. But introducing such a thought at an advanced stage of a critical round is not the same as starting with it on the first tee. Fear of a quick backswing often leads to a tentative forward swing. In Palmer's case it probably would have been better to continue to play with no swing thought at all, because, as Reasor noticed, trying to slow the swing down did more harm than good. Palmer managed to par No. 11, but Casper birdied No. 13. The lead was down to five.

Then Palmer made the third mistake commonly committed

by golfers under pressure. He started trying to be too bold. The 15th hole at Olympic is a short, heavily bunkered par three, and the USGA had chosen a sucker pin position, just beyond a deep trap. Palmer went for the pin, fell short of the green by inches, and wound up in the sand. He bogeyed the hole. Casper hit to the center of the green, sank the putt, and cut the lead to three.

No. 16 at Olympic is a long par five, playing 604 yards that day. Obviously, at that length, it was unreachable in two shots. The conservative strategy would have been to play a couple of 1-irons down the fairway, then hit a wedge to the green. But Palmer hated playing conservatively. He had used his driver in each of the three previous rounds from the 16th tee.

As he stood there, waiting for Casper to hit, Palmer mulled over his strategy. He thought about a 1-iron. But then he decided that he couldn't do that, that Arnold Palmer would look silly playing safe with a 1-iron, trying to protect a three-stroke lead with three holes to play. So he took out his driver and duck-hooked the ball into the trees and rough.

His ball was buried in thick, wiry grass. But Palmer was still intent on boldness.

"Can I get a 3-iron on the ball?" he asked Reasor.

Reasor thought the lie was too difficult for a 3-iron, that it called for a much more lofted club. But he was afraid to tell Palmer that.

"Only with a perfect swing," Reasor said.

Palmer decided that if a perfect swing was required, he would simply have to produce a perfect swing. He tried the 3-iron. But he barely got the club on the ball, moving it only 40 or 50 yards, still in the rough. He hit a 9-iron into the fairway, then a 3-wood to a greenside bunker. He managed to get up and down for a bogey. Casper, meanwhile, played three safe shots to the green and sank a putt for a birdie. The lead was down to one stroke.

It evaporated completely on the 17th, when Palmer missed the green, played a good recovery, but missed a five-footer for par.

Would the Open have ended differently if Palmer had played conservatively? It's impossible to tell. Mike Reasor points out that the swing Palmer made on the disastrous tee shot at No. 16 would have produced a disastrous shot with a 1-iron as well. But we will never know if he would have made that swing with a 1-iron. There are no hard and fast rules for strategy and tactics.

But it's instructive to compare what Palmer did with what Jack Nicklaus did in a roughly similar Open situation a year later, at Baltusrol.

Palmer and Nicklaus made up the final twosome of the tournament, and as they came to the 18th hole, Nicklaus was four strokes ahead. Not only that, but a birdie would break Hogan's record of 276.

The 18th at Baltusrol is a 542-yard par five, dogleg left, lined with trees, reachable with two good shots. A creek cuts across the fairway about 400 yards from the tee. Nicklaus, of course, wanted the record. But he wanted even more to make sure that he won the tournament.

Nicklaus pulled out his 1-iron.

As it happened, he made a bad swing, much as Palmer had done on the 16th tee at Olympic the year before. He sliced the ball into the rough. He could have tried the heroic shot there. But he played an 8-iron, expecting to lay up short of the creek. He mishit it and moved the ball only about 100 yards, but into the fairway. Palmer, meanwhile, played his second shot just off the green.

At that point, Nicklaus hit one of the great shots of his career, a 235-yard 1-iron to the green. He sank the putt and got the record anyway.

The difference between what Nicklaus did in 1967 and what Palmer did in 1966 is subtle but instructive. Both made some bad shots under pressure. But Nicklaus was playing more conservatively, more within himself. He accepted the fact that once he put the ball into the Open rough from the tee, he would have to play a lofted club. His bad swings, as a result, got him into a little less trouble. And when the time came to make a truly difficult shot, he was in a much stronger, calmer mental state. His success reflected it.

A WEEKEND PLAYER can only imagine what it must be like to stand in Palmer's shoes, trying to hang on to a dwindling lead in the U.S. Open. But the lessons of Palmer's collapse are just as applicable to coping with the pressures of a two-dollar Nassau or the final holes of a club tournament.

First, stay in the present and keep your mind sharply focused on the shot immediately in front of you.

Don't, as Palmer did when he started thinking of the Open scoring record, let extraneous thoughts distract you. If you're ahead, don't start calculating whom you'll play in the next round, or what kind of beer you'll order with the two dollars. If you're behind, don't start thinking about losing the match or about how well your opponent played the last few holes.

Second, avoid mechanical thoughts, such as the tempo thought Palmer allowed into his mind. Instead, strive to become looser, freer and more confident. You should want to feel that you trust your swing more on the 18th tee than you did on the 1st.

Third, stick to your routine and to your game plan.

You set them up to give you a chance to post your lowest possible number by having a conservative stragety and a cocky, aggressive swing. If you make some mistakes and fall behind early, there's no reason to try to make up the deficit with bold, risky strategy, like Palmer's 3-iron out of the rough on No. 16. Don't start firing at tight pins where you'd planned to aim for the middle of the green. Don't hit a driver from a tee where you planned to hit an iron. You're far more likely to come back by playing steadily and well and giving your opponent a chance to make some mistakes of his own.

NERVE-WRACKING DISTRACTIONS are not, of course, peculiar to the U.S. Open. They can occur on any course at any time, even in a casual round.

Some golfers get upset when play slows down in front of them. It's often hard not to. But if you dwell on it, you can convince yourself that the delays are going to throw off your rhythm and ruin your round. You may even come up against a player who will deliberately agree with you that the slow play is aggravating and damaging and take quiet delight in destroying your composure.

The only effective response to bottlenecks on the course is a decision that they will not bother you. You can even try to enjoy the languor of it. If you have to wait, keep walking around to make sure that the body stays active and warm. If you must sit, be certain that a few minutes before your turn to hit finally comes around, you stand up, stretch a little, walk around, and get the body limber again. Then go through your routine once or twice in your mind. Get yourself focused back on golf.

Even if there are no undue delays, much of the time in a

round of golf will be consumed by things other than shotmaking—walking to your ball and watching your partners play theirs. I recommend getting your mind off of golf between shots. It's easier for most people to concentrate totally for a minute or so at a time, as they execute their shotmaking routines. Trying to stay that focused between shots can be too taxing. Some players, like Lee Trevino and Fuzzy Zoeller, chat constantly between shots as a way of staying loose. Brad Faxon will sometimes step behind the gallery ropes to chat with friends who are following him around.

If you or your partners don't want to talk, try something else. Look at the birds or trees or weeds. Jack Nicklaus used to scan the gallery for pretty girls and joke about setting up his caddie, Angelo Argea, on dates with them.

Of course, Zoeller, Trevino, Faxon and Nicklaus all switch their attention completely to the task at hand once it's time to play a shot.

If there's a rain delay, it's even more essential to unwind and distance yourself from golf. Read a book. Change clothes. When the rain stops, make up your mind that the delay is going to help you. Warm back up by going through your routine on a few practice swings, simulating a real shot as closely as possible.

Finally, the play of your opponents can be a nervous distraction. Many a player has been cruising along in a match until his opponent suddenly and unexpectedly sinks a long chip or comes out of the woods to make par. Surprised, he loses his focus, starts to feel pressured, and fouls up his own game.

A golfer should always assume that his opponent will hit the best possible shot. Then, if it happens, he'll be prepared to cope with it. I saw a great example of this some years back at the Tournament Players' Championship. Tom Kite and Chip Beck were leading the tournament going into the final round, and they formed the final twosome.

Chip started out horribly, making four bogeys on the front side and shooting 40. Tom seemed to have a comfortable lead. But Tom did not assume that Chip would keep playing that badly, or even that he would play the back nine in par figures. Instead, he assumed that Chip would get as hot on the back side as he had been cold on the front. And Chip did, shooting 31. Tom, however, was ready for that kind of charge. He stuck to his game plan, and he held Chip off until the final hole. There, Tom teed off with a two-stroke lead.

They both reached the green in regulation figures. Tom was 50 feet and two tiers of green away. Chip had a tricky, downhill putt of 25 feet.

Immediately, Tom told me later, he assumed Chip would make that putt, difficult though it was. He rolled his first putt to about five feet.

Then, sure enough, Chip made his birdie putt.

If Chip's putt had surprised or unnerved Tom, his next putt would have suddenly become much harder. But because Tom had prepared himself mentally, his emotional state did not change when Chip's ball disappeared into the hole. Things were still going as he had planned. He was still in control.

And he holed his par putt and won the tournament.

19.

When the Scoreboard Looks at You

ONE OF THE most common mental errors committed by golfers under pressure is letting the score distract them from what they ought to be thinking about.

No one paid more dearly for this mistake than Sam Snead in the U.S. Open of 1939 at Spring Mill, outside Philadelphia. Snead set the Open pace that year with rounds of 68, 71 and 73. As he stood on the 17th tee in the final round, he added up his own total. He knew that par on the final two holes would give him a 69 for 281, tying the Open record Ralph Guldahl had set two years earlier.

In those days, tournament courses had no leaderboards. Nor were the leaders always paired in the final rounds. News of other players' scores flitted around the course by word of mouth, and the news was not always accurate. Byron Nelson, Snead's closest pursuer, had come in at 284. Snead erroneously thought, however, that Nelson had finished a stroke or two better than that.

Not knowing he had a 3-shot lead, he decided to go all out on 17 and hit a 300-yard drive. But his second shot was in the rough, and his chip was short. He bogeyed the hole.

Walking to the par-five 18th, thinking that he had probably fallen into a tie with Nelson, Snead completely lost his natural serenity. He had nervous physical symptoms; his teeth, he recalled later, were chattering. The gallery distracted him. The rush of people coming over to 18 from 17 forced him to wait. He started thinking about the money he stood to blow. He thought about the annoying gallery. He thought about avoiding humiliation. He thought he needed a birdie to win. He thought, in short, about everything but the right way to play No. 18.

Half a century later, Snead still was angry with the gallery, still wondered why no one told him that the score to beat was 284, not 282 or 283. He needed only a bogey to win the Open. But the fact of the matter is that he himself let extraneous thoughts dominate his mind. He let the score distract him. He let the gallery distract him. He did not focus intently on a game plan for No. 18, take each shot as it came and stick with his routine.

Trying to hit another huge drive, he hooked the ball into the deep Open rough. Still thinking he needed a birdie, he tried to hit a 2-wood out of the rough, rather than taking a midiron. He hit, in other words, the shot he thought he should hit rather than the shot he knew he could hit. He topped it.

The ball came to rest in a fairway trap, a hundred yards from the green, half-buried. Snead was desperate to reach the green. He took an 8-iron, rather than a sand wedge. The ball hit the lip. His fourth shot found a greenside trap. He blasted out and, thoroughly discombobulated, three-putted, for a total of eight strokes. He had given the Open away, and after that he never would win one.

Would he have won if he had known the correct score? Perhaps. If thinking about the score accurately can be a dangerous distraction, thinking about a false score is even worse.

But he almost certainly would have won if he had not paid attention to the score. Once he started thinking about it, he introduced a host of distracting thoughts. He let the score, rather than common sense, dictate club selection and strategy. Sitting in the rough after his tee shot at No. 18, Snead was 260 yards from the green. He could have hit a 7-iron and a wedge, leaving himself a putt for the birdie he thought he needed. Instead, he tried for the shot that was too bold, too difficult, and in the end disastrous.

Pressure frequently doesn't do nearly as much damage to a golfer's swing as it does to his course management.

IN FOCUSING SO much of his thinking on his own score and those of the other players, Snead did something I advise golfers to avoid, whether they're in the final round of the Open or just a friendly round.

The minute you start thinking, "If I shoot bogey for the last three holes I'll break 90," or "if I shoot par for the next two holes I'll win the Open," you get ahead of yourself. Your thoughts leave the present. You start worrying too much about fouling things up. You get careful. You get tight. You start steering the ball instead of getting looser and cockier. You play the golfing equivalent of pro football's prevent defense. And disaster often strikes, whether your goal is to break 90 or win the Open.

High-handicappers as a rule pay much closer attention to

their scores than pros do. They can't wait to write down the number after every hole. They're always adding up their strokes and using the number as a way of evaluating how they're doing. If they start to approach a goal, like breaking 90, they're instantly aware of what they have to do on the remaining holes to reach it. It's one of the reasons they're high-handicappers. They make it much harder on themselves.

Professionals, when they're playing at home, rarely use a scorecard. When the round is over, they recollect each hole, add up the strokes and determine their score. That's what the average player should do.

I know it's not easy. Golfers have ingrained the habit of writing down the score after every hole, adding it up after 9, and projecting the total over 18. Playing partners often will do this for them if they don't. If there are bets on the match, that adds to the tendency to keep constant track of the score.

I can only say that you'll shoot a lower score, on average, if you keep your mind in the present and take it one shot at a time.

For modern professionals, the task is harder because there are leaderboards everywhere on the courses they play, and they have to make a conscious decision not to let them distract them.

Jack Nicklaus was excellent at this. Angelo Argea, his longtime caddie, wrote that as a rule, Nicklaus did not want to know how the field was faring and rarely looked at a leaderboard. Once, Argea said, Nicklaus started a final round leading a tournament by several strokes. He ordered Argea not to tell him what the leaderboards said. The caddie stayed mum. But on the 16th tee, Nicklaus suddenly turned to Argea and demanded to know where he stood.

"You're nine strokes ahead," Argea told him.

Nicklaus double-bogeyed the hole.

There are players, of course, who do keep an eye on the leaderboard and want to know where they stand, particularly in the final holes of a tournament. Nick Price is one of them. They like the challenge of knowing the entire situation and dealing with it. If they are successful players, though, you can be sure that they take the score information in and then refocus their attention entirely on the next shot. For most players, it's easier, in my opinion, to pay no attention to the score.

VAL SKINNER TELLS me she has won several tournaments without knowing, until she holed her last putt, that she had won. She's won tournaments knowing, from the way the crowd applauded her, that she had the lead, but not knowing by how many strokes. She makes a deliberate effort to avoid looking at leaderboards. She counts on her caddie to tell her, on the final few holes, if there's anything critical she needs to know about the standings. This means, for instance, that if she's a stroke out of the lead on a par-five final hole, she wants to know. It could affect her decision on whether to lay up or try to reach the green in two. Otherwise, she understands that there is nothing she can do to affect her opponents' scores. She maximizes her chances to win by refusing to think about anything but her own routine and her own game plan.

At the Atlanta Women's Championship in 1994, at Eagle's Landing, Val started the final round two strokes behind Liselotte Neumann. Neumann tripled-bogeyed the first hole, and Val, in the final threesome with her, knew she was close to the lead, if not leading. She decided to pretend, however, that someone in the group in front of them had the lead. She refused to look at a leaderboard. She stuck to her game plan. She played a round that verged on brilliance. Neumann, however, steadied herself and kept pace with Val.

On the 17th, a dogleg par four, Val hit her drive a little left of her target, into a bunker. She tried to hit too much club out of the bunker, and barely got on the green in three. She had a 20-foot putt for par. Neumann had a 3-foot putt for par.

An enormous leaderboard stood behind the green. Val tried to keep her eyes from focusing it, but suddenly, she could not. The numbers and letters, as if of their own volition, pulled into sharp clarity.

The board said she was leading Neumann by one stroke.

The information did not help her concentration as she stood over the 20-footer. It was a slippery, downhill putt with perhaps an 8-foot break. Once she knew that missing it could cost her the tournament, it started to look even slipperier, as if she were trying to bank the ball off a green, marble cliff.

She left her putt 8 feet short.

Fortunately, at that point, all the work Val had been doing to learn to control her thoughts and discipline her mind paid off. She confronted the challenge to set aside all of the distractions. She forgot the standings. And she made her 8-footer.

Then Neumann missed her 3-footer.

The scoreboard, in effect, had given Val a false picture. She had assumed that Neumann would make her 3-foot par putt and tie for the lead if she missed her own par putt. It was a false assumption. But that false assumption, plus the information from the leaderboard, made her own par putt harder than it needed to be and nearly cost her the tournament.

Of course, it's very difficult to block out the score.

"Doc," Val told me later, "I didn't want to look at that leaderboard. But it was like that leaderboard was looking at me."

20.

Competitors

SOME MONTHS AFTER I started working with Tom Kite in 1984, he started recommending me to other golfers on the tour. One of them got to wondering.

"Wait a minute," he said to Tom. "If this guy Rotella helps you, why do you want him to help us? We're your competitors."

"The way I see it," Tom replied, "there's more than enough money out here for all of us. You guys are going to help me get better. And I'm going to help you get better. We're all going to help each other have fun seeing how good we can get."

Tom had the ideal attitude toward competition and his fellow competitors.

He recognized that the other people on the golf course are not the real opposition that a golfer faces.

The first opponent is the game itself. The course, the club

and the ball are all idiosyncratic and unpredictable foes, and they will humble the best golfer more than occasionally.

The second opponent is the golfer himself. Can he discipline his mind to produce the best score his body is capable of?

Only after those two foes have been confronted do the other people on the course come into the picture.

The best athletes realize that if they win the battle with themselves, they have done all they can do. The golfer who can look back on a tournament that he lost and say, "I played as well as I could. I had my mind where it was supposed to be on every shot," will be satisfied and happy.

This is true in all sports. When I worked with professional baseball pitcher Greg Maddux I suggested he approach pitching in much the same way a golfer approaches a golf course. He needed a plan for facing each hitter. He needed a target for each pitch, and a velocity. If he delivered a pitch precisely as he wanted to, he should be satisfied. If Bobby Bonds then hit the ball out of the park, Greg did not consider himself a failure.

Big-league hitters could do that. That's why they were in the big leagues. Testing himself against the best, Maddux would not get everyone out. But testing himself against the best would help him find out just how good he could be.

The best golfers have much the same attitude. Their primary concern is performing as well as they can, or as close to their potential as they can get. If they do that, and lose, they shrug and go on. They know that if they keep performing as well as they can, the wins will come. And they do.

That's why a player like Tom Kite can want to help his competitors play better. He realizes that if they improve their games, it will motivate him to do what it takes to get better. He will move closer to finding out how well he can play.

Most of the touring players I work with come to me because

another player advised them to do so. Typically, two friends will sit down for dinner during a tournament, and one will ask the second why he or she seems to be playing better. This happened a lot in 1993 and 1994 to Nick Price, for obvious reasons. Nick would always be happy to share with players how he had learned to discipline and focus his mind on the golf course. And if they wanted to know more, he gave them my number.

The point is that it never occurred to Nick not to want his competitors to get better. Nor would it occur to any of the players I work with.

So it distresses me when I run into players, usually lesser players, who think it's smart to use gamesmanship to throw off opponents in competitive tournaments. They're always pointing out water hazards or swing flaws.

Such players must be treated as unfortunate distractions, like a slow foursome in front or the greenskeeper's lawn mower roaring to life across a fairway. A golfer simply has to put them out of his mind, get on with his routine, and tend to his business.

Gamesmanship experts hurt themselves. If they are touring players, they will soon be subtly or not so subtly warned to cut it out. If they fail to heed the warning, they will be shunned. The tour, no matter how much money they make, will be a lonely and unhappy place for them.

If they are amateurs, they risk foregoing one of the great joys of the game, friendships with fellow players.

So I advise players at all levels to cherish their competitors. It's better for their games. It's better for them.

Never decide that you can't stand another golfer, because you might find yourself paired with that golfer for the most important round of your life.

On the other hand, a golfer can't let admiration for a competitor intimidate him. A golfer has to choose someone to believe in. It had better be himself.

I work occasionally with some of the players on the Senior Tour, like Larry Laoretti, who spent their twenties, thirties and forties working as club pros and watching players like Jack Nicklaus and Lee Trevino on television. Nicklaus, in particular, was their ideal. Now, they have to be prepared to face a Nicklaus or a Trevino over the final holes of a tournament.

I tell them that if they want to keep Nicklaus on a pedestal, if they want to look at him as a hero, they ought to buy a ticket and watch the tournament instead of entering it. If they want to step onto the golf course with him, they have to believe they can beat him.

I sometimes tell golfers a story about a basketball player I worked with at Virginia named Olden Polyniece, who is presently in his ninth year of playing in the National Basketball Association. He had one of the best minds for sports I've ever encountered.

In 1984, Olden's first year, the basketball team got off to a mediocre start, breaking even in its first few games. The coaching staff decided to put Olden in the starting lineup, at center. His first game would be against North Carolina, in Chapel Hill. The Tar Heels had a fair team that year. It included Michael Jordan, James Worthy and Sam Perkins. They were undefeated and ranked first in all the polls.

Olden learned that he would be starting against them at the team's weekly Sunday night dinner in the back room of a local restaurant. After the players left, Olden walked back into the room, where the coaches and I were still sitting and talking. Olden stepped up to me and said, "Hey, Doc, I've got a question. How am I supposed to believe in myself if this is my first start ever, and we're going up against the No. 1 team on its home court, and we're playing against guys I loved to watch on television when I was in high school?"

I was impressed with the candor of Olden's question. He didn't care that the coaches were listening. All he knew was that he had to get ready to play Jordan, Perkins and Worthy.

"You've got to go in there with the attitude that you're better than they are until they prove otherwise, rather than the attitude that they're better than you are until you prove otherwise," I told him. "Put the burden of proof on them."

"That's a good idea," Olden said.

He went down to Chapel Hill and played a beautiful game. He had something like 15 points and 18 rebounds. The team lost by a point at the buzzer. Then, with its confidence buoyed, it went on to record a string of upsets in the NCAA tournament and reach the Final Four. Olden may not have been quite good enough that night to lead his team to a victory but he had begun to demonstrate an attitude that would assure him of future success.

Golf is much the same. Great players lose more tournaments than they win because players with just a bit less talent got more out of their talent in a particular week. Certainly, Nicklaus at twenty-five was better than Larry Laoretti at twenty-five. But that doesn't necessarily mean Nicklaus will be better at fifty-five. Some golfers progress. Some regress. Some get hungrier and double their commitment. Some lose their hunger, develop other interests, or develop other priorities. The USGA Junior champion rarely goes on to become the Open champion.

And what someone did to you in last year's club championship—or what you did to him—has nothing to do with what happens if you meet in this year's tournament.

21.

Practicing to Improve

THE GOOD PLAYERS I work with don't have to be told to practice. Most of them have grown up believing that hard work and dedication pay off in success. When something goes wrong with their games, their first instinct is to head for the practice area. Then they start working on fixing their problems.

This kind of attitude has won them praise all of their lives. Americans believe in the work ethic. They believe that practice makes perfect, and the best players are the ones who practice the most.

So good golfers grow up thinking that time spent on practice is automatically time well spent. And that attitude takes them a fairly long way. If they have enough talent, it can make them scratch golfers. It can win them college scholarships.

But it rarely can take them to the next level, the level required to win on the PGA Tour. To do that, a lot of them have to learn to back off a little, to stop investing all their time and energy in the fruitless pursuit of mechanical perfection. They need to learn to practice in a different way.

In golf, working hard does not guarantee success. It can even make things worse. Doing the wrong things in practice can ruin your golfing mind.

To improve, you must practice. But the quality of your practice is more important than the quantity.

Go to any practice tee or driving range and watch the way most golfers hit balls.

Many of them don't even bother to select a target before they hit a ball. They would laugh if you suggested that they practice shooting a basketball without using a basket. But they bash golf ball after golf ball into the ether, blithely unconcerned with hitting a target. When they get onto a course, focusing on a target is a new experience for them.

Others spend an entire practice session trying to break the swing down into its component parts and work on one or more of those parts. They may focus on their swing planes, or their hip turns, or their right elbows. But their practice sessions are entirely mechanical. When they get onto a course, they tend to think mechanically.

To understand how to practice you must first understand that there are two states of mind in practice—the training mentality and the trusting mentality.

In the training mentality, a golfer evaluates his shots critically and analytically. In the trusting mentality, the golfer simply accepts them.

In the training mentality, the golfer tries to make things happen. In the trusting mentality, the golfer lets things happen.

The training mentality is very thoughtful. The trusting mentality feels like reckless abandon.

The training mentality is impatient. The trusting mentality is patient.

In the training mentality, a player may just rake ball after ball into position, working on something mechanical. In the trusting mentality, he goes through his shotmaking routine with every ball he hits.

This distinction is not a matter of good versus bad. Both the training mentality and the trusting mentality have their places in a golfer's practice sessions.

The training mentality is essential for incorporating swing changes and for working on the swing fundamentals. Even at the top levels of the game, players constantly work on maintaining their setup and preshot fundamentals as well as basic swing mechanics. The best athletes in the world always spend a portion of their practice time in the training mentality.

One of the things that separates a pro like Tom Kite from the average golfer is that Tom doesn't wait until his game goes sour to try to remedy things. As soon as he detects the slightest problem with any of the fundamental shots, with setup and routine, or with his mental game, Tom drops whatever else he's doing and heads to the practice area to fix it. That's one reason he's such a consistent money winner. When he does this, he's immersed in the training mentality.

Professionals, as they practice in the training mentality, evaluate themselves harshly. An iron shot may go precisely where they aimed it, but if the trajectory is not what they wanted, they will pick apart the swing and remain dissatisfied until the ball flies to the target with the exact arc and curve they want.

BUT THE TRUSTING mentality is essential for getting ready to play competitively. If you want to be able to trust your swing on the golf course, you have to spend time doing it on the practice tee. Human beings are creatures of habit. They cannot, as a general rule, spend all of their practice time in the training mentality and then switch to the trusting mentality for competition. Under pressure, an athlete's dominant habit will emerge. An athlete who spends most of his practice time in the training mentality will generally fall into the training mentality when he least wants to, when the pressure is greatest. He will start thinking analytically, judgmentally and mechanically. He will not be able to trust his swing and let it go.

The dominant habit is the one an athlete practices most. Therefore:

You must spend at least 60 percent of your practice time in the trusting mentality.

This means, in general, that if you hit a hundred balls in a practice session, at least sixty should be hit in the trusting mentality. This isn't easy, because it requires that you shut your mind down except for thoughts of target and routine. The second an imperfect shot leaves your clubface, you will confront the temptation to evaluate and criticize the swing that produced the imperfect shot, to rake another ball up, and to try to fix the problem. If you can't learn to resist this temptation, your practice time will be less productive than it should be and you will never be as good as you can be.

The 60 percent rule is a general guideline. There should be some practice sessions where you spend more time in the training mentality and others where you spend nearly all your time in the trusting mentality.

You may spend more time in the training mentality at the beginning of the season, when you're trying to restore the mechanics and rhythm that tend to slip away during the winter.

You may spend more time in the training mentality when you're trying to fix a problem that has cropped up in your game.

Conversely, the closer a player gets to competition, the more practice time he must spend in the trusting mentality. A player preparing for a tournament should hit 70 to 90 percent of his practice shots in the trusting mentality in the last days before the competition begins. He needs to accustom the mind to the style of thinking that works on the golf course—to thoughts of target, of routine, of acceptance.

This is particularly true of the warm-up period just before a round. This is preparation for competition, when trusting works. At this stage, a player ought to strive to hit all of his shots in the trusting mentality. If he lets himself revert to the training mentality and starts trying to fix swing mechanics, it will be very difficult to get back into the trusting mentality on the first tee. For a competitive round, a player should get to the course at least an hour ahead of time so he can spend his warm-up period steeped in patience and trust. This is not a time to be rushing from practice tee to putting green to first tee, stuffing a candy bar into your mouth on the fly.

While no good pro that I know of tries to fix his swing while he's warming up before a round, a lot of them do work on their mechanics after a round, trying to fix flaws that they noticed during that day's play. If a player wants to do this, I let him. It certainly is better for him than going back to the hotel and brooding about the mistakes. I hope he leaves the practice area with his confidence restored, ready to trust his swing the next day.

But Tom Watson told me that he made the big breakthrough in his career after he learned to stop working on his mistakes after a round. Suppose he'd played a round where he mishit a couple of wedges. Earlier in his career, he might work for an hour and a half on wedges. But the next day, he'd find that he was concentrating so much on wedges that some other facet of his game suffered. So he changed his postround practice habits. He started working for forty minutes on a little bit of everything, not just on the clubs and shots that had been less than perfect that day. He realized that a single day's results, no matter how bad, never justified trying to overhaul his swing mechanics in the middle of a tournament.

Regardless of how close a player is to competition, I'm not a great believer in hitting bucket after bucket with the full swing just for the sake of hitting them. It's an easy way to develop bad habits.

An amateur, particularly, would be far better off hitting a couple of dozen balls three times a week, going through his routine on every ball, picking out a target, and trusting. He would at least be on his way to ingraining mental discipline and getting the best score out of the swing he has.

And any player, whether touring pro or weekend duffer, should spend the majority of his practice time on the short game, on shots of 120 yards and less.

I'd begin by going to a practice green and starting on the fringe. I recommend that good players practice chips every day until they sink two. This does two things. First, it forces them to think about holing chips rather than just getting them on the green in the direction of the hole. And it boosts their confidence. It's amazing how sinking a couple of chips every day can persuade a player that he has a great short game.

Weekend players may not be able to practice long enough to sink two chips. Darkness or divorce proceedings would intervene. They can still drop a dozen balls at various spots around the green and see how many they can get up and down, using their full routines with every shot.

The weekend player ought to make sure he has a few fundamental short shots in his arsenal. One would be the chip from the edge of the green. The second would be the flop shot from a little farther off the putting surface. And the third would be a sand explosion that got up in the air, traveled about 15 or 20 feet, and could be relied on to get out of any greenside bunker.

Once he has practiced those shots, he should move to the practice tee and start working at shots from 40 to 120 yards. Hit lots of different shots: pitch-and-runs, knockdowns, different trajectories. Always have a small target. This will develop feel and touch.

The short shots around the green save pars. The longer wedge shots, from 120 yards to about 40 yards, make birdies. Players can't practice them too much.

I like to see players competing at short-game drills. Bet a nickel, a beer or a soda. Drop balls at varying distances, into varying lies. Award five points for holing a shot and three for hitting it within tap-in distance. It introduces competitive pressure, it sharpens the instinct to hit the target, and it makes practice fun.

A player ought to spend, as a general rule, no more than 30 percent of his practice time on the full swing. And of this time, the bulk should be spent with the club—anything from a driver to a 3-iron—that he uses when he absolutely has to put the ball into the fairway. How much time should be reserved for the long irons and midirons? Almost none, especially if practice time is limited.

I also don't believe a golfer should spend hours practicing

putts. Good putting is primarily a function of attitude and routine. Once a player masters those two, he really doesn't need to hit a lot of practice putts. Bobby Locke didn't. Ben Crenshaw doesn't.

But there are several practice drills I find quite useful in putting.

I encourage players I work with to use a chalk line. This is a device that uses a reel of chalked string to lay down a line on a flat section of green, from the hole to the ball. A lot of players find that this helps them make putt after putt. The image tends to become so vivid that they can then go out on the golf course and see the line much more easily.

Often I ask a player to go to the practice green with a ball and place it 8 to 12 feet from the hole. I ask him to take nine putts and to try a little bit *less* with each putt, until he finds just the right amount of intensity. When he's found it, I ask him to try to maintain that level for five putts.

I also ask players to go to the practice green and putt to the fringe from all possible distances, merely looking at the fringe and reacting to it with each stroke. The idea is get to the edge of the green without going into the fringe. This helps players develop a feel for pace, which is the key to long putts. This drill avoids the pitfall of putting at a hole from long distances, which is that a golfer is bound to miss most of these attempts, eroding his confidence.

If a player wants to practice his putting mechanics, I suggest that he do it without a ball, indoors. Tie a piece of string, about six inches off the floor, to a couple of chairs. Step up until your eyes are over the string and the alignment line on your putter is underneath and parallel to the string. Then practice your putting stroke, trying to make the line on the putter blade stay parallel to the string. Think about the mechanical ideas you want to work on. But don't think about mechanics when you're actually putting a golf ball. Then you want to think only of the target.

Regardless of what putting drills a golfer uses, he should be certain, if he uses a ball and a cup, that he practices making putts. Practicing misses does no good. Yet I see lots of players standing 15 feet from the cup, missing nine out of ten practice putts. They may tell me that they don't get bothered by practice misses, that they're only putting for mechanics and pace, but their eyes see the misses and their minds record them.

So, work hard on putts from two to four feet. Make putt after putt. I sometimes ask players to make twenty-five in a row from that distance.

This is particularly important in the preround practice period. Putt to the fringe from every distance and angle until you are confident you can judge the pace of any putt you will encounter on the course. Then sink a few from short range, using your full putting routine.

Then go on to your long shots. If you find, as you warm up with longer shots, that you're hitting the ball well, you must believe that this is the way you will hit the ball once the round begins. If, on the other hand, you can't find your clubface as you warm up, you must believe that you're saving your good shots for the golf course.

Years ago, when I broached this idea to a group of touring players, Roger Maltbie raised his hand and said, "Wait a minute, Doc. You can't have it both ways. Either you play like you warm up or you don't."

I answered by asking what the goal was. The goal was to play well. That being the case, you have to have it both ways.

This is what Tom Kite did recently when he set the scoring record in the Bob Hope tournament out in Palm Springs. As he warmed up for the final round, he couldn't hit the ball very well at all, at least not by his standards. He reacted by making up his mind that his play on the course would be just the opposite of his play on the practice tee.

He had to do this. Otherwise, as I said to Roger Maltbie, his best option would have been to drop out of the tournament and go home.

YOU WILL CERTAINLY spend more time in the training mentality if you're taking lessons and trying to make changes in the way you swing. No one knows how long it takes an individual to learn a new physical technique—say, a new backswing plane—well enough so that it becomes a habit that repeats itself when he swings without thinking of mechanics. It depends in part on how ingrained the old habit was. It depends in part on how well the individual practices. Does he make the new move correctly each time he practices it? Certainly, if he hits every practice ball with a teacher present, giving him accurate feedback, he will incorporate the improvement that much faster.

Ideally, if you were trying to make a change in your swing, you would stop playing golf for a few weeks while you worked on the practice tee in the training mentality. You would know you had mastered the change when you could switch to the trusting mentality and count on the new swing to repeat itself reasonably well. Then you'd be ready to go back out on the course and play.

I know that this may be more than a lot of amateurs are prepared to do. They want to improve their swings, but they also want to play their regular Sunday morning matches with their friends. Their habit is to take sporadic lessons. Since they are sporadic, their pro may figure he's only got one hour to convey everything these pupils need to know. He overloads them with fixes for all the flaws in their swings.

The golfers then try to incorporate all those changes as they play. Almost inevitably, their scores initially go up, because they are out on the course thinking about their mechanics, particularly about the changes the pro has suggested. After a week or two of frustration, they often react by consciously or unconsciously forgetting about the new techniques and going back to what they have always done. Their scores drop back to their normal range, because they begin to trust their swings again. But they wind up roughly where they started. They make no progress.

A good golfer seeks help differently. David Frost, who never took a lesson until he was a scratch golfer, tells me that he mentally filters what he hears from any teacher he consults. "When I take a lesson," he says, "my teacher can say eight or ten things to me, and I'll be saying to myself, 'Nope. Nope. That's not it. Nope.' But one of those eight or ten things will appeal to me. I'll know it will help, and I'll incorporate it and play better."

Players without Frosty's knowledge of his own swing would be smart to let their pros know that they want to commit themselves to a long-term plan of regular lessons and improvement. The pro, if he's good, would respond by giving this kind of pupil no more than one change per lesson and one swing thought to help incorporate that change. The player would use that swing thought—but only on shots of more than 120 yards—until the new habit was ingrained. He would spend at least twelve hours on the practice range, working on the new move, before taking the next lesson. Then he would go on to the next change and a new swing thought. Over a year's time, any player would improve under this regimen. And eventually, he or she would acquire a fundamentally sound swing and could play without swing thoughts.

The particular swing mechanics a pro teaches matter much less than the confidence he or she engenders in the pupils. If you encounter a professional who conveys the idea that you don't have the talent to play well, drop him or her. You have to expect some awkwardness for a while as you try to master new movements. But if, after six months or so, you still feel awkward and still lack confidence, it may be time to consider switching teachers. Find a teacher who believes in you, who encourages and supports you, who makes certain you leave the lesson tee feeling better about your game than you did when you arrived.

In my experience, a model for all golf teachers is Bob Toski. He's a great player. He's also a trick-shot artist, a singer, a dancer and a raconteur. That's not why he's a great teacher. He's a great teacher because he believes in his students and will do whatever he has to do to help them improve.

I first met Bob when I started working with the staff of the week-long *Golf Digest* schools, adding a day or two of talks on the mental side of the game to the instruction on the swing that Toski and his colleagues gave. At one of the first of these collaborations, I arrived at about 3 A.M. on Thursday morning. As I walked wearily into my hotel room, I heard a voice from the next room:

"Rotella, get in here!"

It was Bob. He was sitting up in his king-sized bed, looking like a little pea against the pillows.

"I've been waiting for you. Sit down," he said. "We've got a seventy-eight-year-old lady with a thirty-five handicap here this week. I've been trying everything with her, and I can't get her to swing inside to out and draw the ball. Give me some ideas.

We have two days left to get her to do it. I won't be able to stand it if she doesn't."

Two things impressed me right away. The first was that Bob, a former PGA champion and tutor to some of the best professionals in the game, was willing to ask a twenty-eight-year-old sport psychologist to help him. His ego wasn't so big that he couldn't try to learn something from someone with perhaps one percent of his experience in the game. The second was his utter refusal to consider the possibility that this woman was beyond help.

We talked for two hours or so about various approaches that we could try with her. And by the end of the week, she did draw the ball. I trust that she happily hit draws to the end of her days and got her handicap under 30. I suspect, however, that I learned more from Bob Toski that week than she did.

This is the kind of attitude you should look for in a golf professional. When you find one with that attitude, stick with him or her. Don't spoil what he or she is trying to do by going to another teacher and perhaps getting different advice.

YOU CAN MAKE your head a practice range. There is a technique that uses the imagination to fool the mind and body into reacting as if what is in reality nerve-wracking is familiar, safe and comfortable. It's a form of daydreaming that is conscious and purposeful.

Sports psychology has adapted this technique from studies of two natural phenomena: nightmares and nocturnal orgasms. In both cases, nothing is really happening to the individual. He is merely dreaming, of something frightening in the case of nightmares, or of something sexually stimulating in the case of nocturnal emissions. But the dream causes a genuine physical reaction. The body stiffens and trembles with fear from a nightmare, just as it would stiffen and tremble if faced with a genuine fright. The sexually stimulating dream causes a real orgasm.

A golfer can mentally simulate the experience of reaching his goal, whether it be winning a tournament or breaking 100. If he does it vividly enough, he can in effect fool the mind and body into thinking that the experience actually happened. Later, when he actually comes close to that goal on the golf course, he will not experience discomfort or disorientation. He will instead have a sense of déjà vu, a comforting and calming feeling that he has been in this situation before and handled it successfully.

If a golfer tells me he wants to win the U.S. Open, I tell him to try to imagine that experience as vividly as he can. He needs to create, in his brain, all the sensory messages that would bombard him as he actually played the last holes of the Open, in contention to win. He needs to smell the grass and hear the murmur of the crowd. He needs to feel the tackiness of his grips, the way the sweat trickles down his forehead and the churning in his gut. He needs to see the way the rough pinches into the fairways, to see the television towers and to see, in his own mind, his golf ball soaring high against the blue sky and landing on the short grass. He needs to imagine something going wrong, to hear the way the crowd noise changes when a ball kicks into the sand, and to imagine himself taking a bogey but retaining his equilibrium. He needs to imagine hearing a roar from some other part of the course and to imagine his response to a competitor reeling off a string of birdies.

If a golfer tells me his goal is to break 90, I tell him to imagine himself on the way to shooting an 86. Like the professional striving to win the U.S. Open, he would try to simulate all the sensory experiences. He should imagine himself calmly refusing to get distracted when his buddies tell him after nine holes that he's on track to shoot in the eighties. He should imagine staying with his routine and game plan. He should see the shots he will play on all of the final holes, both good and bad.

This technique can be very helpful to professionals who have trouble maintaining a hot round. Sometimes a player finds that whenever he makes two or three birdies on the first few holes, he loses momentum. He can't use that good start as a springboard to a really low score. One reason is that he doesn't see himself as the kind of player who shoots 70, or 69 at best. When he gets to three under par, he unconsciously believes that he's reached his limit. He starts to look for something bad to happen. He plays defensively.

If this kind of golfer prepares his mind for shooting lower scores, he'll have an easier time staying focused and making even more birdies the next time he gets off to a quick start.

But the technique won't work if your approach to it is perfunctory, any more than you would trick your body into a fright reaction simply by saying to yourself, "Okay, there's a burglar coming through my bedroom window." You have to imagine in vivid detail, much as a novelist draws the reader into a setting by describing the sensory experiences of his characters.

Val Skinner used this technique just hours before she won in Atlanta in 1994. Because of rain delays, the players had to finish their Saturday rounds early Sunday morning. Val had several hours before she was supposed to tee off for the final round, in a group with Liselotte Neumann, the leader, and Judy Dickenson. She went back to her hotel and lay down. She imagined the way her round would go. She could see everything vividly, right down to the colors her opponents would wear. In her daydream round, she was thirteen under par. The holes had a vivid clarity. On one par-three, for instance, she imagined that she almost got a hole-in-one, but the ball lipped out of the cup and she had to settle for a birdie. Her daydream ended as she accepted the winner's check on the 18th green. Then she got up and went to the golf course.

She did not, of course, shoot thirteen under par. Nor did she almost make a hole-in-one. But she made up a two-stroke deficit and won the tournament. Her daydream, she thought, gave her a feeling of serenity that lasted throughout the round. So intently did she feel that she had won the tournament before she started her final round that when it came time to accept the winner's check, she felt a bit deflated. She had a sense that she had been there and done that.

In the evening, before your next important round, make a regular habit of lying down, closing your eyes, and trying this technique. It should help you. It certainly will be more pleasant than pacing around the room and worrying.

22.

What I Learned from Paul Runyan

A FEW YEARS ago, I was in Toronto to speak to a meeting of 800 teaching golf professionals. I followed Paul Runyan on the schedule.

Paul, who is in his eighties, stood up and began his talk by saying, "I must apologize to each and every one of you."

Every one of the pros came to attention.

"A year ago," Paul went on, "I spoke at your annual meeting and I told you I would work out forty-five to fifty minutes a day, without fail, every day of the year. I'm sorry to tell you that I got lazy two days last year and did not work out. I want you to know that I didn't live up to my commitment, and I promise you that it won't happen again this year."

Everyone in the audience looked startled. Some of them might have thought this was a rhetorical ploy of some kind.

But I knew that it wasn't. He was just telling them the truth about the way Paul Runyan lives his life and the way he honors his commitments.

Doing instructional schools for years with Paul has given me a chance to observe him. He gets up each morning at 5:30. He stretches, exercises, and goes for a substantial walk before breakfast. Then he eats something healthy—oatmeal, perhaps. He's basically a vegetarian.

He gets to the golf course by seven o'clock or so, an hour before the instructional school starts. He goes to the practice green and chips, pitches and putts for forty-five minutes or so. He can drop ten balls in the fringe around a green and get all of them into the hole in less than twenty strokes; he'll chip in more often than he'll fail to get up and down. Then he goes to the range and hits wedges for ten or fifteen minutes, followed by maybe four or five drivers. He's ready to teach.

He teaches until noon, when he goes home and has a light, healthy lunch with Bernice, his wife. Then he teaches again until 4:30. After that, he's likely to want to play nine holes, carrying his own bag. Paul's only concession to age is playing a two-piece ball. As an octogenarian, he's succumbed to the yen for distance that infects most golfers in their teens. His touch around the green is so acute that he can afford to give away the backspin and control most pros get from a balata ball.

After hours, Paul and Bernice still compete in fox-trot contests and cribbage tournaments. They embody an old Satchel Paige aphorism. Someone once asked Paige, the great African-American pitcher who was in his forties before segregation ended and he got to the big leagues, if he could still pitch at that advanced age.

"How old," Paige replied, "would you be if you didn't know how old you was?"

A firm, balanced commitment has been the hallmark of Paul Runyan's life. When he was fourteen or so, he competed in a golf tournament for the first time. He was short and scrawny, and most of the boys in the tournament could drive it 40 yards farther than he could. He reacted by deciding that he would develop a short game so good it would make up for his lack of distance. It did. In his prime, he won tournaments against the likes of Sam Snead, giving away 60 yards off the tee. He was so good around the greens that his nickname was "Little Poison."

Paul's example shows what commitment should mean, and commitment is the final component of a good golfing mentality. To play the best golf you can play, you have to make a healthy, balanced commitment to the game and to improvement.

SOMETIMES, WITH PROFESSIONALS, I find problems of overcommitment. A player is so intent on performing well that he starts to forget that trying harder is not always trying better. And he starts to forget that the game is supposed to be fun.

Mark McCumber, when I started working with him, needed to learn to relax a little. Mark was a fine golfer, but his desire to win and improve was starting to consume him. He was too tense and too serious about the game and life. And he knew it was not helping either his performance on the course or his relationships off it.

"None of us are going to get out of here alive," I told Mark. "You might as well have some fun while you're here."

He had to stop thinking so much about money and titles and start thinking again of golf as the game he just loved to play when he was a kid. He had to stop feeling guilty about easing up on himself a little. I told him that more often than not, good things come to people who stop trying to force them to happen. And good things have indeed come to Mark. He won three times in 1994.

I don't advise people to commit their lives completely and exclusively to golf. That would be like deciding to eat only cookies. It would be bad nutrition. And it would soon spoil your taste for cookies.

This issue arises sometimes when the parents of a youngster ask me for advice. Their child is tearing up the juniors. Her dream is to make millions on the LPGA Tour. So, she reasons, why does she need to study? She should spend all her time honing her golf game.

Well, she needs to study. She could sprain her back getting out of bed some morning and have nothing but her education to support her. Or she could just decide at the age of twenty-two that she's tired of golf and wants to do something else with her life. Studying requires discipline and concentration, two qualities important to anyone.

Some parents, though, are concerned about their child's golf dreams for another reason. They know the odds against success. They want to shield her from disappointment and failure.

I tell them not to worry. Certainly, if a child dreams about becoming a professional golfer, she will encounter disappointment and failure along the way. But why worry about that? People develop pride and find satisfaction, not from doing things that are easy, but from trying things that are difficult, that most people don't even dare to aspire to. I never tell a youngster or anyone else to put aside a dream. Suppose Nick Price had given up on his dreams in 1990, after six winless years? If you give up your dreams, you'll never know if everything might have fallen into place the next week.

The answer for anyone, of any age, who is propelled by a

dream is a balanced commitment. No one should spend all of his time chasing the dream of becoming a great golfer. But during those hours that he sets aside each day to pursue that dream, he has to give golf his undivided attention and energy. And he has to put those hours in every day, regardless of heat, humidity, cold and wind. He has to put them in on the days when he seems stalled on an infinite plateau as well as on days when he feels the gratification of noticeable improvement.

And he needs to realize that commitment need not warp his personality and behavior. Sometimes golfers think they're supposed to be angry and depressed if they have a bad round or a bad tournament. They've been taught that the proper reaction to this kind of misfortune is to get mad and go to the practice tee and beat balls until it gets dark. Then they think they're supposed to brood about their mistakes all night. They think this shows they're committed to the game.

That's not the kind of commitment I'm talking about. For one thing, to flourish on the Tour, a golfer needs the support of friends and family, if not of a spouse. If she wants that, it behooves her to show that she can be an enjoyable human being regardless of what happens on the course.

Some golfers think they should be committed to somehow mastering the game and keeping it in the palm of their hand, as if it were a car or a piece of property that they could own. They can't. They have to recognize that there will be times when they hit the ball beautifully and times when they hit it abominably. And they have to understand that even at their best, they will not come close to mastering the game. Nick Price, as well as he was playing in 1993 or 1994, was perhaps reaching six on a scale of ten, with ten being perfection.

• • •

ON THE OTHER hand, I sometimes run into people who think they can become scratch golfers without making a commitment.

They can't. And I take pride in never saying "can't"!

If you haven't been thinking properly on the golf course, just reading this book and adopting its suggestions can help you. If you have a handicap of 25 and you make up your mind that, henceforth, you will trust your swing when you're on the course, you will follow a sound routine and you will learn to accept your results without getting angry, you can make a quick and noticeable improvement in your scores. You might, for instance, lower your handicap over a summer from 25 to 15 by learning to think well.

But if you want to become a low-handicap golfer, it's not going to be enough simply to read this book, or any other book. You have to make a long-term improvement plan and a commitment more like the one Paul Runyan made. Your plan should include how many times a week you will practice, what you will work on, and for how long. It should include lots of time for short-game practice. Then you must execute that plan.

If someone tells me that he wants to lower his handicap to 5 but he can't find time to practice, I can only tell him that people who consistently play in the mid-70s generally do find time to practice. They get out a few evenings a week after work to hit balls, chip and putt. Or they get to a course early in the morning. They find time at home to work on grip, posture and alignment. They spend a few moments every day visualizing their routines. Most important, they never waste practice time mindlessly hitting balls. They practice with a purpose.

If you want to become a low-handicap golfer, you have to remember what I told Nick Price, Tom Kite, Pat Bradley, and many others about free will. You have the power to make choices. You have the power to think in ways that will help your game. You have the power to make a commitment and keep it.

The happiest people have a sense of commitment in everything they do, whether it's playing golf, running a restaurant or selling hardware. They approach their undertakings with passion.

Golf can give you this happiness whether it's your profession or your hobby. It doesn't matter if you never win a tournament. Golf will challenge you, will give you a chance to test yourself. If you take the ability you have and do the best you can with it, you'll be happy.

No matter what happens, you will find wonderful people who love golf and will be happy to share your commitment with you. They are part of the game's rewards.

In the end, you will realize that you love golf because of what it teaches you about yourself.

Appendix

ROTELLA'S RULES

- A person with great dreams can achieve great things.

- People by and large become what they think about themselves.

- Golfing potential depends primarily on attitude, skill with the wedges and the putter, and how well a golfer thinks. Great golfers are simply ordinary people thinking well and doing extraordinary deeds.

- Free will is a golfer's greatest source of strength and power. Choosing how to think is a crucial decision.

- Golfers who realize their potential generally cultivate the three D's—desire, determination and discipline; the three P's—persistence, patience and practice; and the three C's—confidence, concentration and composure.

- There is no such thing as a golfer playing over his head. A hot streak is simply a glimpse of a golfer's true potential.

- A golfer must train herself in physical technique and then learn to trust what she's trained.

- Before playing any shot, a golfer must lock her eyes and mind into the smallest possible target.

- To score consistently, a golfer must think consistently. A sound, consistent pre-shot routine makes it easier.

- The correlation between thinking well and making successful shots is not 100 percent. But the correlation between thinking badly and unsuccessful shots is much higher.

- Golfers must learn to quiet their minds, stay in the present, and focus tightly on the next shot to be played.

- The loss of focus on four or five shots a round makes the difference between great golf and mediocre golf.

- A golfer must learn to enjoy the process of striving to improve the short game.

- Attitude makes a great putter.

- As ball-striking skills improve, it becomes a greater challenge to love putting and the short game and to maintain a positive attitude toward them.

- It is more important to be decisive than to be correct when preparing to play any golf shot, particularly a putt.

- Confidence is crucial to good golf. Confidence is simply the aggregate of the thoughts you have about yourself.

- A golfer cannot let the first few holes, shots, or putts determine his thinking for the rest of the round.

- A golfer should strive to be looser, freer, and more confident with every hole. This will combat the tendency to get tighter, more careful, and more doubtful.

- Being careful, tightening up, and trying to steer the ball will likely cause disaster. Good golfers gain control over the ball by feeling that they are giving up control.

- Golfers need selective memories, retaining the memory of great shots and forgetting bad ones. Selective memory helps a golfer grow in confidence as he gains experience and skill.

- Golf is a game played by human beings. Therefore, it is a game of mistakes. Successful golfers know how to respond to mistakes.

- Golfers must learn to love the challenge when they hit a ball into the rough, trees, or sand. The alternatives—anger, fear, whining, and cheating—do no good.

- Patience is a cardinal virtue in golf. To improve, a golfer must learn how to wait for practice and good thinking to bear fruit.

- At night, a golfer can program her mind with great expectations. But she must throw them away when she steps onto the first tee.

- On the first tee, a golfer must expect only two things of himself: to have fun, and to focus his mind properly on every shot.

- Players with great attitudes constantly monitor their thinking and catch themselves as soon as it begins to falter.

- A good competitor never allows herself to intensely dislike another player. She might be paired with her for an important round.

- The quality of a golfer's practice is more important than the quantity, particularly for better golfers.

- If a golfer chooses to compete, he must choose to believe that he can win. Winners and losers in life are completely self-determined, but only the winners are willing to admit it.

- Courage is a necessary quality in all champions. But an athlete cannot be courageous without first being afraid.

- In sport, the bad news for the present champion is that tomorrow is a new day, when the competition starts again from scratch. But that's the good news for everyone else.

- On the course, golfers must have the confidence of a champion. But off the course, champions must remember that they are not more important than anyone else.

Acknowledgments

I HAVE BEEN BLESSED WITH A LOT OF PEOPLE TO THANK.

I've had the opportunity to associate with many of the greatest golfers and golf teachers of this era. Most of them are mentioned in the text of this book. I want to thank them all. Without their contributions, my work would be a laboratory exercise.

Three players in particular—Tom Kite, Brad Faxon, and Val Skinner—took extra time to share thoughts and experiences that make this a more informative book, and I am grateful to them.

I also want to thank Dr. Bruce Gansneder for his hours of tireless help with golf psychology research over a period of many years.

I owe great debts as well to my father, Guido Rotella, and to my brothers, Drs. Jay and Guy Rotella, for hours of listening and discussion. Each of them read the manuscript and made valuable suggestions.

I also wish to thank Tony Carroll, Steve Grant, Bruce Stewart, and Rod Thompson, all of whom read this as a work in progress and contributed questions and ideas for its improvement.

I am grateful to Bob Carney and Andy Nusbaum for their encouragement over the years. Dominick Anfuso at Simon & Schuster and Rafe Sagalyn, my literary agent, helped conceive the book and helped me find Bob Cullen as a collaborator. My special thanks go to them.

Also by Dr Bob Rotella

Golf Is Not a Game of Perfect
Golf Is a Game of Confidence
Putting Out of Your Mind
Life Is Not A Game of Perfect

THE GOLF OF YOUR DREAMS

BY DR BOB ROTELLA
WITH BOB CULLEN

POCKET BOOKS

LONDON • SYDNEY • NEW YORK • TORONTO

This edition first published by Pocket Books, 2005
An imprint of Simon & Schuster UK Ltd
A Viacom Company

Copyright © Robert J. Rotella, 1995

This book is copyright under the Berne Convention.
No reproduction without permission.
All rights reserved.

The right of Robert J. Rotella to be identified as the author of this work has been asserted by him in accordance with sections 77 and 78 of the Copyright, Designs and Patents Act, 1988.

1 3 5 7 9 10 8 6 4 2

Simon & Schuster UK Ltd
Africa House
64–78 Kingsway
London WC2B 6AH

www.simonsays.co.uk

Simon & Schuster Australia
Sydney

A CIP catalogue record for this book is available from the British Library

ISBN 1-4165-0200-9

Printed and bound in Great Britain by
Bookmarque Ltd, Croydon, Surrey

To Mom and Dad,

for being the best

Contents

Introduction 9

1. The Golf of your Dreams, and Why Few Attain It 17

2. Picking a Pro 29

3. Getting Committed 47

4. The Hard Part 59

5. The Improvement Cycle 73

6. A Playing Lesson from Bob Toski 85

7. One Stroke at a Time 99

8. The Psychology of a Swing Change 113

9. Bonefishing and Other Distractions 127

10. The Psychology of Practice 133

11. When You Need Another Teacher 149

12. Parents and Children 159

13. The Money Factor 169

14. The Discipline You'll Need 173

15. A Philosophy of Golf and Life 181

Appendix A: Rotella's Rules 189

Appendix B: Your Improvement Program 193

Acknowledgments 203

INTRODUCTION

Of all the statistics kept by the United States Golf Association, the most sobering are these: Fifteen years ago, the average American male golfer's handicap index was 16.2. The average woman's was 29. As I write this, the average American male golfer's handicap is 16.2. The average woman's is 29.

In those fifteen years, golf has seen the introduction of drivers with big heads fashioned from metals once used for rocket ships. They promised to make the ball go further. Golf has seen the advent of perimeter-weighted, game-improvement irons. They promised to make the ball go straighter. It's seen new putters with long shafts that promised steadiness and plastic-blade inserts that promised feel. Every week, it seems, golf has seen the introduction of a new longest ball that promised to shatter windows miles from the golf course.

In those fifteen years, computers and videos have come along to enhance our understanding of the golf swing. They're available not just to touring pros and their swing experts; you have to travel pretty far into the country nowadays to find a driving range that doesn't have a video camera to tape your swing, and a software program that will compare it to Nick Faldo's.

The statistics don't lie: Despite all the billions of dollars they have spent on new clubs and balls, despite all the lessons they have taken, American golfers have not, by and large, gotten any better.

I've played and coached many sports. I got my first taste of how people learn new skills when I was an undergraduate and taught mentally handicapped children how to swim and tumble at the Brandon Training School. While in graduate school, I coached high school basketball and college lacrosse. Since getting my doctorate in sports psychology, I've spent more than two decades helping football teams, baseball teams, and basketball teams. I've helped equestrians, skiers, stock-car drivers, and tennis players.

One thing I've learned is that no other sport would tolerate the stagnant skills that golf tolerates. If a pro-football owner invested heavily in his team and saw no improvement over fifteen years, he'd fire the coach, get new players, or both. But golf is peculiar. There are no owners insisting on performance. Every player is his own master. Teaching professionals, the coaches of the sport, are often judged more on the basis of how smoothly they run the annual member–guest tournament than on how they improve, or fail to improve, the quality of play at their clubs.

I often speak to groups of PGA teaching pros. When I do, I sometimes ask how many of them know more about the golf swing now than they did at the age of 16. Almost everyone raises his hand. Then I ask how many of them are more confident now than they were at 16 that they can drive a ball down the middle of a tight fairway with a match on the line. Very few raise their hands.

It's symptomatic, I think, of the way that the golf-teaching profession has gotten a bit lost. Somehow, the teaching of the golf swing has supplanted the teaching of golf. It's as if a football coach taught his quarterbacks to throw perfect spirals, but not to pick out receivers, analyze defenses, and pass for touchdowns. The team would lose. The coach would either be fired or he'd change the way he coached his quarterbacks.

If the pro at your course faced similar pressure, if he were paid on the basis of how well your club did in interclub matches, I suspect he would begin to change the way he taught. I suspect he'd do whatever he could to change the approach his members took to lessons and improvement.

If the members' livelihoods depended on how well they played, I suspect they'd welcome the change.

But as it stands, the system in golf is all but designed to evade the truth about improving golf performance.

This book will give you that truth. My previous two books, *Golf Is Not a Game of Perfect* and *Golf Is a Game of Confidence,* covered the mental aspects of the game. This book will tell you what you need to know to develop all facets of the game.

It will not, in and of itself, make you a better golfer. It will not teach you how to swing the driver or how to putt. If you read it on a Friday night, you will not go out to the course on Saturday morning any more capable than you were the previous Saturday.

But reading this book will make you aware of what you have to do to play the golf you've always sensed you were capable of playing.

The fact is that you can't make the journey from average player to scratch player in an armchair. You can't do it by reading books, and you can't do it by watching videos. You can't do it by going to the pro shop and buying new equipment and new balls. You can't do it by spending a few days in a sunny clime at a golf school, nor can you do it simply by spending more time practicing and playing. There are no quick fixes, no secrets.

But you can do it.

The good news about golf is that great physical ability is not required to play well. You don't need the height, weight, or speed specifications they look for in the National Football League. In fact, I'm convinced that the vast majority of the population has the physical talent necessary to play golf at scratch or close to it. I'm not promising that you can become a tour player regardless of your age and ability. I am promising that you can improve dramatically if you're willing to put in intelligent effort, substantial time, and diligent practice. You can start to play a kind of golf that feels simple, effortless, and fun.

In fact, I dare you to follow the program outlined in this book for three years and not make great progress.

What you need, first, is the right attitude. All the great coaches have understood this. They develop players and teams by demanding and nurturing characteristics like desire, patience, and persistence. These characteristics, more than physical talent, enable athletes in any sport to improve their performance.

If you doubt it, look at basketball. The playgrounds and minor leagues are full of guys with springs in their legs and fancy dunk moves. There is only one Michael Jordan. He is very talented, but what sets him apart is his attitude toward improving himself. Michael Jordan is committed to a plan. He lifts weights to improve his strength and avoid injury. He stretches. He watches what he eats. He practices two or three hours a day. And he does these things consistently. He is prepared to do whatever is necessary to keep himself and his game in shape.

Jordan involuntarily proved this in the spring of 1995, when he came back to the NBA after a fling at baseball. It was obvious to all that his skills had deteriorated due to lack of practice. Without the time he needed to hone his game and his body, he was just another player. His raw talent alone couldn't carry the Bulls. But the next season, after he had given himself time to return to his self-improvement plan, he was again invincible.

I see the same principle at work in golf. Nick Faldo has been one of the best players of the past decade. It's not because he is supremely talented. It's because he has spent 12 years with the same teacher, taking the same approach to the golf swing. His intense desire and his commitment to that program have made him great.

The minitours in Florida are full of players who are supremely talented. They can all hit the ball over the fence at the end of the range. What they frequently lack, what separates them from great golfers like Faldo, are the same attributes that separate Michael Jordan from the rest of the NBA: desire, commitment, and persistence.

If you have desire, commitment, and persistence, you have the prerequisites for improved golf. You can be a scratch player or close enough to it that you will have a marvelous time seeing how good you can get.

This book is like a map of the route from New York to Los Angeles. The map doesn't carry you there. It shows you how to direct your own efforts. Similarly, this book shows you the path that leads from average golf to excellence.

Whether you make the journey is up to you.

Chapter 1

The Golf of Your Dreams, and Why Few Attain It

I have no quarrel with someone who wants to play indifferent golf.

Millions of people want to play a round of golf once or twice a month. They want to enjoy the fresh air, the sunshine, and the company. They don't want to practice or take lessons, and they may have valid reasons. Perhaps young children demand most of their time and energy. Perhaps their careers demand seventy hours a week. They may just not care very much how well they play golf. That's fine, as long as they understand the limitations they place on themselves, and admit they don't want to play as well as they can, at least not now. If this makes them happy, they're welcome to play their way.

This book isn't written for them.

This book is for the golfer who's stopped being indifferent, the golfer who puts or is ready to put a lot of time and energy into the game, the golfer who's puzzled and frustrated that his time and energy don't produce lower scores. It's written for the golfer who is determined to get better, but hasn't figured out how to go about it.

The fact is that improving your golf is more difficult than, say, improving your cycling. Once you've learned to ride a bicycle, your improvement in speed and endurance will correlate more or less directly with the time and effort you put into training. But with golf, time and effort are not sufficient. The quality and intelligence of the effort you put in are more important than the quantity. What I see as I travel around the country playing golf, consulting with players, and holding clinics, is that most amateurs unintentionally undermine the quality of the effort they put into the improvement of their games. They do so in many ways.

Some players have convinced themselves that talent determines who becomes good at golf, and that they don't have that talent. I'm not going to say that talent doesn't exist. I've seen a few players who have never practiced take to the game so naturally that they got to scratch, or very close to it, with little or no effort. On the other end of the spectrum, I've seen a few people who took up the game as adults, having never done anything athletic in their lives. They can improve, but usually slowly and gradually.

These people, though, are the exceptions, a small percent

of the total population. The vast majority of golfers falls in between. They have the talent required to play well. But their talent must be developed properly.

A lot of golfers don't want to know this. It's more comfortable for them to think that lack of talent limits their potential. They spend a lot of time at golf without getting better, but they can blame their mediocre play on God, on their genes—on anything besides themselves.

This is a universal human tendency. I have a friend who does business in Russia. He decided that his work would be more successful if he spoke Russian, so he took Russian language courses and worked with tutors. For several years, he carried index cards in his jacket pocket with Russian words written on one side and the English equivalents on the other. Whenever he had a few minutes, he'd pull out the cards and study them. After a long while and a lot of practice, he learned to speak pretty good Russian.

But when he meets people who discover that he speaks Russian, the most frequent response he hears is, "You must have an ear for languages. I don't. I have a tin ear."

People would rather believe in tin ears than acknowledge that the reason they don't speak Russian is that they didn't put in the hours of study and practice.

The problem with this is that, as the pioneering American psychologist William James realized long ago, people tend to become what they think of themselves. If you're going to get better at golf, at speaking Russian, or at anything else that requires disciplined effort, you must first think of yourself as capable of doing so. You must believe that you have the talent to succeed.

A friend of mine, Robert Willis, recently sent me a videotape of a golfer named Mike Carver playing nine holes on a course in Grenada, Mississippi. Carver shot 35, or even par. The remarkable thing about the tape was not the score, although it was very impressive to see a player being videotaped for the first time sink a 15-foot birdie putt on the last hole to come in at even par.

The remarkable thing was Carver himself. He was born with a right arm that ends just below the bicep. He has only three fingers on his left hand and his left wrist is fused. His right leg ends just above the knee; he wears a prosthesis. His left ankle is fused.

When he plays golf, Mike puts the club in his left hand and addresses the ball with his hand way out in front of the clubhead. He takes the club back with his left arm, rests it briefly on the stump of his right arm, then swings through the ball one-handed. He steps through as he shifts his weight, à la Gary Player. Then he hobbles off and hits it again. He usually hits a nice, controlled draw, and he can produce about two-hundred yards of distance.

His short game enables him to shoot around par. He takes a practice swing, then lets the chip go, and he almost always makes crisp contact. His nickname is Stoney because he so often chips it up stone dead.

At the end of the tape, Mike is seen putting his clubs into

his car, which has the vanity tag "Stoney 2," but no handicapped sticker. Mike, it turns out, doesn't want one. He doesn't see himself as handicapped.

And that's why Mike Carver can play par golf. He reminds me of one of the insights that John Wooden contributed to sport: "Don't let the things you can't do stand in the way of things you can do." Most people, looking at him, would think him not just lacking talent, but severely handicapped. That is not the way Mike sees himself. He thinks he's got talent. He thinks he can be an excellent golfer. And that belief, coupled with patient practice, has made him one.

Without that belief, without faith that you can become an excellent player, you won't have the motivation required to stick with it when progress is slow. And, in learning golf, there will be times when progress is not just slow but nonexistent. There will be times when you seem to be going backwards.

This fact relegates another large group of dedicated golfers to perpetual mediocrity. They may believe they have the talent to improve. They may take a lesson or two with good intentions. But then their pros tell them they must change their grip or their backswing. They feel very uncomfortable with the change at first; quite frequently, they can barely make contact with the ball. But they won't work on the change to make it feel comfortable and natural. They don't accept the fact that this will take time. And they don't let anything deter them from playing their usual tooth-and-toenail two-dollar nassau on Saturday morning.

Along about the twelfth hole, they're five down, they've just hit two poor shots, and another press is looming. Suddenly they're not very enthused about the process of improvement. Maybe they abandon the new grip or the new backswing then and there. Or maybe they stick with it for the rest of the round, fork over their lost bets, and go to the locker room grousing about how the damned pro has ruined their (15-handicap) games. They talk themselves into believing this, they stop taking lessons, and they finish the season just about where they started. The only thing they got from their lessons was, perhaps, a couple of high scores that bumped their handicaps up a few notches and allowed them to win back some of the money they lost. They are too concerned with short-term results to persist in a long-term process.

Yet another group of nonimprovers subscribes to Ben Hogan's maxim that the golf swing is in the ground and a golfer just has to dig it out. They want to teach themselves how to play the game, and they're prepared to hit thousands of practice balls to do it. This is not impossible. It's true that Hogan and some other great players essentially taught themselves. But keep two things in mind: You never heard of all the lousy players who tried Hogan's learning method and found that all they accomplished was to ingrain a bad swing. And, you didn't, if you were a golf fan, hear much about

Hogan until he was in his 30s. He took up the game as a caddie when he was about eleven years old. It took him more than twenty years of constant effort to build a swing that he could rely on.

On the other hand, look at the examples of the other two main contenders for the title of greatest American golfer: Bobby Jones and Jack Nicklaus. Each of them had a teacher who helped him learn the game and remained his mentor well into adulthood—Stewart Maiden in Jones's case and Jack Grout in Nicklaus's. Both Jones and Nicklaus were contending for national championhips while still in their teens. Each won a U.S. Open in his early twenties.

So, while I may admire the persistence and dedication of the ball-beating golfers down at the end of the range who are trying to teach themselves the game, I would say that the evidence suggests their method is neither the most effective nor the most reliable. A good teacher will save you time. He'll help pull you out of troughs of discouragement. He'll stop you before you can let mistakes become habits.

Even the best of athletes have realized this. I was recently at East Lake Golf Club in Atlanta, where Bob Jones learned the game. In the locker room, there's a picture of Babe Ruth playing golf. The caption quotes him as saying that to play golf well, you need good coaching.

Babe Ruth epitomized the natural athlete. And even he didn't think he could learn the game by digging it out of the ground.

There is a mistake worse than trying to learn on your

own. I'm thinking of the players who flit from teacher to teacher and tip to tip. These are the golfers who read all the magazines and devoutly watch the swing tips on the golf telecasts. Unfortunately, the backswing tip they see on television probably isn't appropriate for the grip they read about in the magazine, and neither of them may be applicable to their particular swing.

They compound the problem if they go from one pro to another, taking a lesson here and a lesson there. Confronted with a pupil he knows he may see only once, the typical golf pro will try to apply a Band-Aid that will help the golfer get through his next round somewhat less likely to hit a ball out of bounds. He won't—he can't—fix the fundamental problems in one lesson. He feels no responsibility for the way such a pupil plays.

Pretty soon, the golfer who wanders from teacher to teacher has a game that's all Band-Aids, which is to say a game that doesn't hold up. His mind is cluttered with different swing theories. He's the kind of person who can chatter impressively about Pro A's latest article on the one-piece takeaway, about Pro B's follow-through, and Pro C's ideas on the position of the hands through the impact zone. Most likely, he adds to the mix a suggestion from his buddy, Player D, who's never broken 80 in his life. One from Column A, one from Column B, one from Column C, and one from Column D may work out fine in a Chinese restaurant, but it doesn't work in golf. Put a club in this player's hands and he looks like a pretzel maker with fleas in his pants, but he loves to chatter about swing theories.

Then there are players whose mental game, or lack of it, limits their ability to improve. Now, I'm a sport psychologist, and the mental game is what I teach. But I'm not going to tell you that golf is played strictly between the ears. Golf is a game of body and mind. You can't play it unless you can swing the club. You can't play it well unless you have a reasonably consistent, repeating swing; unless you can play wedge shots; unless you can putt. However, the mental game is important. In the upper-handicap ranges, I've seen players go from handicaps of about twenty to handicaps of twelve or thirteen just by improving their mental games. In the lower-handicap ranges, the difference between a scratch player and one who plays to a two or three is very often not a matter of ability to swing the club. It's a matter of recognizing the right shots to hit in certain situations, of picking the right targets, of maintaining composure throughout a round. Those are all aspects of the mental game.

The most common shortcoming in the mental area is a failure to appreciate and develop the short game. If you've read *Golf Is Not a Game of Perfect* or *Golf Is a Game of Confidence,* you already know the facts of life as they pertain to the short game. In brief, they are these: The great majority, perhaps two-thirds, of all shots are played from within one-hundred yards of the hole. No one, not even the best players on tour, has refined the full swing to the point where he averages hitting more than 13 or so of the greens he plays in regulation figures. The scoring payoff for a great putt or a great wedge shot is far greater than the payoff for a great drive. These are not secrets. They've been known for generations, and my books are hardly the only source of this information.

Nevertheless there are legions of players who, if they practice at all, spend far more time practicing drivers and five-irons than they do wedges. If you confront this kind of player with the facts about the importance of the short game, he may well agree. However, he is likely to say that he wants to perfect his full swing before he turns to the short game. This is rather like a college kid who declines to date any of the women on campus because he expects someday to meet and woo Cindy Crawford. He might be praised for setting lofty goals, but he is not likely to have much of a social life.

A golfer who wants to perfect his swing before addressing his short game is trying to turn golf into a game of perfection, which it can never be. He doesn't really like golf as it is—a game of imperfect swings redeemed by good chips, pitches, and putts. He will lie on his deathbed someday, wondering when his swing is finally going to come around.

There's one final category of frustrated hackers—those whose deficient mental games sabotage their efforts on the course. They don't have consistent preshot routines; consequently, they don't hit consistent shots. They can't accept that golf is a game of mistakes, and they regularly lose their composure after hitting a bad shot, turning bogies into double and triple bogies.

If you fall into one of these categories, you should now have an idea of why your golf game has failed to improve. And, if you have reasonable powers of deduction, you've probably already started to understand what's required if you want to play the golf of your dreams.

First, you have to admit to yourself that you want to be good and that you have the talent to play well. Second, you must commit yourself to a process that will, over time, improve your game. You will need patience. You will need perseverance. But you can improve. Maybe you can get to scratch; maybe you'll only get to the respectable single digits. I don't guarantee what your final number will be, and you should stop trying to predict how far your talent will take you. I *can* guarantee that if you fall in love with the process of improvement, you'll find out how good you can get.

I recently played a round with Ivan Lendl, the tennis great, that reminded me of how satisfying the process of improvement can be. Ivan doesn't play competitive tennis any more. He's devoting much of his time to seeing how good he can become at golf. This is a man who's won major championships and millions of dollars. He has all the fame and glory anyone could want, and he has the means to choose whatever he wants to do with his life. He chooses to try to get better at golf. What he learned from tennis and is applying to golf is what's applicable to you:

The satisfaction is in the striving.

If you think about it, you'll realize that getting good at golf is not so different from getting good at anything else that's complex, difficult, and rewarding.

Suppose you're a lawyer, and a good one. You didn't start out that way. You started out, in fact, when you were a child and learned to read and write. Slowly, you assembled the skills a lawyer needs. In high school, perhaps, you were on the debate team and learned to present an oral argument. In college, you picked up research skills and people skills. In law school, you took all those fundamental skills and added specialized legal training. Finally, having passed the bar, you entered a firm and worked under a partner as an associate, observing how he or she conducted business.

Along the way, your confidence in your vision grew. You developed a firm belief that you could be a successful lawyer, which helped see you through all the tedious nights of study.

And, though you did the work yourself, all along the way you had mentors who helped you learn more quickly and more thoroughly than you could have on your own.

Golf is the same way. It helps to have a mentor.

CHAPTER 2

Picking a Pro

How do you find a mentor?

You start as you would if you were looking for a doctor to perform elective surgery. You would not walk into a hospital and ask the first person with a stethoscope to cut you open. You would probably try to gather some intelligence first. Who is reputed to be the best surgeon in the field in which you're interested? Once you had a few surgeons' names, you might try to talk to some of their former patients to see if they were satisfied with the results of their surgeries. You might narrow the list of candidates down to two or three, and go to see each of them, trying to get a feel for their methods, their fees, and their personalities. Then you'd pick one.

You can do some of the same intelligence gathering about golf pros. Who in your area has helped some players along the road you want to travel? If you know someone who started with a handicap close to your present level who has dropped to a handicap you'd like to have, ask that person. Who helped him get where he is now?

You generally don't have to be a member of a particular club to take lessons from the pro at that club. Most pros are permitted to give lessons to nonmembers. Nor do you have to take your lessons from the pro at your own club. If you don't feel the pro at your own course is right for you, don't be embarrassed about it. It's his job to sell himself to you.

All other things being equal, there are benefits to working with someone who teaches at the course or range where you intend to practice. This pro is likely to see you much more often than someone you visit a couple of times a month to take a lesson. Even when you're not taking a formal lesson, he'll see what you're doing on the practice range. He might be able to correct a flaw quickly, before it becomes a habit. It will be easier to arrange playing lessons with him.

But proximity and convenience are not as important as your trust that this is the person who can teach you what you need to know to improve. If it requires a little commuting to find someone in whom you can place such trust, be prepared to do the commuting.

Once you have narrowed your list to two or three pros, talk to each of them. Too many golfers fail to do this. They schedule a lesson instead. They show up at the lesson tee, club in hand. They start talking about swing mechanics without ever getting to know the teacher, or letting the teacher get to know them. The process should be more like the way colleges recruit athletes, with each party sizing the other up and talking things over. Don't feel as if you're the supplicant here. A good pro should be eager to get pupils who want to make the commitment you're prepared to make.

Tell each of the pros you call that you're looking for a teacher who can help you play the kind of golf you want to play. Tell her you're willing to put in the time, effort and energy to do it. See how she responds to that. Remember, you're looking for someone who is comfortable teaching players at your level and bringing them lower. There are some teachers who really don't like to work with average golfers. Ask the pro if this describes her. Ask her what her teaching philosophy is. Ask about her rates. Ask whether she intends to stay in the area or might move on. Ask how frequently she'd be able to see you and how much she'd expect you to practice between lessons. Ask if she believes that a person of your age and ability can get to scratch or whatever your dream is. Ask what she thinks it will take to get there.

Remember that a teacher's expectations can have a major influence on a pupil's performance. This has been demonstrated in studies of elementary-school pupils. Teachers in these studies were told that one-half their class had high IQs and one-half had low IQs. They were given the names of the supposed smart kids and the supposed dullards. In reality, the two groups the teachers were given were selected randomly. Each had some smart kids and some not-so-smart kids. By at the end of the year, the experimental premise had become a self-fulfilling prophecy. The kids the teachers thought had high IQs were doing better than the kids the teachers thought had low IQs. The studies showed that teachers taught differently, and better, when they expected a lot from their students. This is called the Pygmalion Effect.

Golf pros are subject to the Pygmalion Effect, too. A pro who thinks you can get to scratch will teach you the things a scratch player needs to know. He'll take the time to correct fundamental flaws rather than applying Band-Aids. He'll teach you the short-game skills and the course-management skills you'll need. Obviously, no reasonable pro is going to tell you the first time he sees you that he's certain you can become a scratch golfer. He'll need to evaluate your skills, your work habits, and your dedication before he can evaluate your potential. But during your first talk and first couple of lessons, you ought to be assessing the pro's attitude and enthusiasm. If he seems pessimistic, if he conveys a belief that you really can't improve, then you ought to look for another teacher. The process of improvement is a long and difficult one. You'll be more likely to stick with it if you know that your teacher believes you can do it.

You'll notice that I have not suggested that you must go to the most exclusive club in your area, or to a resort where the pro is world famous and charges hundreds of dollars per hour for lessons. Top-flight clubs often have excellent teaching pros. Some of the teaching pros with grand reputations, have in fact earned those reputations and deserve every dollar they charge. But a good pro is where you find him and he's not necessarily expensive.

To take a golf lesson from Gene Hilen, you drive out Highway 60 from the center of Frankfort, Kentucky, pass a couple of roadhouses and a filling station, and turn into a city park called Juniper Hills. You pass a swimming pool and some picnic tables, and park your car by the little brick pro shop. You enter through a glass door with a sign, required by law, that says you can't carry a concealed weapon in a city facility.

Not that concealed weapons are really a problem at Juniper Hills. In all the years Gene Hilen's been the pro there, he's seen only one man pull a gun, and he was not a golfer. He was a fellow from the countryside who was upset because his woman had taken up with someone who was playing in a tournament at Juniper Hills, and he figured if he caught them on the course, he could shoot them both.

Gene handled it. He gave the gunman a version of The Gene Hilen Egomania Treatment—soothing, flattering words that make a man feel confident he can iron out the kinks in his golf swing or, in this case, his love life. Pretty soon, the man gave up the gun and got down on his knees with Gene on the floor of the pro shop and prayed for guidance. In the end, Gene helped effect a reconciliation.

But, normally, all you'll see when you walk through the glass door is a bunch of guys playing nickel-dime card games at a table in the corner, some hats and shirts and clubs and balls on sale, and a friendly lady behind the cash register taking the ten-dollar greens fee, which seems to be a tremendous bargain. Juniper Hills is a wide-open, fairly short, municipal golf course, but the turf is thick and the greens are inverted saucers, just like on a Donald Ross course. When the local pros play in the Governor's Cup that Gene runs there each September, a couple of rounds in the mid-60s are usually good enough to win.

On busy mornings, you might find Gene next to a microphone helping to call players to the first tee. If it's Sunday, he sings "Amazing Grace" a capella just before the first group goes off. Other times, you might hear his amplified voice announcing, "That was the worst shot I ever saw. Take a mulligan."

On a weekday, you're more likely to find Gene on his lesson tee. Juniper Hills has no practice range, but there is a little strip of ground between the first and eighteenth fairways. At the top of it, under a tree, Gene has a couple of patches of Astroturf with a mechanical contraption that feeds balls to the rubber tee. He's 61 years old now, and he doesn't like to bend over to tee balls for his pupils the way he once did. He's got an old truck tire that he uses for an impact bag when he wants to show someone the proper position of the hands when the club hits the ball. But that's about as high tech as Gene gets. There are no video cameras, no computers.

If you take a lesson from Gene, the first thing he might ask you to do is throw a golf ball as though you were skipping a rock on a pond. That's something he learned to associate with golf nearly half a century ago. Gene, the youngest of 14 children, went to work when he was nine years old as a caddie at the Lexington Country Club. He and an older brother used to sleep in the bunkers on hot summer nights, using towels pilfered from the pool area in lieu of sheets and blankets. That way, they'd be certain to be at the club at first light so they could sweep up the caddie yard and shine the clubs, all to impress the pro, a Scot named Alec Baxter. They wanted him to let them carry bags for two rounds instead of just one, for maybe 75 cents or a dollar per bag per round. The Hilen family needed the money.

Gene noticed, when he shagged balls for Alec Baxter on the practice range, that the way a golfer moves his right side when he swings is very similar to the move you make skipping rocks. He was skipping rocks on a pond near one of the greens one day when a rock hit a duck and decapitated it. That was deemed destruction of club property, and Alec Baxter fired Gene Hilen.

When he went home and told his widowed mother what had happened, she was not sympathetic. She cut a switch from a willow tree and flayed his backside. She marched him back to the Lexington Country Club, and confronted Alec

Baxter. "My boy will do whatever it takes to make up for the damage he caused," she said. "But he has to work."

Alec Baxter rehired Gene Hilen.

Gene stayed at Lexington Country club for a number of years, managing to complete high school, get married, and start a family as he rose through the ranks to assistant pro. He got to be a pretty good player, though the closest he ever came to making substantial money from his golf turned out to be a blown opportunity.

It happened when he was playing in a local tournament and had a five-foot putt on the final green to shoot 67. Gene started thinking that Larry Gilbert, who was in the tournament and is now doing pretty well on the Senior Tour, might shoot 68 and force him into a playoff if he didn't make this putt. With those kinds of ideas in his mind, he froze and missed the five-footer. It turned out that his 68 still won the tournament by several shots. The big payday was lost the next day, when Gene went to the racetrack. Gene's racetrack custom was and is to play his last golf score in the daily double, and the daily double combination of six and seven paid $7,200 that day. Gene, of course, had bet six and eight.

He learned something from it, though. He learned that a golfer must stay in the present and not let his mind wander to future things, like what might happen if he misses a putt.

Gene got his first chance to teach when a little nine-hole club in Mt. Sterling, Kentucky, made him the golf pro, course superintendent, and swimming-pool maintenance expert. He still knows a lot about greenskeeping and he could no doubt fix your pool filter if it broke down—but what he really got good at was teaching.

When he was called upon to give lessons, Gene read and reread Ben Hogan's book on the golf swing, and plunged in. Through the years, from Mt. Sterling to Juniper Hills, he studied film of the great golfers from Bobby Jones on. He attended seminars. He picked up bits and pieces about the golf swing from a dozen very knowledgeable sources.

What Gene does when he teaches is try to keep things as simple as possible. He'll spend a lot of time with a pupil trying to get the set-up correct—particularly the stance and weight distribution. He'll work on getting the club back properly. After that, Gene tries not to give his pupils too much to think about. He tells them to fire the right side, just as though they were skipping a rock.

"If you have the coordination to put the ball in the washer and wash it, you have the coordination to play golf," he says. "Although, I've noticed that it's hard to teach bow-legged people."

I first heard about Gene from a friend of mine named Rob McNamara. Rob started learning from Gene as a 13 year old. Rob's grandfather had been a golf pro, and his father was an excellent amateur who belonged to the local country club. When Rob was ready to start playing golf seriously, his father took him to Gene Hilen.

Gene has a way with kids. He usually gets them started at clinics, throwing golf balls and singing and dancing, to get the feel of shifting their weight at the same time as they use their hands. Then, he starts them swinging a golf club. For those who can't afford one, he has a barrel full of old ones at the back of the pro shop.

He teaches them basic etiquette and rules of the game. Then he lets them start in a four-hole league. If they shoot 26 for the four holes three times in succession, they're permitted to move up to a C League, and then a B, and so on. Boys who can break 100 for eighteen holes may play in the Men's Golf Association events.

With boys or girls who show some commitment, Gene becomes a mentor. He has them write letters to him describing what they've learned about golf. He monitors their report cards. He finds little jobs for them to do around the course so they can hang around and play a lot of golf. They clean carts or rake bunkers or pick weeds. "They learn that if you want something free, you have to work for it," he says.

Although it's officially against the rules for anyone who's not taking a lesson to hit off the lesson tee, Gene generally turns his back when one of these kids hits practice balls off the tee, as long as the kid picks them up.

Rob McNamara does not remember taking many formal lessons from Gene, but he had a steady stream of informal ones. "He never said he didn't have time to show me something," Rob recalls. "If I said I was having trouble in the bunkers, he'd walk out to the practice green with me and drop a few balls in the bunker and tell me to go ahead and start hitting them.

"He'd watch and then he might say, 'Okay, Pahds, you're too flat.'" ("Pahds" is a derivative of Partner, and when Gene Hilen calls you that it means he either likes you, or he's giving you the Gene Hilen Egomania Treatment, or both.)

"Feel like you're picking those thumbs up to the sky, Pahds," Gene would continue. "And blast it! Splash that sand!"

Rob would, and his bunker play would improve.

A lot of what Gene did with Rob was directed more at his head. Like most golfers, Rob went through times of near despair. "I used to quit every six days," he recalls now.

The toughest times for him came when he turned 14 and then, four years later, when he turned 18. In each case, age bumped Rob up to a new, tougher level of competition. And for a while, he had a hard time coping with it.

"Gene was always encouraging," Rob remembers. "It was always, 'All right, Pahds, you're still the greatest, it's ridiculous to think of quitting.'

"When things were going good, Gene could be critical of me. But when things were down, he would find something positive for me to feed on. I was so hard on myself. He'd point out where my perception was off."

Gene kept the attention of Rob and young players like him because he knew how to make the game fun for the people who played at Juniper Hills. He might, on a cold day, let them organize a putting game on the floor of the pro shop, starting balls at the back door and trying to roll them some fifty feet, past the shirts and the irons, until they stopped just shy of the wall where the new bags were displayed.

He might, late in the afternoon, let them play "cross-country golf," starting on the first tee, say, and playing to the third green, and then from the fourth tee to a green on the back side. Or he might organize a match in which the best player would have to take on the others using only an old two-iron. If a small plane was coming in to the adjacent Capital City Airport, he'd let everybody rush outside to the lesson tee, whip out their drivers, and try to hit it. (No one ever did.)

This is not to say that there wasn't some serious teaching going on. There was. Over the years, Gene Hilen has started thousands of people in golf, and he's sharpened the games of some of them to a fine edge. Some fifty of his kids have won college-golf scholarships. A dozen have won Kentucky high-school championships. When Rob McNamara was 21, after eight years with Gene, his handicap was plus five—five strokes better than scratch.

What's most important about a pro, then, is not what he charges. It's the joy he takes in helping golfers develop. It's his dedication to the game and his profession. It's what he knows, and his skill in communicating it.

In fact, honest communication is the first essential in a successful mentor–student relationship. Good teachers realize this.

A friend of mine named Hank Johnson, the director of golf at Greystone Golf Club in Birmingham, Alabama, tries to have his first encounter with each new student over a cup of coffee. Knowing that a lot of people might object to paying on an hourly basis for this, Hank usually does it *gratis*. He has a checklist of things he wants to find out about each pupil. It covers the usual data about a person's age and golf background. Generally there's some talk about a particular flaw that has prompted the pupil to seek help—slicing, inconsistency, or whatever. But Hank wants to know more than that. He wants to know the pupil's goals. Does he or she just want to be able to feel comfortable playing an occasional round of customer golf? Does she want to win club championships? Or are the aspirations still higher—regional and national amateur competition or the pro tours? More important, how much time is the student willing to commit to lessons and practice?

With that information in hand, Hank suggests a program to the student. Only when that program is agreed upon do they head to the lesson tee.

This is extremely important. A smart pro realizes that a student will make much better progress if he feels that he's following a plan he helped devise. An old coach's saying applies here: "Plan your work and work your plan."

Other pros and pupils establish communications less formally. A good example of this comes from a young teaching pro I know, Pete Mathews, and one of his best pupils, Paul Buckley. Pete is the head pro at New Orleans Country Club, where Paul is a member.

A few years ago, Pete had just taken the job at New Orleans. He and Paul, whose handicap was in the midteens, were partners in a pro–am in Hattiesburg, Mississippi. After the tournament, they drove home together, and Paul asked Pete what he thought of his game.

It was a critical moment in their relationship. A lot of pros, particularly young ones, would have taken the politic way out and said something polite and evasive. Most pros are acutely aware that if they don't keep the members happy, they can easily wind up selling clubs in a department store. They become masters of diplomacy rather than masters of communication.

Pete, however, did not become a golf pro to act like a diplomat. He wanted to teach golf. And he had correctly sized up Paul Buckley.

"I think your short game stinks," Pete said. In fact, he used a verb that was a little more blunt than "stinks."

Pete knew Paul would not take offense. Paul is a man who likes his news straight. And he had heard worse. He had taken over the New Orleans Hilton in 1986, when it was losing $9 million a year, and turned it into the biggest profit center in the Hilton chain. Then, in the late 1980s, he developed Crohn's disease, a form of inflammatory bowel disease. He nearly died from it. One treatment his doctors ordered was hyperalimentation, in which the patient enters the hospital and spends 36 days being nourished by an intravenous drip. The patient takes no food during this period.

Paul decided to use that time to improve his golf game. Until then, golf had been a casual hobby. But he had a putting strip made of Astroturf, and he bought a book on putting. He spent his 36 days of confinement learning to roll the ball into the hole, an intravenous tube dangling behind him. He left the hospital with a pendulum stroke.

Unfortunately, the treatment was not as effective in helping his Crohn's disease as it was in helping his putting. After another year or two, Paul's doctors recommended an ileostomy, and he had that surgery.

A lot of people would have given up golf at this point. Not Paul Buckley. Like a lot of psychologically hardy people, he looked around for someone to serve as a role model for the life he intended to lead. He hit upon Al Geiberger, who was playing competitively on the Senior Tour after an ileostomy. Paul became a Geiberger fan. He got a copy of the scorecard from Geiberger's legendary 59 in the 1977 Memphis Classic, and had it mounted on one of the walls at the Hilton's sports bar.

That was where Paul was when he met Pete Mathews. He

was playing golf, which was itself an achievement. But he wasn't improving. Paul welcomed Pete's candor. He resolved to do something about his short game.

For a year, Paul took regular short-game lessons from Pete. He practiced nothing but the short game. To fit this into his schedule, he often went to the club at dawn, practiced, and then went to work. His weekend partners couldn't understand why he was suddenly starting to get up and down to beat them. They never saw how much he worked.

Paul's handicap reflected the progress he was making. It went from 14, to 12, and then to single digits. Paul is not an overwhelmingly long hitter, but he gets the ball about 220 or 230 yards off the tee pretty consistently, and he keeps it in play. That and a good game around and on the greens, is all anyone needs to play in the low eighties or the seventies on most courses.

I got a note from Paul a little while ago. He plays each year in an event called the Metairie Seniors Invitational. A few years ago, he was in the fourth flight. This year, he made it to the championship flight. In his first round match he shot 77 and, getting no strokes, beat an opponent with a handicap of five. "It was the most exciting event in my entire sporting life," Paul said.

It shows what someone can do if he refuses to limit himself, makes a sensible plan, and sticks to it. If Pete Mathews had not taken a calculated risk and opened communications, none of that progress might have happened.

Communication, of course, has to flow both ways. The pupil has to feel comfortable talking to the pro. He must be able to tell the pro when he doesn't feel right about something the pro is trying to teach him; maybe the pro needs to find another approach. The pupil must be able to speak up when he doesn't understand a concept the pro is trying to get across. The pro ought to be the sort of person who takes such questions not as a challenge to his authority, but as opportunities for further instruction.

This kind of good communication fails to happen, I suspect, a thousand times a day on lesson tees across America. The pro says something in golf jargon—perhaps about the club being laid off. The pupil thinks laid off means someone has lost his job. He doesn't know how that pertains to a golf club, but he nods gamely, unwilling to admit his ignorance.

And nothing is learned.

I have always felt that if the pupil isn't learning, the teacher isn't teaching. But both the teacher and the pupil need good feedback for learning to take place. I think it's a good idea, near the end of every lesson, for the pro to ask the pupil to recapitulate, in his own words, what the pro has just taught. If the pupil can't do it, then the pro, like Lucy Ricardo, has some "'splainin" to do.

And you will find, I am sure, that good communication is always easier if both the pro and the player have made a commitment.

Chapter 3

Getting Committed

I recently met a golfer named Alice Hovde whose story says a lot about the importance of commitment in the process of finding a pro and lowering a handicap.

Alice is a slender, exuberant woman in her early fifties who lives part of the year near the Old Marsh Golf Club in Florida and part of the year in Indiana, where her husband, Boyd, has been state amateur champion.

Alice had never played golf when she married Boyd in 1981. In fact, she didn't know how much the game meant to him until after they were married. And she had no athletic background at all. Her parents had cared nothing for sports. When Alice was in high school, girls were offered a choice between taking gym class or helping out in the school's front office. Alice chose the office.

But she soon figured out that her marriage

would be easier if she learned to play golf at least passably well. It was not just a matter of playing with Boyd. It was a question of being able to engage in conversation with his friends.

"I figured," she says, "that if I took up the game, at least I would understand what they meant when they talked about pitching wedges and five-irons."

So, Alice became a golfer. Her goal was to learn to play well enough not to embarrass herself with her husband. He played in the low seventies. She figured that if she averaged about one more stroke per hole than he took, she would be playing well enough to be decent company.

For a few years, she took lessons and practiced. It was not easy. At first, she could barely get the ball off the ground. She persevered until she could play in the nineties. Once she had reached her goal, she stopped taking lessons, stopped practicing, and stopped improving. She enjoyed the game but, for nearly a decade, her handicap stayed around 20.

Several years ago, a couple of happy coincidences helped nudge her off that plateau. For one, her husband and other people she played with told her that she had the potential to be a better player than she was. For another, Todd Anderson became the head pro at Old Marsh.

Todd is one of the brightest young teachers in golf. When he was a student at the University of Alabama, he got to watch some of the best older teachers conduct schools for *Golf Digest*. He learned from all of them.

As a pro, he developed a quiet, even-tempered teaching

style, and a knack for helping pupils understand what they need to improve, how the improvement should feel, and how they can practice to ingrain a new technique. He drives around Old Marsh in a cart that looks as if he stopped by a garage sale and suffered a bout of low sales resistance. It's full of devices, from mops to lengths of surgical tubing to a video camera, that he uses in the course of his teaching. (Drag a mop across the practice tee and you'll have the feel of the hands leading the clubhead through the hitting area.)

Alice decided to take a lesson from Todd, but she was chary about it. Like a lot of people, she got nervous when a pro asked her to hit a few balls.

On a rational level, this kind of nervousness makes little sense. If your car developed a rattling sound under the hood and you took it to a mechanic, the last thing you'd want would be for the rattling noise to disappear just as he started to check the car. (Which, perhaps, is why it usually does.)

But a golfer who, say, suffers from a slice, is liable to want desperately to hit the ball straight when a pro is watching him. He has the sense that he's being evaluated, and he doesn't want to seem completely hopeless. So Alice's anxiety was understandable.

Then there was the issue of her age; she was 48.

In my experience, no one is too old to learn. Age may make learning harder. But this is usually because people who are older tend to be less receptive to new ideas and new ways of doing things. It's their minds that get inflexible even more than their bodies.

Age may have made them too smart for their own good. They think they know what they can and cannot learn. They put limits on themselves. They sabotage themselves. Then, when they don't improve, they think they've demonstrated how smart they are. The truth is that they fear putting in effort and getting no results.

I'm reminded of Satchell Paige, the great black baseball pitcher. Because of segregation, Paige couldn't pitch in the major leagues until he was past 40. Some people looked on this as a tragedy, but Paige refused to. "Age is a question of mind over matter," he said. "If you don't mind, it don't matter." With that attitude, he helped pitch the Cleveland Indians to the American League pennant in 1948, when he was 42.

A golfer who is middle-aged or older may have to do things that a younger golfer can get away with ignoring. He or she may have to pay more attention to fitness, especially exercises to strengthen the golf muscles and improve flexibility. He or she may have to pay more attention to nutrition. But there is no reason why he or she cannot learn.

The truth is, though, that anyone who puts real effort into an intelligent program will improve. And she will enrich her life finding out just how much.

But Alice wasn't sure about that.

She put up a tough front when she took her first lesson from Todd. She told him that she didn't take lessons well. She told him she didn't intend to practice.

You can imagine the reaction coaches in most sports

would have to this kind of announcement. If the coach were, say Pat Riley of the Miami Heat or Pat Summitt of the University of Tennessee, a basketball player who said he didn't take instruction well and didn't intend to practice would soon be dribbling for another team.

But a golf pro generally doesn't have the same power in the teacher–student relationship that a basketball coach has with his players. He has to keep the members or the customers happy.

So, Todd didn't argue with Alice. Instead, he tried to work on some things that she could improve with minimal practice. At address, Alice had been listing a little to the left. He suggested a more balanced posture. She was gripping the club tighter than he liked, so he advised her to lighten her grip pressure. That was about it. He finished the lesson with a few words of encouragement and told her to have fun. He didn't know if she would be back.

Alice remembers that first lesson as a nerve-wracking experience. She felt as if she were grinding on every swing, but she also picked up Todd's sense that she could improve. She returned for a second lesson, and hit the ball a little better this time. Todd offered her a little more encouragement. He said that if she decided to do so, she could improve. She would have to make a commitment, a commitment to regular lessons and at least some practice.

Alice agreed. And from that moment, their relationship changed.

First of all, Alice felt differently about her lessons.

"I had been so tense. But after we made that agreement, I relaxed, because it was like we were doing something together," she recalls. She started to look forward to her lessons.

Todd's attitude also changed. As a golf teacher in a resort area, he finds it hard to avoid giving sporadic or one-time lessons. If a member calls to say a dear friend is visiting for a week and would like a lesson, Todd tries to be accommodating. The only students he turns away are those whom he knows flit from one teacher to another in search of an instant, magical cure for their golf problems. He tells them he doesn't want to waste their time.

But, what Todd, or any good teacher, really likes is a pupil who's committed to doing the right things for an extended period of time. Alice didn't promise to become a golf zealot, but she did promise to practice a couple of times a week. She and Todd agreed that she would take a weekly lesson provided she had been able to practice. If she hadn't practiced, she would postpone the lesson.

So, Todd's approach to her changed. He started helping her set goals. He figured that before she left for the summer in Indiana, Alice could get her handicap down to 15. She agreed to try. They started working methodically on her swing, trying to improve her turn and quiet her lower body. The improvement started to come quickly. In five months, her handicap indeed dropped from around 20 to 15.

The next season, Todd urged Alice to take a playing lesson. Alice, again, was nervous about it, but she agreed. The playing lesson spotlighted for both of them the shortcomings in her wedge game. As her swing had improved, she found herself more often within wedge distance of the greens on par fours. In such cases, she had tended to try only to put the ball somewhere on the putting surface. Todd told her she needed to play more aggressively, to think about birdies when she had a wedge in her hands. They started to spend more of their lesson and practice time on her short game.

Alice's handicap continued to improve, though more slowly. This is common: It's often relatively easy to knock a few strokes off an average player's game by fixing a big swing flaw that has been causing a few topped shots or shots out of bounds every round. After that, a golfer has to work harder for every saved stroke, and those incremental improvements often occur in the short game. The better you get, the more patient you have to be.

Todd's lessons with Alice by now are not usually concerned with overhauling her swing mechanics. They tend to be about fine tuning—making sure, for example, that her setup with her wedges gets the blade aimed squarely at her target. They frequently go back to fundamentals and make certain Alice is executing them properly. This is common to all sports. NBA practice sessions quite often return to the fundamentals of defense and shooting. Pro-football teams practice blocking and tackling drills that the players have been doing since they were ten years old. Good golfers are always checking things like grip and alignment.

Alice has continued to make progress. When I met her, she and Todd had set new goals for the season. She wanted to get her handicap into single digits, and she wanted to break par for nine holes. I soon heard that she had accomplished the latter, shooting 35 on the back nine at Old Marsh. A few months later, she sent word that she'd gotten her handicap under ten.

Her commitment—to Todd and to a process—was the key factor in Alice's improvement. At some point, any golfer who wants to get better has got to do what she did. She must make a commitment to a teacher. And she must make a commitment to a process of improvement.

A commitment is not a casual thing. I sometimes use the example of a chicken, a pig, and their relative contributions to a bacon-and-eggs breakfast. The chicken is involved in the breakfast. The pig is committed to it.

Sticking to an improvement plan is not easy. If it were, we'd all be slender and shooting in the seventies. It requires a commitment and it requires honoring that commitment. Obviously, you won't want to make a commitment lightly. You may need to take several lessons from a pro before you're certain that he or she is the one to guide you. But, at some point, you have to stop searching and make a decision. The teacher you choose will be your mentor.

This is no different from other sports. I never heard of a basketball coach who allowed uninvited visitors into his practices, visitors who said, "No, let's not play your man-to-man defense. Let's play a match-up zone!" To teach effectively, a coach knows he has to get his players to believe in what he's teaching them and to practice it without distraction.

Similarly, your commitment will require you to shut out other voices. You're going to have to stop paying attention to tips from your playing partners, to teaching segments on television or in golf magazines. If you do see something that grabs your attention and seems pertinent, you're going to talk to your teacher about it before you try to make any changes in your game.

Tom Kite had that sort of relationship with Harvey Penick. Harvey, obviously, couldn't travel on the tour with Tom. And Tom couldn't absolutely shut out the advice that every tour pro gets, largely unsolicited, whenever he steps onto a practice tee. But before he changed anything, Tom ran it past Harvey. He might, for instance tell Harvey that a pretty knowledgable teacher had suggested he needed a slightly bigger hip turn. He'd ask what Harvey thought, and Harvey would listen, think the matter over, and then tell Tom what he thought. Maybe, he would say, that the change could be good for him—but it would mean he'd have to change two other elements in his swing. Or, perhaps he'd say that the change might be good for some people, but not for Tom because of the particular characteristics of Tom's swing. If Tom made the change, it would start changing the character of his misses. Tom made the final decision as to whether to change things, but he respected Harvey's opinion above all others.

That's the kind of commitment I'm talking about.

When you put yourself in the hands of a teacher, you are relying on him to filter all the information and misinformation that is disseminated about the golf swing. He'll be the one to decide what can be helpful to you and how to present it to you.

What you get from this commitment is not just sound instruction, although if you've taken some care in picking your pro, the instruction will be sound. You get a basis for trusting what you've been told. And, if you trust what you're told, if you believe it will work, then you're way ahead of someone who takes the club back with doubts in his mind. In golf, there are so many conflicting opinions tossed about on how to swing, chip, putt, or even hold the club that you have no prayer unless you can focus on one source of advice and trust that source.

Your commitment will also be a commitment of time. Working with a pro will reduce the time you must spend to improve. This book will suggest some ways to compress time, to practice at home, and to get more out of the time you put in, but it will not eliminate the time requirement. To be honest, I have never met anyone who got to scratch by playing on Saturdays and Sundays and practicing for an hour a couple of times a week. I wish I had. Players who get to scratch spend more time than that. They find an hour to practice or play virtually every day. Most people, if they really want to, can find that hour somewhere in their schedules, even if it means getting out to the course for practice at dawn, the way Paul Buckley did, or giving up a favorite TV show or the evening news.

If at present you can't spare that much time, you ought to scale down your expectations until you can. If you can only find three or four days a week to practice or play, you might want to think in terms of getting down to the four to seven handicap range. If you can only find two or three days a week, the best you might be able to do is around ten.

I can't predict exactly how long you'll have to honor this time commitment, except to say that I've never known anyone to get from an average handicap to scratch in much less than two years. It may take you four or six years and, along with the moments of great joy and satisfaction, you will experience plateaus and setbacks along the way.

Commitment to a long-term process will yield one immediate benefit to help you cope with this. It should give you more patience. Because you know you're embarked on a process that you know could take years, you will find it easier to get through days and weeks when you're not only not getting better, you're getting worse.

Great coaches and athletes have this patience. My friend John Calipari has taken over two moribund basketball programs, the University of Massachusetts and the New Jersey Nets of the NBA. In each case, he developed and committed himself to a long-term plan for improvement that he believed in. His plans anticipated that the early years would be rough, but his belief in his plans gave him patience. He built a powerhouse at Massachusetts and I believe he will do the same in New Jersey. I'm not sure exactly when, and neither is John. If you have patience, you continue doing things properly every day and, sooner or later, success comes.

I can't predict when your commitment will give you the golf game of your dreams. But, if you make the commitment, I can guarantee one thing. You'll experience hope and despair, elation and disappointment. You'll test your reserves of patience and persistence. You'll learn a lot about yourself and, in that way, your quest to improve at golf will enhance your life.

CHAPTER 4

THE HARD PART

If you've read this far, you might well be thinking: *Find a pro, make a commitment, and take lessons, huh? It can't be that simple, that easy.*

You're half right. It is that simple. But it's not that easy.

If it were that easy, golf would not be the game that it is. Everyone would play at or near par. Titanium factories could resume selling sheet metal to the Air Force. The folks who make the latest slice-curing club would have to find honest work. People in search of a real challenge might have to take up something like figuring out the origins of the universe or understanding the tax code.

But golf is a hard game to play well. The hard part, of course, is not finding a pro, making a commitment, taking lessons, practicing, or anything else I've discussed thus far.

The hard part is honoring your commitment. I

learn this over and over again from nearly every successful client I have. One of them is Dan Grider. Dan is an open, amiable man, white-haired and blue-eyed, in his mid-50s. He was born in a small town in Minnesota and he lives now in Sioux Falls, South Dakota. Maybe growing up in the upper midwest, where the winters can seem eternal, taught him perseverance. Maybe the economic vicissitudes of his boyhood, when his father went broke, and the family had to move to a house without plumbing, taught him to handle adversity. I don't know.

I do know that Dan is a man who understands the value of patient effort. When he was younger, he went to work in sales for an industrial corporation, and quickly increased the company's business in his territory. His sales secret was simple. He made at least four calls on a client, listening patiently all the time, before he even tried to close a deal.

Dan's first dream was financial security, and he achieved it in the same slow and painstaking way. He worked hard, saved, and invested his savings in real estate. He branched out into sandwich shops, then into an interest in a casino in Deadwood. (His weekly poker games in Sioux Falls are not for the faint of heart.) Today, it's safe to say that there is no chance he'll ever have to move back into a house without indoor plumbing.

He took the same approach to golf some years ago when he sold his Deadwood casino interest and returned to Sioux Falls. Dan was a pretty good athlete as a boy, and he'd played a fair amount of golf when he was in his thirties and forties.

He had never been better than an eight handicap, and his aspirations were higher than that. First of all, he wanted to beat his buddies at the Minnehaha Country Club. Second, he wanted to make an impact in tournament golf. He had ample time and ample resources. He was ready to work hard at the game.

He turned to Terry Crouch, Minnehaha's head pro, for help. Terry is a second-generation golf pro. His father, Max, was a caddie who rose through the ranks in Omaha to become head pro at the Field Club for many years. Terry started out cleaning clubs, washing carts, and picking up range balls for his father. When he finished college, he joined the PGA by apprenticing under his father.

Max Crouch, like a lot of old caddies, was not much for swing theories. He taught the way a swing should feel. If he were teaching today, you could bet he wouldn't own a video camera. Terry, as a young man, went the other way. He delved into the theoretical aspects of the swing, and he studied under some great teachers: Jack Grout, Bob Toski, and Jimmy Ballard. Over time, he developed a teaching philosophy that tried to blend his father's old approach with some of the newer theories.

When Dan came to him, Terry started giving him occasional lessons. He decided that Dan's fundamental problem was a reverse pivot. For a long time, they worked on getting Dan to make an athletic movement through the hitting area. Dan, as is his wont, listened carefully. His college degree is in engineering, so he could understand and appreciate the mechanics Terry was teaching him. He practiced diligently for a year. He did flexibility exercises and lifted weights. He improved his diet and stopped drinking.

His health improved a lot faster than his handicap. It fell a stroke or two, but that was as low as he could get it. He was frustrated. Worse, he felt embarrassed. He sensed that some of his friendly rivals at the club were snickering behind his back, talking about all the effort he was putting in just to remain their pigeon on Saturday mornings. This is the way, unfortunately, of golf buddies everywhere. They'll always cock an eyebrow at someone who works hard to improve. They'll take covert (and sometimes not covert) satisfaction from seeing their friend fail to improve, since this suggests that their own haphazard approach is not responsible for the state of their own games.

Dan was so discouraged that he went to see Terry, and talked about giving up. "The game is just so hard for me," he said. He was thinking that if he continued to play at all, he'd do it casually, without taking lessons and without practicing so much. He'd just try to have fun and forget about that dream of doing well in tournament play.

Terry reacted as any good coach would react. He bucked Dan up. "You've improved more than your handicap shows," he said. This was true. Dan had begun to develop a swing that gave him a nice, consistent draw, which produced a lot of run on South Dakota's dry summer fairways. Part of his problem was that in trying to improve his swing, he had neglected to work on his short game. He was hitting the ball better, but he wasn't always getting it in the hole in fewer strokes.

Terry suggested that they change their lesson and practice approach to try to make Dan's approach less mechanical. Instead of analyzing Dan's swing and thinking about particular positions he needed to get into, they agreed to try a series of practice drills. These drills, such as hitting the ball with the feet together, or stepping as you swing like a baseball player, were designed to inculcate in Dan a smooth, athletic motion without requiring him to think about it.

Dan had another idea. His girlfriend, Carla Clay, had listened to him talk about his golfing troubles quite a bit. Carla is not a golfer, but she is a horsewoman, and she knew enough from equestrian sports to know the importance of the mind in athletic performance. She had suggested Dan might want to talk to a sports psychologist. So Dan brought that idea up to Terry.

Terry agreed. He knew of me because one of Minnehaha's members is the father of Kris Tschetter, the LPGA pro with whom I had worked. Terry thought I might be able to help Dan get off the plateau he was on. This, again, is one role a player's pro should fill. If the player needs special help, whether it be in psychology, strength and flexibility, diet or whatever, the pro helps him find it.

Terry called and asked if I had time to work with Dan. I asked him to have Dan call me. It took Dan a few weeks to work himself up to placing that call. When he finally did, he told me he wasn't sure that someone who works with tour players would be interested in trying to help a six-handicapper.

"I'll work with anyone who's committed," I told Dan. That was and is my policy. I don't care if a player is trying to break 65 or 95. If he's committed to doing what it takes to reach his goal, I'm happy to help with the mental side of the game. On the other hand, I don't want to waste my time on someone who's looking for a quick headshrinking session that will solve his problems for him.

Dan agreed to meet me in Ft. Worth, where I was working with some players in town for the Colonial. We went to a range and hit some balls. He was clearly nervous, but once he relaxed, he started hitting it well. I could see that he had a swing that was capable of much better results than he'd been getting. I could also sense his passion for finding out how good he could get at golf. I generally don't know when I first meet a client whether the individual is truly committed to improvement or only talks about improving. But, with Dan, I felt a willingness to honor his commitment. By that, I mean that he would give his golf a sufficient priority to attack the problems in his game and solve them. He would be in it for the long haul.

A lot of his problems were in the short-game area. Although Terry had given him instruction on the various chips and pitches a golfer encounters around the greens, Dan had a hard time trusting his skill enough to execute those shots. In particular, Dan had a sand phobia. He had little or no confidence in his ability to get out of a bunker, let alone put the ball close enough to the pin to save par. We talked a lot about the need to start thinking about getting the ball in the hole from around the green and trusting that he had the skills to do that.

It would be nice to report that after talking with me, Dan immediately took his game to another level and kept it there, but it would be inaccurate. Worse, it would be misleading.

Dan went back to Sioux Falls determined to work not only on his mechanics, but on his mental game. He made some incremental progress on his handicap, getting down to the five range. He had a significant competitive success, winning the first flight of the South Dakota Match Play.

But, there were also times when he and Terry would try some new drills to refine his swing and Dan's game would take a temporary step backward. There were times when he couldn't break 80 and times when he thought again of giving up his dreams and just playing weekend golf.

If you want to improve your golf game, you have to accept that this is the way it will be. There will be long periods when your efforts can seem wasted, when your scores don't reflect the effort you're putting in. These will be the times when patience and perseverance will be the most important traits you can have.

Dan and I met again the following winter. He'd made progress in trusting his swing and in his short game. We talked a lot about focusing his mind on the target before every shot, about visualizing the ball going where he wanted it to go.

Still, Dan's progress was uneven. Impatient with the length of the South Dakota winters, he began renting a place in Palm Springs each March for spring training. There, he worked on his drills. He developed a habit I would commend to anyone: He recorded some of his practice results.

He might, for instance, hit ten pitches from twenty yards to a tight pin. He'd record the percentage he got within four feet. The next day, he'd do the drill again and again record the results. Or he might do the compass drill—hitting short putts to a hole from four different directions. He'd record how many he could make in a row. Usually, he would see steady progress in his training diary. If he started the month hitting 60 percent of his shots close, by the end of the month he'd be up in the eighties or even nineties.

This is a variation of something athletes do when they lift weights. Typically, a strength coach has a pupil record his workouts—how much weight, how many sets, and how many repetitions—each time he lifts. If, after a few months, the athlete (as athletes sometimes do) complains that he doesn't see any results on the field and doesn't feel any stronger, the strength coach opens the notebook. Almost invariably, it shows a substantial increase in strength or stamina.

Charting practice drills can serve the same function. If, after several months of effort, you don't see any improvement in your golf scores, you might check the log of practice drills. If you've been diligent, you will no doubt see some improvement in the number of consecutive putts you can hole in the compass drill or in the percentage of balls you get up and down from around the green, or the percentage of drives you hit onto an imaginary fairway on your practice range. This evidence of improvement can help sustain your morale during difficult times.

And, Dan was having difficult times in the spring of 1996. He was practicing assiduously, doing the drills that Terry had prescribed, but he wasn't getting better. In fact, he was getting worse. He couldn't break eighty. His handicap rose to around seven, about where it had been when he'd starting working hard on his game five years before.

Then, as they sometimes do in golf, things fell into place. The timing of this phenomenon can be inexplicable. I can't tell you why someone's game comes together in a given week. But the event itself is not inexplicable: It's the result of hard work.

Dan woke up one morning, went out to the course, and shot 75. He started to play much better—not always in the low seventies, but significantly better than he had in months. He went back to Sioux Falls and, since he had just turned 55, entered the South Dakota State Seniors championship, a 36-hole event at Lakeview Country Club in Mitchell.

He played a few practice rounds on the course. He made a good game plan. He felt prepared. He felt ready to win.

And for the first nine holes, he shot 42.

"I was unsettled on the front nine," he would say later. Some people would have given up on the tournament then and there, but Dan is a scrapper. He is the kind of golfer who will go into the trees, manufacture a shot, and scramble to save par for the sake of a one-dollar nassau. He was not about to mail in the last 27 holes.

He shot 37 on the back side, then drove home to Sioux Falls and the practice range at Minnehaha. He worked on wedge approach shots. The next morning, he got up, did his calisthenics, and drove back to Mitchell. On the road he listened to the audio tape of *Golf Is a Game of Confidence,* particularly the segment on how Brad Faxon shot 63 in the final round of the PGA to make the Ryder Cup team. He noted how Brad had, even during one of the great rounds of his life, fought with distractions and nerves.

All I ask, he thought, *is a chance to be nervous.*

By the time Dan teed off, the wind was blowing, as it often does in South Dakota. It was gusting to 25–30 miles per hour. He reminded himself of the need to relax and not worry about things he could not control, like the wind, or what the other players were doing.

He didn't hit the ball very solidly at number one, and wound up three-putting for a bogey. But Dan's mind was where it had to be that day. He accepted what had happened; he didn't get angry or brood about it. He parred number two and then hit a brilliant three-iron into the wind and within a few feet of the hole on number three. He sank the putt and he was off.

Dan played brilliant golf that day. It was not that he scored brilliantly, though he scored very well. His brilliance lay more in the way he kept himself calm and focused under trying circumstances—trailing in the tournament, fighting the wind. While most of the field got discouraged, Dan got looser and freer with each passing hole, which is the way a golfer ought to feel.

He made double bogey at number 13 and bogey at number 14, when his chipping and putting briefly deserted him. The wind, by now, was howling. Dan hit his drive on the par-five fifteenth into some trees on the left rather than risk being blown into a pond on the right. He punched out, hit a five-iron onto the green and made his par.

The sixteenth hole was a 388-yard dogleg, into the wind, with water on both sides. Dan, feeling the wind blowing at his hair and trousers, fought hard to keep his mind on where he wanted his ball to go, rather than where he was afraid it would. He played the hole perfectly, hitting a five-iron to a spot 25 feet below the hole.

When he reached the green, he noticed that the head pro at Lakeview was talking to one of his playing partners. For a second, Dan wondered whether they were being warned for slow play. That couldn't be it, he decided. They'd had to wait on the last tee. His partner came over to him.

"He wanted to know if anyone in our group was playing

well," Dan's partner said. "I told him you were. He said to hang in there, because all the leaders are falling back. You're right in the middle of it."

"I'm just going to do the same thing I've been doing all day—take it one shot at a time," Dan said.

He two-putted for par, feeling relieved that he had escaped from a hole that could have cost him dearly.

He hit a five-iron at number 17, a 210-yard par three playing downwind. He hit it too solidly. It came down in the middle of the green and rolled to the back fringe, 40 feet from the hole. "This will be the longest putt I'll make today," he said, feeling now comfortable and relaxed. He stroked the putt, heard someone say it was going in, and looked up to see it disappear into the hole.

For a man who had just rolled in a 40-footer after being told he was in contention to win the tournament, Dan remained remarkably calm. His thoughts moved immediately to number 18. He described himself later as "excited but calm," a seemingly oxymoronic state that I think typifies winning golfers under pressure. They know their adrenaline is pumping. They can feel the physical reaction, yet they have the discipline in the midst of all this to stick with their mental and physical routines and execute their shots.

Dan picked out his target on the left side of the rough at number 18, drew back his club—and stopped. He had seen someone's shoe out of the corner of his eye. He asked the person to move, then restarted his routine from the beginning. He hit it well, leaving himself in the middle of the fairway, 140 yards out. He would normally have hit an eight-iron, but he decided that in his nervous condition, he could get it there with a nine-iron. He hit the shot a little heavy, and left himself 15 feet short of the green.

Here, his work on the short game paid off. He told himself to forget about his mechanics, to trust his abilities. He hit the chip to about four feet above the hole. He picked the line for his putt, stroked it, and looked up in time to see it plop into the center of the hole.

Dan turned in a 71. The first day leaders had all struggled in the wind, and he was tied for first at 150. There would be a sudden-death playoff involving four players. He reminded himself that all he had asked for was a chance to be nervous.

He drove into the left rough on the first playoff hole, then played a fine wedge that started right and moved, with the help of the wind, toward the pin. He wound up 10 feet from the hole. He waited for the other three to play. None holed out. Dan's hands were shaking. He thought of how Brad Faxon's hands had tingled on that day at Riviera. He stroked the putt. It was on line. It fell in.

He pumped his fist into the air and tears came to his eyes.

One of the first things Dan did was call Terry Crouch. He didn't get him, so he left a message:

"Terry, this is Dan Grider. Terry—I won! Shot 71! Birdied the first playoff hole! Stayed right with the process, and won! I can't wait to tell you about it. I'm really, really happy. Thanks."

Dan would go on that year to win the senior division of

a world two-man team championship in Scotland. He would make his first hole-in-one, see his handicap drop to three, and be selected the South Dakota Senior Player of the Year.

He would continue to have his down times, too, times when the ball didn't go where he wanted it to, times when it was once again a struggle to break 80.

"You don't ever own golf," he would say. "You just get to borrow it sometimes."

Dan is a great example of what a golfer of any age can accomplish if he masters the hard part—honoring the commitment.

Terry Crouch, of course, is still his coach. He still devises new drills for Dan to use on the practice range. And he has yet to erase that message that Dan left on his answering machine last summer. He takes too much pleasure in listening to it.

Chapter 5

The Improvement Cycle

You've picked a pro. You've made a commitment. You've vowed to honor it.

Now it's time to sit down with your pro and plan your first 12-week improvement cycle.

An improvement cycle is a three-month program of lessons and practice that can be repeated indefinitely until you are playing the golf you're capable of. It's based on the knowledge of how people learn athletic skills, coupled with the practical aspects of most people's lives. It's designed so that an individual can improve at golf while continuing to make a living and maintain a family life. It is, of necessity, presented in a one-size-fits-all fashion in these pages, but it may be modified to suit individual circumstances.

One key concept behind it came to me first from Davis Love, Jr., father of the touring pro. Davis was a great teacher. He believed that the optimal amount of practice between lessons was somewhere between six and ten hours. Practice less than that, and you probably haven't done enough to ingrain the new skill you've been taught. Practice more than that, and you raise the possibility that you'll lose your way and revert to old habits without your teacher being around to correct you.

If you're committed to practicing an hour a day, and you play once or twice a week, this means that the approximate time between lessons for you will be two weeks. So, in each improvement cycle, you'll take five or six lessons.

As I said, individual circumstances vary. I believe the optimal practice time for most people is about an hour or an hour and a half. Beyond that, they start to lose their concentration and get sloppy. But, if your schedule lends itself to practicing on a different basis—say, three days a week for two hours at a time—don't worry. You'll just have to make an extra effort to assure that you don't slip into the habit of mindlessly beating balls.

The main thing is that you practice between lessons. If something disrupts your schedule and you can't practice, you may find that it's a good idea to let your teacher know and postpone your next lesson until you have done your practicing and are ready for the next step. Some people, though, prefer to go ahead with a scheduled lesson even if they haven't been able to work on their own. Hank Johnson calls this kind of lesson "supervised practice," and it's a lot more expensive than a bucket of range balls. But if you have the means and your teacher doesn't mind, go ahead.

Here, in outline, is what a typical cycle might look like.

LESSON ONE
Practice i
Practice ii
Practice iii
Practice iv
Play
Play
Practice v
Practice vi
Practice vii
Practice viii
Play
Play

LESSON TWO
Practice ix
Practice x
Practice xi
Practice xii
Play
Play
Practice xiii
Practice xiv
Practice xv
Practice xvi
Practice xvii

Play
Play

LESSON THREE
Practice xviii
Practice xix
Practice xx
Practice xxi
Play
Play
Practice xxii
Practice xxiii
Practice xxiv
Practice xxv
Practice xxvi
Play
Play

LESSON FOUR
Practice xxvii
Practice xxviii
Practice xxix
Practice xxx
Play
Play
Practice xxxi
Practice xxxii
Practice xxxiii

The Improvement Cycle · 77

Practice xxxiv
Practice xxxv
Play
Play

Lesson Five
Practice xxxvi
Practice xxxvii
Practice xxxviii
Practice xxxix
Play—charted round
Play—charted round
Practice xl
Practice xli
Practice xlii
Practice xliii
Practice xliv

Lesson Six—Playing lesson
Five days off

There's an extended version of this outline in Appendix A, with room for you to make notes on your lessons and practice sessions and to chart a couple of rounds.

You'll notice several things.

First, I am not going to try to specify what your lessons ought to be about. That's something for you and your teacher to decide.

Early in the process, you'll no doubt want to cover some fundamentals. You need to decide on a grip, a stance, a posture, a ball position, a distance from the ball, an alignment with the target, and equipment that fits you. These are the fundamentals of the setup and you have to learn them, practice them, and periodically check them with your teacher.

The importance of the setup is one reason I advise the touring pros that I work with to avoid scheduling themselves for more than three or four consecutive tournaments. After that much time on the road, their setups usually start to erode. A slight glitch in the setup can lead quickly to major changes, not for the better, in the way the ball flies. So the smart thing for them is to get together with their swing teachers once a month or so to review and check their setups. It will be smart for you as well.

I have no way of prescribing what you and your teacher ought to work on first. That will depend on the flaws in your game and on your teacher's philosophy. Some teachers may see a problem in something fundamental, like your swing plane, and decide to attack it immediately and directly. Others might prefer to work on relatively easier things like your stance and grip before they worry about things that happen behind your back.

Second, you should keep playing rounds of golf during the process. I don't believe in staying off the golf course while you're trying to improve your game. That tends to lead a player to think subconsciously that the goal of the game and the goal of this process is the perfection of his technique. It's not. The goal of the game is to get the ball in the hole in the fewest possible strokes. In the end, your scores and your handicap are the true measure of how well you're doing. To learn to lower them, you have to play.

You'll want to play in what I call the trusting mode. That is, when you're out on the golf course, you do not think about the mechanics you've been working on. You think about getting the ball to your target. You trust that your swing will get it there. Even if your new technique is not yet perfected, you'll have a better chance of executing a shot if you trust your mechanics than if you let your mind wander into the practice mode, where you think about such things as the way your weight is distributed, or the angle of your right wrist, or whether your swing plane is properly upright.

The time to think about mechanics is during lessons and practice. Even then, you must spend a good part of your practice time hitting shots in the trusting mode. The precise percentage will vary. Right after a lesson, you might hit more balls with your mind on mechanics. Just before you play or compete, you'll want to spend most, if not all, of your practice time in the trusting mode.

You'll notice that playing does not count as practicing. Nor does warming up before you play count as practicing. Only practice counts as practice.

During an improvement cycle, you may want to modify the format of the matches in which you play. Avoid bets or tournaments where someone else's success depends on how well you do. If you've got a partner pushing you to play well, you're more likely to abandon the new technique you're working on if it isn't working well at the moment. That may help salvage a nassau, but it won't help your game. Stay away from this pressure. You might ask your friends to play skins games instead of better-ball nassaus.

You should try to make sure that you play in a format that requires you to hole everything and count all strokes. This means avoiding match play, which can breed some habits you don't want. If your five-foot bogey putt can't win or halve the hole, you pick it up. If you're gettting a stroke on a tough par four, you may play for a bogey instead of trying to make par. If you hit your drive out of bounds and your opponent puts his in the fairway, you may mentally concede the hole and play sloppily—remember, you're trying to become a golfer who makes the critical five-footer, who makes par on tough holes, and who knows how to recover from a bad shot.

So compete, but on a stroke-play basis. You can modify your usual two-dollar nassau so that the payoff is for total strokes on the front nine, total strokes on the back, and total for the round. You can press if the gap gets to four strokes.

Start trying to play at least some of the time with golfers who are better than you are. If you're a 15-handicapper and you play consistently with other 15-handicappers, it's going to be more difficult for you to improve than if you play at least some of the time with single-digit handicappers. You want the habits, the techniques, and the expectations of better players to rub off on you.

This has gotten more difficult to arrange, unfortunately, as clubs and courses have become more crowded. It used to be that people would head to the golf course and pick up a game when they got there. They played with a random selection of golfers, including better players.

Nowadays, nearly all public courses and many clubs have gone to a system of reserved tee times. People have to form groups ahead of time, and they tend to play with the same people week after week. Usually, those people are about as good as they are.

So, you'll probably have to take some initiative if you want to play with better golfers. Don't be shy about asking them. I've known enough tour players and top-flight amateurs to be confident that good players generally don't mind playing with average players so long as they keep up the pace and are pleasant company.

Toward the end of every cycle, I suggest that you chart a couple of rounds. This is a way of assessing your game. Like the tests that a teacher periodically gives to schoolchildren, it will help show what you've learned and where your weak spots are.

To chart a round, sit down when you've finished playing and write down every shot you played and the club you used to play it. Then, circle all the shots played with the eight-iron through the putter—the scoring clubs. This will help you get an idea of how important those clubs are. A round I recently charted for a college player I work with, Gilberto Morales of the University of Nevada–Las Vegas, showed 49 of 73 strokes made with the scoring clubs.

Next, take a look at the tee shots you hit with a driver or a three-wood. There should be about 14 of them. If you kept them all in the fairway or on the first cut of rough, those clubs aren't hurting you. On the other hand, if you hit a few out of bounds or into the woods, that's a sign that you and your teacher have work to do on your swing.

Next, go over the putts you made and check every one that you missed inside of five feet. Then go over the chips and pitches you made from within five feet of the green. How many of them did you fail to get up and down? If you find more than one or two in each of these categories, it's a sign that you need to work on your short game.

Gilberto, for instance, lost six shots on short putts and makeable up-and-down chances. They made the difference between shooting 67 and shooting 73. That's an enormous difference at the top competitive levels. If you shoot 67, you're on the leader board if not atop it. You feel good about your game. If you shoot 73, you're back in the pack and people are asking you what's wrong with your game.

I'm not saying that you should never miss a five-footer or

blow an easy up-and-down chance. But I know that when one of the tour players I work with shoots 67, he's not missing many such opportunities, if any. If you aspire to play scratch golf, neither can you.

Some players might not feel comfortable with the idea of a chart. That's all right. The important thing is that periodically you do an honest assessment of your game to find out where you're losing strokes, and that then you work on those weaknesses.

The next thing you'll notice in the model improvement cycle is the requirement that you take at least some time off. It's important to take five days away from golf every three months or so to keep from getting stale, bored, or both. And you can certainly modify the sample schedule to give yourself one or two days per week when you don't touch a club. You want, as much as possible, to look forward to your practice sessions. Time off will help you do this.

If you live in a state with cold winters, the fourth quarter of each year might, of necessity, be spent away from a golf course. This would be a good time for work on your fitness and flexibility. It would also be a good time for working on your swing without a golf ball. We'll discuss that in a later chapter.

I can't prescribe the specific techniques you and your teacher will work on, but I can proscribe an error that pros and their pupils commonly make. You will not improve very much, or very rapidly, if you confine your lessons to the practice tee and the long swing. To play the golf of your dreams, you'll need to take short-game lessons, and you'll need to take playing lessons.

Chapter 6

A Playing Lesson from Bob Toski

One look at Bob Toski and it's not hard to understand why one of his nicknames is "The Mouse." He's one of the smallest of the great golfers; when he led the PGA Tour in money earnings back in 1954, he weighed about 118 pounds. Jimmy Demaret, who knew that Bob was the eleventh of twelve children, used to kid that "his father ran out of high test before he got to Bob."

Bob has an elfin smile, wispy gray hair that he generally hides under an immaculate white cap, and brown eyes that turn down at the corners and give him, fleetingly, the look of a melancholy priest. That look disappears when he opens his mouth and starts telling stories. He's a great raconteur, full of tales about the days before the PGA Tour was a rich and luxurious enterprise.

He's also a great teacher whose skills have been honed over six decades. Bob has done just about everything in golf instruction that there is to do. He was a founder of the *Golf Digest* schools, and he now has, in partnership with Gary Battersby, his own teaching center near Pompano Beach, Florida.

His teaching roots go back to his boyhood. Bob got his start in golf as a caddie at a nine-hole club in Northampton, Massachusetts, during the Depression. His older brother Jack was an assistant pro there. Bob was deemed too small to be a Class A caddie. As a result, he carried women's bags, either for elderly ladies or for Smith College students. In those days, a candy bar was a good tip, and Bob soon learned that he got more tips when he helped the ladies get around the course in fewer strokes.

So, if he noticed that a woman's left wrist was breaking down as she chipped, he would politely correct her. Even at the age of ten, he had an understanding of the golf swing, a knack for picking out flaws, and a good idea of how to fix them.

His brother Jack taught him both the fundamentals of the swing and the fundamentals of how to teach it. By the time Bob was 16, he was a pretty good player, but, like a lot of small kids, he had learned to play with a very strong grip. It was the only way he could whip the clubhead through the ball and generate decent power. Jack could see, though, that if Bob wanted to go further in golf, he would need a more orthodox grip. The very strong grip would cause him to hit too many low, uncontrolled hooks off the tee.

However, young Bob didn't want to change. He was getting away with the strong grip by hitting his tee shots with a three-wood that had a shallow face and got the ball up in the air quickly. He sensed he would get worse before he got better if he changed his grip.

So, Jack found a way to force him to change. He bought Bob a very flat-faced Wilson driver and laid down an edict. "This is the only club you can practice with." The only practice area available to Bob was the ninth fairway at Northampton. It was right under the window of Jack's pro shop, so Jack could enforce his command.

"But I can't get the ball up in the air with this club," Bob protested.

"That's why you'll have to change your grip," Jack replied.

Bob, with no alternative, took a bag of shag balls and walked out to the practice area. He started trying to hit them with the new club. He hit duck hooks. He hit shanks. He finally broke down, and started to cry in frustration.

He got no sympathy from Jack. "When you're finished crying," Jack said, "you can practice some more and, gradually, you'll change your grip. You're stubborn and you have to learn the hard way."

It took Bob nearly six months of work to master the grip

change. He won almost nothing for an entire summer but, in the end, he had a golf swing that would win at levels much higher than the amateur circuit in western Massachusetts.

He also gained an understanding of some of the problems that confront a golf teacher. A lot of pupils, even when they say they want to improve, refuse to make the changes they need to make because they fear that, in the short run, they'll get worse. So it's not enough for a pro to point out a flaw and demonstrate the correct method. He has to find a way to cajole the student to swing the right way. Bob can't, of course, be as draconian as his brother was with him but, as a teacher, he's devised dozens of little tricks and drills that do the same thing—force a student to break his or her old pattern and do things properly.

"People fear change," Bob says. "You have to shock them to force them to change."

Bob's own golfing development slowed in 1944, when he entered the army. He became an expert rifleman. After his discharge, he turned pro and started winning some local events in Massachusetts. Jack arranged for him to play in an exhibition with three touring pros: Doug Ford, Ted Kroll, and Milan Marusic.

Bob played well that day. "This kid is good enough to play on the tour," Kroll told Jack Toski. So, in 1948, under the wing of Kroll and Marusic, Bob tried the winter tour.

It was not the sort of life that a rookie like Tiger Woods enjoys today. Bob traveled in the back seat of Kroll's Studebaker, nestled behind the clothes rack. They ate at White Castles, where the little hamburgers sold by the dozen in a greasy sack. Bob slept on a cot in rooms where Kroll and Marusic had the beds. Marusic snored all night; Kroll ground his teeth. Bob made $500 that first winter.

"These kids today," Bob says, "don't have a clue what it was like. They want private rooms, private planes. But I wouldn't change it for all the money in the world."

Kroll and Marusic made Bob their protégé. On the tour in those days, there was no money for personal swing teachers. The players helped one another. A lot of the help, Bob discovered, was given not on the practice tee, but on the golf course during practice rounds.

Bob, for instance, used a pitching wedge from bunkers when he first went on tour. Kroll told him, correctly, that he would need to learn to use a sand wedge to cope with the deep, heavy sand they would encounter on some of the courses. He taught Bob how to use the club. Bob remembers getting another lesson, this one from Dutch Harrison, on how to play a dirt explosion shot from a bare lie near the green. There were dozens of other new things to learn.

Bob was getting, in an informal way, playing lessons.

Bob left the tour to become a teacher in the mid-1950s, not long after he won the money title. There wasn't as much money in tournament golf in those days; the players sought recognition and respect, and Bob had earned that. He had a young wife and three small children, and he didn't like being away from home. Of course, he brought what he had learned on the tour to his teaching. He became the best I've ever seen at giving playing lessons.

I heard not long ago about a playing lesson Bob gave to a 12-handicap golfer we'll call Ben. Ben had gone to Bob's teaching center in Florida complaining about his tendency to slice his driver. Bob had, understandably, given him a lesson on driving the ball. Ben had started to hit straighter, longer tee shots—even to draw a few.

The next day, they went to the Palm-Aire Country Club for the playing lesson. Like a lot of south Florida courses, Palm-Aire has an abundance of water but fairly wide fairways. It's not too long, befitting a course where a lot of the golfers are older, but the greens complexes are tricky. The first hole at Palm-Aire is a par five that bends to the left around the shore of a lake.

"The trouble on this hole is all on the left," Bob told Ben. "Set your tee on the left side of the tee box and aim away from the water to increase your margin of error. Our objective in this round is to take no penalty strokes."

He was conveying an elementary principle of course management, one that a lot of players either never learned or have forgotten. Some golfers think it's better never to mention a hazard, lest they introduce a negative thought. In a practice round, though, I think it's best to observe the hazards, talk about them, and pick targets that consciously avoid them. Then, in a competitive round, the golfer can focus solely on the target.

Ben did as he was told and managed to put a three-wood into the fairway. But, still nervous, he hit his next two shots a little fat, catching the turf before the ball, and barely cleared the water with the third, leaving himself a long pitch to the green off wet sand.

Bob, meanwhile, was putting on a display of relaxed golf. He cracked an easy fairway wood for his second shot, aiming right, away from the lake and drawing it gently back into the fairway, leaving himself a short iron to the green. The pin was cut on the right quarter of the green, close to a bunker.

"I'm going to land this about 10 feet left of the pin," he said, and did precisely that. In a good playing lesson, part of what the pro does is set an example. He gives the student a firsthand idea of how an expert plays and thinks.

Ben, though he was taking this in, was still tense in the presence of a professional. He chunked his sand shot and left himself with a short pitch to the green. He shanked that, nearly bouncing it off Bob's kneecap. That left him deep in the bunker, and he couldn't get the ball out. He managed to put the second effort on the green, then sank the putt to save an eight.

Bob said nothing.

Ben pulled his approach to the elevated second green and left himself with a tricky pitch. "You put the ball in a position that cost you—downwind, over a bunker, and blind," Bob said. His own shot had missed the green, but to the right side, which presented a simple, unimpeded chip toward the pin. Bob got up and down. Ben, worried about another shank, barely put the ball on the green, then three-putted. Ben learned something else about course management. Early in a golfer's development, course management skills don't always produce results, because even if the golfer tries to hit smart shots, he can't always do it. Nevertheless, the skills are important to acquire.

Ben plodded along, making a couple of more bogeys with sloppy chips and pitches. He found it difficult to relax. He felt embarrassed, though he shouldn't have. A teacher like Bob Toski doesn't care how well a pupil plays. He only wants to help that pupil improve, and the more of the pupil's flaws he sees, the better.

Slowly, Ben stopped worrying what Bob Toski thought about his golf and started to play the game. He hit a five-iron from under a tree to 15 feet from the pin at number seven. Bob, standing in the fairway, applauded.

"If nothing else, I'll have the memory of Bob Toski applauding one of my shots," Ben said.

"It was a good shot," Bob said. Then he dropped his own approach shot five feet inside Ben's. Bob is still competitive.

They reached the green. Ben missed his birdie putt, pushing it right. Before Bob hit his, Ben asked him what he thought about when he faced birdie putts in competition.

"You want them to break four-and-a-half inches," Bob said, and paused for dramatic effect. "Down."

He holed his birdie putt and smiled as it rattled at the bottom of the cup.

Ben pushed his approach to number eight a little bit and wound up six feet off the green, but still on the collar. Ben's own course has narrow collars, so he asked Bob for advice.

"Putt it," Bob said, perhaps thinking of the chips Ben had chunked earlier in the round. "The objective is to make four."

Ben putted, but he overcompensated for the friction of the fringe and rolled it seven feet past. He missed the par putt coming back.

"It's all right," Bob said. "You're trying to adapt to conditions you haven't played before. Chalk it up to that."

Relaxed now, Ben began playing his normal game of pars and bogeys. At number 14, a 120-yard par three into a breeze, he asked Bob for some help on club selection. "It's between a nine-iron and an eight-iron for me," he said.

"Use the eight-iron," Bob replied. "The front bunker is very deep, but you can putt out of the back bunkers." Again, it was an elementary principle of course management—stay clear of the worst trouble. But it was not a principle that had occurred to Ben. Relieved of concern about club choice, he hit a smooth eight-iron pin high and made his par.

At the next hole, a long par four into the wind, Ben hit his best drive of the day. Then he hit a three-wood that stopped about ten yards short of the green, perhaps 80 feet from the pin. Ben's mind filled with thoughts of the chips he had chunked earlier in the round.

"I'd love to be in your spot needing to get up and down to win a tournament," Bob said. "I'd be licking my chops."

Ben realized at that moment the difference between his thoughts and the thoughts of a great golfer.

He started visualizing the ball going into the hole. He chipped with a pitching wedge and the ball hit the green just where he had intended it. It rolled up, seemed likely to stop, then caught a downslope that gave it enough energy to cover the last 15 feet. The ball broke slightly left as it neared the pin, and stopped a couple of feet away. Ben knocked the putt in for his par.

"Congratulations," Bob said. "That's the toughest hole on the course today."

They hit their drives on number 16, Bob about 40 yards longer than Ben. There was a delay while they waited for the group ahead of them to putt out. They sat in the cart, watching.

"What is it that's kept golf alluring to you for 60 years?" Ben asked Bob.

Bob stepped out of the cart and looked around. "It gives me peace of mind like nothing else," he said. "It's got beauty, sunshine, and fresh air. And it's challenging. Each hole is different. I don't need a lot of people cheering. I just need to be out here figuring out how to play each shot."

He stepped up to his ball with a five-iron and hit a low line drive that never got more than ten feet off the ground. It landed ten yards in front of the green, took one big hop, then rolled gently up onto the green and stopped hole high.

"That's a lost art, that shot," Bob said, pleased with himself. "It's not taught anymore. Now it's all hit it high, bomb the green, and sink the putt. But I like the artistry of the game. There are so many shots you can play. It's like playing all the instruments in a 14-piece orchestra. If you recorded them all separately and then blended the recordings, people would say, 'That's great music. Who's in the orchestra?' And I'd tell them, 'Bob Toski plays every instrument.'"

He laughed.

They finished numbers 16 and 17 with a par and a bogey and a bogey and a par. Ben had learned a lot about the way a pro manages his game and how he thinks. He had seen a little bit of the shot repertoire of a great golfer. He had learned something about his own swing flaws. He asked Bob what he ought to be concentrating on in his next five lessons.

"Short game, bunker game, putting," Bob said.

Ben nodded, thinking that he still wanted to work on his slice. And the next two lessons?

"Short game, bunker game, putting," Bob repeated. "Your short game doesn't hold up under pressure."

Thinking back, Ben had to agree.

• • •

The last exchange between Bob and Ben suggests one of the biggest benefits of the playing lesson. It's not just what it teaches the pupil. It's what it teaches the pro about the pupil. The playing lesson is a great diagnostic tool. It shows the pro what his pupil's game is really like. It shows both of them where they ought to focus during upcoming lessons. In fact, Bob Toski has told me that if he could start his teaching center over again, he would try to get enough land to build three or four practice holes around its perimeter, just for playing lessons.

Yet, most pros and most golfers rarely give or take playing lessons. Imagine a basketball coach who drilled his team during the week and then went fishing on game day. How could he know his team's strengths and weaknesses if he didn't watch it in competition? How could he convey the nuances of strategy if he wasn't there? He couldn't. He would be employed about as long as a member of the Flat Earth Society would last at NASA.

Pros and pupils have given me various reasons why the playing lesson is as rare these days as a persimmon driver. Courses are crowded. Playing lessons take longer; a busy teacher can't see as many pupils. They cost more.

All of those things are true, but they don't justify leaving playing lessons out of any intelligent plan of improvement. Serious pupils and serious teachers find the time for them. They go off early in the morning, on the back side of their course, or they do it in the twilight hours of summer. A playing lesson need not be 18 holes. Six or nine holes is long enough, but you need to take one every few months, as indicated in the outline of the improvement cycle.

At first, your playing lessons will be disproportionately diagnostic. They will give your teacher a chance to familiarize himself with the real strengths and weaknesses of your game—which may not be the ones you perceive. They'll give you both something to go on as you plan the lessons you'll be taking in the next improvement cycle. That's why I recommend taking one early on in your relationship with your teacher, and then at the end of each improvement cycle thereafter.

As time goes by, the character of your playing lessons will change. They'll start to focus more on special situations you may encounter in a round of golf—hilly lies, thick rough, and so on. They'll help the pro deal with things like your preshot routine. They'll focus more on analysis and strategy—the essence of course management. Above all, they'll help you to learn the myriad of skills you'll need if you want to have the short game of a scratch player.

Chapter 7

One Stroke at a Time

A Florida golfer named Patty Pilz knows a great deal about how playing lessons can help develop the short game, and how important the short game is. That's partly because the short game almost caused her to give up golf.

When Patty was a little girl, she played a lot of golf with her father, who was a scratch player. They owned a big half-vacant lot, and her father used to mow some rudimentary greens and tees into the grass there. On long summer evenings, she'd go out with her father and bang balls around. She was an all-around athlete, involved in swimming and tennis as well as golf, and she got to be pretty good. In fact, she was far and away the best player entered in the girls' junior championship at Brookside Country Club the summer she was 12 years old.

Patty was cruising in that nine-hole, stroke-play event when she got to number eight, an uphill par four. She hit her approach shot into a deep sand bunker to the right of the green.

And she couldn't get it out.

She took her wedge and tried to explode the ball up over the lip.

Whump.

It hit the bank in front of her and rolled slowly back to her feet. She tried again. Whump. Same result. She tried again, and again, and again. It didn't occur to her to chip out backwards and play to the green from a grass lie. She flailed at the ball until finally, she managed to lift it over the lip and onto the green.

It had taken her 12 strokes to get out. She lost the tournament, and the trophy, by a stroke.

Traumatized, Patty played no competitive golf for ten years. She stuck to tennis, and she was good enough at it to get a college scholarship. But, in her senior year, because she had transferred from one college to another, her tennis eligibility was gone. She decided to give golf another try and made her college team. Within a year or so, just by dint of playing more, she got her handicap down to about 13.

She kept playing after college. She resettled in Florida, where her parents had retired. Some eight years ago, her handicap was about ten. She heard from a friend about a pro named Bill Davis at the Jupiter Hills Club, which her parents belonged to. For Christmas, she asked them to give her some lessons from him.

Bill Davis, as it happens, is one of the great short-game teachers. He works with touring pros, including Jerry Kelly, a client of mine. He works, of course, with the members of his club. And he takes on a limited number of pupils from outside the club. These nonmembers are some of his best pupils, because Bill doesn't have to accept them. He works only with those who are willing to follow his ideas about the right way to improve their golf games.

When people call about lessons from outside the club, Bill has long conversations with them on the telephone. He finds out how long they've been playing golf, how often they practice, how often they've taken lessons, what their goals are.

Then, if he likes what he hears, he offers them a deal. He will give them them ten lessons, but they must pay for all ten in advance. They must practice between lessons, following a practice plan he will draw up for them. If, after ten lessons and the concommitant practice, they have not improved, he will refund their money.

No one, Bill says, has ever asked for the refund.

That's partly because, very early on in this process, Bill emphasizes the short game.

Not enough pros and players do this, in my opinion. That's partly because of the nature of most pro–pupil relationships. The pupil typically controls the lesson agenda because he comes for one lesson at a time, and with a specific complaint. If he says, "I want help adding distance to my tee shots," the pro generally doesn't feel he can say, "No, let's have a lesson on chipping."

This, I suspect, will be increasingly true now that Tiger Woods has arrived on the scene. Tiger is going to persuade a lot of people, including tour pros, that distance is the key to success. They are going to ask their teachers to help them add distance. There's no doubt that the person who can hit the ball three hundred yards and keep it in the fairway has an advantage over the person who hits it two hundred and fifty yards.

But it's not a decisive advantage. Don't forget that Tiger Woods came to Augusta at the age of 19 hitting the ball every bit as far as he did when he won the Masters at the age of 21. The difference between 1995 and 1997 was that Tiger had polished his scoring game. He hit his short irons and wedges precise distances. He putted better. His course management was smarter.

Many great players learned the short game first and then polished the long game. In an earlier era, they were caddies who spent their spare time playing chipping and putting games with the other caddies for pocket change. Nowadays, I see players like Jose Maria Olazabal and Phil Mickelson, who polished their shorts games early because they had backyard greens or, in Olazabal's case, lived on a golf course where his father was superintendent.

Most team sports have an analogous dichotomy between flashy skills that are fun to practice and subtler skills that a lot of athletes don't want to work on. This problem is solved by giving authority to a coach or manager. A baseball team can't come to spring training and decide to spend all of its time playing home-run derby in batting practice against fat, three-quarter speed pitches. The manager, if he knows what he's doing, is going to insist that the team spend many hours working on throwing to the right cutoff men, sacrifice bunts, and hitting behind runners. Those are the little skills that win baseball games.

A basketball coach, if he knows what he's doing, will not let his team spend all its practice time on run-and-gun scrimmages. He will insist that every day the team work on defense, rebounding, and free throws. He knows that a team will have nights when its shooting is off, when all of the players lay bricks. Good teams win on those nights because they always play defense, always rebound, and always hit a high percentage of their free throws.

Most golf pros don't teach the short game enough because they don't have the authority of a baseball manager or a basketball coach. But Bill Davis, with his outside pupils, has that authority. Once they've paid for ten lessons, they are in his hands. He devises the curriculum. And he makes sure it includes lots of short-game lessons.

This leads to a certain irony. The nonmembers who take lessons from Bill at Jupiter Hills are on a more certain path to improvement than the members who pick and choose what they want Bill to teach them. That's the way golf is. Most people don't choose to learn the short game.

Once he gets a player into his program, Bill is not quick to teach putting mechanics. He believes that touch, a feel for distance, is what most average players need to learn first on the greens. To help them develop it, he has a number of practice drills. In one of them, he has players stroke putts to a hole with a club shaft set down on the grass an inch or so behind it, perpendicular to the line of the putt. They win an imaginary dollar for every putt that goes in the hole or winds up resting against the shaft. But they lose three dollars for every ball that runs over the shaft. They lose fifty dollars for every shot that doesn't either touch the shaft or go in the hole. Bill tells them that after they've won a few hundred imaginary dollars in this touch drill, they can have a lesson in putting mechanics if they still want it.

Of course, not many players do. If they've worked on their sense of pace enough to earn lots of imaginary dollars in his touch drill, they're generally delighted with how much their putting has improved.

This drill is not the only one that can improve touch. Nor will all pros decide to work on touch first. Others may want to fix a player's putting mechanics right away. It depends on the player and the teacher. The most important thing is that the pro and pupil agree on a putting-improvement program that the player makes part of his practice routine from the outset.

To teach other facets of the short game, Bill likes to take his pupils out on the golf course for a slightly different type of playing lesson than the one Bob Toski gave in the last chapter. He gets in a cart with them, and they drive from one potential playing situation to another. Not long ago, he gave this kind of lesson to Patty.

They stopped near a green and he dropped some balls about twenty-five feet from the putting surface, at a spot where players departing the green had matted down the rough with their feet. Bill dropped his hat on the green to simulate a tight pin.

"What's the best way to get to this pin?"

"Putter," Patty said. It was a creative answer, and Bill felt it was the correct answer. The lie was tight, and the footsteps had matted the grass and made it possible to roll the ball through the rough. Using a wedge from that spot, Patty felt, would have brought into play the possibility of chunking it or skulling it.

Other players and teachers might feel a different shot was best in that situation. It would depend on their skills and the condition of the greens they play. But saving strokes from odd spots around the green is frequently what enables a player to pare those last few strokes off her handicap. The important thing is not so much what type of shot you choose to play. The important thing is that, whatever the situation, you have a shot that you've practiced and that you feel you can put in the hole.

Bill stopped at another hole about 40 yards from the green and dropped a few balls into heavy rough. To make sure the lie was bad, he tamped them down with his feet.

"Put one on the green," he challenged.

Patty looked at the green and the two bunkers lying beyond it. She swung—and lofted the ball short. It plopped down in the fairway about five yards in front of the green.

Then she swung harder, and the ball floated out and onto the putting surface. "When the ball's deep in this Bermuda rough, the grass is going to slow the clubhead down," Bill explained. "But most people forget that when they see the bunkers behind the green. They don't hit it hard enough."

He dropped some more balls, much closer to the green but, again, deep in the heavy rough. He showed Patty a "pillow shot," which she could play in such situations, treating the rough like sand and exploding the ball out.

Then, he dropped a couple of balls in the fairway about 20 yards short of the slightly elevated green. He showed Patty a bump-and-run shot she could play if she didn't want to hit a lob off the tight lie. Bill believes that getting the ball on the ground and rolling it is often a wiser choice around the greens than flying it to the pin.

And that is what his on-the-course short-game lessons are largely about—recognizing situations and picking the smartest shot. This is one of the abilities that distinguishes a player with a handicap of six from a player with a scratch handicap. There may not be much to choose from in the two players' long games. Both can hit the ball pretty well and both might hit, say, eight, ten or 12 greens per round.

It's on the holes where they don't hit the greens that the scratch player often separates himself from the six-handicapper. The scratch player is usually better at recognizing different situations, choosing the smartest shot to play, and executing it.

Bill extended this kind of teaching to the green and back into the fairway as he and Patty rambled about the course, looking for gaps between groups playing regular rounds. They stopped in the fairway of one hole and dropped some balls about 150 yards from the center of the green on a downhill lie. The wind from the nearby ocean was blowing stiffly into Patty's face. What, Bill asked, was the right shot to play?

Patty, as it happened, didn't have an iron she could hit into the wind far enough to carry the yawning bunker in front of the green. She hits the ball solidly and consistently, but not particularly long. She could reach the green with a fairway wood. If she did, Bill pointed out, her ball wasn't likely to stop on the shallow putting surface. It would most likely wind up in one of the back bunkers, leaving her with a treacherous shot back.

In this situation, he told her, the smart play was to aim away from the green. Her target would be the fairway area just in front and to the right of the green. Aiming there would take both the front and rear bunkers out of play, and it would give her a reasonably easy chip to the pin and a better chance to make par than she'd have from either of the bunkers.

This wouldn't be the right play for everyone. Longer hitters, obviously, might be able to get an iron high enough into the air to clear the front bunker and still hold the green.

On days when the wind was blowing from another direction, it might not be the right play for Patty, but on this particular day, from this particular spot, it was.

On another hole, Bill dropped some balls in the fairway about 150 yards from an L-shaped green with the pin tucked in the back right quadrant, protected by a large bunker. He asked Patty to pick a target. Correctly, she chose the left side of the green. She would have a long birdie putt if she hit it there, but she was still more likely to make par than she would be if she went for the pin and missed. Again, this kind of judgment is one of the things that separates good golfers from excellent golfers.

In the beginning, of course, not all of Patty's lessons went this way. She came to Bill with a weak, high fade as her characteristic shot.

"She didn't have much motion," Bill recalls. "She could have swung in a phone booth."

Though they worked from the inception on the short game and course management, they initially spent a greater proportion of their time on the long game than they do now. Bill wanted Patty to hit with a lower trajectory. It was not easy, but she came out of the process with a more powerful, consistent shot.

She also came out with what golfers call a predictable miss. In Patty's case, it is to the right. If she mishits a shot, it might fade more than she'd like, but it will not go to the left.

Most scratch players have something similar. They want to know that if they step on to the tee of the toughest hole on a given golf course, with a match or a tournament on the line, they can play the hole knowing that whatever else might happen, they are not going to miss in one direction or the other. Some players know they're not going left. Jack Nicklaus, Ben Hogan in his prime, and Bruce Lietzke are good examples. Arnold Palmer and Brad Faxon, on the other hand, know they're going to hit draws in most tight situations. It helps with planning a strategy. It helps with confidence. Once Patty had a predictable miss, she could make the kinds of judgments Bill was asking for. She could aim for the left side of a green knowing that she would not miss on the left side.

Their work on the swing gave Patty something else to make her more consistent, something she and Bill call medicine. Bill and Patty know that with her swing, the most common problem she will have on the golf course is blocking the ball to the right, because she doesn't properly shift her weight through the hitting zone. When this happens now, though, Patty has a way to recapture the feel of the right movements. She stands off away from the ball, a club in her hands, and makes a couple of baseball swings. Then, with the right feel restored, she begins her normal preshot routine and swings without thinking of mechanics.

This is the best way to handle mechanical problems during a round of golf. You will only know the proper drill to restore feel if you work one out with a pro who knows your swing and its tendencies.

Of course, Patty's progress only looks smooth and easy in

retrospect. Like any improving player, she suffered her share of reversals. She can remember times, playing in club tournaments, when her new mechanics were so awkward that she could barely get the ball off the tee. This is one of the testing moments awaiting most golfers who try to improve.

Her friends and playing partners, she recalls, would quietly suggest that she do things that amounted to going back to her old way of swinging. This is, again, the feedback a lot of golfers get from their friends. There is a strong, perhaps unconscious, urge on the part of most golfers to see everyone they play with conform to a norm. When they see someone trying to rise above the norm, it makes them uncomfortable. At the first opportunity, they're liable to make suggestions that amount to giving up and going back to the old way of doing things.

Patty responded to this kind of peer pressure with an inner strength. She learned to smile, nod, and continue to do what Bill had taught her. She had faith that in the long run, it would work. She honored the commitment she had made.

It took a while, because Patty was holding down a job as she went through this process. She could not practice every day. She practiced on her days off. When she played golf, she tried to go out in informal situations where she could sometimes hit two or three shots from the same spot and work on what she was learning.

Then, suddenly, her game came around and she had the pleasure of hearing the Doubting Thomases reverse themselves. Instead of suggesting that she swing the way she once had, they were asking where she had learned to hit the impressive shots she was hitting.

As her swing and game became more fundamentally sound and her handicap dropped, the nature of Bill and Patty's relationship evolved. She took lessons less often. When she did, she spent less time working on her swing and more time on her short game and on her mental game. This is a natural progression.

It took Patty six years of effort, but she finally reached scratch a year or so ago.

"What winds up happening in going from nine to scratch," she says, "is that you do things in ones. You start taking one fewer putt per round. You start getting up and down one more time. You pick out a better target once per round. And gradually, you get there."

In the past few years, she's won her club championship and played twice in the U.S. Mid-Amateur. Bill has helped her banish whatever lingering doubts there were from that disastrous tournament round at Brookside Country Club when she was 12 years old.

Last year, Patty was playing in a major women's amateur event in south Florida, the Tri-County. She had the lead going into the final round, but she was nervous, afraid she would blow it in the final holes, just as she had as a youngster.

"I'll make you a bet," Bill said. "The stakes are one dollar times the number of the hole you're playing. If you par the hole, no blood. If you birdie it, you win a dollar times the number. If you make bogey, you lose a dollar times the number of the hole."

Patty took the bet. The next day, she didn't think too much about where she stood in the tournament; she thought about her bet with Bill. As she came down the stretch, she only wanted to make sure she didn't lose money to her coach.

Bill got a call that night. "Sit down," Patty said. "You owe me five-seven dollars."

"Great," Bill said.

"And, by the way," Patty continued. "I shot seventy-six and won the tournament by six strokes."

Bill paid off that night, throwing in a bottle of champagne. Patty still has the $57 in a scrapbook. That's the kind of joy and satisfaction that can come to both sides of the pro-player relationship.

Chapter 8

The Psychology of a Swing Change

A major swing change is a little like surgery. I don't know too many people who would elect to go under the knife before they'd tried other, less drastic, alternatives for getting better—medicine, diet, physical therapy, fitness. In much the same way, I think players and teachers should, in most cases, look for the simplest and least drastic ways to get better.

This certainly means that they'll go to work on the player's short game from the outset of the player's improvement program. It usually means that they'll wring whatever improved scoring they can out of enhanced basics like grip, posture, and alignment. It will often mean that the pro will look for shortcomings in the player's strength and flexibility. If she's not an expert in those areas, she'll send the player to someone who is. Many swing flaws are actually due to stiffness or weakness in some part of the anatomy. A lot of golfers can improve by getting stronger and more flexible.

It certainly means that a player and his pro will want to assess the player's mental game. Does he have a consistent, sound preshot routine? Does she pick out small targets and think about getting the ball to them? Does he trust his swing when he plays? No one has a perfect swing. No one needs a perfect swing. There are many golfers playing at scratch or better despite flawed swings because they trust the mechanics they have.

But, in some cases, after all of these questions have been addressed, the pro and player will decide that a swing change is necessary.

They should not embark on a swing change without discussing it thoroughly.

First of all, is the change appropriate? If the player is, for instance, a tournament player, will the new ball flight that can be expected from the change be effective on the courses he has to play?

Second, how does the pupil learn best? Some players are analytical thinkers. They respond best to a long discussion of the new techniques and why they work. Others are visual learners who might respond best to a video that shows their current swing and how it deviates from the better swing the pro wants to teach them. Others might be "feel" learners who want to know how the new movements are supposed to feel. Most of us are a combination of all three, weighted in one direction or another. We all want to get to the stage where we are feel golfers, who perform the right movements without thinking about them, because they feel right.

This discussion ought to encompass two more points. One is how long the pro thinks the player will need to make the proposed change. Two is whether the player is prepared for the possibility of getting worse before getting better. This is very likely, because any fundamentally new movement will feel awkward for a while.

Good communication about these pitfalls will make the swing change a little bit like wading across an unknown river in the daylight, as opposed to wading across in pitch darkness. In the daylight, the wader can see the bank on the other side. Even if the water starts rising, he strides ahead. If it rises over his head, he's prepared to swim for a while because he can see that bank and knows roughly how long it will take to get there. The wader who starts out in darkness is likely to panic if the water gets high, because he doesn't know where he's going. He'll turn back or, worse, thrash around and drown.

So, you ought to have a plan and, if possible, a model. It's helpful if the teacher can show the pupil pictures or film of a touring pro who makes the move the pupil needs to master. That's like having the bank on the other side of the river to look at.

As you embark on a swing change, it's important to know that two of the chief challenges you face are habit and comfort.

Most golfers have a dominant habit or tendency. This is a deeply ingrained physical pattern that probably has its roots in childhood. Bob Toski, for instance, thinks that most right-handed golfers tend to slice the ball because they began in infancy to reach for things with their right hand, and reaching with the right hand is not a sound way to commence a downswing. He may be right. Or, it may be that most golfers start out without instruction and develop bad habits unconsciously and haphazardly. I don't know and it's not important unless you're trying to develop a golfer from infancy.

The fact is that dominant habits exist, and they will show up. Each time you swing, your dominant habit is trying to assert itself. This is especially true under pressure. You need good, sound, dominant habits.

So, you must find a way to break the dominant habit you have, assuming it's one that is impeding your golf swing. You must replace it with the correct habit. This can be a long process, longer than the process of developing a new habit where none existed before.

In general, people learning new sports skills or breaking old habits go through three stages. In the beginning, they are unconsciously incompetent: That is, they're doing it wrong, but they're not aware of it. After instruction, they pass through a long intermediate stage, where they are consciously competent. This means that they know the right movement and can execute it, but only if they think about it and direct their body with their conscious mind. Finally, they reach the advanced stage of unconscious competence. In golf, this means that a player swings correctly without thinking about it. In other words, his dominant habit has become a correct habit. It will show up under stress. He can focus on his target with trust that his body will perform properly. And his body, in most cases, will do what he wants it to. Until you reach this automatic stage, you haven't really learned your new move.

Comfort is the enemy of this process.

No matter how bad a person's swing might be, it usually feels pretty good to that individual. He's done it thousands of times. He's used to it. He just can't understand why this comfortable motion keeps producing bad shots.

Take, for instance, a player with a problem on short pitches from tight lies. Sometimes he chunks them. Sometimes he blades them. He's reached the point where he doesn't trust his wedge, which exacerbates his problem. He goes to a pro for help.

The pro might see that the player has two bad habits. He takes the club back too far inside the proper plane of the swing, and he's got too much lower body motion.

The player may have a hard time believing what the pro is saying to him. It doesn't feel to him as if he's taking the club back inside. It doesn't feel to him as if he's moving too much from the hips down. In fact, he feels quite graceful. Of course, he can't see where the club goes once it leaves his field of vision, which is centered on the ball. He can't see what his legs are doing.

Even if he trusts his pro, or the pro shows him his movements on videotape, it will not be easy for him to change. That's because human beings are not objective judges of their own motions. If the player in question changes his backswing path so that the club moves just half an inch further to the outside, it will feel to him as if it's moved a foot. If he quiets his legs just a little bit, it will feel to him as if he's swinging with stiff, locked knees. To make the new, correct motion, a player will most likely have to feel as if he's exaggerating the movement. If he's trying to nudge his swing path a few inches to the outside, he'll have to feel as if he's pushing the club out somewhere in the vicinity of the next station on the practice tee.

This is one reason why it's more difficult to improve on your own than it is to improve with a coach. You need someone to observe you, to tell you what you're really doing, as opposed to what it feels like you're doing. Even experienced players with excellent, thoroughly understood, swings can use this help. I've stood on the practice tee with Tom Kite and watched him ask Mike Carrick, his caddie, where Tom's club is on his backswing. Sometimes Tom will have Mike hold the shaft of another club at a particular point off Tom's right hip and make certain that his shaft passes over the shaft Mike is holding as he draws the club back. Despite all his years of playing golf, and despite all he knows about his own swing, Tom still isn't precisely certain where his backswing is when he practices. So how can you be? You'd need another pair of eyes.

In making a swing change, of course, the problem is that beyond Tiger Woods and Nick Faldo, few of us can afford to have a teacher next to us each time we practice. Thus, you and your teacher will have to discuss ways to make sure that when you practice your new technique on your own, you're doing it properly.

One method good teachers use is to make certain, during the lesson, that the player gets acquainted with the right feeling. That's why teachers often use an impact bag. It helps players understand what proper hand position at contact feels like.

Another method is based on the principle that Bob Toski's brother Jack used to induce him to change his grip. The teacher devises drills that force the player to perform correctly. Bob may tell a player who has trouble rotating his left arm properly through the hitting zone to spend practice time letting go of the club with the right hand at impact, which forces the left arm to turn properly. There are a thousand drills for all the myriad problems in a golf swing, and any effective effort to change a swing will no doubt use some of them.

• • •

It will probably help in this effort if you can find ways to practice without a ball.

Wait a minute, you might say. Golf is about hitting a ball and making it go into a hole. Practicing without a ball might seem ridiculous—unless you know Hank Johnson and two of his star pupils, David and Greg Belcher.

I've known Hank for many years. We met at a *Golf Digest* school where he was teaching the swing and I was teaching the mental game. Later on, he moved to Greystone in Birmingham, Alabama.

A few years ago, Hank was struggling with a problem that faces many pros. He had some pupils who didn't have time to practice. They were professional people who were chained to their jobs every day, all day. They wanted to get better, but they wanted to play golf, not practice it, on the weekends.

Hank started to think about ways that these pupils could practice the correct motions at night, at home. He began to devise exercises for them, using some rudimentary, homemade tools. He had them practice the golf swing holding a soccer ball rather than a club in their hands. He had them practice the putting motion without a club or a ball, but with the left hip pressed against the frame of an open door—which forced them to move their hands with their shoulders.

He had each of them build a plane board out of plywood. A plane board, if you're not familiar with it, is simply a flat board about six feet long and three feet high, constructed with legs, so that it can be propped up at any angle to the ground from zero to ninety degrees. A player sets it to the correct angle for the plane of the club he is swinging. He stands behind it and lets the club shaft rest against the front of the board. If he swings along the board, it helps him learn how the correct plane feels.

Hank devised a series of plane-board exercises, most of which the pupil does holding a kitchen broom rather than a golf club. They're all designed to help the player practice the correct motions at different points in the golf swing. I won't go into all of them here because Hank has published a book that includes them, *How to Win the Three Games of Golf*.

Hank was inclined to think of these exercises as poor substitutes for practicing on a range with clubs and balls—until he noticed something. The pupils who had no daylight hours for practice, who worked strictly with the home exercises, were getting better faster than pupils who worked regularly and exclusively on the range.

This puzzled Hank for a while, but the more he thought about it, the more he believed he understood it. He theorized that the act of hitting a golf ball is not necessarily the best way to learn a new swing movement.

When a player hits a golf ball, even a practice ball, he wants to hit it well. He wants to see it fly in the direction he intended. Whether he realizes it or not, he quite often wants that satisfaction more than he wants to execute his new move properly. The feedback for trying to execute the new move properly, after all, may in the beginning be a lousy shot.

Most players with bad swings, Hank knows, have developed ways to compensate for them. If their swing path, for instance, is out-to-in, they may have learned, subconsciously, to try to close the club face as they move it through the hitting zone. Sometimes, this works well enough to produce a decent shot. But they can't do it consistently enough to be good golfers.

On the practice range, a lot of players hit the ball better with their flawed swings and compensating movements than they do with the new movements their teacher is trying to instill. They get, in effect, misleading feedback from the way their balls travel. Consciously or not, they start practicing their bad swings. They make no progress.

Hank's pupils who practiced in their basements and garages, however, had no concern with how a ball traveled. They were focused solely on training to make a new, proper motion. Consequently, they learned it better and faster.

As he studied these results, Hank would occasionally call me and ask whether his thinking was in accord with what researchers in kinesiology and sports psychology were finding as they studied the way the best coaches instill new skills in athletes in all sports. I told him it was.

My good friend Dr. Bob Christina of the University of North Carolina at Greensboro conducts research in how individuals master athletic skills. Along with Dr. Daniel Corcos of Rush Medical College in Illinois, he published his findings in a manual, *Coaches Guide to Teaching Sport Skills*.

Among the things that Bob advocates is breaking a complex skill into smaller parts. You wouldn't, for instance, try to teach a young diver to perform a triple somersault with two full twists all at once. You'd break the movement down. Away from the pool, you'd teach the technique of springing off the board, perhaps using a trampoline and safety ropes. Far from any water, you'd work on somersaulting and twisting. Only when the diver had mastered all of those separately would you ask her to put them all together and try it at a pool.

That, in essence, was what Hank was doing with his home exercises. Each of them focused on a portion of the golf swing.

Bob Christina has also found that fear of failure is a big obstacle to learning new skills. That, too, corresponded to what Hank had learned. Practicing on the driving range introduces an element of anxiety, if only because the golfer wants to see the ball fly properly. That makes him more inclined to fall back on old, imperfect methods rather than stick with new and better, but still awkward, ones. By having his golfers practice at home, without a ball, Hank eliminated that anxiety.

Hank's method also corresponded to other things I'd heard. Julie Inkster, the LPGA star, told me that she learned the golf swing as a girl in a squash court. The late Harvey

Penick liked to have golfers do things like swinging at dandelions with a weed cutter to master the right movements.

Hank has demonstrated the effectiveness of this method with some pupils who have made excellent progress. Two of his best are the Belcher brothers. David and Greg are shortish, athletic guys in their thirties. Davis is a welterweight and Greg a middleweight. They both work in the automobile business with their father and, in that business, they're expected to play a lot of customer golf. They were both decent but not outstanding players, largely self-taught, until a few years ago. David's handicap was 15 and Greg's was 18. Then, they decided they wanted to shoot in the low 70s instead of the high 80s.

They knew Hank from their church, and approached him about taking lessons. "Do you really want to learn this game?" Hank asked them. "Or do you just want to fix a few things and get better?"

Assured that they wanted to learn the game, Hank told them it would be a long process. He gave them each a copy of his book and asked them to clear some space in their garages, basements, or offices for practice gear. Then he installed a plane board and other apparatus for each of them and taught them the exercises they were to perform.

Hank's method, of course, did not rely solely on indoor exercise. Both David and Greg practiced outdoors as well. When they did, though, it tended to be on exercises and drills Hank had devised. He likes his pupils, for instance, to practice hitting short pitches by placing the ball a foot or so inside the T formed by a bunker rake laid flat on the ground. They have to take the club back high to avoid the rake head, and have to swing it straight to avoid the handle. The drill reinforces the method Hank teaches for that shot.

David and Greg continued to play rounds of golf, though generally with each other and not in tournaments. The fact that they were both in the same program helped them. They reinforced each other.

Their progress was sometimes slow and sometimes nonexistent. At their second lesson, Hank changed David's grip and address. When David tried to hit balls with the new grip and posture, he couldn't hit them more than sixty yards. On the course, he couldn't break 100. But he stayed committed.

"We're going to take three steps backward, but when it comes, it will come fast," Hank promised.

It did. Soon both Greg and David showed improvement. But David improved faster. Hank asked, and learned that David was much more faithful than Greg about doing his indoor exercises. As a result, his swing improved faster and with less conscious effort. Greg had to struggle to improve his plane and overcome a tendency to slice.

David can remember many evenings when his wife would come out to the garage and shake her head over what her husband was doing with that broom and that odd-looking board. The payoff has come in vastly improved golf. David now carries a three handicap. His driving accuracy and distance have both improved. He hits more greens and he putts better. Greg is a six. When they play customer golf, they impress the customers.

The ironic thing about what Hank has learned about teaching golf is how few of his pupils take advantage of it. He estimates that perhaps one in 20 people who come to him for lessons undertake his complete program. The rest are looking for a quick fix—and there are none. Swing changes take time and effort.

The things that Bob Christina and Hank Johnson have learned can reduce the time and pain involved. Anyone who is contemplating a major swing change ought to consider their methods. If possible, they should embark on the change in the autumn, after the competitive golf season is done, and do a full winter of indoor work without a ball to make the progress come faster the next spring.

Chapter 9

Bonefishing and Other Distractions

A year or so ago, a friend of mine named Dick Kreitler was well on his way to a low, single-digit handicap. Then something happened, something which can be very instructive for you.

Dick is a financial consultant who realized about fifteen years ago that modern communications technology meant that you didn't have to live in New York to be a player on Wall Street. He moved to Ketchum, Idaho. There, he managed his own portfolio and those of his clients quite well, well enough that he was able to retire in his early fifties.

He had moved to Ketchum to take advantage of the skiing at Sun Valley. Shortly after he arrived there, he discovered that a golf school was taking up residence in the resort during the summer months. Dick had not played much golf until then, but he took it up, getting his instruction in periodic visits to the golf school. Gradually, skiing paled and golf became his sport. He whittled his handicap down to about 15. When he retired, he wanted to play as much as he could, which meant Florida in the winter. Dick and his wife took a place in Vero Beach and joined the Orchid Island Golf & Beach Club. There, he met teaching pro Mark Heartfield.

Mark is a smart young teacher who was born and raised in Massachusetts. He divides his time between Orchid Island in the winter and Sankaty Head on Nantucket during the summer months. He has some progressive ideas about instruction. He likes pupils who commit to a series of lessons. Once they do, he tries to devote one-third of the lessons to teaching the swing on the practice tee; one-third to teaching the short game; and one-third to playing lessons, emphasizing course management.

When Dick decided to make Mark his teacher, he committed himself to this program. It involved more than just golf lessons. Dick is a stocky, muscular guy, and Mark thought he needed more flexibility, so he introduced him to a physical therapist, Gary Kitchell, who began working with Dick on stretching exercises.

Dick took a golf lesson from Mark every week, and was a model pupil. He practiced diligently, and came to each lesson with an agenda, something he wanted to work on. Mark finds this kind of pupil much more apt to learn than someone who simply shows up and says, "Okay, pro, what do you want to work on today?"

Not surprisingly, Dick improved quickly under this regimen. His short game got a lot sharper. His ball-striking became more consistent, primarily because he and Mark worked on improving his preshot setup, and taking some tension out of his swing. Thanks to the course-management lessons he was taking, Dick made fewer foolish mistakes when he played. As a result, his handicap dropped in the course of one winter season from about 15 to nine.

That's tremendous progress. Dick was playing a lot of rounds in the 70s, and was enjoying golf as never before. He returned to Vero Beach this past winter determined to get even better, and resumed his program with Mark.

This time, he and Mark decided on a swing change. Dick tended to hit a high fade with an upright swing, and he played a lot of his golf in windy places. If you've ever tried to play a high fade on a windy day, you know how difficult it can be. The wind turns fades into slices and makes balls balloon and fall well short of their normal distance. Mark felt that to get his handicap down to the next level, around five, Dick would have to learn to hit a draw with a lower trajectory. To do that, he thought Dick would have to develop a flatter swing plane; that is, the path of the club is somewhat lower and further out behind the player's back.

They started to work on it, and several things happened.

First, Dick became quite determined to master the change, which was fine. But his determination caused him to prod Mark to spend more of their lesson time on the practice tee, working on the new swing. They spent less time working on Dick's short game, even though Mark felt there was still ample room for improvement in that area.

Second, Dick's scores started to go up. Orchid Island has water on nearly every hole. It can look tight, even claustrophobic, and can be a tough place to work on a new swing. Dick was hitting more balls into the water. As a result he got a little tight. Mark could see this as they played together. Moves Dick executed on the practice tee didn't come off on the course.

Dick's handicap rose from nine to eleven. At about that time, he discovered bonefishing.

I'm not a fisherman, but I will take the word of Dick and others who testify that it's an exhilarating experience. "It's a riot," Dick says.

Suddenly, he was gone from Orchid Island for weeks at a time on bonefishing trips. His golf practice became sporadic. His progress stopped.

Dick did not consciously think, "My golf isn't going so well, so I'm going to get interested in something else." He just did. It wasn't until recently, upon some reflection, that he decided there was a connection between his rising handicap and his interest in bonefishing.

The connection between Dick's golf swing and his interest in bonefishing is an example of what causes many golfers to fall short of their goals. They stay enthused and committed while they're seeing progress, but their commitment and enthusiasm wane when the progress stops. Since virtually no one makes smooth, steady progress in golf, this helps assure that most people fail to stick with an improvement program.

Mark Heartfield sees this all the time. A lot of the members at Orchid Island are people who suddenly have more time to devote to golf than they ever had before. They've retired, or cut back on their work. They still have their health, and they have the means to take as many lessons and hit as many range balls as they'd like. Of the pupils who come to him, he estimates that about half say they want to embark on a long-term improvement program.

But Mark estimates that only 15 percent stick to it. The rest find that other interests seem more compelling. They've got out-of-town guests. They've got volunteer work. Or, as in Dick's case, they've got some other sport.

What they've got, I think, is a lack of patience. The fact is that you probably won't stay the course if you can't be patient, if only a falling handicap can motivate you.

If you want to stay the course, it will help if you can fall in love not with improvement, but with the process of improvement. Improvement is not something you can tightly control. It will come, but you can't decide when and how much you'll get better.

You can control your immersion in the process of improvement. If you decide that you love striving to get better, you can always make yourself happy by working at your game.

This is what you must do if you expect to honor your commitment.

A good teacher, like Mark Heartfield, will try to help you. Mark does whatever he can to make his lessons fun. He's softspoken and encouraging. When a pupil hits a frustrating patch, he tries to simplify things, to make the changes the pupil is working on easier. But, there is only so much the teacher can do to help you. The rest has to come from within you.

"The people who stick with the program tend to be organized, systematic people," Mark observes. "They have a desire to be better and a love of the game."

And, I think, they love the improvement process.

Dick Kreitler, I am sure, will bounce back. He had the discipline and organization required to work as a financial consultant two thousand miles from New York, getting up every morning at 4:30 to be ready for the opening of the markets. He understands now why he hit a frustrating patch last winter. He understands what he'll have to do if he wants to both improve at his golf and indulge his new love for bonefishing. Mark will try to make sure that he devotes more time to his short game, which ought to improve his scoring.

It's now just a matter of whether he has the patience to stick with it.

CHAPTER 10

THE PSYCHOLOGY OF PRACTICE

Golf is a great social sport. But as I study the habits of great golfers, I'm often struck by how many of them found it a solitary endeavor, especially as they practiced.

The archetype, of course, is Ben Hogan. Whether it was due to the harsh circumstances of his childhood or just a sense of what would help him learn to play golf, Hogan liked being alone. He even had a fictitious alter ego, Henny Bogan, to keep him company.

When Hogan practiced, he went to the far right end of the driving range so that he could turn his back on the rest of the players. I spent some time with Hogan in Ft. Worth several years ago, and I asked him why he did that. He explained that he simply didn't want to watch what anyone else was doing. He was working as hard as he could to monitor and refine what *he* was doing. In the prime of his career, after his swing had become the model for American golf, people often gathered to watch him practice. Hogan, conscious of the fact that he was paid to let people watch him play golf, tolerated this. But he insisted that no one speak to him as he worked. A business executive, he pointed out, would not be expected to tolerate people barging into his office to ask him questions. So, why should a golfer?

I've heard other stories of the way great golfers worked, and solitude is often a part of them. Byron Nelson got his first professional's job in the depths of the Depression. On weekdays, almost no one had the leisure to come out to the club for play or lessons. So Nelson practiced, hitting irons to one end of the practice area, walking after them, and hitting them back. Paul Runyan had a similarly lonely job at a club in Arkansas, and took advantage of it to hone his short game.

Ken Venturi, when he was growing up in San Francisco, had a stammering problem. It was so bad that he was ashamed to play a sport where he might have to talk to his teammates and risk being teased. That was why he took up golf—he could play alone. He spent hours at the practice area in Harding Park, hitting balls and talking to himself. He pretended to be an announcer, describing how his own next shot could decide the Open championship. In fact, he believes that learning the rhythm of the golf swing and harnessing it to his speech was the key to overcoming his stammer.

Mark O'Meara, to take a great player of the present day, has said that from the time he was 13 or so, golf became his best friend.

I don't think it's coincidental that all of these great players liked to practice alone. Practice doesn't have to be a solitary pursuit; in fact, it can be done profitably with a like-minded friend, the way David and Greg Belcher do it. But the great players' penchant for practicing alone can help you understand the difference between practice and quality practice. If you're working hard at your golf game but not getting better, learning this distinction can help you resume improving.

I see too many players who make one or both of two common mistakes in their approach to practice: The first is that they socialize too much on the practice tee. They're chatting about business or the movies or the putt that got away the last time they played. Their minds are not on the golf shots they're practicing. The second common mistake is beating balls. Beating balls is a mindless exercise. There's nothing wrong with mindless exercise if the sport is, say, jogging. If it's golf, your mind has to be on the task at hand. Otherwise, you're liable to be ingraining bad habits.

One way to determine whether you're beating balls is to compare your mental processes on the course and on the range. On the course, I assume, you have a mental routine.

It includes assessing the variables like lie and wind. It also includes picking out a small target. It includes envisioning the ball going to the target, or, if you're not the type of person who graphically envisions things, waiting until your mind is focused on the target and you're confident the ball is going to go there.

If you don't go through each of those mental steps each time you hit a practice shot, you're probably beating balls.

It would be helpful if players went through their full routines, both mental and physical, each time they hit a practice shot. Not many players have the discipline to do this. After all, on the range, the club they want to hit with is usually in their hands already and the lie isn't likely to change much from one shot to the next. And sometimes, you may be working in such a way that your on-course routine is impossible. You may, for example, be using a club laid on the ground to help make sure your alignment is correct. So I don't criticize a player who truncates his physical routine a bit as he practices, as long as he goes through the steps he needs to focus his mind on every shot.

Remember, you're not practicing to be able to hit good shots on the driving range. You're practicing to be able to hit good shots on the last hole of the biggest match of your life. Your dominant habit will show up there, and it had better be a good one.

You'll notice that practicing with this kind of mental discipline takes time. Hogan was legendary for the number of practice balls he hit. Not many people remember that he didn't hit them all at once. He'd hit a small bag and then stop, maybe drink a little water, and think about what he was trying to accomplish. Then he'd hit another small bag.

If you take your time as you practice, and your time is limited, you will hit fewer balls. That's all right. I would rather see a player hit fifty practice shots with his mind focused on every one, than hit two-hundred shots with his mind wandering.

It might help if you try what Ken Venturi found worked for him long ago in Harding Park. It's the same thing that works for a lot of kids who let their imaginations help them as they practice. Try pretending that instead of standing on the range with a seven-iron in your hand, you're standing in the eighteenth fairway at Augusta, 150 yards from the pin, on Sunday afternoon with the Masters on the line. Let yourself really believe it. (Or, if your imagination isn't that supple, pretend you're standing in the final fairway of your own course, 150 yards out, needing par to win two dollars from your best friend.) Prepare for the shot as you would if your imaginary situation were real. Then hit it.

This will have two benefits. It will help focus your mind on your practice shot. And, it will help you prepare for encountering the real situation. The next time you're in the fairway 150 yards out needing a good shot to beat someone, you won't find the situation abnormal.

Another practice habit that good players employ is switching clubs and distances frequently. You may be able to hit pretty good practice drives after you've had the club in your hand for a few minutes, you've warmed up, and you've gotten used to it. However, on the golf course, you never hit a driver twice in a row. You put the club in your hands after you've hit an iron, perhaps a chip or pitch, and a putt or two. That's a different challenge, and it makes sense to practice for it.

A lot of players I've worked with play a course in their imaginations as they practice. They try to envision how the fairway of the first hole would fit on the practice range, and where the hazards would be. Then, they hit their tee shots. They estimate what they'd have left for their second shots and the hazards they'd face. They select a club and hit that shot. If they think their approach would have been short and right, they pull a wedge and pitch the requisite distance.

This, too, makes sense. Hitting balls on the driving range without imagining fairways and hazards and greens is like practicing jump shots without a rim, just bouncing the ball off a backboard. You wouldn't try to improve your jump shot that way and you shouldn't try to improve your golf by hitting aimless practice balls.

Ben Hogan told me that he used the shag caddie to bring the practice range to life. Hogan and his caddie both wanted the caddie to be able to field every shot Hogan hit to him on the first or second bounce. This gave Hogan a small target to aim at. And if, as he worked his way through a bag of 20 balls, he hit 17 right at the caddie, Hogan felt some pressure on the last three to make it a perfect practice bag, which helped him learn habits of concentration that carried over from the range to the golf course.

Seve Ballesteros told me that in the years when he was playing well, he'd always have his clubs strewn about him on the ground when he practiced, because he was always imagining holes and situations and the shots he would need to play them. He believes that it's no coincidence that in recent years, as his play has gotten spotty, he's often found himself on the range with one club in his hand and the rest neatly stowed in his bag. He's been trying to hit perfect shots with one club instead of practicing to play golf.

Imagining a golf course may help you with one of the practice challenges of a player on an improvement program—spending the right amount of time in the trusting mode. As you go through a series of lessons, you're going to be learning some new mechanics. They may involve a significant swing change, or they may be subtler alterations, like an adjustment in your putting stance. But, by virtue of the fact that you're taking lessons, your mind will be engaged to some degree with mechanics.

As I've said, immediately after a lesson, you may want to spend most of your practice time with your mind in the training mode. That is, you consciously think about the new moves you've been taught. You might be hitting the ball with your mind on your swing path or your weight distribution or something else that your pro has suggested you change.

As the time between lessons goes on, you must gradually increase the number of practice shots you take in the trusting mode. That is, you're not thinking about the mechanics of the stroke. You're thinking about your target and the ball getting to that target. On the golf course, your mind should always be in the trusting mode.

On the practice tee, this isn't easy to do if you're trying to learn a new technique and you mishit a couple of shots. Suppose you're trying to cure a slice by drawing the ball. Suddenly, you hit a couple of big left-to-right fades on the practice tee. The temptation is to stop trusting your swing and start trying to fix it. It's a temptation that, most of the time, you must resist. Practice is, after all, intended to rehearse what you want to do on the golf course. If you set out to practice in the trusting mode and revert to trying to fix your swing when you mishit a ball, that's very likely to be what you'll do on the course. Continuing to trust your stroke as you practice is part of the discipline you have to learn.

This is especially true as tournament play approaches. I don't mind if, during the off-season, a player decides to abandon the trusting mode and go back to the practice mode to work on something that doesn't feel quite right. This is especially true if his teacher is around, which is one of the advantages of working with someone from your own club or course. Your teacher might be able to take a quick look at what you're doing and make a suggestion that will fix it on the spot.

But as competition approaches, I advise against trying to fix anything that goes wrong. Within a week of a tournament, you don't have time to fix any fundamental flaws. You want to be training your mind for tournament pressure.

The best thing you can do if you hit a skein of bad shots during pretournament practice is put the club away and go work on some other part of your game. You simply have to believe that you hit the bad shots because you got careless with some part of your routine and that your normal stroke will return once competition starts.

Practicing in the trusting mode will also help you know when you've mastered a new skill. If the shot doesn't work in the trusting mode, then you haven't mastered it: You haven't reached the level of unconscious competence.

Your goal ought to be an overall ratio of roughly six practice shots in the trusting mode for every four shots with your mind focused on technique. So, if you hit all, or nearly all, of your shots in the training mode in the days immediately after your lesson, you ought to be hitting the vast majority of them in the trusting mode as your next lesson draws near.

Your practice plan ought to include a lot of work on the kinds of lies that trouble you. If you're having problems with, say, downhill lies, make sure you go over the adjustments they require with your pro, perhaps during a playing lesson. Then, find a way to practice from that lie. It might mean going out on the course very early in the morning or late in the evening, but I can assure you that the reason good players seem to handle those tricky lies with ease is because they've practiced on them.

They've also practiced with focused minds. As you plan your practice, remember the examples of Hogan, Nelson, and Runyan, as well as some of the modern players I've worked with like Brad Faxon, Davis Love III, Pat Bradley, and Billy Mayfair. Think about ways you can make practice an excursion into your own little world. It might entail practicing at certain times when the facilities on which you practice will be less crowded. It might entail going down to the far end of the range, as Hogan did. However you manage it, practicing with a focused mind will make your practice more efficient and beneficial.

How much should you practice? It depends, of course, on the time and enthusiasm you have.

Bill Davis has a couple of pupils, Jay and Arline Hoffman, who have decided they want to see how good they can get at golf and are prepared to devote a lot of time to it.

Jay started out in golf in a way that taught him to associate the sport with hard work—as a caddie. At Washington Golf & Country Club in northern Virginia in the mid-1950s, caddies got $2.50 per bag and maybe a fifty-cent tip for walking a hilly course in the fetid humidity that is Washington in the summer. If he carried two bags for two rounds, he could earn maybe $11 for a day's work. After a couple of years of caddying, he switched to carrying bricks at construction sites. After serving in the army, he went into the construction business. He played golf a bit, with his caddie's swing, but not often enough to get good at it.

Over the years, though, Jay reached the stage where he owned enough real estate and radio stations to begin to set his own schedule. He and Arline started spending a lot of their time in Florida and they joined Jupiter Hills Golf Club.

Arline had never played until her child went off to college, but when she took it up, she found she liked the challenge of controlling the golf ball. They began taking a joint weekly lesson from Bill Davis.

When he gets pupils who are eager to learn and willing to put time into the effort, Bill will prescribe their practice sessions, writing down the shots he wants them to try. Here is what one of Jay and Arline's recent practice regimens looked like:

1. PUTTING:

   a. Seven-point compass drill from one, two, three, four and five feet, five times per week.

   b. Putting with eyes closed, three balls from three, six, and nine feet, seven repetitions, five times per week. (This drill is intended to focus the pupil's attention on how hard he's hitting the putt, not on his line or putting mechanics.)

c. Putting from one cup to another set 20 feet apart, ten repetitions, five times per week.

2. CHIPPING:

a. From three yards off the green with seven-iron, nine-iron, pitching wedge, and sand wedge, five with each club, five times per week.

b. The same drill from six yards off, eliminating the seven-iron and adding a lob wedge, five times per week.

c. The same drill from nine yards off, using the three wedges, five times per week.

3. SHORT PITCHES:

a. From 15 yards off the green with the three wedges, five balls each, five times per week.

b. Same drill from 20 yards, five times per week.

c. Same drill from 25 yards, five times per week.

4. LONGER PITCHES:

a. From 50 yards, five balls each with pitching wedge and sand wedge, five times per week

b. The same drill from 60 yards, five times per week.

c. The same drill from 70 yards, five times per week.

5. Bunker play:

a. 15 shots each with the sand wedge and the lob wedge from different lies in the practice bunker, five times per week.

6. Full swing:

a. 10 balls each with nine-iron, seven-iron, five-iron, a fairway wood and a driver, two repetitions, three times per week.

This means that in a week's time, Jay and Arline would each hit 300 long shots, 590 putts, and 795 chips and pitches. Bill anticipates that they'll also play four rounds of golf per week and take two days off to keep fresh.

Not surprisingly, the Hoffmans have improved by following this regimen. Jay, who was a 22-handicapper when he started with Bill a few years ago, recently played 12 consecutive rounds in the 70s. Arline's handicap has dropped to about 12.

"We like to practice," Jay says. "And we have faith in Bill. We know what he's teaching us will help us."

This is a strong practice schedule and I realize that not everyone can take this sort of time, but it's exemplary in several respects. First, it places proper emphasis on the short game. Second, it's a plan that Bill and Jay and Arline have mutually agreed on, even though Bill takes the role of prescribing the drills and shots he wants them to practice. They all believe it will help them. And, finally, the Hoffmans enjoy it.

It's important to try to make practice enjoyable. For some people, this is not a problem. They love getting out to practice and they'll do it in the rain if necessary. For others, it's a partial problem. They like certain kinds of practice—perhaps hitting drivers—but they don't care for others, like putting.

This is where a buddy system of the sort that Jay and Arline have may be helpful. I know I've pointed out the solitary practice habits of many great golfers, but remember that they sought solitude not for its own sake but because it helped them focus and concentrate as they practiced.

Two people can do this as effectively, perhaps more effectively, than one—if they're both committed to the same program. They can reinforce one another. They can prod one another. When they practice together, they're not socializing. There's a sense of companionship, of camaraderie, that comes from being engaged in a joint enterprise, but they're both concentrating on the task at hand.

David and Greg Belcher, Hank Johnson's star students, have this sort of relationship. They compete with one another, but they both take pride and pleasure in the other's achievements. When they play a round of golf together, each urges the other to stick with the techniques Hank has shown them, even if those techniques are as yet unpolished and are not helping their score on this particular day. Jay and Arline play together in much the same way.

If two people are supposed to practice, it may increase the likelihood that they'll do it. If one is not in the mood, the other may prod him to practice anyway. You'll have to decide, based on your own personality and circumstances, whether the buddy system is right for you.

There's one other way that effective practice can involve more than one person. I like to see players compete with one another on the practice green or at the practice tee. If one of your friends happens to be working on his putting at the same time you are, it's fine to make a little bet on who can hole more putts from a given spot. If you're on the range, compete to see who can hit an iron closest to the various target pins that are out there.

You'll be doing what practice ought to do: focusing your mind in the same way you want to focus it on the golf course. That is quality practice.

Chapter 11

When You Need Another Teacher

One of the first mentor-pupil relationships I ever observed in golf involved a girl named Kandi Kessler and a young teaching pro named Phil Owenby. They taught me something important about handling one of the most difficult and sensitive aspects of anyone's relationship with a teacher. They showed how to bring another teacher into the improvement process constructively.

Kandi took up golf when she was 11 or 12 years old. Up until that time, horses were the love of her life, but she developed some allergies and her doctor told her she couldn't hang around barns any more. To fill the void, her father, Frank, introduced her to golf.

Kandi took to it with passion. She was a shy girl and liked the fact that she could play golf alone.

Her Dad would drop her off in the mornings at Farmington Country Club in Charlottesville, Virginia, and she'd spend the day there. She'd start on the practice range, move to the practice green, then head for east nine, the least played of Farmington's 27 holes. She'd play it two, three, sometimes four times, then she'd hit balls until it got dark.

Within a year or two, she could shoot in the 80s. She had a few lessons that helped her with the fundamentals of grip and posture, but had no regular mentor until Phil Owenby came along.

Phil is a tall, soft-spoken golfer from North Carolina. He'd played college golf at N.C. State, but when he went up against Curtis Strange and Jay Haas, who were over at Wake Forest, he realized teaching would be his niche in the game.

The day after graduation, Phil started working as an intern in the pro shop at Farmington, doing the things people do on the bottom rung of the teaching ladder—looking after the range, the carts, and the bag room. He soon noticed Kandi.

"She had a thirst to get better," he recalls now, nearly twenty years later. "So we hit it off."

This is an important factor in the forging of a strong relationship between any pro and any golfer. If the pro is convinced the golfer has that thirst to do better, that will to work, he or she will naturally respond more favorably than to someone who conveys a lackadaisical attitude. It's one of the things that separates good players from average players.

Good players have a knack of showing teachers that they're eager to improve. One of your jobs as a player is to make sure your teacher knows how much you want to get better.

Phil started tutoring Kandi. On summer evenings, after his regular work was done, they'd take a cart out onto the east nine. She drove, which is always a treat for a youngster. Their lessons were not unlike the ones Bill Davis gives to Patty Pilz. As they played, Kandi would sometimes hit her ball into difficult situations—deep rough, uneven lies—and Phil would teach her how to cope with them. Sometimes he'd let her hit several balls from each spot. Sometimes he'd ask her to play with one ball and they'd try to get a lot of holes in before dark.

"She was a natural mimic," Phil recalls. He only had to show her something once or twice and she would start to incorporate it into her own game. Teaching on the course that way kept it fun for her, he remembers. It also taught her to think about things like shot trajectory, working the ball left or right, and course management.

They worked on her swing as well. Kandi had a tendency to take the club back too far inside, and Phil gave her drills designed to prompt her to make a more upright swing. Sometimes he would have her swing with her rear end against a wall. Sometimes he'd put a club behind her on the practice tee and and she'd try to take her club back toward the club on the ground behind her.

Under this tutelage, Kandi improved dramatically. Her

handicap dropped from the high teens to two or three by the time she was a junior in high school. She won the state junior amateur three times. When she was 16, she won the state amateur. She started thinking seriously about a career on the LPGA Tour. Around this time, I started helping her with her mental game.

Kandi and her father decided that if she were going to play professionally, she would need a better short game than she had. They wanted her to get it from the best instructors available. They tried a couple, and then I suggested they talk to Davis Love, Jr.

But we never cut Phil Owenby out of this process or did anything behind his back. He was consulted. The Kesslers invited him to come along with them to Sea Island, Georgia, where Davis Love, Jr., taught.

Phil, at this point, could have declined and bowed out, but he was smart enough to realize that as a young and relatively inexperienced teacher, he could learn a lot from someone like Davis Love, Jr. So he went with the Kesslers.

He absorbed an enormous amount just by watching Kandi's lessons.

"The first thing I learned was how he handled people," Phil recalls. "He'd have Kandi hit balls for maybe 15 or 20 minutes, not saying anything, until she started to relax. He had a way of making her feel very good about herself. When he was about to teach her something, he'd start off by saying, 'This will be easy for you, as good an athlete as you are.'"

Davis Love, Jr., taught both Phil and Kandi things they hadn't known about the short game. Once, it was a discourse on the design of the various wedges, how they're supposed to penetrate turf and sand. On another occasion it was a discussion of controlling the distance on short pitches by varying the length of the backswing, allowing the downswing always to be firm and accelerating.

Whatever he taught, he was always supportive of Phil. "He'd always be saying, 'When you go back, Phil should work with you on this or that,'" Phil recalls.

"I think Mr. Love actually liked having Phil watch the lessons, because I lived so far away from Sea Island," Kandi remembers. "He knew somebody would be reinforcing what he taught me and I'd have less tendency to revert to old habits."

Kandi went on to become a Curtis Cup player for the United States. She played in five U.S. Opens, finishing fourteenth in her best year. She turned pro and had some success, but eventually opted to give up touring in order to marry and have a family. Now Kandi Kessler-Comer, she's the director of golf at Glenmore Country Club near Charlottesville, the same post Phil occupies at Roanoke Country Club. They stay in touch.

The kind of candid, constructive relationship they had is all too rare. Too often, if someone decides to see another pro, he does so secretly. Maybe he thinks his regular pro will be angry or offended at the implied lack of confidence. Maybe he just wants to avoid a conversation he fears could be unpleasant. Doubt and confusion usually ensue. A player seeing two teachers tends to tune out what the older teacher says to him. The relationship of trust they once had is spoiled.

No two pros, even two pros who agree on the fundamentals of the swing, teach the same. They have differences of nuance, differences of emphasis, differences, perhaps, of terminology. The player who sees two or more pros will inevitably zero in on whatever slight differences exist between them. Right away, he loses some confidence in his swing. How can he trust his swing when he hears, or thinks he's hearing, two different ways to do it? He can't. A player who doesn't trust his mechanics swings tentatively, stiffly, gracelessly. His results get worse. Pretty soon, he's lost.

This can be a big problem for some of the tour players I work with. Of necessity, they're on the road a lot, away from their swing teachers, and the practice tees at tour events are full of people who would like to make a reputation as a teacher by giving tips to a star. They're full of fellow playing pros, many of them well-meaning, who know a lot about the swing and are all too happy to share what they know.

A player who misses a cut or two is tempted to start listening to this free advice. Or he hears about Teacher X, who's helped a certain player turn his fortunes around. There are vogues in golf teaching, and there is always someone who seems anointed, for the moment at least, as the man who knows the secret.

My friend Brad Faxon worked through a problem of this sort early in 1997. Brad's 1996 season was, by most standards, a fine one. He finished second in four tournaments and eighth on the money list and led the tour in putting. But he didn't win an event, and he was down the list in driving statistics. Brad wanted to improve his long game and he worked hard at it.

Early in 1997, though, his hard work wasn't paying off. He missed a couple of cuts in California and Florida. When his long swing wasn't grooved perfectly, he fretted about it. He started listening to too much advice on mechanics. He got a bit confused.

We talked before the Player's Championship in late March. I suggested a few things to Brad. I thought he needed to go back to the basics of his game. While it was fine to try to improve his long swing, he had to remember that no one swings perfectly. He had to remember that wedges and putting are the strengths of his game and he should enjoy using them. He had to filter out the conflicting advice he was getting and settle on one method, and only one method, to believe in.

When Brad did that, he went on a tear. He finished fourth at the Players' Championship, won at New Orleans, tied for second at Hilton Head, was second at Greenboro, and tied for second at the Colonial. In a single month, he won hundreds of thousand of dollars and put himself in a strong position to make the Ryder Cup team. Setting aside doubt and confusion helped him do it.

The need to avoid doubt and confusion must guide you as well.

It's not outside the realm of possibility that you will reach a point where the advice of another pro can be helpful to you. After all, no one goes through an academic education with just one teacher. In kindergarten and the primary grades, one teacher can handle all subjects. By the time high school begins, a student goes to different teachers, each of whom specializes in a different subject. If he goes to college or graduate school, he may have a particular faculty member who serves as his advisor. However, that teacher's job may include referring the student to other teachers and courses for the knowledge he needs.

It may be that after you've progressed beyond the golfing equivalent of elementary school, you'll feel a need for specialized instruction in some facet of the game—wedge play, perhaps, or psychology. You'll want to consult specialists. If you're serious about becoming a tournament player, perhaps a touring pro, you may need to put together a team of sorts: a primary teacher; perhaps a fitness expert to help with strength and flexibility; a sport psychologist to help with your mental game; and maybe one or two specialized teachers.

If and when that happens, be smart. Handle it as Kandi Kessler and her father did when they decided she needed some specialized short game instruction from Davis Love, Jr. Talk it over with your regular teacher. You may be surprised at his reaction. He may agree with you. He may have some good ideas about people to consult. He may even be willing to go with you and observe your lessons. He ought to be willing to review any videotape you bring back from the lesson.

Whatever happens, share with your teacher the things you learn from the specialist. Let him help you integrate them into the game you've been building. Even if your principal teacher and the specialist disagree about how to hit a particular shot or perform a particular part of the swing, and you decide to take the specialist's advice, tell your principal teacher what you're doing and why. You'll still need his help and guidance and he'll be in a better position to give it if you keep him informed.

There's always a possibility, when bringing in new teachers, that egos will collide. Everyone involved with a golfer ought to realize that they're in it not to enhance their own reputations and egos, but to help the player. Unfortunately, that's not always the case.

Not all teachers and consultants know what Bear Bryant knew about apportioning credit. When Bryant's Alabama teams won big, he always told the press that the boys played well. When Alabama lost, he always took the blame for himself. That's one reason he was a great coach.

If not everyone you're working with is as instinctively wise as Bear Bryant, you have a management problem. The last thing you need is to have one teacher disparaging the other, trying to undermine someone else. The best way to avoid this is to be open with everyone you work with and demand that they integrate their advice into the package you're putting together.

Chapter 12

Parents and Children

The man may wear his cap with the peak turned out over his forehead, the way the designer intended, while the boy's cap is turned backward, the way baseball catchers wear them. The man may wear his trousers cinched with a proper belt, while the boy's shorts droop fashionably low, hanging precariously between his hips and his shins. The man may hum snatches from a Beach Boys tune as he walks while the boy whistles something from Fugazi.

But, if they are playing golf together, they are, for a while at least, comrades.

Few things in our culture can bridge the gap between generations as well as golf. It's a game that fathers and mothers introduce to their sons and daughters. It's a game that families can play together when the kids are growing up and after the kids are grown and have kids of their own.

The link between generations doesn't even have to be from older to younger. I helped my own father and mother take up golf when they were in their sixties. Now, some of the most pleasant time we spend together is on a golf course.

It's hard to think of an outstanding golfer of the past half century or so, from Arnold Palmer and Jack Nicklaus down through Pat Bradley and Davis Love III, whose game was not intertwined in a close, loving relationship with a father.

Most often, what I hear these players say when they talk about the contributions their fathers made to their games has nothing to do with the grips they passed on, or the backswings. It has to do with character. Jack Nicklaus recounts how his father cured him of throwing clubs. Davis Love III talks about how his dad taught him to be honest about reporting his scores. "Pap didn't just teach me how to play golf," Arnold Palmer once said. "He taught me discipline."

So, if you teach your children to love golf and to play it well, you're not just giving them a game that can reward them with pleasure and exercise for the rest of their lives. You have an opportunity to teach traits like honor, discipline, and perseverance that will help them in whatever they do.

It's not as simple as having a child, cutting down some clubs, and doing what comes naturally. I've seen athletes whose careers and lives were damaged by parents who didn't know where to draw the line between support and interference, between loving and smothering, between encouraging and pushing. I'm sympathetic toward them, because there can be no clear rules about where that line ought to be. Each child is different—what seems pushy and smothering to one child may seem warm and supportive to another.

I'm working right now with a young man, Mike Henderson, whose father, Dan, has been very active in his golfing development. When he was 16, Mike was selected the Rolex Junior Golfer of the Year from a field that included Tiger Woods, so he and Dan must be doing something right.

Mike is the youngest by ten years of Dan and Glenda Henderson's four children. By the time he turned ten, the other children were more or less out of the nest. Dan, who has a business distributing vitamins, was then in a financial position to set his own schedule.

One day when Mike was 10 years old, Dan cut down a club and took him to a driving range. Dan, who carried about a four handicap, taught his son a few of the fundamentals of grip, stance, and swing; Mike started popping straight shots into the range.

None of his other children had become serious golfers, but Dan saw potential in Mike, and he immediately began to cultivate it.

They were, in fact, getting a late start. Lots of juniors start much earlier. About a month after he played his first round of golf, Mike entered a junior tournament, the North State, at his home course, North Ridge Country Club in Raleigh, North Carolina.

"How many tournaments you played in?" Mike's playing partner asked.

"This is my first," Mike said, politely.

"I've played in about a hundred," the other 11-year-old said. "Know how many trophies I've won?"

"How many?"

"About a hundred," the kid said.

Unintimidated, Mike shot a 92 and finished fifth.

Mike and his father were just getting started. Dan started coming home early from work, picking up Mike at school. They lived near the seventh green at North Ridge, and there was a six-hole loop that began near their back door. They played it every night, but they did more than play holes. They stopped around idle greens and chipped and putted extra balls. They practiced.

Dan did not want Mike just hanging around the club. "My philosophy was to help him get good fairly quickly," Dan recalls. "But parents who just drop their kids off at the club aren't doing that. Those kids' first focus is social. They don't get better."

Dan gave up his own golf game in favor of supervising Mike's. "Most parents choose to spend their time playing themselves or drinking at the nineteenth hole," he says. "I chose to spend it with Mike. I was there enough that he could stay focused."

Dan did not try to be Mike's swing teacher. He sought out good instruction. He first took Mike to Austin, Texas to see Mike Adams. There was a trip to Florida to see Jimmy Ballard and a trip to Maryland to see Kent Cayce at Congressional Country Club.

Mike was improving rapidly. At the age of 12, he shot a couple of rounds in the sixties, from the red tees. He's a pleasant, teachable kid, and he learned from each of the pros he and his father went to see. He practiced what they showed him, under Dan's watchful eye. Dan videotaped his lessons so they could refer back to them if some question arose.

Dan was still not satisfied they had found the teacher they could commit to. He read an article about David Leadbetter in *Golf Digest,* tracked down Leadbetter's phone number, and persuaded David's wife to schedule a one-hour lesson for Mike, even though David at that time was not taking new students. When Dan sees something he wants, he is not easily deterred. When the time came, he and Mike drove ten hours to Orlando.

The one-hour lesson stretched to five hours. Both Dan and Mike liked the way David analyzed his swing and liked even more the way he helped Mike correct his flaws. "I knew I was home if David would work with Mike," Dan recalls.

It was not easy to get a commitment from David, who could easily work 24 hours a day with all the golfers who would like to take lessons from him. For a couple of years, they saw David occasionally, but took lessons from other teachers. Finally, they reached an agreement. David would see Mike every month or six weeks, and he would review videotapes Mike sent him.

From that point, David has been Mike's only swing teacher. Mike has been a conscientious pupil. David, for example, taught Mike to check on his setup position in a mirror. Mike has faithfully stood in front of a mirror for 15 minutes or so each day, practicing getting into the correct posture. He's developed a beautiful golf game.

The important thing is not that Mike has worked with David Leadbetter, although David is certainly a great teacher. The important thing is that he found a teacher he believed in, he committed himself to taking instruction only from that teacher, and he has faithfully done what the teacher has asked.

Dan, for his part, did what fathers need to do in this process. He recognized his son's potential and desire to improve. He found his son a teacher he believed in, and he let the teacher teach. Dan observes Mike's lessons and makes the videotapes, but he would never try to contradict something David has taught Mike. His role is to support David when David isn't there.

This is the right approach for a parent to take. Parents ought to lay down certain rules of behavior for their young golfers. They ought to require that a child meet minimal standards for behavior, temper, sportsmanship, and grades in school if he or she is to continue playing and taking lessons. But they ought not try to teach the backswing.

Dan took on another role on Mike's behalf. Mike is naturally a warm, friendly, and personable kid, the kind of kid who will politely chat with anyone about golf. Once he started to win junior championships, he became something of a celebrity. People wanted to talk to him when they saw him on the range. They wanted him to explain what he was doing, and they wanted him to watch what they were doing. Mike didn't have what Ben Hogan had, that ability to get curt when he had to practice.

So, Dan became the watchman. He accompanied Mike when he practiced. He diverted the people who wanted to talk to Mike. They could talk to Dan.

"A lot of people thought that I was standing over Mike, making him practice," Dan says. "I never had to make him practice. I just had to make sure he had a chance to practice."

Still, it was a tight relationship between an adolescent boy and his father and there were times when it chafed. The Hendersons got through those times with love and good communication. Dan has always allowed Mike to voice any complaint that he has.

"There were times when I'd get angry with him or he'd get angry with me, but I always knew it was never something important enough to sacrifice our relationship," Mike says. "You understand that you both love and care for each other, and you get over it."

As Mike grew older, Dan stepped back a bit. "From the time he was about 16, I was there less," Dan recalls. This is a natural step, but one that some parents and children understandably find difficult. Almost of necessity these days, a parent is going to be heavily involved in the development of a young golfer. There are almost no caddie yards anymore where kids can learn the game on their own.

But there will come a time, in the midteens, when the parent–child relationship has to change and become more collegial. The parent has to start doing less talking and more listening. The child has to have room to grow up.

For Dan Henderson, the hardest part was seeing Mike go off to college. Mike chose Brigham Young University, a couple of thousand miles from home, because he liked the campus atmosphere, and because his coach there was happy to let David Leadbetter remain the only one to correct Mike's swing. The Hendersons, who are Mormons, were happy with the choice, but there are times, when Dan knows Mike is playing in a tournament out west, when he finds it hard not to be there.

Mike has done well at BYU. He was Western Athletic Conference freshman of the year in 1996, and was first-team all conference in 1997. He aspires to win some major amateur events, and then make his mark on the PGA Tour.

He knows what he has to do to accomplish that. Mike is not a big guy. His tee shots average about 260 yards, and he won't outmuscle anyone at the professional level. His success will depend on how sharp he gets with the scoring clubs, particularly the putter. It's a big jump from junior golf to the tour.

The Hendersons' development formula might not be suitable for everyone. A child who wasn't instantly passionate about golf might not be able to accept, as Mike did, Dan's level of involvement—and certainly not every child needs to take lessons from David Leadbetter.

There are two key things in the upbringing of any junior golfer that the Hendersons did right, that are appropriate for anyone. Dan found his son a teacher they both believed in, a teacher who could credibly promise to take Mike to the level he sought. Later, as Mike became competitive at the national level, Dan sought out other experts to help with other aspects of his development. That's when I became Mike's sports psychologist. Dan, though he was always present, never dominated Mike, never forced him to do anything.

Any junior who travels to tournaments is going to have a parent for a companion, and that parent had better let the child voice his or her opinion. That parent should respect the child's opinion to the degree that the child's maturity warrants, and facilitate, not block, the child's desire to make friends with the other kids.

Otherwise, the outcome might not be as good as it was with Mike Henderson. The outcome could be burnout and the loss of the opportunity to enjoy the benefits that golf can bring to the relationship between a parent and a child.

Chapter 13

The Money Factor

Here are two truths about the relationship between money and the golf of your dreams:

You can't buy a game.

You can't learn for free, either.

There are indeed people who act as if they think they can buy a game. They go to golf schools at resorts where the range attendants wear white gloves. They buy all the best things: clubs, balls, clothes, gadgets. The first time some company comes out with a ten-thousand dollar driver, they'll buy that, too.

Their spending by itself won't make them much better, if at all. While it's nice to have good equipment, the fact is that good players can shoot par with the old set of rusted MacGregors they inherited from Uncle Jack and stashed in the garage on the off chance that they might one day be antiques.

There are also people who let money keep them away from the kind of improvement that would make the game more enjoyable for them. They're not about to pay some golf pro fifty dollars for a lesson, to say nothing of one hundred fifty dollars.

If they're the sort of people who play a few times a year on days when the greens fees are discounted, that's fine—so long as they know that their golf budget is constraining their ability to play well, and they accept that fact.

However, there are lots of people who fall somewhere between these two extremes. Their means are not unlimited, yet they spend a fair amount of money on the game by the time you add up their club dues, their new irons, their fresh Titleists, their vacation tabs at nice golf resorts, their greens fees. They spend a lot of time on the game, too. They want to improve, but they balk at spending money or time on a systematic improvement program.

All I can say to them is that they ought to decide how much getting better at golf is worth to them. If they have to work within a budget, should their priority be a new set of irons or learning how to play better?

The cost of improvement is substantial but not outlandish. Short-game practice costs nothing. Range balls aren't too expensive. There are lots of good teachers like Gene Hilen out there, giving lessons for twenty-five dollars. And, if you come to a pro ready to commit yourself to a series of lessons, you're in a decent bargaining position. Most pros will offer you some kind of package rate.

If you're a parent looking for lessons for your child, be aware that most teaching pros are delighted to come across a child with a little talent and a hunger to learn and practice. They are often willing to cut some deals that can reduce the cost of lessons to almost nothing, especially if the child is old enough to do odd jobs, like picking balls up off the range or cleaning clubs.

All in all, it should be possible to pay for a three-month improvement cycle for about what it takes to play a single round of golf at Pebble Beach. You could spend a lot more. You could probably spend a little less.

What is it worth to you?

Chapter 14

The Discipline You'll Need

When Rocco Mediate walked out to the tee for a shoot-out exhibition prior to the Las Vegas Classic in the autumn of 1993, he had no inkling that he was about to both alter his career and demonstrate the key to self-discipline. His only intention was to have a good time and maybe win a little money in an event the tour put on for the customers kind enough to buy tickets for practice rounds.

But, when Rocco hit his three-wood off the tee on number 16 that afternoon, he felt a twinge just below the middle of his back. He told his caddie that something didn't feel right, and by the end of the round, he was limping a little bit. A couple of days later, he could barely walk. He withdrew from the tournament.

Rocco had qualified to play in the Tour Championship the following week at the Olympic Club in San Francisco, and he did not want to miss that. On Monday of that week he felt all right. He began to believe that his back pain had been just some kind of sprain. But after 14 holes of his practice round, the pain returned. It was almost unbearable. On the fifteenth tee, he hit a seven-iron toward the green, but it went no more than 120 yards. It took him an hour to hobble the three-hundred yards or so to the clubhouse.

I'll condense what Rocco went through for the next eight months. Anyone who's had a herniated disk knows the story. He consulted specialists. He tried to rehabilitate his back through exercise. There were occasions when the pain eased, and he was able to play. There were times of debilitating agony. He had to call the Masters and withdraw. He managed to play in the U.S. Open at Oakmont, where he was paired with Arnold Palmer in Palmer's last Open. After three rounds, he had to withdraw.

He had back surgery a month after the Open. When he awoke from the anaesthesia, his surgeon told him the operation had gone well. A portion of the disk had been removed, but the nerves in the spine were undisturbed.

That was not the way Rocco felt. The pain from the disk area was gone, but he felt an intense, overarching pain from the surgery, and his back felt stiff, as if encased in something. For a few moments, he doubted he would ever play golf again.

He put that thought aside and started working on his surgeon's plan for rehabilitation. The first thing on the list was six weeks of rest. Rocco complied. He did nothing more active than walk during that period.

As soon as he could, he began working with a trainer, Frank Novakoski. At first, it was a matter of being rubbed down and trying to break up some of the scar tissue that had formed around his spine. But fairly soon, Rocco was on a four-hours-per-day exercise regimen.

I should add here that before his injury, Rocco was not, by his own account, in very good shape. When he won at Greensboro in 1993, he weighed about 245 pounds, and he stands just a little over six feet. He had always figured if he was in shape to walk the golf course, that was good enough.

His initial, presurgery attempts to rehab the disk injury got him into somewhat better condition, but his postsurgery workouts transformed him. The hours of abdominal exercises, stretching and flexibility exercises, stair-climbing exercises, a stationary bike, and other workouts took five or six inches off his waist and about 45 pounds off his body.

He still had lots of work to do before he could play competitive golf again. The first time he was allowed to pick up a club, he took an iron into the back yard and tried to chip a ball about 10 yards, from the kids' swing set to the porch. It hurt so much that he fell to his knees.

He persisted. Six weeks later, he played, and not badly, in the Diner's Club matches. He went to Peter Kostis and Gary McCord for help in changing his swing to place less strain on his back.

He became a regular denizen of the fitness trailer that moves along with the players from tour stop to tour stop. To help motivate himself, he put together a tape of music from the *Rocky* movies. When he played that tape, he could hear some muted snickers. He used them as motivation. "Go ahead and keep laughing, boys," Rocco would say to himself. "I'll step all over you when I go past you."

He nearly lost his card because he won very little money in 1995. He got a medical extension and needed to win quickly as the 1996 season began. He responded brilliantly, winning $42,088 with a sixth-place finish at Phoenix to assure his place on the tour. He went on to finish fortieth on the 1996 money list. Rocco has not yet regained the form he had before his back injury. He's sometimes depressed and frustrated, but he's getting there.

The key to Rocco's recovery, I think, could be discerned in his answer when a journalist asked him whether he had ever thought about what he would do for a living if he couldn't play golf again.

"I never thought about doing anything else," Rocco replied. "I didn't have time."

Now this is a man who, many people would think, had nothing but time to think about a future without competitive golf. He had six weeks of enforced rest after surgery. He had all those hours on the stationary bike and other exercise equipment, but in Rocco's recollection, he had no time.

That, I think, is why he stuck so religiously to his rehabilitation program. His mind was dominated by a vision of himself back on the tour, playing great golf. With that image in front of him, he did his exercises. When his career encountered a crisis, Rocco found that he had the self-discipline, the will, to do what he had to do.

In my experience, self-discipline is not a quality, like blue eyes, that people either have or don't have at birth. Every time they face a situation requiring discipline, people either talk themselves into sticking with a plan or they talk themselves out of it.

Rocco talked himself into it.

You might think that it's easier for a professional athlete, whose livelihood is at stake, to find the discipline he needs to stick with a regimen, but I could show you examples of dozens of athletes who didn't have the discipline to rehabilitate after surgery and who cut their careers short. Mickey Mantle was one.

Money wasn't the motivation you might think. Rocco had put himself and his family in a solid financial position. He was well established as a golfer, and he would have found ways to make a living in the game if his back had prevented him from returning to the tour.

What motivated and still motivates Rocco was his vision. He sees himself winning golf tournaments again. People who can retain that vision, that image of the self they want to be, tend to remain on improvement regimens. People who lose faith in that vision tend to give up, usually after two to eight weeks, once the initial burst of enthusiasm has faded. That's the way it is with most New Year's resolutions.

That's because most improvement programs, if they have any validity at all, produce an immediate, beneficial impact for someone who has, until he begins the program, been floundering.

If you, for example, are an average golfer and you begin the program I've outlined, you'll probably notice some quick results. Your short game will improve because you've begun taking lessons and practicing it. Your course management will improve as well. Your scores will be lower. But somewhere in those first few months, you'll hit your first plateau. You may even, as Dick Kreitler did, find that your scores are going up again as you work to master a swing change.

That's when your discipline will be tested, as Rocco's was.

You'll find, after some discouraging round, that you're beginning to wonder whether the effort you're putting in is worth it. You might have played against someone who never practices, never takes a lesson, but who nevertheless beat you.

You think, *Why should I spend all this time on lessons and practice? I'm always going to be a hacker. All of my friends are going to see me working, and not getting better, and they'll kid me.*

That's when your discipline starts to break down. You put aside the vision of yourself as a fine golfer, a scratch golfer. Instead, you choose to see yourself as duffer. You start to believe that talent determines golfing ability, and that you have no talent. You are on the way to talking yourself out of your commitment to improvement. It becomes easy to find a reason to skip the next practice session, to cancel the next lesson. Very soon, you're back where you started.

Real talent is not what most people think it is. It's not a natural ability to hammer the ball down the range. It's not some extraordinary gift for putting. Real talent is what Rocco displayed when he hurt his back. Real talent is patience. It's persistence. It's the ability always to keep in mind the vision of yourself as you want to be. Real talent leads to discipline, and discipline leads to a sustained effort over a long period of time. That effort is what produces, in the end, long drives down the middle and extraordinary putts.

Everything in this book is designed to help you tap your real talent, to find the discipline you need to get better. If you follow the program, you will have a mentor, your pro, who will help you through the rough spots. You will be working on aspects of the game that will improve your scoring.

But the pro can't learn the game for you. He can teach you, but you must learn it for yourself. That's one of the great things about the game.

Just as I can guarantee that if you stick with this plan for three years, you will play the golf of your dreams, I can guarantee that you will encounter, during those three years, periods when it all seems useless and you're tempted to give up, when other claims on your time suddenly seem more important.

That's when you will have to find the strength within

yourself to stay the course. That's when you have to keep your dream in the front of your mind. That's when you have to arm yourself with reasons to continue.

If you can do that, then, like Rocco Mediate, you can talk yourself into being disciplined.

Chapter 15

A Philosophy of Golf and Life

Why should you begin the program I've outlined? Why should you commit yourself to it? Why persevere in that commitment?

The answer, I think, lies partly in the nature of human beings. To be fully human is to struggle with adversity, to overcome it. A few generations ago, our ancestors faced challenges that were simple and primal. If they wanted to eat, they had to plant crops, work the soil with their hands, and hope that the rains came. If they wanted shelter, they had to cut trees and build it. If they wanted to go somewhere, they had to walk. They survived because they thrived on challenges. If they had not been this way, if their first reaction to a challenge was to roll over and give up, they would have perished before they got a chance to *become* ancestors.

It's reasonable to think that they passed this trait, this tendency to confront and overcome challenges, along to us. We humans are beings with an innate need to be challenged.

But humans also love play. You may have to work to teach a child to read or pick up his room. You generally don't have to work to teach her to play. It comes naturally.

I think this has to do with the natural unity between body and mind. Our modern culture tends to separate the mind from the body. Much of what we do is categorized as either mental work or physical work. In fact, people sometimes ask me where the mind ends and the body begins. They think there must be a point, somewhere between the jawbone and the collarbone, where this separation occurs.

I don't think they are separate, and I think we we are most content when our minds and bodies are working in harmony. Play both allows and requires us to do that, to seek that synchronization.

That, I think, is why so many people play golf and why golf is the greatest game in the world. It is an endless challenge. And it is play.

You will search long and in vain, I suspect, for an endeavor that combines the challenges and pleasures of golf. It tests your body, not for brute strength but for strength tempered by coordination and grace. It tests your mind for the ability to learn, to strategize, to remain calm under pressure. It tests you for qualities of character that I greatly admire: persistence, patience, and determination. Golf challenges you to measure yourself against a universally recognized standard of excellence, par. More than that, it challenges you to better not just an opponent, but yourself.

It is the most honest sport I know. You can't fake golf skills. You can't hide behind the skills of teammates. At the end of a round, you can't tell yourself you played well if you haven't.

It is a sport you can never master, never cease to learn. It will never bore you. And boredom, I suspect, is at the root of many of the plagues of modern life.

I think this is why people invented golf. It gives us the playful pleasures of being outdoors in good company, of striking a ball and making it fly a long way—and it challenges us. It satisfies our need to face difficulties and surmount them. Golf makes our lives fuller and more complete—if we maintain the balance between challenge and play.

When I talk to people about the challenge of becoming good at golf, I sometimes promise that if they commit themselves to a process of improvement, they will have a ball finding out how good they can get. One listener recently objected.

"Wait a minute, Doc," he said. "If I practice and take lessons for weeks and weeks and then don't improve when I play, I'm not having a ball. I'm discouraged, disappointed, and unhappy."

True enough. People can and do err in the direction of getting too serious about their golf. I sometimes talk with retirees who tell me how much they looked forward to being able to spend all day, every day, working at their golf. But after a few months, they say, the game doesn't seem like fun any more.

The reason, I suspect, was their approach to the game. They wanted to work at it. They transferred to golf the attitudes they had had toward their jobs, and changed it from a game to a job, from play to drudgery. They expected that their handicaps would drop in response to their efforts with the same regularity that their paychecks rose on the job. When that didn't happen, they stopped having fun at golf. It was their attitudes that defeated them, not the nature of the game or the challenge of improvement.

So, as you progress through this program toward the golf of your dreams, remember that it's not a job. If you are going to honor the commitment you've made, there probably will be times when you have to prod yourself to do your putting drills or your stretching exercises, but you can't let them become drudgery. Remember that golf is something you chose to play. It's something you've admitted to yourself you would like to play better. You're practicing not because you want to work harder than anyone else, but because you know practice will eventually make you better, and you want to savor the joy of playing the best golf you can play. You practice your putting because you know that someday, that practice will allow you to walk onto a green and think, *it's party time*. You practice because practice will eventually make the game easier and effortless. The more you understand golf, the simpler and more instinctive the game will seem to you. The better you play, the less fatigue you'll feel at the end of a round.

When I say you'll have a ball finding out how good you can get, I don't mean that the process will be all smiles and giggles. I mean that you'll experience many of the emotions that life offers, including frustration, disappointment, and despair. I mean that you'll be able to take pride in having the mental tenacity to persevere in the face of those emotions. And I mean that when, having persevered, you finally do your best, when you put things together and play well, you will feel twice as happy about it, twice as proud of what you have accomplished, because of the travail you faced along the way.

If it were easy, you wouldn't experience this joy, any more than you experience joy when you satisfy your hunger by picking up the phone and ordering pizza.

Some people who take up the challenge of golf later object that the game isn't fair. To which I reply, "You're right. Golf is not fair."

It isn't fair that Tiger Woods and Laura Davies got so much more talent than most of us. It isn't fair that some people got expert tutelage early in life and never developed bad swings to overcome. It isn't fair that one player's mishit ball will strike a tree, carom onto the green, and roll up next to the pin while another's will strike the same tree, carom deeper into the woods, and be lost.

So what? Would you like life to be perfectly fair? Would you like to pay the full price for all the mistakes you've gotten away with? Would you like to give back all the advantages you've been given? The fact is that golf, like life, deals us all a set of circumstances, and our challenge is to make the best of them. If you love golf, if you love life, then you love its caprices.

As my friend Tom Kite says, if you love golf, you love it when you've got it in the palm of your hand, and you love it when you can't find it. You love it when you win on Sunday, and you love it when you fall on your face. You love it when it breaks your heart.

And it will, at times, break your heart. You may work on your short game, go to the course, chip and putt beautifully—and shoot the same old score because your long swing has gotten away from you and you can't stop hitting your tee shots into the woods. Or you may put everything else together and find that you can't putt.

That's when you will have to find the strength within yourself to stay the course. That's when you have to keep your dream in the front of your mind. That's when you have to arm yourself with reasons to continue.

That's when you have to say to yourself, *I love golf. I really admire people who get good at it. It's a hard game and it takes time. But I will really feel good about myself when I get there.*

If you can find the strength to think this way, to be patient and persistent and yet always playful, there will be a glorious payoff. It may take longer than you expect or want, but, at some point, things will start to fall into place. The three-foot putts will start falling consistently, rolling firmly into the middle of the cup. The chips and little pitches will start to spring off your club face with crisp, controlled authority. You'll love to watch them roll and curl to a stop by the hole.

Maybe it will be a sudden moment of grace and clarity, a feeling of *ah, so that's it*. Or it might happen gradually and quietly, so that it won't be noticed until you're taking a long walk to a green with a putter in your hand and you realize how many of your irons have been flying straight to the flag.

In a game that is rich with sweet moments, these will be the sweetest of all. These will be among the sweetest moments of your life.

Appendix A

Rotella's Rules

- The good news about golf is that great physical ability is not required to play well.

- Characteristics like desire, patience, and persistence, more than physical talent, are what enable athletes in any sport to improve their performance.

- If you're going to get better at golf or at anything else that requires disciplined effort, you must first think of yourself as capable of becoming a fine golfer. You must believe that you have the talent to succeed.

- What's most important about a pro is not what he charges. It's the joy he takes in helping golfers develop. It's his dedication to the game and his profession. It's what he knows, and his skill in communicating it.

- If the pupil isn't learning, the teacher isn't teaching.

- No one is too old to learn.

- At some point, any golfer who wants to get better must make a commitment to a teacher, and he must make a commitment to a process of improvement.

- If you want to improve your golf game, you have to accept long periods when your efforts can seem wasted, when your scores don't reflect the effort you're putting in. These will be the times when patience and perseverance will be the most important traits you can have.

- Only practice counts as practice.

- The playing lesson is a great diagnostic tool. It shows the pro what his pupil's game is really like.

- It's on the holes where they don't hit the greens that the scratch player often separates himself from the six-handicapper.

- As you embark on a swing change, it's important to know that two of the chief challenges you face are habit and comfort.

- You need good, sound, dominant habits.

- If you decide that you love striving to get better, you can always make yourself happy by working at your game.

- However you manage it, practicing with a focused mind will make your practice more efficient and beneficial.

- Parents ought to lay down certain rules of behavior for their young golfers. They ought to require that a child meet minimal standards for behavior, temper, sportsmanship, and grades in school if he or she is to continue playing and taking lessons. But they should not try to teach the backswing.

- Self-discipline is not a quality, like blue eyes, that people either have or don't have at birth. Every time they face a situation requiring discipline, people either talk themselves into sticking with a plan or they talk themselves out of it.

- Real talent is patience. It's persistence. It's the ability always to keep in mind the vision of yourself as you want to be.

Appendix B

Your Improvement Program

Take notes on each lesson and practice session. They'll help you remember what you've learned and chart your progress. Copy these pages and use them each time you go through an improvement cycle.

Lesson One _____

_____

_____

_____

Practice session I _____

_____

_____

Practice II _____

_____

PRACTICE III _____
_____

PRACTICE IV _____
_____

PRACTICE V _____
_____

PLAY (COURSE AND SCORE)_____

PLAY (COURSE AND SCORE)_____

PRACTICE VI _____
_____

PRACTICE VII _____
_____

PRACTICE VIII _____
_____

PRACTICE IX _____
_____

PLAY (COURSE AND SCORE)_____

PLAY (COURSE AND SCORE)_____

Your Improvement Program · 195

LESSON TWO _____
_____
_____
_____

PRACTICE X _____
_____

PRACTICE XI _____
_____

PRACTICE XII _____

PRACTICE XIII _____
_____

PLAY (COURSE AND SCORE)_____

PLAY (COURSE AND SCORE)_____

PRACTICE XIV _____
_____

PRACTICE XV_____
_____

196 · THE GOLF OF YOUR DREAMS

PRACTICE XVI _____
_____

PRACTICE XVII _____
_____

PRACTICE XVIII _____
_____

PLAY (COURSE AND SCORE) _____

PLAY (COURSE AND SCORE) _____

LESSON THREE _____
_____
_____
_____

PRACTICE XIX _____
_____

PRACTICE XX _____
_____

PRACTICE XXI _____
_____

Your Improvement Program · 197

Practice XXII _____

_____

Play (course and score) _____

Play (course and score) _____

Practice XXIII _____

_____

Practice XXIV _____

_____

Practice XXV _____

_____

Practice XXVI _____

_____

Practice XXVII _____

_____

Play (course and score) _____

Play (course and score) _____

Lesson Four _____

_____

198 · THE GOLF OF YOUR DREAMS

PRACTICE XXVIII _____

PRACTICE XXIX _____

PRACTICE XXX _____

PRACTICE XXXI _____

PLAY (COURSE AND SCORE) _____

PLAY (COURSE AND SCORE) _____

LESSON FIVE _____

PRACTICE XXXII _____

YOUR IMPROVEMENT PROGRAM · 199

PRACTICE XXXIII _____

_____

PRACTICE XXXIV _____

_____

PRACTICE XXXV _____

_____

PLAY (CHARTED ROUND) _____

No. 1. SHOTS: _____ TOTAL: _____

No. 2. SHOTS: _____ TOTAL: _____

No. 3. SHOTS: _____ TOTAL: _____

No. 4. SHOTS: _____ TOTAL: _____

No. 5. SHOTS: _____ TOTAL: _____

No. 6. SHOTS: _____ TOTAL: _____

No. 7. SHOTS: _____ TOTAL: _____

No. 8. SHOTS: _____ TOTAL: _____

No. 9. SHOTS: _____ TOTAL: _____

No. 10. SHOTS: _____ TOTAL: _____

No. 11. SHOTS: _____ TOTAL: _____

No. 12. SHOTS: _____ TOTAL: _____

No. 13. Shots: _____ Total: _____

No. 14: Shots: _____ Total: _____

No. 15: Shots: _____ Total: _____

No. 16: Shots: _____ Total: _____

No. 17: Shots: _____ Total: _____

No. 18: Shots: _____ Total: _____

Total shots: _____
Shots from within 120 yards of the hole: _____

Percentage of tee shots in play: _____

Percentage of putts under five feet made: _____

Percentage of up-and-down chances converted: _____

Percentage of sand saves: _____

Play (charted round) _____

No. 1. Shots: _____ Total: _____

No. 2. Shots: _____ Total: _____

No. 3. Shots: _____ Total: _____

Your Improvement Program · 201

No. 4. Shots: _____ Total: _____

No. 5. Shots: _____ Total: _____

No. 6. Shots: _____ Total: _____

No. 7. Shots: _____ Total: _____

No. 8. Shots: _____ Total: _____

No. 9. Shots: _____ Total: _____

No. 10. Shots: _____ Total: _____

No. 11. Shots: _____ Total: _____

No. 12. Shots: _____ Total: _____

No. 13. Shots: _____ Total: _____

No. 14: Shots: _____ Total: _____

No. 15: Shots: _____ Total: _____

No. 16: Shots: _____ Total: _____

No. 17: Shots: _____ Total: _____

No. 18: Shots: _____ Total: _____

Total shots: _____ Shots from within 120 yards of the hole: _____

Percentage of tee shots in play: _____

Percentage of putts under five feet made: _____

Percentage of up-and-down chances converted: _____

Percentage of sand saves: _____

Practice XXXVI _____
_____

Practice XXXVII _____
_____

Practice XXXVIII _____
_____

Practice XXXIX _____
_____

Practice XL _____
_____

Lesson Six (playing lesson) _____
_____
_____
_____

Five days off

Acknowledgements

The list of people who helped with this book is a long one. It begins with all coaches I have known over the years in many sports. By watching them and listening to them, I have learned much about the dedication, faith, and commitment involved in preparing an athlete for peak performance. I've seen the joy that the best coaches derive from helping human beings honor a commitment, focus their minds, and attain their dreams. I've learned that coaching is truly a noble profession.

I must thank as well the athletes who have honored me with their confidence over the years. They've shown me how to chase a dream doing something they love.

More specifically, I am indebted to the golfers—professional and amateur—whom I've worked with. I suspect I learned as much from each of them as they learned from me about the way people get better at golf. I owe much as well to the teaching pros I have been privileged to call colleagues over the years—at *Golf Digest* schools, at the National Golf Foundation, in the PGA of America.

Then there are the individuals whose names you've read in the pages of this book—Rob McNamara and Gene Hilen; Hank Johnson; David and Greg Belcher; Paul Buckley and Pete Mathews; Alice Hovde and Todd Anderson; Bill Davis, Patty Pilz, and Jay and Arline Hoffman; Bob Toski; Kandi Kessler-Comer and Phil Owenby; Dan Grider and Terry Crouch; Dan and Michael Henderson; Mark Heartfield and Dick Kreitler; Robert Willis and Mike Carver; and Rocco Mediate. Each of them gave generously of time, insight, and, in many cases, hospitality. More than that, they gave inspiration. I am thankful to them all.

I've also benefitted from the advice of a number of people who commented on this project while it was in progress, including Bill Heron, Rod Thompson, and my parents, Laura and Guy Rotella.

I am grateful as well to my agent, Wally Buchleitner, and to my editor at Simon & Schuster, Dominick Anfuso, who is a genius at titles, concepts, dust jackets, and general guidance.

Finally, thanks to Casey and Darlene Rotella for their kindness and patience with the disruptions this project caused.

Also by *Dr. Bob Rotella*

Golf Is Not a Game of Perfect
The Golf of Your Dreams
Putting Out of Your Mind
Life Is Not a Game of Perfect

GOLF IS A GAME OF CONFIDENCE

DR. BOB ROTELLA

with Bob Cullen

POCKET BOOKS

This edition first published by Pocket Books, 2004
An imprint of Simon & Schuster UK Ltd
A Viacom Company

Copyright © Robert Rotella, 1996

This book is copyright under the Berne Convention.
No reproduction without permission.
All rights reserved.

The right of Robert Rotella to be identified as the author of this work has been asserted by him in accordance with sections 77 and 78 of the Copyright, Designs and Patents Act, 1988.

3 5 7 9 10 8 6 4

Simon & Schuster UK Ltd
Africa House
64–78 Kingsway
London WC2B 6AH

www.simonsays.co.uk

Simon & Schuster Australia
Sydney

A CIP catalogue record for this book
is available from the British Library

ISBN 0-7434-9246-3

Printed and bound in Great Britain by
Cox & Wyman Ltd, Reading, Berkshire

Contents

	Introduction	9
No. 1	How Brad Faxon Stayed in the Present	13
No. 2	How Fred Arenstein Broke 80	37
No. 3	How Jay Delsing Kept Trusting	43
No. 4	How Davis Love III Got Back to the Masters	56
No. 5	How Val Skinner Won the Sprint	76
No. 6	How Paul Runyan Beat Sam Snead 8 and 7	84
No. 7	How Patsy Price Broke 90	94
No. 8	How Tim Simpson Battled the Yips	100
No. 9	How Byron Nelson Won Eleven Straight	111
No. 10	How Bill Shean Prepared for the Club Championship at Pine Valley	119
No. 11	How Billy Mayfair Rebuilt His Confidence	138
No. 12	How Dicky Pride Crossed the Fine Line	151

No. 13	How David Frost Learned to Close	164
No. 14	How Guy Rotella Came to Golf	175
No. 15	How Nona Epps Learned to Come Through in the Clutch	184
No. 16	How Pat Bradley Finished Her Victory Lap	194
No. 17	How Claude Williamson Got from Stumpy Lake to the Cascades	204
No. 18	How Tom Kite Honors His Commitment	213
Appendix	More Rotella's Rules	235

Introduction

GOLFERS SOMETIMES ASK ME FOR MY DEFINITION OF CONFIDENCE. I've been fortunate enough to spend more than twenty years working with athletes as a head coach, a trainer of the mind. For about a dozen of those years, I've been teaching and coaching professional golfers. Here is one of the best definitions I've come up with:

Confidence is playing with your eyes.

I hear this from athletes in all sports with targets. Think of the shooter on a roll in basketball. She just looks at the basket and lets it go. Think of a great pitcher when he's sharp. He looks at the catcher's mitt and throws it in there. Think of the trap shooter. He squints at the clay disc and squeezes the trigger.

The eye of the confident athlete zeroes in on the objective. The brain and the rest of the body simply react. The basketball shooter doesn't give herself a lecture on the mechanics of pushing a ball through the air. The pitcher doesn't mentally rehearse the motions of shoulder, arm, elbow, wrist, and finger that produce a slider. The trap shooter needn't ponder how to coordinate the movements of his torso and his trigger finger.

Confident athletes let their brains and nervous systems perform the skills they have rehearsed and mastered—without interference from the conscious mind.

So it should be with the golfer. The confident golfer sees where he wants the ball to go. Sometimes, even after he turns his eyes back to the ball, he continues to see the target with his "mind's eye." He lets his body swing the club. The more confident he is, the better the chance the ball will go there.

I don't know why this is so. I know only that this is the way the human organism was created to function and the way it functions best.

Of course, if everyone were endowed with an abundant, constant supply of confidence, my profession would not exist. But not everyone is.

Most golfers experience confidence only occasionally and only haphazardly. They normally play in a state of barely repressed tension. Their swings and scores reflect it. But now and again, for reasons they do not understand, things fall into place. They hit a couple of good shots, sink a putt or two, and suddenly they feel confident. They begin playing with their eyes, hitting the ball to the target, and they experience golf on an entirely different level. They string pars and birdies together. They glimpse their potential as golfers.

Inevitably, though, the swing falls out of the slot, or a couple of putts slide by the hole, and the spell of confidence ends. These golfers do not control its departure, any more than they control the passing of a thunderstorm over the course. They finish their rounds with their old golf games, warm but wistful memories of their hot streaks, and a gnawing sense of frustration.

The golfers I work with refuse to wait until confidence descends upon them. Most of them are professionals whose dreams and livelihoods depend on finding a way to play confidently. Some are amateurs, from scratch players to high handicappers, who simply want to play golf as well as they can. They understand that this requires confidence.

In all sports, confidence separates winners from also-rans. The best athletes combine confidence with physical competence. But every smart coach I've ever known, if he has to choose between a competent athlete who lacks confidence and an athlete of lesser physical gifts whose mind is ready to maximize his potential, who is confident, will pick the confident player.

I teach all golfers that they are endowed with free will. They can control their thoughts. In fact, they are responsible for their thoughts. They can choose to think confidently. They can take this confidence with them every time they go to the golf course, and they can have it from their first swing to their last.

But it takes an honest commitment to develop confidence.

I have found that simply stating this premise does not persuade a lot of people. They are not accustomed to thinking the way great golfers think. They can't believe confidence is something they can learn and control.

Some of them, in truth, see confidence as a form of self-deception. I frequently meet people who tell me that dwelling on thoughts of what they want to happen—another good definition of confidence—is unrealistic. To me, they've just found a rationalization for the thoughts that defeat them.

I believe that confident thinking, about golf or anything else, is just being honest about where you're capable of going. It at least gives you a chance to find out what you can attain.

Some golfers tell me it's too hard to stay positive and confident. They may try it for a while, but they give it up when they run into adversity.

I reply that it may seem easier to be negative in the short run. But in the long run you're going to waste a lot more energy being negative. You'll flail away at the game, but you'll never find out how good you could have been. So the truth of the matter is, if you intend to invest time and energy in golf, it's a lot easier to be positive.

I've found that stories teach more effectively than do lectures on theory. So I've assembled eighteen stories about players I have known and worked with: eighteen holes, if you will, of a golf course. Some of these players have recorded extraordinary achievements in major championships, like the 8 and 7 thrashing Paul Runyan administered to the great Sam Snead in the 1938 PGA or the 66 Davis Love shot in the final round of the 1995 Masters. Some have just broken 90 or 80 for the first time. These accomplishments, to them, were just as sweet as Davis's 66.

These eighteen golfers have two things in common. They love the game. And they all have something to teach you about confidence, about playing with your eyes.

No. 1

How Brad Faxon Stayed in the Present

THE FIRST HOLE AT THE RIVIERA COUNTRY CLUB IN LOS ANGELES presents a lot of choices. It's a great starting hole, a 501-yard par five. The tee sits eighty feet above the fairway, giving the player a panoramic view of the verdant canyon where the course is situated. For the members, this elevation provides the comforting assurance that the first shot will at least get up in the air. And it means that even if their first couple of strokes are hit with irons or fairway woods, are the product of stiff muscles, and don't go particularly far, they still have a chance to reach the green in regulation and get started with a par.

But to Brad Faxon, standing on that elevated tee at the beginning of the last round of the 1995 PGA Championship, No. 1 looked much more challenging. Brad had played well the first three days of the tournament, getting to five strokes under par. But some twenty golfers had played better; the leader, Ernie Els, was eleven strokes ahead. Brad wants to play well in all the tournaments he enters, particularly majors, but the 1995 PGA was especially important. It was the last opportunity to earn points for the Ryder Cup team, and Brad had been dreaming of playing in the Ryder Cup for a long time. As the tournament began, he was fourteenth in the standings, a few hundred points away from the top ten and a spot on the team. The math was complicated, and nothing would be settled until the last strokes had been played Sunday. But in essence, the situation was simple. To earn enough points to make the team, Brad had to play not just an excellent round but a superb one, a round that would vault him past at least a dozen players and into the top five.

He faced, in short, one of the great challenges of the game. Could he produce his best golf when he most wanted to produce it?

Brad and the thousands of spectators in the canyon below knew that if he were to make the Ryder Cup team, he could hardly afford to start with a comfortable par on No. 1. He wanted to birdie the hole, to eagle it if possible. Doing that would require a long, accurate drive off the tee. But using the driver would bring into play the out-of-bounds stakes that line the left side of the hole and the trees that line the right. He would have to hit the fairway, because trying to reach the green in two from the thick kikuyu grass rough was foolhardy. Without backspin, the ball would never hold the green. So his driver would have to be hit nearly perfectly. It would have to be hit with confidence.

FORTUNATELY, BRAD HAD been preparing to hit that driver for a long time. When I first started working with him, in the late 1980s, he was a young player with a deft short game and an extraordinary mind. Brad is one of the most enthusiastic, optimistic, and playful human beings I have ever encountered. He loves playing games of all kinds, and he is very creative. But he lacked confidence in his driver. When he mishit a wedge or a putt, as even the best players do, he had no trouble forgetting it and believing that the next shot would go in. But when he sprayed a drive off the tee, he felt as if all the energy had been sucked out of his body. Thereafter, the club felt suspect in his hands.

We worked for several years on this problem. To begin with, Brad hit a lot of 3-woods off tees where his fellow competitors hit drivers, sacrificing distance for the sake of confidence. He worked with a swing instructor to fix some minor flaws in his mechanics. He worked at developing the discipline to savor and remember his good drives and the patience to wait as his driving improved. Gradually, he became more confident, and in 1992, he broke through to win twice and finish eighth on the money list. He still was, and probably always will be, most confident with a wedge or putter in his hands. Even the best players find that certain facets of the game come easily to them; they must work at trusting others. But Brad had begun to relish hitting his driver again.

And Brad had done some intelligent things to prepare himself during the week of the PGA. Several times, after leaving the course, he met some friends and went Rollerblading alongside the beaches from Santa Monica to Muscle Beach and Venice—as much as twenty miles round trip. It's probably safe to assume that Bobby Jones, Ben Hogan, and Jack Nicklaus never went Rollerblading during the week of a major championship. It's not a traditional form of golf preparation. But Brad likes the exercise, he likes the fresh air, and he likes the company of the friends he makes in abundance as he travels the circuit. And he's good enough to be confident that he won't fall and hurt himself. Most important, Rollerblading is fun; it relaxes him.

In my experience, a player who spends every minute at a tournament site, beating balls and worrying, trying to grind his way to a peak performance, is likely to do worse than the player who looks at preparation as a long-term process, who gets in a reasonable amount of practice at the tournament site, and then finds a way to relax and forget about golf.

Brad also chose to dwell on thoughts that would help him. He had not played particularly well in the weeks preceding the tournament. He started well in the British Open, but finished fifteenth. Then he went home to New England to play in the New England Classic. By chance, he was paired the first two days with Lanny Wadkins, the Ryder Cup captain. He wanted very much to impress Wadkins, and he put a lot of extra pressure on himself. He missed the cut. He made the cut the next week, at the Buick Open, but he finished back in the pack. Nevertheless, as he headed to California, Brad thought he was playing well. He simply wasn't pulling his game together and scoring.

Fortunately, he's always liked Riviera. It's a course whose holes are visible; there are no blind shots. The architect, George Thomas, believed in confronting a player with challenges rather than surprising him. Brad feels most comfortable on a tee that helps him visualize the shape of the shot he wants to hit, and at Riviera, the design clearly suggests fades on some holes and draws on others. He reminded himself that he likes the course.

The Riviera greens were still soft from a partly successful reconstruction job during the previous year. Brad knew that they were bound to spike up, and that lots of players would gripe about it. He decided to think of that as an advantage. If he could will himself to take the greens as he found them, without complaint, he would have a huge advantage over all the players who would whine, moan, and convince themselves that the condition of the greens meant they weren't going to make any putts.

As we often do, Brad and I took a walk together on the eve of the tournament's final round. This time, it was a short walk, up a staircase at the home of a friend, Peter Lomenzo, to a little deck with a bench and a view of the Pacific. We sat and talked. He knows by now that there are no magic words, no parlor tricks that a sports psychologist can perform to put a player into the right frame of mind before a crucial round. He knows that there are no startling new breakthroughs in behavioral science that I can reveal to help him to play better. He knows, and even enjoys, the fact that our conversation will revolve around two basic and interrelated ideas that we have discussed many times before. One is staying in the present. The second is committing to the process. A large part of this book will be devoted to elaborating on those two ideas.

Staying in the present sounds simple, so simple that even some teaching professionals can't understand how it can be difficult. I did a clinic recently for PGA members in the Boston area. One of them raised his hand and asked a question.

"What's the big deal about staying in the present?" he wanted to know. "How can it be hard for tour players to keep their minds in the present on Sunday?"

I asked him whether he played many tournaments himself. He said no. I asked what his name was. Let's say that he said "Joe."

"Okay, Joe," I continued. "Who do you think is the sexiest woman in America?"

Without hesitating much, he named Cindy Crawford.

"Wow, Joe," I said. "What an incredible coincidence! As I was leaving my hotel this morning, the phone rang and it was Cindy. She told me you'd be at my workshop today. She wanted me to tell you that she wants very much to meet you afterwards. She's in room 201, and she said that precisely at seven o'clock, she'll be slipping out of her bath and into something more comfortable. That's when she wants you to be there. She wants to take maybe half an hour for a little conversation, and then from seven-thirty till ten, she wants to make mad, passionate love to you."

Joe was blushing.

"But there's one catch, Joe," I went on. "If at anytime between now and seven-thirty you think about her, the deal's off."

"That's impossible," Joe managed to say.

"And you've only been thinking about Cindy for five minutes," I replied. "These guys have been dreaming about winning golf tournaments for most of their lives."

Then they began to understand the mental discipline a successful tour golfer needs to stay in the present.

To play golf as well as he can, a player has to focus his mind tightly on the shot he is playing now, in the present.

If the golfer thinks about anything else, that pure reaction between the eye and the brain and the nervous system is polluted. Performance usually suffers. This is just the way human beings are constructed.

A player can't think about what happened to the last shot he hit, or the shot he played with the tournament on the line a week ago. That's thinking about the past. He can't think about how great it would be to win the tournament, or how terrible it would feel to blow it. That's thinking about the future.

In Brad's case, I told him on that Saturday night, it meant that it would do him no good to think about how badly he had played with Lanny Wadkins in New England two weeks previously, or how very few putts had fallen for him during the first three rounds at Riviera. That was the past.

Most especially, it would do him no good to think about making the Ryder Cup team, or the fact that he'd probably need to shoot in the low 60s to do it. That would be thinking about results, the future.

He already knew that there was no way he could decide simply to ignore the Ryder Cup. All summer, interest in the team had been building. The point standings were posted in every locker room; at every tour stop, reporters asked the players in contention how they felt about it. The Ryder Cup was an unavoidable distraction of the type that tour players have to learn to cope with.

Brad and I had already agreed that there was no way he could avoid thinking about the Ryder Cup from time to time. But he couldn't afford to think about it on the golf course. If Ryder Cup thoughts occurred to him while he was competing, he had to catch himself, stop, and return his mind to the present, to the shot at hand.

Brad had resolved to turn the Ryder Cup hubbub into an asset instead of a distraction. Every time someone asked him about it, he would answer that, yes, he wanted to make the team; as he did so, he would remind himself that his best chance of doing that lay in keeping his mind in the present, focused on the shot ahead, every time he competed.

Throughout the week of the PGA, he made certain to avoid falling into the trap of trying to calculate where he stood in relation to the other players with a chance to make the team and what he would have to shoot to beat them. Trying to sort that out would have taken his mind so far afield that he might never have found his way back. When he teed off on Sunday morning, he was deliberately unaware of what place he was in.

I told Brad on that Saturday evening that he was doing everything right with his mind. He just had to be patient and trust that the results would come. I told him that his goal ought to be simple: to be able to stand in front of the mirror on Sunday night with a big grin on his face, able to tell himself that he had

20 • GOLF IS A GAME OF CONFIDENCE

trusted his swing all day, that he had had fun playing a meaningful round of golf.

And then I said good-bye and got ready to catch an early flight from Los Angeles on Sunday morning. One of the great things about golf is that once a player steps onto the first tee, no coach, no swing doctor, and no sports psychologist can help him. He is alone with his mind and his caddie. He has to do it himself. I watched on television what Brad did in the last round of the PGA.

STANDING ON THE first tee, Brad told me later, he immersed his mind in the process of hitting good shots. The process varies from player to player. Some players visualize the shots they want to hit and see everything about them—the flight, the trajectory, the bounce, and the roll—in their mind's eye. Some players don't visualize. They simply identify a target, then think about the ball going there. Others just look at the target and react.

But a player who is committed to the process of hitting good shots will never draw a club back until he knows where he wants the ball to go and believes that the club in his hands will send it there.

Good players typically have a physical routine wrapped around this mental process to make sure their alignment and posture are consistently correct. Physical routines can vary. Brad, for example, sometimes takes a practice swing and sometimes doesn't. But the mental routine at the heart of the process cannot vary.

Brad had, in fact, been thinking about the first drive since going to bed Saturday night. He had seen the shot he wanted over and over again. He stepped up, addressed the ball, and replicated the shot he had seen in his mind. The ball flew straight and far, hung up against the sky, and then dropped into the middle of the fairway, three hundred yards out. He felt a surge of excitement as he walked down the hill to the fairway below.

Brad's caddie, Cubby Burke, set the bag on the fairway and gave him the yardage. He had 195 yards to carry the big sand bunker that guarded the front right portion of the green, where the hole was cut. He had 201 yards to the hole. The wind, as it generally does at Riviera, was coming off the nearby Pacific, blowing softly from right to left.

It would, Brad knew, be a 4-iron shot under normal conditions. But these were not normal conditions. He could feel the adrenaline pumping. His first instinct was to hit a hard 5-iron, with a draw, right over the trap.

Just to see what Cubby thought, Brad asked him.

"Solid four," Cubby suggested.

Brad knew Cubby couldn't tell how excited he felt, how strong.

"Cub, I'm going to hit a hard draw, with a five," he said.

"Well," said Cubby, pulling out the 5-iron. "See your shot. You know what you want to do with it."

This is one reason why Cubby is a good caddie. Some caddies take great pride in their job of measuring yardage and recommending clubs, so much so that when the golfer wants to go against their recommendations, they argue. Cubby knows that the best thing he can do for Brad is to help him feel decisive before every shot. He said the right thing.

Brad went through his process again and swung. The shot was flawless, exactly as Brad had envisioned it, a shot that started high, drew into the pin, and cleared the bunker with a few yards to spare. It rolled to a stop about fifteen feet past the hole.

Walking onto the green, Brad was pleased. The putting surface had dried out and firmed up somewhat since Saturday. A mid-iron that carried the bunker and reached the green was bound to roll some. He had put it about as close to the pin as he possibly could.

Now he faced an eagle putt. If there was one thing Brad had found fault with in his play for the first few days, it was his putting. He had not, he felt, been free enough.

When I speak of a player being loose and free on the putting green, I don't mean careless. But most players err in the other direction. They don't trust their instincts and abilities. They doubt whether they've read the green correctly. They try to force the clubhead to stay on line. They try to steer the ball into the hole. They putt worse by being too careful than they would if they were careless.

When Brad is putting well, he comes close to having the ideal mind. He never thinks about speed. He feels that thinking about speed is like thinking about how far to throw a ball when you're playing catch. The outcome is likely to be an awkward toss. In the same way, thoughts like "Don't run it too far past" or "Get it there" lead to lots of three-putts.

Brad's putting process starts with a thorough examination of the green. On a day when he is particularly sharp, he can see at a glance things that most golfers would never notice—the grain, how closely the grass has been cut, patches where the grass is a few millimeters longer than others. He gauges the slope. Sometimes he gets Cubby's input. He is looking for the line on which the ball will roll into the hole. As soon as he thinks he has that line, he steps over the ball, makes a practice swing or two if he feels the need for it, and then lets the putt go, trusting his first instincts.

Once he's over a putt, Brad doesn't think specifically about getting the ball into the hole. He's already picked out a line that he's convinced will do that. He concentrates narrowly on the task at hand—getting the ball rolling well on the line he has selected. Then he waits to see what happens, letting the green take care of everything else. He knows that when his mind is right, his system and his senses will take care of touch and direction much better than he would if he tried consciously to control those variables.

Conversely, when a golfer thinks about results instead of process, the mind doesn't know where the hole is.

On the first hole at Riviera, Brad's eagle putt went right into the hole.

He was on his way. And he was brimming with confidence.

Some people might say that it's easy to be confident when you've just holed an eagle putt. But what if the putt had missed?

To be sure, success breeds confidence. But great players don't depend on success at the first green for their confidence. They strive to maintain the same attitude whether or not the first putt falls. Brad, for instance, deliberately avoids measuring how well he is putting by how many putts fall. He knows that too many variables, some of them beyond his control, can influence that. He tries to monitor whether he is putting confidently and getting the ball rolling well on his intended line. If he does that, and the ball comes close to the hole, he feels that he is putting well. If the first one or two don't fall, he believes that only increases the chances that the third or fourth ones will.

Still, it was great to nail that first putt.

No. 2 at Riviera is the toughest hole on the course, a 460-yard par four that calls for a long fade off the tee and a long iron second shot to a narrow green. Again, Brad shaped his shots just as he envisioned them. But this time his 22-foot birdie putt ran just past the edge.

At the third, Brad again drove into the fairway. This time, he found himself somewhere between a 7-iron and a 6-iron. Without much thought, he asked for the six. Brad was playing by feel, trusting his instincts. His instincts at No. 1 had told him to take less club, to hit the hard 5-iron. At No. 3, they told him to hit a little six and not to work the ball, to go straight for the pin over a bunker.

Brad was smart enough to trust himself and go with his instincts. He knows that being trusting and decisive have more to do with the success of a shot than calibrating the distance. Almost invariably, a player's second thought about club selection is based on doubt. Predictably enough, it rarely works as well as the first idea.

Brad's 6-iron went dead straight and stopped five feet from the hole. His playing partner, Jose Maria Olazabal, was a foot outside him, and Brad got a good read from watching Olazabal's putt.

Lining up that putt, for the first time that day he let his mind wander from the present. He thought, for a moment, that if he made the putt he would be three under after just three holes, off to a brilliant start.

Some people have the impression that players with great minds never experience distracting thoughts, doubts, or fears. As a matter of fact, they do. Brad is no exception. Players with great minds don't stay in the present on every shot; they only strive to. The good ones constantly monitor themselves and catch themselves when their minds start to wander. This is what Brad did. He reminded himself to get back into his putting process. He used a physical cue—lining up the "Tour Balata" line on his Titleist with the line on which he intended to roll the putt. And he knocked it in.

He parred the fourth, a 230-yard par three. At the fifth tee, he pulled out his 3-wood to play a 419-yard par four.

This choice suggests the difference between a confident player and a reckless player. Brad was hitting his driver beautifully; there was no question about his confidence. But No. 5 is a tight hole, with out-of-bounds right and trees left. Brad was playing with a game plan, and the plan called for a 3-wood. He had the discipline to stick with his plan.

We'll consider game plans in more detail later on. Suffice it to say now that a good game plan helps a player to swing confidently and decisively, because he knows he's already made the most rational, intelligent strategy choices.

He hooked his tee shot at No. 5, into the first cut of rough. But the 3-wood did its job, leaving him short of more serious trouble and able to play a 7-iron into the green, which he did, leaving himself a 30-foot putt. Brad had not been making many 30-footers during the tournament, but as he lined this one up, he was thinking he was due to make one. He got the ball rolling on his intended line and at the last moment, it dove left, into the hole. He was four under for the day.

No. 6 is Riviera's signature hole, a 175-yard par three with a little pot bunker in the middle of the green. In practice, this means that the hole has alternate greens, one to the left of the bunker and one to the right. The pin on this day was back left. Brad could immediately see the perfect shot—a 6-iron, starting at the left edge of the pot bunker and drawing in toward the flag. He hit it and left himself a 15-foot putt with a right-to-left break.

The cup, he could see, was cut into a slope. And the green looked shaggier to him. He sensed that this putt would be a little slower than the previous ones. Again, he hit it perfectly. Again, it went in.

That birdie brought some new potential distractions. The crowd roared, and he could see that his gallery was beginning to swell. He glanced at a leader board and saw that his name was on it. He had jumped from five under to ten under, and he had moved up into the middle of the top ten.

I don't generally recommend that players look at leader boards during a round. I think it takes them out of the present and diverts their minds into thoughts about results, outcomes, and other things that can do them no good. But some players look at them anyway; sometimes they're unavoidable. I tell them that if they're going to do it, they had better be prepared to ward off any distraction and return to the kind of thinking that got their names up there to begin with.

I'm not the only one who recomends this, and golf is not the only sport where it's a good idea. A couple of years ago, I was in Phoenix with Billy Mayfair, and we had sideline passes to the Fiesta Bowl. Notre Dame fell behind in the first half. We listened to what Lou Holtz told the team at halftime.

"Okay, guys, I don't want anyone looking at the scoreboard," Holtz said.

The principle is the same.

AS THE RIVIERA crowd roared, Brad could feel his body responding, starting to feel more nervous and excited. At the same time, he felt acutely sensitive to everything around him. He hit a 3-wood off the tee at No. 7, a 408-yard par four, and left himself 151 yards to the pin. The wind was at his back and he felt strong. He hit a 9-iron. So sharp was his feel for the ball that while it was in the air, he thought it might be a bit short, and he said "go" to it. It landed three feet short of the hole. The putt had a six-inch break. Brad knew better than to linger over it, to think too much, and to get careful. He stroked it in.

Now the crowd was big and loud, and his friends in the gallery were screaming. He could see people who had been watching other pairings streaming toward the eighth tee. He felt buoyed by the noise and excitement.

Brad, again following his game plan, pulled out a 3-wood. No. 8 is a tight 370-yard par 4 with overhanging trees blocking approaches from the right edge of the fairway. Brad played down the left side, but he hit the ball a little too hard. He was in the rough with a decent lie, but without much chance to spin his approach.

His wedge flew up from the rough, wobbled a little in the air, and bounced once in the kikuyu rough before rolling onto the green and stopping eight feet from the hole. The crowd roared, thinking that Brad had planned it that way.

Now distractions were assaulting Brad's mind. He thought that making the putt would move him to seven under for the day, and perhaps into the tournament's top five. Not coincidentally, for the first time that day, he overread a putt. He played a break that wasn't there, and the ball slid by the hole.

He walked to the ninth tee. Spectators clapped him on the back, told him how well he was doing. The breeze was again at his back and he aimed his drive at the pair of bunkers that guard the fairway. Someone in the crowd told the ball to hurry, but Brad knew there was no need. His ball carried about 280 yards, well over both bunkers, and left him between a 9-iron and a wedge to the green. He hit the 9-iron about twenty-five feet past the hole.

He had another birdie putt, and now he could not ignore the physical symptoms of nerves. His fingers and hands were tingling. The yelling of the crowd rang in his ears.

I teach players to welcome these nervous symptoms rather than fear them. They work and practice all their lives to make it to a situation like the one Brad was in, a situation that gets the adrenaline flowing. Nerves will only make them choke if they

28 • GOLF IS A GAME OF CONFIDENCE

fear the symptoms and start to focus their attention on their hands rather than on their targets, if they start to worry and wonder why their hands are shaking. Once they do that, players tend to tell themselves that they can't putt with shaking hands. They have to remember that lots of tournaments have been won by players in that condition.

Brad welcomed his symptoms, and rolled the birdie putt. It seemed to have missed, but it was breaking so sharply at the end that it half turned around and fell in at the top of the hole.

The crowd, in this situation at a major championship, becomes part of the action. It emitted a roar unlike any Brad had ever heard for himself. He jabbed at the sky with his fist. He got goose bumps. His heart started to pound. He had gone out in 28 strokes. It was the lowest nine-hole total ever in a major championship.

As Brad walked off the green, spectators yelled things like "Ryder Cup!" and "59!" Someone close to the path where the players walk got in his face and said, "You could win this thing."

Fortunately, Brad has always liked playing for a gallery. He has spent his entire career making friends with the people who watch him play; as a consequence, the fans almost always are pulling for him. Some players find that a big crowd makes them want to avoid mistakes, avoid being ridiculed. A big crowd turns Brad into an entertainer. He feeds off its energy.

But he had to be careful not to let the gallery's support turn his mind away from the present. There was more than enough temptation to do that in any case. As Brad made the turn, the leaders were just starting their round, passing by him on adjoining fairways. As he glanced at them, the notion that he could win the tournament flashed through his mind.

Brad worked hard not to get carried away by the excitement. At No. 10, a 315-yard par four, he opted for a 3-iron off the tee, because the wind was not helping him, although he knew that some of the big hitters would try to drive the green. His sand wedge second from 80 yards out in the fairway was 10 feet short of the hole, and he missed his birdie putt.

At No. 11, the wind was behind him and he decided to try to reach the green, 564 yards away, in two shots. His drive was perfect, finding the narrow landing area about 285 yards out. He crushed a 3-wood that carried 245 yards and bounced up to the green. The eagle putt stayed out this time, but the birdie pulled him to eight under for the day and 13 under for the tournament.

Now he let his thoughts edge ahead of himself. After two strong shots at No. 12, he had an eight-foot birdie putt. But as he told me later, with his characteristic humor, "I thought about a bunch of other things—going to nine under, winning the tournament, my acceptance speech."

The hard fact is, any player on the back nine who's thinking about his acceptance speech is not likely to have a chance to deliver it. He pulled the birdie putt, missing by four inches. The crowd gasped as if the putt had just missed, but Brad knew he had hit it badly. Four inches on an eight-foot putt is a canyon-sized miss for a player of his caliber.

Then he did the only thing he could do in the circumstances. He quietly laughed at himself for allowing all the extraneous influences to affect him. And he began working to draw his attention back to where it had to be.

He did a good job parring Nos. 13 and 14, and now there were two conflicting thoughts running through his mind. *Don't,* he told himself, *let a couple of missed birdie putts discourage you. Stay with the process. Stay in the present.* But at the same time, he was thinking that he had only four holes left. He needed some birdies to make a run at the championship.

No. 15 is one of the toughest holes on the back side, a 447-yard dogleg right. Still feeling powerful, Brad blew his drive right over the fairway bunker that marks the dogleg's turn. Though in previous rounds he had been hitting 3-irons and 4-irons into the green, he had only a 6-iron left. But he had the wind in his face and a hanging lie, with the ball above his feet, the kind of situation that promotes a hook. He pushed any thought of a hook out of his mind and decided instead to hit what he calls a "punch-and-hold fade" into the breeze. It went where his mind had envisioned it, leaving him a 15-foot birdie putt.

His putting stroke faltered here, and he hit the putt too hard. It was the first putt of the day, he would recall, that felt wrong leaving the putter. But his mental mistake came on the second putt, a three-footer, downhill, with a small break to the right. He had a clump of spike marks between his ball and the hole, and he thought about the spike marks instead of trusting his stroke. He missed, and made bogey.

Players sometimes tell me that they can't trust their putting stroke if they see spike marks on their line. When they do, I put a putter shaft down on the green, across their line, and ask them to putt over it. If they hit the ball just a little harder than normal, it jumps over the shaft and goes in the hole. Even then, some will say the putter shaft is round and a spike mark isn't. So I'll take a nickel and stand it in the turf and make them putt through that. They generally can. Spike marks don't deflect putts off line nearly as often as they deflect players' minds from the trusting state they ought to be in.

Now Brad faced yet another challenge to his mental discipline. When a player in the midst of a hot round hits a bad shot or two and makes a bogey or worse, all sorts of useless thoughts are liable to flit through his mind: *There goes 59.* Or *There goes the Ryder Cup.* Or *How could I have missed that putt?* All of those are thoughts focused on the past. The only useful thought for Brad to entertain at that moment was about where he wanted to hit his tee shot on No. 16.

As he walked to the tee, buoyed by the continuing applause and encouragement from the gallery, Brad tried to do that. *Don't let the bogey distract you from what you're supposed to do,* he told himself. *You can still hit a good shot here.*

Which is what Brad did. No. 16 is an old-fashioned kind of island green par three, the kind virtually surrounded by sand. Brad hit a 7-iron with a draw that checked up about twenty-five feet short of the hole. Again the physical symptoms of nerves were undeniable as he stood over the putt. Again he willed himself to concentrate on his putting process. The ball broke hard left to right and dove in. He pumped his fist again and moved through the roars to the tee at No. 17.

He was again eight under par for the day and he wanted another birdie. But No. 17 is a long par five, 578 yards, unreachable for Brad. That did not undermine his belief that he could make birdie. All he wanted to do was lay up to give himself a good wedge shot to the green, then trust his putter. He hit a fine wedge, but it caught the slope leading to the upper tier of the green, where the pin was. A foot or two farther and it might have been knocked stiff. But it rolled backwards, down the slope, and left him thirty feet away. That did not bother him. He believed that he could make the next putt, and he hit it beautifully. It stayed right on the edge of the hole. He could not believe it didn't fall. Days later, looking at the videotape, he still couldn't.

Standing on the tee at No. 18, he knew that whatever slim chance he had had to win the tournament was probably gone. He had no idea where he stood for the Ryder Cup team. He got under his drive for the first time that day, popped it up, and left himself twenty or thirty yards short of his accustomed spot in the eighteenth fairway. He tried to hit the same kind of hard 5-iron he'd hit at No. 1. He didn't catch it as well, and he wound up about five yards short of the green, looking at an uphill chip.

The eighteenth green at Riviera is in the middle of a natural grass amphitheater, and by now it was filled with people. There was an enormous scoreboard on the hillside, and Brad looked at it. He saw he was in fourth place. He still didn't know exactly what he needed to do to make the Ryder Cup team, but he knew it was extremely important to finish his round by remaining focused until his ball was in the hole.

He hit his chip a touch too hard. It rolled over the dry, crusty back half of the green and didn't stop until it was twelve feet past. Brad thereupon forgot about the Ryder Cup and the standings. He thought only of making his twelve-footer.

He read the green from both sides of the hole and noticed that there were three or four spike marks in his line, about two feet short of the hole. This time, he told himself that there was nothing he could do about them. He told himself to start the ball on its line and trust that it would hold that line as it got to the hole.

It did. The roar of the crowd reverberated around the amphitheater. It was the loudest sound Brad had ever heard on a golf course.

Brad had closed with a 63, the lowest final round score ever in a PGA Championship. No one has ever shot a better score in a major championship.

He made his way to the scorers' tent through a throng of screaming people and signed his scorecard. Someone from CBS invited him to climb up to the announcers' booth and talk about his round. And it was only there that he learned, from the CBS producers, that the Ryder Cup team was within his grasp.

A few minutes later, Davis Love III and Fred Couples called the locker room to let him know he had made it. That was typical of the way so many golfers, though remaining competitors, find ways to support and encourage their friends on the tour.

IF YOU'VE GOTTEN the impression that a great round of golf comprises dozens of skirmishes in the mind of the golfer, not all of which are won, you're right. I have recounted this round in detail because it illustrates that even the best players, playing as well as anyone has ever played, wage constant war with doubts and fears and distractions. Some weeks it's easier than others. But if they don't conquer the doubts on a particular shot, the best players pick themselves up and gather themselves to work on the next one. That's what Brad did in the final round of the PGA. He wasn't perfect; he was merely striving for perfection. He disciplined his mind to give himself the best chance he could to play as well as he could. And he saw how good that could be.

Of course, it doesn't always work out that well.

Thinking well can't guarantee shooting low scores or winning. It only gives a player the best possible chance to score well and win. If it were foolproof, golf would not be a game. It would be a laboratory experiment.

Fortunately, it's a game. Brad's results in the Ryder Cup demonstrated that.

The Ryder Cup is not, I think, as significant for a player as winning a major championship. At least, I've never had a player tell me he's dreamt for years about winning a singles match at the Ryder Cup. But I do often hear that players have been dreaming of winning the Masters or the U.S. Open since they were five years old.

34 • GOLF IS A GAME OF CONFIDENCE

The Ryder Cup is, however, a tremendous television spectacle, and it confronts its players with a unique set of mental challenges. First, of all, they're representing their countries rather than playing for themselves. If a player has an off-week in a regular tournament, he slams the trunk shut on Friday, goes home, and few people care except for his family and friends. He can try again next week. If he has a bad week at the Ryder Cup, all the golfers of two continents know and care about it. More important, he's let down his teammates, the peers whose opinions and esteem he values most highly. And there is no next week.

Brad and Davis invited me up to Oak Hill to watch them play in the 1995 matches, and we talked about the team aspects of the event. I reminded them of their days on college golf teams, Brad at Furman and Davis at North Carolina. They made their best contributions to their teams by taking care of themselves and their rounds. Once that was over, they could cheer and concern themselves with what the rest of the team was doing. They ought, I thought, to approach the Ryder Cup the same way. Take care of their own games, and then enjoy being part of the team.

But neither the team format nor the outside pressure affected the essence of the challenge. They had to do the same thing they have to do in every competitive round: stay in the present and commit themselves to their routines.

They both responded well. Davis split four matches over the first two days of foursomes and four-ball play. Brad split two. Davis won his singles match over Costantino Rocca, 3 and 2. Brad lost his to David Gilford, 1 down.

Brad tried to blame himself for the loss of the Cup, since he had a chance, by parring the eighteenth, to halve the match with Gilford and salvage half a point.

But I knew, and he knows, that he had nothing to blame himself for. He trusted his driver very well for the entire round on a very tough driving course. He putted well, burning the edge of the hole half a dozen times. But Gilford, who is supposed to be a better ball-striker than putter, putted better. He was one up going into the last hole.

On the eighteenth tee that Sunday afternoon, some very good players found they could not trust their swings and they hit ugly, awkward tee shots. Brad hit an excellent drive, long and in the fairway. Gilford was well behind him, and hit a 4-wood long and left of the green, behind the grandstand. Brad hit a 5-iron that perhaps caught a gust of wind and fell just short, in a bunker.

From his drop area, Gilford had no chance to pitch to the green and hold the ball on the putting surface; the ground was too hard. He tried to run the ball down to the green, but it got caught in the heavy rough. He was lying three.

Davis, who had finished his match, was in the crowd behind Brad, exhorting him. "Hole it, Fax!" he yelled.

Brad envisioned a low, running sand shot that would feed toward the hole. And he hit it, but just a smidge too hard. The ball stopped seven feet away.

Gilford then chipped poorly, stopping his ball about twelve feet below the hole.

Then Gilford sank his putt. He was down in five. Brad needed his putt to win the hole and halve the match.

It was no easy putt. It was going to break, and the amount it would break would depend on the speed. Brad needed to get both the speed and the break precisely right.

He read the putt and stepped up to it. He thought the right thoughts. He hit the ball well.

And it hung up on the high side of the hole.

That doesn't mean that Brad didn't play well, that he wasn't mentally tough and that he won't take some very positive memories from his Ryder Cup experience. It means that Oak Hill, set up as it was that day, was an extraordinarily difficult golf course. And golf is an extraordinarily difficult game. If you love golf as Brad does, you love the fact that it is this way.

All a player can do is stay in the present, commit himself to the process of hitting good shots, and give himself the best possible chance.

No. 2

How Fred Arenstein Broke 80

PROFESSIONALS LIKE BRAD FAXON ARE BY NO MEANS THE ONLY GOLFERS who can benefit from paying full attention to the business at hand—staying in the present—and from an unwavering commitment to the process of hitting good shots. Both concepts are as beneficial for weekend golfers as they are for touring pros. A golfer I know named Fred Arenstein demonstrates why.

Fred is an accountant who lives in northern New Jersey. He started playing more than thirty years ago, when he was a kid in Albany, N.Y. In those days, the Albany municipal course would let a boy play unlimited golf, all summer long for twenty dollars.

The course became Fred's summer camp. He and his buddies used to hop on bicycles every summer morning, ride out to the course, and play eighteen holes. The back nine was hilly and long, and there were no motorized carts in those days. Consequently, older golfers stayed away in the heat and the boys had it almost to themselves. They would hang out there and play more holes each day.

As a boy, Fred never took a lesson. He generally hit a big

slice. Like a lot of players with flawed swings and a zest for competition, he developed a good short game to compensate for his errant long shots. He spent a lot of time around the practice green, chipping and putting.

As he got older and more serious about the game, Fred took a few lessons to straighten out his slice. He developed a technique in which he cocks his wrists early in the backswing, very deliberately setting the club on an inside-to-out path. When it's working, he hits a reasonably reliable high draw.

Though he's a burly guy, Fred doesn't hit the ball particularly long, and he doesn't even carry a driver. He tries to keep the ball in the fairway and around the green and relies on his chipping and pitching to bail him out of trouble. His handicap for years has ranged from 12 to 18, placing him in the broad middle of the golfing spectrum.

About ten years ago, he settled in New Jersey and started playing at Francis Byrne Golf Course. Byrne is a fine old public course, a former private club that was deeded to Essex County years ago. The sand in the bunkers can get a little muddy and the tees can be a little bald. But it's 6,653 yards from the back tees, and it's an honest test of golf.

Fred has a regular game there, on Saturday mornings, with his friends Larry Pinilis and Barry Forester. To get a Saturday tee time, at least one member of the group has to rise early Thursday morning and show up at the course well before dawn; the line starts forming at around 4 A.M.

But that's not such a hardship in the summer, because there's enough warmth and enough daylight to tee off at 6:30 A.M. and get in a round before work. Fred's boss doesn't mind if he comes in at 11 on Thursday mornings as long as he stays late to compensate.

That's Fred's summer golfing regimen: a round on Saturday, maybe a round on Thursday morning, some chipping and putting practice, and maybe a trip or two to a driving range in the evening.

Fred's game last summer was pretty consistently in the 80s. He'd shoot 86 or 85 most of the time. On a good day, he'd get into the low 80s. On a very good day, he might go out in 37 or 38 strokes. But invariably, when that happened, he'd balloon a little on the back side, bringing it home in 44 or 45 strokes. Once, he'd needed only a par four on the eighteenth hole to shoot 78. One of his partners mentioned it, and, unnerved, he made six.

That frustrated Fred. Like a lot of golfers, he saw 80 as the border that separates the kingdom of golfers from the kingdom of duffers. Mathematically, there's not much between 80 and 79; it's a difference of less than two percent. But in Fred's mind, and I suspect in the minds of hundreds of thousands of others, 80 seemed as big a barrier as the Atlantic Ocean did to pre-Columbian Europe.

It was, in fact, a mental barrier. Fred's swing and touch were sufficient to get him into the high 70s. But to do it, he had to refine his mental game.

In mid-season, he picked up a copy of *Golf Is Not a Game of Perfect*. I'm pleased to say that he found some ideas in the book that helped him. The first group of ideas concerned the process of hitting good shots.

First of all, he learned to play with whatever swing he brought to Francis Byrne on a given day. In his occasional practice sessions, Fred tended to be very analytical about his full swing. He thought about where his clubhead was, whether his swing plane was correct, and other mechanics.

Francis Byrne had no practice range, so Fred's first long shot of any day at the golf course was taken from the first tee. If it went awry, he typically fell into the same frame of mind he had at the driving range, trying to analyze and fix his swing.

This is one of the worst things a golfer can do. Not even

professionals who study and teach the swing for a living can consistently tell what went wrong in their own bad swings. Most of the key movements happen behind them, out of sight, so they can't see them.

Even a pro who's watching someone else swing, if he's honest, will admit that he can't diagnose swing flaws with certainty unless he can look at slow-motion videotape.

So how is a weekend player supposed to diagnose his own swing glitches?

He can't.

But most amateurs try to. They start thinking about how far they turn, or how their hips uncoil, or squaring the clubface as they bring it through the impact zone. And those kinds of thoughts tend to make a swing tense and arrhythmic.

Instead of trying to fix his swing, Fred started dropping down to a club he felt he could trust. If that meant hitting only 7-irons for a few holes, he hit only 7-irons, until he felt he was warmed up and ready for the longer clubs.

This is a very sensible approach for weekend players, but not many have the nerve to use it. I see so many amateurs who pull the driver out on every par four and every par five because they think that's what a man's supposed to hit. They play it, even though when it's time to swing they're scared to death of hitting it out of bounds. As a result, they often do hit it out of bounds. They'd be much better off playing a shorter club that they felt confident about and playing the course 150 yards at a time. Their scores would be lower.

Fred started to pick out specific targets for his shots. And he developed a pre-shot routine that he tried to employ before every stroke.

His process, then, involved trusting his swing, picking out a target, and repeating a routine.

All of those things helped him to focus his attention on the present, on the shot at hand. In fact, he came up with a thought that reinforced this good tendency.

Okay, Fred, he would say to himself. *Just make one more good shot, like it was the last shot you were going to hit.*

He had been a player who kept close track of his score, as an accountant might, adding up the numbers as he went along, multiplying and dividing. He was the type of player who knew that if he shot 28 for the first six holes and kept to that pace, he would have an 84.

That was the last aspect of his mental game he needed to change.

Nearly all golfers would be better off if they forgot about the score as they played.

Fred's breakthrough came in a casual round, just after dawn on a midsummer Thursday morning. Barry and Larry had come down to Francis Byrne to join him.

No. 1 at Francis Byrne is a good starting hole for a course with no practice range. It's a short par five, 456 yards from the white tees, with a flat, generous fairway and no water. It's a hole on which three decent shots will find the green and get the player started with a par.

But Fred started off badly. His tee shot at No. 1 was in trouble, and he made six, a bogey.

In the past, Fred had always figured that he needed a par at No. 1 to shoot a good round, particularly since No. 2 was one of the tougher holes on the course, a 211-yard par three guarded by a deep bunker on the left side.

But it's significant how wrong these kinds of assumptions often turn out to be. Players who make great scores often get their birdies on holes they consider very tough. They par the easy ones. And I've often seen a player shoot a good score after botching the first hole, because he lowers his expectations and relaxes.

Fred did the right thing at No. 2. He took out his 7-wood and picked out a target, a tree on a hilltop behind the green. He hit a great shot that rolled up onto the green about fifteen feet from the hole. He made the putt for a birdie.

That settled Fred down. He made fours on the next four holes. He knew that he was one over par as he stood on the tee at No. 7. He pulled his tee shot into the woods there and made bogey. That set him off on a string of bogeys that left him seven over par as he reached No. 13.

He didn't play No. 13 particularly well, either. His approach shot found a bunker. But he blasted out to within a foot of the hole and saved his par. That set off another string of fours that lasted the rest of the way in.

The string of bogeys in the middle of the round had proven to be a blessing, the last key to breaking 80. For after making a few of them, Fred forgot about the score. He stayed in the present and just tried to go through his routine on each shot. Throughout the back nine, he didn't know where he stood in relation to par or to 80.

He was pleasantly surprised when one of his buddies added up the numbers. He'd shot 78.

THERE'S A WIDESPREAD misimpression among weekend golfers that to shoot in the 70s, a player must have a swing that a pro could envy. It's not true.

On the average golf course, from the white tees, a lot of players could break 80 at least once in a while. All they need is a swing they can repeat with fair consistency, a good short game, and the right mental approach. Like Fred Arenstein, they need to stop keeping track of their scores and focus their attention exclusively on the present.

No. 3

How Jay Delsing Kept Trusting

NOT MANY OCCUPATIONS HAVE SANCTIONS AS FINAL AND AS DAUNTING as the cut that comes after thirty-six holes of every professional golf tournament. If I have a couple of bad days in the classroom, I can go back and try to do a better job the third day. But a golfer who isn't on his game for the first thirty-six holes has no such luxury. He gets no second chance and he earns no money. He can only tote up his lost expenses and get out of town. Miss a skein of cuts, and a sense of failure and foreboding can infest a golfer's mind the way termites infest a home—unwanted, hard to get rid of, and very destructive. Missing cuts can cause a golfer to start playing to not miss cuts, which is a sure way to miss more of them.

In the first few months of 1995, my friend Jay Delsing missed nine in a row.

I started working with Jay in 1990. He was a player with obvious talents. He'd been an outstanding junior golfer in St. Louis, where he grew up. He played on some excellent UCLA teams with players like Corey Pavin, Steve Pate, and Duffy Waldorf. Once in a while, on tour, he would burn up a golf course.

He's set or tied course records at a couple of PGA Tour stops with scores like 61 and 62. But in the first five years of his pro career, he hadn't been able to win a tournament, and he'd had to go back to qualifying school twice in order to stay on tour.

In those five lean years, Jay often fell victim to a confidence-debilitating syndrome that can destroy the careers of players who don't win soon after they join the tour.

He would generally arrive at a tour course on Monday and play a practice round. He'd practice again on Tuesday. And during those rounds he'd play well, shooting in the 60s.

But on Wednesday he couldn't play a practice round because Wednesday is pro-am day, and Jay wasn't ranked high enough to be invited to play in many pro-ams. Being diligent and ambitious, he would resolve to practice hard. He would go to the practice tee early and stay late. And that was a dangerous place for him to be.

Practice tees on the PGA Tour are crawling with people obsessed with the mechanics of the golf swing. Some are players. Some are teaching pros who want to make a name for themselves and offer unsolicited lessons. Some are even less qualified—equipment company representatives or fans. Hang around a tour practice tee for an hour or two and you're likely to hear a dozen theories about how to execute a particular portion of the golf swing, half of which conflict with the other half.

I certainly understand the importance of sound swing mechanics. But there is a time and place for working on mechanics, and it is not on the eve of a tournament. Lots of the players I work with have decided, at one time or another, that they need to improve their swings. The smart ones take some time off from the tour, go to a teacher they trust, and work on the new movements until they can execute them without thinking about them. Then and only then do they return to competition.

It's tough even for a successful player to shut out the buzz of swing tips and theories that is in the air on a tournament practice tee. Ben Hogan found a way to do it. He would go to the far right end of the practice tee and keep his back turned to the rest of the players. He didn't want to see how other people swung; he knew his swing was different from the norm of the day, and he didn't want anything undermining his belief in it. And he didn't want to discuss or debate swing mechanics as he practiced. But not many golfers have Hogan's discipline. They're gregarious people, and the practice tee is one place where they can loosen up and be friends with their fellow competitors.

It's even harder for a player who's been missing cuts to ignore the buzz. Missing cuts can undermine confidence. This is particularly true if the player doesn't have what is considered a classic swing and wasn't taught from childhood by a respected pro. Jay fell into that category. He started playing golf on a public course in St. Louis called North Shore Country Club. Then he picked up a few things caddying at a club called Norwood Hills. He learned a lot from his father, Jim Delsing, a former major league baseball player who carried a single-digit handicap but was not a teaching pro. Jay has a good swing and lots of athletic talent to back it up. But even though his ball goes to its target when he's playing confidently, Jay's is not a swing many people would point to and say "That's a beautiful golf swing."

Certainly, the people on the practice tee weren't saying that. More often than not, by the time the sun set on Wednesday, Jay would be trying to fix something in his mechanics. He would be thinking that his swing wasn't good enough to win on the tour. And in that frame of mind, he would go out on Thursday and shoot something ugly—a 75 or a 78. The next day, thinking that it barely mattered, he might relax and shoot a 66 and make the cut by a stroke or two. Or he might shoot another 78 and miss it. But he was not consistently scoring well.

So when Jay came to Charlottesville to work with me on his mental game, one of the first principles we discussed was one that applies to every player:

A golfer cannot score as well as possible if he is thinking about his swing mechanics as he plays.

Research in sports psychology is only beginning to reveal why this is so. The best I can say is that the human organism performs repetitive physical tasks best if the brain is not consciously trying to guide the process. It performs best when an individual focuses on a target or a goal and doesn't think about how to execute the movement.

Consider, for example, the bucking, stalling effort of a novice driver who is trying to learn how to handle a manual shift. The movements are not that complicated. You push the clutch pedal in, you shift the gear, you let the clutch pedal out. But because the novice driver is thinking intensely about how to perform each step, he has no rhythm, no grace. The car lurches down the road like a drunk bouncing off lamp posts. On the other hand, consider the experienced driver. On the road, he never thinks about how to change gears. He thinks about how fast he wants the car to go and in what direction. He changes gears smoothly, effortlessly, without even being consciously aware that he's doing it. It's the same way on the golf course.

A golfer has to train his swing on the practice tee, then trust it on the course.

This applies as much to professionals as it does to an amateur like Fred Arenstein.

Sometimes, amateur players will hear this and say that it sounds fine for a professional who has a flawless swing. But they don't think their swings are good enough to trust.

First of all, none of the great professionals has had a flawless swing. Nobody would teach Walter Hagen's lunge through the ball. Nobody would teach novices to regrip the club as Bobby Jones did at the top of his backswing. Nobody would teach the flying right elbow of Jack Nicklaus. And nobody would teach Lee Trevino's swing plane. But they all won championships trusting those swings, even taking pride in their idiosyncrasies.

I was walking in a gallery with a teaching pro not long ago, watching Fred Couples play a competitive round. "Fred Couples," the teacher said, "blows my mind."

He was vexed that Fred, with his seemingly simple, unanalytical approach to the game, was one of the top players in the world, while he, who understood the swing so well, was helping hackers straighten out their slices.

"What you have to understand," I replied, "is that university professors, who are really good at thinking analytically, got to write the definition of 'genius.' They chose to define a genius as someone who thinks as they do, who breaks things down to figure them out, who makes the simple complicated. That'll make you a genius in academia.

"But if you want to be a genius in sport, you must be able to make what some people think of as complex into something simple. Because simplicity works under pressure. It lets you have rhythm and feel.

"Fred's a lot more honest than you are," I said. "If you wanted to get better and play as well as he does, you'd first have to stop deceiving yourself."

He looked at me and said, "What?"

"You heard correctly," I said. "You keep pretending that every time you hit a golf ball that doesn't go where you wanted it to go, you can analyze why it didn't, and that you can correct it after you've analyzed it. That's not true. It doesn't work. It hasn't worked. Yet you keep right on doing it.

"If I asked you to get on the golf course and be like Fred, just hitting it to your target time after time, even if some shots miss, you might try it for a little while. But if it didn't work right, you'd want immediately to go back to your old way of analyzing and correcting, as if that worked.

"Fred, if he misses a shot, just shrugs and accepts the fact that he missed. He doesn't think it's a big deal, because he trusts his swing and doesn't think he'll miss again. He doesn't try to figure out what went wrong and correct it. And because he trusts, he misses much less often than you do."

It's true that few amateurs have swings like Fred Couples or Jay Delsing. A lot of them have serious swing flaws that will, uncorrected, prevent them from ever becoming scratch players. But a lot of people who play in the 90s have swings good enough to score in the 80s, if they would trust them. It's a matter of getting the best possible scores out of the swings they have —be they in the mid-60s, as in Jay Delsing's case, or in the mid-90s. To do that, they have to trust.

This means, on long shots, that they think about where they want the ball to go, not about keeping their heads down, or keeping the left arm straight, or pronating at the top of the backswing. On putts, pitches, and chips, it means thinking about getting the ball into the hole, not about keeping the putter blade on line.

I prefer that golfers play without swing thoughts. The ones who fully trust their swings can do that. But I know that lots of golfers have been playing with swing thoughts all their lives and feel naked without them. I tell such players that they can have one, and only one, swing thought per round. Any more than one and they are liable to bog their brains down in a welter of mechanical thinking.

Some swing thoughts are better than others. In general, the less mechanical, the better. Reminding yourself to have a nice, even tempo is a good swing thought. Thinking about keeping the clubhead behind the hands on the downswing is not.

Once Jay understood this, his consistency improved and he had several years where he comfortably kept his tour eligibility.

But trust is not a collectible, like a rare postage stamp, that you can buy, mount, and own forever with no additional effort. Every golfer needs to work on trust in every competitive round he plays.

And in Jay's case, there can be a fine line between trusting and being reckless. Jay is instinctively an aggressive player, with a talent for shaping iron shots. Sometimes, though, he would get too aggressive. He would go for sucker pins and pay the penalty if he missed. He might find himself in the woods after an errant drive, with 190 yards and a few acres of sand between him and the green. He might then try to carve a 5-iron under a branch, through the glade, and over the sand, when the wise play was to lay up and trust in his wedge and putter to salvage par.

We talked a lot about having a game plan and sticking to it. There is nothing wrong with hitting a 1-iron instead of a driver off the tee on certain holes, I would tell him. The important thing is to trust the swing you put on the 1-iron.

For a variety of reasons, Jay was not playing well when I saw him at the Kemper Open in June. We talked a lot about keeping his equilibrium. I reminded him that missing cuts had nothing to do with the kind of man he was. And it doesn't. The difference between missing a cut and making a check can be one bad bounce in thirty-six holes of play. A golfer in a slump has to keep that in mind.

Jay missed the cut at the Kemper, but I thought he was making progress. The proof came a few weeks later in Memphis, at the FedEx St. Jude Classic, his next tournament.

The Tournament Players Club at Southwind is one of the tour's new stadium courses, designed for tournament golf with high drama in mind. Water is in play on about half the holes, and disasters are nearly always possible. But so are birdies. All the par fives are reachable in two shots and the winning scores are low. Winners at Memphis average better than 16 under par.

Jay got off to a solid start with a 69, but that score wasn't low enough to give him any assurance he would make the cut. His Friday round began on the tenth hole, and as he teed off, he was trying to trust his swing and stay in the present. We've often talked about the importance of trying to play great golf on Fridays, rather than trying to make the cut, and that was what he wanted to do.

No. 10 is a 447-yard par four; he drove well and put his approach shot only ten feet from the hole. Putting downhill, he ran his first putt four feet by. He missed the second.

At this point, Jay faced a crisis. He could have reacted by blowing up. A lot of golfers do this. They let the results of the first hole or two determine their attitude for them. If the results are bad, they lose their confidence and play badly the rest of the day.

But a good player, faced with some bad results, remembers that he determines his attitude. It is not determined by what happens to him. It comes from within.

Jay reminded himself that he had done everything right, mentally, on No. 10. He had believed each of his first two putts would go in, and he'd stroked them that way. The fact that they didn't, he told himself, was just the sort of test that golf throws up periodically to make itself challenging. In that frame of mind, he got the bogey back and then some. He turned in 33 and then burned up his back nine, coming in with a 63. He easily made the cut, but he was five strokes back of the leader, Jim Gallagher, Jr.

It rained again the next day, and once again, Jay started at No. 10. He played another solid round, and he was a couple of strokes under par when he came to his last hole, the course's ninth, a 450-yard par four, dogleg right. A pond guards the left side of the green.

Jay drove badly and found himself behind a tree, two hundred yards from the green, with the last sixty of those yards over water. The pin was cut in the front of the green. But he had a good lie, and he thought that he could hook a 4-iron around the tree and over the pond and still make birdie, despite the bad drive. Then he caught himself.

Trusting your swing doesn't mean that you have a go at every high-risk shot presented in a round of golf. It means, rather, that you prefer the strategy that gives you a shot you know you can make. Taking those shots enhances trust. It's easy to make a bold decision and then, as the downswing starts, become doubting and tentative. It's hard to be trusting if you know there's a 50–50 chance your swing is going to send your ball into the water.

Jay took out a 9-iron, played out into the fairway, and then hit another 9-iron to about twelve feet. He made the putt for his par. He thought about how, earlier in his career, he might have tried the 100–1 shot and taken a six, and he left the course feeling very confident, though he was still six shots back. In his hotel room that night, he made a commitment to himself. Although he had barely made any money all year, he was going to play Sunday's round with his head exactly where it had to be on every shot. He was going to trust every swing. He was going to play without fear.

And he did. On No. 3, a par five, he exploded out of a greenside bunker and holed his shot for an eagle. He birdied the fifth and happened to glance at a leader board. He was, remarkably, still six shots off the lead. He told himself to forget about what Gallagher was doing and keep his mind focused on each shot as it came. He parred along until he got to the fourteenth, a long par three. There he reminded himself to trust every swing from that point forward. He stroked a forty-footer that broke about twelve feet over a hump in the green. It skipped its way over some spike marks and went in.

At No. 15, a 385-yard par four, he hit his approach about twelve feet past the hole. As soon as he walked onto the green and saw the putt, he was seized by the knowledge that it was going in. He caught the eye of Kathy, his wife, who was walking in the gallery. He winked at her. And then he drained the putt.

Jay drove well off No. 16, a par five. As he walked down the fairway to his ball, he saw another leader board, the first he had looked at in ten holes. Gallagher, he learned, had been coming back to the field. With his birdies at fourteen and fifteen, Jay was only one stroke off the pace.

He had 250 yards left to the hole, which would normally call for a 3-wood, but he knew he was filled with adrenaline, and a 1-iron felt right. He hit it hole high, but well left of the green, leaving himself a tricky lob shot over a sand bunker.

Before he set up for the shot, Jay said a silent prayer. *Oh Lord,* he thought, *let me stay in the present and keep having fun.*

Someone ought to needlepoint this prayer and put it on clubhead covers. He didn't ask for divine intervention to get the shot close. He didn't pray that he wouldn't chunk it into the sand. He asked for precisely the attitude he needed to give himself the best chance to make a good shot.

He reminded himself that he had worked for years to put himself in precisely this sort of situation—playing with a tournament on the line. Then he walked up, went through his preshot routine, focused on his target, and hit a lovely little lob that stopped six feet from the hole. Jay has great touch with his wedge when he's trusting his swing.

How Jay Delsing Kept Trusting • 53

He sank the putt, and he was tied for the lead.

The TPC at Southwind closes with two long par fours. No. 17, 464 yards, has a creek running across the fairway and a green flanked by three traps. No. 18, 440 yards, is a dogleg left, with water hugging the entire left side of the fairway and a lot of sand on the right.

Jay's tee shot at No. 17 went left. He couldn't tell if it landed in the fairway or the rough, but it caught a mound and kicked farther left, then caromed off a golf cart being used by CBS television and came to rest under a bush. He had to punch the ball out short of the creek. He caught a bad lie and couldn't get his third shot close to the hole. He made bogey. He was one back.

Now came the test. Could he stop thinking about the bad breaks and bad stroke on No. 17? Could he continue to trust his swing? Many golfers, after hitting into trouble on the left off the tee at No. 17, would take a look at the trouble facing them on the left side of No. 18 and start thinking furiously about how to prevent another hook. Others might reach for an iron, because on No. 18, the creek that runs down the left side broadens to a pond about 250 yards out. Jay had ample reason to think about those things, because in his years of playing at Memphis, he had put a few sixes down for No. 18. Some thoughts of those past disasters flitted, unsolicited, into his mind.

But he refused to entertain them. He took out his driver and focused on his target, which was the corner of a distant greenside bunker and a tree trunk behind it. And he let the shot go without thinking of how, mechanically, he wanted to hit it. The ball soared out over the middle of the fairway. It hung in the air a long time before it came down and stopped about 290 yards out. Jay picked up his tee, quietly joyous. This, he realized, was the kind of moment he had been living for. As he walked down the fairway, lined on both sides with spectators, he had the curious sense that he was fifteen years old again, playing in a Missouri junior tournament, about to birdie the last hole and win. He hit a smooth little 8-iron to about eight feet.

On television, announcer Gary McCord was telling people that Jay was at a disadvantage, because he didn't have any recent memories of good finishes on the last hole. When Jay heard about that later on, he snorted. He had lots of good memories. He had made hundreds of eight-foot putts. He drew on them.

People sometimes tell me that they can't control which memories rise to the surface of their minds before they hit a shot. Sometimes they think about a drive they hit pure and long down the middle; sometimes they think about one they sliced out of bounds.

This is normal. But I tell them that people can choose to develop long memories for their good shots and short memories for mistakes. And they can certainly choose which memories to dwell on. They can use their memories to help, not hurt.

Jay was determined to dwell on the good memories. As soon as he marked his ball, he felt certain he knew how the putt would break. He knew he was going to make it. It felt almost as if he had already made it. He went through his routine, stepped up without delay, and hit the ball right where he wanted to.

The ball slid just below the cup on the left side. Jay fell to his knees in disbelief.

He tapped in for his par and then waited for Gallagher to finish. Gallagher stumbled at the eighteenth. He was on in three and had about a twenty-foot putt. His went in. That's how tournaments are decided.

But Jay knew better than to feel like a loser. He felt good about trusting himself throughout the final round. He knew he had done everything he could to win. He had won the battle with himself by trusting his swing down the stretch while in contention. A player who wins that internal battle knows how to win. He knows his game will hold up under pressure. He simply has to wait for the next opportunity.

Buoyed by that feeling, Jay went on to have an excellent second half of the 1995 season, winning almost a quarter of a million dollars. He remained hopeful that his turn would come.

I think it will.

No. 4

How Davis Love III
Got Back to the Masters

DAVIS LOVE, JR., HAD TWO OF THE SOFTEST HANDS I HAVE EVER SEEN on a golfer, and a temperament to match. I met Davis when we were both on the staff at *Golf Digest* schools. He was the first person I ever saw who looked like his hands got softer through impact when he hit a golf ball. After I got to know him, I started calling him the King of Smooth. I liked him very much.

He was, in some respects, a country boy from Arkansas. Shortly after we got to know one another, he invited me to his home. He wanted to show me some of the volumes in his library of golf books, the ones that showed how some of the great players of the past had approached the mental game. But the first thing that caught my eye was an old, yellowed newspaper clipping, framed and hanging on the wall.

It told how a teenager named Davis Love, Jr., had made it to the quarterfinals or semifinals of the U.S. Amateur. The reporter had observed that this qualified him for an invitation to play in the Masters, and he asked if Davis planned to go.

"I don't know," Davis replied. "Where they playing it this year?"

He went on to obtain an excellent background in the game. He played at the University of Texas for Harvey Penick, whom he revered. He worked hard at the game. Too hard, perhaps. Davis Love, Jr., was one of those players who put a lot of pressure on themselves.

He decided that what he really wanted to do was what Harvey Penick had done: teach. And he was a wonderful teacher—demanding, yet patient.

As we got to know one another, I heard more and more about his two sons, Mark and Davis III. Teaching them had been his priority since they were old enough to hold clubs. I heard stories about twilight rounds of golf. Davis would come home tired from a long day on the lesson tee and the boys would greet him at the door.

"C'mon, Dad, let's go golfing!"

So off he'd go, walking on his tired legs, because the boys wanted to walk. They'd play four holes. And the boys would want a soda. So into the clubhouse they'd trudge. Davis might suggest that they resume on the first hole again. But the boys would have none of it. So he'd walk back out to the fifth hole with them, and finish from there.

Not surprisingly, they grew up loving the game.

But it was Davis III who had the yen to become a professional, and as the years passed, the game got more serious for both father and son. Davis, Jr., taught his namesake a long, fluid swing of enormous power. And through long hours of drilling in the hot Georgia sun, Davis III developed into a golfer with the potential for greatness.

As a teenager, Davis III saw his father in a different light than I did. Davis, Jr., was a grinder, a man who believed, for example, that the way to make sure you didn't miss short putts was to practice them—four hundred from two feet and then four hundred from three feet and then four hundred from four feet. He had, of course, picked up some sound ideas from Harvey Penick about the mental game. Penick taught Davis to be patient and to play one stroke at a time. But Davis III's perception was that his father was intent on the mechanics of the stroke, and believed that the best players got where they were by practicing until their hands bled.

In my conversations with Davis, Jr., I saw a different side. He told me that he didn't think he'd gotten as much from his own ability as he might have if he had known better how to relax and take pressure off himself. And he wanted his son to be better at it.

So he would sit with me, long into the evening, and we would talk about the psychology of golf at the highest levels. My ideas were not the ones he'd grown up with. But intuitively, he said, they made sense.

In 1987, when Davis III had been out on the tour for a year, Davis, Jr., suggested that he see me, and we got together. The immediate problem was Davis III's short game. He had led the tour in driving distance his rookie year and ranked high in greens hit in regulation figures. So father and son concluded, quite reasonably, that he needed to learn to get the ball into the hole better.

Davis III had the requisite mechanical skills with the wedge and putter; Davis, Jr., had seen to that. But he didn't have a consistent routine. Sometimes he would look at the hole, bring his eyes back to the ball, and tense up, thinking about the mechanics of his stroke. That became clear when I asked him to talk out loud about what he was doing as he prepared to putt or chip.

Davis was a big basketball fan and a friend of Michael Jordan, who had attended the University of North Carolina at about the same time. So we talked about the way a good basketball player's head operates. He could see that Jordan didn't stop in the middle of a move to the basket to think carefully about mechanics. Jordan locked his eyes on the rim and let the ball go. I wanted Davis to react to his targets in the same way.

To help break his old habits, I asked him to try a new putting routine. At its core, any good routine has three elements: a last look at the target, bringing the eyes back to the ball, and the start of the swing. They should be performed rhythmically and sequentially, so there is no significant delay between bringing the eyes back to the ball and beginning the swing. I want the brain and nervous system reacting to that last look at the target. A lot of players' routines are flawed because they let mechanical thoughts, like taking the putter head back on a certain line, interfere with that reaction. So I suggested that Davis start taking the putter back as he brought his eyes to the ball.

Davis understood the concept, and he adopted the new routine. The next time I saw him, at the Byron Nelson Classic in Dallas, he felt relieved to be free of the old ways that had had him standing over the ball a long time and getting tight before he hit the putt. He felt, he told me, like he was just walking up to the ball and hitting it. It felt good, and he was hitting the putts solidly. He was "freeing it up." The new problem was that he was hitting too many putts six feet past the hole.

"What are you freeing it up *to?*" I asked.

"I'm not," Davis said. "I'm just looking at the hole and hitting it."

He was so into freeing it up that he forgot to free it up to something in particular. That was like a pitcher throwing freely toward the south end of the ballpark, instead of to the pocket of the catcher's glove. Davis had to focus on the tiniest possible target—on the line that would take the ball from its spot on the green to the back of the cup. He had to be thinking about its end point in the hole.

He had, in effect, gone from being too careful to being careless with his putts. Freeing it up to nothing is sloppy golf; it's too loose. Getting careful and trying to steer the ball is too tight. It's easy to fall into either habit. But they don't work.

In putting, the challenge is to make a free stroke to a specific target. Guiding, steering, or being careful with a putting stroke are faults bred by doubt.

Davis went back to the practice green. A week or two later, at the Colonial National Invitation in Fort Worth, it came to him. He started dropping putts from all over the golf course.

For Davis, the image that solidified the happy medium was an unusual one. He thought about one of those little executive desk toys that have a row of five stainless steel marbles suspended from strings. Set the marble on the left in motion and it swings back, hits the stationary marbles, and knocks the right-end marble into mirror-image motion. The right-end marble, in turn, swings back and starts the sequence in the opposite direction. A rhythm begins as they bounce off one another. Click-click-click. He said he felt that he replicated that rhythm as he looked at the hole, looked at the ball, and took the putter back.

Over the years since then, that rhythm has been the key to Davis's putting routine. Some people depart from their routines by getting too tight and careful; Davis tends to lose his touch by overemphasizing being loose and free and forgetting about the target. At the British Open in 1994, he found that he was swinging the putter well before he got his eyes back to the ball, rather than following that click-click-click rhythm that helps him lock into the target. But the memory of the rhythm helped him correct himself.

Davis and I worked on the same principles for his full swing routine. Again, his problem was that he tended to get a little careless. I asked him to make sure he took time to decide precisely what kind of shot he wanted to hit before he took his practice swing. Then he needed to make that swing serious, as if he were really hitting. When he does those things and looks at a specific target, he's a great striker of the ball.

We talked about practice regimens and preparing for tournament play. I'm not a believer in hitting hundreds of practice balls, especially putts, just for the sake of hitting them. I'm much more interested in the quality of a player's practice than the quantity. If one of my players walks onto the practice green, drains four ten-footers in succession, and knows that his routine is sound, I see no reason why he should stay on the green and keep putting just so he can say he hit his daily quota. He's only likely to miss some, tarnish his confidence, and get the urge to start working on his putting mechanics.

A player has to know himself. He has to know how much and what kinds of practice he needs to be at his best. And he has to put that practice in. But going past that point can be counterproductive. It's analogous to the twin pitfalls—being too tight or too sloppy—Davis had to learn to avoid in his putting routine. A player needs to find the happy medium.

This notion appealed to Davis. He has always wanted to be as good as he can be. He dreams of winning major championships and he is willing to work as hard as necessary to fulfill those dreams. But he wants to be his best as efficiently as possible. Partly because he's had wrist problems, he's not interested in practice for the sake of practice, not interested in the quantity of balls he hits. He has other interests that are important to him—his family and his hobbies. He loves to hunt and fish.

I told him that was fine. He could even use his hobbies to reinforce what we were striving for in his golf game. A fisherman who sees a spot in a stream and reflexively casts toward it has a lot in common with a golfer who sees a hole and putts to it.

But Davis also thought, erroneously in my opinion, that his father wouldn't have agreed. He remembers the taskmaster in his father, and he hears the whispers that he could be even better if he worked harder.

There is tragedy in this. Davis Love, Jr., died in a small-plane crash in 1988. Davis III felt the pain that any son feels at the loss of a father who loved him, and whom he loved. But he also felt, very keenly, the loss of a mentor. He often wonders about the conversations he and his father would have had. He's learned a lot about himself and about golf in the past seven years. He wishes he could chew over what he's learned with his father.

Based on my own conversations with Davis, Jr., I know several things. One is that he would be thrilled to see how much Davis III has accomplished. Another is that he would agree on the importance of his son's being relaxed and confident about his golf. He would, I think, say that Davis III is doing great and getting better. He would understand that his son might get tight, anxious, and worse if he started living and breathing golf twenty-four hours a day.

TIGHTNESS AND ANXIETY largely account, I think, for the problems that Davis used to have playing well in major championships. After he'd won on the tour half a dozen times, writers started including him on their perennial lists of "best players never to have won a major." Publicly, Davis always responded that since he had never contended in a major, it was impossible for anyone to say that he was capable of winning one. He was trying to reduce the pressure on himself, to lower everyone's expectations.

But privately, Davis's expectations were higher than any sportswriter's. He felt that major championships should be the easiest for him to win, because they're played on difficult golf courses. The difficulty of the courses, he reasoned, should eliminate the chance that an inferior ball-striker will get a hot putter and win. The majors, he thought, were made for a player like himself, a superior ball-striker who can also putt well. In particular, he saw himself winning the Masters. U.S. Open and PGA courses, which tend to have tight fairways and heavy rough, give an advantage to accurate hitters, even if they're not as long as other competitors. They would always be a tough challenge for him. But Augusta is made for long hitters. So his failure to contend there became a source of growing frustration. He didn't relax and play his best golf.

Going into the 1994 season, playing well in the majors was Davis's top priority. He arrived at Augusta thinking that he was playing well and putting well. But, as often happens when a player is too tight, he played badly. He missed the cut.

It hurt, and Davis went into a tailspin that lasted the rest of the summer. Golf stopped being fun for him. Worse, he stopped doing the things he needs to do to play well. At home, he practiced less. He'd fly to a tournament site on Tuesday, go to the practice range, and start trying to figure out where his swing was and what he needed to do to get ready. His native ability helped him get by, but after finishing second on the money list in 1992 and twelfth in 1993, he fell out of the top thirty and failed to win a tournament. At the time, he didn't realize what was happening. He thought he was the victim of some bad breaks and was very close to where he had been in 1992 and 1993. But he wasn't.

Davis started to come out of this funk at the President's Cup in the fall of 1994. Energized by the challenge of team competition, he got focused on his game again and played well. But it was too late to salvage the season. He missed the Tour Championship. He didn't qualify for the Masters.

I was only one of several people who told Davis that autumn that his commitment had slipped. So did Jack Lumpkin, Davis's swing teacher. So did Penta, his mother. And for that, Davis deserves some credit. Part of the trick of staying at the top in golf is surrounding yourself with people who are supportive, but who know how to tell you when you're off track. And part of the trick is listening to them. Davis did both.

Jack told Davis that he'd gotten a little careless with his setup and alignment; his swing had gotten a little too upright and loose at the top and too "handsy" at the bottom. I told him that he needed to stop thinking so much about winning major championships and commit himself to doing the best job he could of following his mental routine on every shot, from the first day of the first tournament to the last day of the year.

Starting in November and December of that year, Davis worked hard. This didn't mean he beat balls all day and wore himself out. But he did the work on his fundamental skills needed to lay a strong foundation for the next season. And he didn't return to the tour until he was confident that he had fixed his swing glitches and was mentally ready to play well.

He skipped a few of the early tournaments that he normally plays, in Hawaii and Tucson, and jumped in at Phoenix. It was clear he was much sharper than he had been in 1994.

But he no longer had the luxury of working his way back into peak form in relative anonymity. Because of his play in 1994, he had not qualified for a Masters invitation. The only way he was going to get one was by winning one of the first tournaments of the year. As the tour left California and reached Florida, this became a running sidebar for the golf press. Could Davis do it? The reporters pressed him at every stop.

He came close, finishing well at Phoenix, Pebble Beach, and Doral. The next-to-last chance came at the Players' Championship. With the TPC Stadium Course set up to be very difficult, he opened with a 73, then shot 67 and was tied for third. On Saturday, he shot 74, but he was still tied for fifth, three strokes back of Corey Pavin and Bernhard Langer. With the wind up, the greens dried out, and the rough high, he managed a 72 on Sunday. He was three strokes short of Lee Janzen's winning total. There was just one chance left, the Freeport McMoRan Classic at English Turn Golf Club in New Orleans.

The challenge of winning the one tournament he had left to qualify for the Masters was an extraordinary one. First of all, no one controls the outcome of a tournament. A player can only play his best; the rest depends on how others do. Second, no one can play his best if something deflects his attention from the process of hitting each shot well. The task Davis faced was like trying to perform brain surgery in the middle of a circus. The Masters was that distracting.

Moreover, he had to cope with the conflict between what he thought his father would have advised him to do and what his own experience told him was best. He thought that his father would have been on him to grind hard—to be on the range early Monday morning for a videotaped practice session, working on swing flaws; to fly to New Orleans Monday night, not wasting time traveling during the day; to play a practice round Tuesday morning and spend Tuesday afternoon on the practice tee and the putting green; to play in the pro-am Wednesday morning and then have another full afternoon of practice.

I suspect Davis, Jr., would in fact have had a different attitude. I think he knew that the grinding, practice-till-your-hands bleed attitude is great for a player who's trying to go from average to very good. But it's less effective for a player who's trying to go from very good to excellent. At the top levels of golf, the best players have an element of aristocratic nonchalance. They practice hard until they feel they're playing well. Then they know that it's time to ease off a little bit, to relax.

Davis, as he left the Players' Championship, felt he was in fact playing well. So he did what he and his wife, Robin, had planned to do. He drove home to Sea Island, Ga., with house guests—Fred Couples and his fiancée. He didn't touch a club on Monday. On Tuesday, Davis and Fred played a casual round on a new course Davis had helped to design, Ocean Forest. The range wasn't open yet, so they couldn't warm up or practice. Fred shot 68 and Davis 66. He and Fred flew to New Orleans and learned they'd been the only ones in the field able to play at all on Tuesday. It had rained in Louisiana, and it continued to. The pro-am was washed out on Wednesday. Davis had never played English Turn before. Now he would have to start learning the course in competition. He decided that he could figure the course out as he went along.

When the tournament started, Davis was still playing well. He opened with a 68, four off the lead. On Friday, his 69 moved him into a tie for third. And on Saturday he made two eagles and three birdies and shot 66 to take the lead.

Now Davis truly was like Odysseus sailing past the Sirens. As soon as he took the lead, the distractions intensified. People in the crowd were yelling, "Masters tickets! I need Masters tickets!" In the press room, reporters barraged him with questions. Did he think he could win and make the Masters? What would it mean to him to make the Masters? We had talked about these kinds of distractions in the past, and Davis knew what to do. Every time someone mentioned the Masters to him, he needed to think, *If I want to win this tournament and get in the Masters, I have to concentrate on my routine on every shot. I can't start thinking about the Masters.*

But it wasn't easy.

I called Davis at around that time. As frequently happens, we talked about college basketball. Part of my job is to find the most effective way to talk to an individual. A lot of athletes, including Davis, respond well to analogies drawn from other sports that they follow. In addition to Michael Jordan's shooter's mentality, I've often talked to Davis about Dean Smith. I'll point out that Dean, no matter what the other team does, has a plan that he executes. Davis needed to emulate that. And talking about basketball is a form of relaxation; I wanted Davis to relax.

Mike Heinen made a tremendous run at Davis that Sunday, shooting a 62. Just before he made the turn, Davis looked at a leader board and saw that he had fallen two strokes behind. As I've said, I don't recommend that players look at the boards. They're better off paying exclusive attention to a good game plan and a good routine; what others are doing can only be a distraction. But a lot of players can't or won't avoid the leader boards, and Davis is one of them. If that's the case, they had better be able to use the leader board as a cue to focus tightly on their own games, their own routines.

Davis did that. He was standing on the ninth green, waiting to try an eight-foot birdie putt, and he told himself, "O.K. Let's just play ten holes focused on routine. Just go through the routine and get freer every time."

Thinking that way, he knocked in the putt. The chase was on. He eagled the eleventh, birdied the twelfth and fifteenth, and regained the lead by two strokes.

At which point Davis listened to the song of the Sirens for a moment and nearly ran his boat on the rocks. His thinking moved from a tight concentration on the present, on his routine, to the future, to the allure of the Masters. He told himself, "All right, just par in and you go to Augusta."

He hooked his drive into a trap on No. 16, but managed to

reach the green and make his par. No. 17 is a par three, 207 yards, with water and a long bunker guarding the left side. Davis took a 6-iron and told himself, "Just put it somewhere in the middle of the green." He hooked it into the bunker, and though he hit a pretty good sand shot, he couldn't get up and down.

On No. 18, a watery, sandy par four of 471 yards, he aimed his drive at a letter in the "Freeport McMoRan" sign behind the green and blasted the ball more than 300 yards down the fairway, leaving himself no more than 150 yards to the hole. For him, this was a 9-iron. But then he thought, *No, I'll hit a smooth eight, just play it somewhere to the right side of the green. I've got the whole green to work with.* And he quit on the shot and pushed it into a bunker. Another bogey, and the tournament was tied.

Although Nos. 17 and 18 are tough finishing holes, a lot of armchair critics were doubtless thinking that Davis had choked, that he was afraid or lacked confidence.

Choking, though, is nothing more than being distracted by something. In Davis's case, focusing on the Masters had distracted him from two vital elements of his pre-shot routine. The first was picking out the smallest possible target.

A golfer's brain and nervous system perform best when they're focused on a small, precise target.

I like players to aim at something as small as a particular branch on a tree, not just a side of the fairway or the green. I like them to aim for a small spot in the cup or a particular blade of grass when they're putting.

When Davis aimed for vague targets like an area of the green on No. 17 and a side of the green on No. 18, he was setting himself up for trouble. As he told me afterwards, "The most dangerous thing you can do is hit a ball without knowing where it is going."

The second vital element he forgot was decisiveness. His first instinct told him to hit a 9-iron to the eighteenth green. Ninety-nine percent of the time a player will do better if he follows that first instinct and hits a decisive shot than he will if he reconsiders and goes to another club. Even if that second choice is technically the correct one, his swing is likely to be affected by doubt and indecision.

Fortunately, Davis had the self-awareness to figure out his mistake. He had never won a playoff before, but he knew what he had to fix to win this one.

He and Heinen each parred No. 16, the first playoff hole. They came again to No. 17. This time, Davis picked out a tiny target. He'd been drawing his irons that day, so he picked out a leg of the television tower behind the green, about fifteen feet right of the hole. He swung, and the shot took off, drawing toward the flag just as he had envisioned it. It nearly went in, but it stopped three feet away.

As Davis walked up to that seventeenth green, his face was red and twitching. Fans could see his lips moving. They could see he was talking to himself. It was a good thing they couldn't hear him, because the language was not pretty. He was berating himself for having forgotten about the small target and for his indecision on the seventy-first and seventy-second holes.

But he got over it in time to tap in the birdie putt and win the tournament. It was, I think, a turning point in his career. The next time we talked, he had things in the proper perspective. He was pleased and proud that he had reacted to the pressure of the last two bogeys and the playoff—not by getting upset but by correcting his error and getting back to his mental routine. He *should* have been pleased and proud.

. . .

BUT HIS SATISFACTION was unsullied for only an hour or so. The people at Augusta faxed their invitation to English Turn and let him know they were glad he'd be coming back to the Masters. His wife, Robin, planned a victory party. Jeff Sluman and Fred Couples called and offered to share the houses they'd rented in Augusta. Then, as he was leaving English Turn, someone broke the news that Harvey Penick had died.

The golf world knew what Harvey Penick had meant to Tom Kite and Ben Crenshaw. Not so many knew of his link to Davis. Harvey Penick had been Davis Love, Jr.'s college coach, but more than that, his ideal. "My Dad," Davis III would say, "basically thought Harvey Penick was the greatest man who ever lived. He *was* golf to my Dad."

Davis III had visited Mr. Penick several times. Each time, Harvey talked graciously with him and invited him to take an informal lesson. And each time, Davis III had the sense he was hearing again the things he had heard all his life from his father, only now from the original source. So when Harvey Penick died, it was, to Davis, as if another link to his father had gone with him.

He was no longer in a mood to celebrate. He didn't even want to follow his normal practice routine at Augusta. He wanted to fly to Austin Tuesday night, attend Harvey Penick's funeral on Wednesday, and fly back to Augusta just in time to hit a few practice balls Wednesday night.

Ben Crenshaw, ironically, talked him out of it. Ben had played with Davis on Thursday and Friday in New Orleans. And Ben had played badly. His toe was bothering him and he couldn't drive straight. His putting was so bad that he disgustedly putted the last three holes on Friday with his 1-iron. He missed the cut and went home to Austin, and he was there when Mr. Penick died.

On Monday night, Davis called Ben about the funeral. "Look, Davis," Ben said. "You've just won New Orleans. You're on a high and you need to be practicing and getting ready. We'll tell everyone you send your respects and you'll come out some other time to see Helen and Tinsley (Mr. Penick's wife and son)."

Davis was not convinced, but his wife and his mother both seconded Ben's advice. And, of course, there was a side of him that couldn't wait to get to Augusta. That side of him felt like a kid in bed on Christmas Eve, agog with the thought of the great things in store. It was not just that he could tell that his swing and his putting stroke were grooved. It was the way he had won in New Orleans—recovering his composure and coming back to win the playoff. He had proven something to himself.

In a sad, ironic way, his grief over Harvey Penick's death helped Davis. It eliminated any possibility that he would be euphoric or giddy after New Orleans. It helped him avoid the letdown that players often suffer the week after winning a tournament, when their thoughts tend to linger in the immediate past rather than focus on the present. It reminded him of many of the wise things that he had heard from both Mr. Penick and his father. Equally ironically, of course, grief similarly helped Ben Crenshaw to focus.

I spoke with Davis briefly before each round of the Masters. I tried to remind him to keep thinking the way he had in the New Orleans playoff—to let it go to a precise target, to follow his routine on every shot, to stay patient.

Davis was a little shaky in the first round, shooting 37 on the front nine. But it was a mark of his improved confidence that he did not get discouraged or impatient and turn that mediocre start into a round that would eliminate him from contention. He played the back nine in 32 and finished the day tied for ninth.

Another 69 on Friday left him tied for seventh. A 71 on Saturday gave him a 209 total, tied for eleventh with Greg Norman, but only three shots behind the fifty-four-hole leaders, Crenshaw and Brian Henninger.

He came to the course Sunday morning excited. When Davis is excited, he walks faster, he talks faster, he thinks faster. He has butterflies in his stomach and he is hungry, but he can't eat and he has a feeling akin to a runner's waiting at the starting line before an Olympic final. He is ready to go.

He knew that he had to find a way to slow himself down a little, to take deep breaths, to amble from place to place instead of striding. So he found a few old friends from home, got the appropriate passes and badges, and sat down with them on the front porch of the Augusta National clubhouse and had lunch. They talked about what they might do back at Sea Island after the tournament. Maybe it was that plantation atmosphere, that sense of leisure. Maybe it was the thought of fishing. Davis relaxed a little.

When lunch was over, he warmed up with Jack Lumpkin at the practice range, and then came over to the putting green, where I found him. I was thinking of something I'd heard recently about the UCLA basketball team. In the NCAA championship game, the Bruins had had to play without their great little point guard, Tyus Edney, who was injured. Despite Edney's absence, UCLA played a great game and won. Afterwards, one of the players credited their loose, confident attitude to something Ed O'Bannon had said to his teammates in a huddle early in the game. "Forget that it's the NCAA Championship," O'Bannon had said. "It's only a pickup game. Play street ball."

Davis and I had talked about something similar in the past. He knew how Michael Jordan liked to come back to Chapel Hill in the summertime and play in pickup games with other former

Carolina greats. Jordan always seemed to light it up in those games, even though the opposition was composed of all-Pro players. What made Jordan Jordan was that he would do exactly the same stuff the next spring, in the playoffs against the Knicks or the Lakers. Other, lesser, players would get the idea that playoff basketball was too serious to approach with the same attitude that worked in Chapel Hill in July. And that was one of the reasons that Jordan would dominate them.

So as Davis left the putting green and headed for the first tee, that was what I told him: "Remember, it's just a pickup game."

Davis and Norman, paired together, both parred No. 1 and birdied No. 2, a reachable par five. Davis birdied No. 5 and Norman birdied No. 6, sinking a putt from off the green. No. 7 became a key hole for Davis after he hit a bad drive into the trees on the right side of the hole. No. 7 is a short par four, only 360 yards, but the green and its surrounding bunkers and swales are treacherous. Davis had only 130 yards left, but no direct shot to the green. He had to hit a low fade under and around the trees, then over a deep bunker that fronts the green. He cut a 7-iron into the green and saved his par. Then he birdied No. 8, the second par five, and parred No. 9. He turned in 33. He and Norman were momentarily tied for the lead.

No cliché in golf is hoarier or truer than the maxim that the Masters begins on the back nine Sunday afternoon. Starting with Amen Corner, the course provides nine opportunities for drama, heroism, and disaster. The winner is usually the player who handles his game and his emotions best under this intense pressure.

"All right," Davis told himself. "You've got a challenge ahead of you. You've got a long way to go. Let's play the best nine holes you ever played. Get into the routine. Have some fun."

He hit two fine shots to within ten feet of the hole at No. 10.

Norman's approach was left of the green, down in a swale amid some pines. He looked like he would have to play well just to make bogey. But Norman bounced his chip off the slope and onto the green. It slammed into the pin and fell in. The crowd exploded. *Oh, gosh, here comes Norman,* Davis thought.

Routine saved him. Though he was transparently nervous and excited, he felt a kind of peace as he settled into the familiar chain of actions: reading the green, selecting the target and the line, aligning his body, taking one last look, and letting it go. Click-click-click. The ball rolled in.

He parred eleven and twelve, not easy holes to par in those circumstances. But No. 13, the 485-yard par five that is wrapped around Rae's Creek, has always been a difficult hole for Davis. His long tee shot always makes it possible to reach the green in two and make a birdie. But the second shot must always be hit from a sidehill lie that makes it impossible to hit his bread-and-butter approach shot, a high fade. He thought of the times he'd misplayed that shot; and he misplayed it again, hitting a 7-iron to the left of the green, way too far left, seemingly miles from the hole. He three-putted for a par that felt like a bogey. Norman birdied the hole, and now Davis was behind both him and Crenshaw.

He was, he would recall later, nervous. Very nervous. But over the last five holes, he forgot his mistake on No. 13. He learned how well he could play nervous.

At No. 14, he hit a wedge approach to two feet and made birdie. His drive on the 500-yard fifteenth was so long that he needed only a 9-iron for his second shot. It stopped ten feet from the pin, and he almost holed the eagle putt.

At No. 16, he hit a 6-iron almost exactly where he wanted it. It flew over the water and landed on the green, 190 yards away. The ball needed to be about two feet farther left. If it had been, it would have caught a slope and rolled down toward the pin, probably stopping within five feet. Instead, it hung on the upper terrace of the green, 60 feet away. Davis made a good run at the putt, but it was impossible to stop it close to the hole. He bogeyed it.

He told himself that he was not out of it, if he could birdie the last two holes. No. 17 is a 400-yard par four. For professionals, the drive past the Eisenhower Tree is not a problem. The approach shot is. Unless it's struck precisely, the ball can roll off to the left or right of the hole, leaving treacherous chips and making bogey a distinct possibility. Standing in the fairway after another long, straight drive, Davis thought briefly of some of the disastrous shots he had seen there. Then he reminded himself of all that he had learned that spring, of the discipline he had acquired. He said to himself, "Let's hole this shot," and focused tightly on the pin. He swung his wedge. The ball stopped six inches from the hole. He made the putt.

And, of course, he didn't win. He played the eighteenth bravely, getting up and down from the left side of the green for his par. He shot 66, and his total of 275 would have won sixteen of the previous eighteen Masters. But Crenshaw, playing behind him, was just as brave and a little better with the putter. Crenshaw won by a shot.

But Davis didn't lose. He had not only played his way into contention in a major championship for the first time in his career, he had played well down the stretch.

More important, he had learned a great deal about himself and his game during the ordeal of coming back from an off year and qualifying for the Masters. Those lessons carried him through some tough situations the rest of the season—he played very well at the U.S. Open and was one of the bulwarks of the American team in the Ryder Cup. He can only get better.

No. 5

How Val Skinner Won the Sprint

FEW PLACES ON A GOLF COURSE DEMAND BETTER THINKING FROM A golfer than the short, reachable, but dangerous par five. The eighteenth hole at the new LPGA International course in Daytona Beach is just such a hole—452 yards, with a lake lining the left side of the hole from tee to green.

When Val Skinner arrived there in the final round of the Sprint Championship last year, the need for clear, confident thinking could hardly have been more acute. Val had begun the day one stroke back of the third round leader, Kris Tschetter. A string of three birdies at Nos. 2, 3, and 4 had given her the lead, and she reached No. 18 ahead of Kris by two strokes.

Val, of course, wanted to win. She already had five wins on tour; she had her best year ever in 1994, capturing the Atlanta Women's Championship and more than $350,000. But from Atlanta through the first few months of 1995, she had experienced the frustration of playing well enough to win, but not winning.

And Val sometimes gets impatient when she doesn't win. She grew up in Nebraska, the daughter of a golf pro who put her first clubs in her hands when she was barely old enough to walk. She developed a very strong game. As a senior in high school, she won twenty titles. Her success continued in college. At Oklahoma State, she was the Big Eight female athlete of the year, twice led the nation in scoring average and was collegiate player of the year.

When she turned pro, she had to learn patience. No professional wins as often as Val had grown used to doing. After I started working with her, I noticed that she played best in the weeks when she could put her mind in a calm and quiet state.

But mellow serenity doesn't come naturally to Val. She's got an enthusiastic, outgoing personality, and she really loves the game of golf. She loves thinking about it and analyzing it. Combine those qualities with the frustration that seeps in when there's a long time between wins, and Val has a challenge. She has to work hard to cope with the high expectations she has of herself, to refrain from tinkering with her swing in competition, and to trust that adhering to her mental and physical routine will see her through to her best results. And she has to work hard to have the discipline to stick to her game plan.

Val is a long hitter. She averages about 240 yards off the tee, but she can crank her tee shots 270 yards under favorable conditions. Being a long hitter is an advantage, of course, but not an unalloyed one. Since she's long, she's frequently got a relatively short iron in her hands when she approaches a par four; she might have a 7-iron when the bulk of the field hits 5-irons. This increases the temptation to shoot for the pin. That's no problem when shooting for the pin is the smart play. But it can be disastrous when the pin is cut in a sucker position, next to a hazard.

Likewise, her length makes it feasible for her to try to reach a lot of par fives in two strokes. And in a lot of cases, this is exactly what she ought to do. You don't win many golf tournaments shooting even par. Most often, it takes something like 10 or 15 under. That means making birdies, and a reachable par five is the natural place for a long hitter to make them.

I don't teach any hard-and-fast rules for making decisions about strategy on par fives. But there are a couple of constants. First, a player must always weigh risks against rewards. What's the worst that can happen if a long second shot goes awry? If it can go out of bounds, with a stroke and distance penalty, that increases the risk side of the calculation. If a lateral water hazard is the worst penalty, the risk is reduced. A player could drop at the water's edge, pitch to the green and still make par if she sinks her putt. And if the worst hazard is sand or rough, the risk is minimal. In those cases, the potential for an eagle or birdie almost always outweighs the risk.

The second constant is the game plan. I want professionals to make their decisions about par fives on Tuesday and Wednesday, during practice. That way, their decisions are more likely to be coolly taken than they would be in the heat of competition. Of course, a plan has to have some flexibility, taking into account such things as the presence or absence of favoring winds. But in general, a player who thinks she is executing a plan is more likely to be decisive than a player who walks onto a tee wondering what to do. And decisive players, by and large, hit better golf shots.

Val, of course, had a game plan for LPGA International. And her plan called for playing No. 18 as a two-shot hole.

She had a lot of time to think about it on the tee. Play had slowed down ahead of the final threesome. The delay seemed interminable. Val had tried, during a previous delay, making small talk about the weather. But neither Kris nor Beth Daniel, the third member of the group, was in the mood for chit-chat.

So she noticed things. She noticed the crowd. She noticed

the television cameras. And she deliberately kept her eyes off the leader board.

Val generally doesn't want to know where she stands in a tournament. She has her game plan, which is designed to produce her lowest possible score. She wants to execute that plan. Any other information is extraneous and potentially distracting.

But there are a few situations where she wants to know. One of them is when she's standing on the tee of a hole like No. 18 on Sunday afternoon, in contention to win a tournament. She could tell, from the way Kris had played and the reactions of people in the crowd, that she had the lead. She didn't know by how much. She turned to her caddie.

"How're we doing?" she said.

"Great!" he replied.

"What do we need to do?"

"Par is fine."

That didn't settle her mind much.

There were, she thought, at least three clubs she might use off the tee: driver, 3-wood, and 3-iron. She'd been hitting the driver all week on this hole, playing the ball down the right side of the fairway. Twice, the strategy had worked and she'd reached the green in two. Once, she'd buried the ball in one of the fairway bunkers on the right side.

She thought about the shorter clubs. If she hit one of them, she'd have to hit a lay-up shot with an iron to the narrowest part of the fairway. That could easily leave her with a third shot to the green from a difficult lie in the rough. With the driver, she calculated, the worst that could happen would be a shot blocked right of the fairway traps. And if that happened, she could wedge back into the fairway and still have a short iron for her third shot.

So she went with the driver. As soon as she pulled the club

from the bag, she could detect a reaction. Peter Kostis, the television color man who was walking with the group, looked like he had just seen her pull out a ceremonial knife for hara-kiri. She could sense that she was flouting the conventional wisdom.

In this case, the conventional wisdom says that with a two-shot lead, you play safe with an iron off the tee, play for the easy par, and protect the lead.

In this case, the conventional wisdom was wrong.

I am a believer, and always have been, in a conservative strategy and a cocky swing. But the important half of that phrase is not the conservative strategy. It's the cocky swing. A conservative strategy is the means to an end. The end is a confident, decisive frame of mind as the golfer swings at the ball.

The right choice is the decisive choice.

And Val, following her game plan, made that choice.

Her mistake came in what happened next. As she drew the club back, the last thought that flashed through her mind was of the bunkers on the right-hand side of the fairway, the ones she'd plugged in earlier.

Keep it away from those bunkers, she thought.

Her brain and nervous system reacted to that thought. Her body stiffened on the downswing. Her hips held back and she yanked the ball left, into the water.

Afterwards, of course, all the sportswriters wanted to second-guess her. She'd flouted the conventional wisdom and hit it into the water. Second-guessing is their job. But they forget how often someone pulls out a 3-iron, gets conservative and careful with her swing, and pulls the ball into the water anyway.

Val walked off the eighteenth tee seething. But then she made an excellent decision, a champion's decision.

She decided that the only constructive thing for her to do was accept what had happened, put aside her anger, and go on from there.

Acceptance is critical after a bad shot. An angry player can't really execute a pre-shot mental routine.

A smart player knows that bad shots happen, often at the least convenient times. That's part of golf. The smart player accepts this, as Val did.

One of the ironies of the game is that bad players have a harder time accepting bad shots than good players do. Show me a foursome of once-a-month players who can't break 100, and the chances are I'll be able to show you a dozen instances per round of muffled curses, shouts of "I can't believe it!" and thrown clubs. And these are people who never practice and have swings that look like steam shovels falling off a ledge.

Winning professionals have much better grounds to get angry when they mishit a ball. After all, they've practiced for years. They have good swings. And their livelihoods are at stake. But if they're winners, they know better than to indulge in anger. They know that they're going to mishit some shots. They accept it when they do. They forget the bad shot and think about hitting the next one as well as possible.

Readers with long memories may be thinking right now, *Wait a minute. Didn't Tommy Bolt throw clubs into the water? And didn't he win the U.S. Open?*

Well, yes he did. But here's Bolt's considered opinion on the subject:

"Anger destroys both concentration and coordination, and that compounds both the strokes and the anger, and it's one helluva mess."

He was right. If high handicappers learned nothing else about the mental side of golf, they could improve just by learning to accept the result of any shot with equanimity. And they'd be more pleasant company.

. . .

FORTUNATELY, BY THE time she got to the edge of the water and took her drop, Val had put aside her anger. She walked along the edge of the lake, telling herself, "I am not going to let this tournament go. I am not going to give it away." And she drew on her reserves of strength and composure.

She had to, in effect, make a new plan for the hole. And the first thing the plan had to take into account was the lie she was facing. She had dropped the ball into thick rough, and because of the slope leading down to the water, the ball was well above her feet.

Had she remained angry, had she failed to accept her bad tee shot and put it behind her, Val could well have transformed a mistake into a disaster. The setup invited her to do just that. Thick Bermuda rough tends to grab the club's hosel and close its face as it comes through the ball. The sideslope tends to produce a flat inside-to-out swing. All the ingredients were there for an angry golfer to hit another hook into the water.

Val adjusted. She forgot about going for the green. It was too far away, particularly from that lie. She would have to plan to reach the green in two more strokes; she wanted her approach shot to be a full wedge. That meant that the next shot, her third, could be hit with a lofted club.

Too often, players who are in trouble on a hole fail to do this. They see that they're, say, 250 yards away from the green, and they pull out a fairway wood, though they can't hit the green. They're mad and they want to hit the ball as far as possible. But even if they hit the wood well, they'll leave themselves a half-wedge of some kind, which many players find troublesome. They'd be much better off in this situation hitting a 6-iron and a full wedge.

This is what Val decided to do. She didn't want her third stroke to put her in position to have to hit a little finesse shot with her wedge to the green. She could feel the tension affecting her body. She was aware of her own breathing; she could feel herself tightening up. She wanted to take only full swings in that state. So she pulled out a 6-iron.

Next, she adjusted for the lie. She took a stance that placed the ball closer to her right foot than she normally would. She opened the face of her 6-iron a little. She picked out a target, went through her routine, and hit a sound recovery shot, well clear of the water—in fact, into the rough on the right side.

This time she caught a good lie. She reminded herself that she'd hit this kind of wedge from the rough thousands of times before. And she hit a beauty, about five feet from the hole.

She strode to the green confidently. After Kris Tschetter missed her eagle putt, Val could have made six and still won. But she had no intention of making six. She lined up the putt and knocked it in for her par. She won in style.

After the victory ceremony, and after the press had grilled her, Val called me. She was wondering whether she made the right choice on the eighteenth tee.

"Maybe I should have just hit a 3-iron. Maybe I should have bunted it down the fairway," she said.

I told her that she and other great players with high expectations of themselves had to be careful to not let other peoples' criticism turn a victory into a defeat. I told her to remember that she had shown a winner's mind when she accepted the results of her tee shot and went on from there to par the hole. And I told her not to second-guess her club selection.

It's more important to be decisive than to be correct, I said. Because as far as I'm concerned, if you're decisive, you are correct.

No. 6

How Paul Runyan Beat Sam Snead 8 and 7

When the finalists in the 1938 PGA Championship at Shawnee Country Club began making their way to the first tee, it would have been hard to find a spectator or sportswriter who didn't think the outcome was a foregone conclusion. One of them, dressed that year in a floppy newsboy's cap and a long-sleeved white shirt, was Sam Snead. The other, a natty wisp of a man with precisely combed blond hair, was Paul Runyan.

The seemingly essential difference between them had been apparent on the practice tee when they warmed up. Snead, then twenty-six, was in a couple of respects the John Daly of his day. He was a rawboned country boy, and he launched the ball. His tee shots regularly went 280 or 290 yards, gargantuan drives with the equipment of those times. Runyan, in contrast, looked Lilliputian. He was about five feet seven with his golf spikes on and weighed maybe 120 pounds right after breakfast. He would be giving Snead fifty or sixty yards off the tee.

And the golf course seemed to favor Snead. Shawnee was the first course designed by A.W. Tillinghast, the Philadelphian whose later work included some of America's classic championship layouts, among them Winged Foot and Baltusrol. It's hard to say now whether the Shawnee course was as good as those were. The band leader Fred Waring bought the place in 1943, added nine holes, and tore up a lot of Tillinghast's original design. But one aspect of the Shawnee course remains clear from old scorecards.

The course had relatively short par fives. Sam Snead could reach at least three and possibly all four of those greens in two shots. Paul Runyan, whose best drives traveled maybe 230 yards, couldn't reach any of them.

But there were a few other factors, a little more subtle, that gave Runyan a chance.

The first was the rough. Most of Shawnee's holes were on an island in the Delaware River. It had rich alluvial soil, and the rough grew thick and lush. A few years prior to the 1938 PGA, Runyan had played in a lesser event at Shawnee. He remembered that Bobby Cruickshank had found his ball in the rough, laid his bag down beside it, and then gone to help a competitor find his ball. A few moments later, he turned around—and couldn't find his bag. If a golf bag could briefly disappear in the Shawnee rough, there was going to be a premium on staying in the fairway. Runyan would do that.

The second—more important—factor in Runyan's favor was his short game.

From his earliest days in golf, Paul Runyan had understood the importance of chipping, pitching, and putting. He'd had to.

He was born in 1908, the son of a poor dairy farmer in Hot Springs, Arkansas. When he was a boy, the Hot Springs Country Club was founded not far from his family's farm. He began caddying there, though it was sometimes tough to persuade people that he was big enough to carry their bags. And he started to play whenever he could. He'd practice swinging in his father's pasture. He'd sneak into the club and play a couple of holes on the way to school. At recess, he'd take his one club and climb over the fence to the fifth hole and play that until the greenskeeper caught him.

On those occasions when the club permitted it, he would compete against the other caddies. He soon found that lots of caddies could outhit him. In self-defense, he began to focus on the shots where strength and size didn't matter, the short shots. He watched the members at Hot Springs and copied the putting technique of a man who believed that the hands had to be directly opposed to each other and the elbows bent, one directly behind the shaft and the other directly in front of it.

The same technique, Runyan found, served him well from off the green. Southern greens in those days were not green. They were made of oiled sand, because agronomists had yet to develop strains of Bermuda grass that could be shaved to putting length and still survive the summer heat. Oiled sand was inconsistent. Pitch to a soft spot and the ball would sit down and stop. Pitch to a hard spot, and it would take off, out of control. Runyan determined that it was best to hit low chips and get the ball rolling on the ground as soon as possible. To do that, he adapted his putting stroke and used it with his chipping clubs.

One day he played a match with two big, strong farm boys, the Lanoy brothers. On virtually every hole, they outdrove him. And on nearly every hole, Runyan would use his chipping and putting to get the ball in the hole before they could. When the Lanoys started snapping clubs over their knees in frustration, Runyan realized he was on to something. He had discovered that an athlete who wants to win badly enough will usually find a way. His way was the short game.

At the age of fourteen, he became the apprentice of James Norton, the pro at Hot Springs, and he learned the art of making clubs. Norton advised him to grow a mustache to make himself look a little older, and within a couple of years, Runyan began giving lessons; he is still giving them as this is written, seventy-one years later. In 1927, he got a big break. The Jewish community in Little Rock founded its own golf course, a nine-hole layout called the Concordia Country Club. Paul Runyan was hired as head professional. Membership was small, and the club was busy only on Wednesday afternoons and weekends.

This gave him the opportunity to practice, and he seized on it five or six hours a day. More than half of that time he spent on chips, putts, and short pitches. Nowadays, golf has more than enough statisticians charting rounds to demonstrate the importance of the short game. We know that in any round, the majority—as many as 70 percent—of all shots will be struck within one hundred yards of the hole. And we know that the wedges and the putter are the scoring clubs, that a pitch hit stiff to the pin or a long putt sunk saves a stroke, while a well-hit drive leaves a player with lots of work left to make his par. Anyone who fails to understand the importance of the short game today has only himself to blame.

But when Paul Runyan fell in love with his wedges and his putter, he was pioneering. He intuitively understood their importance in a day when relatively few players did. And he honed his short game to a new standard. From around the green, he started thinking not just about getting his chips close, but about holing them. He very often did hole them. By the time he began playing in professional tournaments, he was good enough to average less than two strokes into the hole from around the green. In other words, he holed out his chip more often than he took three strokes to get down. He calculated that in a seventy-two-hole stroke play event, if he could stay within ten shots of a long hitter like Snead from the tee to the green area, he could win. He figured he was at least ten strokes better within fifty yards of the hole.

That gave him a confidence that infused his whole game. If a player thinks that he can get up and down from anywhere around the green, he can relax and swing confidently on his approach shots. He won't be tempted to overswing at his tee shots. All facets of his game improve.

Any player I work with will testify that these are the same principles I teach today. Golf was and is a game where winners have to have excellent short games. If anything, the short game is more important today than it was sixty years ago, because the depth of competition is greater now than it was then and everyone can drive the ball pretty well.

I want players to fall in love with the short game as Paul Runyan did, to devote at least half their practice time to it, and to delight in their ability to use the wedge and the putter to defeat and confound players who are, ostensibly, better ballstrikers. I want them, as they go through their routines for short shots, to think about the hole as their target.

That holds true, and then some, for the average amateur. If someone brought me a group of randomly selected 25-handicappers, took us to a golf course, and told me I had a week to get all their handicaps under 20, I would first confiscate all their woods and long irons and lock them in the bag room. Then we would spend the week practicing chips, putts, and pitches. We'd play competitive games around the practice green. I wouldn't care whether they used Paul Runyan's chipping technique or one of the more standard methods. Around the green, whatever works, works.

I would teach these amateurs the same concepts I teach the pros, with one exception. A professional's threshold distance for trying to hole a shot ought to be about 120 yards. From 120 yards and in, a professional playing from a decent lie generally has to be able to shoot at any pin, even if it's cut close to a hazard. If he can't, he ought to consider another line of work. For the amateur, the threshold distance for using the hole as a target may be somewhat less—sixty yards, or forty. And there may be instances where prudence will tell the 25-handicapper that wedging the ball onto the green will have to suffice. Suppose, for instance, that he's facing a delicate little pitch over a yawning bunker to a hole cut only a few yards on the other side of the lip of the trap. He'll still have a small target, but it might not be the hole. It might be a spot closer to the center of the green, assuring that the shot clears the bunker.

But I suspect my imaginary class of 25-handicappers would be amazed at how often they would chip and pitch with the hole as their target and at how many strokes they would start to save by doing so—and by practicing.

There are, unfortunately, golfers who don't want to hear this. They want to believe that golf is about hitting the longest tee shots or learning to have a reliable draw on the 4-iron. They rebel against this fact of life:

As long as the rules reward getting a ball in a hole in the fewest strokes, golf will be about playing well with the wedges and the putter.

Such types existed in Paul Runyan's heyday as well. In 1933, Gene Sarazen and some other touring pros decided that there was entirely too much emphasis on the short game, particularly putting. They wanted to redesign golf to favor "shotmaking." So they prevailed on the organizers of some winter tournaments in Florida to expand the diameter of the hole from 4¼ inches to 8 inches.

The first tournament conducted with the big hole was called the Florida Year-Round Open. Most players began charging every putt. It didn't work. Sarazen had several three-putt greens. Runyan had no three-putts. He played his normal game on the greens, and he won by 11 strokes.

The advocates of the big hole decided this must have been an aberration. They staged another big-hole tournament, this one in Tampa, at match play. The finalists were Paul Runyan and Willie McFarlane, who was also a great short-game player. Runyan won again.

The experiment with the big hole ended abruptly that day. It proved only that there is no getting around the importance of the short game.

Snead and Runyan proved it again on the third hole of their match at Shawnee. They halved the first two holes, both with par fours. No. 3, a 458-yard par five, was supposed to be the first hole where Snead's superiority would show. It ran along the edge of the island, bounded by a strip of thick underbrush on the left side and guarded all around by rough. Runyan hit a driver and a brassie and was still short of the green. Snead hit a driver and an iron, but he pulled the approach slightly and failed to hold the green. Runyan pitched from the fairway and got his ball close to the pin. Snead, from the thick rough, couldn't get close with his shot, although it was shorter. He missed his birdie putt. Runyan made his. Snead was one down.

It may have helped that Runyan believed in a theory of match-play psychology that gave an advantage to the competitor "playing the odd." Under this theory, the important thing was to be the first to hit onto a green—the third, or "odd" shot played by a twosome on a standard par four. The idea was that by sticking the ball close, you could put more pressure on your opponent, especially if the opponent had begun to think complacently that he was going to win the hole because his tee shot was longer.

Walter Hagen, Runyan recalls, believed devoutly in this theory and had even developed some wily ways to use it. On a short par four, for instance, Hagen might use a tee shot that was analogous to a baseball pitcher's change-up. He'd take what looked like a full swing, but he wouldn't hit the ball very hard, ensuring that he'd have the shorter drive and would be first to hit his second shot. Then he'd stick the approach close to the pin. The opponent, startled by this seeming reversal of fortune, would then get so tense over his own approach that he was liable to botch a shot he might otherwise have executed easily. Or so the theory went.

I'm not sure how effective this kind of gamesmanship would be today. Touring pros rarely have match-play events anymore, and when they do, I advise them to play their normal games.

But I know that Paul Runyan thought that Snead's superior length off the tee made him vulnerable to the psychology of "playing the odd." That's the right kind of attitude to have. His alternative was to buy into the conventional wisdom that Snead's length gave Snead a huge advantage. If he had thought that way, he would have walked off every tee silently bemoaning his fate. He would have played worse. Winners find ways to think about the strong parts of their game and to believe that those assets will prevail.

If there were any lingering doubts in either player's mind about the power of the short game, the fifth hole erased them. No. 5 at Shawnee was called the Punchbowl Hole, a 108-yard par three to a slightly concave green. Snead put his tee shot inside Runyan's, which missed the green. Runyan chipped to about two-and-a-half feet. Snead's birdie putt slid about a foot past the hole and stopped directly between the hole and Runyan's ball. Runyan was stymied.

Under the rules at that time, players didn't necessarily mark their balls on the green to make way for someone putting from farther away. If the balls were within eleven inches of one another, or if either ball was within eleven inches of the hole, the closer ball was marked and removed. Scorecards of the time had an eleven-inch stripe on them called a stymie measure to gauge the distance. But if the stymie measure didn't save him, the player whose ball was away was out of luck. He had to play next. Sometimes, he might have a breaking putt that would give him a way to play around the closer ball. But quite often the hole was lost because of the stymie. This seemed unfair to a lot of people, and the rule was changed a few years later.

But that was the situation Runyan faced. Distances were measured. Snead's ball was fifteen inches from the hole, and Runyan's ball was thirteen inches behind it. Both putts were flat and straight. It looked like Snead would win the hole and square the match.

Runyan had no choice. He took his 9-iron and chipped for the hole. His ball hopped neatly over Snead's, rolled forward, caught the edge of the cup, and plopped in. In an instant, a hole that Snead thought was his had been snatched away and halved. Runyan got his ball out of the hole. Then he nonchalantly picked Snead's up and flipped it to him, conceding the putt.

"I have no idea what that did to Snead psychologically," he recalled recently. "But it certainly didn't help him."

Indeed not. Slowly, the thirty-six-hole match became a rout. Runyan took the greatest satisfaction from the results of the par-five holes. Of the seven that he and Snead played, Runyan won three, each with birdies, and halved the rest with pars. He went eight holes up with a birdie on the 472-yard par-five tenth in the afternoon round. The match ended when both players parred the next hole and Runyan had an insurmountable lead, eight up with seven to play.

"I saw it," Snead said at the presentation ceremony, "but I don't believe it."

He should have believed it. The importance of the short game should be engraved on the mind of every golfer.

FORTUNATELY FOR ME, Paul Runyan always considered himself first and foremost a teacher of golf. Nearly half a century after his triumph over Snead, he was still teaching at *Golf Digest* schools, which is where I got to know him and started to learn from him.

He remains a model for any golfer. At eighty-seven, he is spry and active. He gives lessons at a course near his home in California. And he still plays. He shot a 73 in one round with his friends recently—a 73, he added, that was not helped by a single long putt. He had a five-dollar bet with one of his friends that he would break 70 at least once before the end of the year.

He's still working on his short game. Paul tells me that he recently decided that the overlapping chipping grip he'd been using for about sixty years wasn't necessarily the best way to equalize the grip pressure from each hand. It put four fingers of one hand on the shaft against only three from the other. So he went to an eight-finger grip, which he reports gives him a firmer stroke. I can't wait to find out what innovations he comes up with when he's in his nineties. Such is his zest for golf and for life.

I hope I can be like him when I grow up.

No. 7

How Patsy Price Broke 90

PAUL RUNYAN'S INTUITIVE UNDERSTANDING OF THE IMPORTANCE OF THE short game goes double for people with handicaps over 20.

If a good player like Runyan, who hit a lot of greens in regulation, figured that his short game could make up ten strokes per tournament against players like Sam Snead and Byron Nelson, how much would a good short game be worth to golfers who shoot in the 90s?

Enough, in most cases, to make them players who shoot in the 80s.

The statistics are simple. A player who shoots in the 90s generally hits no more than one or two greens per round in regulation figures. That means that on sixteen or seventeen holes, he or she is going to face a chip or a pitch to the green.

Most high handicappers, by definition, rarely get up and down; sometimes they take four strokes, because they leave a shot in a bunker or stub a chip. If they learned to get up and down even a third of the time, they would save enough strokes every round to play in the 80s at least part of the time.

And improving the short game doesn't require any complicated swing changes. All it usually takes is a few fundamentals, the right attitude, and regular practice.

I've seen this proven by a lot of golfers. One of the most recent was Patsy Price, a Californian who got in touch via the Internet after she read *Golf Is Not a Game of Perfect*.

Patsy took up golf as an adult, when she started dating her husband, Dave, a golfer with a seven handicap. One of their first dates was at a driving range.

Patsy knows what she wants. When she saw Dave walking to the tee with a bucket of balls, she asked him, "Where's my bucket?" And he went back and got her one.

He gave her a 5-iron and she started to swing. From that bucket, she hit one perfect shot. And that was enough to hook her.

Patsy had always been an athlete, specializing in softball. In golf, she found a sport where even a person of her size—she stands two inches over five feet—could propel a ball almost out of sight. That struck a deep chord within her.

Patsy is an engineer by profession, and she approached learning the game as an engineer might. She wanted to know the mechanics of the golf swing—where the leverage and the power came from. She wanted to smack the ball.

This is not a bad attitude for a beginner. Studies have shown that it's a mistake to teach a beginner to strive for accuracy in most sports. It's better to strive for speed. But, typically, little girls are taught to throw for accuracy. Little boys are taught to throw hard. That's where the expression "throws like a girl" originates.

Later on in an athlete's development, it's possible to teach someone who's learned to throw hard, or swing hard, to perform with more control. But it's nearly impossible to teach speed once the pupil has learned to throw or swing for control.

Patsy, fortunately, had no patience with teachers who patronized her and told her to think of simple things like rhythm and concepts like "open the gate, shut the gate." She especially disliked teachers who didn't take her seriously because she is a woman.

She kept looking until she found teachers who responded when she asked them to describe in detail things like the action of the wrists through the hitting zone. Her present teacher uses videotapes and computers to analyze his pupils' swings in minute detail.

And Patsy worked assiduously at her game. She developed a strong, fluid swing and she learned to hit the ball a long way off the tee—as long as a lot of women professionals. Within a couple of years, she was shooting in the 90s.

She and Dave got married and established a golf-oriented household. They have a putting green and a practice net in their living room to keep the muscles loose during the winter.

Patsy had big dreams for a golfer who started after her thirtieth birthday. She wanted to have a single-digit handicap. She wanted to play in the California State Amateur.

Her progress halted a few years ago, when she had a baby. For three years, she stopped playing. When she started again, she found she still had a few bad habits she'd picked up during her pregnancy. She tended to cast the club and hit a slice.

She went to work again on her swing, but her scoring didn't improve with practice the way it had when she first took up the game. She hit a plateau when her handicap reached 20, and for a long, frustrating time, she couldn't get past it.

A large part of the reason was Patsy's determination to improve her swing so that she could compete on a high level. It's great to have long-range goals and a commitment to work toward them. It's great to try to develop a better swing.

But sometimes, golfers forget that the object of the game is not to have a great swing, but to put the ball into the hole.

In competition, how you score is more important than how you swing. And Patsy tended to neglect work with the scoring clubs, particularly her wedges. She loved hitting tee shots—that was a problem in mechanics. She loved putting—that was an intellectual exercise that challenged her. She didn't bring the same intensity to her short game.

A round that she played on her birthday last year showed how much her scoring could improve if she did. To celebrate the occasion, Dave took her to a resort called Tan-Tar-A, in the Ozark Mountains. It has a tough Pete Dye course called the Oaks.

On the day they arrived, Dave and Patsy had time for nine holes. They played from the blue tees, which is something Patsy often does. She likes to compete with men, and she thinks she sees the whole golf course from the back tees.

She shot 50 for the nine holes.

The next day, she and Dave were paired with another couple. Patsy and the woman partner played the yellow tees, typically the senior men's tees. She shot a typical round: 50–45 for a total of 95.

That afternoon, she persuaded Dave to play again. This time, she played the red, forward tees. At the end of nine holes, she asked Dave what she had.

"Fifty," he told her.

As it turned out, he'd made a calculation error. She had actually shot 47.

But Patsy was livid. As far as she knew, she'd shot 50 for the front nine from the back tees; 50 from the yellow tees and 50 from the red tees, even though the nine played about 500 yards shorter from the red tees than it did from the blues.

It dawned on her that something she'd recently read in *Golf Is Not a Game of Perfect* was true. Scoring didn't depend much on how far the ball went off the tee. It depended a great deal on how well she hit the ball from within one hundred yards of the hole. And in that range, she had been playing sloppy golf.

She resolved to try some of the things I'd recommended. She focused tightly on getting the ball into the hole from around the green. "If I missed the green," she told me later, "I looked at that flagstick and I thought to myself, *this chip's going down*."

When she putted, she thought the same way. Patsy had believed that anytime she putted from more than forty feet, she was in three-putt territory. She started thinking about holing her long putts instead of trying to get them in the general vicinity of the cup.

It helped, by the way, that when Patsy plays with Dave, he keeps score. When she plays by herself or with others, she keeps her own score, and she treats the card like an engineering data base. She keeps track of strokes taken, greens in regulation, length of first putt, etc. With Dave keeping score, she stopped counting all those things.

It also helped that she thought she'd shot 50 for the front nine and therefore had no realistic chance to break 90. She forgot about the score and simply played, focusing on each shot as it came, particularly the short ones.

She toured the back side in 39 strokes. When she reviewed the card and corrected the addition for the front nine, she realized she had not only broken 90, she had shattered it. She'd shot 86.

Just to prove it was no fluke, she shot an 86 the next morning.

Not every golfer, of course, will see the immediate benefits Patsy did when she changed her attitude toward the short game. Improvement is rarely so dramatic.

But if a person with a 20 handicap like Patsy's came to me and asked for just one tip to lower her scores, I'd tell her to do what Patsy did—to get enthused about that short game. Falling in love with the short game and playing golf confidently are intimately linked.

No. 8

How Tim Simpson Battled the Yips

A LOT OF GOLFERS HAVE TOLD ME THAT THEY HAVE THE YIPS, THAT putative disease that turns strong men jelly-kneed in the face of four-foot putts. There have been so many that sometimes I think you could staff all the pro shops around the country with players who mastered the art of striking the golf ball well enough to go on tour but could never get over their fear of putting. And of all the golfers I've tried to help with putting woes, none has fought the battle more tenaciously than Tim Simpson.

Tim's is a story of triumph and tragedy that's still being written.

As a boy, Tim was a good putter. He'd taken up the game when he was seven years old; his father gave him a putter to play with. He set records in high school and college. He grew up into a stocky bear of a country boy, and he made it to the tour at the age of twenty-one. He practiced his short game diligently. In rain, sleet, and snow. It didn't matter. He believed he could be the best player in the world, and he set out to do it. He was not afraid of winning.

But at some point, he started to lose confidence in his putting.

Tim can pinpoint the moment when his putting problem seemed to crystallize. It was in the final round of the Players' Championship in the spring of 1978, his second year on the tour. A gale was blowing off the Atlantic that day, with gusts strong enough to knock over a big tour golf bag. Tim had a one-foot putt on the seventeenth hole. The wind blew him off balance as he stroked the putt, and he missed.

The missed putt preyed on Tim's mind. It cost him several thousand dollars at a time when he was struggling to establish himself as a professional. It reinforced a notion that he had begun to develop that his putting wasn't tour quality. He fell into a spiral of bad thinking and bad putting habits.

Tim always thought of himself as a grinder. The code he was raised by held that you overcame your problems with hard work and determination. He started to spend long hours on the practice green. He was always one of the first to arrive at a tournament course on Monday.

He decided he needed to perfect his putting stroke. First, he concluded that the wind had affected him because he'd been standing up too straight. Tim is a very sturdy player, but he began to crouch over his putts more.

The leading money winner on the tour in those years was Tom Watson. Tim had heard that Watson, like Bobby Jones, advocated a short putting stroke, like driving a tack into the back of the ball. Tim had always been a putter who moved the club with his shoulders and had a long, smooth stroke. But in those days, copying Tom Watson's putting style didn't seem as self-evidently dangerous as it might seem now. Tim tried to change, to be more like Watson.

His search for the perfect mechanics prompted him to get tighter and more careful on the green. He started to feel very shaky, very uncomfortable—anything but the way an athlete should feel before he does something. That led to more missed putts.

And given the time and emotion he was investing in his putting, Tim's tolerance for missed putts dramatically diminished. He started to get angry just about anytime he missed a birdie putt under fifteen feet. Putting became almost a life-and-death battle for Tim. He walked around the course telling himself he simply had to make this, had to make that, couldn't afford to miss this. So every time he did miss, his frustration and anger grew.

The irony was that Tim's ability from tee-to-green remained constant or even improved. His confidence with all the clubs in the bag except his putter remained high. Tim became a player who could boldly thread a 3-iron between bunkers and over water to within a few feet of a dangerous pin position. Then he'd let the short birdie putt scare him.

The archetypal Tim Simpson hole, in his mind, became a long par four. He'd crack a tight, controlled draw down the middle about 280 yards. His opponent would be in the trees right. The opponent would be short and left with his second. Tim would draw a 7-iron in around four feet from the hole. The other guy would wedge onto the green to about thirty feet and make the putt. Tim would miss his four-footer. They'd both have pars for the hole, and Tim would be muttering to himself that somehow the scores weren't fair.

His putting, in short, was threatening to ruin him. It ate at him. It looked as if it might thwart his quest to realize his dreams. Some weeks were better than others, but he never felt confident that his putter wouldn't betray him. It was like trying to stay in a marriage with an unfaithful spouse. He couldn't relax.

He tried most of the putting cures that float around the locker rooms and practice greens of the tour like the magic elixirs they used to sell at county fairs. He fiddled with his setup. He fiddled with his stroke. He thought about keeping his head still. He thought about accelerating the putter blade through the ball. He thought about holding his follow-through.

Tim talked to Jack Nicklaus, who told him that he always stood over the ball until he knew it was going in. Then and only then did Jack start the blade back. But that didn't help Tim much, because Tim had always putted best when he took little or no time over the ball, when he just looked at the target and hit it.

He started to suspect that the problem was in his mind, and he went to see a psychiatrist. He did the Rorschach tests. The psychiatrist said he was perfectly normal.

But he was feeling lost and discouraged. In 1983, his friend Carol Mann of the LPGA Tour suggested that Tim might get some help from me, and we started to work together.

ONE OF THE first things I told Tim was this:

The disease called the yips doesn't exist, except in the mind.

For one thing, the yips are supposedly a condition of the nerves brought on by aging. Tim's problems had begun when he was twenty-two years old, so old age had nothing to do with them.

For another, research has failed to find any scientific, neurological basis for the proposition that age robs us of any of the physical abilities involved in putting.

But there are lots of golfers who either never had or somehow lost the right attitude about putting. They prefer to believe that they have the yips. Tim was certainly one of those.

I told him that he wasn't as bad a putter as he thought he was.

No one who gets to the PGA Tour and stays there is a bad putter. Some are better than others, but no one is bad. Putting is just too important a component in a golf score.

Tim thought he was a bad putter for several reasons. He was a good wedge player, good enough that he expected to get up and down whenever he missed a green. If he left himself a six-foot putt for par and missed it, he blamed his putting rather than the iron shot that missed the green in the first place.

Second, Tim hit a lot of greens because he was, indeed, very good with his woods and irons. That gave him a lot of birdie putts in the range of seven to fifteen feet. No one makes all of those. But Tim dwelt morosely on the ones he missed.

It's a natural trick of perception. If you're hitting the ball badly, you generally come into the clubhouse thinking that your putting wasn't so bad, and perhaps even saved you from a miserable round. If you're hitting the ball well, you're likely to focus on your putting as the only thing standing between you and a string of 62s. Tim frequently came off the course with a 69 or 68, feeling unhappy because he thought it should have been 64 or 65.

That, in turn, caused him to put more pressure on himself when he was putting.

I tried to get Tim to see his yips problem not as something that had happened to him, like a virus entering his system. It was a function of his own mind. It didn't own *him*. He controlled *it*.

I told him he had to be patient. He hit the ball well enough that he didn't have to make as many putts as some of the other players did. All he had to do was make one or two good putts per round to be in contention at most tournaments.

He needed, I thought, to master the trick of working less at his putting. His grinding—the long hours of practice, the effort to master a perfect stroke—was hurting his attitude rather than helping it. He was trying too hard to control everything that happened on the green. He had to understand the paradox that in golf, to gain some control over what happens, a player has to abandon the notion that he can control everything.

One day on the practice green at the New England Classic, Tim was telling me how badly he was putting. He was unhappy with what I'd been telling him. And all the while, he was stroking twelve-footers into the cup.

I put a foot in front of his putter, stopped him, and pointed out how well he'd been rolling the ball when he wasn't thinking about it, when he was thinking about what he wanted to get off his chest with me.

I told him that the next day, he ought to try to get into the same thoughtless frame of mind on the greens. I wanted him to simplify his routine—to read the green, then step up, take a look at the target, and stroke it. If it missed, wherever it went, tap it in and go on. All he could do on any putt was calm his mind, focus on his target, go through his routine, and roll it. Then he could accept what happened. That had to be all he tried to do.

If he wanted to think about putting, I said, he should start thinking of thinking himself as a good putter. He should start thinking only about making putts. His persistent complaining about his putting had become part of his problem.

Tim tried it. It wasn't an instant cure. In my experience there are no instant cures. But it was a turning point. He putted better for the rest of that tournament.

As he explored this new approach to putting, Tim found it feeling more and more natural. He talked to some of the best putters on the tour and found that only a few of them spent as much time practicing putting as he had been doing. That helped him to ease off the putting practice. Some days, he went to the course, warmed up, and then hit no more than a handful of practice putts to get the speed of the greens. Then he would go play.

He played with the attitude that the best thing that could happen on a given putt was he'd make it. The worst was he'd miss it. The best wasn't so great; the worst wasn't so bad. He stopped trying to force putts to fall and started trying to let them fall.

In short, his attitude toward putting became more like his attitude toward the long game. With the long clubs, he'd always been a player who saw a target, hit the ball, found it and hit it again. Mishits didn't bother him, because of his firm faith in his ability to hit the next shot. As he started to think that way on the greens, his putting improved. So did his scores.

In 1989, he was sixth on the money list. In 1990, he was eighth. In those years, he was not near the top of the PGA putting statistics, finishing about sixtieth each time. But he made a lot of putts.

Any golfer who considers himself a chronically bad putter can learn from Tim's experience. No doubt it's true that some players have a greater natural gift for putting than others. But, after all, how much of putting is physical? How hard is it to roll a ball along the ground?

Putting, perhaps more than any other stroke, is affected by attitude, by how the player thinks about putting, by his confidence. And no one is afflicted by nature with a bad attitude. That's something golfers choose to develop entirely on their own. Conversely, they could choose to develop a positive attitude about it. When Tim did, he won a lot of money and several tournaments.

I remember how excited he was when he won at New Orleans in 1989 and qualified for the Masters. I remember how proud he was when he won back-to-back at the Disney tournament in 1989 and 1990, giving him matching trophies for his kids, Christopher and Katie.

He had become one of the top players in the world.

BUT THE ROAD to the top isn't straight. Nor are there any guarantees about staying there. In April 1991, Tim missed the cut at the Masters and accepted an invitation from some friends to go turkey hunting in the Georgia woods. He spent a night in a hunters' cabin and during the middle of that night, he woke up covered with ticks. Most likely, some hunter the previous week had gone to bed with his hunting clothes still on and infested the bedding.

Within three days, Tim felt as if he had the flu. Worse, his hands were shaking. He was listless. He had no energy.

He went to his physician and had a blood test. It was negative. The symptoms persisted, although they varied in intensity. Sometimes he was wracked with arthritic pain. Sometimes he seemed almost well again.

He rarely had enough energy to practice. He kept playing the tour, but he was no longer the golfer he had been in 1989 and 1990. He wound up missing the 1991 Ryder Cup team by a sliver.

Tim went to more doctors. In 1992, he was diagnosed with Lyme disease; it caused arthritis to hopscotch unpredictably around his body. He went on courses of antibiotics and cortisone injections. Last year, a doctor told him he had Epstein-Barr virus.

Whatever the diagnosis, his golf continued to suffer. After the 1994 season, he lost his tour card. In 1995, he played the Nike

Tour. He hoped it would be a year of rehabilitation, after which he would rejoin the PGA Tour. But he missed the top ten on the Nike money list and he didn't get one of the spots available at the tour qualifying school.

There was nothing I could do about Tim's physical problems. I was concerned, though, with their effect on his attitude.

Sometimes, working with college athletes, I've seen cases where a kid breaks an ankle, can't play—and his grades plummet.

Logically, one would expect the opposite. Free of the obligation to practice for several hours every day, a kid ought to have more time to study, and his grades should go up.

But it turns out that athletes' minds don't work that way. Once an athlete is injured, his mind and mental energy tend to focus on healing, sometimes at the expense of everything else.

It seemed to me that Tim's illness affected him that way. During the years he played great golf, Tim's commitment to becoming the best was constant and consuming. Whenever I suggested something I thought would help, Tim was ready to do it, as long as it made sense to him.

After his illness came on, that wasn't always the case. I thought that in his situation, he ought to be careful to not risk exacerbating his health problems. I thought he ought to give up chewing tobacco, give up drinking caffeine, and get himself in the best possible physical condition. He's older now and he has to change some bad habits he could get away with when he was in his twenties.

He told me that he felt the tremors in his hands much less when he experimented with a long putter, the kind where the butt presses against the golfer's rib cage. I suggested he use it in competition. But Tim didn't want to do that. He would say that no one makes a lot of putts with the long putter. I'd reply that I'd seen Bruce Lietzke and Brett Ogle win with the long putter. And, besides, the ball doesn't know anything about the length of the shaft of the club that hits it.

For a long time, Tim and I butted heads about how he should respond to his illness. When I suggested changes in his lifestyle, he took it as an effort on my part to deny the reality of his symptoms.

I never doubted the reality of his illness. But I believe that people must do as much as they can to take personal responsibility for their health and success. I couldn't guarantee him that changes in his diet and habits would make him feel better and play better. But I felt they were well worth trying. He could find out if they'd help only by trying them.

Tim had reached the top by applying his will to the problem of his putting. The power of will has been the engine of every great athlete I've ever coached, of all the great people I've met. Success, I believe, is self-determined, even though there are times in life when it's easy to think that it's not.

Tim's illness brought on such a time. He would try to practice and hone his skills, but his body would get tired. He would start telling himself that the effort wasn't worth it. But it is at such times that a person finds out how badly he wants something.

Sometimes players who have been on top and had the ground crumble beneath them don't think they should have to start all over again. They don't want to face again the intense effort, hard work, and sacrifice they once were prepared to sustain.

Every individual goes through periods when he does a lot of the right things—practicing efficiently, thinking well—and gets no immediate, tangible results. This is the point where successful people bring to bear the powers of faith, patience, persistence, and will. Faith is the ability to believe without any tangible evidence.

. . .

I WISH I could end this chapter with the story of a great tournament Tim played to climb back onto the tour. I can't. He hasn't done it yet.

But I've seen signs recently that his old commitment is coming back. He's decided to play with the long putter. He's getting into better physical condition. He failed to make it through the PGA Qualifying School last fall, but he told me it wasn't because he putted poorly. His swing was just a little off that week.

I thought that was a good sign. Tim wasn't blaming his putting for his problems. And he knows that his swing will come back. His thinking is starting to remind me of 1989.

When Tim and I talk now, it's about how he has no other choice but to decide that he loves the challenge of overcoming his illness. I tell him that I have seen lots of players struck by injury or illness. Two results are possible. It can make him stronger, or it can make him weaker. He has to believe that in the long run, his illness will make him a better player, because it will make him twice as tough, mentally and emotionally.

More than ever, because of his illness, Tim needs to get back to the things he did well before he got sick. He has to spend some time each evening visualizing the great round he will play the next day. He has to get back to believing in himself.

He has to believe that there's nothing he can do about his illness other than the treatments his doctors prescribe. But he can still control his thinking. He can decide that this illness is going to tell him a lot about himself and his character. He can decide that whatever else happens, he is going to be proud of himself when it's all over.

If he can do that, then his illness cannot really defeat him. Nor will illness or injury defeat any golfer who can honestly tell himself that he did everything in his power to overcome it.

No. 9

How Byron Nelson
Won Eleven Straight

EVERY NOW AND THEN A SPORTS WRITER WILL MENTION MY ROLE IN helping a player prepare his mind to win a tournament. Quite often, the writer will imply that there is something new or mysterious about what I teach. I sympathize with the journalist's search for novelty, but nothing could be farther from the truth. I teach principles that great golfers have always known and practiced.

I know this because whenever I talk to the great golfers of the past, that's what their stories tell me.

Of all the records in the long history of the game, the two most impressive are Bobby Jones's Grand Slam of 1930 and Byron Nelson's streak of eleven straight victories in 1945. Unfortunately, Jones is no longer around to talk about what went through his mind in 1930. But Byron can talk about the 1945 streak, and if he is asked, he will.

I had a chance to visit with him not long ago at Fairway Ranch, his home in Texas. Of all the great players of his era, Byron is the one who strikes me as the happiest, perhaps because he knows the joy of sharing and giving. He shares himself and what he has learned, and he is always conscious of an obligation to give something back to the game. The day we spoke, he had just finished hosting an annual fund-raising pro-am for a golf scholarship in his name at Abilene Christian University. He wants to get the scholarship's endowment up to a million dollars, so it will be self-sustaining. He also is a very visible and active host at the Byron Nelson Classic each spring in Dallas. And he makes it a point to attend the Masters and the Ryder Cup and the other major tournaments each year, although he's now eighty-three. He knows that his presence at a tournament symbolizes the game's continuity and best traditions, although he's far too unpretentious ever to put it that way himself.

I knew that Nelson's streak must have demanded an enormously effective golfing mind. And I knew that perhaps the most arduous tournament of the eleven he won that summer was the PGA Championship at Moraine Country Club in Dayton, Ohio.

In those days, the PGA was a match play event, but it began with a thirty-six-hole qualifying tournament. Byron tied for the qualifying medal with Johnny Revolta at 138. He didn't have to qualify, but he played because there was a cash prize that went along with the medal. Byron's share of that pot came to $125, which he calculated would pay for a few more acres of the spread that eventually became Fairway Ranch. Then there were five rounds of match play, each at thirty-six holes. Byron beat Gene Sarazen, Mike Turnesa, Denny Shute, and Claude Harmon to make the finals, where he faced Sam Byrd, the former New York Yankee outfielder who switched sports and became an excellent professional golfer. By the end of the tournament Byron had played 204 holes, the equivalent of nearly three regular tournaments. He was 37 under par.

All of this occurred in sweltering August heat, compounded

for Byron by an aching back. Every night, he received heat, massage, and osteopathic treatment. "It was the toughest tournament I ever won," he said.

The key hole of the final match, Byron recalled, was the ninth.

Moraine's ninth hole is a 416-yard par four. In both the morning and afternoon rounds, Byron went for a pin that was cut in the back right portion of the green. Both times, he missed long and faced a difficult downhill chip from the rough. Both times, Byrd put his approach shot within ten feet of the hole. Both times, Byron could not stop his ball on the downslope and he wound up lying outside Byrd in three while Byrd lay two.

Both times, Byron curled in his putt. Both times Byrd, unnerved, missed his.

"I made those putts because I could see the line they were going to follow," Byron said.

That got my attention. Did Byron Nelson visualize his shots back in 1945?

"I could visualize the flight of my ball just like you could draw a string," he replied.

I asked him to elaborate.

Well, Byron said, he might walk up the fairway, facing an iron shot to a pin cut in the back right portion of a green and protected by a bunker.

Even though his normal ball flight was a draw, he didn't try to draw the ball over the bunker and into the pin. "I had learned in my practice how to fade it," he said, "I just thought about that, and—funny thing—my body did it.

"In my early years," Byron explained, "I thought a lot about mechanics. I was trying to learn a new way of swinging, because steel shafts had just been introduced. I thought that swinging those clubs required you to take the club straight back and turn and use the feet and legs and get away from pronation and taking the club too much inside, which you did with the old hickory shafts.

"My first job as a pro was in Texarkana, Texas, back in 1933. People wouldn't start to play till after lunch. So I had the whole morning to practice. There was nothing much else to do.

"I didn't have anyone to shag balls, and I couldn't have paid them if I did, because I wasn't making that much money. So I'd hit some 3-irons or 8-irons or whatever and then I'd take the club down and hit them back. I thought very hard about mechanics in those days.

"But I found that as my game got better, starting in around 1936, I'd practiced and worked enough so that it was like you were going to sit down at the table and eat a piece of steak. You take your piece of steak and your knife and fork and you don't think about how you cut your steak or how you feed yourself, any more than you would about how you put on your shoes and tie them. That's automatic. And I felt that was the way my game was. Automatic.

"I think that's the reason I played as well as I did—because I trusted my swing," he concluded.

I asked him if he had what today would be called a pre-shot mental routine.

"I always felt that I didn't have a very creative imagination," Byron said. "But now I look back on the way I played, and I did have a creative imagination. Golf was so different then. On one golf course there might be two or three greens that were real hard, two that were real soft and so on. You played a practice round to learn these things. Then, during the competitive round, you'd walk up to the ball and visualize, concentrate, whatever word you want to use.

"I looked for a faraway target—a tree, a house, a barn, a flagpole, maybe a bunker in the distance that I couldn't reach. And I'd look at that and I'd take the club away from that. And then, when I came back through, I'd try to make sure that the back of my left hand was going right to that target."

Was that his only swing thought?

"Yeah," he replied. "Basically it was. On short shots, I taught myself to think as if it was like pitching coins to a line the way boys do. I'd look at the target, and I never thought to myself, *Take a three-quarters back swing.* I looked at the target and relied on feel."

Between the time he felt he had mastered the swing and the time he reached his peak as a player, there were two more things Byron had to learn about the mental game.

One had to do with acceptance.

"If all good players would tell you the truth about it, when they were young and learning how to play, they got mad when they missed shots," he said. "I mean *mad*. Bob Jones had a terrible reputation as a kid—throwing clubs, and awful stuff. I never was bad about throwing clubs, though I won't say I never did it. But I would get upset—kind of boom-boom, though not ugly at anybody."

I asked how he had learned to get rid of his anger.

"When I was the pro at Texarkana, there was an older man there named J. J. Wadley, who had learned to play golf from Jim Barnes, the 1916 PGA Champion. He was a wealthy man and he liked me because I was a good, staunch Baptist and I didn't smoke and didn't cuss. And he was a good player for his age and he would, just by his example, kind of shame me once in a while.

"And then when I went to work as an assistant for George Jacobus at Ridgewood Country Club in New Jersey, I still had a little problem, and he would tell me, 'Byron, whenever you play, you need to not get upset and get mad. Don't ever let it carry forward to another shot.'"

And he took the counsel of his parents.

"My father and mother were a big help. They didn't play golf. They knew nothing about golf. But they could tell I was upset when I came home from a bad round. I wasn't being ugly about it, but they could tell I was upset. So then they'd talk to me about it, and they said, 'You're going to have to learn to get over it.'

"I believed my parents. They were wonderful parents. They were smart parents. And, also, you know, I believed in the Bible, and it said, 'Let not the sun go down upon your wrath.' It doesn't say you can't get angry. But don't harbor it.

"So it was a process of gradually educating myself."

After he learned to control his temper, Byron said, he felt as if he were cruising on the golf course. He felt as if he were driving his car at 60 miles per hour on an open road. He was comfortable and in control, even when adrenaline was pumping.

He still missed shots. But he realized that everyone was going to miss some shots. The key was to accept that fact and forget about the misses.

"I still think that players who are consistent are players who forget what happened," he said. "The next shot is what counts, not what happened. I see players who are going along real good and they mishit a shot and they'll be standing in the fairway, swishing that club back and forth, trying to figure out what they did wrong. That's a mistake."

He had one more refinement to add to his mental game before the streak began. At the end of 1944, Byron was already well established as a player, but he wanted to get better. He took inventory after that season and found that his mistakes tended to fall into two categories—poor chips or "careless" shots. He might, for instance, miss a short putt because he failed to follow his routine every time. So he made up his mind to practice harder on his short game, and to make sure his mind was completely focused on every shot in 1945. The result was the streak.

During 1945, Byron told me, he was so focused on the process of hitting good shots that he never knew how he had scored until after his round. He felt as if he played in a trance.

"I would come in and I'd have to go hole by hole on my scorecard, carefully, to realize what I'd shot. I didn't ever know if I was five under, three over, or whatever it was. I never carried that in my conscious mind," he said. "I never knew where I stood in a tournament."

That peak concentration lasted, he said, through the first two tournaments of 1946. One of them, the Los Angeles Open, was a semi-major in those days, and one Byron had always wanted to win. When he won it, and then won again at San Francisco the next week, he realized he had fulfilled all of his goals. He had won every important tournament there was to win. And he had amassed enough prize money to buy the ranch he had always dreamed of. He kept playing through the end of 1946, mainly because he had an endorsement contract with MacGregor. But the trancelike state of concentration that had carried him through the streak was gone. And then he retired from tournament golf.

It was clear that Byron had, through experience and some helpful teachers, picked up virtually all of the fundamentals of golf psychology that I teach today. He had learned to trust his swing and not to think about mechanics as he played. He had learned to visualize his shots. He had learned the importance of his short game; he had learned to rely on feel near the greens. He had learned to accept the results of any shot and let go of anger and frustration. He had learned to stay in the present and not to worry about outcomes.

118 • GOLF IS A GAME OF CONFIDENCE

Only one thing still puzzled me. Byron had published a couple of golf instruction books in his heyday. Both were full of photographs and text about swing mechanics. Both ignored the mental aspects of the game that had obviously helped him reach the top. Why?

"Aw," he said, and smiled, almost sheepishly. "People didn't talk about that sort of thing in those days."

No. 10

How Bill Shean Prepared for the Club Championship at Pine Valley

NOT MANY PEOPLE THINK OF AN AIRLINER AS A PLACE TO PRACTICE GOLF. But that is where an old client of mine, Bill Shean, did his best work getting ready for the 1995 club championship at Pine Valley.

I first met Bill about eight years ago. By that time, he was already an accomplished amateur golfer.

Bill started in the game the old-fashioned way, as a thirteen-year-old caddie at Hinsdale Golf Club, in his hometown in Illinois. His first weekend on the job, he made eight dollars. The following day, Monday, was the caddies' day to play. Using some old clubs that belonged to his father, Bill played with them—and lost twelve dollars. He decided he had better learn something about the game, and fast.

So he went to a drugstore and bought a paperback copy of Ben Hogan's *Power Golf*. Bill was a good athlete, adept at any game he tried, and inside of a year, with his self-taught swing, he was scoring in the high 70s. He was short and wiry, and he was constantly seeking ways to compensate for his lack of length. To this day, he tees the ball extraordinarily high because he once read a magazine tip from Arnold Palmer that suggested this was a way to get an extra ten yards.

He played high school golf, but he was not one of those boys who are groomed for the pro tour through lots of early lessons, the USGA junior program, and a college powerhouse. He went to the University of Michigan with an Evans Scholarship, provided by an educational fund for former caddies. When he graduated, he went into the insurance business. He became a true amateur golfer, balancing his passion for the game against the demands of a business, a growing family, and a church which he served as treasurer. He rarely touched a club from October to April, but his game slowly, steadily improved. He was a contender in club championships, and won a number of them.

But he could never push his game to the next level, the national level. He tried, but never qualified for the U.S. Amateur. After a while he decided that part of his problem was psychological. With his caddie's swing, he never quite felt he belonged in national competition. "I would," Bill said, "beat myself before I started."

About eight years ago, Bill read something I had written in *Golf Digest* and called me up. I invited him to come to see me in Charlottesville. We talked, as I usually do with a new client, and he told me what he thought of himself and his game.

I took him to the practice tee at Farmington Country Club and handed him a 5-iron. I asked him to picture a big banana slice and then step up to the ball and hit it. He did. Then I asked him to picture a draw. He did, and he hit that. Then a tight, controlled fade. Then a straight ball. He hit them all.

"Your skills are fine," I told him. "You hit the ball as well as any amateur I work with. You just have to believe it."

Some people, when they hear that sort of thing from me, may

be a little suspicious that I'm patronizing them. I'm not. I'm honest with people. If I start with a player who has a dysfunctional swing and a yen to break 70, I tell him that he needs to take swing lessons. But, quite frequently, the player who comes to me is someone, like Bill, whose physical skills are more than adequate for his aspirations. When I tell him that, though, I am often met with skepticism. It's intriguing that people are quite willing to believe a swing teacher who tells them their mechanics are all wrong. They have a hard time believing someone who tells them their mechanics are all right, but their mental game is not.

Bill, however, was receptive. So we talked a lot about two things: pre-shot routine and game plan.

Like most good players, Bill had worked hard on the physical aspects of a pre-shot routine—grip, stance, posture, and alignment. They are all extremely important for consistent shotmaking, and the professionals I work with regularly check them. But they do it at home in front of a mirror, or on the practice tee. On the course, they want to be able to set up their bodies without much thought. Bill had reached the stage where he could do that.

Less accomplished players, though, should not shy from making meticulous, conscious attention to grip, stance, posture, and alignment part of their routines. It will pay off.

But Bill had little or no sense of the mental side of the routine, and that is the side I care more about. Even more than grip, stance, posture, and alignment, a sound, consistent mental routine is the foundation of consistency. So we worked on it. Before every stroke, I asked him to stand behind the ball and observe the situation. Assimilate the information about lie, wind, yardage, and anything else pertinent. Choose a club, trusting his first instinct. Pick out a target. Picture the shot he wanted to hit.

Bill, as it happens, has the kind of mind that readily visualizes a shot. Some players do. They can visualize as readily as they can turn on a VCR. Some players, though, do not. This is not a disadvantage. They simply have to look at their target and believe that the ball is going there.

Once Bill had the picture firmly in his mind, and believed in it, I asked him to take his address without delay, take one more look at the target, and let the shot go without permitting thoughts about his mechanics to interfere with his concentration on where he wanted the ball to go—in short, to trust his swing.

Those are the fundamentals of a good mental routine. They are the process that a good player commits himself to think about and to follow on every shot.

Then we talked about game plans. Golfers should have a game plan for every competitive round they play. A game plan breaks down the course hole by hole. It designates the club to hit on every tee and the target to aim at. Frequently, it designates the section of the green a player wants to hit with his second shot—or his first on par threes. For good players, it establishes threshold distances on par fives. Within a certain number of yards, the player will try to reach the green in two. If his tee shot falls short of the threshold, the plan tells him where to lay up to give himself the best third shot into the green.

It often helps to formulate a plan if a player looks at a hole from green to tee rather than the other way around. This perspective suggests where the sucker pin placements are and where it's best to aim for the center of the green. It suggests what type and length of shot a player wants to hit into the green. And that, in turn, suggests the best length and placement of the tee shot.

On a typical 490-yard par five, for instance, the weekend player may decide that he wants to hit his third shot from a level spot in the fairway, 100 yards short of the green, which is his normal wedge distance. How to negotiate the first 390 yards? It may be that the course architect has placed hazards that influence the choice. But all other things being equal, is the best strategy to try to hit a driver 240 yards on the first shot and leave 150 for the second? Or would the smart approach be a 3-wood off the tee, for 200 yards, followed by a 4-wood for 190?

It depends on the player. The important thing is to think these things through ahead of time, during the planning process.

Game plans, obviously, take into account a player's strengths. Bill, for instance, feels that the driver is the straightest and most reliable club in his bag. So he plans to use it often. For other players, an intelligent game plan might require ignoring the driver and teeing off with a 3-wood or an iron on certain par fours and fives. Short, tight holes, in particular, may call for less club off the tee. Why drive the ball on a 310-yard par four that's lined with woods, water, or sand? A 3-wood or 3-iron may keep the ball on the fairway more often and still leave only a comfortable short iron to the green.

Sometimes, golfers confuse a conservative game plan with lack of trust in their swing. On the contrary, a conservative game plan is designed to enhance the golfer's confidence on every swing. First of all, it removes the decision-making process from the heat of the moment. Once he's out on the course, he has the feeling he's just carrying out a plan he already knows is designed to give him the lowest possible score. He knows that every shot in his plan is within his capabilities. That eliminates a lot of potential doubt.

A conservative strategy joined to a cocky swing produces low scores. Reckless boldness joined to a doubtful swing is a formula for disaster.

Obviously, a game plan has to have some flexibility. You can't select a club for certain par threes until you know where the wind is coming from, and how hard. You can't hit the ball as far if the weather turns cold and damp as you can when it's warm and dry. In effect, a golfer has to have a Plan B and a Plan C for different weather conditions. But there must be a plan.

Bill Shean listened attentively to what I told him and went home to Illinois. Later, he reported what happened. The first dozen or so rounds he played, he was highly disciplined. He followed his pre-shot routine religiously. He stuck to his game plan. And his scores were lower—below the course rating for each of the twelve rounds.

But he discovered something else. Normally, Bill is a gregarious, pleasant golf partner. If he has guests, he wants to make sure that they enjoy themselves. But when he immersed himself in his pre-shot routine and his game plan, he felt he couldn't do those things. He became quiet and detached. It felt, he said, like he was working. He decided that he wasn't quite ready for the commitment I was asking for. And he by and large stopped doing what we had talked about.

This happens sometimes, and I understand when it does. Personalities differ. Brad Faxon and Lee Trevino can be gregarious and still concentrate; in fact, being gregarious helps them. Bantering with the gallery between shots relaxes them. Ceasing the banter delineates sharply the moment when their pre-shot routines begin. But others, like Ben Hogan, have to stay quiet and deliberate throughout a round.

Situations also differ. I don't have the same mental approach for a Sunday afternoon round with my wife and daughter that I have for a tournament round. Football teams aren't as intense for an August exhibition game as they are for the Super Bowl.

I advise amateurs to designate a few weeks of every year as their competitive weeks. They might be the weeks of the club championship or some other competition. For a few days prior to those competitions, they need to find a way—either a prep tournament or some serious practice rounds—to reestablish the habit of immersing themselves in process and game plan. The rest of the year, they can play casual golf. But serious amateurs have to understand that in top-flight competition, they'll be going up against people who play no casual golf, who try to play with competitive discipline every time they step on the course. Such people will have an advantage.

Bill understood that. At that time, in his late forties, he wanted most of his golf to be casual. That was fine with me.

AT ROUGHLY THE same time he first met with me, Bill was invited by an Illinois friend named Jay Berwanger (yes, the same Jay Berwanger who won the first Heisman Trophy back in 1936) to play a few rounds of golf at Pine Valley Golf Club in Clementon, N.J.

Pine Valley is not so much a country club as it is a retreat for golfers. The ambience is almost monastic, except that in this cloister, the services are held outdoors, on the golf course. There is no pool and there are no tennis courts. The clubhouse is an unpretentious two-story building with plain green curtains, a lot of bare wood furnishing, and a sign near the front door that prohibits Mulligans off the tee at No. 10. It is not the sort of club that is likely to hold a Fiesta Night at fifty-five dollars per couple.

The course this simplicity serves is widely regarded as the most demanding test of golf in the world. It was planned and built, with some help from the British architect H. S. Colt, by a businessman and avid amateur golfer named George A. Crump. In 1912, Crump decided that the players in the Philadelphia area needed a new club, with a course that might be open and playable a couple of months longer than the rest of the courses around, a course that would challenge them and sharpen their skills for national competition. Crump found a large, empty tract of land in the pine barrens of southern New Jersey, served by rail from Philadelphia. The soil was sandy and it drained quickly, so it would have the playability he wanted. The land rolled, providing lots of elevation changes. And there were marshes and ponds for water hazards. It was a beautiful canvas on which to design a golf course.

And Crump had very exacting design ideas. He wanted holes of every kind: a couple of drive-and-pitch par fours; a couple of long, heroic par fours; doglegs left and doglegs right; holes that played in every direction relative to the prevailing wind; holes with plateau greens and holes with greens set in valleys; a little lob of a par three and a long, stern, uphill, everything-you've-got par three. He wanted some open tee shots, where all the hazards are visible. And he wanted some blind tee shots, where the golfer looks out at an acre of sand, juniper shrubs, and pine scrub, aims at a tree on the horizon, and trusts that there is a fairway somewhere out there beyond the forecaddie.

Most of all, Crump wanted the course to be uncompromising. Every tee shot at Pine Valley must first carry an expanse of sand or water one hundred to two hundred yards long. There is, in fact, so much sand on the course that the club doesn't bother with rakes; there would have to be too many of them. Players simply smooth over their sand divots and leave their footprints. The fairways are velvety and reasonably generous, and there is little rough. But missing the grass is like entering a Siberian prison; extrication is likely to be difficult, unpleasant, and costly. Many of Pine Valley's holes seem to be shaped like bottles with the flag at the lip; the closer you come to the greens, the tighter

How Bill Shean Prepared for the Club Championship • 127

they get. As time has gone by, and trees have grown in around each hole, the course has become still tougher. Its slope rating, from the back tees, is 153. Every now and then, during the club's annual Crump Cup competition, some guest will come in with a handicap of one or two and fail to break 100.

Bill Shean liked Pine Valley immediately. It was challenging. It was, he thought, a club for players, not a chief executives' club. When he was invited to join, he accepted.

Most years he made time to fly in for the President's Cup, the annual August stroke play championship for members. But though he played well on occasion, he never won. The 1995 President's Cup did not seem likely to change that. Bill's business had kept him busier than usual. He hadn't had as much time as he wanted to sharpen his physical skills.

So he decided that he would have to make up for that with his mental game. On the plane from Chicago to Philadelphia, he took out an index card and a yellow legal pad. And he recommitted himself to a sound pre-shot mental routine and a game plan.

On the index card, he wrote down his mental routine:

"1. Have fun. Focus on every shot."

This was a general reminder.

"2. Observe."

By that, he meant checking the lie, the wind, the yardage, the pin sheet and anything else that was relevant.

"3. Target. Club. Kind of shot."

He would pick out a target, pick a club, and decide how to work the ball—high or low, fade, draw, or straight.

"4. See it."

He would envision the shot, see it going through the air and landing. From short iron distance, he would envision the ball going into the hole.

"5. Feel it."

He would envision swinging the club. Sometimes he might take a practice swing. Sometimes he wouldn't. But he would not make a shot until he felt that the right swing was inside him.

"6. Trust it. Commit to it. Let it go. Give up responsibility for what happens to it."

He would refrain from thoughts about swing mechanics and believe in his ability. He would be decisive. He would step up and hit the ball without delay. And he would never berate himself for a bad shot.

Bill's mental routine was a sound one. It included a lot of steps that made it easier for him to be decisive.

To reinforce his commitment to it, Bill decided to keep a different, private kind of score. He would, of course, write down the number of strokes he had taken. But after each hole, he would also write down the number of strokes he had taken after faithfully following his routine. He might, for example, make four on a par three. But if he had followed his routine on each shot, he would write "4–4" on the scorecard and grade himself at 100 percent. Or he might par the hole but lose his concentration on his first putt. Then he would write "2–3" and grade himself at only 67 percent for the hole. He vowed that the percentage score was the only one he would keep running track of and care about.

This is not a system that would be used by a lot of the touring professionals I work with. They work hard on adhering to their processes, and writing additional numbers down would only distract them. But there are some highly organized, structured people for whom this can work. Bill is one of them. It's a matter of individual preference.

Then, on the yellow legal pad, Bill wrote down a plan for every hole. He made some general decisions first. He would not, for instance, plan on drawing the ball off any tee. His natural shot is a fade, and he didn't feel confident, given his lack of practice time, that he could work the ball right-to-left. Whenever he got in trouble, he would choose a safe, conservative route back to the short grass, even if it meant playing backwards. There is, for example, a small, nasty pit bunker in front of the green on the par-three tenth that the members, when they're in mixed company, call the Devil's Aperture. A ball that finds the D.A. generally comes to rest on a downhill lie. The golfer has a constricted swing because of the walls of the bunker. He's got to clear a ten-foot lip. And there is no relief backwards, since there is nothing between the bunker and the tee besides sand and scrub. Bill decided that if he hit into the D.A., he would simply declare it unplayable, tee another ball, and hit his third shot. The worst hazard at Pine Valley, he knew, was panic. He planned to avoid it.

Here is his plan for each hole, and how he executed it during the first round:

No. 1, 427 yards, par four.

This is a dogleg right, but Bill's first notation was "drive to the center." Since he normally fades his tee shots, there's a temptation to try to shorten the hole by playing close to the corner. In the past, he found that this kind of aggressive tee shot sometimes led to trouble, a big opening number, and a feeling, for the rest of the round, that he was playing from behind. So he opted for a conservative tee shot and hit one into the middle of the fairway.

Steep banks, sand, and trees flank the green. He decided to play for the middle of the green no matter where the pin was cut. His 6-iron was a little thin, leaving him on the fringe, short and right. His pitch up was weak, but he holed a fifteen-footer to save his par.

No. 2, 367 yards, par four.

This tight, straightaway par four is one of the longer 367-yard holes in the world, because the green sits atop a ridge, high above the fairway, guarded by a necklace of bunkers. Bill planned to aim his drive at a tree branch behind the left side of the green and fade it into the middle. He did. He wanted to leave his second shot on the green below the pin placement he anticipated, and he did, smacking a 7-iron to twelve feet. He made the putt.

No. 3, 181 yards, par three.

As with all but one of Pine Valley's par threes, the green here is an island in a heaving sea of calamity. Bill expected the pin to be toward the back of the green during the tournament, and his main concern was to make sure he did not go long or left trying to stick his tee shot close. He wanted to play for the center of the green and have an uphill putt. He did, and got his par.

No. 4, 444 yards, par four.

This hole features a blind tee shot, over a sandy waste and the crest of a ridge, to a fairway that veers right and drops sharply downhill. The second shot can be anything from a fairway wood to a 7-iron, depending on whether the tee shot catches the downslope. Bill planned to hit an aggressive left-to-right tee shot, carrying 235 yards to catch the downslope. That's about as far as he can hit it. His drive found trees on the right. Following the plan, he eschewed a risky shot toward the green and chipped back into the fairway, leaving himself a long iron to a back left pin.

Bill's plan called for an aggressive shot to a pin in that position, but the 3-iron he played was too much club, and the ball ran over the green. He chipped back close and made the putt for a bogey. In his second scoring column, he gave himself 3 of 5, judging that he rushed himself on the tee shot and made a mental error by overclubbing on his approach to the green.

No. 5, 232 yards, par three.

This is a titanic par three, over a chasm and a pond, sharply uphill, to a green set in the side of a slope. Anything that misses right winds up either in a pine thicket or a series of tough little bunkers that look like shark's gills cut into the side of the slope. It's a hole where a lot of balls are picked up.

Bill planned to play a driver and aim at the staircase that leads up to the sixth tee from behind the left side of the green, minimizing the chance of missing the green to the right. If he hit it straight and missed left, he would still have a chip to the pin and a chance for a par.

He hit it eighteen feet right of the pin and two-putted.

No. 6, 388 yards, par four.

Bill prefers to play this dogleg from the back of the tee area, because that eliminates any temptation to cut the dogleg off by driving down the right side and fading the ball. He planned instead to start his drive down the left side and cut it a little, making it to the corner and leaving a medium iron, slightly uphill, to a narrow green that slopes severely from right to left.

He hit his drive roughly where he wanted to and played a knock-down 6-iron that caught the green's slope and rolled toward the hole. He made a ten-foot putt for his birdie. On the card, he gave himself 3 for 3.

No. 7, 578 yards, par five.

The fairway on this long hole is essentially two grass islands, lined by woods and divided by sandy wastelands; the second, called Hell's Half Acre, begins about 300 yards from the tee and stretches for another 120 yards or so. Bill had a Plan A and a Plan B, one for a windless day and one if the wind was in his face. Into the wind, he would try to hit a straight, hard drive so he'd be able to carry the sand with his second shot. With no wind, he'd play a cut drive, which he felt was a little more reliable. Then he planned to hit whatever club would leave him a full wedge into the green.

There was no wind, but his routine broke down on the tee shot. He recalled afterwards that he had failed to make a decisive hip and shoulder turn into the ball. He pulled it left, into some trees. Again, he played conservatively on the recovery, chipping sideways back into the fairway. A lot of players, in his situation, might then have pulled a fairway wood out of the bag and banged it as far as they could. But Bill stuck with his plan, and played a 3-iron that stopped 120 yards—a full wedge— from the green. He pitched it to thirty-six feet and two-putted for a bogey. He gave himself 5 of 6.

No. 8, 319 yards, par four.

This is a tricky short hole. The second shot is invariably from a downhill lie to an undulating, narrow green that can look as though it's set on a low pedestal with beveled edges, surrounded by sand and rough. Bill had once seen an excellent player, a man who had been runner-up in the British Amateur, take a 12 at this hole, chipping futilely from one side of the green to the other. His plan reminded him that no matter where the pin was, he would ignore it and aim for the center of the green. He did, even though he was only seventy-two yards away. He took his par, and walked to the ninth tee content.

No. 9, 427 yards, par four.

The view from the tee is a trompe l'oeil, because the fairway looks narrower than it actually is in the landing area. Bill's plan was to aim for the right-center of the fairway. The green slopes from left to right, and holding it from the left side of the fairway almost requires a long draw, which he didn't want to hit. From the right-center, he was able to hit a 6-iron and keep it under the hole. He made his birdie putt from eighteen feet.

He was one under par again, but he didn't know it. Walking to the tenth tee, he focused instead on his percentage score. It was good, he decided, but it could be better on the back nine.

No. 10, 146 yards, par three.

A small green, surrounded by trouble. Bill's plan anticipated a pin cut short and right—perilously close to the Devil's Aperture bunker. He resolved to ignore it and shoot for the middle of the green, which he did, dropping an 8-iron eighteen feet past the hole and two-putting.

No. 11, 392 yards, par four.

Though this hole bends gently right, Bill planned to hit his drive as straight as he could, because trees to the left of the tee discourage a fade. From the middle of the fairway, he wanted to plant an iron just short of the pin and leave himself an uphill putt. He did, and parred the hole.

No. 12, 344 yards, par four.

This dogleg left is considered the birdie hole at Pine Valley, a hole that George Crump thought of as a pitch-and-run. But when he got there, Bill found that it had gotten harder by getting shorter. A front tee was in use, and the hole was playing about three hundred yards. That meant that a good drive would be followed by a half-wedge. Some players would have laid up with an iron to give themselves a full wedge, but Bill has great confidence in his driver, and used it. His sand wedge to the green left him thirty-six feet away, and he two-putted. As he walked off, he reminded himself not to let the failure to make birdie distract him, because three of the best and most challenging holes on the course were coming up.

No. 13, 448 yards, par four.

A long dogleg left, by way of green islands surrounded by woods and bleak, sandy wasteland. Bill planned to play this hole aggressively, because he rarely hooks the ball. The player who tries to shorten the hole by driving the left side and hooks it can easily find himself in an unplayable lie. Bill hit his drive long and straight. The second shot here, like the first, is designed to punish severely anyone who plays down the left side and misses even slightly. The safe route, for a lot of players, is to lay up short and right of the green and try to chip close for a par. But Bill had only a 6-iron into the green, from a lie that left the ball slightly above his feet. He aimed for the middle and let the lie curve the ball gently left, toward the pin. He had only twelve feet for his birdie, but missed the putt. Nevertheless, he gave himself 4 of 4.

No. 14, 184 yards, par three.

The builders of Pine Valley placed this green on an island in the middle of a marsh and set the tee on a hill high above. They filled in the water behind the green to make it a peninsula, now surrounded by trees. But it is still a hole with no margin for error and a hole that can quickly ruin a medal round. Bill's plan was to minimize the chance that the swirling winds above the hole could blow a good shot into the water. He hit a knockdown 5-iron to the green and two-putted.

No. 15, 591 yards, par five.

Bill planned to play this hole defensively. It's a long one, with a tee shot over water to a fairway that rises steadily, cants left to right, and narrows considerably as it goes. Only a handful of players have ever reached it in two. Bill had no chance to do this, so he thought carefully about where he wanted his second shot to end up. The farther the second shot goes, the steeper and more difficult the lie for the third. Bill decided to lay up a little short and leave himself between a 4-iron and a 7-iron into the green, but from a relatively flat lie. He did. On his approach, he ignored a sucker pin at the back right corner of the green. His thirty-foot birdie putt found the cup. That, he thought, was a bonus. But just such bonuses often accrue to players who stick to a conservative strategy that allows them to swing confidently.

No. 16, 433 yards, par four.

This hole tests the confidence a player has in his driver. It bends right, but the sandy waste in front of the tee is aligned so that a player who wants to favor the right side off the tee has to carry more than 200 yards of trouble before hitting the fairway.

A player can aim farther left and have to carry only 170 yards, but that leaves a much longer, downhill second shot to a green guarded on the right by the edge of the pond that's in play on Nos. 14 and 15.

Back in the airplane, Bill had felt the hole was made for his hard fade off the tee; he expected to hit anything from a 4-iron to a 6-iron into the green. But he was excited after his birdie at No. 15, and he cracked a long drive that left him only a 9-iron into the green. His ball stopped ten feet away, and he made the putt for another birdie.

No. 17, 338 yards, par four.

For the first time, Bill deviated from his game plan. He had intended to hit his driver again and cut it to follow the bend in the fairway. But the tees were up and he thought that another exceptionally long drive might run through the fairway into the woods. So he used a 3-wood instead.

This is the only kind of deviation I like to see from a game plan, a deviation in a conservative direction. A golfer who changes to a more aggressive strategy has usually got some doubts in his mind when he gets ready to swing.

Bill hit his 3-wood dead center, but it settled in a divot. Again, he changed his plan slightly. He had intended to hit a short iron to the front of the green, keeping the ball below the hole. But to make certain he got out of the divot, he hit a 9-iron and landed fifteen feet past the pin. He two-putted.

No. 18, 428 yards, par four.

The last tee box, high over the fairway, offers a view that can be either intoxicating or intimidating, depending on how a round has gone. The fairway is framed by woods, sand, and shrubs. In the distance, the green is visible atop a mesa, beyond a road, a stream, and a wreath of bunkers. There's a temptation to just belt away off the tee, but Bill's plan reminded him to hit more thoughtfully than that. He wanted to start the ball toward a yellow hazard stake in the distance and cut it into the middle of the fairway, well short of some bunkers that guard the right side. Then he would have a medium iron over the course's last sandy waste, the road, the stream, and the greenside bunkers to a green that slopes sharply, left to right and front to back. He hit the fairway with his drive and left a 6-iron twenty-five feet under the pin.

As Bill reached the green, a distraction ambushed him. Someone near the first tee called out that another competitor had shot 69. Bill started adding up his score. He realized that if he made his putt, he would have 66. Thinking about that, instead of his putting routine, he left his birdie putt well short. He managed to pull himself back into the present and finish with a 67.

It was easily the lowest competitive round he had shot at Pine Valley. But it was not a perfect ball-striking round; he'd been in the woods twice. He'd made some excellent putts, but holed only one from more than twenty feet. It was simply a solid round in which a good plan had helped him stay with his routine, avoid panic, and let the strengths of his game carry him.

He would go on to follow up that round with a 69 and a 73 and win the tournament by seven strokes. In the process, he established new competitive course records for thirty-six and fifty-four holes.

The tournament would be, he would later reflect, one of the warmest memories of his life. It would be a weekend when all the effort he had put into golf—improving his swing and his mind—came together and bore fruit. It would be a weekend when he proved to himself that his balanced commitment to family, work, and sport was compatible with excellence. It would be a weekend that told him the best things in his life were still ahead of him.

But none of those things were on his mind as he stepped off the eighteenth green that morning. An assistant pro, Jason Lamp, asked him what he had shot.

"Eighty-three percent," Bill said.

He had, he calculated, stuck with his mental routine and his game plan on 56 of 67 shots. It took him a moment to realize that Lamp wanted to know how many strokes he'd taken.

No. 11

How Billy Mayfair Rebuilt His Confidence

BILLY MAYFAIR, WHO WON MORE THAN $1.5 MILLION ON THE PGA Tour in 1995, keeps a notebook in which he jots down ideas that emerge in the conversations we have over the course of a season. Here is what he wrote after our first session of 1995, a few hours before the start of the Phoenix Open:

"Enjoy what you're doing. Have fun."

This may seem like belaboring the obvious. Golf is a game. It's supposed to be fun. Any little boy knows that.

In fact, Billy Mayfair knew it when he was a little boy. But two weeks into the 1995 season, he'd almost forgotten it.

The previous season had not been a good one for Billy. He fell from 30th on the money list in 1993 to 113th. After January, he did not have a top-ten finish. He missed a lot of cuts.

In his first two events of 1995, at Hawaii and Tucson, he shot an 80 and a 79 and missed the cut both times. By the time we got together in the study of his new home in Scottsdale, Billy was in serious distress.

"I feel like I'm holding on by a thread, Doc," he said to me as we sat down. "I'm afraid I'm going to embarrass myself out there today."

Once he had said that, Billy's doubts and fears spilled out in a torrent. He was afraid he would never play well again. Or if he did play well for a few rounds, and got in contention, he was afraid he would blow his lead. He had a new bride, a new home, and he was afraid he was going to play his way off the tour.

He was particularly anxious about playing in Phoenix, where he grew up. Once, when he'd been the hot young phenom out of Arizona State, he'd felt as if he owned Phoenix. Now he felt that it had become Phil Mickelson's town.

All of this was said, of course, in a room that belied his words, a room filled with trophies he had won playing golf. Billy was a good player. I knew that. The problem was, he didn't know it anymore.

We would not, I realized, be leaving for the golf course immediately. We had some work to do right there before Billy could play tournament golf. He had to find his way again.

For Billy, the way started in the backyard of his parents' home when he was a toddler. He remembers his father putting a sawed-off club in his hands and teaching him to chip plastic balls around the backyard.

As a very young boy, he tried a variety of sports. But swimming competition paid off only in ribbons. Golfers won trophies, and Billy liked trophies. He was hooked.

The way led next to a great old municipal course in Phoenix called Papago Park. Built in the desert on the western edge of the city under some striking red rock cliffs, Papago was a tough, straightforward course with a driving range, and, most important, a big, rolling, crowned practice green.

The practice green became Billy Mayfair's playground. Every day after school, his mother would pick him up and drive him to Papago Park. He'd stay there until dark. Then it was back home, dinner, homework, and into bed.

Mondays through Fridays, Billy chipped and putted. That's all he did. From the practice green at Papago, he could look down at the practice tee and see boys his age whaling away with drivers. Look toward the south, and he could see the first tee, and there might be boys starting actual rounds of golf. It didn't matter.

Mondays through Fridays, Billy Mayfair was there to chip and putt. It was partly because the Mayfairs didn't have a lot of money to spend on greens fees and range balls. But it was mostly because Billy knew that chipping and putting would make him a better golfer.

There was one other kid at Papago Park who did the same things Billy did. That was Heather Farr, who grew up to be a star on the LPGA Tour before her life was tragically cut short by breast cancer.

It was no coincidence that the two kids who spent all their time on the practice green were the ones who went on to professional success. Skill with the wedges and the putter is what separates money winners from touring pros.

On weekends, Billy had a different routine. On weekends, the course's pro, Arch Wadkins, would let Billy pick up balls along the range and hit them for free. That was where he learned his long game.

And from a very young age, Billy competed. The Mayfairs scraped together money for travel and tournaments every summer and school vacation. Once, when he was a teenager, Billy spent Christmas Eve and Christmas alone in a Miami hotel room, because there was only enough money to send one member of the family to Florida for the Orange Bowl tournament.

He didn't mind that much. Billy was a shy, quiet, towheaded

kid, never a social butterfly. He knew that tournament golf was what he wanted to do, and he was willing to do whatever it took to play.

He went to Arizona State, and there he started to win national championships. In 1986, he won the U.S. Public Links Championship and in 1987, the U.S. Amateur. He was the college player of the year. Then he turned pro.

Billy knew what his amateur credentials meant as a pro. The PGA Tour players who had graduated from Arizona State had apprised him of that. "Here's a quarter," one of them had told him. "Go call someone who cares what you did as an amateur."

But he did well in the qualifying school and hung on to his card after his rookie year, 1989.

When I first noticed him, Billy was much like the unobtrusive kid who used to hang around Papago Park, chipping and putting. He wasn't one of the outgoing players on the tour practice tee. He kept to himself, said very little, and practiced a lot. You didn't see him out at night.

One of the big lessons he learned in his first year was taught, inadvertently, by Tom Kite. Tom won at Bay Hill that year. Billy finished back in the pack. Billy drove to the next tournament venue, the TPC at Sawgrass, and went out to the course Monday morning.

There was Kite, on the practice tee, less than eighteen hours removed from his win at Bay Hill, working hard on his game.

That, Billy decided, was someone to emulate.

The next year, 1990, his hard work started to pay off. He won nearly $700,000, more money than any second-year player in PGA history. He was a fixture on the tour for the next few years, winning for the first time in Milwaukee in 1993.

But in 1994, it started to go sour. The problem was that Billy tried to perfect his golf swing.

There is no bigger canard in golf than the old saw that practice makes perfect. It doesn't. Golf is a game played by human beings, and no matter how much they practice, they will remain imperfect. They will make mistakes.

Athletes who become self-critical perfectionists are flirting with trouble.

When their skills, inevitably, fail to meet their expectations, they can get tense and frustrated. They can begin to doubt their abilities. The more they practice, the worse they perform.

That was what happened to Billy in 1994. Moreover, in his determination to perfect his golf swing, he started to neglect his short-game practice. He'd stay at the range and beat balls until he was exhausted. In the little time he had left, he might hit a few putts, but that was it. He got away from the regimen of chipping and pitching that had brought him success as a boy.

ALL OF THAT, of course, was not something that could be remedied in the few hours we had before Billy's Phoenix Open tee time. I appreciated the candor and courage Billy displayed in confiding his fears to me. A lot of players would have been too proud to do it. I knew that as long as he recognized his problems, he had a good chance to solve them.

But at that particular moment, he didn't need a long-term program. He needed something to latch on to, a thought that could get him through the day and the week. He needed a ray of hope.

That's when I suggested that he resolve to enjoy himself.

Golf, after all, was a game he had always loved. He'd loved it when he was a boy, spending all those hours on the practice green at Papago Park. He'd loved it enough to want desperately to make it his career.

He could rediscover the pleasures of the game—the texture

and smell of freshly clipped grass on a sunlit day, the click that the ball makes when it's struck solidly, the deliciously long seconds watching a well-struck drive soaring against the sky, or a good putt rolling toward the hole. He could enjoy the camaraderie of competition and the friends he'd made on the tour.

That, in fact, is what I'd recommend to any player who is suffering a crisis of confidence. The first step ought to be the rediscovery of the joys of the game.

A golfer who actively appreciates the essential pleasures of the game is insulated from the ups and downs of competition. If he scores badly, it's not so terrible. If he scores well, that's great. But he doesn't need to score well to enjoy himself.

Billy went out and enjoyed himself in the Phoenix Open. And, not coincidentally, he started to play better. He played so well, in fact, that he almost won. He tied with Vijay Singh and lost in a playoff.

When he called me that Sunday night, though, he didn't sound like a loser. He was thrilled. He'd won enough money to assure himself of keeping his card. More important, he'd proven to himself that he could still play.

I wish I could take credit for that, but the truth is that even a player who thinks his confidence is totally shattered, or his swing is totally fouled up, can in reality be just a half inch away from his old self. It can be a literal half inch, if we're talking about the swing plane. Or it might be a figurative half inch, if we're talking about confidence. Billy really didn't have as far to come back as he thought he did.

And I wish I could take credit for the next step that he took to restore his game, but again, I can't. Billy went out to San Diego two weeks after the Phoenix Open. He was paired the first two days with Peter Jacobsen, who'd just won the AT&T at Pebble Beach.

"You haven't done that well in five years," Billy asked Peter. "What happened?"

Nothing magical, Jacobsen replied. He had just dedicated himself to his short game over the winter months.

I, of course, had often mentioned the short game to Billy. He'd known about it since his youth. But there's nothing like hearing it from a player who's just won. Billy rededicated himself to his short-game practice regimen. Within a couple of months, he started to feel that his short game was back.

And the short game is usually great medicine for an ailing golfer. **The best remedies for a golfing slump, I've found, are putting things back in perspective, dwelling on the positive, looking for something good to happen—and rededication to the short game.**

THE IMPROVEMENT WAS immediate and noticeable. Billy found that on days when his long game was not perfect, good chipping and pitching helped him score decently. On days when his long game was on, it helped him go low. He finds that a lot of the par fives on the tour are just beyond his reach in two shots. That leaves him with a lot of twenty- or thirty-yard pitches. He started to get a lot more of them close enough to make birdies.

He rediscovered that a good short game helped take the pressure off his long game and his putter. He found that when he missed a green, he would calmly hand the club back to his caddie and walk toward the hole thinking that he might chip his third shot into the hole, and that he could at least make par.

He stopped thinking, *Oh gosh, here comes another bogey.*

He changed his practice philosophy. If his swing didn't feel exactly right, he stopped fighting it, figuring that it would be better to let it rest overnight than to keep on beating balls and ingraining his mistakes. He spent the extra time practicing his chips, putts, and pitches. He decided that true discipline, at times, meant that he stop hitting balls and get some rest rather than keep practicing until he was exhausted.

In July, he won the Western Open, his first victory in almost two years. He had several more top tens and a couple of near misses.

He had a good chance to win the World Series of Golf in September. After three rounds, he was in fourth place, three behind Vijay Singh and one behind Jose Maria Olazabal and Jim Gallagher, Jr.

He scorched the front nine with a 32, and he opened a three-stroke lead on the field by the time he reached the tee at No. 15.

And there, he suddenly started thinking that he was going to lose the golf tournament. He had a premonitory vision of himself sitting in front of his locker, head down, sad and disgusted.

He bogeyed the next three holes. He missed a six-foot par putt on No. 15. His sand wedge approach to No. 16 was perhaps too aggressive, and he bounced off the hard surface into the rough. He was over the green on No. 17. He was tied for the lead with Greg Norman and Nick Price, who were coming on strong.

Billy steadied himself and played No. 18 beautifully, hitting his approach to eight feet. His birdie putt, which would have won the tournament, was well struck. It veered right at the last instant and lipped out.

On the first playoff hole, Norman chipped in from sixty-six feet away for a birdie that neither Billy nor Nick could match. Ironically, it was someone else's short game that beat Billy.

"I had the golf tournament in my hand," Billy told the press afterwards. "And I lost it."

• • •

THE LOSS WAS still fresh in Billy's mind when he came to the Tour Championship at Southern Hills Country Club in Tulsa in the last week of October.

Conditions were tough in Oklahoma that week. It was cold. The wind, as Rodgers and Hammerstein would have put it, came sweeping down the plain. The greens were dry and hard to hold. It was not the same course that Nick Price had played in 11 under par in the 1994 PGA. Even par was going to be a very good score.

Billy was ready. He had spent the previous week thinking about Southern Hills and thinking about playing it in cold, windy weather. When he got to the course and saw the flags stiffly snapping in the gale, he thought to himself, *Yeah! This is what I prepared for.*

I talked to Billy by telephone just before the tournament started. We talked about the usual pretournament ideas: staying in the present, staying committed to routine, being patient. We talked about the thoughts he had to change if he wanted a better outcome than he'd had at the World Series. We talked about being ready to win.

Billy opened up with a 68 and stayed near or in the lead for the next two days. On Saturday, he shot a 69, and the second-round leader, Brad Bryant, struggled to a 73. Suddenly, Billy was the fifty-four-hole leader, and by the same three-stroke margin he had lost at the World Series.

We talked each night during the tournament, and I emphasized how a tough golf course like Southern Hills, especially in unfavorable conditions, demands patience. There were going to be bogeys. Players had to resist the urge to get too bold in an effort to make up for them.

Billy was nervous about his three-stroke lead. He had never

had that kind of margin after fifty-four holes. He felt it put more pressure on him and reduced the pressure on everyone else.

"Is there," I asked, "anyone in the field who wouldn't trade places with you? Anyone you'd trade places with?"

"No," Billy said.

"Well, then," I said, "let's be glad you have that three-stroke lead. And let's be totally prepared to win tomorrow."

It wasn't easy for him to do that. A lot of players who think perfectly well in run-of-the-mill tournaments have the misimpression that it takes something different to win a big event—a major championship, a World Series, a Tour Championship. It doesn't. The players who win big events are usually players who are comfortable enough to think exactly as they do in lesser events, to stay with their routines and stay in the present.

Billy had to literally talk himself into being that way. When he woke up Sunday morning, he told himself, "This is your golf tournament. You're going to win this golf tournament."

He stepped to the window and looked at the flags outside the hotel. The wind, he estimated, was already blowing at 30 miles per hour.

"No matter how the wind's blowing, you're going to win this golf tournament," he told himself.

When he stepped onto the first tee, and when he stepped up to virtually every shot that day, it was the same thing. "You're going to win," he told himself.

Normally, this kind of thought might not be helpful. It's oriented toward results, toward the future. But in Billy's case, I would make an exception. He wanted to avoid a repetition of the World Series. He didn't want to think about losing. Telling himself he would win was a way of preempting such thoughts. Then he took care to return to the present and get into his routine.

The first tee at Southern Hills, like the first tee at Riviera, sits high above the valley, where the bulk of the course is. The wind had blown Billy's drives into the rough in each of the first three rounds. But on Sunday, it had shifted behind him, and he needed only a 3-wood. He hit it down the middle, 110 yards from the green.

The ball came to rest in a divot. He hit a wedge, but he couldn't spin it, and it rolled to the back edge of the green. "One shot at a time. Stay in your routine," he told himself.

He chipped to about six feet, made the putt for par, and he was on his way.

At No. 2, with the wind howling from left to right, he drove the ball into trees on the right side of the hole. He felt surprisingly unruffled. He thought he had an opening to the green and he went for it. His ball hit a tree and bounded out into the fairway. Still unperturbed, he hit a sand wedge to ten feet and made that putt.

It's amazing how patient and composed you can be if you believe you're going to win. When a golfer is in the right state of mind, missed shots mean little to him.

Billy told me later that if he hadn't prepared his mind to win, he probably would have stepped up to those first two putts worried about making bogey, worried about letting his lead slip away. Instead, he addressed them thinking only of making them, of finding a way to score well.

He kept making pars as the rest of the field slipped back. At No. 15, he hit a good drive, but it kicked off a mound and into a tough fairway bunker. He had two choices. He could hit a sand wedge and make sure he got out into the fairway. Or he could try to reach the green with a 4-iron. The latter was a risky shot. If he got the ball to the green, but left it a little right, he could face an impossible chip downhill and be looking at the possibility of a double-bogey.

How Billy Mayfair Rebuilt His Confidence • 149

For the first time that day, he decided he needed to know where he stood. He asked his caddie.

"You're five strokes up," the caddie replied.

Billy put the 4-iron back in the bag and hit the sand wedge. He made bogey, and another bogey at seventeen.

Still, he had a comfortable lead on the eighteenth tee. He picked out a tower on the horizon, aimed at it, and went through his routine. Then he let the shot go. It was down the middle. He had 185 yards left, over a bunker, and he picked out a pillar in the clubhouse as a target. He swung and watched the ball clear the bunker. The celebratory roar from the crowd told him all he needed to know. The ball was on and close.

He had, indeed, won the golf tournament.

AFTERWARDS, BILLY PHONED and told me about something he'd seen on television in Phoenix. Charles Barkley of the Phoenix Suns, a good friend of Billy's, had been on. The interviewer asked Barkley what he thought about his friend Billy Mayfair's "dream season."

"I wouldn't call it a dream season," Barkley said. "That makes it sound like he won't have another one."

That answer pleased Billy. In fact, in the season of his dreams, he wins all four majors. So he won't be content with what he achieved in 1995. He has a lot left that he wants to accomplish.

He's certainly in a stronger position to try to achieve those dreams than he was at the beginning of 1995. He has been through the fire.

All great athletes, I think, have had to go through a period of fire, a period of despondency and near despair. The fire is like the smelting process that burns ore and turns it into precious metal. Without the fire, the process cannot happen.

An athlete who has gone through what Billy did and come out the other side is stronger. He knows that come what may, he is tough enough to bounce back.

And that, like a good short game, is an enormous asset.

No. 12

How Dicky Pride Crossed the Fine Line

GOLF IS A GAME OF SMALL GRADATIONS. THE DIFFERENCE BETWEEN A good drive and a drive out of bounds can be a few millimeters of change in the swing plane. The difference between making a living on the tour and looking for another line of work can be as small as a stroke a round.

So it is with the mental game. Players who win may think only slightly differently from those who don't. They trust their swings absolutely; others occasionally entertain a few little doubts. They marshal the right thoughts and attitudes on nearly every shot; others admit distractions several times a round. Those subtle differences can have an enormous impact on results. A good mind can be the difference between struggling in golf's minor leagues and winning on the PGA Tour.

In fact, it frequently is the difference. If you were to go to Florida sometime and happen upon one of the golf courses where the Tommy Armour mini-tour events are held, you might be hard-pressed to tell what level of golf you were watching. The players on the Tommy Armour Tour nearly all have impressive games and swings. They hit the ball a long way. They have all the shots. They sink a lot of putts. The only quick way to distinguish them from PGA Tour players would be the accoutrements of their game: They ride in carts, because they can't afford caddies, and they probably haven't sold advertising space on their shirt sleeves.

The difference between them and PGA Tour players is largely mental. Tour players have learned to think in ways that enable them to win. Mini-tour players by and large haven't. Good thinking can make a difference of a stroke or two a round, and that is all that separates minor leaguers from major leaguers in golf. It's a fine line.

Dicky Pride can testify to that.

I first saw Dicky years ago at the North River Yacht Club course in Alabama, where *Golf Digest* held some schools. He was always out on the practice range, hitting balls. He wasn't the sort of young golfer who would impress casual watchers as someone with great potential. Most people are impressed by great length on the practice tee, and Dicky didn't have that. He's of average size, and his good drives generally went 250 or 260 yards, with a little fade. He looked like the kind of kid who would have to scramble to make a good college golf team.

In fact, that's what he was. Dicky grew up in Tuscaloosa, where his father was in the real estate business. Dick Pride was a good amateur golfer and for a few years the coach at the University of Alabama. He taught Dicky the fundamentals.

Dicky was a fine basketball player in high school and a good golfer, but not good enough to get scholarship offers from any major colleges. He enrolled at Alabama, in his hometown. For a year or so, he never touched a club.

In the summer between his first and second years in college, Dicky got the bug again and started playing. He tried out for the golf team that autumn as a walk-on. He made it. He averaged 78 that season and never made the traveling squad.

But he kept plugging away. He spent a summer working at the Elk River Club in the North Carolina mountains, where he met his swing teacher, Todd Anderson. He read books by Tom Kite and Bob Toski. He took one of the critical steps a golfer who wants to get good has to take: He realized he had to improve his short game, and he started spending more time on chipping and putting than he did on his full swing.

He tried out for the golf team again and made it. But the first time the coach held qualifying for the traveling squad, Dicky shot 87. He was still terribly inconsistent, but he kept at it. The next semester he averaged about 75 in competition. He got his scholarship.

Dicky never thought of playing professional golf until his last year at Alabama. He started to display a talent for playing well on tough courses. He qualified for the U.S. Amateur in 1991. He got to the semifinals—a remarkable performance for someone who had been a questionable choice to make the Alabama golf team a year earlier. He might have gotten to the finals, except that on the seventeenth hole, he let his thinking escape from the present.

He was one up. He hit his drive into the fairway and his opponent drove into the rough. Like a temptation from the devil, a distracting thought entered his mind: *Wow! Win this hole and you go to the Masters.* (The finalists at the U.S. Amateur automatically get invitations.) Just as Davis Love III stopped playing well when he started thinking about the Masters, Dicky started making mental mistakes. He pushed his 7-iron lay-up shot to the right and into a bunker. His next shot flew the green. He made a double-bogey and lost the match in a playoff.

Dicky went back to school and played well in his senior year, though not well enough to be an All-American. No one thought of him in the same class as Phil Mickelson or David Duval, who were the top collegians at the time. Except Dicky. He had started to believe he could do something in golf.

In 1992, he qualified for the U.S. Open. He went to Pebble Beach and shot 83 and 88. But that experience was enough to persuade him that he could compete on the highest level. Dicky had a good mind.

He turned pro later that year, went to Florida, and joined the Tommy Armour Tour. After he won his first event down there, he came north to Charlottesville to see me.

Not many people would have bet much money on Dicky's chances of making it to the PGA Tour at that stage. But I didn't care what his credentials were. First of all, it's not my job to care. It's my job to help people realize their potential, and to do that, I have to treat each of them as if they have unlimited potential. As I told Dicky:

It's not very important where you've been. Life is about where you're going.

And I could see that Dicky had some talent. The ground was covered with snow, and it happened that Brad Faxon was visiting. I took them down to the University, to the gym where I have my office. We did some putting on an indoor course. Brad had to drain two long putts on the last two holes to beat Dicky. And Brad was one of the top putters on the tour.

More important, I could tell from the stories Dicky told me that he had a good attitude about himself. Given his scant accomplishments as an amateur, he had to have a good attitude just to think he had a chance to make it on the tour.

Dicky already understood some of the fundamentals of the mental game. He already had a sound routine. He didn't burden himself with thoughts about swing mechanics while he was on the course. He thought about where he wanted the ball to go.

We talked about a long-range philosophy that could carry him from the mini-tours to the big tour. Dicky is an intense, wired young man. He needed to understand that golf is a game that rewards steady, continuous effort far more than short bursts of passion. I suggested a goal for him: to improve a little every day. If he could do that, the rest would take care of itself.

I told him that success wasn't a matter of how much he knew about the mental game. Lots of people know the principles. It's a question of who applies those principles consistently and who applies them at the right moment. Psychiatrists and physicians, for instance, get great educations about the ailments, mental and physical, that afflict human beings. They understand how to stay healthy. Yet their suicide rates are among the highest in the country. Knowledge isn't much good unless you use it.

Of course, we talked a lot about the challenge he would face that fall in the tour's qualifying school. Every year, nearly a thousand very good young golfers pay their entry fees and embark on the q-school process. After a round of regional qualifying tournaments, the best of them spend six tough days in the final stage. At the end, the top forty and ties get cards that entitle them to play the tour.

I told him it would actually be a little easier to do well in the qualifying school than it was on the Tommy Armour Tour. That's because a lot of players think they can do well on the Tommy Armour Tour. Not so many really believe they can do well at the qualifying school.

That fall, Dicky had his mind in the right place during the first stage of the school. He called me up one night and recounted how he'd almost gotten into a fistfight with someone who wanted to talk to him after the third round about what he would have to shoot to make the finals.

"You're in great shape. All you need to shoot tomorrow is—" the man said.

"I don't want to know," Dicky said. He was determined not to start playing with one eye on the scoreboard.

"But, Dicky, all you have to do is—"

"I don't want to know," Dicky interrupted him again.

After a few more, increasingly louder, exchanges, the man finally got the message. Dicky didn't want to know.

He played excellent golf in the final stage, opening with a 70 and following that with 71, a 64, a 72, and a 68. He faltered a bit in the final round, three-putting several holes in a row. But Tim Simpson, who was playing with him, told me he was impressed by how well Dicky buckled down, stuck with his routine, and kept his composure. He birdied the sixteenth hole and came in with a 77, for an overall total of nine under par. He got his card. He was no one's All-American, but he had made it to the tour ahead of a lot of players who were All-Americans.

LIFE ON THE tour was a challenge of a different order. It was not so much a question of nerves as of intimidation. In Dicky's first tournament, in Hawaii, he felt as if he had held his breath through the first nine holes, waiting, perhaps, to wake up. He missed the cut in his first six events.

He made a cut and a three thousand dollar check at Bay Hill, then missed a couple more cuts. He took a few days off to go to the beach with his fiancée, Kim Shearer. He told her how depressed he was. He told her how hard he'd been practicing and how little it seemed to help. He told her he didn't think he had the talent to play on the tour. He was nearly in tears.

Kim did a wise thing. She told him to stop whining and start acting like the guy she'd met when he was playing the Tommy Armour Tour. Back then, Dicky had been cocky. He needed to get cocky again, she said, and start playing the way he was capable of playing. Dicky went to Houston and made another cut and another check. His confidence was slowly coming back.

I saw Dicky shortly after that at Byron Nelson's tournament. We talked for a while about his putting. I told him he had to stop thinking so much about whether the ball was going into the hole and stop caring whether he struck the ball perfectly and gave it the classic overspin roll as he sent it on its way. He needed to concentrate on getting the line and the speed and letting the results take care of themselves.

Dicky finished in the top twenty at the Byron Nelson, which was shortened by rain. He was slowly getting more comfortable, but he was still on a roller coaster. He was up one week and down the next. The New England Classic was a down week. He missed the cut again. His wrist was sore. He missed his plane out of Boston on Friday night and didn't get into Memphis until Saturday.

Dicky's exempt status was low enough that he wasn't certain he'd get into the field at Memphis. On Saturday, he didn't try to play a practice round. He just walked the course, making notes for his game plan. He carried a putter and a few balls, and he made certain to hole at least five short putts on every green. That day, he must have watched 150 of his putts roll into the cup.

He kept practicing, but he didn't learn for certain that he would be in the field until Lee Janzen dropped out on Tuesday. I think that helped him. It kept his thoughts focused on his desire to play, not on whether he could make the cut. His attitude was, "I'm hitting the ball well. I just need a chance to show it."

In fact, there was a concatenation of good influences on his mind: the putts he made on the first day he walked the course; the wait to see whether he could play; and even the playing partner he drew for the first two rounds, Howard Twitty. Howard is tall and lanky, with a slow, ambling stride. Dicky let that slow, steady walk set a calm, deliberate mood for him that lasted nearly all week.

He opened with a 66, despite bogeying the last two holes. He kept playing well, though not without some misadventures. He snap-hooked the ball into the water on the eighteenth hole on Saturday, but he was still tied for the fifty-four-hole lead.

Dicky was a self-described nervous wreck on Saturday night. He called me from his hotel room.

"Doc, the eighteenth hole is driving me crazy," he said. "I've hit it in the water there twice. I can't get myself to stop thinking about it."

There was only one thing he could do, and that was to confront his fear of the eighteenth. I told him to visualize the tee shot he wanted. He needed to see the club he would use, the swing he would make, the flight of the ball, the spot where it landed. He needed to hear, in his mind, the hush before he let the shot go and the reaction of the crowd as the ball took off. He needed to smell the grass and feel the sweat trickling down his neck.

That helped a little bit. He went to bed, but he felt hot, so he got up and turned the air conditioning on. Then he remembered he can't sleep with air conditioning on. He couldn't get back to sleep. At breakfast time, he could barely eat. Then he had an unanticipated delay before teeing off, and by the time he addressed the ball for the first time, he felt as if he were inhaling a strange gas—certainly not oxygen.

Dicky pushed a weak tee shot right of the bunkers on the right side of the fairway. Then he hit a 5-iron that jumped long, winding up on a downslope behind the green. He was looking at a chip that he would normally have felt lucky to stop within ten feet of the hole. As he addressed the ball, he didn't feel right. He considered, for a second, backing off. Then he caught his attention and forced it back to the business at hand, imagining the target and the ball going in. He swung fearlessly and flopped the ball onto the green. It trickled in.

There's no question that holing out like that on the first green can ignite a round. It's not just being lucky. Holing a shot like that can inject confidence into a nervous player's mind. It can help him to play his best golf the rest of the way.

Dicky was still struggling a bit, driving into the rough and laying up in the wrong spots. But he managed to hold his round together through the turn.

On No. 10, he hit a good drive into the fairway and had a 6-iron left. For the first time that day, his mind slipped out of the present. He thought about everything that would come to him if he won, beginning with the trip to the Masters. It was the same distraction that had beguiled him a few years earlier at the U.S. Amateur, and his mistake had similar consequences. He hit a poor shot over the green into a nearly impossible position.

Dicky lost his composure.

"I'm not going to let myself do it again!" he yelled at his caddie. "I did it to myself once and I thought myself out of the Masters, and I'm not going to do it again!"

His caddie, of course, had no idea what Dicky was yelling about.

He hit a lob wedge that only reached the fringe of the green. Then he made the putt. As with his chip-in on the first hole, the putt from the fringe helped him recover his focus. It did not waver the rest of the way.

He birdied eleven and lipped out putts on thirteen, fourteen, and fifteen. He told himself that the near misses only showed that he was putting well. He birdied No. 16 and tied for the lead again. On No. 17, he hit a 3-iron into the green, thinking that he would cut it and work it in toward the flag from the left side. The ball went dead straight. He caught a bad break in the rough. His ball was on an exposed root. He couldn't get his chip closer than thirty feet, and he made bogey.

That's all right, he told himself. He had made a bogey, but not a mental error. His pre-shot routine was still exactly what it should be.

So he came to the eighteenth tee needing a birdie. The tees were up, the fairways were hard, and the hole is a dogleg left. A long drive, from the forward tee position, could go through the dogleg. Dicky pulled out his 3-wood. He called to mind all the positive images he had conjured up the night before, went through his routine, and hit a perfect tee shot, into the center of the fairway, 167 yards from the hole.

He was excited, and he realized it. So he took a bit less club than he might otherwise have done, a 7-iron, and hit it twenty feet from the hole.

Jay Haas was Dicky's playing partner. He had fallen out of contention, but did something elegant on that last hole.

"Enjoy this," he said to Dicky as they stood on the green. "This is what you play for."

It was exactly what a rookie would want to hear from a veteran at that moment.

Dicky lined up his putt, went through his routine, and stroked it. For an instant he thought he had left it short. But it struggled up to the hole and fell in. For about ten seconds, he screamed his jubilation at the top of his lungs, letting out the accumulated tension of the final round. No one could hear him over the roar of the crowd.

He had shot 67 for a 17-under-par total of 267. He was in a playoff with Hal Sutton and Gene Sauers.

Dicky played the playoff hole, No. 18, exactly as he had a few minutes before—3-wood, 7-iron to twenty feet. Sutton and Sauers also reached the green in regulation. Sauers missed his putt, leaving it an inch or so short.

As he prepared to hit, Dicky felt awash in confidence. He knew his target should be the right lip. He knew if he got the ball to the hole on that line, it would go in. He thought, he later told me, about something I'd once said: that golfers under intense pressure tend to hit woods and irons long and leave putts and chips short. He thought about getting freer and cockier. He told himself, "nothing but net." And he stroked a firm, bold putt that hit the center of the hole, popped against the back of the cup, and fell in.

Sutton missed his birdie putt, and Dicky had gone from being a nonentity to a winner on tour.

He received a photograph in the mail shortly afterwards. It was a picture of the scoreboard at a 1992 amateur event called the Cardinal Invitational. It showed Dicky Pride in forty-fourth place with scores of 72, 79, and 73.

"What a difference a couple of years make," the tournament organizers wrote.

I thought they should have written, "What a difference the right state of mind makes."

BUT AS QUICKLY as Dicky got himself into the right state of mind, he got out of it. He recorded no more top-ten finishes in 1994, and he did not win in 1995. Were it not for the two-year exemption he got for winning at Memphis, he would have had to go back to qualifying school.

After winning, Dicky's expectations of himself were higher. He wanted so badly to do it again that he tried perhaps too hard.

When he hit a shot that didn't measure up, he tended to become self-critical and impatient. This happens quite often after a player wins a first tournament or a first major. Dicky had to learn to leave his new expectations behind when he stepped onto the course.

And there were changes in his life that affected his game. He bought his first home and his first car. His success led to invitations for outings and other distractions that he'd never had to deal with before.

We've talked recently about ways that Dicky can manage his schedule to enhance the chances that he will regain that optimal mental state he attained in Memphis. He's scheduled checkup visits with Todd Anderson every four to five weeks, primarily to make certain his setup and posture are correct. That way, he shouldn't find himself trying to compete when he's got doubts about his mechanics. We're going to see each other every month or so and talk periodically on the phone to make sure his mental game is where it should be.

He's scheduled periodic rest breaks. We've tried to make certain that his wife and his career are his top priorities. The time he has for socializing with his friends has to be subordinated to those priorities.

And we've talked about being consistent about practice time. He has to work out a schedule that gives him time around a practice green every day, or his short game won't be where it has to be.

If he doesn't feel ready to play great golf, he's going to stay at home until he does. He won't show up just because there's a tournament.

We want to make certain that when he competes, he's ready to trust equally in all parts of his game. Last year, it seemed that every week there'd be some part of his game he wouldn't trust

—his driver, his wedges, or some aspect of his putting. That has to end.

But even if he does all those things, he will not automatically recapture the mental edge he had in Memphis.

The hard fact is that the optimal state of mind isn't an object that a golfer can acquire, own, put on a shelf, and take down for use whenever it's required.

Rather, it's a condition that can be fragile, ephemeral, and maddeningly elusive. It emerges from the confluence of a lot of factors, some very subtle. And the factors vary from golfer to golfer. The best a golfer can do is ascertain as best he can the factors that work for him and strive to make certain they are present every time he competes.

The optimal state of mind is something a player must work on patiently, every day.

No. 13

How David Frost Learned to Close

ONE OF THE HIGHEST COMPLIMENTS A PROFESSIONAL GOLFER CAN receive is to be known by his peers as a closer. A closer is someone who puts tournaments away, who wins when he gets into position to win.

My friend David Frost is a closer.

Frosty is by no means one of the longer hitters on the PGA Tour. The Nike Tour or the NCAA Tournament, for that matter, are full of players who can outdrive him. But he is an excellent putter, an accurate iron player, and a deft wedge player. Those are skills that assure him of making the cut in nearly all the tournaments he enters. When he's putting particularly well, he's a threat to win.

And nowadays, when he can win, he does. He won at New Orleans in 1990 by holing a bunker shot on the eighteenth hole to edge Greg Norman. He won the World Series of Golf in 1989 in a playoff against Ben Crenshaw. He's won other tournaments by building an early lead and then steadily pulling away.

But it wasn't always this way for Frosty. In his early years on the tour, he finished second eight times before he finally won. He lost playoffs. He blew putts. He got the shakes.

Frosty had to learn to close, to handle pressure. So do most golfers.

HIS GOLF CAREER began at the age of fourteen in his native South Africa, where his father owned a vineyard near Cape Town. Frosty and his brother started caddying for their father on weekend afternoons at the Stellenbosch Golf Club. When the old man was done, he'd head for the grill with his friends. Frosty and his brother would take his clubs and play until darkness fell.

Frosty liked the game and had an evident talent, particularly for putting. He took the first forty dollars he earned as a caddie and bought a mixed bag of used clubs: an old Bullseye putter, some irons, and a ladies' 1½ wood.

He took no lessons, apart from a few clinics conducted by the South African Golf Foundation, where kids learned the rudiments of a proper stance and grip.

He just played and practiced a lot, working particularly on his short game. At school, he didn't always have time or opportunity to get to a course to practice. So he'd take some balls, a 7-iron, and an old tire, set the tire upright in some grass, and practice chipping through it. At home, his father brought a truckload of beach sand up to the farm and made a practice bunker out of it.

He played in junior tournaments during school vacations. But there was very little parental pressure to compete. Frosty feels, and I agree, that this helped him. Parents who prod a child to compete and win before he's ready can instill in the child a dread of close competition and pressure situations that carries over into adult life.

Instead, Frosty's father gave him a natural incentive. If he broke 80, his father would buy him a new set of clubs. By the time he was sixteen, Frosty was coming close.

One day, he and his father and the Stellenbosch pro played a round. After sixteen holes, Frosty needed only two pars to shoot 78.

He started thinking of the score. His swing got tense. He bogeyed the seventeenth and double-bogeyed the eighteenth.

It was his first experience with pressure, and he had failed to handle it well.

Yet Frosty chose not to think badly of himself. He decided that while he hadn't broken 80 that day, it would inevitably happen sooner or later.

Frosty attributes this attitude to a naturally optimistic personality. I'm not so sure I would call it natural.

People choose their attitudes. He could have chosen to think of himself as a choker, to believe that he would always tense up and perform poorly under pressure. He didn't. He chose to think that with experience he would get used to the pressure.

That kind of attitude makes an enormous difference in how people respond to the setbacks, disappointments, and wretched performances that inevitably attend the game of golf.

His next opportunity came at a course called Clovelly, in a junior tournament. He shot 38 on the front and thought to himself, *This is easy. I've been here before.* He brought the round home in 38 for a 76. He and his father went straight from the course to a sporting goods store, where he picked out his promised set of clubs.

Over the next two years, he brought his handicap down to one. When he had done that, he took his first personal golf lesson, from a Johannesburg pro named Phil Ritson. Shortly after, he got to scratch, and then below scratch, to plus one. He was one of the top amateurs in South Africa.

David has often mentioned to me that he became a scratch golfer, or nearly so, before he took his first formal lesson. It's an important part of his golfing personality.

He has always intuitively appreciated the fact that it's more important to learn to score than it is to learn to swing. As a boy, he learned first how to get the ball in the hole. He developed creativity and imagination, especially around the green. Then he decided it was time to clean up his swing.

In taking lessons, he's always let his feelings guide him. He might hear eight or ten different bits of advice in the course of an hour's instruction. He's always had enough confidence to nod his head in agreement on all of them while internally saying "No, that's not for me" on most of them. He'll leave a lesson with one or two things he wants to work on. After a couple of days of practice, he will boil those two things down to one glimmering feeling he tries to incorporate into his game. He's the opposite of the player who leaves a lesson trying to incorporate ten changes into his game, and after a few days of practice has expanded those ten things into a couple of dozen new moves. That kind of player hasn't got a chance on the golf course. Frosty's kind of player always has a swing he can play and score with.

I've told Frosty that it's important to take the same selective attitude toward the mental tips I give him. Some of what I teach he has always done well. He doesn't have to pay much attention to it. Some of what I teach may not feel quite right to him. In that case, he feels free to reject it or modify it. A golfer has to know himself well enough to know what is going to work for him under pressure.

Frosty had to do two years of uniformed service, and he did them in the police force, where he walked a beat and served as a court orderly. When he finished with that, he got a job as a marketing representative for a cigarette company. He played golf on his weekends, squeezing seventy-two holes of tournament play into two days of thirty-six holes each.

Again, this differed from the environment in which most American golfers develop today. Typically, the best juniors get college scholarships. The best college players immediately turn professional. They never experience the discipline of earning a living outside of golf the way that American players of earlier generations did.

Frosty feels this, too, made him a better competitor. He knows what it's like to survive on a junior cop's pay; he's done it. He knows that his life wouldn't end if his golf career did.

In fact, he didn't aspire to play professionally until he was twenty-two. He might have remained a top-flight amateur had not the South African golf authorities chosen to leave him off the national team for a test match against Taiwan. Miffed, he turned pro.

In the Southern Hemisphere summer of 1981–82, he played South Africa's December-to-February tour. He earned $16,000. He decided to try his luck in the United States.

Using his $16,000 in winnings, he flew to the United States and signed up to play one of the Florida mini-tours. But he had recently taken another swing lesson and didn't play well. He spent $5,000 on entry fees and didn't make a dime.

Again, Frosty chose to see this experience positively. He wrote off his bad play as the result of his swing change and went on to Europe's summer circuit.

He qualified for a few tournaments and won a few modest checks in Europe and returned to South Africa. He finished third on the South African Order of Merit that season, and that won him an exemption to play in Europe in 1983.

He got his first good chance to win in Europe in the summer of 1984, at a tournament in Leeds. He had the lead after the third round; he was paired Sunday with Nick Faldo. But after Saturday's play, he stopped into a golf shop and saw a 3-wood that caught his fancy. He bought it and put it into his bag the next day.

The 3-wood's shaft was much too stiff for Frosty, but back then he knew almost nothing about club specifications. He pulled the club out on the second hole and whipped a shot out-of-bounds. He finished the day with an 80.

Characteristically, though, he refused to be traumatized. He simply decided that he would never again stick a new club in his bag without understanding its specifications and testing it thoroughly.

In the fall of that year, he came to the United States to try to qualify for the PGA Tour. It was a big gamble; the plane fares and entry fees as he shuttled back and forth for the two stages of qualifying school ate up most of his bank account. But he shot a 68 in the final round and got his card.

The next spring, at the Houston Open, he had his first chance to win in the United States. Frosty was in the penultimate group, a couple of strokes behind the leader, Ray Floyd. He was also just about broke; the expense of buying a new car had wiped out his savings.

The eighteenth at the TPC at the Woodlands course is a tough finishing hole, a 445-yard par four that bends gently to the right around a lake that extends virtually from tee to green. The Sunday pin position, of course, is on the right side of the green, bringing the water dramatically into play.

After driving into the fairway on the eighteenth hole, Frosty chose to be bold. He hit a beautiful 3-iron, slightly cut, that landed on the green and stopped about six feet from the pin.

As he walked toward the green, the possibility of winning reached up and grabbed him. As a foreigner, Frosty felt keenly the importance of winning in America. It was, in his estimation, the ultimate proving ground.

The pressure was such that he felt he could barely stand. For the first time in his life, he felt his hands shaking. He thought he could see his putter fluttering and jerking in his hands like a fish on a dock. When he drew the club back, he felt no flow, no connection between his hands, the putter, and the ball. He missed the putt.

As it turned out, the putt would probably have put him into a playoff, because Floyd bogeyed the eighteenth and still won.

Golfers often ask me a variant of the chicken-and-egg question:

Which comes first, confidence or winning? The implication, in some minds, is that you can't win until you have confidence, and you can't get confidence until you've won. But if that were the case, no one would ever win for the first time. The fact is that the confidence required to win can be learned.

Frosty started learning. He chose to see the bright side of what had happened in Houston. He had hit a great 3-iron under pressure. He'd made $40,000 for finishing second, which eased his money worries. He had not accomplished everything he wanted, but he decided that the next time, he would be better prepared to cope with his nerves.

At about this time, Frosty came to see me. He had been working on his swing with David Leadbetter, and David felt that Frosty needed some help with his mental game to make sure that he got the most from his talent.

So at Leadbetter's recommendation, Frosty flew to Charlottesville to see me. We talked about some concepts that were new to him that would help him produce his best golf under pressure. They will, by this time, be familiar to you.

He had never had a consistent mental routine. Nor had he

learned the importance of focusing on a small target before each shot. We worked on incorporating both into his game.

We talked about the importance of relaxing between shots. Frosty didn't need to try to concentrate for five consecutive hours every time he played a tournament round. I encouraged him to think of other things while he waited between holes or walked after his ball. He learned to bring his attention back to golf each time he started his pre-shot routine.

We also talked about the importance of regular rest. Being so close to the edge financially and being away from home, Frosty tended to play a lot of tournaments. And he practiced a lot. I had to get him to understand that as he became better and better it was going to become more important to take time off, to stay fresh. Absence makes the heart grow fonder. When you've been away from the one you love for a while, you're twice as glad to see her when you come home. A professional player may love the game, but he has got to get away from it regularly if he wants to be excited and ready to play every time he tees off on Thursday morning.

IT WOULD BE nice to report that immediately after he started working with me, Frosty started to win. But he still had many trials to endure.

In 1987, he tied for the Western Open title with Tom Kite, Nick Price, and Fred Couples. The playoff began on the sixteenth hole. Frosty drove into the fairway. The flag was tucked to the right, next to a bunker. Frosty followed his game plan, which called for him to aim for the center of the green in that circumstance. He did, and hit his approach accurately.

Tom Kite, though, aimed for the pin and made birdie. He won the tournament.

Frosty learned from that experience. He decided that in a sudden-death playoff, he had to be more aggressive.

That same summer, in the British Open at Muirfield, he learned another lesson. He started the final round one shot off the lead, paired with Paul Azinger in the final twosome. Azinger made a couple of birdies on the first four holes.

Frosty thereupon forgot that there was much more golf to play. He decided he had to chase Azinger. He got too aggressive with his birdie putts and ran several of them far enough by the hole that he three-putted. He fell out of contention.

Ironically, it was Nick Faldo who won that day, making pars on every hole. Azinger came back to him. He would have come back to Frosty too, had Frosty been more patient.

That's all part of learning to win at the highest level. A golfer has to have a finely honed sense of when to be aggressive and when to be patient.

Frosty's sense of it required just a little more honing. The next spring, he was at Hilton Head, playing well in the MCI Classic. He was in Sunday's last group, and he held the lead briefly around the turn. But he bogeyed the twelfth hole, and Greg Norman overtook him.

Down the stretch, Frosty hit every green and missed every birdie putt. He wound up losing to Norman in a playoff.

He decided after that that he'd been too anxious to sink those birdie putts. He needs to be just a bit indifferent and nonchalant to hit them as well as he can. He adopted a new thought for his putting routine: *It doesn't matter*. It relaxed him.

We talked a lot by phone on Sunday evenings during those years. I always tried to remind Frosty that although he might not have won, he'd played solid rounds. He'd proven he knew how to win, knew how to handle his mind and emotions. Someone else had happened to have a great day. Even so, he'd learned from it. We were able to take near misses and turn them into something positive.

He was ready to win.

AT THE SOUTHERN Open later in 1988, Frosty had a two-shot lead at one point on the back nine. But he three-putted the fourteenth and sixteenth holes to fall one behind Bob Tway.

The final hole was a long par five, downhill, with a stream that cut across the fairway about thirty yards in front of the green. Frosty hit a good drive, but he was still too far to reach the green.

He thought he could, however, get over the stream and leave himself with a short little chip to set up a birdie. It was a risky, aggressive shot, but he played it well. His pitch, though, was about eight feet short of the pin.

He slammed the club into the ground. But it was not, as some spectators surmised, because he was displeased with his pitch. He was pumping himself up to make his birdie putt.

Frosty walked onto the green. This time, there were no tremors. This time, he had a routine that was focused solely on putting the ball into the hole. This time, he made the putt. And he won the playoff.

It had taken three years and seven second-place finishes for Frosty to develop from the golfer with the shaking hands who missed a crucial six-footer and lost at Houston into the confident, aggressive golfer who shrugged off his mistakes and won the Southern Open by sinking a crucial eight-footer.

Frosty managed this because he chose to believe that each loss was a beneficial experience. He drew the lessons he could from them and then forgot about them. That's the way any golfer should approach a loss.

It's not what happens to golfers, but how they choose to respond to what happens that distinguishes champions.

Since the Southern Open, he's won eight more tournaments in the United States and several others in South Africa. He continues to learn how to close.

At the 1989 World Series of Golf, he hit a bad 7-iron approach to the eighteenth green in the final round, pulling the ball into the gallery area and leaving himself an awkward chip from a sidehill lie.

But he realized, as he walked toward the green, what he had done wrong. He had stood too long over the 7-iron, trying to be too fine with it. He should have stuck to his routine, stepped up to the ball, and swung without delay. Delay, he realized, only made his muscles tense.

He returned to his routine for the chip shot, hit it stiff, and went on to take the title in the playoff.

He still feels nervous in tight situations. But he doesn't let his nerves overcome him as he did earlier in his career. At the 1990 Million Dollar Challenge in Sun City, South Africa, he took his second straight title with a birdie on the eighteenth green that defeated Jose Maria Olazabal. He putted it with shaking hands.

Occasionally, he doesn't close well. In 1994, at Phoenix, he had the lead with ten holes to play, when he hit a bad shot and lapsed into trying to fix his mechanics. He shot 42 for the back nine.

And there are still situations he has yet to conquer. He's never won a major championship. That's a level of pressure that the professionals can feel only four times a year. It may take him longer to learn how to deal with it.

But, as ever, he learns and goes on.

No. 14

How Guy Rotella Came to Golf

When I visit with my father, Guy, we talk sometimes about the golfers I've met. I remember telling him once about something said during the course of a day I spent with Ben Hogan. I had asked Hogan what his adolescence was like.

"I never had an adolescence," Ben replied.

The bleakness of that response stuck with me, and I was curious to know my Dad's reaction.

"Well, I didn't have an adolescence either," Dad said.

That startled me, because I had never once heard my father, who was then seventy-six, complain about his life.

He had, he explained, never thought there was anything to complain about. His generation had a different understanding of adolescence. The average teenager in his time and place worked, studied, went to sleep. He didn't think he had an inalienable right to play sports, to go to parties. Anything of that sort was a windfall.

My dad was born in 1919, in Rutland, Vermont, one of eight children. My grandfather worked at the Rutland Marble Finishing Plant. Weekends he worked a second job, chopping trees and selling firewood so he could pay down the mortgage on the family house.

When my father was nine, my grandfather was promoted to yard foreman at the marble plant. Shortly thereafter, he was in the yard supervising the movement of some heavy marble blocks, when one of them fell from the crane and crushed him, killing him instantly.

My grandmother was left with eight kids and a mortgage-free house. There was no Social Security or workmen's compensation back then. Somehow, she made do. She took in boarders. Every night after dinner, she and her daughters would do finishing work on belts from a Rutland garment factory. She had a chicken coop and a garden.

And she got help from the community. Every autumn, men who had come from my grandfather's village in Sicily would go out into the woods and bring back enough firewood to keep the Rotella family warm through the winter. In the spring, they would come with shovels and spades and work the garden soil so the family could plant vegetables.

Another friend of my grandfather called and said, "Send the boy to my barber shop and we'll look after him." And that was how my father learned the trade that sustained him for much of his life.

He continued going to school, to Mount St. Joseph's Academy, where my brothers, sisters, and I would eventually go. He cut hair and he studied. At nine o'clock each night, my grandmother would take the fuse out of the fuse box so he would have to stop reading and go to sleep. She was worried about the electric bill.

After high school, he bought a barber shop, and he ran that for two years until he had saved enough money to enroll at the University of Alabama, where tuition was only thirty dollars per semester and a room was a dollar a week. He was there until 1941, when the war broke out. He went into the Navy, and then he met my mother. They married and started a family, and that was the end of his formal education, though he never stopped reading and learning. He and my mother helped put five kids through college, three of them through graduate school.

I recount all this partly because I admire what my father has achieved, and partly to explain why he came late to golf.

Dad was sixty-three when I persuaded him and my mother to try golf. Until that time, they had never set foot on the grounds of the Rutland Country Club. But I believe that you're never too old to learn to play golf, as long as you're not afraid to try. And I had never seen my father fail to accomplish something he set his mind to doing—gardening, plumbing, or any other chore around the house. I remember he once built a stereo receiver out of what seemed to me to be a million tiny pieces. All he needs to do is see a way to reach a goal. Then he'll get there.

It took a while for them to see the goal. They took no lessons, and for the first few months, they played mainly with each other. But within a year, they both loved the game. My mother had a rhythmic, repeatable swing from the start. Dad read everything he could get his hands on about the game. He discovered that he had a good natural putting touch. And when he realized he was good enough to play with his brother and some of his other lifelong friends, he was like a kid with a new toy.

His first year, he scored in triple digits. Over the next ten years or so, he brought that score down slowly and steadily.

His progress came to an abrupt halt three years ago. He was playing in a tournament, and his shoulder was sore from a fall he'd taken. Someone he was playing with suggested that he could loosen the shoulder up by windmilling it. Dad tried it.

Never accept free medical advice from somebody you meet on the golf course.

Dad tore his rotator cuff apart. The likelihood is it already was damaged, perhaps from the years he spent with his arm extended, cutting hair. But windmilling completed the process. He couldn't raise his left arm.

He waited for a couple of months to see if it would get better with rest. It didn't. He needed surgery. Just before he went under, he told the surgeon to make certain he left a golf swing somewhere in that shoulder. But when the operation was over, the doctors told my mother that they couldn't predict the range of motion my father would regain.

There were people my father's age in Rutland who had undergone rotator cuff surgery and hadn't regained full use of their shoulders. He chose to assume that they were disabled because they hadn't done their rehabilitation exercises. He was going to do his exercises. He wanted to play golf again. He understood that a person is never too old to improve his physical condition, never too old to dream and improve. Golf had become the new challenge and the new toy of his retirement, and he was not about to give it up.

Three times every day, he did those exercises. At first, the effort exhausted him so much that all he could do afterwards was sit and rest until it was time to do them again. Gradually, he got stronger. One day he walked into his surgeons' office and raised his arm over his head. They were as excited and surprised as kids at the circus to see how well he was doing.

A few months after the surgery, I was home for a visit and he drove me to the airport in Burlington. There was an indoor driving range nearby, and I asked him to stop there. He wasn't supposed to be doing anything athletic that early, but I gave him a 7-iron and put a ball on a tee and told him to hit it with a three-quarter swing. He did. Then he hit one with a smooth, full swing. He said it felt fine.

"That's enough for now," I said. "Use this as fuel for motivation to keep working on those exercises. You're going to play golf again."

He continued to work hard on his rehabilitation, and still does. By the next spring he was playing and improving once more. That's one of the great things about golf. Until the end of a person's life, it affords pleasure, exercise, and goals to work toward.

Dad's goal became breaking 80. He's still working on it.

In his case, the mental nature of the barrier was evident when he played his best round to date at Rutland. He was out with his regular group: Frank Esposito, Sal Salerni, and my uncle Roy. They're compatible players. Uncle Roy carries a 13 handicap, my dad's an 18, and Frank and Sal are somewhere in that region as well, although my dad tells me that Sal's game has slipped a bit since he started spending a lot of his spare time on flying lessons. They usually play a two-dollar Nassau, with a little extra money for birdies and greenies.

It was July, the peak of the golf season in Vermont. People have played enough to get their swings grooved. It's warm enough to get the muscles loose.

Rutland Country Club is a beautiful, tight old course, not very long. The greens are slick bent grass, among the finest anywhere. It's a course that demands accuracy and good putting.

Fortunately, those are Dad's strong suits. He's not very long, maybe 180 yards with the driver. But he's usually in the fairway. And he's a confident putter.

On this particular day, Dad felt great. The weather was good and everyone was happy. It was one of those days, he recalled later, when the shots don't take any effort. Everything feels smooth. He was picking out small targets and thinking about making the ball go there. That was all he was thinking about, save for a general feeling that it was good to be alive and playing golf on such a glorious day with three good friends.

He parred the first, then got up and down from off the green to par the second. He kept making pars or bogeys until the front nine was done. Then it happened.

"Geez, Rotella," Sal said. "You shot a 39!"

At that moment, Dad's thinking snapped out of the present. He stopped thinking about the next shot and started thinking that he could break 80.

He started thinking he was on a hot streak, which wasn't exactly true. He was simply playing up to his potential. Thinking *I'm on a hot streak* can be harmful if the subconscious corollary is *I'm bound to cool off.*

Sal's announcement that Dad had shot 39 was the equivalent of those people at the PGA Championship screaming "Ryder Cup!" at Brad Faxon.

Just as Brad had to keep the Ryder Cup out of his mind, Dad had to keep breaking 80 out of his.

Ideally, no one would add up his score and no one would think about it until the round was over. But in the real world, lots of people are going to keep track of your score, if only to figure out who won the two-dollars for the front side. And lots of people can't seem to avoid adding it up for themselves, even if they're playing alone.

Those people have to treat the knowledge of a partial score the same way Brad treated those cries of "Ryder Cup!"—as a stimulus to keeping their minds in the present and thinking about their routines.

Dad didn't quite manage this. He hit his approach into a trap on No. 10 and couldn't get up and down. He bogeyed the next three holes, although on a couple of them he could have saved par with some good wedge play.

By that time, he was thinking that he was in danger of blowing his good start.

I find this a common problem with players trying hard, perhaps too hard, to put together a great round or a great tournament. Sometimes I ask them what their attitudes would be if I told them that I had just been visited with a divine revelation. It was already written in heaven that they were going to win three times this year on the tour, or break 80, or whatever their goals might be.

Guaranteed.

In the bag.

All they had to do was enjoy watching it happen.

If that were true, they all would be a lot more patient, a lot more accepting. If they hit a bad shot, their attitude would be, "Wow! I hit it into the gunch on this hole and I'm still going to win! What a great story this is going to make!"

If they had that attitude, they'd win or break 80 a lot more often.

But Dad got a little anxious and went for the green with his second shot at No. 14, hitting a 3-wood. That's a hole he normally lays up on.

He missed with the 3-wood, and then went into what he might call his Jimmy Piersall syndrome. He gave up on the hole, got angry, wedged badly, and made a double-bogey.

This is proof enough that golf is a confounding and intriguing sport. My dad is a tough man. When he was in the Navy, he won boxing and wrestling championships. Golf is the only thing I've ever seen that can grab his emotions, excite him, and shake his composure that way.

He finished with 44, for an 83. It was an excellent round for an 18-handicapper, but it could have been better. It could have been under 80. It was a near miss.

Of course, my Dad's miss was leavened by the fact that whatever happens on the course, he walks off the last green pleased that he had a chance to play. That's a great thing. It's one reason I'm confident he will make it into the 70s sometime soon, so long as he remembers to stay in the present. I'm thrilled that he has the game, and proud that I introduced him to it.

I WISH THAT I set a better playing example for Dad. But staying in the present can be much harder to do than it is to say.

I played with him recently in the Member-Guest Tournament at Rutland, a four-ball, best-ball event. We were even going into the eighteenth hole in our semifinal match. No. 18 at Rutland is a long par four, a dogleg left with a tee shot over water.

We seemed to be in good shape to win. I reached the green in two, though I left myself a downhill, sidehill putt of maybe sixty feet. Dad was just off the green in three. Our opponents looked out of it. One of them had picked up. The other was over the green in three, facing a pitch to a green that sloped severely from back to front. It looked as if either of us could win the hole—Dad by getting up and down, me by two- or even three-putting.

This was when I stopped thinking about the present and started thinking about the future. I thought about how neat it would be for Dad to make the putt that won the match. He'd been playing well that day. I thought about how pleased he would be.

Dad chipped up for his fourth shot, and it stopped about five feet below the hole, the kind of putt he usually handles well. Our opponent hit his fourth shot. He caught the ball very thin and hit a low line drive. It looked like it would certainly fly over the front of the green and make our situation even easier. But it hit the flag stick and stopped an inch from the hole. We conceded his putt for a five.

Suddenly, I had to try to jerk my thoughts back into the present. I couldn't quite do it. I left my first putt about six feet short. I missed the second. Dad missed.

We lost the playoff.

I thought, *Great. I spend my days teaching people to stay in the present. But today I don't do it myself.*

That's part of the challenge of the game. It's not enough to learn what to do. You need the discipline to make yourself do it every day.

Fortunately, every new day is a fresh chance. So I'm hopeful that Dad will invite me back to the Member-Guest. If he does, I plan to redeem myself.

No. 15

How Nona Epps Learned to Come Through in the Clutch

It sometimes seems to me that there are but two kinds of parents: those who want their kids to play golf, and those who want their kids to play golf better.

Some parents seek me out because they have kids who don't seem interested in the sport, which the parents love. Understandably, the parents want to pass along to their children the pleasures and benefits of their game.

Others have kids who started playing the game, showed some ability, and then abruptly decided to give it up.

Still others have kids who have truly promising games: They've won the junior club championship, or something on the high school level, and now these parents can see college scholarships and maybe a professional career ahead, if only the child would just apply herself.

I'm tempted to refer all of these parents to a friend of mine named Charlie Epps, because Charlie is a proven expert in raising a young golfer the right way.

We got to know each other as colleagues. Charlie is a teaching pro from Houston, but he has done a lot of work for *Golf Digest* schools where I've been on the staff. Charlie loves the game and is an excellent player as well as a teacher. He believes firmly in the importance of a golfer's attitude, and we spent a lot of dinners chewing over ideas on the best ways to think about golf.

He had a personal as well as a professional interest in the subject, for he had two daughters, Nona and Mimi. Over the years, he's asked me a lot of questions about kids, parents, and golf.

He wanted to instill in his girls a love for the game and a confident attitude that would help them maximize whatever talent they have.

To start with, Charlie understood two key principles. One is that no parent is going to make a kid like golf. And the second is that it will do no good to restrict a child to golf at the expense of other sports.

The best way to introduce a kid to golf is casually.

Let him come out to the course with you once in a while, preferably late in the day when it's not so crowded. Let him drive the cart. Around the greens, give him a ball and a chipping club and a putter. Most kids instinctively understand the notion of putting a ball into a hole.

Remember that the child's attention span will be short, probably way too short for an eighteen-hole round. A parent has to recognize that the first objective in taking the child to the course is for the child to have fun. When the child stops having fun, it's time to go home.

In short, let the child dictate the nature and duration of the experience. If the kid wants to walk, don't take a cart—or vice versa. If the child wants to drop a ball in a bunker just to see what hitting it out of there feels like, let him. If he wants to take time out to see if there are tadpoles in the creek by the third fairway, that's fine too. If he wants to quit and go swimming after five holes, quit and go swimming.

This means that the parent has to recognize that his or her own game has a lesser priority when a child is along. If you're determined to get in eighteen holes or if you're interested in shooting your best score, leave the child somewhere else.

Too often, I see or hear about parents who do just the opposite. They take the child to the course, walk onto the first tee, hand him or her a driver, and expect the kid to hit the ball with it. When the child dribbles the ball off the tee, the parent counts, "one." And the parent then makes the child endure this for another five hours, until a proper round has been played.

Or I see parents who give the child no reason to think that golf is enjoyable. They moan and groan—or worse—when one of their shots is less than perfect. Why would a child want to play a game that demonstrably makes his father or mother unhappy, frustrated, and angry?

On the other hand, what kid wouldn't want to play a game if he sees that players celebrate their good shots and laugh off the bad ones?

Some parents want to play Joe Expert with the kid, constantly correcting his swing. Especially in the early stages, I think this is a mistake. No kid wants to spend hours being lectured and corrected. Let the child learn by imitation for a while. Let her swing however she wants to swing.

There is, of course, one exception to the rule of letting the child do what he wants and have fun. And that concerns etiquette. Any child who wants to throw clubs or other sorts of tantrums should be immediately and firmly set straight. Generally, though, that shouldn't happen if the child isn't kept out on the course longer than he or she wants to be.

A little farther down the road, you might want to teach a child a sound grip. And a little beyond that, it might be time for lessons. I think group lessons are best, particularly if they lead to a child's playing and competing against other children.

This was the basic approach Charlie Epps took with his older daughter, Nona. Since he was a teaching pro, she was always around golf courses. As a youngster, she'd occasionally go out with her dad because she liked to drive the cart. And she took group lessons with other kids.

But though she was the daughter of a pro, Nona Epps never played a full eighteen-hole round of golf until she was a freshman in high school.

She played volleyball and softball and ran track most of the year. Charlie encouraged her to do it. He let her know that whatever sport she wanted to play was fine with him. Golf was available, but only to the extent she wanted it.

She started to take to the game when she entered high school and found that her school had a golf team. She liked being part of a team. She liked competing.

At this point, Charlie started to become more active with her. He made sure she had good mechanical fundamentals—the grip, the stance, the swing. The important thing was that he taught them to her when she was ready to learn them, instead of trying to force them on her when he, not she, was ready.

And he always remembered the importance of helping her develop a good attitude and a good mental game.

He and Nona started sharing what Charlie called "positive notes." When she played in a high school event, he'd give her a small piece of paper to carry in her pocket. It might say "Smile. Relax. Play in the present. Have fun. No omars."

An "omar" is the Epps's code word for a mental mistake like forgetting your routine.

And she'd prepare notes for him when he played. She might write "Good grip. Good stance. Good swing," on a piece of paper that he'd carry.

It's great if a parent can recognize that communication with a child is a two-way process. I like it when parents let kids give them advice on things like reading putts. I think parents would be amazed at how much they could learn if they let themselves see the game through the imaginative eyes of a child once in a while. Most important, it helps in building a good, amicable relationship with the child.

In Nona's freshman season, she made good progress. Her first competitive round was about 123. By the end of the spring, she broke 100 for the first time, winning a fifty-dollar prize from her grandparents.

At this point, her interest in golf shouldered aside her other athletic pursuits. She started playing golf year round.

When this happens with a child, it's great, as long as the desire comes from the child, not the parent.

A child of almost any age can't spend too much time playing golf and practicing. But children burn out if they're doing it because someone requires it and they're not having fun.

At this stage in his kids' development, Charlie and his wife started taking the girls to the golf course for a regular Sunday round. They'd invent small competitions for Nona and Mimi: who could chip closest, who could drive farthest.

Charlie started to be a little more demanding of Nona. He'd show her a shot and expect that she'd work at it on the range. He might even let a little frustration show if she didn't.

But he didn't push her too far or too fast. At the high school age, a lot of parents want their children to enter national competitions. For one thing, they know that college golf coaches scout those competitions and hand out scholarships to children who do well in them.

There's even a certain amount of reverse sandbagging that goes on. The USGA, for instance, might say that only girls with handicaps of five or less can enter a certain event. Some parents will do what they can to finagle their children's handicaps under the limit or get them a waiver.

Charlie didn't do that. Nona never played in the USGA junior competitions.

I think that's a sound idea. Boxing managers, it seems to me, have always had a wise strategy for bringing along a promising young fighter. They don't overmatch him. In fact, they lean over backwards to give him easy opposition. They let him pile up a lot of wins against tomato cans, building confidence, before they ask him to step in against anyone remotely comparable in ability.

Young golfers can benefit from the same kind of easy early competition. I think a boy or girl is a lot better off winning local tournaments than losing badly at the national level. Losing is no fun for a lot of kids. It's a proximate cause of burnout. There'll be time enough later on to learn that it's a competitive world and no one wins all the time.

In her sophomore season, Nona did something quite remarkable. She was scoring consistently in the 90s, until one day she shot 80. She improved her previous best score by better than ten strokes.

This tells me a lot about the attitudes Charlie taught her.

First, he taught her to play in the present. She didn't know how many strokes she was taking until she added them up at the end of the round.

Thus, she had no comfort level to break through. When a golfer has been playing for a while, he can start thinking of himself as a 90s shooter, or an 80s shooter. If he starts to play significantly better than that, and fails to keep his mind focused tightly in the present, he can become distracted by his own score, perhaps by a feeling that he's playing over his head and is bound to come back to his "normal" level, his comfort level.

Nona didn't have that problem. When she found herself playing well, she just continued to play well.

Not only that. Charlie never emphasized scores with her. He certainly never let his attitude toward Nona be affected by the scores she posted. She knew that whether she shot 80 or 180, he would still ask only whether she had fun and whether she stayed committed to her routine.

The next year, Nona broke 80 for the first time in competition, shooting 78. She still wasn't consistent, but she started to emerge as one of the better girls in Texas high school golf. Her scoring average was in the low 80s, and she had the occasional 74 or 73.

Golf was by no means the only priority in her life. Nona wanted to go to Texas Christian University, and that is where she went, even though she wasn't offered a golf scholarship. She got some letters from smaller schools interested in recruiting her for their golf teams, but they didn't interest her. That was fine with Charlie. He didn't particularly want her to have the pressure of justifying a golf scholarship.

Nona didn't even play golf in her freshman year at TCU. She wanted to get acclimated to university academics. She wanted to join a sorority and have some fun. She did those things.

At the beginning of her sophomore year, she tried out for, and made, the golf team. Then she faced a four-round qualifying competition for girls who wanted to make the traveling squad that was headed to a big intercollegiate event in Nebraska.

Nona shot 77 and led the field after the first day. She followed that with a 79. But in the third round, she ballooned to an 88. Her chance of making the traveling team suddenly seemed remote.

When she called home after shooting 88, Charlie just said, "Go get 'em tomorrow."

How Nona Epps Learned to Come Through • 191

The TCU women played the final qualifying round at Mira Vista Golf Club, a tough new Tom Weiskopf–Jay Morrish design outside Fort Worth.

Nona hit a 3-wood and a 5-iron to the fringe of the first green. She sank the long putt and felt a surge of confidence. She followed that with another birdie putt on the third hole. She was trusting her putting stroke. She saw a line and she hit the ball.

On No. 4, she hit to eight feet, giving herself another birdie putt, one that would have put her three under par. "Take 'em when you can get 'em," she remembered her father saying. Then another thought entered her mind: *I'm two under. Maybe I've used up my supply of birdies.*

With that in mind, she missed that putt. Then she did a smart thing. She chastised herself for letting her mental routine break down on the birdie putt, for hitting it while in doubt. And she resolved not to repeat that mistake.

She had a bogey and a birdie the rest of the way out and made the turn at two-under 32; par for the front side was 34, since one par four had a temporary green and was being played as a par three.

It was the first time she had ever played nine holes under par. But she put that idea out of her mind and drove well on the downhill tenth, a 363-yard par four. She had a 9-iron into the green.

Nona went through her routine. She stood behind the ball, visualizing her shot. Then she tugged on the bill of her visor. She looked at her target and found an intermediate target on the same line, a few feet in front of her ball. She put the club in her right hand, aligned it, and took her stance and grip.

And at that point, she had a little epiphany. She remembered once playing a round with Charlie, and she could almost hear again something he had said when she executed a similar downhill pitch: "I'm impressed with the way you play that shot."

With that compliment from her father in mind, she swung and lofted the ball into the air. It hit a foot from the pin and stuck.

Parents, I think, would be amazed at how often something they've said will pop into their children's brains at a critical moment. If they knew how often this happened, they might take care to improve the odds that it would be something positive and helpful.

Nona made her putt and she was three under. She picked up another birdie at No. 11, then bogeyed the thirteenth, a very long, tough par four. She pitched in from seventy yards and eagled the fourteenth.

Two holes later, her round was interrupted. By prearrangement, Nona had to drive a teammate back to the TCU campus for a late class.

A lot of golfers would have used this as an excuse to play badly for the remaining two holes. They would have dwelt on how unfortunate they were to have such a great round broken up, right on the verge of breaking 70.

Nona didn't. She played rhythm and blues on the car radio as she drove back and forth to the campus, thinking that this would help her maintain the good rhythm she had going that day. As darkness neared, she drove back out to the course and finished up clean.

In the first critical round of her college career, she broke par for the first time in her life. She broke 70 for the first time in her life. She shot 65.

As I said, her Dad raised her not to know comfort levels.

• • •

Of course, one round does not a career make. Nona made the TCU traveling squad and went to Nebraska for the tournament. The weather was cold, and so was she. She couldn't break 80. She still has a lot to learn about consistency and playing in adverse conditions.

The next challenge she'll face is keeping her loose, optimistic attitude even if she makes a true commitment to see how good she can get at golf. It's relatively easy to stay positive if golf is something you regard as a hobby. If it becomes your main work or passion in life, it gets harder to smile at bad bounces and stubbed chips.

But she and her father have built a great foundation.

No. 16

How Pat Bradley Finished Her Victory Lap

THE MOST INTENSE ATHLETE WITH WHOM I HAVE EVER WORKED MIGHT not draw a second glance walking through the average shopping mall.

Our media stereotype of the intense, mentally tough athlete is a masculine one—maybe a linebacker, shot full of pain killers, laying waste to quarterbacks on Sunday afternoon. Not many sportswriters associate intensity and toughness with the image of a slightly built woman, prematurely gray, with a shy, unassuming demeanor. But mental toughness has no gender. Pat Bradley is slightly built, shy, and unassuming. But Pat has an intensity that can sear you when she chooses to reveal it. She is as mentally tough as any human being I have ever known.

When Pat first came to see me, she had been a fixture on the LPGA Tour for about ten years. She'd already won a number of tournaments, including the U.S. Women's Open. But it was what she had to say about herself that impressed me.

She didn't want to talk about the tournaments she'd won. She wanted to talk about the times she'd finished second. She wanted to know how she could convert those second place finishes into firsts. She understood that no matter how good a player is, she faces two choices. She can get better. Or she can stagnate.

And Pat wanted to get better, because she had great dreams and huge ambitions. She wanted to win more tournaments, especially major championships. She wanted to be Player of the Year. She wanted to be in the LPGA Hall of Fame. I love to work with athletes who dream.

What impressed me most was why Pat thought she could do such things. She had never been a prodigy, one of the USGA's golden girls. She grew up in New Hampshire and Massachusetts, the daughter of a man who owned a ski and sports shop. Golf seasons are relatively short in New England, and as a junior player she didn't rank with her peers from California and the South, who got to play all year round. She was, she likes to say, a "local yokel." It wasn't until she was halfway through college at Florida International that she thought her game might be good enough for the LPGA.

Even then she didn't have any flashy physical talent to set her apart. She drives the ball about 230 yards, which was average for the LPGA. She didn't have the silken roll that marks a great natural putter like Ben Crenshaw or Nancy Lopez.

What Pat did have was an appreciation for the power of her own mind. She felt she was capable of seeing every shot before she hit it, of willing herself to get the ball in the hole. And that kind of resolve can more than make up for a little bit less than optimal length off the tee.

Pat had already figured out most of what I teach golfers about the mental game. It was a challenge to me to find ways to help her get even better.

She mentioned that when she got into position to win, she started to feel the physical symptoms of nerves. She got butterflies. And she feared that.

I told her to embrace the butterflies. They signified that she was where she was supposed to be. She had worked hard to be good enough to get into contention. The onset of nerves only verified that her hard work was paying off.

Pat liked that idea, and she used it to help herself get comfortable either in the lead or challenging for it.

She liked another idea I mentioned to her. I told her that our bodies and brains are, in one sense at least, like computers. The data that a computer receives will inevitably be reflected in the data it puts out.

This reinforced her ability to see her shots before she hit them. She believed that she could win because she had the strongest mind, the best ability to visualize successful shots. She gave her mind only positive input.

And then she went on a tear. In 1986, she won the Dinah Shore, the LPGA, and the du Maurier. She lost the U.S. Women's Open by a few strokes. It was the closest any LPGA player has ever come to the Grand Slam. She fulfilled her dream of being Player of the Year. Then she did it again in 1991.

Pat in those years played with her eyes. No matter where she hit the ball, she thought calmly and confidently about getting the next shot where she wanted it to go. She rolled in putts from all over the green. She made par from woods, from water, from sand. It didn't matter. She saw herself as Houdini, able to escape from anything. No matter how many shots she fell behind, she believed she could come back. And with that attitude, she often could. At one 1986 tournament, with an elite field of sixteen players, she started the final round almost in last place, seven strokes off the lead. She shot 63 and won.

She had a lot in common with Ben Hogan. Neither one was a great player at the outset. They needed a long time to get to the top. Like Hogan's, Pat's discipline was so intense that she had no attention to spare for small talk. She had a reputation as a grim player, and a silent one. Of course, that was a distorted perspective. As Pat once told me, "From the time I teed off to the time I finished, I was always talking. I was in constant, silent communication with myself."

It was just that people couldn't hear it, couldn't share it.

AT TIMES IN those years, I worried about how hard Pat drove herself. She couldn't leave the game at the golf course. As soon as one round was over, she started thinking about the next one, planning every shot on every hole. More often than not, she ate dinner by herself in her room. For company, she might have an occasional Red Sox or Celtics game on television.

As Pat herself will tell you, she had an intense fear of failure. She worried that if she played badly, she would be letting people down—her father, the rest of her family, even her fans. It didn't matter that the truth was that her family and friends would have felt the same about her no matter how she played. No matter how much she achieved, she was unrelentingly self-critical. If she shot 68, she was all right. If she shot 75, she was a bum—in her own mind.

I told her that she should be clapping herself on the back more often for the great things that she'd accomplished. But Pat found that very hard to do. There was no denying that her intensity was helping her win golf tournaments. And she wanted very much to win golf tournaments.

In 1987, she fell ill with Graves' disease, but she continued to whip herself to perform. Graves' disease is an illness of the thyroid gland. In Pat, it manifested itself as shaking hands, body tremors, and general weakness. On the course, she had to change her position at address, because she was afraid her shaking hands might inadvertently cause the club to move the ball. She turned away from other competitors when she took a drink of water, for fear they would see the liquid sloshing in the cup. At airports, she could barely make it up the first step into a rental car courtesy van.

But she confided in no one, fearful of showing weakness. For nearly a year, she told herself that she just needed a rest, that she was trying too hard, or even that she was creating the symptoms psychosomatically.

Finally, on a layover in Dallas in early 1988, she called a friend, Dr. Skip Garvey. He listened to her describe her symptoms for about five minutes. He ordered immediate blood tests. The next day, when he told her she was physically sick, Pat felt as happy as if she'd just won a golf tournament. At least there was something really wrong with her. At least *she* had not failed. It was just her body. And there was a cure.

Her illness demonstrated that no matter how mentally tough an athlete might be, calamity can still befall her. Toughness is not invulnerability. But toughness can help to overcome calamity. It did with Pat.

She took radiation treatment and started on a medication regimen. Gradually, she and her doctors brought the disease under control. By 1989, she started to win again. Her ultimate goal hove into view—the LPGA Hall of Fame.

The LPGA Hall of Fame is the most exclusive shrine in sports. No one is elected. To make it in, a player has to win thirty LPGA tournaments, including two majors. By way of comparison, if the same standard were in use for the men's tour, only one currently active player—Tom Watson—would have enough wins to qualify. No one else would be close.

In 1991, Pat went on another tear, winning five tournaments and Player of the Year honors again. In the autumn of that year, she won two tournaments back-to-back, for her twenty-ninth and thirtieth victories. The penultimate victory, the Safeco Classic, was an archetypal Bradley triumph. She birdied the seventy-second hole to tie Rosie Jones at 280. They went back to the tee at No. 18, a par five, for the playoff. Pat sliced her drive into a creek. She dropped, hit a wood, then a full 9-iron fourth, and sank an eighteen-foot par putt to keep the playoff going. She birdied the next hole to win. She really was like Houdini.

When she won the next week, she was in. She had nothing left to prove.

And as soon as that happened, she stopped winning.

"I was exhausted," Pat has told me. The mental effort that enabled her to win golf tournaments, the ascetic discipline, had taken a lot out of her. Making it into the Hall of Fame enabled her to tell herself she could rest.

She looked around and decided that there were other things in her life that she wanted to pay attention to. Her relationship with her fellow competitors had always been respectful, but generally distant. She started cultivating friendships, going out to dinner. She chatted a little on the golf course. She even enjoyed the faint look of shock on the other players' faces when she talked and smiled during a round.

The slight change in her personality, however, affected her golf. Putts she would have made in 1986 and 1991 lipped out in 1992 and 1993. Her confidence in her ability to get the ball in the hole wavered. Without that bright, flaming intensity, her physical skills were just average. For three seasons, she was winless, and she finished no higher than nineteenth on the money list.

I told her not to worry. She was taking the psychological equivalent of a victory lap. It's only natural that a person's desires change as her life progresses. When it was over, when she'd smelled the flowers long enough, she would know what to do to get back to winning.

A couple of years after her Hall of Fame ceremony, Pat called me up. She had decided her victory lap was over.

"This has been fun, Bob," she said. "But I don't want to drop off the earth. I don't care if I win all the time, but I want to be one of the top ten players again."

So we started talking about ways to balance an intense approach to golf with being the sunnier, friendlier golfing personality she had become since 1991. We started talking about ways she could still win, but without exhausting and isolating herself. If she could adapt, we decided, she could have it both ways.

Step one was a slightly curtailed schedule. During her best years, Pat played a lot of tournaments. Typically, she'd go on tour for six weeks in a row. And she felt she usually reached her peak in the last three weeks of that stretch.

We discussed playing no more than three consecutive weeks without a rest. The trick, I said, was to forget about using the first tournament or two to warm up. She had to be at her best from the first day of the first tournament.

We talked about learning to leave the game at the golf course. I encouraged her to keep developing friendships, to help younger players, to share what she'd learned. She would be giving something back to the game by doing so; she'd also be helping herself. She could still take a limited time each evening to think about the next day's round, visualizing her shots.

On the course, I felt she needn't spend the whole day in an isolation chamber. She could continue to talk to her fellow competitors and to the gallery and still play well if she could learn to modify her pre-shot routine. She needed to insert a step in the routine that consisted of shutting out all the outside distractions and getting into her old, intense mode of thinking. She had to learn to turn it on and turn it off.

This is an important lesson for anyone who hopes to play competitive golf and maintain a family and a social life.

A golfer has to learn to compartmentalize. The happiest players are the ones who do.

OVER THE LAST year or so, Pat has worked hard on finding this balance in her life. It is starting to pay off.

She started last season with her game in great shape after a winter of practice. She had taken to heart my advice that if she was going to play a curtailed schedule, she had to be ready to play whenever she teed it up. She could not afford, as some players do, to play her way into competitive shape.

On the practice range before that first round of the season, at the Chrysler-Plymouth Tournament of Champions at the Grand Cypress course in Orlando, Pat was hitting the ball beautifully. She was thinking, *Sound the bell! I'm ready.* She was cocky.

And she shot 79.

That night, she shed tears of frustration. Then she rallied. "Pat, there are three more days," she told herself. "You can bounce back. You've done it before."

For the next three days, she used the pain of that 79 to goad herself, and she played excellent golf. She finished the tournament tied for third.

The players stayed in Orlando for the next tournament, the HealthSouth Inaugural at Disney World's Eagle Pines Course. Pat opened with a 71 and a 72, but the course was playing very tough in cold, windy weather. She was only two shots off the lead held by Beth Daniel.

Entering the final round of the fifty-four-hole event, she felt relaxed and free of pressure. After three winless years, she thought, no one expected her to overtake Daniel. Only Pat knew how close she was to regaining the form she had had in 1986 and 1991.

She struck the ball beautifully on the front nine, hitting every fairway and every green. But the greens on the course were chewed-up Bermuda grass, and she made only one birdie putt, although she had several of about four feet and half a dozen inside fifteen feet.

Pat stayed patient. It seems almost contradictory, but during her intense, winning years, she was always able to stay patient. During her victory-lap years, when her intensity wasn't as good, she had less patience. She found herself slamming the putter back into the bag when she was unhappy with her performance on the greens.

In fact, there is no contradiction. When she was at her most intense, Pat was also her most confident. A confident player shrugs off a missed birdie putt and figures that the miss only improves the odds that the next one will go in.

That was how Pat felt that Sunday afternoon in Florida.

She birdied Nos. 11 and 12 to take the lead at four under. But Daniel, playing behind her, regrouped with birdies of her own at Nos. 14 and 15. She drew even.

Pat hit a perfect drive on No. 17, a nasty par four with a large, shallow green that sloped from front to back, fronted on the left by a lake and on the right by a bunker.

Her second shot would have to be just as good, long enough to clear the lip of the bunker, but not so long as to roll down the slope and off the back of the green. The wind was behind her, making it even harder.

Pat went through her routine, visualized the shot she wanted, and hit what she later described as a "career 6-iron, pure as the driven snow." It landed softly on the green and stopped fifteen feet past the hole. She had an uphill right-to-left putt, and she hit it aggressively. It was her margin of victory.

She was back.

. . .

PAT WENT ON to do almost exactly as she had told me she hoped she would in 1995. She limited her stints on the road to three or four weeks. She finished eleventh on the money list. She was in the top ten nearly a dozen times. She made a run at the U.S. Open. And she kept her life in balance.

Now, in her mid-forties, she's taken up weight training during the weeks she's not on the circuit. She tells me she feels stronger than she did when she started as a professional.

I think the autumn of her career may turn out to be an Indian summer.

No. 17

How Claude Williamson Got from Stumpy Lake to the Cascades

WHEN A GOLFER I KNOW NAMED CLAUDE WILLIAMSON WALKED ONTO THE first tee for a quarterfinal match in the Virginia Senior Amateur championship last summer, he had already come a very long way.

The challenges he faced that morning were formidable. First of all, the tournament was being played on the Cascades course at the Homestead, up in the mountains in Hot Springs.

The Cascades is one of American golf's classic courses. It started hosting USGA national tournaments back in 1928. The fairways are narrow and canted, the greens are slick, and there's a creek in play on half the holes. It demands a good strategy, a confident swing, and a lot of patience.

More important to Claude, his opponent was Moss Beecroft, a man whose lineage in Virginia golf is almost as long and distinguished as the Homestead's. Moss had been playing and winning tournaments on courses like the Cascades for years. He was the defending champion.

But the challenges posed by Moss Beecroft and the Cascades, Claude might have said, were small in comparison to those he had surmounted just to become good enough to be there.

How Claude Williamson Got to the Cascades

• • •

CLAUDE WILLIAMSON GREW up in Virginia's Tidewater area, but he never set foot on a golf course as a boy. He graduated from Virginia Tech with a degree in chemistry and went into the Army. The Army sent him to New York City, where it had a medical laboratory. He married, lived in Queens, and commuted to Manhattan.

There have probably been hundreds of Virginians who played golf as youngsters, moved to New York, and had to give up the game. There have no doubt been thousands of New Yorkers who never played as youngsters, moved to Virginia, and took it up. But Claude may be the only Virginian who's ever moved to New York City and taken the game up there. One Christmas, his wife bought him a set of irons. He embarked on his golfing career at twenty-four.

Like thousands of other New York golfers, Claude and a friend took to rising well before dawn on weekend mornings and heading out to a scruffy public course in Brooklyn, where they stood on line for a tee time. He took no lessons. He hit the ball, chased it, and felt frustrated. His scores were usually between 110 and 120.

When he left the Army, he moved back to Virginia, into a neighborhood where a lot of men played golf, getting together on weekends for a game and some beer. Claude soon joined them. They played at public courses in the Norfolk area, places like Lake Wright, Suffolk County, and Stumpy Lake. This was where his golfing education began.

He started taking lessons from an old touring pro named Claude King. His form improved, and he began shooting in the low 90s and high 80s.

Then he started playing at a course called the Bide-A-Wee

Golf Club, owned by another old pro named Chandler Harper. The caliber of players at Bide-A-Wee was a notch higher. Claude Williamson kept taking occasional lessons and practicing, and within a few years his handicap was down into single digits.

He had discovered, more or less by good fortune, several of the secrets to improvement. He took lessons and paid attention. He practiced a couple of times a week after work. He recognized that improvement was a long-term process. Most important, he did what he could to surround himself with players who challenged him to get better.

Claude's progress into the 70s demonstrates some hopeful truths for golfers who take up the game as adults and find themselves on public courses, unable to break 100.

It's true that they start out way behind those fortunate enough to have learned the game as kids. But it's also true that they have no bad memories weighing them down. They don't remember years of missed putts, sliced drives, and misery. They have no bad habits.

They haven't formed a fixed picture of themselves as golfers. I see a lot of people who have played golf for a while and stagnated. They see themselves as congenital 80s shooters, or 90s shooters. They put limits on themselves.

Claude didn't.

He recognized early on that he had to work on both his physical skills and his mind, and he was open to tips that would help him think better around the course.

One day he was playing with Chandler Harper at Bide-A-Wee. Claude hit a bad shot, and he started cussing himself.

"Claude, what's your handicap?" Harper asked.

"Seven," Claude replied.

"Well, after you've hit seven bad shots, then you can get upset with yourself," Harper said.

Claude remembered that advice, and he followed it for years.

He would count his bad shots and remind himself that he had no right to get angry until they exceeded his handicap. Not coincidentally, he found that this started to happen later and later in his rounds.

He discovered that he could improve his swing mechanics by watching television. At first, he would watch televised tournaments. He'd observe the positions that good players got into at various stages of their swings. And he would try to copy these positions.

Then he ran across a swing video by Al Geiberger and decided to make that his model. He got a video camera and taped his own swing. Then he'd play Geiberger's tape on one television and his own on another and watch them simultaneously. He tried to match Geiberger's takeaway, hand position, follow-through, and tempo.

I don't recommend this kind of use of videotape for everyone. Some people look at themselves on tape and say, "I can't believe my swing is that bad." The tape undermines their confidence. Others, like Claude, find it helps them. The important thing was that he found something that worked for him, that didn't confuse him, and he stuck with it.

As a result, his handicap continued to fall, until he was just about a scratch player. It had taken him twenty years of consistent effort to get there, but he made it.

At around the same time, Claude moved to Charlottesville, which is where I got to know him. We competed in some city tournaments. We talked a few times, casually, about the kinds of attitudes that would help him continue to improve.

I ran into him just last summer at a tournament, when he asked me to autograph his copy of *Golf Is Not a Game of Perfect*. Claude was later kind enough to say that the book had helped him.

First, it reminded him of the importance of a pre-shot routine.

After reading it and thinking about what worked best for him, Claude had developed a mantra he called "aah," an acronym for "align, aim, and hit." That's as good a summary of any of the basic components of a good routine. He set his body up the same way every time. He picked his target and aimed at it. And without further ado, he swung.

Second, the book reminded him to pick out small targets. Claude had been in the habit of aiming at general vicinities, like the middle of the fairway. He started aiming at particular branches or bunker corners.

Third, the book reminded him to trust his swing when he played. If he hit a bad shot, rather than start to question his mechanics and try to fix them, Claude resolved to try harder to stick with his mental pre-shot routine.

Finally, the book refreshed his memory of what Chandler Harper had told him years ago about accepting the results of any shot, regardless of what happens to it. He stopped letting missed putts make him angry and affect his concentration on the next tee.

As a result of all these things, he got a little more consistent.

CLAUDE FINISHED READING *Golf Is Not a Game of Perfect* just as he was getting ready to leave for the Homestead and the Virginia Senior Amateur.

He had not been able to put in the practice time he usually does before an important tournament. Claude works for an insurance company. Six weeks before the tournament started, his company had been asked to take over the University of Virginia employees' disability insurance policy. The ensuing deluge of work had meant he'd had little time to practice. In fact, Claude had had to withdraw from the State Amateur because he couldn't get away.

I've seen, quite often, that such circumstances can actually help a player who is fundamentally well-prepared. Given a lot of time to practice, this kind of player can work too hard to be ready for a particular tournament. He can get too tight and too perfectionistic.

But if circumstances prevent him from doing a lot of pretournament practicing, this kind of player can lower his expectations, get looser, and actually play better. It depends on the individual.

When he arrived at the Homestead, Claude followed another tip he'd gotten from *Golf Is Not a Game of Perfect* and walked the course backward. Looking at holes from green to tee, he could better see the optimal angle of approach to each green and the optimal landing area for each drive.

He could also see where the slope of a fairway meant that the landing area was in fact more restricted than it looked from the tee. On the first two holes, for instance, the fairways fell sharply from left to right. That meant that a drive down the right side might bounce into trouble. He brought along a yardage book and marked it up with a pencil, based on the way he wanted to play each hole.

Claude shot 75 and 78 in the stroke-play qualifying segment of the tournament and finished eighth. He closed out his first two matches 7 and 5. That brought him to the quarterfinals against Moss Beecroft.

It's often tough for a player without credentials of one kind or another to face a player with extensive credentials. It might be the club championship; you're the last player into the top flight and you go up against the guy who's won it the past three years. It could be the U.S. Senior Open and you're Larry Laoretti competing against Jack Nicklaus. The problem is the same.

If it's someone you've never played before, you had better

not let paper credentials beat you. You need to think that you're better than he is until he proves otherwise.

I sometimes ask tournament golfers who tell me they don't think they can win. "Well, who is it you think is going to win? Who do you believe in more than yourself?"

It's a waste of time to make a commitment to becoming good, to practice consistently, and then go out and believe in someone else more than you believe in yourself. At the very least, a player has to enter a tournament with the attitude that he's better than anyone else until someone proves otherwise. Put the burden of proof on the competition.

If it's someone who's beaten you the past ten times you've played, you have to believe that you can bring a new attitude and, hence, a new game, to the match. Maybe you lost with your old game and old attitude. But that doesn't mean you will with your new ones.

Moreover, you can remind yourself that you are your real opponent. **If you can win the battle with your mind and emotions and play your best game, then you can't really lose**. You may simply find out that on this particular day, someone had a better golf game than you had, or that you ran out of holes.

Claude worked on thinking that way. He told himself that Moss Beecroft had only fourteen clubs, the same as he did. But he didn't get much sleep that night.

And he didn't have the chance to build up confidence on the practice tee before the match. The Homestead's practice range is a long way from the Cascades course's first tee, and the match began early in the morning. Claude went to the tee without hitting any warm-up balls.

This is a problem a lot of amateurs encounter. They have a match they badly want to win. But they can't get to the course in time to warm up. Or the course doesn't have a practice tee.

The best way to handle this situation is to find time to visualize the tee shot you want to hit. Take a lot of practice swings and make sure your muscles are as loose as you can make them. Pick up a club you can trust; if your driver has been balky of late, or the hole is tight, it might be best to leave the driver in the bag for a few holes. Concentrate on your target and your pre-shot routine. And no matter what happens, don't assume that the first tee shot, good or bad, will have any influence on the shots you play thereafter.

Claude had been hitting his driver well, so he pulled that club out of the bag and hit it exactly where his game plan specified. He hit his approach shot to six feet. Though he didn't make the birdie putt, he easily parred the hole. Beecroft bogeyed it.

Something like this frequently happens when a player with credentials meets a player without credentials. The favorite can come to the first tee complacent. If the underdog is ready to play from the first stroke, he can often jump out to a lead.

They halved the next ten holes. No. 12 is one of the toughest holes on the Cascades, a 476-yard downhill par four. The creek crosses the fairway and then runs along the left side all the way to the green.

Claude, still with the honor, busted his best drive down the middle, about 210 yards from the green. Beecroft reached back for a little extra distance and pushed his tee shot to the right, into the rough. He couldn't reach the green, and made bogey. Claude hit a 7-wood, which he carries in place of a 2-iron, almost stiff. He coddled the six-foot birdie putt, knowing that he needed only a par. He made the tap-in and he was two up.

They halved the next four holes with pars. No. 17 at the Cascades is a great par five to play toward the end of a tight match. It's 491 yards, a dogleg left, with the creek running all the way down the right side of the hole. It's reachable, by experts, with two great shots. But the risks are high.

Claude, with the advantage of being dormie, hit a driver down the middle. Beecroft hit his drive into the creek on the right. Claude made a routine par, and the match was over.

The tournament, of course, wasn't over. Claude still had two matches to play; he warned himself not to start celebrating early. Despite a slight letdown in the semifinals, he won 3 and 1 again. And he won the final match 5 and 4.

It took Claude a while to appreciate fully what he'd done. Then he started to savor it. Claude had lifted himself, rung by rung, from the bottom of the ladder in Virginia golf to the top. The view from there was very satisfying.

Most dreams are attainable if the dreamer is ready to devote consistent, intelligent effort to them.

No. 18

How Tom Kite
Honors His Commitment

ONCE IN A WHILE, SOMEONE WILL APPROACH ME AT A GOLF TOURNAMENT or clinic and tell me what a relief it is to learn that he can become a first-class golfer just by changing the way he thinks.

Or someone out on the tour will come to me because he's heard that I help players get better just by changing the way they think.

They might even bring up an example, saying that they observed the way Tom Kite improved after he started working with me—just by changing the way he thinks.

I am at once flattered, embarrassed, and slightly irritated by this kind of compliment.

It's true that a lot of golfers who are presently averaging 95 could drop that average under 90 by improving their thinking: staying in the present, trusting their swings, picking out small targets, accepting the results of their shots, following intelligent routines and game plans.

They are weekend players who don't want to practice and who will be content to break 85 or 80 on occasion. I'm happy to be able to help them develop that kind of game to its fullest by thinking effectively.

But there are others who have reached that stage and are tired of it. They want to press ahead, to test themselves. They shoot 85 and would like to regularly shoot 75. They shoot 75 and they think it should be 69. They want to play well consistently. Some of them, unfortunately, would like to believe that all this requires is a psychological massage, a quick and easy change in their thinking. This bothers me, both because it's inaccurate and because it undervalues the work done by players who do improve.

The difference between a dream and a fantasy is commitment.

I wish that I could take all of the fantasizers with me some day to watch Tom Kite practice. Then they might begin to understand the commitment required to find out how good they can be.

A typical day at home in Austin during the golf season begins with Tom rising early and seeing his children off to school. Then he goes to the course. He stretches, carefully and thoroughly.

He'll hit wedges and work his way up through his irons and his woods. Then he'll work on his short game some more. This might take two or three hours. He's not counting.

Nor is he paying much attention to the weather. If it's a sunny day in July, it might be 98 degrees out on the practice tee. He will stay out there until sweat plasters the shirt to his back and the trousers to his thighs, take a short break to towel off and drink some water, and then practice some more.

In fact, there is a side of Tom that relishes the heat, a side that is thinking, "Good. It's so hot that a lot of guys won't practice. But I'll build up strength, discipline, and endurance, and the next time the U.S. Open is at Oakmont or Congressional or someplace where it sizzles in the summer, I'll have the advantage."

Then Tom might play a round, but he'll play it competitively, trying to simulate tournament conditions as closely as possible.

After the round, he'll go back to the practice tee and work on whatever facets of his game did not meet his standards when he played.

Up until this point, I could be describing the practice regimens of any number of first-rate players.

What separates Tom from the rest is the quality of his practice, not the quantity. Some players just beat balls. They work, but they don't improve.

Some players even set themselves up for failure as they practice. They fear failure. Even more, they fear the guilt they will feel if they fail without having practiced. So they hit balls until dark, thinking subconsciously that no one, including themselves, will be able to say they missed the cut or lost their tour cards because they didn't work. Players who fear failure generally play with fear, and consequently generally play badly.

Some people work hard, but they are unable to see themselves as successful, as winners. Their hard work never bears fruit.

Tom does not fear failure. He hates to lose, and he loves to win, but he's not afraid of failure. His love of winning drives his practice habits. He doesn't see practice as an exercise in self-denial or sacrifice. He sees it as an integral part of the process of improvement and winning. He sees himself as a winner.

He knows that the competition is working hard; some are getting better. He will do whatever is necessary to be as prepared as he can be, because that is how he maximizes his chances of winning.

To improve, a player must practice in the right way, working on both his swing and his mind.

As he practices, Tom is constantly challenging his mind and his creativity in an effort to do both.

A lot of this he picked up as a boy, first in Dallas and then in Austin. His father belonged to River Lake Country Club in Dallas, where Tom first started to play. And I use the word "play" advisedly. Golf was never work for Tom or the other kids. They spent all summer long at the course and on the practice tee. But it was always a game.

The boys constantly invented contests to amuse themselves. Who could hit it highest? Who could hit it lowest? Who could hit it the shortest distance using a full swing with a driver? Who could hit it farthest with a wedge? Who could slice it the most? Or hook it the most?

On the golf course, there were more games. The boys might call each other's shots. Tom's opponent could stand on the tee and tell him that his drive had to start off over the right rough and draw into the fairway. Then Tom might make his opponent hit a 90-yard bump and run onto the green.

Some of these games might seem silly and even harmful. To win a long wedge contest, for example, you have to learn how to blade the ball. It's not a shot you'd likely want to hit on the course. But it teaches control of the club. It teaches a boy to envision a shot and then trust his brain and body to hit it. It teaches how to play under pressure. It trains both the swing and the mind.

In fact, it often strikes me that adults would be better off if they let kids teach *them* how to practice, rather than the other way around. Kids are more creative and instinctive.

In Tom's case, the child was indeed father to the man. He still plays games that train his swing and his mind concurrently. When he's on the range, he reminds me in many ways of city kids playing basketball—playful, competitive, joyful. This does not mean he's one of the guys who wander around the tee, kibitzing. He's there to accomplish something, and his attitude toward people who drop by to schmooze is the same as a businessman's might be toward someone who barged into a business meeting to chat. He doesn't welcome it.

But people see this concentration and they mistake it for something robotic, even obsessive. In fact, just the opposite is true. On the practice tee, Tom might deliberately hit two big slices and then pure the next ball, just to know he can do it. When I'm around, he asks me to give him challenges. I might tell him to start a driver at a tree in the distance and draw it eight yards. Then start a 5-iron at a bush by the edge of the range and hit a high cut. Hit a wedge over a tree or punch a 7-iron under a branch and make it stop. Then take ten balls and aim for a pin sixty-five yards away. Hit the pin at least once, and I buy dinner. Miss with all ten, and dinner's on Tom.

He rarely buys dinner.

Tom finds ways to inject fun—and tension—into short-game practice. He'll seek out a thin, sandy patch of worn-out grass, drop some balls, and hit lob wedges to a high pin. From such a lie, his misses look awful, plopping weakly into the bunker or flying low over the green like frightened quail. But he knows that when he can handle this drill, he is hitting the ball precisely. Sometimes it amazes me just how precisely. When he practices putts, I ask him to tell me which side of the hole the ball will enter, and how fast. He does. I have seen him stand eight to ten feet from the hole on a flat section of the practice green and chip in eight consecutive balls. With a sand wedge. Without scuffing the green.

Tom also constantly tries to simulate the pressure he will feel in competition. In 1993, during his four-ball match at the Ryder Cup, Tom hit a marvelous 3-wood to the green of the short par-four tenth hole, a shot that had to fade precisely over a stream, between two large trees, and hold a small green. It was a pivotal shot in securing the match for the United States. It was a shot that Tom had practiced over and over on the range. And every time he did, he would tell himself that he was standing on the tee with the Ryder Cup on the line, the European crowd quietly eager to see him fail, the television cameras focused on him, his partner anxious. In short, he tried to experience all the emotions and stress he would feel in the actual competition. When the big moment came, he had a feeling of déjà vu, a feeling of confidence.

MOST OF ALL, Tom's commitment is such that he treats setbacks as goads to get better.

If he could play one shot from his career over again, it probably would be the ball he hit into the swollen waters of the creek on the fifth hole of Rochester's Oak Hill Country Club during the last round of the 1989 U.S. Open. Going into that day, he had recorded masterful rounds of 67, 69, and 69. He led by a stroke over Scott Simpson and three over Curtis Strange. Mentally, he felt as sharp as he ever had.

The fatal shot at No. 5 was a block to the right. After the penalty, Tom reached the green of the par four in four and, upset, three-putted from twelve feet. The Open slipped away.

As soon as the tournament was over, Tom reflected honestly on his mental state at the time he hit the ball. Had his mind been in the present? He thought that it had. Had he believed in the shot? Yes. Had he doubted himself in some way? No. Mentally, he had done everything he was supposed to do.

There was only one other conclusion to reach. His swing had broken down.

It was not, in fact, the first time that he had blocked a ball right of right under pressure. Earlier that year, he had almost lost at Bay Hill when he put his approach to the eighteenth green into a lake.

Tom looked at film and talked with two teaching professionals he trusted, Chuck Cook and John Rhodes. He decided that under pressure his swing was prone to deliver the clubhead to the ball on an inside-to-out path that was too pronounced. (This sometimes happened on the range too, but you tend to forget those.) It was the same problem that plagued Greg Norman and Johnny Miller at certain stages of their careers.

Tom and his teachers agreed to make a significant swing change, widening his stance and flattening his swing plane, so that he could square the clubface with his body rather than his arms.

A lot of players of Tom's stature would be chary of making this kind of change, knowing that their games might regress for a while. But Tom did not want the thought of possible blocked shots hanging over him. He was still on a quest to see how good he could be, and if that quest required a swing change, so be it.

He started working on the change during the off-season at the end of 1989. He spent countless hours on practice tees. As Tom says, he doesn't watch the clock when he's having fun. For him, improvement is fun. He enjoys nothing more than the feeling of getting better.

He practiced his new swing into 1990, and in spurts, it worked very well. But just as he thought he was getting it down, he overdid it a bit by getting through the ball too much with his upper body. And because he had never played with this flaw, his misses went everywhere. So at the end of the 1991 season, he went back to the range for more refinement of his swing.

Finally, early in the 1992 season, it all fell into place. Golf started to seem easy. If he wanted to hit it high, he hit it high. If he wanted to turn it right-to-left, he turned it. His wedges were sharp. He putted confidently. And he felt no threat of disastrous misses like the one at Oak Hill hanging over his head. He won the BellSouth Classic in Atlanta, his first title in sixteen months. Heading into the early summer and the U.S. Open at Pebble Beach, he felt like a pilot who has broken through the clouds to find smooth air and a tailwind. Everything was copacetic.

Pebble Beach is one of Tom's favorite courses. He'd won the Bing Crosby there; he holds the course record. Pebble Beach embodies the kind of challenge and tradition he respects most in golf. It is no coincidence that players of the caliber of Jack Nicklaus and Tom Watson had won the previous opens at Pebble Beach.

But for some reason, at Pebble Beach Tom found that his swing had gone slightly awry. It was nothing awful, except by the high standards Tom had set for himself, particularly in the previous few weeks. He could not consistently get the ball to start on his intended line and go right-to-left. Instead, he was hitting a ball that started a little left and faded slightly.

A lot of people who had spent the time and effort Tom did to modify their swings would have reacted by spending the whole week trying to find that tight, beautiful little draw again. Worse, they might have persuaded themselves that there was no way they could play well without it. Tom, fortunately, knew better.

We talked on Tuesday night, two days before the tournament started. We agreed that he had to decide that he could win the U.S. Open without his A-plus swing, that he could use the swing that he had that week, plus his mind and his short game, to find a way to prevail. And he did. He played that whole week with a swing that felt far less than perfect, not the one he had practiced and worked on. Of the sixty-six players who made the cut, fifty-three hit more fairways than Tom; thirty-one hit more greens. No one took fewer strokes.

A rundown of Tom's final round shows how this was possible.

How Tom Kite Honors His Commitment • 221

Tom arrived at the course Sunday morning one stroke behind the leader, Gil Morgan. The practice tee at Pebble Beach is inland a bit from the ocean and protected from the brunt of the wind, so Tom did not immediately realize what the conditions would be like on that day. He warmed up with his long clubs, then made sure to spend some time practicing flop shots at the chipping and pitching green the USGA had installed for the Open. Then he went to the putting green.

There, he felt the wind start to freshen and blow hard off the Pacific, up to 30 miles an hour. He saw the sun shining, and he realized that the combination of sun and wind would dry the greens until they had the resilience of billiard tables. It would be a brutal day for scoring. The wind would affect every shot. Some greens would be nearly impossible to hold, and a lot of pins would be inaccessible.

Tom left his woods in the bag for his tee shot at No. 1, a 378-yard par four that gets a round at Pebble Beach off to a gentle start. He hit a 3-iron into the fairway and a 9-iron to the green. He poured in his birdie putt, a breaking 20-footer.

Oh, boy, he thought, *this is going to be fun.*

Any premature jubilation was tempered on the next few holes. At No. 2, a short par five where good players count on birdies, he hit a mediocre pitch to the green for his third shot and missed his putt. His par felt like a bogey. Despite being one under, he felt as if he hadn't gained anything on the field.

On No. 3, though, he got an inkling of what the field would be doing that day. His playing partner, Mark Brooks, four-putted from about twelve feet. The greens were that treacherous. Tom made a routine par.

He got into trouble himself by being a little aggressive on No. 4, a short par four that is the last of the easier, inland holes. The wind caught his tee shot and pushed it a few feet into the rough. Nevertheless, Tom elected to shoot at the pin, which was cut in the back right corner. His pitching wedge from the thick grass jumped a little, landed on the back of the green, and bounced like a basketball into a small bunker behind the green.

The ball settled on a downslope, and Tom faced the kind of penalizing situation that characterizes the U.S. Open—a sand shot from a downhill lie onto a crusty little green that sloped sharply away from him. There was no way to stop the ball close to the pin; he did well to keep it on the green, forty-five feet away. He then compounded the error with a poor putt that he left four feet short. His six left him one over par for the day.

This was perhaps the critical moment in Tom's round. A lot of players might have started feeling sorry for themselves, thinking that the USGA had tricked up the course. Tom could sympathize with that point of view. He was not happy, and as he passed his wife, Christy, on the way to the fifth tee, he said, "Well, it looks like the USGA has really done it to us today."

But he did not succumb to self-pity or anger. Nor did he think about what had happened at almost the same point in the final round in 1989 at Oak Hill. He didn't stop worrying that he was going to let another Open slip away. He reminded himself that based on what had happened to Brooks and him, there were going to be a lot of disasters during the final round. Everyone would suffer. He had to be patient.

Trying to gauge the wind at No. 5, a par three, he came off his 5-iron a bit and hit the ball into a right-hand bunker. When he reached it, he saw that the ball was buried in the sand.

"Oh, man," he said to himself. "I've just made double-bogey from a bunker at No. 4, and now I've got another bunker shot."

But he dragged his mind away from No. 4 and back into the present, hit a great explosion, and stopped the ball eight feet from the hole. Then he hit his par-saving putt into the heart of the hole.

There isn't much room for spectators at the fifth hole, and television rarely covers it. So when people talk about Tom's round at Pebble Beach, they rarely mention this hole. But the two short shots he hit to save his par at No. 5 were as important as any he struck that day.

At No. 6, Pebble Beach turns toward the ocean, into the teeth of the wind. Tom hit two beautiful wood shots and still barely made it to the top of the hill at the par-five sixth. He needed a knock-down 6-iron third shot to cover the last 115 yards to a green that's reachable in two on calm days.

He faced a twenty-foot putt, one that normally would have been very fast. But he realized that the wind would slow it down, and he gave it a firm stroke. The ball was going a little faster than he'd wanted, but it dove into the cup like a rat going into its hole. He was back to even par.

The tiny 113-yard seventh presented a harrowing shot. It's at the tip of a promontory, with an elevated tee. The wind was howling off the ocean. The only way to hit the green would have been to hit the ball out over the water and trust the wind to bring it back. The approximate aim point would almost have to be Yokohama. One player among the last thirty that day pulled the shot off.

Tom hit another 6-iron on a hole that is generally no more than a sand wedge shot, trying to keep it low, under the wind. But from the elevated tee, that was impossible. He watched the wind catch the ball and drive it left, left of the bunker, into thick rough by the eighth tee.

He faced his next shot calmly. The wind, directly in his face now, would help him this time, holding the shot and helping it land softly. He had been practicing his flop shot all week just for a moment like this. He swung confidently and lofted the ball over the bunker. It landed on the green, rolled directly to the hole, and fell in.

He did not celebrate. He breathed a sigh of relief, knowing how much hard golf he had yet to play.

At No. 8, the classic par four that spans a Pacific inlet, he faced a club selection problem. Normally, he hit a 3-wood to the landing area about 265 yards out in the fairway. But the gale behind him suggested that a 3-wood might be too much. So might a 4-wood, which would get up into the wind. A 3-iron seemed right. Then an even harder gust blew in from the ocean.

"Mike," Tom said to Mike Carrick, his caddie. "Do you think a 4-iron would be enough?"

"Maybe it is," Mike said.

It was. Tom blew the 4-iron 260 yards up the fairway into perfect position. Then he hit a beautiful 8-iron over the cliffs and brine and into the green. It landed just short of the pin and caromed as high as the flag. He wound up in the rough behind the green.

It left him much the same little flop shot he'd had at No. 7, and he hit it almost as well. He made a four-foot putt for his par.

No. 9 is a long par four, strung along the edge of a cliff, playing even longer because of the wind. Tom hit a fine drive, but the gale gave him a tough club choice. He wanted to hit a 4-wood to the green, but he was afraid of what the wind would do if he got the ball up in the air, which he tends to do with his 4-wood. So he opted instead to try to hit a low hook with his 3-iron. It's always tough to hit a shot when a player is in doubt about club selection. But at Pebble Beach in a 30-mile-per-hour gale, there are no easy club choices. Tom blocked the 3-iron right, into a patch of gnarly kikuyu grass halfway down the cliff to the beach. He was fortunate enough that a marshal saw where the ball went, or he might not have found it.

He had two choices. Since the cliffs and beach play as a lateral hazard, he could penalize himself a stroke and drop the ball forty yards or so in front of the green; or he could try to hit it out of the kikuyu. He had enormous confidence in the 62-degree Hogan wedge he'd been using for all his recovery shots that day, and he blasted this one out of the thicket and onto the green. He made five. But, as he told Mike as they walked off the green, "some bogies are better than others."

At No. 10, which wends its way further along the cliff, he pulled his drive left, conscious of the close brush with disaster he had survived on No. 9. His lie was terrible, and he could only hack a 7-iron out into the fairway. But he hacked it to the perfect yardage for his lob wedge, sixty-eight yards. He knocked the pitch stiff and made par.

At No. 11, with the wind finally behind him, he drove long and had only a sand wedge to the green. He knew better, this time, than to shoot for the pin. To reach the pin, he would have had to clear a bunker, and a shot that cleared the bunker would likely not hold the green. So he played left of the bunker, to the middle of the green, leaving himself twenty feet away but safely on. His putt almost went in. As he walked off the green he reminded himself that in the prevailing weather conditions, pars would be more than adequate. A remarkable number of players that day failed to break 80.

At No. 12, a par three, with the wind blowing fiercely from left to right, he took a 4-iron, closed the face a little, and tried to hit a big hook. The ball started out at the left edge of the green; on a calm day it might have hooked twenty yards left. But the wind blew it twenty yards right, onto the green about thirty feet right of the hole. The crowd around the green exploded with applause as if he had knocked it right up against the pin.

"Listen to that," Tom told Mike. "No one's hit this green for a long time."

He was right. Behind the twelfth green, he got a look at a leader board. He was the only player in the field under par.

Tom had always liked the green at No. 12. Over the years, in various tournaments, he'd made a number of birdies on it. With those thoughts in mind, he stroked his putt and holed it.

The crowd, of course, erupted again. He walked to the thirteenth tee feeling, as he said later, "super good about everything."

He parred No. 13 and then started down the long fourteenth, an uphill par five. Normally, the second shot at No. 14 is a lay-up, designed to give a player his most comfortable wedge shot for the approach to the green.

At this point, he remembered a chance encounter he had had the night before with two friends from Austin. Tom and Christy had been walking in Carmel after dinner, when they bumped into Lance and Hailey Hughes, who had come to California to watch the tournament.

They had sat by the fourteenth green most of the third round, watching golfer after golfer try to pitch on from ninety or one hundred yards, a pitch that had to clear a yawning bunker in front of the green. Invariably, their pitches either came up short in the bunker or hit the hardened green and kicked off the back and into the rough. That, in fact, had happened to Tom in the third round.

The only players who had held the green in three, Lance said, were the ones who tried to reach it in two and left themselves only a chip shot.

Remembering this, Tom took out his 3-wood and tried to hit it right of the bunker and long. He pulled it a bit and landed in the left rough, close to the green but with the bunker to negotiate.

He flopped the ball onto the green and stopped it two feet from the hole. He told me later that it never crossed his mind that he would hit anything but a great shot.

The birdie at No. 14 gave him a substantial lead. He was at

five under par; he didn't realize at the time that Jeff Sluman was having a good round and would finish at one under. He felt in control. He'd gotten past the worst holes on the golf course.

I don't recommend that players look at leader boards, although a lot of them do. They tend to distract players, to break their concentration on the shot at hand. For the leader in a major championship, that concentration is hard enough to keep. The mobile television crews are taking pictures of the grass where his ball lies. The crowds are yelling and screaming support as if this were a coronation instead of a golf tournament. It's hard not to start thinking about the people you'll thank when they hand you the trophy.

But Tom had looked at the leader boards and knew were he stood: If he played solid golf on the remaining four holes, the tournament was his. He had to take in that information without letting it change the way he'd been thinking up till that point.

At No. 15, he hit a good tee shot with his 3-wood, but he hooked it a little too much, trying to hold it against the wind. It landed in the left rough. He knocked a great iron shot to the edge of the green, stroked a 40-foot putt to within six inches, and made his par.

The crowd was roaring, and for a few seconds Tom was tempted to celebrate with them. But he reminded himself that he had three tough holes left to play, gave them a smile and a tip of his hat, and tried to focus on business.

At No. 16, still contending with the wind, he hit another 3-wood into the right rough. His 6-iron approach caught the back of the green and rolled off. He hit his chip shot a little heavy, and then hit a mediocre putt. He made bogey. He was down to four under.

No. 17 presented him with yet another of Pebble Beach's club selection dilemmas. The pin was in the left side of the back half of the hourglass-shaped green, about as far from the tee as it could get. The wind was blowing so strongly in his face that he thought he might need a driver to reach it. But a driver, if the wind slacked off as he swung, could fly the green and put him on the one place that could jeopardize the tournament, the beach.

He opted for a 3-wood, and put the ball into the bunker that fronts the green. He got a bad break. The ball came to rest on the left edge of the bunker, on a side slope. He would have an awkward stance, with one foot out of the sand and one foot in. The wind was in his face, and he had a long carry. Double-bogey was certainly a possibility.

Oh, man, he thought. *Why couldn't I have gotten a plain vanilla bunker shot?*

It was time for yet one more recovery shot with his wedge, and he hit a good one, not giving himself time to think about what might happen if he chunked it or bladed it. It landed on the green about ten feet from the pin. He missed the putt, but all he needed, at this stage, was a bogey.

This putt was the only mental error he made on the finishing holes. Thinking he had the tournament in hand, he lost his concentration. But he turned that lapse into a positive factor. He used it to remind himself to concentrate exclusively on his routine as he played the critical tee shot at No. 18.

All week long Tom had been hitting a 3-wood off the tee at No. 18, the famous par five that stretches 548 yards along the ocean's edge. But his last three shots with that club had failed to find short grass. He wanted a club he could hit confidently.

"What do you think about a driver?" he asked Mike.

Mike, probably trying to avoid looking at the ocean, gulped and said, "Yeah, that's fine."

Tom fell back on the pre-shot habits he had practiced for so many years. He picked out his target. He confined himself to one swing thought: *slow.*

He took the club back as slowly as he could. On tape, later, he would see that there was nothing particularly slow about the swing. But he felt like a figure in a slow-motion movie. He swung.

"That's a tee-picker-upper," Mike said.

It was. It was the kind of drive that's hit so well that the golfer doesn't have to watch and see what happens to it. He can bend over, pick up the tee, and start walking.

It was straight, and it was long. He could have, if he had had a big lead or was a stroke behind, gone for the green in two. He laid up with a 5-iron, leaving himself once again with seventy yards left to the hole—the perfect distance for his lob wedge. When he knocked his third onto the green, he knew that his long quest for a major championship was over.

His triumph demonstrated so many things. It showed the importance of the short game. Even though he missed a lot of fairways and greens, he was able to play well because of his wedge and putter. He hit ten lob wedges during his round.

It showed the importance of staying in the present. Except for a few minor lapses, Tom would tell me later, his round had no past and no future. He was always thinking of the shot at hand. He never once thought about what had happened to him in 1989 or all the other times he had been in contention at a major championship.

It showed the importance of commitment: commitment to improvement, commitment to doing whatever you can do to win.

FOR A PERIOD of about a year, until the spring of 1993, Tom was the best player in the world. He won the Los Angeles Open. At the Bob Hope, he nearly lapped the field, setting a scoring record that still stands, 35 under par for ninety holes.

Then, on an off day, he took his kids to an amusement park. One of them jumped on his back to see a passing attraction. The next morning, Tom's back felt wooden and sore. Eventually, he went to a doctor and had an MRI exam. He had three bulging disks—one, perhaps, caused by the accident with his child, and the other two much older.

Tom tried to continue playing. The next month, I flew down to Augusta to stay with Tom during the Masters. Normally, when he invites me to meet him somewhere, he picks me up at the airport himself. But this time, his father met me, and I knew something was wrong.

We drove to a strip mall in Augusta, to the dark, dank little office of an acupuncturist. We found Tom lying on a table with sixty or eighty needles sticking out of him—from his torso, his ears, even around his eyes. He turned over and there were just as many stuck in various places on his backside.

That was how much he wanted to play in the Masters.

The acupuncture did little good, and he did not play well in the tournament.

Tom went home for a while to work on his rehabilitation. No one knew then whether the back injury would be chronic. But I knew that if there was any way to prevent that, Tom would find it. He would refuse to let the injury become an excuse, refuse to pity himself. He would seek out the best advice he could find. And whatever those advisers prescribed, he would do. He would take control of the health of his back. He would attack the rehabilitation process. No matter how many hours a day they told him to exercise, he would. He would even find a way to look at the injury as a blessing, as a goad to get stronger and fitter and thereby prolong his career.

But the road back has been long and daunting, even for Tom. His back healed, but when it did, his command of his game was not quite the same. He didn't win for the rest of 1993 or the following year. And 1995 was, by Tom's standards, a terrible year. He didn't win a tournament. He finished 104th on the money list.

There were reasons. He and Christy were building their dream house. That distracted him. He didn't put in quite the same amount of time practicing, particularly with his wedges. He lost his patience at times and let his frustration affect his game.

But Tom has had down years before. And each time, he's discovered and rediscovered that he intensely dislikes playing poorly and will do anything he can to get back on top.

When the season ended, he looked forward to going home. He thought of the off months as a time for purging the traces of 1995 and rebuilding himself and his game for 1996.

In contrast to his post-1989 reconstruction period, Tom did not feel a need to change his swing. That, he thought, was solid.

Instead, he concentrated on his body and his mind. From Thanksgiving through Christmas, he planned to leave his clubs in the closet most of the time. But every day, he would be exercising—lifting weights, jogging, using the StairMaster. His routine varies each day, because he doesn't want to get bored with it. But there is always something. Winter, Tom feels, is when a player has to build up the strength and endurance he will need to carry him through the next season.

This is why the writers and commentators who have suggested Tom is simply over the hill at forty-six are wrong. Physically, he is in better shape now than he was in college. He weighs less, and he's stronger. He didn't lift weights until fairly recently. Now, like most players who want to be competitive, he's a firm believer in it.

And Tom will spend a lot of time in the office he's built in his new home, a sanctuary of dark wood paneling and warm memories. The walls are covered with memorabilia—magazine covers, photos, plaques, and trophies. They remind him of important milestones in his golf career and of the people who helped him achieve them.

The room has a television set, a VCR, and a cabinet that contains videotapes of every tournament Tom has won or played well in. He has a cassette called the "Tom Kite Highlight Film." He has another of the Tom Kite model swing.

I suggested that Tom compile the highlight tapes and watch them, because I have always felt that Tom was, at times, too demanding and judgmental of himself. Some of that he inherits from the upright work ethic of his father, who was a supervisor for the Internal Revenue Service. Mr. Kite was the kind of man who never stopped trying to improve the efficiency of the offices he managed. If his employees were doing 95 percent of their work properly, Mr. Kite worried about the remaining 5 percent and how to fix it. That was no doubt a good attitude for an IRS supervisor to have. But it will take a golfer only so far. A perfectionist, self-critical attitude can help someone become a good player. But it won't help him take the next step and become a great player, because once on the course, great players think more about what they can do well than about what they do poorly.

Tom started learning this in his boyhood from Harvey Penick, who relentlessly emphasized the positive aspects of every pupil's game. Tom learned more by watching the great players of the generation that preceded his—Arnold Palmer, Lee Trevino, and Gary Player, his boyhood idol. He noticed the way they carried themselves and talked.

But this was still something I thought Tom needed to work on when he and I first got together in 1984, just before the Doral tournament in Miami. We talked a lot about how effective persons know how to appreciate their own best attributes. They value their achievements. They acknowledge their shortcomings and they work to improve them, but they keep them in perspective.

Even the best golfers lose more tournaments than they win. And even when they win, they make mistakes. I told Tom that he had to realize that mortals attain perfection only fleetingly. The rest of the time, they are well advised to accept being human, to accept the fact that humans make mistakes. I told him not to forget that he is one of the best golfers on the planet even if he misses shots.

Tom won the 1984 Doral Open, beating Jack Nicklaus down the stretch. At eight o'clock the following morning he called me to thank me for my help. For a little while, he talked about how great it had felt to play well and beat a champion as great as Nicklaus.

Then he said, "God, I must have made a total fool of myself when I jumped up and threw my visor on the eighteenth green."

I laughed. "You son of a gun," I said. "If you can't have fun making birdie on four of the last five holes and rolling in a forty-footer on the eighteenth to beat Nicklaus, then you can't have fun. The world wants to watch you have fun playing golf!"

If Tom had a tendency to be critical of himself within twenty-four hours of one of the best days of his career, it's not hard to imagine how much playing badly gnaws at him. He works very hard to maintain the positive, optimistic attitude that Harvey Penick instilled in him when he was a boy.

That's what the tapes are intended to help him do. Seeing himself hit spectacularly good shots under pressure refreshes Tom's mind. It reminds him of how well he can play. As he says, "It's an ego boost in a sport where your ego needs a lot of boosting."

• • •

So he will watch the tapes, and lift the weights, and when the times comes to practice again, he will practice hard. That is the nature of his commitment.

Then he will return to the tour, and everyone in the golf world will be watching to see if he can come back. Tom once said that playing in a golf tournament is like walking out in front of the public buck naked. He feels as if he's vulnerable to every critic, every second-guesser. He does it because he loves the feeling he gets when he comes through. It is a feeling he never gets tired of.

But I think that whatever happens on the course, Tom cannot really fail. He does not, at the beginning of each year, set the standard goals for himself. He does not say that he wants to win a certain number of tournaments or dollars. He has dreams—dreams of winning major championships. And now, I'm sure, he dreams of being the playing captain who leads the United States to victory in the 1997 Ryder Cup.

His objective, every day, is the same: to do whatever he can to become the best player he can be. Because of the way he honors his commitment, Tom is bound to continue to succeed. When his career finally ends, maybe after the Senior Skins game in 2015, he'll be able to look back and take pleasure in something that he and some other fortunate people have learned: It's the striving that gives a person pleasure and satisfaction. Or, as Tom puts it, "I enjoy improving. Big time."

He will know that his commitment made him happy and content nearly all the days of his life.

That's the happiness I wish for every golfer.

Appendix

More Rotella's Rules

• To play golf as well as he can, a player must focus his mind tightly on the shot he is playing now, in the present.

• A player who is committed to the process of hitting good shots will never draw a club back until he knows where he wants the ball to go and believes that the club in his hands will send it there.

• Nearly all golfers would be better off if they forgot about the score as they played.

• A golfer cannot score as well as possible if he is thinking about swing mechanics as he plays.

• A golfer has to train his swing on the practice tee, then trust it on the course.

• In putting, the challenge is to make a free stroke to a specific target. Guiding, steering, or being too careful with a putting stroke are faults bred by doubt.

• A golfer's brain and nervous system perform best when they're focused on a small, precise target.

- The right choice is the decisive choice.

- Acceptance is critical after a bad shot. An angry player can't really execute a pre-shot mental routine.

- As long as the rules reward getting the ball in the hole in the fewest strokes, golf will be about playing well with the wedges and the putter.

- Sometimes, golfers forget that the object of the game is not to have a great swing, but to put the ball into the hole.

- The disease called the yips doesn't exist, except in the mind.

- Every individual goes through periods when he does a lot of the right things—practicing efficiently, thinking well—and gets no immediate tangible results. This is the point at which successful people bring to bear the powers of faith, patience, persistence, and will. Faith is the ability to believe without any tangible evidence.

- A conservative strategy joined to a cocky swing produces low scores. Reckless boldness joined to a doubtful swing is a formula for disaster.

- Athletes who become self-critical perfectionists are flirting with trouble.

- The best remedies for a golfing slump are putting things back in perspective, dwelling on the positive, looking for something good to happen—and rededication to the short game.

- It's not very important where you've been. Life is about where you're going.

- The optimal state of mind is something a player must work on patiently every day.

- It's not what happens to golfers, but how they choose to respond to what happens, that distinguishes champions.

- Which comes first, confidence or winning? The implication, in some minds, is that you can't win until you have confidence, and you can't get confidence until you've won. But if that were the case, no one would ever win for the first time. The fact is that the confidence required to win can be learned.

- The best way to introduce a kid to golf is casually.

- A child of almost any age can't spend too much time playing golf and practicing. But children burn out if they're doing it because someone requires it and they're not having fun.

- A golfer has to learn to compartmentalize. The happiest players are the ones who do.

- If you can win the battle with your mind and emotions and play your best game, then you can't really lose.

- Most dreams are attainable if the dreamer is ready to devote consistent, intelligent effort to them.

- The difference between a dream and a fantasy is commitment.

- To improve, a player must practice in the right way, working on both his swing and his mind.

Acknowledgments

ONCE AGAIN, WE HAVE BEEN BLESSED WITH MANY PEOPLE TO THANK

Every golfer featured in this book cheerfully contributed hours of time and candid recollections. We are in their debt.

Students and faculty in the Curry School of Education at the University of Virginia generously afforded time to research and complete the book.

Dominick Anfuso and Cassie Jones at Simon & Schuster provided encouragement and a title. Rafe Sagalyn, our literary agent, came up with the format. Guy Rotella, Jr., read the manuscript as it progressed and helped straighten out our syntax and clarify our thinking.

Finally, our families—Darlene and Casey Rotella and Ann, Peter, and Catherine Cullen, lovingly forgave the absences from domestic duties that the book required.

B.R. and B.C.
FEBRUARY 1996

About the Authors

DR. BOB ROTELLA, Director of Sports Psychology in the Curry School of Education at the University of Virginia, has been a consultant to some of the top golf organizations in the world, including PGA of America, the PGA Tour, the LPGA Tour, and the Senior LPGA Tour. A writer for and consultant to *Golf Digest,* he lives in Charlottesville, Virginia, with his wife, Darlene, and daughter, Casey.

BOB CULLEN is a journalist and a novelist. Since he began collaborating with Bob Rotella, he has reduced his handicap by nine strokes and broken 80 for the first time. He lives with his wife and children in Chevy Chase, Maryland.